BRITISH SOURCES
for
IRISH HISTORY
1485–1641

COIMISIÚN LÁIMHSCRÍBHINNÍ NA hÉIREANN

BRITISH SOURCES
for
IRISH HISTORY
1485–1641

*A Guide to manuscripts in
Local, Regional and
Specialised Repositories in
England, Scotland and Wales*

◆

BRIAN C. DONOVAN
DAVID EDWARDS

DUBLIN
IRISH MANUSCRIPTS COMMISSION
1997

For
Kenneth Nicholls &
James Lydon

Printed by ColourBooks Ltd.,
Baldoyle, Dublin 13, Ireland
1997

Design by Dunbar Design

Indexes by Helen Litton and Brian Donovan

HARDBACK ISBN 1 874280 10X
PAPERBACK ISBN 1 874280 24X

CONTENTS

ACKNOWLEDGEMENTS

This book would not have possible without the assistance of the archivists, librarians and general staff of the record repositories throughout Britain. They went out of their way to find relevant documents for us, and were always professional and generous with their help. Without them this project could hardly have begun. Moreover it would have been almost impossible in the absence of adequate catalogues and indexes. Our gratitude to the army of anonymous archivists and listers who compiled them is immense.

Being able to actually visit many of the repositories dealt with in this book would have been unfeasible without the financial assistance provided by the Trinity College Association and Trust, Grace Lawless Lee Fund, Dean of Graduate Studies, and the Department of Modern History at Trinity College, Dublin. The Irish Manuscripts Commission and the Department of the Taoiseach helped us complete the task with a generous travel grant for our final (and longest) journey to Britain.

We are also grateful to the owners of the manuscripts cited in this work for permission to publish descriptions and extracts of them here.

Travel through Britain was made far less of an ordeal by Nuala Duffy and Fay Holman who graciously provided accommodation in Glasgow and London. Back in Dublin, Ben Klaasen helped resolve numerous computer related problems in the months before publication. During the course of our work we received practical support and useful suggestions from academic colleagues, particularly Professor Nicholas Canny, Professor Aidan Clarke, Dr. Raymond Gillespie, Dr. James McGrath and Bríd McGrath. Dr. Mary O'Dowd kindly read through an early draft, and Dr. Brian Trainor looked over the final work carefully.

Our debt to Mr. Kenneth Nicholls and Professor James Lydon is evident from the dedication.

ABBREVIATIONS

A.P.C.	J.R. Dasent et al (eds.), *Acts of the Privy Council*, 39 vols (London, 1870–1964).
B.R.S.	Bristol Record Society.
C.S.P.I.	*Calendar of State Papers relating to Ireland*, 24 vols (London, 1860–1912).
Cal. Carew Mss.	J.S. Brewer and W. Bullen (eds.), *Calendar of the Carew Manuscripts preserved in the Archiepiscopal Library at Lambeth*, 6 vols (London, 1867–73).
Cal. Fiants Ire.	Calendar of Fiants of the reigns of Henry VIII ... Elizabeth I, in 7th–22nd *Reports of the Deputy Keeper of the Public Records in Ireland* (Dublin, 1875–90).
Cal. Ir. Patent Rolls, James I	*Irish patent rolls of James I: facsimile of the Irish Record Commissioners' calendar prepared prior to 1830*, with forward by M.C. Griffith (I.M.C., Dublin, 1966).
Cal. Patent Rolls, Ire.	James Morrin (ed.), *Calendar of the Patent and Close Rolls of Chancery in Ireland*, Henry VIII–Elizabeth, 2 vols (Dublin, 1861–2).
Complete Peerage	G.E. Cockayne, *Complete Peerage* (ed. V. Gibbs) (1910–49)
Griffith, *Cal. Inq. Dublin*	Margaret C. Griffith, *Calendar of Inquisitions formerly in the Office of the Chief Remembrancer of the Exchequer Prepared from the MSS of the Irish Record Commission: Co. Dublin* (I.M.C., Dublin, 1991).
H.M.C.	Historical Manuscripts Commission.
H.M.C., *Guide to the Location of Collections*	*Guide to the Location of Collections Described in the Reports and Calendars Series 1870–1980* (Guide to Sources for British History 3, HMSO, London, 1982).
Hayes, *Sources*	R.J. Hayes, *Manuscript sources for the study of Irish civilisation* (11 vols, Boston, 1965–75).
I.M.C.	Irish Manuscripts Commission.
N.A.I.	National Archives of Ireland.
N.L.I.	National Library of Ireland.
Proc. R.I.A.	*Proceedings of the Royal Irish Academy.*
P.R.O.	Public Record Office of England and Wales, London.
P.R.O.N.I.	Public Record Office of Northern Ireland.
S.R.S.	Southampton Record Society.

INTRODUCTION

In a sense, this book is a response to the worst archival disaster ever to
befall students of Irish history – the burning of the Public Record
Office in Dublin in 1922, at the height of the Irish Civil War. Because
of the 1922 fire a huge amount of irreplaceable historical evidence was lost.
Knowledge of all periods of Irish history was dealt a devastating blow, as
entire categories of official government records dating back to the Middle
Ages disappeared overnight in the 'singeing flames' of conflict –
testamentary records, deeds, patents, evidence of customs administration
and taxation, church court records, sheriffs' returns, parliamentary papers,
records of local assize courts, gaol delivery rolls, and of course, the records
of the four central government courts of Exchequer, King's Bench,
Common Pleas and Chancery. Add to this the burning of many Anglo-Irish
Protestant country houses during the War of Independence and the Civil
War and the loss of the private records they contained, and it is clear that
the shadow of the early 1920s has been destined always to loom large as a
forbidding spectre over the work of Irish historians. Because of the
destruction then, historians have struggled against the scarcity of
information ever since. To adapt a metaphor used by E.H. Carr, since the
1920s Irish historians have been condemned to work in the manner of a
builder whose raw materials, documents, have been severely rationed,
thereby forced to render and re-render the same old sections of a run-down
building until the sudden discovery of fresh supplies of documents permits
the commencement of work long overdue in other sections. For students of
the period 1485–1641 this book is meant to open up the prospect – so long
delayed – of extensive construction and renovation work, from the
foundations of the building to the very rooftop, and all places in between.

It should come as no surprise that the new supply of documents
contained in this book comes from Britain. The destruction of the '20s made
many Irish historians more dependent upon British archives than they had
been before; this certainly was the case with historians of late medieval and
early modern Ireland, who suffered, perhaps, more than most from the loss
of materials. With no major national archive to rival the richness of the
holdings of the London Public Record Office or the British Library,
scholars of the period 1485–1641 grew accustomed to conducting much of

their research outside Ireland, especially in London, Oxford and Cambridge, but also in some of the many local record offices and archival repositories that have mushroomed across Britain since the 1950s. For example, the work of many of the leading authorities on sixteenth and seventeenth century Ireland, through D.B. Quinn and T.W. Moody to Nicholas P. Canny and beyond, has been as much based on documents available only in Britian as those accessible in Ireland.

This book began life in the late 1980s when the present authors were both postgraduates in the Department of History at Trinity College, Dublin. To further our research we both needed to follow in the footsteps of our forerunners by looking to Britain for additional sources of information, as there was too little material of relevance to our studies surviving at home in Ireland. Indeed, the fact that we were both occupied in the field of local studies, writing theses on the early-modern history of two Irish counties (Cos. Wexford and Kilkenny respectively), meant that we had to locate and examine a wider range of archival materials in Britain than was usually the case for students in our position. We both had cause to rue the devestation of the past, having discovered, among other things, that most of the local government records of Wexford and Kilkenny had perished in the 1922 fire. With so little material remaining, how were we going to write up the histories of either county? Unless we found more evidence to flesh out our inquiries in Britain, it seemed that our work might become just two other Irish history theses seemingly destined to remain unread, confined to the shelves as well-intentioned cul-de-sacs, academic dead ends. To write worthwhile Irish local history covering the sixteenth and seventeenth centuries, we had to travel to Britain.

The problem that confronted us when planning our first sorties to Britain was essentially the same as that which had confronted all our predecessors since the 1920s: blinding ignorance of the British archive network. Apart from the vast collections of papers that are held in the British Library, the London Public Record Office, and the college libraries of the universities of Oxford and Cambridge, we knew of precious little material that was held elsewhere. We were aware of the existence of a regional archive network across Britain, but we had no idea how large it was, let alone how many British regional archive centres held Irish material.[1] However, despite this state of near-blindness, we were still very optimistic that we would find our way to major new sources of information on Wexford and Kilkenny (we were young). We blame our naivety on the work of previous pioneers,

---

[1] For example, R.Dudley Edwards & Mary O'Dowd, *Sources for early modern Irish History, 1534–1641* (Cambridge 1985) was largely useless for our purposes, containing just two pages discussing British regional archives.

which encouraged us greatly. For his study of *The Londonderry Plantation*, published in 1939, Theo Moody had drawn attention to the records of the London livery companies that survived in London. Twenty years later, in *Strafford in Ireland* (1959), Hugh Kearney had highlighted the importance for seventeenth century Irish studies of the Wentworth Woodhouse Manuscripts housed in Sheffield City Library. Since then other scholars had discovered some valuable smaller holdings. The Ards colonisation papers of Sir Thomas Smith held in Essex Record Office had been noted in Nicholas Canny's *The Elizabethan conquest of Ireland* (1976). Michael MacCarthy Murrough's book on *The Munster Plantation* (1986) had drawn upon a whole range of minor collections of manuscripts kept in the county record offices of Devon, Hampshire and Kent, as well as in Nottingham University Library, and the possibility of discovering fresh material in Scotland had been hinted at in Michael Perceval-Maxwell's *Scottish Migration to Ulster in the Reign of James I* (1973) and Raymond Gillespie's *Colonial Ulster* (1985). Most encouraging of all, however, was Richard Hayes' *Manuscript Sources for the History of Irish Civilisation* (4 vols., Boston, Ma., 1965; supplementary volume, 1975). Though primarily a guide to the collections of documents kept in the National Library of Ireland, Hayes had greatly expanded the scope and value of his work by mentioning material of Irish interest from all over the world – including, crucially, the first attempted (though highly tentative) listing of Irish manuscripts in Britain that included reference to archives held in provincial record offices and town libraries. We decided to follow up Hayes's leads to see just how extensive this material was and to discover if other materials existed across the British local archive network, a network that had grown enormously since the completion of his work in 1975 when a supplement to *Manuscript Sources* was published.

We have a confession to make. Had we realised the scale of the task we had undertaken, we would probably not have proceeded with it. It seems incredible to us now, some seven years later, that we were once naive enough to think that (a) we might find only enough material for a short article in *Analecta Hibernica* or some similar periodical, and (b) that somehow within a space of two years we could have completed a thorough survey of all the local archive centres in Britain. Oh, the foolishness of youth! Our hopes of getting quick results were utterly shattered in 1989 when we discovered the second edition of *British Archives* by Janet Foster and Julia Sheppard.[2] Having consulted it we realised that far from writing to perhaps seventy or eighty archive centres – our original estimate – we

---

[2] The third edition of this invaluable work was published in 1995.

would need to contact between four and five hundred places if our search was to be thorough. The sin of Lucifer (and a little healthy competitiveness between the authors) soon won the day. With each of us trying to outdo the other as an exponent of positive thinking, pretending to be undaunted by the task that suddenly confronted us, we carried on into the great unknown with much bravado. If the book that follows is an accident, it is also a testament to the power of rivalry and blind stubborn optimism. Instigated in order to help both authors improve their Ph.D. dissertations, it became a major added burden that prevented both of us from finishing our theses inside a normal timeframe. At the time of going to press we have both yet to hand in our dissertations. We are glad the book is finished.

SURVEY PROCEDURE

The procedure we followed in putting this book together was dictated by the work of Foster and Sheppard. Based on the listings that they supplied in *British Archives* we realised that an initial two-part correspondence survey would be necessary before we could even consider visiting any archive centres – there were just too many repositories that might hold Irish material for us to harbour ambitions of ever visiting all of them. Moreover, finally aware of the vast number of local record offices and town libraries that apparently had never been contacted by Irish historians, we decided right from the start to exclude the five main national archive repositories in Britain from our project, i.e. the Public Record Office, London, the British Library, the Scottish Record Office, the Scottish National Library and the Welsh National Library. The content of these was already quite well known to Irish scholars, and there seemed little point in expending our limited financial resources revisiting familiar territory when so much unfamiliar territory lay within reach.[3] Following a similar line of logic we included the college libraries of Oxford and Cambridge universities mainly because we did not wish to exclude other university libraries, many of which had not been properly searched for Irish materials. Finally, we also decided to exclude collections of documents that were still in private hands. We were only concerned with material that was accessible to the public through an archive office.[4]

---

[3] In the event of this book receiving a second edition we would expand it to include lists of Irish material in the National Libraries of Scotland and Wales, the Scottish Record Office and the British Library.

[4] Anyone seeking further information on documents of Irish interest that are still held in some of the great ancestral homes of the British aristocracy should consult Historical Manuscripts Commission, *Guide to the Location of Collections described in the Reports and Calendars series, 1870–1980* (H.M.S.O., London 1982), or else write to the National Register of Archives in London.

All books are only as good as the limitations of their authors; this one is no different. It confines itself to the period 1485–1641 because that is the period of most interest to the present writers, both of whom specialise in the history of late medieval and early modern Ireland. The book, then, is offered as a guide only to those documents of Irish interest from the late medieval/early modern era that are kept in the non-national archive centres of England, Scotland and Wales, because that is all that the authors felt capable of achieving.

Having decided to exclude papers in private keeping and those in the five British national archive centres, we were determined to make amends by finding as many references to late medieval and early modern Ireland as possible from within our designated catchment area – county and regional record offices, and local and college libraries. Accordingly in 1988/9 the first letter we despatched was sent to more than 450 archive centres across Britain which Foster and Sheppard had indicated held historical collections dating back as far as the 1400s. The letter was deliberately couched in very general terms; like a begging letter, it emphasised the paucity of surviving documentary sources in Ireland in order to make the point to British archivists that any document in their care that referred to Ireland, no matter how insignificant it seemed, would be a welcome addition to our knowledge.

The response to this, the first letter, was very encouraging. Of the total of 461 repositories that we had contacted, only 47 failed to reply. Most important, more than one in six (82) of the archive centres confirmed that they had Irish material. Sometimes the material they held was not immediately relevant to our survey, belonging either to the pre-1485 or post-1641 periods, but still we had reason to be pleased, as over eighty British archive centres claimed to possess material that referred to late medieval and early modern Ireland – a major increase on the number of British archive repositories that had been noticed in Hayes's *Manuscript Sources*.

Nevertheless, for all that we had discovered many new sources of information, it was clear that many other archive centres might still possess material of interest. Our first letter had been much too general to encourage British archivists and librarians to examine their indexes very carefully for Irish references. Indeed, many of those who had replied had not looked beyond 'Ireland' in their place-name index. Unless we could find a way to get them to check right across the full range of their indexes, checking up Irish people – or British people in Ireland – as much as Irish places, then much material might evade our grasp. Our problem was compounded by the fact that some archivists had written back to explain the essentially local priorities of their archive offices: most of them served a fixed region of Britain, and the indexes and catalogues they held were usually intended only to fascilitate local studies. In short, Ireland was of only peripheral interest. The Irish references that were recorded in their indexes probably did not represent the totality of Irish-related material in their possession; the only way that more material might be unearthed was if we could supply a wider range of Irish-related names to be checked. Ms A.M. Wherry, the county archivist at Hereford & Worcester Record Office (Worcester) provided some particularly helpful advice in this regard, suggesting how we could help her discover more Irish material if we would meet her half-way by supplying a list of Worcestershire families who had held land in Ireland or served in Ireland in the period that interested us. Encouraged by her suggestion we decided to particularise the second batch of survey letters by compiling individual searchlists for each archive district, thereby making the history of sixteenth and early seventeenth century Ireland relate more specifically to the counties and regions of Britain.

We spent the summer and early autumn of 1989 – nearly six months – researching familial links between late medieval/early modern Ireland and the British localities, drawing up lists of individuals and families from different parts of England, Scotland and Wales who had contacts with Ireland during the period 1485–1641, either directly through working in the Irish administration, serving in the army, acquiring Irish land, trading with Irish ports, and inter-marrying with Irish families, or else indirectly, through general involvement in British politics or a variety of other activities. In order to compile these lists we relied on a wide range of standard authorities, from G.E. Cockayne's *Complete Peerage* and Burke's *Landed Gentry of Britain and Ireland* to the *Victoria County History of England* and various Heraldic Visitations of English counties dating from the sixteenth and early seventeenth centuries that have been published by the Harleian Society. As a result of this research we were able to proceed with our plan of including detailed localised lists of colonists, politicians, soldiers, merchants and landowners as part of a second series of letters to the archive centres of Britain. Although the lists varied enormously in size and quality, with some (such as those for Yorkshire and Gloucestershire) containing the names of up to thirty persons/families with known Irish connections, while others had as few as seven or eight, overall we were satisfied that we now had enough to subject the archive network to a much sterner test than before.

The second batch of letters was sent to nearly 400 British archive centres over a period of half a year between the autumn of 1989 and the spring of 1990. Despite the shortcomings of some of the local searchlists, the response was excellent, a tribute to the professionalism and magnanimity of archivists all across Britain. The great majority of those we had contacted had taken the time to go carefully through their indexes and catalogues in search of the people we had identified. The results were very good. Approximately ten archive centres that had previously reported nothing of Irish interest now gave a positive reply, having discovered references to Ireland that had gone unnoticed at the first time of asking (among this group was Warwickshire Record Office and York City Library). Equally significant, many of the repositories that had responded positively to our first letter now wrote back to report that more material of interest had been found. As a result of all this to-ing and fro-ing of correspondence, by the summer of 1989 it was at last beginning to become clear which archive centres we should target for the second phase of our survey – the travel phase.

Only by travelling to as many archive centres as possible could we hope to produce a reliable guide to Irish-related documents in Britain. Though numerous archivists had gone out of their way to notify us of items of interest, their comments continued to warn us that much more material probably existed. Despite their willingness to help, there was only so much that the archivists could do to answer our queries; after all, some archives were better funded than others and had better indexes than others. Moreover, those archive centres that possessed large collections covering the period 1485–1641 could only tell us of the Irish material they contained if the collections had been fully catalogued. It was often the case, however, that large holdings were only partly catalogued; sometimes they were not catalogued at all. In short, there was a clear need for historians from Ireland to deal with many of these larger collections themselves.

Beginning in July 1989, and continuing over the next four years until December 1992, we made a series of research trips to various regions of Britain. Because of the generosity of the Trinity Trust and the Grace Lee Lawless fund at Trinity College, Dublin, and later that of the Irish Manuscripts Commission and the Department of the Taoiseach, we received enough financial backing to enable us to visit 55 separate archive centres in England, Scotland and Wales. The route we followed was a circuitous one. In 1989 we started in Kent, at the Kent Archives Office in Maidstone, and then travelled to south-western England, the north of Wales and north-western England, taking in Avon County Library, Bristol City Record Office, Cornwall County Record Office, all three Devon Record Offices (at Exeter, Barnstaple and Plymouth), Hampshire Record Office, Southampton

City Archives Office, Southampton University Library, Somerset Record Office, South Glamorgan Archive Service, University College of Swansea Library, University College of North Wales Library, and Cumbria Record Office, Carlisle. Before returning home, we also managed to visit the University of London Library. In 1990 we headed first to Chester, visiting Cheshire County Record Office and Chester City Library, before travelling inland to inspect the archives of ten midlands archival centres – Cambridge University Library, both Cambridgeshire Record Offices (at Cambridge and Huntingdon), Leicestershire Record Office, Northamptonshire Record Office, Nottinghamshire County Archives Office, University of Nottingham Library, the Bodleian Library at Oxford University, Oxfordshire Archives Office and Warwickshire Record Office. From the midlands we headed north to Manchester, Leeds and Sheffield, visiting John Ryland's University Library, Sheffield City Library, Leeds District Archives and the Yorkshire Archaeological Society. In 1991 we began our researches in Scotland, taking in Ayr Burgh Archives, Dumbarton District Library, Edinburgh City Archives, Edinburgh University Library, Glasgow University Library and Strathclyde Regional Archives before turning south, returning to the Bodleian Library at Oxford on our way to London to visit the Corporation of London Record Office, the Greater London Records Office and the Guildhall Library. Before going home we also visited Guildford Muniment Room in Surrey and Bradford District Archives in West Yorkshire. Our final research trip, in November–December 1992, was the most taxing of all. Intending to take in as many places as possible in order to bring the survey to an end, we frequently separated to head out in opposite directions from our base in London. Possessing a BritRail Flexi Pass, which entitled us to 15 journeys a month each, we travelled far and wide across England, paying visits to Bedfordshire Record Office, Berkshire Record Office, Buckinghamshire Record Office, Dorset Record Office, Gloucestershire Record Office, Lincolnshire Archives Office, Lambeth Palace Library, the National Maritime Museum and the Victoria & Albert Museum in London, Shropshire Record Office, Staffordshire Record Office and Wiltshire Record Office. Fittingly enough our last train trip took us back to where our survey had started, at Kent Archives Office; after four years we had come full circle.

The book took on its present bulky shape mainly because of these journeys. Had the authors proceeded to publish a guide to British archives without visiting so many places, the book might have run to little more than 150 pages. The visits transformed the project and revealed to us the limitations of surveys by correspondence only. Quite simply, there is no substitute for actually testing an archive firsthand. In many of the places that we visited we not only filled out enormously the references passed onto us by archivists during correspondence, but we also uncovered a great quantity of material that had previously gone undetected. At Northants Record Office, for instance, we discovered two collections of pre-1641 Irish material – the O'Brien of Blatherwycke Manuscripts and the Ormond (Kilkenny) Manuscripts – that the archivists had overlooked when writing to us earlier (largely because most of the material in both collections post-dated 1641 and related mainly to property in the English midlands, i.e. they had not been indexed under Ireland). Likewise, having decided to visit Warwickshire Record Office only because it was on the train-line to Oxford, we were delighted to discover a good deal of Irish material among the Greville of Warwick Castle Manuscripts and the Fielding of Newnham Paddox Papers, material that had not been brought to our attention during correspondence. Travel also enabled us to turn around some of the negative responses to our first and second letters – centres with Irish documents that came to our notice only through travel included Ayr Burgh Archives, Cornwall Record Office, the Victoria & Albert Museum, Nottinghamshire County Archives Office, Cambridgeshire Record Office (Cambridge) and Swansea University Library.

The advantages of being on the spot were enormous. Though it was time-consuming and often tedious, being able to thumb through the card indexes of the archives to look up as many Irish-related names as we could remember, led us to the whereabouts of many more documents than we otherwise would have found. The Irish material in the Fuller Collection at the University of London Library was only discovered because we requested permission of the archivist to run through the uncatalogued documents belonging to the collection that are kept in cabinets (the catalogued documents – containing few pre-1641 Irish items – are kept in boxes). Usually access to the uncatalogued material is limited, reserved for students of palaeography at the university, but our presence on the spot, having come all the way from Ireland, gained us access and resulted in the rediscovery of many documents relating to Co. Cork that had been feared lost. Finally, it should also be pointed out that visiting so many archive centres allowed us to fill out the catalogue entries for Irish-related documents which sometimes left a lot to be desired as aids to historical interpretation. Occasionally, depending on the amount of time available to us, we even enjoyed the luxury of transcribing entire documents verbatim, some of which are included in the book below.

Early in 1993 we decided to bring the survey to an end and begin writing up our results. During the spring and early summer we posted a final batch of letters to just over 150 archive centres in order to tidy up some loose ends. We would have liked more time to visit more archive centres, but we had exhausted the academic travel funds available to us. However, as it was we had easily accomplished our original goal of improving the knowledge of Irish-related documents for the period 1485–1641 held in British archives. Having begun the survey hoping to find hundreds of documents of interest, we had ended up with files of notes that listed thousands. Nonetheless, one thing did concern us greatly – the unevenness of our findings. Despite our best intentions the survey had become an essentially English project, in that the vast majority of the documents we had discovered were held in archive centres in England. Our findings from Scotland and Wales were paltry by comparison. This was due to circumstances quite beyond our control. As much as anything else that we learned, our travels revealed to us the profound infrastructural inequalities that exist between the different regions of modern Britain. In contrast to record offices and repositories across England, most of which possess full-time professional staff and properly trained archivists, local archive centres in Scotland and Wales are in a perilous state, hopelessly under-resourced by the state. Sadly, unless devolution manages to loosen the purse-strings for culture in Britain, we do not anticipate a time in the forseeable future when Scottish or Welsh archive centres will become much more accessible to students of Irish history.

ADVICE FOR FUTURE RESEARCHERS

For anyone interested in conducting a search of their own for undiscovered historical documents, we would advise that they begin with what is already known. One of the principal lessons of our survey was that famous collections of manuscripts, especially those that have received extensive calendars, often contain a mine of previously unnoticed material. Time and again during our work we learned that published calendars were only as exhaustive as their calendarers; they were usually highly selective, concentrating on material perceived to be of major importance (e.g., the correspondence of monarchs, statesmen and famous political figures), and this to the exclusion of other types of documentary material. For whatever reason, documents of interest for Irish social, economic and legal history – deeds and leases, rentals, account books, inventories, trade records, court records and legal memoranda – have rarely made it into calendars of historical documents based on major manuscript collections in Britain. With only this lop-sided printed heritage to go on, Irish historians have largely been unaware of the existence of a great deal of extra untapped evidence lurking among such well known collections as the Maxwell of Pollok Papers at Strathclyde Regional Archives, the De L'Isle & Dudley Manuscripts at Kent Archives Office, the Fitzwilliam (Milton) Manuscripts at Northants Record Office, the Strafford Papers among the Wentworth Woodhouse Muniments at Sheffield City Library, and the Temple Newsam Manuscripts at Leeds District Archives, all of which have provided the basis for the publication of extensive calendars in the past. Add to this the fact that bundles of entirely Irish documents lurking amidst the great collections have often been specifically ignored by the British historical press (frequently on the assumption that Irish publishers would publish them), and so it is that the Irish documents have continued to go unused, forgotten because they belong to collections that many scholars thought had been mined in full. In short, we discovered that where much was found before much more remained to be found. In the book that follows we have often listed documents that previous listers chose to ignore.

Anyone wishing to follow in our footsteps for the period prior to 1485 should be able to complete a survey a good deal faster than we did for our period. For one thing, we have already done some of the work in this area, having prepared a handlist of documents of a medieval date from thirty-eight British archive centres that accidentally came our way during our survey; this will be published in *Analecta Hibernica* No. 37 (forthcoming). For another, it should be much easier to find Irish-related medieval material than later (post-1485) material, for the older the document the more it is prized: collections that date back to the Middle Ages tend to be catalogued more carefully than those that do not (this is why we made so many accidental discoveries). Nothing should prevent Irish medievalists making our *Analecta Hibernica* handlist redundant in the next few years.

For those interested in the post-1641 period we would likewise advise that they begin a separate survey as soon as possible. Quite simply, the amount of Irish documentary material dating from the middle of the seventeenth century onwards that survives in Britain is tremendous. Almost everywhere we went we came across collections of estate papers, accounts, correspondence, etc, that included an abundance of post-1641 Irish references. Indeed, many of the collections that we drew upon for this book also contained much material that could be used for a book dealing with later early modern Ireland. Moreover, a lot of the ground-work has already been done by Dr. Anthony Malcomson and the P.R.O.N.I., who have spent many years acquiring microfilms and photocopies of eighteenth century collections held in British local record repositories.[5]

Perhaps students of later seventeenth century and eighteenth century Ireland could begin work on similar projects to ours, covering the periods c1642–1700 and 1701–1800?

HISTORICAL POTENTIAL

Because of the broad range of material sought out by us – to repeat, we looked for any reference of Irish interest we could find, no matter how slight – we hope that knowledge of all aspects of Irish history between 1485 and 1641 will be greatly enhanced, if not actually transformed, by our findings. The documents we found embrace all the great issues of late medieval and early modern Ireland, covering the Kildare ascendancy, the Tudor reintervention, the Elizabethan wars, the age of plantations, the centralisation of English power and the growth of arbitrary government, and the increasing colonialisation of Ireland's economy and society. Although what follows could never make up for what was lost in the 1920s, at least students of late medieval and early modern Ireland will have several thousand more documents to work with than used to be the case – more than enough new material for a major re-examination of one of the most tumultuous periods of Irish history.

New insights into the Kildare ascendancy and the age of aristocratic autonomy (c1485–1534) are provided by documents among the Talbot de Malahide Papers in the New Bodleian Library at Oxford University, and among the Strafford Deeds at Sheffield City Library. Though mainly concerned with the region around the Pale, nonetheless the items in these collections provide some of the most valuable information we have on the Irish feudal order as it existed on the eve of the English reintervention under Henry VIII. At last it might be possible for historians to peer beneath the Fitzgeralds of Kildare to examine the complex political and social fabric of the Pale prior to 1534, by shifting attention away from the Fitzgeralds and their cronies to include the likes of the Talbots, the Cusacks, the Harrolds, the Bowdens, the Nettervilles and the Britts in future analyses. For important areas outside the Pale, extracts from long-lost state documents concerning the Fitzmaurices, barons of Kerry, during late medieval times can be found at the Inner Temple Library in London, while conditions in south Co. Cork, around Cork City, Youghal and Kinsale, can be traced in

---

[5] Their extensive copying programme has also seen the publication of two volumes of Irish official papers, A.P.W. Malcomson, *Eighteenth Century Irish Official Papers in Great Britain: Private Collections* (Belfast, 1990).

the Fuller Papers at the University of London Library, which provide information regarding the Ronans, the MacCarthys, the Coursys, the Barrys and many other Munster families.

The growth of the English presence in sixteenth century Ireland following the collapse of Kildare power in 1534 can be detected in many different documents listed in the book, and some important gaps in our knowledge have been plugged. Much more can now be known about the workings of the court of Exchequer following the discovery of a commonplace book of c1640 at Essex Record Office which contains dozens of transcripts taken from the sixteenth and early seventeenth century records of the Irish Remembrancer of the Exchequer (the records of which were destroyed in 1922). New details of the introduction of government garrisons into the Irish localities by the Tudor state can be found among previously unnoticed sections of the De L'Isle & Dudley Manuscripts at Kent Archives Office. More information has also been uncovered about the beginnings of the provincial presidencies during the reign of Elizabeth I, and as a result certain interpretations of the presidencies currently in vogue will have to be revised – for instance, a royal warrant of Queen Elizabeth at Glasgow University Library concerning the second Lord President of Munster, Sir John Pollard, shows that by June 1569 Pollard had gone to Ireland to take up his post, a fact that has long escaped the attention of Irish historians and has led some authorities to speculate that the presidency remained underdeveloped as a civil institution until the 1570s.

However, more than anything else for the Tudor period, the book that follows contains a huge amount of material concerning the expansion of the English military machine in Ireland before 1603. All across England and Wales, local archive centres contain an abundance of documents outlining the raising and financing of troops for service in Ireland, particularly during the period of the Desmond rebellion (1579–83) and the Nine Years War (1594–1603). The sheer bulk of this material indicates the extent to which securing Ireland against rebellion or foreign invasion (or both) was crucial to the English monarchy. Evidently, the Irish wars had to be won at any cost, and there is no doubt that by the latter days of the reign of Elizabeth I the spectre of Ireland had begun to loom large over the English countryside. Levies of troops for service in Ireland became a major demographic drain on the English population, so much so that every attempt was made to circumvent the queen's orders and 'dodge the draft'. Chester was one of the main ports of embarkation for Ireland and details of how ordinary able-bodied men deserted the ranks can be found among the Mayor of Chester's Military Papers at Chester City Record Office. Though other collections are also very valuable, we anticipate that the Chester Military Papers will soon become one of the main sources for the history of the Elizabethan army in Ireland. Another archive centre worth special mention is Lambeth Palace Library which holds the Bacon Manuscripts, a collection of papers which include a large number of documents dealing with the activities of government spies in Ulster at the start of the Nine Years War – remarkable material by any standard, the sort of papers that usually do not survive.

The suffering and dislocation experienced by Englishmen as a result of the sixteenth century Irish wars are revealed in a number of ways by the documents we unearthed. Among the earliest references we found was an award made by Welsh officials relating to Edward Griffith, a captain in the Irish service who died of dysentry in Dublin in 1541; this item is held in the University of North Wales Library. Of related interest is the number of references we found in local archive centres to maimed and crippled ex-soldiers from the Irish campaigns. A typical example of this can be seen in the parish records of Market Deeping at Lincolnshire Record Office which contain details of money paid to maimed soldiers returning from the wars in Ireland in 1603; such was the scale of the problem, however, that even local authorities in western Scotland like the Ayr Town Council had occasionally to dip into public funds to ease the plight of those English military refugees from Ulster who put ashore within their jurisdiction, often in a desperate state, during the course of the conflict. Both the Mayor of Chester's Letters and the Mayor's Military Papers at Chester City Record Office contain letters of commendation on behalf of crippled veterans returning to England from Ireland in need of charity. It is little wonder that there was an increase of anti-Irish prejudice in England and Wales at this time.

English soldiers, of course, were not the only people reduced to extreme poverty by the Irish wars. Documents concerning the displaced Irish poor abound in British local record offices, a testament to the fact that Irish refugees were a major British problem. All too often these unfortunates were deemed 'undeserving poor' by local authorities in Britain and left exposed to the rigours of contemporary anti-vagrancy legislation. A typical example of what happened to them is outlined in the 1587 Reportory of the London Court of Aldermen kept at the Corporation of London Record Office, when all the 'Irish roagues & vagabonds' then living within the liberties of London were hunted down, captured and sent to Bristol for deportation back to Ireland. Harsh treatment continued to be meted out to Irish vagrants long after the end of the Elizabethan wars; peace did not bring an improvement in attitudes. Only those Irish who held begging licenses (or passports) could escape harsh treatment by the authorities after

1603; often Irish people were found guilty of forging such licenses, which seem to have been in short supply. The Essex Quarter Sessions Rolls at Essex Record Office contain several detailed cases retailing the usual treatment of the vagrant Irish, noting how they were publicly flogged and beaten before being sent home.

As well as enhancing awareness of the wars of the Tudor reconquest, we hope that this book will improve knowledge of the British colonisation in Ireland before 1641. Collections of papers concerning plantation projects and life on plantation estates turned up in many of the archive centres we contacted. On the government side, there is a large collection of official papers dealing with the political state of the Jacobean plantations in Ulster, Munster and Leinster among the Cranfield Papers at Kent Archive Office; this collection is of major importance, filling in many of the gaps that exist in the State Papers of the early seventeenth century. The listing we have given to it below does not do it justice (it was too large for us to examine thoroughly in the time available during our visits to the office). A priority should be made to have it calendared and published, for in addition to the plantations, its contents afford a detailed examination of the entire workings of the Jacobean state in Ireland. Apart from material in the Cranfield Papers, perhaps the most valuable material on the nature of British colonialism that we found were the private estate papers of some of the planters. At Clywd County Record Office in Hawarden there is a seventeenth century survey of the tenancies on Lady Aungier's estate in Sligo and Leitrim. A similar document exists for the Ulster Plantation estate of Burleigh and Orwell in Co. Donegal which gives a schedule of all the tenants on the estate circa 1637; this apparently unique item is kept among the Basil Manuscripts at Buckinghamshire County Record Office in Aylesbury. Information regarding tenant conditions on another plantation estate – that of the earls of Londonderry at Galin-Ridgeway in Queen's County – is available in documents at Bedfordshire Record Office and Nottingham University Library, while the development of the Annesley estates in the Wexford and Ulster plantations can be traced in the Valentia collection at Oxfordshire Archive Office. With all this material now available we hope that the time has finally arrived for a major re-evaluation of the impact of British colonialism in early modern Ireland.

In the final analysis, however, our book is above all a testament to the breadth of Ireland's relations with Britain during the late medieval and early modern period. Obviously, given the current fashionability of 'British history', we hope that the multifaceted nature of Ireland's position in the British state after 1603 can be explored in great detail by historians using the many new documents cited in this book. Something that has been hitherto underappreciated, and which this new British history might redress, is the extent to which Irish men and women comprised an important marginal element of local society in England, Scotland and Wales both before and after the establishment of the British state under James VI and I in 1603. There is more, much more, to the history of the Irish in Britain than the spasmodic appearance of Irish beggars and refugees in British towns and villages. More commonly, the Irish were semi-legitimate outside participants in British society, an accepted (if not always popular) component of everyday life. Many British ports had sizable Irish communities and Irish merchants were often deeply involved in British commercial affairs. Information about Irish merchants abounds for the west of Britain, from Southampton through the Welsh ports to Carlisle and on to Ayr and Dumbarton in Scotland – but Irish traders did not confine themselves to the west. It is striking to see how far east the tentacles of Irish contact stretched into the British interior. Take, for instance, the will of Robert Dale of Dublin, who died in the city of Durham in 1637, having gone there on business, or the evidence, also from 1637, of money owed by Thomas Whyte, another Dubliner, to an English grain merchant from the area near Berwick on Tweed (both of these references come from items in the possession of the Department of Palaeography at the University of Durham). Perhaps future researchers could trace the limits of this economic contact by questioning the extent to which Irish merchants were integrated into the ranks of their English, Scottish and Welsh counterparts: did they join them as trading partners? Did they inter-marry with them? Or did they only participate in British commerce from without, failing to become fully integrated in the larger community because of their peripheral colonial status? The sources exist for such a study. Equally significant, it should also be possible, using some of the documents listed below, to measure the increasing influence of British merchants in Ireland during the early seventeenth century and to determine whether or not the Irish economy was colonialised on their behalf before 1641.

Although it is self-evident that mounting British (i.e. English, Welsh and Scottish) colonisation in Ireland after c1540 increased the level of contact between Irish and British people, it has not generally been noted that this led to more Irish people travelling to Britain. Yet this was entirely predictable. If an Englishman held land in Ireland then his Irish-born estate officials might sometimes follow him back to England. This was the case with Walter Weldon of Kildare, a man whose family had been in Ireland since Anglo-Norman times, and who in 1628 (according to documents in

Bedfordshire Record Office) turned up in Bedford as party to a transaction concerning his employers, the Savages of Cardington, who held the manor of Reban in Co. Kildare. Often, however, Irish people went to Britain to settle there; this was especially true of migrants to London, where a large community of Irish exiles developed before 1640. References to these have been found at the Institute of Heraldic and Genealogical Studies in Kent, the Guildhall Library in London and the University of Southampton Library. Likewise, details of the Irish community in Bristol appear in the archives of Bristol City Record Office.

These are just some of the main areas of inquiry that we feel will benefit from the documents listed in this book. Many other areas could also be mentioned. Clearly, biographical studies of individual politicians, noblemen, rebels, soldiers, planters and officials should profit a great deal from what follows. So too should local studies of the counties and regions of Ireland; indeed, we are pleased to report that that the book includes notice of important new sources for nearly every Irish county (our own studies of Wexford and Kilkenny were greatly enhanced by our discoveries). Aspects of the history of the Reformation and Counter-Reformation, such as details of clerical appointments and the Catholic and Protestant clergy's involvement in politics, should also be boosted by our findings. But it is impossible to draw attention to everything. Ultimately, students will consult this work only for what interests them, and some will find it more useful than others. We wish them luck. All that remains to be said is a few words about how to approach the book.

SOME WARNINGS ABOUT USING THIS BOOK

Readers are warned that despite our best intentions the listings of documents that follow are not definitive. In all likelihood a huge amount of material still remains undiscovered. The clearest indication of this can be seen in the difference between the entries for those archive centres that we visited and those we did not. While we would be quite surprised if many further references materialise at Essex Record Office, where we spent several days, we entirely expect that more references will emerge at those major county record offices that we were unable to visit, such as Lancashire Record Office and Norfolk Record Office. Perhaps the best indication of the limits of our knowledge is that, although the book contains entries for 111 archive centres, we only visited 55 of them. Furthermore, we would not claim to have compiled a definitive listing of documents even for those repositories we did manage to visit. Too often we found that collections dating back to sixteenth and seventeenth centuries were poorly catalogued –

as a result, our findings have a hit and miss quality concerning them. Add to this the fact that each year more and more material is catalogued and indexed, and that all the major record offices are constantly in receipt of new materials, and it is clear that this book is in danger of going out of date almost as soon as it is published. We strongly urge that future researchers using this book contact the relevant British archive centres themselves to check our findings. Ideally we *will* soon be out of date and new documents unknown to us will come to light. (We intend to prepare a second edition of the book in fifteen or twenty years time to draw attention to any new discoveries; with this in mind, we would greatly appreciate it if future researchers could keep us informed about new materials that come to light).

It should not be assumed that all the material listed below is easily accessible. Some collections are only available on limited access. Although most of the Lords Bray of Stamford Hall Manuscripts at Leicestershire Record Office are readily available to readers one section of the collection is not, i.e. those papers dealing with the trial on charges of rape and sodomy of the second earl of Castlehaven in 1631, which can only be consulted with the permission of the owners of the collection, the Bray family. At Kent Archives Office the permission of Viscount L'Isle & Dudley is required before readers can consult the Sidney papers in the De L'Isle & Dudley collection. Research can be hindered in other ways too. Students wishing to examine the Middleton Papers at Surrey Record Office in Guildford have to order material several days in advance, as the documents have to be transported to the record office from a warehouse situated elsewhere in the county. A similar situation pertains regarding the papers of the O'Briens of Thomond and Orrery at Petworth House – these can be consulted at West Sussex Record Office in Chichester provided documents are ordered in advance, although available catalogues are not very good, so that it is difficult to know exactly which sections of the collection one should ask to see. Problems of inaccessibility of a quite different kind exist in Scotland, where some of the outlying local archive offices are only opened on request; otherwise they remain shut, with no permanent staff to sort or catalogue their holdings.

Finally, it is quite likely that professional archivists who consult this book will be horrified by the methodological inconsistencies we have shown in compiling our listings, as we veer from one standard to another with random abandon, giving brief catalogue-style summaries of some documents, calendar-style descriptions of others, even verbatim transcripts in places. We make no apology for this. From the very beginning we decided we would be deliberately inconsistent. We saw little point in following archival procedures that might sacrifice the amount of historical information available in the book in order to obey principles of archival procedure that only confuse us. All we ask is that archivists show us a little tolerance. We are historians, not archivists, and our book is meant for students of Irish history who have long suffered from a shortage of available information. The one rule we have tried to follow consistently is in trying to give more detailed entries for single documents than for collections, and this on the grounds that students are less likely to travel across Britain to check a single stray reference than to consult a large number of documents.

CONVENTIONS

Archive centres are grouped by country and listed alphabetically by county. It should be noted that the structure of the book is defined by the boundaries of the counties and regions of Britain as they stood at the time the text was completed and sent to press. It is quite possible, given the frequent modification to regional administrative borders in Britain since 1974, that some of the counties and districts mentioned below will disappear in future years, either merged with another district or abolished. Clearly, we cannot anticipate such changes. Readers should check these details for themselves by cross-referencing this book with the most recent edition of Foster and Sheppard's *British Archives*.

Telephone and fax numbers are given for all the archive centres included in the book. The numbers given are internal British numbers. To phone from abroad one must use the relevant international access code, and remember to drop the 0 on the local code.

Copyright for the material listed in this book lies either with the owner of the collection to which it belongs or else with the institution in which it is deposited.

Modern dating (year beginning 1 January) is used throughout. Single or 'stray' references are listed first in the entries for each archive centre, followed by collections. For the purposes of our survey we defined collections as any group of documents that held more than one Irish-related reference. Archive centres marked with an asterisk (*) represent centres which were visited by the authors.

BRIAN C. DONOVAN, TRINITY COLLEGE, DUBLIN
DAVID EDWARDS, UNIVERSITY COLLEGE, CORK
SEPTEMBER, 1997

ENGLAND

AVON : Avon County Library *
Central Library, College Green, Bristol BS1 5TL
Tel: (0117) 929 9147

COLLECTIONS

MSS of the Society of Merchant Venturers of Bristol (microfilm no. 25306)

This collection remains in the private keeping of the Society. The documents available on microfilm include the Book of Trade for 1598–1693, which contains two early seventeenth century references to Ireland (pp63–4 and 139), both of which have been published by the Bristol Record Society in Patrick McGrath (ed.), *Records relating to the Society of Merchant Venturers of the City of Bristol in the seventeenth century* (B.R.S., xvii, 1952).[6]

AVON : Bristol City Record Office *
'B' Bond Warehouse, Smeaton Road, Bristol BS1 6XN
Tel: (0117) 922 5692
Fax: (0117) 922 4236

LOOSE ITEMS

1509   (17 Apr.) Photograph of fol. 54ᵛ of the *Liber Primus Kilkenniensis* concerning an enrolment in the Bristol City records of a charter of Henry VIII by which freemen of Kilkenny were also made free of Bristol. (08804)[7]

1558   (21 Aug.) The contents of a boat 'laden for Carlyngford', valued at £14 10s., consisting of salt, fish and iron. (This appears in a merchant's account, DC/A/6/3)

1579   (24 Nov.) Letter from the Privy Council ordering payment to the Mayor of Bristol for feeding and clothing soldiers sent to Ireland. (8029/5)[8]

1598   (9 Ju.[9]) Account of money laid out by John Webb, Mayor of Bristol, in equipping and transporting 700 troops to serve in Ireland. (16080/3)

1601   (31 Aug.) Acknowledgement by Captain Nicholas Browne of the payment by John Hopkins, Mayor of Bristol, of the expenses of 195 men going to Ireland, with details of same. (8029/6)

1636   (Nov.) 'An account of tabaccos out of the Eagle of Bristol and the Fortune of Wexford'. (Southwell MSS 12964/13)

---

[6] The Society of Merchant Venturers can be contacted at Merchants' Hall, The Promenade, Bristol BS8 3NH. There is a published guide to their holdings by Elizabeth Ralph, *Guide to the Archives of the Society of Merchant Venturers of Bristol* (Bristol, c1988).

[7] See Charles McNeill (ed.), *Liber Primus Kilkenniensis* (Dublin, 1931), p118.

[8] There is a note of the warrant for payment in *A.P.C.*, 1578–80 (London, 1895), p319.

[9] Date given as 'Ju' in document.

1

COLLECTIONS

Bristol City Archives (various refs.)

Most of the principal civic records of the Tudor and early Stuart period are available in print. Various references to Bristol's close economic ties with Ireland (especially with Waterford) and to provisions for the Irish army can be found in the following publications of the Bristol Record Society: Elizabeth Ralph (ed.), *The Great White Book of Bristol* (B.R.S., xxxii, 1979); Maureen Stanford (ed.), *The Ordinances of Bristol, 1506–1598* (B.R.S., xli, 1990) (ref. 04272–4); Lucy Toulmin Smith (ed.), *The Maire of Bristowe is Kalender* (Camden Soc., 1872) (ref. 04720i), and Francis Bickley (ed.), *The Little Red Book of Bristol* (Bristol, 1900) (ref. 04718). The City Record Office also holds many wills proved in the diocese. These have received a comprehensive listing for the Tudor period in S. Lang & M. McGregor (eds.), *Tudor Wills Proved in Bristol, 1546–1603* (B.R.S., xliv, 1993). Other series have received only partial listings in print, as follows:

Apprentice Books (ref. 04352/1–6)

The Record Office holds extensive apprenticeship registers for the period 1532–1658. The documentation up to 1565 has appeared in Denzil Hollis (ed.), *Calendar of the Bristol Apprentice Book*, Pt. I, 1532–42 (B.R.S., xiv, 1949); Elizabeth Ralph & Nora M. Hardwick (eds.), *Ibid*, Pt. II, 1542–52 (B.R.S., xxxiii, 1980), and Elizabeth Ralph (ed.), *Ibid*, Pt. III, 1552–65 (B.R.S., xliii, 1992). Typescripts are available on the Record Office open shelves for the period 1565–78, and on call for 1600–30 (ref. 2102). There are a great many references throughout to Irish apprentices (who came mainly from the south).

Great Audit Books & City Chamberlain's Accounts (ref. 04026/1–155)

These financial records include receipts from the Crown of moneys due for the charges incurred by the corporation when billeting and transporting Irish troops. D.M. Livock (ed.), *City Chamberlain's Accounts of the sixteenth and seventeenth centuries* (B.R.S., xxiv, 1966), contains two full accounts for 1556–7 and 1628 (refs. 04026/6 & 04026/19), as well as extracts from 'The State Book of the Mayor and Cominalty' (ref. 04108) and 'The Book of the Citties Accomptes' (ref. 04118) concerning ships patrolling the Irish coast and Sir Piers Crosby's Irish regiment in 1628. However, the entire series of City Chamberlain's Accounts or Great Audit Books cover the period from 1532–1785, and without doubt contains further material concerning Ireland which has not been published.[10]

Proceedings of the Common Council (ref. 04264/1–25)

This series begins in 1598, and includes mention of the activities of Irish army victuallers, and payments by the corporation for the passage of vagrants back to Ireland. One Irish reference in this collection, concerning the activities in 1584 of John Bland, the Queen's Surveyor of the victuals (ref. 04264 (1) 3), has been published in Jean Vanes (ed.), *Documents illustrating the overseas trade of Bristol in the sixteenth century* (B.R.S., xxxi, 1979), p48. The existence of this document amongst these records indicates that there are at least a few stray references to Ireland prior to 1598.

Smyth of Ashton Court MSS (ref. 32835 & 36074)

The sections of this collection which contain material relating to early modern Ireland have been published by the Bristol Record Society. Jean Vanes (ed.), *The Ledger of John Smyth, 1538–1550* (B.R.S., xxviii, 1974), has references to trade with Waterford and other Irish towns (ref. 32835 AC/B63). Similarly, J.H. Bettey

---

[10] There is also a Little Audit for 1628 (04048) which may contain Irish material.

(ed.), *Calendar of the correspondence of the Smyth family of Ashton Court, 1548–1642* (B.R.S., xxxv, 1982), includes several letters regarding the movement of Irish soldiers in 1582 and some early seventeenth century letters concerning the earls of Thomond and Castlehaven (ref. 32835 AC/C13/4–8; 36074/105, 110–11, 114, 125 and 139a).

BEDFORDSHIRE : County Record Office *
County Hall, Cauldwell Street, Bedford MK42 9AP
Tel: (01234) 228 833/363 222 ext. 2833
Fax: (01234) 228 619

LOOSE ITEMS

1617   (29 May) Family settlement (for 75 years) between Sir Thomas Rotherham of Luton, councillor of state in Ireland, and Sir James Evington, reciting a bond of statute staple *circa* 1615–16 concerning the marriage portion of Sir Thomas's daughter, Elizabeth Rotherham [badly damaged]. (D.D.DW 121)[11]

1633   (18 Dec.) Conveyance by Robert, 2nd Earl of Londonderry, of two messuages in Ballinekill in the manor of Galen Ridgeway, Queen's County, to Seafoule Gibson, gent., for a consideration of £300. With a note of consent by ten named persons. (D.D.FN 871)

COLLECTIONS

Whitbread Papers (ref. W)

1600   (8 Dec.) Pardon granted under royal letters patent to Sir Arthur Savage for all offences committed by him in England or Ireland before 29 Nov. 1600; enrolled on the patent roll of the Irish Chancery. (W90)

1616   (12 June) Indenture endorsed 'A deed of mortgage ... to save harmless Sir Arthur Savage', whereby Savage, one of the King's Privy Council in Ireland, mortgaged the manor of Hill Hall in Beds. to William Plomer, and Plomer agreed to pay money on Savage's behalf to Lady Dorothy Wharton and Barrentine Mollins. (W2362)

1616   (27 Nov.) A lease for 21 years of lands at Scattywood in Beds. by Walter Dayrell of Gray's Inn and Richard Miller of London, goldsmith, to George Blundell of Cardington in Beds., with a proviso that Blundell must pay an annual rent of £21 to the use of Sir Arthur Savage, one of H.M. Privy Council in Ireland. (W325)

1619   (21 June) Articles of agreement concerning a post-nuptial settlement (in the sum of £2,000) between Sir Arthur Savage and Sir Thomas Snagge, re the marriage of Thomas Savage, son and heir of Sir Arthur, to Douglas Snagge, daughter of Sir Thomas. Thomas Savage is to receive four annuities, each for £300, one of which is to come from the castle and manor of Reban, Co. Kildare. (W95)

1625   (22 March) Statement concerning legacies paid to William Smythes, gent., one of the sons of George Smythes, late alderman of London; includes a note that William has received the sum of £280 12s 0d from Sir Arthur Savage in Ireland. (W230)

---

[11] According to the Record Office catalogue, this item is unfit for production.

1625   (31 May) A receipt by the Clerk of the Hanaper for the sum of £60 paid by Sir Arthur Savage for the alienation of Reban manor, Co. Kildare. (W 3261)

1628   (7 July) Deed to create an entail whereby Sir Arthur Savage of Cardington and Dame Sarah his wife grant the pasture grounds and arable lands of Scattywood in Beds. to their son and heir Sir Thomas Savage and Walter Weldon of Kildare, esq. (W331)

1628   (16 Aug.) Appointment of attorney by Sir Arthur Savage nominating Richard Goodwin of Bedford, gent., to receive the property recited in W331 above on behalf of Sir Thomas Savage and Walter Weldon of Kildare in Ireland. (W333)

1629   (10 Feb.) Letters patent given at Dublin granting license to Sir Arthur Savage to travel and transport his necessary goods from Ireland to England and there remain 'until his business shall be concluded, or until we notify our will and pleasure to the contrary'. (W97)

1640   (18 Jan.) Indenture of bargain and sale between Anthony Abdy of London, alderman, and Sir Thomas Carey of Meath in Ireland[12], whereby in consideration of the sum of £1,401 8s 8d paid by Carey to Robert Bateman, Treasurer of the City of London, Abdy agrees to sell the Park Grange estate in Beds. to Carey, to hold in fee farm of the Crown, at a rent of £41 4s 8d. (W2301)

1640   (20 Jan.) Lease by William Wakefield to Sir Thomas Carey of Meath in Ireland of property in Beds. for 75 years, which mentions *inter alia* that William's mother Mary Wakefield had given Carey a loan of £800. (W2302)

1641   (5 April) Copy of the last will and testament of Sir Thomas Savage of Covent Garden, including a bequest to his two younger children, William and Douglas, specifying that they should receive £500 a piece from his son and heir Francis, the money to be raised from his Irish estate. (W274)

BERKSHIRE : County Record Office *
Shire Hall, Shinfield Park, Reading, Berkshire RG2 9XD
Tel: (01734) 233 182
Fax: (01734) 233 203

COLLECTIONS

Downshire Estate Collection (ref. D/ED)[13]

The extensive Irish estate records of the Marquess of Downshire are presently housed in the Public Record Office of Northern Ireland (P.R.O.N.I. ref. D.671). However, the records concerning their English estates were deposited with the Berkshire County Record Office, and include a few items of Irish interest, viz

---

[12] Carey had earlier been one of the Masters of Chancery in Ireland; see *C.S.P.I.*, 1625-32, p274.

[13] The Trumbell papers, which once formed part of this extensive collection, but are now in the British Library, are currently in the process of being listed and published by the H.M.C. (*Downshire Mss.*, 5 vols (1936–88)). So far volumes 2–5 of this series have included the manuscripts of William Trumbell the elder from 1605 to 1616. A further volume, vol. 6, is forthcoming and will complete the Commission's calendar of William Trumbell's papers. It includes numerous documents concerning Ireland, general Irish affairs and Irish troops in Flanders and the Netherlands.

1585	(15 May) Letters patent granting to Ever Mac Rorye of Kilwarlyn, chief captain of his nation, various lands in the lordship of Kilwarlyn (named), to hold for ever by knight's service. Recites his surrender of same. (D/ED T300)[14]
1608	(26 May) Letters patent of James I, granting to Sir George Colley 93 acres of land in Ardkill and Collinston, and the rectories of Carbury and Ballimorehir, Cos. Kildare and Westmeath. (D/ED T301)
1620	Letters patent creating Sir Francis Blundell a baronet. (D/ED F27)[15]
1620	(1 Oct.) Conveyance by Sir William Alexander, one of the Masters of Requests, to Walter Alexander, servant to the prince, and James Alexander of Stirling, Scotland. Stating that the King granted to Sir William 1,000 acres of land in Co. Longford, parcel of the late plantation. Now Sir William, in consideration of £555 (stg) sells same to Walter and James Alexander. (D/ED T302)
1626	(27 Nov.) Bargain and sale of a third part of the ship *The Eagle of Bangor* (120 tons) from Nymian Barkley of Bangor, Co. Down, merchant, and Sir Archibald Atkinson, to Sir William Alexander. In consideration of which Alexander is to buy ten guns, various pieces of ordnance, stocks, carriages and furniture for *The Eagle* (presently at Dover). Once this has been completed Alexander will own a third of the ship (the other two thirds being owned by Barkley and Atkinson). (D/ED F33)
1628	(7 July) Bond of Malcolm, Archbishop of Cashel, to Sir William Alexander, in £80 (stg). Reciting a deed dated 20 February 1617 by which Sir James Cunningham conveyed two water mills, portlage and other customs in Cargan, Co. Donegal, to Sir William Alexander for £400. Also reciting the King's letter to the Lord Deputy and Commissioners for the Plantation dated 9 May 1627, to settle Alexander and Sir Archibald Atkinson in possession of above. Now Alexander, in his interest and the interest of Dame Katherine Cunningham (widow of Sir James) and George Cunningham, deposits the deed of conveyance of 1617 in the hands of Malcolm, to be available at all times and to be shown to the Lord Deputy and Commissioners. Bond for performance of same. (D/ED F34)
1637	(26 May) License of alienation granted to Arthur Hill to alienate the lands he purchased from the Earl of Antrim and Edmund MacShane, being a moiety of the manor of Clanagheskie *alias* Fortescue (Co. Antrim). (D/ED T303)

Lenthall Papers (ref. D/ELl)

c1598	(n.d.) Accounts entitled 'The Queens Majesties allowance for 100 men sent to the realm of Ireland', from Worcester. Detailing costs of £44 for coats, entertainment on the march to Chester, and other expenses. (D/ELl O5/4)
1599	(21 March) Copy of the Queen's letter to the Earl of Nottingham, Lord Lieutenant of Surrey, for the levying of £90 for the furnishing of 30 men into Ireland. (D/ELl O1)

---

[14] A full version of Ever MacRory's surrender and regrant of 1585 is in *Cal. Fiants Ire.*, Eliz.I, nos. 4649–50.

[15] This item has been withdrawn to the British Library.

1599   (22 March) Copy of Privy Council's directive to the Earl of Nottingham 'for the filling up and supplying of certain decayde bands' in Ireland. (D/EL1 O1)

1599   (23 March) Copy of the Earl of Nottingham's orders to the deputy lieutenants of Surrey 'for the spedy levyinge of a certaine nomber of men for the fillinge uppe of certayne decayde bands' in Ireland. (D/EL1 O1)

1599   (17 May) Copy of the Privy Council's letter to the Earl of Nottingham, for the raising of men in Surrey towards 'the suppressing of the great insolence of the Rebells in Ireland'. (D/EL1 O1)

BERKSHIRE : Eton College Collections
College Library, Eton College, Windsor, Berkshire SL4 6DB
Tel: (01753) 671 221
Fax: (01753) 671 244

COLLECTIONS

Con O'Neill's school bills (ref. Mss. 272b–c)

1616–17   (25 Dec. 1616–25 March 1617) The school bills and expenses of Con O'Neill at Eton, from Christmas 1616 to the feast of the Annunciation 1617.

1617   (25 March–24 June) The same, from the feast of the Annunciation to Midsummer 1617, signed by Fulke Greville on 4 August.[16]

1617–18   (25 Dec. 1617–25 March 1618) The same, from Christmas 1617 to the feast of the Annunciation 1618.[17]

1618   (24 June–25 Sept.) The same, from Midsummer to Michaelmas 1618.

BUCKINGHAMSHIRE : County Record Office *
County Hall, Aylesbury, Bucks HP20 1UA
Tel: (01296) 382587

LOOSE ITEMS

1627   (January) Copy of letters patent, granting to George Villiers, Duke of Buckingham, lands in Borris, Dorrivargan and Ballyvorgill, Queen's Co., and elsewhere, to hold for ever. (D104/53)

COLLECTIONS

Basil MSS (ref. D/X 776)

1637   (23 Nov.) Articles of agreement between Robert Harrington of Leytonstone, Essex, and Martin Basil of Lincoln's Inn, Middlesex,

---

[16] This item first appeared in print in Francis J. Bigger, 'Young Con O'Neale's School Bill', *Ulster Journal of Archaeology*, 2nd series, iii (1897), pp140–3, and was re-published with various minor corrections in T.W. Moody (ed.), 'The School-bills of Con O'Neill at Eton, 1615–27', *Irish Historical Studies*, ii (1940–1), pp189–204.

[17] *Ibid*, p198. There is a photograph of this item in the Ulster Museum, Belfast.

whereby Harrington will sell to Basil the manors of Burleigh and Orwell in Co. Donegal, in consideration of £2,050 (stg) paid, and £3,800 to be paid. It is a complex and detailed document, with eight points of agreement. Appended is a schedule of all the tenants and leases presently in force on the estate (a total of 53 tenants are named). (D/X 776/2)

1638 (26 April) Bond of observance of covenants, between Martin Basil and Elizabeth Basil, and Patrick Acheson of the Strand, Middlesex, regarding payment on the above agreement. (D/X 776/3)

Verney of Claydon House MSS (ref. M11)

Parts of this collection contain the correspondence of Sir Edmund Verney with his Irish acquaintances between 1626 and 1640, as well as letters from James Dillon, later Earl of Roscommon, to his friend, Sir Ralph Verney. These papers are still in private hands and access to the original letters is not permitted, but microfilm copies exist in Bucks. R.O. (ref. M11/1–4) and in the British Library. There is an analysis of the collection in H.M.C., *7th Report* (London, 1879), and it also forms the basis of F.P. & M.M. Verney, *The Verney Memoirs* (2 vols., London 1892), chapters 9 and 10 of which deal extensively with the Irish material.

CAMBRIDGESHIRE : County Record Office, Cambridge *
Shire Hall, Castle Hill, Cambridge CB3 0AP
Tel: (01223) 317 281
Fax: (01223) 317 201

LOOSE ITEMS

1506–7 Computus roll of the bailiff of Thomas, 7th Earl of Ormond, Michaelmas 22 Henry VII – Michaelmas 23 Henry VII, for the Earl's manors of Zouches, Colvilles, Maneys and Shardelowes in England. (R 52/15/1)

CAMBRIDGESHIRE : County Record Office, Huntingdon *
Grammer School Walk, Huntingdon PE18 6LF
Tel: (01480) 425 842
Fax: (01480) 459 563

COLLECTIONS

Manchester of Kimbolton Castle Collection (ref. DDM)

This collection has been widely dispersed since the H.M.C. compiled a report on it late in the nineteenth century (*8th Report*, App. II). Most of the Irish material mentioned therein (nos. 172–202a) was bought by the National Library of Ireland.[18] However, many other Irish administrative papers (that had been overlooked by the H.M.C. commissioners) remained with the Manchester family until well into the present century, when they deposited the rest of their muniments with the Huntingdon Record Office. This material is listed below, and

---

[18] These records are now housed at N.L.I. Mss. 8,013–8,014, and include the item published by R.J. Hunter, 'Catholicism in Meath, c.1622', *Collectanea Hibernica*, xiv (1971), pp7–12. For an introduction to the location of other parts of the Manchester collection see H.M.C., *Guide to the Location of Collections*, p42.

it is worth mentioning that much of it was microfilmed for Queen's University, Belfast between 1954 and 1955, and photocopied for the P.R.O.N.I. in 1971. It is likely that other Irish manuscripts are still lurking somewhere among the less well catalogued boxes of estate records, particularly those concerning the Bernard family, though the authors were unable to locate them when they visited the Record Office.[19]

1614	Note signed by James Ware giving the amount of the King's arrears of revenues in Ireland. (DDM 70/1)
1617	Declaration of the King's annual revenues from Ireland. (DDM 70/2)
1618	Names of persons to whom annuities, pensions and perpetuities (figures given) were granted from Irish revenues, which often gives the date of the grant and records whether the annuity has been assigned [12pp]. (DDM 70/3)
1618	The establishment of the Irish army [7pp]. (DDM 70/4)
1618	Schedule of the 4th Plantation of Wexford with names of undertakers and natives, acreages and Crown rents [5pp]. (DDM 70/5)
1618	Tables of the total of the establishment of the war's payments from April 1st. (DDM 70/6)
1620	Articles relative to the 6th Plantation – Leitrim, Queen's County, Westmeath and part of King's County [15pp]. (DDM 70/7)
1620–1	Abstract of the King's Irish estate – patents, rents in Connaught, Ulster, Donegal, Monaghan, Cavan, Mayo. (DDM 70/8)
1620	A comparison in parallel columns of the composition of Connaught between the composition books and the survey of Sir Charles Coote. (DDM 70/9)
1620	Articles and conditions of the 5th plantation in Longford and Ely O'Carroll [8pp]. (DDM 70/10)
1620	'A Certificate of Monopolies and Greivances' [13pp]. (DDM 70/11)
c1620	Plan of Co. Armagh showing estates and their owners and naming the undertakers and servitors. The plan is coloured with pictures of castles, houses and forts. (DDM 70/52)
1621	Return of the King's income from Ireland (Leinster, Munster, Connaught, Belfast). Covering years 1615–21, signed W. Croxton. (DDM 70/12)
1621	Statement of the composition of Co. Clare. (DDM 70/13)
1621	Brief declaration of the profits of the Court of Wards from 1617–21. (DDM 70/14)
1621	'Answers to the Apostles'. Report on how far recent orders by the King have been carried out [46pp]. (DDM 70/16)
1621	Schedule of the King's Irish revenue. (DDM 70/17)
1621	Charges, payments and arrears of the Court of Wards, 1617–21. (DDM 70/18)
1621	Note of moneys paid for writs of covenant, 1615–21. (DDM 70/18a)

[19] In 1998 or 1999, the I.M.C. plans to publish Victor Treadwell's edition of the papers of the 1622 Commission of Inquiry.

1621–2   (25 March 1621–25 March 1622) A table of exports from Ireland, listed by port and commodity, and giving comparative examples from 1615–6 [2pp]. (DDM 70/30)

1622   (Easter) Particulars of moneys owed to the King's pensioners and others, payable out of the revenues of Ireland [6pp]. (DDM 70/27)

1622   (19 July) 'An abstract of such monies as have been paid into the hannaper to his Majesties use for fines upon writs of covenent in the years 1615–21', by Francis Edgeworth. (DDM 70/57)

1622   (4 July) A note of yearly charges on the former farmers of the King's customs of Ireland (upkeep of customs, establishment in posts, etc.), listed by port. (DDM 70/26)

1622   (28 July) A certificate by G. Rawson on 'Sheriffs that have not yet accounted'. (DDM 70/31)

1622   Certificate by Charles Cooke of the quarters found by the indentures of composition upon the first establishment in the several counties of the province of Connaught, besides the counties of Clare and Leitrim. (DDM 70/15)

1622   Declaration of the state of His Majesty's debts in Ireland. (DDM 70/19)

1622   Statement of the revenue derived from Imposts and Tonnage in Ireland, 1615–22. (DDM 70/20)

1622   An establishment order [3pp]. (DDM 70/21)

1622   Report of the commission set up to enquire into the state of the King's Irish revenue, dealing with the discovery of abuses and offering suggestions for remedy [16pp]. (DDM 70/22)

1622   The charge of the army from July 1616 to Sept. 1622 [3 sheets]. (DDM 70/23)

1622   Report by Mr. John Pitt, collector and farmer, on the reasons why the customs do not improve but decline [3pp]. (DDM 70/24)

1622   Report on the same subject [2pp]. (DDM 70/24a)

1622   An audited book of the payments made to the officers (named) in the Government of Ireland (Court of Exchequer, etc.) [10pp]. (DDM 70/25)

1622   Instructions given by the King to the Irish commissioners. (DDM 70/28)

1622   Table of the King's Hanaper Account for 1615–21 [2pp]. (DDM 70/29)

1622   The King's profits from 1615–21, from fines of patents, originals and Court of Wards. (DDM 70/32)

1622   A table showing the revenue from imports on wines, especially Spanish wines, 1615–22. (DDM 70/33)

1622   A statement of the King's customs in Ireland, 1615–22 [3pp]. (DDM 70/34)

1622   A list of the tenants of the Earl of Abercorn now under the guardianship of the Countess of Abercorn [3pp]. (DDM 70/35)

1622	Articles for the Plantation of Ulster. Also a survey of the present state of the plantation in the counties of Cavan and Fermanagh [9pp]. (DDM 70/36)
1622	Estimate of the King's debts in Ireland. (DDM 70/36a)
1622	Articles and instructions for undertakers and servitors relative to the 3rd Ulster plantation [4 sheets]. (DDM 70/36b)
c1622	Account of the 5th plantation of King's County and Queen's County [24pp]. (DDM 70/46)
c1622	Report of a commission set up to examine into the internal hindrances to Irish trade, with a table of customs illegally exacted by the officers of the ports of Dublin and Wexford [8pp]. (DDM 70/51)
c1622[20]	A list of the names of the Irish customs officers. (DDM 70/44)
c1622	The humble petition of Robert Goodwin, gent., to the Irish commissioners (concerned with Ulster customs). (DDM 70/45)
c1622	Report by a commission set up to enquire into the state of the Irish army [8pp]. (DDM 70/47)
c1622	Complaints of the natives of the 5th and 6th plantations in Longford, Leitrim, Ely O'Carroll and MacCoughlin's territories in Queen's County and Westmeath. (DDM 70/49)
c1622	Petition of the nobility and gentry of Ireland concerning plantations [4pp]. (DDM 70/50)
c1622	A remonstrance by quartermasters to the Irish commissioners for providing arms to be bought in Amsterdam for foot and horse troops. Table given of rates in Dutch, English and Irish currency. (DDM 70/53)
c1622	Indenture of all the land (with names of tenants) belonging to the portion of Francis Sachowell *alias* Sargowell [Sacheverell]. (DDM 70/54)
c1622	A resume of a case of wardship – Nicholas Wynn. (DDM 70/55)
c1622	A memorandum of sums owed by recusants and not recoverable. (DDM 70/56)
1623	A proclamation for the banishment of Jesuits and priests, by the Lord Deputy and Council. (DDM 70/37)
1623	Names and entertainments of all the officers of justice and others in the Irish courts and in the customs administration, etc. [7pp]. (DDM 70/38)
1623	Financial memorandum for 1623. (DDM 70/39)
1623	A schedule giving the establishment payments for Munster and Connaught (Presidents, pensioners, officers, etc.) [3pp]. (DDM 70/40)
1623	An army establishment schedule. (DDM 70/41)
1623	A brief tendering of the King's debts in Ireland, how they may be discharged; computed to March 31st 1623, as it was sent out of England. (DDM 70/42)

---

[20] Though the following have no date, it can reasonably be assumed that they relate to the period of the 1622 Commission.

c1623 Report of the commissioners on the King's revenue in Ireland [23 sheets]. (DDM 70/48)

1624 Appointment of commissioners to examine the state of Ireland with a view to the removal of grievances, the encouragement of trade, etc. [4pp]. (DDM 70/43)

c1624 Enquiry into the state of the King's Irish revenues [3pp]. (DDM 70/43a)

c1624 On the same subject – supplementary to above [2pp]. (DDM 70/43b)

1639 (7 Aug.) An inventory of the goods and chattels of which Henry, late Earl of Thomond, was possessed at the time of his death; taken and appraised by Sir Richard Southwell, Sir Hardress Waller, John Hunt and Adam Cusacke. Compiled in the form of a parchment roll, it lists all of the Earl's plate and goods room by room in the house, his property in the stable and park at Bunratty and on the island of Innishmore, as well as his stock and jewels. The total value of the Earl's moveable goods is given as £3,292 9s 7d. (DDM 7/23)

1641 Notes and documents arising from the trial of Thomas Wentworth, Earl of Strafford and Lord Lieutenant of Ireland. (DDM 28/2)

CAMBRIDGE UNIVERSITY : Cambridge University Library *
West Road, Cambridge CB3 9DR
Tel: (01223) 333 000/333 143
Fax: (01223) 333 160

Most of the Irish documents held by the Library have been listed in M.R. James, *Catalogue of the (Western) Manuscripts preserved in the Library of the University of Cambridge* (Cambridge, 1856–67), which was reprinted in 1980. Although much of this material is quite well known, occasionally James's catalogue listings are partial or misleading, and an effort has been made to fill out some of his entries and identify those items which have been microfilmed for the National Library of Ireland, as follows:

PREVIOUSLY LISTED MATERIAL

LOOSE ITEMS

1536–1603 Two volumes entitled 'Collection of letters and papers relating to the rebellion in Elizabeth's reign', nearly all of which covers the period 1590–1603. However, it also includes a letter dated 21 May 1536 from Francis Herbert to Thomas Cromwell, sent from Dublin, requesting a grant of monastic land. (Ms. Kk. I. 15)[21]

c1541–7 A treatise on the coins of England and Ireland, etc., with drawings of them, presented to Henry VIII by Nicholas Tyery. (Ms. Ff. II. 22)[22]

1564 (17 Sept.) Letter from Sir Nicholas Throckmorton to Sir Nicholas Strange, mentioning *inter alia* the state of Ireland. (Ms. Dd. III. 64)

---

[21] N.L.I. microfilm n.5278. p.5387.

[22] In his catalogue, James mistakenly claimed that this was addressed to Edward VI. The manuscript was published by G.O. White Cooper & F.J.H. Jenkinson (eds.), 'Nicholas Tyrry's proposal to King Henry VIII for an Irish coinage', *Cambridge Antiquarian Society*, Octavo publications, no. xxii (1886).

1568–9   The memoranda book of John Vowell *alias* Hooker (Ms. Mm. I. 32), best known for the diary of the first session of the Irish Parliament held at Dublin between 17 Jan. and 23 Feb. 1569, which has been published.[23] In addition to this, Hooker's book also contains the following material:

fol. 61r   Note concerning the request of Mr. Gosse [Gorst?] of Carlow for a freehold estate in Idrone, mentioning a deed dated 1376. n.d. [c1569].

ff 62r–7v   Journal of Hooker's dealings in Ireland on behalf of Sir Peter Carew, 20 April 1568 – March 1569.

ff 68r–9v   Account of receipts and payments by Hooker while in Ireland, 21 Dec. 1568 – 26 March 1569.

1569   (28 April) A volume of letters belonging to John Parkhurst, Elizabethan Bishop of Norwich, which includes a letter addressed to Parkhurst by the Lord Deputy of Ireland, Sir Henry Sidney, concerning the virtues of the future Bishop of Cork and Cloyne, Richard Dixon. (Ms. Ee. II. 34)[24]

1585–1644   A large bound volume entitled 'Ms. letters from the beginning of the Irish rebellion, 23rd Oct., 1641', which contains copies made late in the seventeenth century 'from the originals at the Duke of Ormond's charge' of approximately 247 letters dated between 25 Oct. 1641 and 8 Aug. 1644 [ff 1–179]. In addition, at the back of the volume there are copies of miscellaneous Irish state papers, 1585–1627, including two letters addressed to Lord Deputy Chichester [ff 214–37]. (Add. Ms. 4246)[25]

c1585   Articles concerning the offers by Elizabeth I for the disposal of her lands in Munster, and a 'platt of her Majesties offer touching the peopling of Munster in Ireland'. (Ms. Ee. II. 12)

1593–8   A volume of original letters, for the most part between Sir William Cecil, Lord Burghley, and his son Sir Robert Cecil, some of which relate to Irish affairs. (Ms. Ee. III. 56)

1596   'A view of the present state of Ireland discoursed by way of a dialogue between Eudoxus and Irenius', by Edmund Spenser. (Ms. Dd. X. 60)

1599–1633   Treatises in Irish on medicine and botany, and c20 poems addressed to the chief of the O'Reillys, written by 'T.R.'. (Add. Ms. 3082)[26]

16th cen.   Two books of the history of Ireland, compiled by Edmund Campion. (Ms. Kk. I. 3)

1616   (c3 May) 'A briefe collection of the state of the 7th proportion, being the Ironmongers and others for the escheated lands in Ulster, and how farr and in what manner the said companies have held their proceedings.' Deals with the financial involvement of the London livery companies in Co. Londonderry. The last receipt of money is dated 3 May 1616. (Add. Ms. 335)

---

[23] C.L. Falkiner, 'The Parliament of Ireland under the Tudor sovereigns: Supplementary Paper', *Proc. R.I.A*, xxv, C (1904–5), pp563–6.

[24] This letter has been published in R.A. Houlbrooke (ed.), *The Letter Book of John Parkhurst, 1571–5* (Norfolk Record Soc., xliii, 1975), p95.

[25] The volume was purchased from Lord Chandos in 1747 by H. St. John, through whom it passed to Henry Bradshaw sometime before 1886, when it was acquired by Cambridge University Library. It is available for consultation in the National Library of Ireland as N.L.I., microfilm n.5327, p.5436.

[26] See *Eriu* (1906), p125.

c1620   Rentals for the town of Coleraine and the manors of Killreagh, Killowen, Macosquin, Aghure, Lisneycourt and Magherafelt in the province of Ulster. (Ms. Mm. III. 3)[27]

1626   Copy of an account of oral evidence taken in 1626 concerning the rents which had been due to O'Donnell from his territories by ancient custom. (Add. Ms. 2766 (20), item 7)[28]

1627   The judgement of the archbishops and bishops of Ireland, concerning the toleration of the popish religion. (Ms. Gg. IV. 13)

1627   The effect of the speech delivered by the Lord Primate of Ireland, Dr James Ussher, before the Lord Deputy and the great assembly at Dublin Castle. (Ms. Mm. V. 9)

1636   (Aug.) Report of a conference between Henry Leslie, Bishop of Down, and the Presbyterian ministers at Belfast. (Add. Ms. 4344)[29]

1640–52   Two copies of 'A Short view of the state and condition of Ireland from the year 1640 to the present time 1652'. (Add. Mss. 4347–8)[30]

1641   (4 Nov.) 'A copie of the King's Commission given to Sir Phelim O'Neill and his proclamation thereuppon' at Newry, 1641. The commission, which was a forgery, was read in Parliament in 1652. (Ms. Mm. I. 46)[31]

c1641   'The rise and progress of the Irish rebellion begun in the year 1641' [12pp]. (Add. Ms. 4353)[32]

17th cen.   'A Collection of the description and division of all the several shires and towns in Ireland with their greatness and large precinctes, shewing also the government in Munster'. Although this manuscript was found in the study of Sir Edward Waterhouse during the reign of James I, most of its contents date to the Elizabethan period, when Waterhouse served as Clerk of the Casualties and Chancellor of the Exchequer in Ireland. The volume also contains a survey of the royal estate in Ireland *temp* Eliz. I, which includes an inventory of crown lands rendering achates to the Lord Deputy's household. (Ms. Dd. III. 84 I)

17th cen.   An argument upon the question of impositions in Ireland, by Sir John Davies, with an answer. (Ms. Ff. III. 17)[33]

---

[27] N.L.I. microfilm n.5278, p.5387.

[28] N.L.I. microfilm n.6244, p.7017. There is a translation of this in the Royal Irish Academy, made by John O'Donovan in the nineteenth century (R.I.A., Miscellaneous O'Donovan Mss., 14/B/7, labelled 'Ordnance Survey, Ireland' (strongroom)).

[29] This item includes additional details to the text of the conference printed in J.S. Reid, *History of the Presbyterian Church in Ireland*, Vol. 1 (Belfast, 1867). It can be consulted on N.L.I. microfilm n.5328, p.5437.

[30] N.L.I. microfilm n.5325, p.5437.

[31] See R. Dunlop, 'The Forged Commission of 1641', *English Historical Review*, ii (1887).

[32] N.L.I. microfilm n.5328, p.5437.

[33] There is another copy of Davies' argument in Ms. Ff. V. 21.

UNLISTED MATERIAL

The following are those items which have been acquired by the library since the publication of James's *Catalogue*:

LOOSE ITEMS

c1542–50   Opinion of Sir Gerald Aylmer, Sir Thomas Lutrell, Sir James Bath and Sir Thomas Cusacke, members of the Irish Council, in a controversy over bribery in a mayoral election in Cork. (Doc. 33)[34]

1546–7   Note of values of prebends belonging to St. Patrick's Cathedral, Dublin, 38 Henry VIII (copied in a notebook of Anthony Dopping, afterwards Bishop of Meath, d.1697). (Add. Ms. 711)

1563   Assignment of a lease by the Dean and Chapter of Trinity Cathedral, Dublin, to Richard Fagan of Dublin, gent., mentioning an earlier lease to John Challoner of Dublin [Removed from a binding, text imperfect]. (Doc. 40)

1569   Eighteenth century note of an indenture made on 23 April 11° Eliz. I, between Sir William Greysley of Colton, Staffs., and Francis Agard of Grange Gorman in Ireland, concerning Blythbury in Staffs. (Add. Ms. 3908, p7)

1584–5   (Aug. 1584–Dec. 1585) Two acts of John Long, Archbishop of Armagh, dated Aug. 1584, and Dec. 1585, contained in the episcopal register of Richard Cox, Bishop of Ely. (Ely Diocesan Records, G/1/8, ff 180^{r-v})

16–17th cen.   Collection of bardic poems dating from the sixteenth and seventeenth centuries transcribed and compiled in 1791. (Add. Ms. 4207)

1626   Copy of a letter from Charles I to Lord Deputy Falkland concerning the poor state of medical practices in Ireland, and discussing the foundation of a College of Physicians. (Add. Ms. 2766 (19))

1641–50   A list of Irish tracts [17pp]. (Add. Ms. 4605)

17th cen.   A copy of verses in praise of Geoffrey Keating by his man-servant. (Add. Ms. 3085, fol. 113)

17th cen.   Miscellaneous copies of poems by and attributed to Geoffrey Keating. (Add. Mss. 4183, ff 49v, 56, 78 and 110; 4205, ff 97–138; 6477, p190; 6516, passim; 6559, fol. 196v, and 7089, p112)

COLLECTIONS

Transcripts from the Papal Archives (Add. Ms. 4878 & 4881)[35]

1555   Copy of a letter by Hugh Curwen, Archbishop of Dublin, to the Pope [possibly Paul IV],[36] concerning his consecration in Dublin. (Add. Ms. 4878, fol. 96)

1578   (5 June) Copy of a letter from Patrick O'Hely, Bishop of Mayo, to Cardinal Comensi. (Add. Ms. 4878, fol. 414)

1578   Two letters by Patrick O'Hely, Bishop of Mayo, to Cardinal Comensi, written from Paris. (Add. Ms. 4881, ff 25 and 28)

---

[34] The dating of this item is determined by the period spent by Cusacke as Master of the Rolls.

[35] Purchased by the Library from Lord Acton in 1903.

[36] Pope Paul was elected on 23 May 1555. However, Curwen may have intended instead either of Paul's predecessors, Marcellus II (d. 1 May 1555) or Julius III (d. 23 March 1555).

1582	James Eustace, Viscount Baltinglass, to the Papal Nuncio, from Madrid. (Add. Ms. 4881, fol. 88)
1582–3	Four letters by Gerald, 14th Earl of Desmond, to Pope Gregory XIII. (Add. Ms. 4881, ff 67, 79, 85 and 99)[37]
1583	'Cornelius Laonensis' [Connor O'Mulrian, Bishop of Killaloe] to Cardinal Comensi, from Madrid, re the progress of the Desmond rebellion. (Add. Ms. 4881, fol. 97)
1583	Gerald Fitzgerald to Pope Gregory XIII, re the Earl of Desmond's campaign in Ireland. (Add. Ms. 4881, fol. 101)
1584	Maurice Fitzgerald to the same, regarding the death of the Earl of Desmond and the state of Irish Catholicism in general. (Add. Ms. 4881, fol. 109)
1585	A note of reasons for appointing Catholic bishops in Ireland. (Add. Ms. 4881, fol. 115)

CAMBRIDGE UNIVERSITY : Corpus Christi College Archives
Trumpington Street, Cambridge CB2 1HS
Tel: (01223) 338 049

All of the pre-1641 Irish material held by the College has been listed in M.R. James, *Descriptive Catalogue of Manuscripts in the Library of Corpus Christi College, Cambridge* (2 vols., 1909–12), to which nothing new has been added:

1502	The protocol/letter book of the notary N. Collys (1454–1504) contains a commission to enquire into the affairs of the archbishopric of Armagh and the aldermen and sheriff of Drogheda in 1502. (Ms. 170, p128)
1560	(30 May) Letter from the Privy Council to Matthew Parker, Archbishop of Canterbury, concerning the vacant sees of Armagh and Meath. (Ms. 114, pp99–101)
1567	(3 Nov.) Letter to Archbishop Parker from Thomas Butler, 10th Earl of Ormond, requesting Parker's favour towards a poor excommunicated priest, sent from the court [2 pp]. (Ms. 114, p65)
1571	A Gaelic ballad printed in Irish characters. (Ms. 12b)

CAMBRIDGE UNIVERSITY : Emmanuel College Library
Cambridge CB2 3AP
Tel: (01223) 334 292/334 200
Fax: (01223) 334 426

The following items of Irish interest are listed in M.R. James, *Catalogue of the Western Manuscripts in Emmanuel College Library, Cambridge* (1904):

| 1576 | (13 Sept.) Letter of condolence written from Dublin to Mary Draycott by Robert and Margaret Bisse and Cicely Fagan. A note on the edge says 'This letter shoeth the death of Olfer Draycott to be in a. 1576'. (Ms. 80) |

---

[37] The letter on fol. 99, dated 18 June 1583, was published in P.F. Moran (ed.), *Spiciliguim Ossoriense*, 1st series (Dublin, 1874), p81.

1594–9   A volume containing *inter alia* several references to the army in
      Ireland during the Nine Years' War (Ms. 53), *viz*

    1594   (June) A notice of soldiers levied in various counties in June
        1594 for service in Ireland.

    1594–9   Further particulars of forces sent into Ireland, France and the
        Low Countries.

    1596   (March) Abstract of the forces bound for Ireland furnished by the
        clergy.

CAMBRIDGE UNIVERSITY : The Fitzwilliam Museum

Trumpington Street, Cambridge CB2 1RB
Tel: (01223) 332 900
Fax: (01223) 332 923

LOOSE ITEMS

1640   Collection of Irish tales belonging to the Ulster cycle, compiled in
      1640 for Dearmuit MacCarthy. (Illustrated Mss, Ms MacClean
      187)[38]

CAMBRIDGE UNIVERSITY : Gonville & Caius College Library

Cambridge CB2 1TA
Tel: (01223) 332 419
Fax: (01223) 332 430

The College holds only a little material of Irish interest, and this has all been
listed in M.R. James, *Catalogue of the Manuscripts in Gonville & Caius College
Library, Cambridge* (1907), to which written communication has added a few
further details, as follows:

1599   'The Discoverie and Recoverie of Irelande, and the Aucthors
      Apologie', probably by Captain Thomas Lee, in which the author
      gives his views on the state of the rebellion in Ireland. (Ms.
      150/200, ff 81–154 and 155–83)[39]

16th cen.   A document entitled 'The Lords as they sit in the Parliament House
      in Ireland, and other Irish names: with coats', part of a sixteenth
      century compilation probably assembled during the 1580s. (Ms.
      552/316)

1600   (29 Nov.) Speeches of the Lord Keeper and Lord Treasurer in the
      Court of Star Chamber touching the service of the Earl of Essex in
      Ireland [7 ff]. (Ms. 197/103, pp285–90)

1627   A volume containing the arms of the Irish nobility, including
      creations, to the year 1627. (Ms. 560/320)

17th cen.   A pedigree of the Butlers, earls and dukes of Ormond. (Ms. 525/697)

---

[38] There is a good description of the contents of this manuscript in Padraig de Brún & Máire Herbert,
Catalogue of Irish Manuscripts in Cambridge Libraries (Cambridge, 1986).

[39] Although there is a contemporary note between the text of the Discoverie and that of the Apologie to the
effect that 'Sr Henrye Lea seemes to be the author of y^s booke', historical opinion normally credits the
work to Captain Thomas Lee. There are other copies of this manuscript in the library of St. John's College,
Cambridge, below, and in the British Library (Add. Ms. 33,743).

CAMBRIDGE UNIVERSITY : Magdalene College, Pepys Library
Cambridge CB3 0AG
Tel: (01223) 332 100

A very detailed calendar of the correspondence collected by Samuel Pepys has appeared in H.M.C. *Pepys MSS* (London, 1911), and it contains thirteen items of Irish interest for the period 1564–99, most notably a number of letters addressed to the Queen and the Earl of Leicester by some of the principal figures in Irish politics during the 1560s.[40]

CAMBRIDGE UNIVERSITY : Pembroke College Library
Cambridge CB2 1RF
Tel: (01223) 338 121
Fax: (01223) 338 163

According to M.R. James, *Catalogue of the manuscripts in the library of Pembroke College, Cambridge* (1905), the library has only two items concerning Irish history before 1641. Correspondence with the librarian has added a little more detail to James's description of both documents:

1595   (2 April) Letter to F. Paris, requesting him to supply one light horseman for service in Ireland, or else to pay £20.[41]

16th cen.   A sixteenth century copy of a document of the reign of Edward II showing the title of Thomas, Duke of Norfolk and Maurice, Lord Berkeley, to the Earl Marshal's estate in Cos. Carlow and Wexford by descent from Thomas Brotherton, Earl of Norfolk. (College Archives, Framlingham A.9)

CAMBRIDGE UNIVERSITY : St. John's College Library
Cambridge CB2 1TP
Tel: (01223) 338 631

The following items were listed in M.R. James, *Catalogue of the manuscripts in the library of St. John's College, Cambridge* (1913), to which further details have been furnished by the College archivist:

1599   'The discovery & recovery of Ireland, with his apology', by Captain Thomas Lee. (SJC Ms. no. I.29)[42]

1641–9   'A copy of the arraignment and indictment of my Lord Maguire, taken by me, William Barnes, in the Court of King's Bench'. The 'Arraignment' and the rest of the title is in French, as is the note that the proceedings are transcribed into English at the request of

---

[40] It should be noted, however, that although the editors of the calendar drew attention to the fact that Vol. III of the Pepys MSS includes a series of ciphers used by Lord Deputy Wentworth, Lord Deputy Leicester and Viscount Sligo between 1638 and 1641, they did not consider them worth printing.

[41] Further details of this letter, part of the Paris family correspondence, can be found in H.M.C., *5th Report* (1876), App., p486.

[42] This was donated to the library by Thomas Baker, historian of the college, and mistakenly dated 1699. James refers to it as Ms. 41.

'one of my friends'. Although Barnes heard the case in Michaelmas, 1644, the document contains a full record of the indictment of Cornelius, Lord Maguire, Sir Phelim O'Neill, Roger Moore and others, on a charge of conspiracy to levy war against the King and to invade and attack Dublin in Oct. 1641, seeking to alter the religion 'by law established'. The pleas, including arguments by the Crown and the defence counsel, are given, as is the final judgement and the dismissal of an appeal on 16 Aug. 1649, after which Maguire was to be executed at Tyburn [21 ff]. (SJC Ms. no. S.8)[43]

CAMBRIDGE UNIVERSITY : Sidney–Sussex College Archives
Sidney Street, Cambridge CB2 3HU
Tel: (01223) 338 800/ 338 824
Fax: (01223) 338 884

The H.M.C. report on the College archives (*3rd Report* (1872), App., pp327–9) gives a few examples of entries in the College register, including the admission of Henry Roper, son of Thomas, Viscount Baltinglass, in 1633. It states that he was born in his father's house called 'Roper's Rest' near Dublin (p328). It is possible that other Irish entries exist in the College register which were not published.

CAMBRIDGE UNIVERSITY : Trinity College Library
Cambridge CB2 1TQ
Tel: (01223) 338 488
Fax: (01223) 338 532

Among the documents listed in M.R. James, *Catalogue of the manuscripts of the library of Trinity College, Cambridge* (4 vols, 1900–4) are the following:

1571	The history of Ireland, by Edmund Campion. (Ms. 754)
1575	(23 Dec.) 'Mr Edmund Tremayne's Inquiry whether Ireland to be governed after yᵉ Irish manner as yᵗ hath been accustomed, or to reduce yt as neare as maye be to English government' [8pp, unfinished]. (Ms. 710, no.6)
1641–9	Proceedings in the case of MacMahon together with the proceedings, arraignments and judgement in the case of Lord Maguire. Mostly dating from 1644. For more details see a similar account (SJC Ms. no. S.8) in St. John's College Library, Cambridge [80 fols]. (Ms. 1175)
17th cen.	A document entitled 'Sopra il regno d'Irlanda et delle genti vi bisognia per acquistarto', held among a collection of seventeenth century Italian political papers [2 fols]. (Ms. 971)[44]

---

[43] Maguire had been arrested on the morning of 23 Oct. 1641, in his lodgings in Dublin. James's catalogue gives Ms. 405 (2) as a reference.

[44] This document is part of a collection of 91 seventeenth century manuscripts donated to the library in 1691 by Sir Henry Puckering.

CHESHIRE : Chester City Record Office *
Town Hall, Chester CH1 2HJ
Tel: (01244) 324 324 ext. 2110
Fax: (01244) 324 338

LOOSE ITEMS

1640   Part of a pedigree of the Hattons of Woodhouse in the parish of
            Frodsham in Cheshire which refers to John Hatton, Mayor of
            Coleraine in 1632–3, who died at Chester in 1640. (G/Mc.4)

COLLECTIONS

Chester City Archives (ref. various)

Chester City Record Office possesses probably the best catalogued municipal
archive in Britain, making research there less of an effort and more of a pleasure
than is often the case elsewhere. The City archives go back a long way, and
contain extensive series of records on many aspects of the City's administration
throughout the fifteenth, sixteenth and early seventeenth centuries. Most of the
major classes of documents to be found here relate in one way or another to
Ireland.[45] Indeed, so close was the contact between Chester and its western
neighbour – it was one of Ireland's main trading points, it normally served as the
main port of embarkation for English soldiers sailing to Ireland, and it was the
first stop on the Dublin-London communications route – that the City Record
Office should soon become one of the main centres for the study of Irish history
in the early-modern period. The principal series are listed below in chronological
order.[46]

1407–1835 Assembly Files (ref. AF)

This series contains 62 files of petitions and other material relating to the City
Assembly. It has only a few references to Ireland, of which the following have
been found:

1625   (13 Dec.) Petition of Philip Watson, merchant, who submits himself
            to the Mayor, confessing that he had brought wool and other goods
            into Chester from Ireland without paying duty on them, being
            ignorant of the City's customs. He does not intend to sell them in
            Chester, but will send them abroad. (AF/12/30)

1629   (n.d.) Petition of Richard Stubbs of Kinderton in Cheshire,
            waggonman, to the Privy Council. Last March he was bringing
            goods belonging to Walter Kennedy of Dublin from London to
            Chester, when they were stolen at Brickell. They are valued at £10.
            He is a poor man, and has been imprisoned for six weeks, and is
            unable to procure bail to answer an action. (AF/14/41)

1633   (5 Oct.) Petition of Francis Knowles, servant to H.M. farmers of the
            Customs, regarding a quantity of skins purchased by him from
            Thomas Talbot of Wexford, which were seized by the sheriffs of
            Chester as 'foreign bought and foreign sold'. He asks that his
            offence be remitted, so he can have the benefit of the sale.
            (AF/17/47)

---

[45] Only the Mayors' Books (ref. MB) barely make mention of Ireland.
[46] John Cordy Jeafferson, in his H.M.C. report on this archive (*8th Report*, App.I, pp355–403), noted a
number of Mayor's letters concerning Ireland. Where possible these items have been identified in our
listing of the Mayor's Letters (ref. ML) below.

1422–1624 Sheriffs' Books (ref. SB)

This collection of 15 large volumes relates primarily to the highly varied activities of the City's sheriffs. The books contain memos and notes regarding the City court pleadings, presentments at quarter sessions, financial accounts, and valuations of goods given as sureties on oath before the sheriffs. However, the most significant part of the books that concern Ireland is the yearly recordings of all customs entries. Makeshift and heavily summarised customs records were entered every financial year from the fifteenth century, but during the reign of Henry VIII these records became more standardised, and mirror the detail of the customs accounts and port books in the P.R.O. For example, the customs entries for the year 1557–8 list all vessels arriving in Chester; the date they arrived (with their port of origin), names the masters and merchants, and gives a breakdown of each cargo (SB/10 ff 110–169).[47] These customs accounts are a very valuable addition to the study of Irish trade, considering that there are few early sixteenth century Chester customs accounts in the P.R.O., and the Chester port books (also in the P.R.O.) begin very late. The Sheriffs' Books appear to have a complete yearly series of these records, and they also include the arrests and fines for non-payment of customs, an aspect often left out of the records in the P.R.O.[48] Overall there are hundreds of entries in these books about Irish ships and merchants.

1477–1818 Murengers Account Books (ref.MUB)

There are four account books (the covering dates of which are 1477–8 & 1551–9; 1559–65; 1618–1801; 1801–1818). These accounts of murage collected from incoming ships relate almost entirely to the coasting trade, and references to Irish merchants are few and far between. For example, in MUB/2 (Account Book for 1559–65), there is only one reference to an Irish merchant, John Challenor of Dublin, who paid murage for three tons of seck on 27 January 1560. It is unlikely that there are many references to Ireland in the other books.

1497–1839 Mayors' Files (ref. MF)

There is no catalogue to this large series (253 files) in the Record Office, but it does contain some documents relating to Irish merchants who were to appear in the City's courts. For example, in 1614 Ralph Wall, a Chester ironmonger, petitioned the Mayor regarding his suit of trespass (to the damage of £11) against Dionysius Byrne, merchant of Dublin. The case was to be heard in the Pentice Court, and Byrne was alleged to have received goods from Wall for which he never paid. Nevertheless, Byrne claimed that he had never received them (MF/47/3,5). It is very probable that there are more documents of this nature throughout the series.

1539–1849 Assembly Books (ref. AB)

These books only contain regular assembly orders and accounts from c1588, and relate chiefly to internal municipal affairs. The books for the period 1603–1642 have been published, Margaret J. Groombridge (ed.), *Calendar of the Chester Council Minutes 1603–42* (Record Society for Lancashire and Cheshire, cvi, 1956). This publication contains many references to Ireland, particularly petitions to the Assembly, regarding trade with Ireland, Irish cattle and yarn, and troops bound for Ireland (see pp23, 30–1, 36, 103n, 137–8, 181, 194). The sixteenth century material, which commences in 1539, has not been published, and includes the following items:

---

[47] The 1557–8 Irish boats came from Dublin, Drogheda, Wexford and Waterford.

[48] For instance, in 1551 Thomas White, a Dublin merchant, was fined for not paying customs on three tons and three hogs of wine (SB/10 fol. 2).

1579   (3 July) Admission of Humphrey Philips, tailor, for 40s., at the request of William Gerard, Lord Chancellor of Ireland.[49] (AB/1 fol. 176)

1590   (3 July) The suggestion of Robert Brerewood, that the selling of Irish yarn should be unrestricted on two days a week, is deferred while the legal points are investigated. (AB/1 fol. 229)

1590   (1 Oct.) The sheriffs allege that Thomas Aldersey, merchant, wrongfully sold a hogshead of 'traun' for one Symon Malone, a merchant stranger (?Irish). The case to be inserted. (AB/1 fol. 230)

1599   (15 Feb.) Note of receipt of letters from the Privy Council giving warning of the arrival of large numbers of troops in transit for Ireland, with instructions to feed and pay them. Assessors are appointed to raise a rate sufficient to meet the costs, until the money is refunded by the Exchequer, and Thomas Lynyall is appointed to organise the feeding of the soldiers. (AB/1 fol. 256)

1599   (1 March) A banquet to be prepared for the Earl of Essex, who will be visiting Chester on his way to Ireland. A silver cup and gold angels are to be presented. (AB/1 fol. 256)

1599   (n.d.) Persons are appointed to arrange for the accommodation of soldiers, and to see to their embarkation to Ireland from Liverpool, Wallasey, Burton Head and elsewhere. (AB/1 fol. 256)

1601   (3 July) Mrs. Knight, widow of the late Clerk of the Pentice, is alleged to be holding certain government money entrusted to her husband for Irish affairs. The City Treasurers are to investigate the matter. (AB/1 fol. 269)

1546–1716 Mayor of Chester's Letters (ref. ML)

This series contains the regular correspondence of the mayors of Chester. Some of these items relate to the army and to military matters in general, and have been listed separately in the Record Office catalogue of the Mayor's Military Papers (ref. MMP). These military items are described with the analysis of the MMP series below.[50]

1550   (1 Feb.) Letter from the Mayor of Dublin to the Mayor of Chester, protesting against the increased severity of customs at Chester. (ML/5/1)

1574   (21 Feb.) Letter from Sir William Fitzwilliam, Lord Deputy of Ireland, to the Mayor, from Dublin, relating to his servant, Richard Rabone, presently in Chester on his master's business. (ML/1/10)[51]

1575   (10 June) Letter from Lord Deputy Sidney to the Mayor. Expostulates on the treatment of the widow of George Wissett, who was arrested after leaving Ireland. (ML/5/16)

1575   (22 Sept.) General pass from the Knight Marshal, to permit William Lee to travel to Ireland. (ML/5/17)

---

[49] There are many other references to Gerard in the Assembly books relating to his activities in Chester while he lived there and after he went to Ireland, but these relate exclusively to Chester history. See AB/1 ff 179, 185, etc.

[50] The items noted in H.M.C., *8th Report*, App.I, pp355–403, are identified below.

[51] Printed in *Ibid*, App.I, p374a.

1576   (5 March) General pass from his commanding officer to John Morgan, a soldier recently discharged from service in Ireland, to travel home or elsewhere. (ML/5/18)

1581   (14 Aug.) Copy of a letter from the Mayor to Burghley. Reports on pirates in the Irish Sea, and encloses examinations of some of their victims. (ML/5/30)

1585   (3 Feb.) Letter from Burghley to the Mayor, sending instructions concerning £1,100 which he will receive from Sir Lucas Dillon for Irish affairs. (ML/5/39)

1587   (8 May) Letter from Burghley to Edmund Gamull at Chester, instructing him to give a receipt for an earlier transaction to the bearer, Thomas Fauntleroye, 'Mr. Tresorers man'.[52] (ML/5/77)

1589   (12 Feb.) Letter from Walsingham to the Mayor. Orders that Charles Trevor, an Irishman held prisoner in Chester, be immediately sent to the Lord Deputy in Ireland. (ML/5/82)

1589   (13 March) Copy of a letter from the Mayor to the Lord Deputy. Covering note for the letter by Walsingham (above), concerning the Irish prisoner who was arrested for removing an Irish lad, [   ] Orkeworth, from the tuition of Dr. Culpeper of Oxford. (ML/5/83)

1590   (14 March) Copy of a letter from the Mayor to [Burghley]. Reports on the staying of sufficient shipping to transport 700 soldiers to Ireland. (ML/5/213)

1590   (25 March) Letter from Walsingham to the Sheriffs, ordering the immediate release of William Maurice, servant to the Lord Deputy, who was arrested in Chester on his way to Court. (ML/5/96)

1590   (31 March) Letter from the Sheriffs to [   ], requesting the release and presence of William Maurice. (ML/5/97)

1590   (4 April) Copy of letter from the Mayor to [   ]. Reporting that he is sending a seminary priest, Richardson, received from the Lord Deputy of Ireland, with the bearer. (ML/5/214)

1593   (19 July) Letter from the Earl of Derby to the Mayor, requesting that interference with the officers of Richard Carmarden, royal patentee for the carrying of Irish yarn, shall cease forthwith. (ML/1/49)[53]

1593   (29 July) Draft letter from the Mayor to the Earl of Derby. Reports that he can find no evidence of interference with Mr. Carmarden's officers (one of whom is Thomas Aldersey). (ML/5/113)

1593-4   (Nov. 1593–Aug. 1594) Letters from Sir William Fitzwilliam, Lord Deputy of Ireland, to the Mayor, requesting that the enclosed letters be forwarded to the Council etc. (ML/1/52, 54–5, 57, 63, 67, 77, 79, 85, 91, 93, 100, 104, 107)[54]

1594   (22 Feb.) Letter from the Privy Council to the Mayor, instructing him to examine and detain all persons travelling to and from Ireland, unless they are well known, or can give sufficient account of themselves. (ML/1/56)[55]

---

[52] i.e. a servant of Sir Henry Wallop, Treasurer-at-war in Ireland.
[53] Printed in H.M.C., 8th Report, App.I, p375b.
[54] Some of these are printed in Ibid, App.I, pp376a–377b.
[55] Printed in Ibid, App.I, p375a.

1594	(24 March–5 Oct.) Letters, examinations, evidences, etc., concerning Irish and English recusants travelling to Ireland. The papers relate chiefly to the case of Edward Cowper and Agnes Mordaunt who were trying to bring two boys, Richard Ody from Ely and John Warnford, the son of a London recusant, to Ireland through Chester, but were caught. A number of Chester recusants are examined, including Robert Sefton, Edmund Day and a 'Mr. Bold'. The two boys and Cowper were sent to London, and Agnes Mordaunt was exonerated.[56] At the same time another Irish recusant, Richard Browne, was found with two well-known Scottish recusants in the town, and they were also detained and examined. Browne was eventually released and sent back to Ireland. (ML/1/59–62, 64–6, 69, 70, 74, 82–4, 88d; ML/5/123–4, 218–243)
1594	(6 May) Note from R. Asheton, Sheriff of Lancashire, that he has received a warrant from the Privy Council, dated 30 April, to muster 200 soldiers for Ireland. (ML/1/76)[57]
1594	(14 June) List of English children sent to Chester by order of the Lord Deputy and Council. (ML/1/89)
1594	(15 June) Letter from the Lord Deputy and Council to the Mayor, regarding recusants arrested in Dublin on their way 'to places of Popish religion'. (ML/1/90)[58]
1594–6	Letters from Lord Buckhurst to the Mayor, relating to Captain Barnaby Rich's accusations against Alexander Coates, who it is alleged assaulted and robbed Rich. (ML/1/103, 105–6)
1597	(1 Jan.) Letter from James Ware to the Mayor, from Dublin, reminding the Mayor about two boat-loads of coal still due. (ML/1/118)
1597	(1 May) Letter from John Leeche, deputy to the Queen's Receiver, to the Mayor, discussing the date when he will pay the Mayor £500 for Irish affairs. (ML/5/145)[59]
1597	(13 May) Letter from Phy. Williams and Francis Mychell, secretaries to the Lord Deputy, to the Mayor. Ask the Mayor to sign a certificate of their expenses in England for Sir Henry Wallop, the Irish Vice-Treasurer. (ML/1/134)
1598	(5 Jan.) Copy of a letter from the Mayor to George Brook, reporting that John Murray and John Garret, Irishmen, who robbed Brook of £100, have been apprehended. (ML/5/156)
1598	(28 Jan.) Copy of a letter from the Mayor to Mr. Gamull, reporting the delayed arrival in Liverpool of *The Popinjay* from Ireland with the body of the late Lord Deputy, Lord Burgh. (ML/5/244)
1598	(16 Sept.) Copy of a letter from the Mayor to the Lord Justices of Ireland, the Earl of Ormond, and the Irish Council, enclosing letters forwarded from the English Council. Asks that the bearer, Robert Harris, master of *The Katherine of Hilbery*, be recompensed for his expenses. (ML/5/250)

---

[56] She was closely related to Lord Mordaunt.

[57] Printed in H.M.C., *8th Report*, App.I, p376a.

[58] Printed in *Ibid*, App.I, p377a.

[59] Printed in *Ibid*, App.I, p379b.

1601   (14 Nov.) Certificate from Arthur Chichester, Governor of Carrickfergus, of the delivery of troops by John Munelly, mariner. (ML/2/171)[60]

1606   (19 Nov.) Letter from the Earl of Salisbury to the Mayor, to pass on enclosed letters to Sir Richard Cooke in Ireland. Endorsed 'hast hast', and the notes of times of arrival at certain places *en route* are given. (ML/2/181)

1606   (27 Nov.) Letter from Sir Richard Cooke to the Mayor, from Liverpool, confirming his receipt of the above. (ML/2/183)

1607   (14 March) Draft letter from the Mayor to Lord Stanhope, regarding two un-named men arrested in Chester *en route* to Ireland, and their examinations. (ML/2/190)[61]

1607   (13 April) Letter from the Earl of Salisbury to the Mayor, to pass on an enclosed packet to Mr. Stroud to bring to the Lord Deputy in Ireland. (ML/2/194)

1607   (27 April) Letter from the Earl of Salisbury to the Mayor, enclosing a letter to be sent to the Lord Deputy in Ireland. (ML/2/195)

1607   (4 June) Letter from the Earl of Salisbury to the Mayor, enclosing a packet to be sent to Ireland. (ML/2/196)

1607   (29 July) Letter from Sir Arthur Chichester, Lord Deputy of Ireland, to the Mayor. Thanks him for sending packets of letters. Asks him to send the most important packets he receives *via* Holyhead which is faster, and the others by the usual route. (ML/2/199)

1607   (2 Aug.) Letter from Richard Al[ ] to the Mayor. Wants him to arrest his servant, Thomas Washer, bound for Ireland, who stole £400 from him. (ML/2/200)

1607   (28 Sept.) Letter from William Angell, *et al*, farmers of the impost on yarn, to the Mayor. Responding to the Mayor's letter dated 4 June, arguing that Irish yarn be allowed into the port of Chester. They accept this, on condition that a 25s imposition be charged on each pack of yarn that is imported. (ML/2/201)

1608   (1 Feb.) Letter from the Mayor to Sir Julius Caeser, relating to charges in sending 400 foot to Dublin in November, and 80 horse more recently. (ML/6/3)

1608   (29 Feb.) Letter from the Lords of the Council to all Mayors, Sheriffs, etc., in England, to assist and protect Henry Reynolds and William Turvin, servants of the Treasurer-at-war in Ireland, in their travel into Ireland with the army's wages. (ML/2/214)[62]

1608   (cApril) Petition to the Lord Deputy of Ireland from John Howe of Chester, who was inconvenienced when forced to carry a packet of letters in his boat to Dublin. Asks for some compensation for lost trade. A note dated 20 April is subscribed by Lord Deputy Chichester, stating that Howe should approach the Mayor for a certificate of expenses. (ML/2/215)[63]

---

[60] Printed in *Ibid*, App.I, p380a.
[61] Printed in *Ibid*, App.I, p380b, but misdated as 13 March.
[62] Printed in *Ibid*, App.I, p381a.
[63] Printed in *Ibid*, App.I, p382a.

1608 (22 May) Letter from Dudley Norton to the Mayor, undertaking to be surety for a debt of Sir Randell MacDonnell of Ireland, owed to Roger Darbisher. (ML/2/218)[64]

1608 (26 May) Letter from the Mayor to the Council, requiring instructions regarding foot soldiers delayed in leaving for Ireland. The town cannot afford the allowance of 6d a day for each man, because of lack of victuals. (ML/6/5)

1608 (16 June) Letter from Sir Arthur Chichester to the Mayor, in reply to his letter concerning Henry Quine, a prisoner. Notifies him that a bond for Quine's appearance, by Thomas Walker of Naas, should be cancelled. (ML/2/222)[65]

1608 (17 June) Letter from the Earl of Salisbury to the Lord Bishop, Mayor, and Sheriff of Chester. Instructs them to send over Quine, the servant of Sir Cahir O'Dogherty, presently imprisoned at Chester. (ML/2/223)[66]

1608 (July) Draft certificate of the Mayor regarding 50 men impressed from Warwick for service in Ireland. Forty-nine arrived in Chester on 14 June last, at which point five were found unfit because of infirmities and one ran away. The company was then delivered to the Earl of Thomond with coats, hose and shoes. Since then (9 July) eight other men have run away.[67] (ML/6/11)

1608 (16 Nov.) Letter from Sir Arthur Chichester to the Mayor, asking him to send over Richard Hocknell immediately, so he can speak with the Lord Deputy. (ML/2/227)[68]

c1608 Letter from the Mayor to the Earl of Salisbury, asking for instructions regarding the Earl of Clanricard's company of horse, and that of the Lord Deputy and Sir Oliver Lambert, presently in Chester. Delay in sending them to Ireland, costing 18d a day. (ML/6/4)

c1608 Rough draft of a letter from the Mayor to the [Council], certifying the transportation of 250 complete arms, levied out of London, to Ireland. (ML/6/6)

1609 (7 Feb.) Warrant from Lord Deputy Chichester to all Mayors, Sheriffs, etc., requiring them to help conduct John Williams and John Lodge, pirates arrested in Ireland, to the Mayor of Westchester. (ML/6/17)

1609 (7 Feb.) Letter from same to the Mayor of Chester, instructing him to keep the above pirates and their examinations safe until he receives further instructions from the Lord Admiral. (ML/6/18)

1609 (8 March) Letter from the Mayor to the Privy Council, notifying the arrival of the pirates Williams and Lodge from Ireland, and requesting instructions. (ML/6/24)

1609 (4 April) Letter from the Mayor to the Lord Admiral, informing him that the pirates sent from Ireland are still imprisoned in Chester and he has received no instructions. (ML/6/25)

---

[64] Printed in *Ibid*, App.I, p382b.

[65] Printed in *Ibid*, App.I, p382b, and misdated as 15 June.

[66] Printed in *Ibid*, App.I, p382b.

[67] There are a great deal of such certificates in the Mayors Military Papers (ref. MMP).

[68] Printed in H.M.C., *8th Report*, App.I, p382b.

c1609   Rough draft of a letter from the Mayor to the Council, informing them that they attempted to suppress the alesellers and 'typlers' within the City because they refused to take out royal licences. However, the Mayor has ceased to stop them because there are large numbers of foot soldiers to be transported to Ireland who need their provisions. (ML/6/21)

1610   (18 Jan.) Warrant from Sir Peter Frechvile of Derby, to all Constables, etc., in Co. Derby. That Robert Butterworth, a wandering soldier, stole his livery coat and gilt rapier, and must be apprehended. Copy of a warrant sent to Chester in case he flees to Ireland. (ML/6/33)

1610   (25 Feb.) Letter from the Lords of the Council to the Mayor and officers at Chester. Notifying them of the plantation of Ulster, and to allow all persons licensed by William Cockayne, William Towrson or John Rowley, to pass freely into Ireland. (ML/2/231)

1610   (22 March) Rough draft letter from the Mayor to [   ], relating that persons intending to travel to inhabit Ulster have been provisioned at their own charge in Chester, but that after leaving, the Justices of the adjoining shire (not named) have refused to provision them, although payment was offered, hindering their journey. (ML/6/43)

1610   (6 June) Letter from James Stafford, Mayor of Wexford, to the Mayor of Chester, concerning goods stayed in Chester belonging to Richard Stafford of Wexford. (ML/6/50)

1610   (2 July) Letter from William Sparke to Mr. Hamer from Manchester. Tells him that he has received instructions to raise the imposition on Irish yarn to 30s. per pack on all yarn imported into Chester, because of the difficulty in collecting the imposition. (ML/6/52)

1610   (7 July) Letter from Sir Arthur Chichester to the Mayor, asking him to victual a ship called *The Lion's Whelpe*, under Captain Owen Wynne, to be sent to seek out pirates off the coast of Loughfoyle. (ML/2/232)[69]

1610   (10 July) Letter from the Mayor and Edmund Gamull to Thomas Gamull and Hugh Glaseour, relating that Irish yarn imported into Chester is being charged at 5s. a pack more imposition than at Liverpool or elsewhere, to the great discomfort of the Chester merchants. (ML/2/233)[70]

1610   (31 July) Letter from the Lords of the Council to the Mayor, notifying him that they have directed the Lord Deputy of Ireland to send him Coward and Barret, two pirates taken in Ireland. (ML/2/236)[71]

1610[72]   (15 Aug.) Letter from Sir Henry Townshend to the Mayor, asking him to release from prison Harry Leighe, as his family is ready to go over into Ireland. (ML/6/60)

1610   (Nov.) Letter from Sir Arthur Chichester to the Mayor, instructing him that he is to receive Gabriel Bunnage (*alias* Bunidge), apprehended for suspicion of piracy. (ML/2/240)

---

[69] Printed in *Ibid*, App.I, p399a.

[70] *Ibid.*

[71] *Ibid.*

[72] According to the catalogue this document is either dated 1610 or 1611.

c1610   (15 [ ]) Letter from Sir Arthur Chichester to the Mayor, concerning a Warden of Dublin Castle arrested for debt in Chester. He is to be sent to Ireland. (ML/2/241)

1611   (26 April) Letter from the Earl of Nottingham[73] to the Mayor, directing him to arrest Richard Hiccocke, sailor, and his men, who have embezzled goods belonging to James Duffe, merchant of Dublin. (ML/2/246)[74]

1611   (cSept) Letter from the Earl of Salisbury to the Mayor, to send an enclosed packet to Lord Carew in Ireland immediately. (ML/2/245)[75]

1611   (2 Oct.) Letter of Sir Arthur Chichester to the Mayor, responding to the Mayor's letter explaining the miserable condition of Gabriel Bannage (see above), who could not be charged of piracy. Chichester informs him that he has sent a letter to the Lord Admiral in Bannage's favour. (ML/2/247)[76]

1611   (14 Oct.) Rough draft of a letter from the Mayor to [the Privy Council ?], relating that they have arrested one Griffith Evans who had a mass book, a surplice and other vestments. He was meant to meet a Mr. Plunkett of Ireland who, he confessed, wore and used these vestments. They are searching for Plunkett. (ML/6/62)

1611   (15 Oct.) Letter from the Mayor to the Lord Admiral, relating to Gabriel Bannage, suspected of piracy. Asks that he either be sent for or released, as he is old and impotent. (ML/6/64)

1611   (1 Nov.) Letter from the Earl of Nottingham to the Mayor. He has received the Lord Deputy's letter, and he instructs the Mayor to set Gabriel Bannage at liberty. Note subscribed that Bannage was discharged on 19 Nov. (ML/2/249)

1611   (16 Nov.) Letter from the Mayor to the Earl of Salisbury, regarding a letter from the Lord Deputy desiring him to pay John Griffith £5 in compensation for bringing a packet of letters to Ireland. Asks that Griffith be paid by the Treasurer, as the City has no money. (ML/6/67)

c1611   Draft letter from the Mayor to the Earl of Salisbury, informing him that the Lord Deputy in a letter dated 29 Oct. asked him to victual His Majesty's pinnace, *The Lion's Whelpe*. This will cost £150, which the City does not have. (ML/6/69)

1612   (25 Jan.) Letter from Sir Thomas Bludder to the Mayor. Questions the accounts submitted for victuals requested by the Lord Deputy of Ireland. He will not accept the £20 demanded for salt and beef, which could not have been more than £6. (ML/2/253)

1612   (14 March) Letter from the Earl of Clanricard to the Mayor, regarding a watch that he lost in Mr. Dawson's house in Chester last May, which has come into the Mayor's hands. Asks for its return. (ML/2/257)[77]

---

[73] Charles Howard, 1st Earl of Nottingham and Lord High Admiral of England.

[74] Printed in H.M.C., *8th Report*, App.I, p399b.

[75] Printed in *Ibid*, App.I, p399b, where there seems to be some confusion as to whether this letter is addressed to the Lord Deputy or Lord Carew.

[76] Printed in *Ibid*, App.I, p400a.

[77] Printed in *Ibid*, App.I, p399b, and there dated 1612[–13]. It is possible that the present Record Office catalogue or the H.M.C. report was occasionally confused with old year-end dates.

1612   (1 June) Letter from the Mayor to Mr Angell and the other farmers of the impost on yarn. Explains that Chester is losing trade because the impost on Irish yarns is 10s per pack in Chester, but only 5s per pack in Liverpool and elsewhere. (ML/6/80)

1614   (19 Jan.) Letter from Richard Forster, Mayor of Dublin, to the Mayor of Chester. Wants more information about a disease, supposed to be pestilent, which is raging in Chester. Worried it will spread to Dublin. (ML/2/261)[78]

1614   (28 Jan.) Letter from the Mayor to Richard Forster, Mayor of Dublin, answering his letter (above). States that Chester is free from all contagious and pestilent diseases, though some persons have lately died from ague and fever. (ML/6/89)

1614   (9 April) Letter from Sir Thomas Ridgeway to the Mayor, to send on a packet of letters by Holyhead, which is the quickest route. (ML/2/264)

1614   (6 Aug.) Letter from the Mayor to the Lord High Admiral, concerning the victualing of a ship and 15 men to bring the Lord Deputy to Ireland, which cost £23 16s 1d. (ML/6/100)

1616   (2 July) Letter from Thomas Jones, Lord Chancellor of Ireland, and John Denham, to the Mayor. Asking him to examine Rowland Johnson of Chester, ironmonger, in a suit between John Johnson of Dublin, gent., and John Taylor of Chester, ironmonger. They enclose the interrogatories to be administered.[79] (ML/6/109–109a)

1619   (Feb.) Letter from William Griffith and John [ ], to the Mayor from Caernarfon, replying to his request for the names of the owners of ships. They mention a merchant, Hugh Davyes, who trades regularly with Ireland but does not own a ship. (ML/6/118)

1619   (17 Feb.) Letter from Edward Glegg to the Mayor, telling him that he cannot appear at the requested time, but has sent warrants to a number of people, many of whom are in Ireland. (ML/6/119)

1619   (18 Feb.) Letter from Humphrey Jones, Mayor of Beaumarius, to the Mayor, replying to his request for names of owners of ships. There are five ships in the town, two of which are owned by Captain Pepper who uses them in his office as post-master to Dublin. (ML/6/122)

1619   (6 March) Letter from same to same, relaying the same information, and stating further that he can give little help in urging ship owners to help suppress Turkish pirates.[80] (ML/6/125)

1619   (2 April) Letter from same to same, stating that Capt. Pepper will not allow his boats to be used against the pirates, because they are generally in service in Ireland. (ML/6/128)

1619   (14 May) Letter from Thomas Betson to the Mayor. Has heard that a popish priest has landed near Chester, from Ireland, in the company of Lady Mountgarret. Sends a description. (ML/6/138)

---

[78] Printed in *Ibid*, App.I, p400a where it is incorrectly dated 19 February; see following item (ML/6/89) which replies to this letter, and is dated 28 Jan.

[79] More documents concerning this dispute are listed amongst the Quarter Sessions Examinations below, QSE/13/4, *et al*.

[80] Presumably, the previous letter by Jones, and that from Griffith in Caernarfon (ML/6/118), also related to the suppression of Turkish pirates.

| 1619 | Rough draft of the answer of the Merchants of Chester concerning the action intended against the Barbary pirates. They will contribute to this, but they detail the collapse of profitable trade in Chester. They discuss the great quantity of iron made in Ireland which has swamped the port, making trade with Biscay less profitable. Furthermore, they state that the owners of small barques make their living by carrying passengers into Ireland. (ML/6/135) |

c1619 (n.d.) List of ports and creeks belonging to the chief port of Chester. Notes that shipping seldom comes into any of the creeks, but that they are sometimes the landing place for small Irish barques. (ML/6/133)

1621 (16 Nov.) Letter from the Council to the Earl of Derby, ordering him to levy 200 foot in Co. Lancaster and 100 in the City and County of Chester for the strengthening of Ireland. (ML/6/157)

1621 (cNov–Dec.) Letter from Sir George Boothe to the Mayor, informing him of the Council's letter of 16 Nov. (above) and asking for 20 men for service in Ireland, to be viewed and mustered by 12 December. (ML/6/159)

1621 (cDec.) Draft letter from the Mayor to the Earl of Derby, informing him of Sir George Boothe's letter (above) and that the City of Chester has always been free of such impositions – he cites letters of Henry VIII to that effect. (ML/6/160)

1623 (14 May) Letter from the Earl of Middlesex and [Carew?] to the Mayor, regarding the working of saltpetre in the City's liberties for the King's use in the realms of England and Ireland. (ML/6/164)

1627 (11 April) Deposition before the Mayor by William Forlicke of Coleraine, master of *The Civill Orange*, concerning the delivery of certain goods by Thomas Pierson of Londonderry to Edmond Clarke of Salop, corvesor. (ML/7/1)

1627 (14 April) Certificate by Sir John Vaughan, Mayor of Londonderry, that Richard Stocke of Londonderry, merchant, deposed that certain goods being aboard *The Civill Orange* of Coleraine were on 10 March 1626 consigned at Culmorie by Thomas Pierson to Edmond Clarke of Salop. (ML/7/2)

1627 (3 Oct.) Depositions of Francis Knowles, former deputy of Chester port, and John Baforne of Chester, carter, in a case between Thomas Akinns, plt. v. Lawrence Ussher, deft. Akinns, the owner of *The Grace of God of Dublin*, is suing Ussher, a merchant from Dublin, for losses incurred when Ussher did not enter goods at the Chester customs house. (ML/7/5)

1550–1679 Mayor of Chester's Military Papers (ref. MMP)

This series is very large, and incorporates 18 sizeable volumes and files. The first 16 of these (MMP/1–16) cover the period prior to 1641, and hold 461 items. Nearly all of these relate to Ireland, making this the biggest collection at the Record Office concerning Irish history. Furthermore, there are over 50 of the Mayors' Letters (ref. ML, see above) catalogued with this series. Although its sheer size precludes a detailed listing, many of the documents are of a similar nature and can be easily summarised. The covering dates for the material is 1550–1616, with the vast majority of documents logically covering the period of the Desmond War (1579–83) and the Nine Years War (1594–1603). In general the manuscripts cover each and every aspect of the journey made by English troops going to Ireland, from the musters in the shires and the embarkation for Ireland to the return of the surviving veterans.

The earliest items are dated 1550, and include a pay-roll of Irish kern in Chester, but thereafter the collection is concerned purely with English troops going to Ireland. A large part of the series comprises letters to and from the Privy Council, the Lord Deputy and the Mayor concerning the arrival of troops in the City, and contains instructions on the continuation of their journey. When soldiers arrived in the City they were inspected and supplied with coats and hose. Often soldiers had deserted during their journey to Chester or were too sick on their arrival to continue any further; there are many inspectors' receipts detailing this information. It was the task of the Mayor and Sheriffs to lodge and feed the soldiers until they could be sent on to Ireland. Most of the items relating to this concern the City's attempts (a) to acquire victuals, and (b) to raise loans from the local merchants and aldermen to cover the expense until it was remunerated by the Exchequer. The slow repayment of these loans often required the Mayor to write to the Irish Treasurer-at-war and the English Lord Treasurer to speed up their payments.

While the soldiers remained in Chester, there were frequent arrests, examinations and court hearings about their desertion, theft, mutiny and occasional acts of violence and murder. Many of these disturbances would not have taken place if it had not been for the serious delays which regularly occurred in transporting the men to Ireland. There are many items concerning the Mayors' problems in acquiring adequate shipping, causing them to regularly impress local merchants' vessels for the journey. Compensation for the merchants' trouble was chronically slow, and there are a few petitions from aggrieved ship-owners in the collection. Even when the soldiers had finally got to Ireland, the army which they joined there still needed to be victualled, and there are a considerable number of documents regarding the activities of state victuallers and the deputies of the Irish Treasurers-at-war. Unfortunately, there are very few manuscripts about returning soldiers; those that do exist are generally limited to licenses to return issued to soldiers who were wounded or sick.

Overall the collection is voluminous and well worth further examination. Research is aided by a detailed catalogue in the Record Office.[81]

1552–1858 Quarter Sessions: Examinations (ref. QSE)

This collection of 20 bundles is very incomplete. However, it includes a number of examinations relating to Ireland, *viz*

1585	(22 Feb.) Examinations of Robert Bries, a soldier levied in Staffordshire for service in Ireland, re a rumour that the Earl of Derby had been captured by the French. (QSE/3/48)
1596	(23 May) Examination of a sailor regarding a rumour of a minor attack on Ireland. The sailor had been held prisoner in a ship from Brittany with a Spanish crew and an Italian captain. (QSE/5/65)
1600	(March–April) Examinations of soldiers bound for Ireland. Fragments only. (QSE/5/142–7)
c1601	(n.d.) Record of examinations taken before Nicholas Barran, Mayor of Dublin, relating to the fraudulent importation of some sadle trees, smuggled to avoid customs.[82] (QSE/3/1)

---

[81] A selection of these items has appeared in print in H.M.C., *8th Report*, App.I, pp396a–399a.

[82] Although this document is in a file of 91 documents dated 1577–88, Nicholas Barran was Mayor of Dublin in the years 1600–1 and 1607–8. See Colm Lennon, *The Lords of Dublin in the Age of Reformation* (Dublin, 1989), p229.

1602	(15 Feb.) Examination of two Dutchmen, Julius Balough of Loughin in Gelderland, and Lambert Hoover 'of Westfoland in Germanie in the Low Countries'. They claim that they were travelling to visit Balough's brother at Loughfoyle in Ireland, who was serving as an 'auncient' to Sir Henry Docwra. (QSE/6/23–6)
1609	(6 & 8 April) Examinations relating to two trunks bound for Ireland, in which were found 'diverse papisticall books ... and superstitous reliques'. The owner, a student at Lincoln's Inn, claims they are law treatises, but admits he is a Catholic. (QSE/8/11–12)
1609	(26 & 28 Dec.) Examinations concerning a child, the daughter of the brother of the Bishop of Down, who was staying in Chester. (QSE/9/20,22)
1609	Examination of two servants of Sir Richard Trevor, Commissioner for Irish affairs. (QSE/8/28)
1610	(5 & 8 June, 2 July) Examinations regarding speeches against one Byfield, the city preacher, accusing him of being no scholar, as he is unfamiliar with Latin, and a renegade on his way to Ireland. (QSE/9/55,59,70)
1611	(23 June) Examination of Walter Carey, an Irish soldier, on suspicion of recusancy. (QSE/10/38)
1611	(26 June) Draft of letter by the Mayor to the Privy Council referring to his examination of Carey, above. (QSE/10/39)
1611	(23 Oct.) Examinations concerning some trunks sent into Ireland. They had been inspected by Mr. Parsons, collector for the farmers of the customs. (QSE/11/4)
1612	(2 July) Deposition pertaining to the seizure of some yarn imported from Ireland. The yarn had not been weighed, making payment of customs difficult. (QSE/11/60)
1615	(4 Nov.) Examination of Richard Chetwood, ironmonger, regarding a debt owed by a Dublin merchant to John Taylor, ironmonger, his former master. (QSE/13/4)
1616	(2 March) Examination of William Smith, half-owner and master of *The Unicorn of Leighton*, who had freighted some corn from Ireland for John Taylor, ironmonger. The grain was in bad condition when loaded and worse when it reached Parkgate. (QSE/13/16)
1616	(12 April) Examinations of Nicholas Welsh, master of *The Mayflower of Chester*, and others, relating to the Irish corn in *The Unicorn*, above. (QSE/13/18–19)
1616	(18 & 22 July) Examinations of Rowland Johnson and Robert Harvie, ironmongers, and others, regarding the release from prison in Ireland of Lawrence Rathburne, ironmonger, in a case at issue between John Johnson of Dublin, gent., and John Taylor, ironmonger.[83] (QSE/13/26–7)

1639–1665 Town Clerk: Protested Bills (ref. TCB)

These are protests (or complaints) about bills of exchange, usually concerning money for goods due or given. Many of these were made in Dublin.

---

[83] For other documents in this lengthy dispute see the Mayors' Letters above, ML/6/109–109a.

1639   (15 Oct.) Dublin. Regarding a bill of exchange by Owen Hughes and John Smith to Ralph Richardson, innkeeper of Chester. Bill of protest at the request of William Edwards, 28 Oct. 1639, that he never had any dealings with these parties. (TCB/1 fol. 2)

1639   (31 [ ]) Dublin. Bill of exchange by John Francis and William Humphrey to Charles Walley of Chester, alderman. To pay £60 (stg) to Edward Evans, assignee of Edward Powell, silkman of Cheapside. (TCB/1 fol. 5)

1640   (10 April) Dublin. Bill of exchange by Percival Williams to his master, Richard Byrd, merchant of Chester. To pay £7 (stg) to William Edwards, merchant of Chester. Protest: that he had no provision in his hands. (TCB/1 fol. 9)

1640   (11 June) Certificate by the Mayor of Chester that the ship *le Anna de Neston* arrived in Chester in May 1640 from Bilbao, laden with various goods belonging to Chester merchants, and also with 14 bags of Spanish wools for the account of James Blake, merchant of Ireland. (TCB/1 fol. 10)

1640   (21 July) Dublin. Bill of exchange by Edward Dickenson to Ralph Richardson, merchant of Chester. To pay £100 (stg) to John Johnson. Protest: that he had nothing to do with the drawer. (TCB/1 fol. 11–12)

1640   (28 May) Dublin. Bill of exchange by Paul Turner to Thomas Throppe. To pay £20 to Richard Bradshaw. Protest, 10 June 1640: that he owed him nothing. (TCB/1 fol. 13)

1640   (26 Nov.) Dublin. Bill of exchange by [ ] to [ ], to pay £30 (stg) to John Johnson , merchant of Chester. (TCB/1 fol. 13)

1641   (26 Feb.) Dublin. Bill of exchange by Thomas Martin to Thomas Butler of Roseley, tanner. To pay £100 (stg) to Thomas Crickley, merchant. Protest, 30 March 1641: the goods which were sent from Martin to him were not to his liking. (TCB/1 fol. 13)

CHESHIRE : County Record Office and Chester Diocesan Record Office *
Duke Street, Chester, Cheshire CH1 1RL
Tel: (01244) 602 574
Fax: (01244) 603 812

LOOSE ITEMS

c1557–60   (n.d.) A short note, *viz* 'Robert Ratclyfe the owner of a barke called the Sunday beynge apoynted to serve under the ryght honorable Earl of Sussex Lord Deputy of Irelande wyth tenne mariners whose names be subscribed. William Pemberton, Rychard Wryghte, Jeore Wryghte, Peter Lunte, Harry Enodalle, William Dyatt, Thomas Betson, Nicholas Pemberton, Robert Stronge'. (DDX 43/34)[84]

1614   (6 Nov.) Deed of feoffment. Sir John King to Henry Peirse of Dublin, esq., of a moiety of the town of 'Clonana' in Ireland, late in the possession of MacDonell in rebellion. Recites letters patent of 9

---

[84] This is the entire text of the manuscript, the dating of which can be deduced from internal evidence. Thomas Radcliffe was made Lord Deputy in 1556, but only titled earl of Sussex in 1557. Furthermore he was made Lord Lieutenant of Ireland in 1560. S.G. Ellis, *Tudor Ireland* (Longman, 1985), p329.

March 1606 of a grant to Sir John King, as well as some earlier deeds of feoffment [badly damaged, faded, in Latin]. (uncatalogued, DBC Accession 261, Box 60)

COLLECTIONS

Cholmondeley of Cholmondeley Collection (ref. DCH)

1612   (16 May–6 Nov.) Seven items relating to a dispute between Sir John Savage and Sir Richard Trevor over the marriage of Magdalen Trevor and Arthur Bagenal of Newry, and the preferment in marriage of Anne Bagenal, daughter of the late Sir Henry Bagenal of Newry. The dispute concerned a bond, dated 5 July 1603, in which Trevor agreed to pay Savage 1,000 marks for the conclusion of the two marriages. The documents include answers by Savage, briefs on behalf of Savage, and a petition of Sir Richard Crow regarding Arthur Bagenal's marriage. (DCH/E/304–9; DCH/O/31)[85]

1632   (10 July) Grant of a lease from (1) Thomas, Viscount Savage, Sir Richard Trevor of Trevalm, Co. Denbigh, Arthur Bagenal of Newry, Co. Down, and Magdalen his wife, to (2) Sir John Danvers of Chelsea, Co. Middlesex, Sir Thomas Waighman of Dublin, Arthur Bassett of Mountjoy, Co. Tyrone, and John Easton of Leeswood, Co. Flint., of the manors, etc., of Sir Henry Bagenal, deceased, in Ireland. (DCH/O/63)

Cowper (Condover) Collection (ref. DCC)

The material in this collection relating to Ireland was accumulated during Thomas Cowper's term of office as Mayor of Chester (1641–2), and consists largely of examinations of people travelling to Ireland after the outbreak of the rebellion. Most of these items have been published by the H.M.C., *5th Report*, Appendix, pp348a–352b.[86] However, there are four documents that were missed :

c1598   (n.d.) Petition of Robert Whitbie on behalf of the Mayor of Chester to the Lords, concerning the transport of troops to Ireland. Gives reasons why the custom of sending ships from Liverpool to collect troops, munitions etc., from the port of Chester, is preferable to forwarding them by land for shipment from Liverpool. (DCC/47/2)

1641   (1 Nov.) Information by Redmond Comen about Arthur Magennis, arrested while returning to Ireland from Germany. Comen supports Magennis's claim that he was merely returning to Ireland to get his pedigree to prove himself a gentleman, for a match he is to have in Germany. (DCC/47/7)

1641   (9 Nov.) Order from the Earl of Northumberland, Lord High Admiral, to the Mayor of Chester, demanding his assistance in enforcing the embargo of all shipping found in Chester's waters that are fit for the transport of troops and horses to Ireland. (DCC/47/15)

1641   (13 Nov.) Letter from Thomas Cowper, Mayor, to the Earl of Northumberland, in accordance with his orders of 4 Nov. (see H.M.C., *5th Report*, p349a). He has arrested one Arthur Progers, who has information against him relating to Ireland. Cowper will do his best to enforce his orders of 9 Nov. above. (DCC/47/16)

---

[85] See below under Gwynedd, University of North Wales, Plas Newydd MSS Series V/1438–9, for the original bond, and further details of this dispute.

[86] A fuller calendar exists in the search room of the Record Office.

Leicester–Warren of Tabley Collection (ref. DLT)

The H.M.C. report on this collection ('Lord de Tabley MSS', *1st Report*, App., pp46–50) mentioned a series of letters to Lord Mountjoy in 1601, as well as a 1613 letter sent to Lord Deputy Chichester. None of these items could be located at the record office, and it is possible that they were disposed of before the collection was deposited here. However, the following material of Irish interest was found in the collection:

1169–1643   'Of the chief governors of Ireland under the Kings of England since the conquest'. The listing goes up to 1643, and forms chapter 5 of a volume entitled 'Collections touching Ireland by me P. Leycester, March 1 1659'. The other four chapters are a history of the conquest of Ireland, taken from Giraldus, Camden, Hoveden, and other authorities, in 22 closely-written folios. (DLT/B/2 ff 262–8)

c1620–30   (n.d.) Plea from John Carville, in the King's service in the Irish Treasury, that Budworth and Cooke be forced to answer for a debt of £1,000 due to Carville [two copies]. (DLT/A/51/13a,b)[87]

1636–40   Volume of private and public accounts of Lord Deputy Wentworth and Sir George Radcliffe (DLT/B/43),[88] *viz*

   1636–9   Account of money paid by Sir Adam Loftus to Lord Deputy Wentworth.

   1637–9   Account between Sir Adam Loftus and Sir George Radcliffe.

   1639   (1 March–1 Sept.) Accounts of Sir George Radcliffe, by Thomas Littell, including Radcliffe's profits of office, his account as farmer of the Irish customs, money he received for pipestaves, money he paid to Littell for an account dated 1635–8, and other expenses.

   1639   (20 March–20 Sept.) Accounts of Lord Deputy Wentworth, including income, expenses on purchases and mortgages, money paid out to his steward and Lady Wentworth, the account for the ship *The St. Patrick of Dublin*, and a separate Sligo account.

   1639–40   (1 Sept.–1 March) Accounts of Sir George Radcliffe, with similar details.

   1639–40   (20 Sept.–20 March) Accounts of Lord Deputy Wentworth, with similar details.

   1640   (1 March–1 Sept.) Accounts of Sir George Radcliffe, with similar details.

   1640   (20 March–20 Sept.) Accounts of Lord Deputy Wentworth, with similar details.

   1641   (11 May) Document headed 'the King's schema', giving reasons for Strafford's probable execution 'tommorrow'.

   c1641   A document entitled 'Sir George Radcliffe's Case', explaining the claims being made against Radcliffe.

   n.d.   'A short schetch of Lord Straffords Life'.

17th cen.   Seventeenth century copy of the First Book of the History of Ireland, by Giraldus Cambrensis, and the Second Book of the Conquest of Ireland up to 1504, author unknown. (DLT/B/76)

---

[87] This person may be John Carroll, appointed Clerk of the Exchequer in 1609.

[88] There is a note inside this volume which reads 'these papers came with Sir Francis Leicester's wife whose father was secretary to Stafford'.

CORNWALL : County Record Office *
County Hall, Truro, Cornwall TR1 3AY
Tel: (01872) 73698/323127
Fax: (01872) 70340

LOOSE ITEMS[89]

1618   (21 May) Sale by Edward Harris, Chief Justice of Munster, of his
            manor of Colquite in Cornwall, to the Earl of Suffolk for £2,000.
            (PH/10)

1640   (18 Aug.) Letter from Francis Sawle to his uncle, Jonathon
            Rashleigh, relating to the 'many flying reports' of who will replace
            the Earl of Northumberland as Lord General. He states that 'som
            great ones stand for my Lord Debitie of Ireland and it is thaught yt
            he will carry yt...' He goes on to say that this issue has been
            rankling the Council, who have been sitting for three days 'and are
            yet hard at it'. (RS/1/1040)

17th cen.   (n.d.) A document called 'Methodus Concionandi', by William
            Chappell, Bishop of Cork (1582–1649), 'written with his own
            hand'. (RS/66)

CUMBRIA : County Record Office, Carlisle *
The Castle, Carlisle, Cumbria CA3 8UR
Tel: (01228) 812 416/812 391

LOOSE ITEMS

1530   (6 May) Letter from Sir William Skeffington to Leonard Musgrave
            and Edward Eglaby, informing them on behalf of the King and the
            Duke of Norfolk that they will receive letters and also money for the
            transporting of soldiers under their command to Ireland. They shall
            make sure that ships will be in readiness so that they can set sail
            with the next favourable wind. Skeffington also announces that he
            will send his brother and some of his men as quickly as possible.
            Written from the Tower of London. (D/AY 1/199)

COLLECTIONS

Pennington (Muncaster) MSS (ref. D/Pen)

This collection was listed by the H.M.C. in 1885, *10th Report*, App. IV, pp223–
98. Most of the calendared material is now housed at this record office. In
particular, the collection includes a number of references to the transportation of
the Graham clan to Ireland in 1606 (pp258–67 of report) which is now housed at
reference D/Pen/216.

Lonsdale MSS (ref. D/Lons)

Many of the items concerning Ireland in this collection have been either
published in full or received a partial listing. The letter books, notebooks, and
some miscellaneous papers of Sir Christopher Lowther of Whitehaven, relating to

---

[89] We would like to thank Todd Gray at the Centre for Maritime Historical Studies, University of Exeter,
for helping us identify whether there were Irish references in a merchant's account book dated 1606–26 in
the Rashleigh MSS (ref. R 4546) in this Record Office. Unfortunately nothing could be found. We wish
him well in his present task of investigating the archival sources of maritime history for England.

trade with Ireland and including his correspondence with the Irish branch of the Lowther family, were published in D.R. Hainsworth (ed.), *Commercial papers of Sir Christopher Lowther, 1611–44* (Surtees Society, Vol. 189, 1977). Part of the collection also received a H.M.C. report (*13th Report*, App.VII) which includes a number of references to Ireland, particularly in the parliamentary journals of Sir John Lowther (1623–4, 1626, 1628, 1629) now housed at D/Lons/L2/1–4. However, despite all this attention the vast bulk of this extensive collection has still to be listed in print; indeed, at present most of the collection is only partially catalogued. The following list represents most (or all) of the remaining material relating to Ireland that could be found; it is possible that there are a few more manuscripts lurking in other uncatalogued bundles.

1618–38   Legal note book of [   ] Lowther (possibly Gerard)[90], student at the Inns of Court (The Temple). It contains lecture notes taken at New Inn and Clifford's Inn, and notes of debates between students. In 1628 the author went back to New Inn, and from 1634–7 there are some accounts that he kept during his residence in London. From 1638 he was employed as a rent collector in Westmoreland. Most importantly, however, Lowther's book contains five pages of accounts that he kept while he was practising in Ireland, which commences with the following introduction, '7 September 1622: I came into Ireland with the L. Deputie Falkland the 7th of September 1622 but what I gott in the course of my practise the first year I kept no account as henceforward I resolve to doe and I beseach god to bless my labors and that I may indeavor to deserve my fees'. The accounts cover the period from 7 Sept. 1623 to Easter term 1624, and include 74 entries of legal fees paid to Lowther. The entries include cases heard in the courts of King's Bench, Common Pleas, Exchequer, Chancery, the Court of Wards, Castle Chamber, 'coram deputato' (i.e. the Deputy's Court), the Dublin tholsel, a court leet, Thomascourt, and mentions his fees for legal advice. Furthermore Lowther, prior to Easter term 1624, worked on the north-eastern circuit of the quarter sessions which heard cases at Drogheda, Dundalk, Downpatrick, Carrickfergus, Armagh and Monaghan. Each entry includes only minimal detail, giving the name of the court and his client and the fee charged, but occasionally further details are given, for example 'Scaccario: of Charles Monke for putting in information upon seisures 20s', and often the name of the other party in the case is given. Overall Lowther made £48 15s 6d during the period, the largest fees being paid by the Earl of Antrim, 50s, and Osburne Clarke, 44s [c100 fols, unfoliated]. (D/Lons/L2/8)[91]

1628–55   Bundle of four deeds entitled 'St. Bees, two leases by Richard Lowther of Ingleton, Yorks, to Gerrard Lowther of Dublin of lands at St. Bees and in Ireland 1628, etc.' (D/Lons/W Sect.III [uncatalogued], St. Bees)[92]

c1630   Account Book of Sir Patricius Curwen. This volume contains numerous entries regarding trade with Ireland in the 1620s and 1630s. (D/Lons/W [uncatalogued])[93]

---

[90] The author states that his brother was Richard Lowther, therefore the book was probably kept by either Sir John Lowther or Sir Gerard, though most likely the latter.

[91] The section on Ireland can be found mid-way through the volume.

[92] Unfortunately this bundle could not be located when the Record Office was visited by the authors.

[93] Nor could this volume be located when the Record Office was visited. The manuscript was, however, used extensively in Colin Phillips, 'Cumberland and Westmoreland Gentry 1600–65' (unpublished PhD

1632–55   Volume (43 unpaginated folios and 137 paginated folios), of accounts used by Christopher Lowther whilst he was in Ireland, 1632–5, and also by his executors after his death, 1644–55. Both of these sets of accounts are interspersed throughout the volume, and the following is a list of those accounts drawn up by Lowther prior to his death. (D/Lons/W1/8)[94]

1632–5   (8 Oct. 1632–24 Oct. 1635) General account of Lowther's business transactions in Ireland. This is by far the longest account in the volume and details many payments, especially for the purchase and transportation of wheat, coal, salt, beef, hops and staves. Furthermore there are payments of rent and many other charges incurred in running a merchant operation in Dublin. The various payments were made to a variety of mostly Dublin-based merchants, particularly Roger Gernon, Richard Balle, Thomas Dodd, Andrew Handcock, John Black, John and Thomas Cheevers, Henry Jones, John Parker, William Barker and John Newman, and many others. The overall figure for payments during these three years was £1,538 12s [unfoliated, 8 fols].

1635   (22 June–Nov.) 'Peticharges upon salt from ye 22nd July'. Short account of small payments incurred in the sale of salt [unfoliated, 1 fol.].

1635   (22 June–28 Nov.) 'Peticharges upon Coales 1635'. A longer account of similar expenses. (ff 19v–21v)

1635   (20–25 July) 'Peticharges upon Tarre Account'. Includes only two entries. (fol. 49v)

1635   (22 June–7 Dec.) 'Pettie Charges General'. This account includes a wide variety of household expenses. (ff 66v–68v)

1635   (22 June–27 Nov.) 'Pettie Charges of Sundrie Wares'. Short account of purchases. (fol. 79v)

1635   (22 June–29 Aug.) 'Voyages to Whithaven Pettie Charges'. Costs in transportation. (fol. 89v)

1635   (30 Oct.–28 Nov.) 'Petty charges upon Blood'. Very short account. (fol. 94v)

1635   (31 July–1 Aug.) 'Charges upon houshold stuff'. Miscellaneous purchases of household supplies. (fol. 99v)

c1632   (n.d.) Copy of instructions to Thomas, Viscount Wentworth, Lord Deputy of Ireland, and President of the Council of the North, on procedures to be followed in 57 articles. With marginal notes in the hand of Sir John Lowther. (D/Lons/L13/2/2)

1633–9   Bundle of bonds and other documents of Christopher Lowther of Whitehaven. The following are the items which make specific reference to Ireland, but in many of the documents the domicile of the parties is not mentioned. Therefore there may be further documents concerning Irish merchants, etc., elsewhere in the bundle. (D/Lons/W1/6)[95]

1633   (10 Sept.) Agreement between Viscount Baltinglass and Christopher Lowther, regarding 192 bushells of salt sent to John

---

thesis, University of Lancaster) to show the considerable trading activity of the Curwen family with Ireland; see especially pp195–201 of his work.

[94] Because the book was only very partially used by Lowther, his executors obviously felt justified in using the volume for their own needs. The executors' material, which makes up the bulk of this volume, does not include any references to the period prior to 1641.

[95] This is the reference for the entire bundle, the individual items do not have a specific reference number.

Williamson, and the 'sinking of one pitt for coles in Henry Davys ground of Corkhill'.

1633   (15 Sept.) Indenture between (1) George Radcliffe of Dublin, esq., and Christopher Lowther of St. Bees, and (2) Viscount Baltinglass. (1) grants to (2) all their interest in a salt works lately in the occupation of Henry Davis, in consideration of the above agreement.

1634   (15 Feb.) Bond of John Hood and Ralph Smith 'two of the horsetroop under the command of the rt. hon Edward Lord Viscount Chichester', in £5 (stg), to pay 50s (stg) before 1 May following to Christopher Lowther of Whitehaven.

1635   (19 June) Bond of Ralph Osborne of Kickestown in Co. Down, salter, in £5 14s (stg), to pay £2 17s (stg) before 29 Sept. following, to Christopher Lowther of Whitehaven. On the dorse is a note that on 5 Oct. Lowther had received only £1 5s (stg) from Osborne, leaving £1 12s (stg) outstanding.

1636   (1 April) Acknowledgement by Patrick White of Dundalk that he received of William Atkinson, for the use of Christopher Lowther, 160 barrels of white salt worth £5[ ][96] (stg), which he confesses to owe to Lowther, and will now pay in 20 days. With a note on the dorse that on 12 June 1637, he still owed £5 2s 7d.

1636   (20 April) Letter from Patrick White at Dundalk to William Atkinson at Christopher Lowther's house in Dublin, regarding Atkinson's letter of 16 April, and that he will be able to pay outstanding moneys on Wednesday next when he has made a sale.

1636   (2 June) Bond of James Lowman of Glanmagowe, Co. Kilkenny, gent., in £30 (stg), to pay £20 (stg) before 10 July following, to Christopher Lowther of St. Bees. With a note to the effect that the 'bill is given for the value thereof in Iron, wyne' which was purchased on Lowman's behalf by Lowther.

1636   (14 June) Demand note from William Atkinson at Carlingford to Patrick White at Dundalk, to repay the long outstanding £5 2s 7d for salt. With reply by White promising to pay.

1636   (16 July) One folio of Christopher Lowther's accounts, listing money owed to him and his outstanding bills.

1637   (5 Aug.) Richard Henry and Patrick Marran of Carrickfergus bind themselves in £6 11s to Henry Bailand of Whitehaven to pay £3 5s 6d (stg) to Christopher Lowther.

1637   (20 Sept.) Ferall Chrystian of Carrickfergus acknowledges to owe Christopher Lowther 25s 4d (stg), to be paid by 20 October next.

1639   (11 March) Edward Guy, servant to Richard Lowther at Dublin, acknowledges to owe 2s to Richard Powlay, and to repay him before the last week of April.

1640   (10 July) Grant by Christopher Lowther of Whitehaven to Thomas Dawson of Moyola in Co. Londonderry, gent., in consideration of 20s (stg), of a parcel of ground near the pier of Whitehaven, on condition of building a house in three years on the land (with stipulation of size, etc.), rent 10s *per annum*, to be held for ever. (D/Lons/W1/31 pp246–7)

---

[96] Only two numbers, second number destroyed, i.e. fifty something.

DEVON : County Record Office, Exeter *
Castle Street, Exeter EX4 3PU
Tel: (01392) 384 253
Fax: (01392) 384 250

LOOSE ITEMS

1488   Petition of John Atwill of Exeter, sent to Ireland with Sir Richard Edgecombe, Royal Commissioner for Ireland, in 1488. (ECA/Book 60 A, L.18)[97]

1590   (6 May) Pardon for Phillip Harte of Exeter, reprieved from the death penalty on condition of serving as a soldier in Ireland. (ECA/Book 55, fol. 187)

16th cen.   A nineteenth century transcript of the manuscript life of Sir Peter Carew, by John Hooker of Exeter. (Z19/7/2)[98]

1601   Letter ordering the Treasury to pay the Mayor of Barnstaple, John Delbridge, the sum of £296 6s 4d, owed to him for the transport of soldiers to Cork and their maintenance. (51/10)

1628   (22 March) Bargain and sale by Baldwyn Carpenter of Curryglasse in Co. Cork, yeoman, and Richard his son, mercer of the same, to William Ham of Tiverton, merchant, of tenements, messuages, etc., in Staford, Coliford and Coliton in Devonshire. (47/59)

COLLECTIONS

Courtenay of Powderham MSS (ref. 1508 M Devon)

1586   Articles for the Plantation of Munster. (Irish deeds/1)

1593   Letters patent to Henry Ughtred of the Castle of Meare, etc., Co. Limerick. (Irish deeds/2)

c1593   Letters patent to Robert Strowde of Muskerry, etc., Co. Limerick, and a copy of same. (Irish deeds/3,4)

1594   Letters patent to Sir William Courtenay of the Castle, town and lands of Castlenoa (alias Newcastle), Co. Limerick. (Irish deeds/5)

1595   Bargain and sale by Robert Strowde of Parnham, Dorset, to Sir Henry Ughtred of Meare, Co. Limerick, of all his Irish lands. (Irish deeds/6)

1611   Grant by Trinity College, Dublin, to Courtenay of Newcastle, of the lands of Ballyrobert, etc., Co. Limerick. (Irish deeds/7)

1613   Feoffment by Sir Robert Strowde to one Harres (and others) of his castles, houses, lands, etc., in Munster. (Irish deeds/8)

1617   Grant by John Dowdall to George Courtenay of Newcastle, of the lands of Kilcolman etc., Co. Limerick. (Irish deeds/9)

1620   Feoffment by Sir Robert Strowde to George Ughtred Courtenay of the lands of Muskerry, etc., in the parish of Cloneltie, Co. Limerick (attainted lands of Gerald, Earl of Desmond). (Irish deeds/10)

1623   Bargain and sale by George Ughtred Courtenay to John Dowdall of lands at Kiltermanleagh. (Irish deeds/11)

---

[97] This item is undated, but Sir Richard Edgecombe's mission to Ireland was in May–July 1488.

[98] For a published version of this see *Cal. Carew Mss.*, i, pp lxvii–cxviii.

1625	Bargain and sale by George Ughtred Courtenay to Dominic Roche of Limerick, of the lands of Cahirleawye, etc., Co. Limerick. (Irish deeds/12)
1627	Grant by George Courtenay to Andrew Comyn of Limerick, of the castle and lands of Portrynard in the parish of Templecley and of the monastery of Nephelagh. (Irish deeds/13)
1629	Feoffment by George Ughtred Courtenay to Richard Harte of the town of Lasneshenegery. (Irish deeds/14)
1629	Deed Poll by George Ughtred Courtenay to Thomas Gibbon of Co. Limerick, of lands in the parish of Mohownagh. (Irish deeds/15)
1629	Marriage settlement between George Ughtred Courtenay and Richard Harte in relation to Katherine Gore and concerning the town of Lasneshenegery. (Irish deeds/16)
1639	Feoffment by George Ughtred Courtenay to Richard Harte of the town and lands of Lasneshenegery, etc. (Irish deeds/17)
1639	Grant of wardship (?) to George Ughtred Courtenay involving lands in Co. Limerick. (Irish deeds/18)
1640	Feoffment by George Ughtred Courtenay to James Bourke of the lands of Rhine (?) and Rathmack in Connolagh. (Irish deeds/18a)
1641	Assignment by George Ughtred Courtenay to Anthony Dowdall, of the lands of Killtenanleigh. (Irish deeds/19)
.1641	Assignment by George Ughtred Courtenay to James Creagh, of the lands of Cloun-lehard. (Irish deeds/20)

Courtenay Additional MSS (ref. 1508 M/Devon add.)

1638	(9 May) Copy of the grant of the manors of Mayne, Newcastle, etc., Co. Limerick, by Charles I to George Courtenay. (Irish deeds/1/1)

Totnes Borough MSS (ref. 1579)

A report and calendar of this collection appeared in the H.M.C., *3rd Report*, Appendix, p341–50, which includes documents relating to troops sent to Ireland in 1601–2 (refs. 1579 A/17/15&18).

DEVON : North Devon Record Office, Barnstaple *
Tuly Street, Barnstaple EX32 7EJ
Tel: (01271) 388 608

LOOSE ITEMS

1632	(12 Oct.) Deed of arrangement and sale between Rowland Colstone of Bristol, merchant stapler, and Edmond Knowles of Minehead, merchant stapler. Colstone sells to Knowles any wool, cloth or frieze that Colstone's factor, Nathan Coggan, shall buy in Ireland under Knowles's advice over the following year. Knowles is to cover all the charges of transportation, customs, etc., and to pay Colstone 10% of his profits for the first shipment, and 11% thereafter. They also bind themselves in £500 for the performance of these agreements. (B1/682)

COLLECTIONS

Chichester of Shirwell MSS (ref. 48/25)[99]

This collection includes nine deeds dated 1459–1625, relating to the English estates of the Flemings, barons Slane, and the Dillon family (ref. 48/25/9&10). The lands involved were the manors of Croyde Hoe, Bratton Fleming, Chumhill, High Bray, Alverdiscott, Ash Rogus, and South Molton, all in Devonshire, and many of the documents pre-date 1485. In 1502, the estate was partitioned between Christopher, Lord Slane's, co-heirs, Amy Bellewe and Anne Dillon (ref. 48/25/9/8), and the remaining documents in the collection concern the Dillon portion. In 1599 Robert Dillon sold this large estate to Robert Chichester of Youlton, for £9,900 (ref. 48/25/9/9), and thereafter a branch of the Dillons continued in residence on part of the estate as tenants.

Incledon–Webber of Braunton MSS (ref. 3704 M)

This collection is very similar to the Chichester MSS above, and includes over 60 items concerning the Bellewe and Dillon estates in Devonshire, 1559–1629. The earliest document, dated 1559, is a deed concerning the 1502 partition of Christopher, Lord Slane's, Devon estate, between Robert Dillon and William Bellewe (ref. 3704 M/TL4/21). Thereafter the collection records the sales made by the Bellewe family to a junior branch of the Dillons, who in turn sold it in lots to the Incledon family between 1625 and 1629 (ref. 3704 M/TL4/37–50).

DEVON : West Devon Record Office, Plymouth *

Unit 3, Clare Place, Coxside, Plymouth PL4 0JW
Tel: (01752) 385 940

LOOSE ITEMS

17th cen.   Two volumes of notes and biographical sketches drawn from original documents entitled, 'Damnonii Orientales Illustres or The Wortheys of Devon', by John Prince (1643–1723), Vicar of Berry Pomery, and author of *Worthies of Devon* in 1701. By the time of his death Prince had collected a great deal of further biographical material for which he could find no publisher. This unpublished work was collected into the two volumes mentioned here which include extensive entries for Sir Hugh Clotworthy with a long digression on the Irish wars (p85), as well as for Benjamin Culme, Dean of St. Patrick's Cathedral in Dublin (p93), and Thomas Stuckley (p579). Curiously, the entry concerning Clotworthy contains a retelling of the old prophesy that five brethren to an earl would be carried into England never to come back, which was seen as a foretelling of the fate of Silken Thomas and his five uncles in the reign of Henry VIII. (WDRO 373/1–2)[100]

COLLECTIONS

Plymouth Borough Papers (ref. W)

The borough archives are extensive, and are listed below under their various sub-sections. Most of the material relates to trade and the borough's tolls and customs

---

[99] This collection was originally housed in the County Record Office in Exeter, but was transferred to Barnstaple when that office was opened in 1988.

[100] This volume was originally part of the Phillips MSS of Cheltenham. For an introduction to these volumes see *Devon and Cornwall Notes and Queries*, xxxi (1968–70), pp67–77 & 171–3.

charges. The documents record trade with many Irish ports, particularly Wexford, Galway, Cork, Drogheda, Waterford and Londonderry. The H.M.C. reports on the collection (*9th Report*, App. I, pp262–84 and *10th Report*, App. IV, pp536–60) include some documents concerning Ireland prior to 1641 (*9th Report*, App. I, p265). The volume containing these items is now catalogued as W359, and is treated below.

Borough Court Papers (ref. W355–6)

This is a large collection of legal papers concerning cases heard in the town courts during the sixteenth and seventeenth centuries, and includes some references to Ireland. There are three documents arising from a case in 1641, when Thomas and Anne Jones, executors of Thomas Scoose, brought Anthony Bazarte of Crookehaven in Co. Cork, merchant, to court over the non-payment of debts (W356 sub 1641).

Bushelage and Keelage Accounts (ref. W139–45)

This series covers the dates 1618–29, and includes seven account books. Irish ships and barques figure prominently with each paying the standard charge of 1s 4d keelage. The accounts for 1618–9 (W139) include nine such boats. However, the listings never actually name the boats or their occupants, and seldom name their port of origin, except for the standard 'a Iresh ship' or 'a Iresh barck'. Notably, there do not appear to be any references to Irish ships paying bushelage.

Cranage Accounts (ref. W149–52)

The port's cranage accounts cover the dates 1620–26, and record the payments made to labourers, called 'Jobers', for removing ships' cargoes to the warehouses situated along the quays. For example, on 20 December 1620, the following entry is given, 'Olyver French, Ireshman for 17 tons beef and talow 6d per tone payd the Jobers 18d Resteth 7s.' (W149 fol. 3r). It should also be noted that the cranage accounts occasionally list the water bailiff's fines on ship owners. In 1624 a fine of 2s 6d was received from David Roche, an Irishman, 'for sweepings thrown into the water' (W150 fol. 5r).

Moorage Accounts (ref. W146–8a)

These account books are dated 1621–31, and concern the charges paid for mooring a vessel in the harbour. Once again Irish ships are prominent, and occasionally the port of origin is stated as well. Though the charge was usually 6d. per vessel, it could vary between 4d. and 1s. In the accounts for Michaelmas 1631 to Michaelmas 1632, a total of 27 Irish ships paid moorage at the port (W148a).

Tonnage and Keyadge Accounts (ref. W153–6)

This series, dated 1621–6, includes many detailed references to Irish merchants, their cargoes and their payments for keyadge. For example in 1627, the following entry appears, 'Received of Thomas Coling of Washford for 9 tones of beames and coopers tymber 4d per tonne, 3s' (W156 fol. 2r). There are similar entries throughout the collection. However, there seem to be no references to Irish merchants paying tonnage.

Town Customs (ref. W162–7)

The Plymouth customs accounts (1620–33) are doubly valuable to historians, for not only do they list incoming merchants who paid the town custom, but they also frequently record the annual moorage, keyadge, cranage, keelage and tonnage accounts. As a result, because the customs accounts series is easily the lengthiest series that has survived, it provides much additional material concerning moorage, cranage and the like.[101] This aspect aside, the Plymouth customs accounts are a valuable historical source in their own right. A typical account gives the name of each merchant who was charged the custom, and lists his cargo as well as the toll paid, e.g. the 1620–1 account book notes that 'Roger Copinger Iresh the 12th March 2 tonnes ½ of tallow 3s 4d per tone … 8s' (W162 fol. 2v) There are many references to Ireland throughout the series.

Miscellaneous Borough Papers (ref. W359)

This is a volume of manuscripts relating to the borough of Plymouth from 1496 to 1800, and it includes the following items concerning Ireland:[102]

1607	(14 Feb.) Letter from the Mayor of Plymouth and James Bagg to the Earl of Salisbury. Relating the arrival on 12 Feb. of a boat from St. Malo bound for Ireland. A passenger on the ship, Thomas Myller, page to Robert Marshall, late of Kelfynon in Ireland,[103] and now resident in Jersey, was searched and arrested. On his person they found a box of letters addressed to various people in Ireland, an 'Agnus Dei' and two other Catholic pictures. These items are sent to Salisbury. (W359/38)
1607	(14 Feb.) The examination of the aforementioned Thomas Myller, aged 18 years, by the Mayor of Plymouth. He explains that he was bringing the letters to Ireland from Jersey, under the orders of his master (Marshall). He was forced to land in Plymouth because of contrary winds. The 'Agnus Dei' was intended to be delivered to Lady Walsh, and the other pictures to Lady Slane. Myller states that both these women are Roman Catholics, and that his master used to own the items. (W359/39)
1607	(18 Feb.) Letter from the Lords of the Council to the Mayor of Plymouth and James Bagge, ordering the release of Thomas Myller and the restoration to him of the box of letters and pictures that had been entrusted to him by his master, Robert Marshall. Marshall is not unknown to the Council 'by reason of his late imployment in his Majesties service in Mounster'. (W359/40)
1607	(24 Feb.) Rough draft of a letter of passport and free passage, signed by the Mayor, on behalf of Thomas Myller, travelling to Cork in Ireland with letters and tokens. (W359/43)
1608	(29 Aug.) Draft letter from the Mayor of Plymouth to the Earl of Salisbury, relating to a ship from the 'Groyne' which has just landed in Plymouth. On board was an Irish youth, who had been put out of service by his master (Sir William Stanton), and is now travelling to London to the Earl of Clanricard. The pilot of the boat, however, stated that the youth had been drunk in Groyne, and had told him that there was a fleet bound for Ireland bringing the Earl of Tyrone to make him King of Ireland. (W359/55)

---

[101] It should be noted that not all the town customs accounts record this information.

[102] It is likely that this volume is the item described by Hayes as 'Ms IV : Items temp. Elizabeth I including items relating to Irish affairs' as no volume or manuscript of this name could be found in the Record Office. This seems more probable when we consider that some of the documents in this volume, concerning Sir William Stanton's ex-servant (W359/55), were noticed in the H.M.C. report on the collection (*9th Report*, App. I, p265), and the H.M.C. identified the volume as 'Ms. IV' of the Plymouth borough archives.

[103] He was 2nd Justice of Munster.

1641   (27 June) Order from the House of Commons to the Mayor of Plymouth, touching the imprisonment of John Poyer of Pembroke, who at the order of the House stayed a certain loaded ship that came to Milford from Galway in Ireland, a town actually in rebellion. Poyer is to be released.[104] (W359/72)

DORSET : County Record Office *
9 Bridport Road, Dorchester DT1 1RP
Tel: (01305) 250 550
Fax: (01305) 224 839

LOOSE ITEMS

Eliz. I   Undated late sixteenth century order to the bailiffs of Bridport to have a soldier furnished with a corselet for the Queen's service in Ireland. (Bridport Borough Papers, DC/BTB/FG 4)

1641   (7 Jan.) A warrant for a commission to the Earl of Strafford to be Lieutenant and Governor General of Ireland. (D/BKL uncatalogued)

1641   A bundle of miscellaneous material, including notes on the trial of the Earl of Strafford, dated 1641, evidently drawn up by one of his accusers (possibly John Pym) after his execution. Among other things, the author states that when Strafford said that laws 'are but ministerial and ought to exact and not dispute the king's writs', he had been drawn to dispute the point, declaring 'I deny those words ... I pray a convenient time for making my proofs ... By managing of the Evidence is meant the ordering, applying and inforcing the Evidence according to ye truth of ye fact' [3pp]. (Lyme Regis Borough Archive, DC/LR/O4a)

COLLECTIONS

The Pleydell–Railston of Whatcombe Archive (ref. D/PLR)

1634–7   A small bundle of deeds relating to the various properties in the barony of Loughty, Co. Cavan, and in the City of Dublin, to which Benjamin Culme, Dean of St. Patrick's Cathedral, was party, viz.

     1634   (4 Feb.) Indenture between (1) 'the worshipfull Benjamin Culme, deane of the Cathedrall Church of St. Patricks, Dublin, and the Chapter of the same', and (2) John Pue alias Aphugh of Dublin, gent., witnessing that the Lords Justice and Council of Ireland have licensed the Dean and Chapter to let two waste plots of ground in St Bride's parish near Sir Thomas Rotherham's house and adjoining the King's pavement in Golden Lane (now in the possession of Captain William Magre and Anne Howard, widow), to hold to Pue for 81 years at a rent of 40s per annum. Witnesses: John Pugh, John Allen, Henry Gwynn and John Ampthill. (D/PLR/T 465)

     1637   (21 March) Indenture between Robert Fferward, Chantor of St. Patrick's Cathedral, and Stephen Stephens of Dublin, gent., witnessing that Fferward, with the consent of the Dean and

---

[104] It is highly unlikely that this item really belongs to 1641, and more probably dates from 1642 at the earliest.

Chapter, has agreed to let to Stephens a garden or waste plot belonging to the chantorship on the east side of St. Bride's Street, for 40 years at a rent of £3 *per annum*. Witnesses: Gilbert Domville, Thomas Parry, William Sweetnam and Nathaniel Hewet. On the reverse is a memo dated 14 Dec. 1637 recording that in consideration of £25, Stephens sold his interest to Dean Benjamin Culme. Witnesses: Philip Culme, Philip Fennelly and Philip Watson. (D/PLR/T 466)

1637 (31 May) Indenture between Philip Culme of London, merchant-tailor, and Dean Benjamin Culme, reciting that in consideration of a certain sum (unspecified) paid to Philip by the Dean, Philip agrees to sell to the Dean all the poles or parcels of land with their appurtenances which he holds in the barony of Loughty, Co. Cavan, *viz.* Dromany, Agarilly, Tallagh & Gortichore, and the moieties of Tullianagh, Killchore, Killanahere, Rahaha and the house of Lissamogan. Witnesses: Edwin Babington, Henry Williams and Hugh Reilly. (D/PLR/T 463)

1637 (1 June) Indenture between same and same, witnessing that Philip Culme, in performance of a deed of 16 July 1634 made with Dean Benjamin, and also in consideration of £600 paid to him by the Dean, has agreed to grant and confirm his property in Loughty, Co. Cavan to the Dean and his heirs for ever. Witnesses as above. (D/PLR/T 464)

The Sherborne Castle Estate Archive (ref. D/SHC)

1563–1635 A bundle of documents relating to the manor and barony of Geasehill in King's County, all of which are in very poor condition,[105] *viz.*

1563 Extract from a grant by Thomas, Earl of Sussex, chief governor of Ireland, to Teige McCahir and Callough McTeige, of a wooden castle and its appurtenances in Derrymollen and the two Brechams in the King's County, together with all messuages, cottages, orchards, etc., in Clonhast, Kepoughe, Ballimolland, Clyncoucorke, Cappekillmore, Kylkelly and Raghenan. (D/SHC/KG 2701)

1563 (25 Oct.) Copy of a grant by Queen Elizabeth to Lysagh McMorogh of the lands and hereditaments of Raynduff, Ballyevell, Ballinoe and Ballycollyn in King's County. (D/SHC/KG 2693)

1620 (1 March) Release by Con McTeige O'Connor of Ballinghamoyne, gent., and Bryan O'Connor his son, to Lady Lettice Digby, Baroness Offaly, widow of Sir Robert Digby, of the lands of Ballenghomoyne and Annagharmoy in King's County. (D/SHC/KG 2694)

1624 (24 Nov.) Petition of Charles Connor requesting arbitration in a boundary dispute with the Baroness of Offaly about the limits of his estate at Killiler in Geashill barony. (D/SHC/KG 2695)

1627 (30 Oct.) Feoffment to uses by (1) Lettice, Baroness Offaly, Robert, Lord Digby, Baron of Geashill, her son, Lord Docwra of Kilmore, Treasurer-at-war in Ireland, Sir John Moore of Croghan, Robert Lloyd of Geashill, gent., and Edward Hammett of the same, gent., to (2) Sir Adam Loftus of Rathfarnham, Co.

---

[105] Of the following eight items no less than five (KG 2693–4, 2696–7 and 2701) are so badly mutilated that they are unfit for consultation. The summary descriptions given here are based on the catalogue descriptions which are available on request from the archivist.

Dublin, Sir Laurence Parsons, Sir Luke Fitzgerald of Tennoghan, Co. Meath, and Walter Weldon of Athy, Co. Kildare, esq., re the barony and territory of Geashill, the advowson of the church of St. Mary the Virgin there, and the dissolved monastery of Killeigh, all in King's County. (D/SHC/KG 2696)

1632   (20 Dec.) Deed of mortgage whereby (1) Robert, Lord Digby of Geashill, Lettice, Baroness Offaly his mother, Sir Adam Loftus of Rathfarnham, Sir Luke Fitzgerald and Walter Weldon agree to convey the property in KG 2696 above to (2) Sir Richard Boyle, Earl of Cork. (D/SHC/KG 2697)

c1635   (n.d.) Petition addressed to Lord Deputy Wentworth by Lettice, Baroness Offaly, reciting that in accordance with an award made by the late King, James I, on 11 July 1619, she is entitled to receive £300 from Elizabeth, Dowager Countess of Kildare. To date she has only received £200, and asks the Deputy to order the delivery of the remaining £100. (D/SHC/KG 2702)

c1635   (n.d.) Loose page of a draft copy of an order by King Charles I to un-named commissioners to 'take such course as you shall thincke convenient that the sayd morgage of Moylagh may ... be produced before you'; the order follows a petition to the Crown by Lady Offaly to settle the ownership of Moylagh manor. (D/SHC/KG 2703)

DORSET : Poole Borough Archive
Museum Service, 4 High Street, Poole, Dorset BH15 1BW
Tel: (01202) 683 138
Fax: (01202) 660 896

The late Mr. D.F. Beamish, assistant borough archivist, believed there were a few fleeting references to trade with Ireland in the borough archives, but did not have any further details. Since his death in 1993 the archives have been in the process of a major reorganisation and extensive listing which have as yet produced no confirmed references to Ireland. It is possible, however, that something will turn up eventually.

DURHAM : University of Durham, Dept. of Palaeography and Diplomatic
5 The College, Durham DH1 3EQ
Tel: (0191) 374 3610
Fax: (0191) 374 7481

LOOSE ITEMS

1636   (28 Nov.) Will of Robert Dale of Dublin. He made his mother, Margerie Dale, executrix, but the administration of his goods was entrusted, on a bond of £40, to two men of the City of Durham. He made a legacy of 12s 11d to the poor of St Bride's parish in Dublin. (Durham Probate Records, sub anno 1637)[106]

1637   Inventory of Ferdinando Crawforth, a grain merchant from Tweedmouth, near Berwick upon Tweed, who died in 1637. The archivist informs us that Crawforth was very wealthy, as his probate bond was for £1,000, a rare sum at this time. Among his debts was

---

[106] He died sometime between the making of this will and August, 1637.

one of £9 10s due by bond from Thomas Whyte of Dublin. (Durham Probate Records, sub anno 1637)

ESSEX : County Record Office *
PO Box 11, County Hall, Chelmsford CM1 1LX
Tel: (01245) 430 067
Fax: (01245) 430 085

LOOSE ITEMS

1632   (30 June) Grant by (1) Sir Richard Wingfield, Viscount Powerscourt, Marshal of H.M. Kingdom of Ireland, and William, Lord Fitzwilliam, Baron of Liffer, to (2) Sir Nicholas Byron of Holborn in Middlesex, of an annual rent charge of £50 out of the manor of Gaynes Park in Essex, to hold to Byron, his wife Dame Sophia and their son and heir William, for life in survivorship, on the death of Richard, Viscount Powerscourt without issue. (D/DCe)

c1641   Extract from the records of Bradfield parish reporting 'The names of all those inhabitants thereof as have freely contributed and given towards the relief of those poor distressed Protestants in Ireland according to that Act to that purpose made by the Honorable House of Parliament'. The document goes on to list a total of 57 people from the parish, with details of how much each gave; altogether £11 3s 2d was collected. (Luckyn MSS, Box 6, D/DH VI A116)

1641–2   (May 1641 – May 1642) Annual churchwarden's accounts for the parish of Waltham Holy Cross, which records the payment of 3d out of the parish funds 'for an act towards the contribution for Ireland'. (D/P 75/5/1, fol. 100r)

SMALL COLLECTIONS

Chelmsford Churchwarden's Accounts[107]

1639   Payment of a shilling to two Irishmen, Stephen Ralfe and Briatt Ralfe, who came to Chelmsford with letters of commendation.

1641   (4 April) Payment of a shilling to four Irishwomen.

1641   (15 April) 'To an Irish man the 15 Aprill ... 1s 0d'.

Clayton MSS (ref. D/DAc)[108]

1635   (11 May) Assignment of the manor of Beaulieu *alias* New Hall, etc., in Essex by (1) Randall MacDonnell, Viscount Dunluce (son and heir apparent of Sir Randall MacDonnell, Earl of Antrim), Katherine, Duchess of Buckingham, and Thomas, Viscount Savage to (2) Philip, Earl of Pembroke & Montgomery and Sir Robert Pye of Westminster. (D/DAc 35)

---

[107] Bound verbatim transcripts of these are available on the open shelves in the Record Office.

[108] The Clayton MSS are widely dispersed throughout Britain, Ireland and the United States. For an introduction and guide to the collection as a whole, which includes the present location of each section, see Frank T. Melton, 'The Clayton Papers', *Bulletin of the Institute of Historical Research*, 52 (1979), pp91–9. Further pre-1641 material was found in the Clayton deposit in the Glamorgan Archive Service, Cardiff (see below).

1635   (11 Nov.) Further assignment of the same estate by the same parties as above. (D/DAc 36)

Essex Sessions Rolls (ref. Q/SR)

1566   (7 Jan.) At Brentwood: 'Received the 16th December last of the constable of Hatton one William Gryffyn and delivered [him] to the constable of Brokestreat to pass into Ireland'. (Q/SR 17/51)

1580   (5 Oct.) Inquiry taken before Sir Thomas Lodge, including the examination of John Tremayn who came lately out of Ireland 'and shows forth his passport which is very like to be counterfeit and says he arrived at Arborough above three weeks past'. (Q/SR 76/56)

1614   (Epiphany) Names of prisoners in the House of Correction, which includes 'Thomas Garrett and Eleanor his wife, with Margaret Roche her reputed sister, of Monton Castle in Ireland, [who] being taken vagrant with a counterfeit passport were committed by Sir Henry Maxey [on] 11 Jan.'. (Q/SR 205/119)

1627   (Easter) Names of same, which includes 'Ellen Barke of Limerick in the county of Munster [sic] in the kingdom of Ireland, who pretendeth that she came into England to be relieved by her uncle William Barke of London (but where he dwelleth she does not know); she was taken vagrant at Great Coggeshall and was committed by Bob Aylet on 28th March'. (Q/SR 257/79)

1639   (Michaelmas) Names of same, which includes 'Margaret Smith and Ellen Smith her sister, taken vagrant at Barking, and begging; committed by Ezechial Kightley, esq., [on] 6th Oct.'. The decision of the court was that they were to be 'well whipped and sent to Waterford in Ireland'. (Q/SR 307/124)

Hill Hall MSS (ref. D/DSh)

The most celebrated part of this collection contains a small bundle of papers relating to Sir Thomas Smith's attempt to colonise Ulster during the reign of Elizabeth I (D/DSh 01).[109] The following list is slightly more detailed than that available in the National Library of Ireland:

1572   (27 July) Quitclaim by Thomas Smith to his father Sir Thomas Smith, for £250, of all the rights and interests in the district of the Great and Little Ards, Clandeboy, towards the south from the castles of Belfast, Nowbrey and Tome, to the late monastery of Masserine in Clandeboy, and in Tyrone and Clandeboy, 'which the said Sir Thomas smyth knight or I the said Thomas his sonne or our heires or assignes, before the xxviiith daie of March ... 1579 against the Yrish shall obtaine, possesse and inhabite', in accordance with royal letters patent, dated 16 Nov. 1571. (D/DSh 01/1)

1573   (1 Dec.) 'Orders set out by Sr Thomas Smyth knight, Chancelor of the noble order of the Garter, princypall Secretary to her highnes and Colonell of the Ardes and sowth Clandeboy, whereby all adventurers for the Ardes may be advertised what and how they may clayme by any booke heretofore set out in his and Thomas Smith esq., his sonne's name, now deceased'. These detailed orders relate to the arms, etc., required of each man, with provisions for

---

[109] For an analysis of the colony based on this collection, see Hiram Morgan, 'The colonial venture of Sir Thomas Smith in Ulster, 1571–5', *Historical Journal*, xxviii (1985), pp261–78.

temporary or permanent loss of land for being 'unfurnished or evill furnished'; the allotment of land to the adventurers in accordance with the number of armed men provided (including the creation of lordships of hundreds, half hundreds and manors with courts leet and baron); the calling out of the soldiers, which is to be limited to one half (except during an emergency) so that 'the courts barons and the leetes may be the better kept'; the division of the freeholds into 'hondreths, fyfties and tenths' over which are to be sent 'centuriers', 'cinquanteners' and 'deceniers' elected at the leets; division of spoils; the execution and fortification of a 'princypall Cytie or towne of strength' which is the 'chief strength to forifie a Colonie'. The document bears the signatures of Sir Thomas Smith and 16 others, 10 of whose names are accompanied by the numbers of horsemen and foot soldiers that they have committed to the enterprise, *viz* Henry Berkeley (25 horse, 50 foot), Jerome Brett (25 horse, 50 foot), William Clayton ('footmen & horsemen to the number of 12 plowland'), Fran. Cary (10 horse, 13 foot), T. Lancaster (6 horse, 12 foot), Edmund Derney (20 horse, 40 foot), Edward Russell (10 horse, 30 foot), Francis Brymynge (50 foot or 25 horse), Thomas Sergeant (10 horse, 10 foot), Thomas Leveke (1 footman). The remaining six signatories were C. Smith, Laurence Nicholson, John Joyce, Edmund Halle, Anthony Stapley and Dutton. (D/DSh 01/2)

1573   (8 Dec.) Deed of covenant between Sir Thomas Smith and Sir John Berkeley of Beverstone Castle in Gloucestershire, by which Berkeley agrees to provide footmen and horsemen in the 'towne or cytie called the Queenes New Colony or Smyths Colen' in return for 40 ploughlands at Comber Monastery and Lough Con, each ploughland containing 253 acres; Berkeley is to pay an annual rent of 42s 2d per ploughland to Smith. In addition there are clauses relating to the loss of men through battle, plague, or other causes; the use of timber for building houses and ships; inter-marriage with 'the wyeld Irysh' or 'Scotishe Irish' is forbidden; likewise Berkeley or his assigns cannot set land to the Irish, except by leashold for a maximum term of five years. (D/DSh 01/3)

1573   (13 Dec.) Bond in £1,000 by Jerome Brett of Leeds Castle in Kent to provide 100 armed soldiers to serve under Sir Thomas Smith in accordance with the orders signed by him on 1 Dec. (01/2 above). (D/DSh 01/4)

1573   (16 Dec.) Deed of covenant between Sir Thomas Smith and Francis Brunyng of Chisinbury in Wiltshire, gent., similar to 01/3 above; although his rent is the same as Berkeley's (i.e. 42s 4d per plough-land), Brunyng's interest covers 50 ploughlands. (D/DSh 01/5)

1573   (18 Dec.) Bond of Francis Brunyng in £500 to provide 50 armed men, similar to 01/4 above. (D/DSh 01/6)

1573   (20 Dec.) 'Offices necessarie in the Colony of the Ardes and orders agreed uppon'. The document lists the qualities and functions required of officials such as the 'Chieftayne or Deputie Colonell, or Setler of the Colony', 'Common Counsell', 'Privie Counsell of martiall affaires', 'Mr. of the horsemen', 'Trybune or Coronell of the footemen', 'The Marshall', 'The Mouster master', 'Chapleynes', 'Faters of the Colony', and other 'aides and assistauntes'. The tithes of the colony are to be divided among the officers according to rank 'tyll the countrie be divided into parishes, half hondreths and hondreths'. Captains are advised not to banquet and feast one another 'for these two yeares', to consult one another before and after dinner, and not to entertain a stranger in company with other captains, on grounds of security and expense. The document states that these orders have been made 'because you must begin as [if] you were all in warre', and it concludes with an 'Advice or admonycion' by Sir Thomas Smith that 'Two things do I wishe most specyallie avoyded now at the beginynge of this Colony, superfluity of fare or delicatree, and excesse of apparel. For yow be com to laye the foundation of a good and (as is hoped) an eternall Colony for your posteritie, not a May game or a stage playe ... And a soldier is praysed rather for his good harnes on a valyante back. A good weapon in his hande, than for his painted and well colored coats or cloake'. The document is signed by Sir Thomas Smith, Jerome Brett and George Smith. (D/DSh 01/7)

1577   (1 Feb.) Grant by Sir Thomas Smith to his nephew William Smith of all the estates in Ireland granted to him by letters patent on 16 Nov. 1571. (D/DSh 01/8)

c1578   (n.d.) Power of attorney from George Smith of London, esq., and John Wood of Greenstead, gent., executors of Sir Thomas Smith, deceased, to William Smith (nephew of Sir Thomas), for the better recovery of debts due in virtue of bonds entered into by various persons, including 01/4–5. (D/DSh 01/9)

1580   (16 April) Grant by George Smith of Mount Hall, esq., and John and William his sons, to Anthony Morley of Lewes in Suffolk, esq., of the site of Arkayne within the Little Ardes in Ulster and a sixth part of all the estates in Ireland granted to Sir Thomas Smith, now deceased, by letters patent in 1571, at an annual rent of a boar and a hogshead of claret, or 40s in lieu of the same. (D/DSh 01/10)

Maldon Borough Archives (ref. D/B 3)

Maldon has an extensive body of records dating back to the reign of Elizabeth I, in particular a long run of chamberlain's accounts. The following references should not be taken as a definitive listing of all the relevant Irish material in the collection:

1598   Annual chamberlain's accounts (D/B 3/3 273), which include the following items of interest:

p6   Under the heading 'Souldyers', the Chamberlain prays to be allowed 12s 2d paid and delivered in prest money for the costs of sending six soldiers to Ireland, over and besides the £10 that was collected for them.

p8   In the section marked 'Foreign payments', the Chamberlain accounts for 2s paid towards the setting forth of light horse into Ireland, which sum was wanting of that collected for the service.

p8   He also accounts for a further 3s paid in prest money to the Irish soldiers, with a note that the sum was not redelivered.

1599   Annual chamberlain's accounts for the borough of Maldon (D/B 3/3 162, un-paginated), with twelve separate references to troops bound for Ireland, all under the 'Foreign Payments' heading, viz.

(a)   For charges laid forth by the bailiff in carrying a letter to Mr Wiseman, and for carrying the money (collected in Maldon) unto Chelmsford when the light horse went into Ireland ... 3s 4d.

(b)   For money laid forth by Edmund Ffrench or Ffrende,[110] the sergeant for horse-hire, and other expenses in riding to London about the town's business and in going to Chelmsford with the soldiers ... 9s 2d.

(c)   For money due to John Pratt for twelve yards of cloth at 9s 6d the yard to make eight soldiers' coats, and other expenses ...£8 6s 10d.

(d)   For money to the bailiff for the making of eight soldiers' coats for the town this year ... 18s 0d.

(e)   For money paid to Thomas Parkys for keeping a sick soldier in his house that was set forth out of the town for the Queen's service in Ireland ... 5s 0d.

(f)   For money paid forth in prest money to the soldiers that went into Ireland, which was not repaid again ... 10s 0d.

(g)   Payment to Edmund Ffrench or Ffrende, the sergeant, to go with the said soldiers to Chelmsford ... 12d.

(h)   Money paid to William Webb the cutler for making the soldiers' swords and daggers, and for lining their headpieces when they went to Chelmsford on 17 August to train before going to Ireland ... 8s 4d.

(i)   Money given to Captain Weston's man bringing a letter to the bailiff for the adjoining of the soldiers when they were appointed to have gone forth ... 12d.

(j)   Money for 'taffaye silk & thread' delivered by Mr Breder unto Robert Pollard for the trimming of the soldiers' coats ... 6s 8d.

(k)   Payment for two girdles for the soldiers ... 4d.

(l)   Payment for cloth to make bags for the soldiers ... 9d.

1603   Annual chamberlain's accounts (D/B 3/3 274), which includes just the one reference to Ireland, again under the heading 'Foreign Payments', *viz.* a payment of 2s to 'divers soldiers' returning from the wars in Ireland.

Mildmay of Marks MSS (ref. D/DMs)

Although this collection was given a brief calendar in H.M.C., *7th Report*, App. (1879), pp 590–1, some of the Irish material which it covered has since been scattered. The following items are all that remain in the Record Office:

1580–3   The accounts of George Hervey the younger for all receipts and payments made on behalf of his brother, George Hervey the elder, from the feast of St. Michael the Archangel 1580 to the annunciation of the Blessed Virgin Mary 1583. The account makes mention of three Irish payments: (1) £20 to Richard Wingfield upon George Hervey the elder's letter for payment to be made to 'a marchant of Develing [i.e. Dublin]'; (2) 2s 'for 3 ells of canvas to trusse your stuff in to send to Yreland'; (3) £10 to Thomas Maria Wingfield upon George the elder's letter. (D/DMs F4, pp 2–3)[111]

1601   Copies of two receipts for sums given to Sir George Carew, Master of the Ordnance, for the supply of ammunition for use in Ireland. (D/DMs O4/1–2)[112]

---

[110] Surname unclear.

[111] Of these, only the payment for canvas was mentioned in the H.M.C. report.

[112] These two items are all that now remain in the collection of the 14 receipts 1599–1600 mentioned in H.M.C., *7th Report*, App., p591.

Myles & Doddinghurst Place MSS (ref. D/DFa)

1564–71   A bundle of papers concerning Richard Stanley, one of the Tellers of the Exchequer in England, 1555–94 (D/DFa O4), which contains the following items of Irish interest:

1564   (29 Jan. – 6 Feb.) Six letters from the Marquis of Winchester to Richard Stanley concerning payments made under Winchester's orders by the Mayor of the Staple to Sir William Fitzwilliam, Vice-Treasurer and Treasurer-at-war in Ireland, to satisfy Fitzwilliam's outstanding wages and other matters. Figures amounting to £5,700 were paid in this way, and Stanley is required to settle the account with the Mayor of the Staple.

c1571   (n.d.) Petitions to the Lord Treasurer of England and Sir Walter Mildmay, Chancellor of the Exchequer, which include: (1) a petition for the sum of £212 12s 10d to cover the allowance of Captain [Nicholas] Malby and Captain Jasper Horsey, dated 27 Sept. 1571 'upon Ireland warrant', as appeared by a constat of the Auditor, Mr Jermyn; (2) a petition for the sum of £261 1s 5d allowed to Sir Peter Carew in April 1571, as appeared by a similar constat; (3) a petition for the sum of £70 allowed to be paid to Callough O'More; (4) and a petition for £56 6s 2d due to Mr [Nicholas] White, as by his bill may appear.

Petre MSS (ref. D/DP)

1583   (After 20 July) An inventory of the household stuff belonging to the Earl of Sussex made shortly after his death on 20 July 1583, which mentions that the late Earl possessed three white Irish mantles, value 30s, one double murrye Irish mantle, value 13s 4d, one blue Irish mantle, value 12d, and one yellow Irish mantle, value 12d. (D/DP F240/1, page 15)

1584   Bond of £47 from Oliver Lambert of Dublin to George Greene of Castlewaring, Co. Kildare. (D/DP Z82)

1622   Quitclaim by Jerome [   ][113] of Lesloe, Co. Cork, to all persons of all his rights in his lands in England (un-named) pertaining to him in right of his wife, or which his wife shall sell or has already sold. (D/DP E93)

LARGE COLLECTIONS

Barrett Lennard Muniments (ref. D/DL)

This vast collection includes the extensive estate and family papers of the Loftus family of Clones, Co. Monaghan. A small part of the collection, comprising some of the legal records of Lord Chancellor Loftus, were published by the H.M.C. in *Various Collections III* (1904), and cover the years 1634–1715. These published items are now catalogued as D/DL L56/1–7. Some of the estate records were also microfilmed for the Public Record Office of Northern Ireland. However, most of the Loftus manuscripts were not published, as follows:[114]

---

[113] Unidentifiable in Ms.

[114] P.R.O.N.I. Mic.170; notably, some of the following items regarding the Clones estate have been used by Philip Ó Mórdha, in a series of articles in the *Clogher Record* from the early 1970s down to the present. Though he was mainly interested in the later 17th/18th century he gives details of a few items of relevance to this survey in 'Some Priests and Parsons of the Clones Area 1620–1840: With notes on Some Families of this Period', *Clogher Record*, ix (1977), pp232–60. The items he mentions are dealt with below.

Correspondence (D/DL C)

1608–41   Memorandum of evidence found among the Barrett–Lennard family correspondence during the nineteenth century, noting a deed of feoffment from William Brouncker to Sir Francis Rush, with livery of seisin, 1 June 1608; a note that the church living at Clones was held by George Stocker in 1634, and a note that Humphrey Galbraith was installed as Archdeacon of Clogher in April 1641. (D/DL C39)

1640   (12 April) Lady Mary Jephson to Sir William Lambach, from Castlejordan in Ireland, re her grand daughter, Anne Loftus, and the organisation of her finances by Sir Robert Loftus. (D/DL C46)

1640   (10 Dec.) Lord Moore of Drogheda to Lady Jephson, from Mellifont, regarding his power to receive the rents for his cousin, Anne Loftus. (D/DL C46)

1640   (14 Dec.) Sir William Sambiggs to Lady Jephson, regarding Anne Loftus's affairs in Ireland, especially the receipt of her rents, and also regarding a deed concerning the lands of Dunsink and Cribbellstown. (D/DL C46)

Ecclesiastical Records (D/DL Q)

1594   (23 July) Document entitled 'A note of such taites of my land of Clones as the Sheriff of Monaghan tenants doither now manure and gave grassed with their cattles, written at Monaghan', after which follows details for Patrick MacEdmund Boy O'Conally, Patrick MacAughe Roo and Christopher MacDowlin. At the end of the document is a note of all the tithes belonging to the coarbe of Clones, etc., which lists details for seven parsonages. (D/DL Q3)

1608–82   Extensive notes on the title to the parsonage of Clones and the Abbey of Clones, giving extracts of documents starting with James I's letters patent to William Brounker in 1608. Thereafter details are given of further letters patent, bishops' deeds, legal disputes, etc. [5 pages]. (D/DL Q3)

1608–1717 A volume written in 1717, giving a detailed history of the title to the parsonage of Clones taken from a variety of generally unnamed sources. Much of the volume concerns the complex legal disputes concerning the land in the 1630s and later [107 pages]. (D/DL Q2)

1617   (13 March) King James I's letter in favour of Sir Francis Rush over his dispute with the Bishop of Clogher concerning tithes, parsonages, etc. (D/DL Q3)

1630   (19 Jan.) Inquisition post mortem into the estate of Thomas Rush, late of Clonish, Co. Monaghan, listing his lands and deeds [4 pages]. (D/DL Q3)

1638   (17 July) Copy of an order of the Lord Deputy and Council, calendared by the H.M.C. (D/DL Q3)[115]

1639   (18 June) Copy of the decree of the Lord Deputy and Council, calendared by the H.M.C. (D/DL Q3)[116]

c1641   (n.d.) Extracts and comparisons from two un-named surveys of values of land in 1641 (probably taken from the Civil Survey and

---

[115] *Various Collections III*, p185.
[116] *Ibid*, p205.

the Down Survey). It lists 43 townlands with a total value of £400 and £482. (D/DL Q3)

Estate Records (D/DL E)

1486–1603   Notes made in the eighteenth century towards a history of Clones, containing extracts from the Annals of the Four Masters recording the deaths of two abbots of Clones (Philip McJames McMahon d. 1486, James McRory McMahon d. 1502) and of Thomas Buidhe, Dean of Clones, in 1506. In addition there is a transcript of an inquisition of 1587 into the abbey lands, and there is a note recording that during the Nine Years' War the chief of the McMahons secured the corbetship or collegiate church of Clones from the Pope for his eldest son, who was then a boy. (D/DL E91)[117]

1622   (12 March) Verified copy of the last will and testament of Cahill duffe O'Connelly of Mathicarney, Co. Monaghan, specifying that he is to be buried in 'the little church called the plen-hill', and bequeathing money to the Catholic clergy of the diocese of Clogher. Original will witnessed by Henry Maignardh, priest; Con O'Connelly; Bryan McMahon and Thomas Connolly. Copy witnessed by Jacobus Connally, Hugh McMahunus and Bryan McMahon. (D/DL E91)

1628–9   Memorandum made in the late seventeenth century regarding the whereabouts of certain deeds relating to the purchase of the lands of Cree-Eustace in King's County [Co. Kildare?] by Lord Chancellor Loftus in 1628 or 1629. Loftus secured possession of the estate despite a bid by the Earl of Cork. At the end the author of the manuscript states that Michael Higan of Knockbarron in Ely O'Carroll had many documents about the Cree-Eustace estate, 'which wrightings if they be got for ye plaintife will carry the busnesse cleare'. (D/DL E91)

c1635   Unsigned letter to Mr [Edward] Aldrige, possibly by Paul Davis, instructing him how to proceed in the negotiations with the tenants at Clones. At the end there is a note of 33 tenants, most of whom appear on the 1637 rental mentioned below (D/DL E87 and E88), and a reminder for Aldrige that those of the tenantry that agree to build on their leaseholds are to be rewarded with longer leases of 40 years. (D/DL E88)

c1635   A fine copy of the proposed new leases which were to be offered to the tenants at Clones, with some additional information to the rentals detailed below (D/DL E87 and E88), most notably the acreage of each leasehold. (D/DL E88)

c1635–40   Undated valuation of the church lands at Clones 'let by the yeare at this rent'; details the lands of Rathmey, Drumroe, Dromalle, Boleghbrene, Tiertonny, Lutkahelen, Clonenele, Drumtrue, Claragh *alias* Agherahin, Dromacegan, Dromederoy, Leaghtell, Shanuologh, Corragh, Gortduanne, Caventate, Tonedyohogg, Edenferone, Mulleneclohe, Carne, Cruiagh, Legmackelly, Clonkirkell, Lisneruh, Clonkine, Clonedergole, Cloncorren, and Tie. On the reverse is a list of the value of 34 tenements held by the tenants in the town of Clones. The document ends with a note by the valuer giving his opinion that the tenements are worth no more than the rates contained within. (D/DL E88)

[117] For further details, see Mervyn Archdall, *Monasticum Hibernicum* (Dublin, 1786), pp582–5.

c1635–40　Undated valuation of the abbey lands at Clones, *viz* Killekeragh, Killo-ly-nan, Corenshoe, Knocke, Cappoge, Killecoghell, Ballintappa, Tolienen, Tatentampell, Killegoremme, Rategolm, Grangemore, Rathgolane, Minelle, Rathlagen, Annaghkilly, Cloneville, Clonnorrell, Larg, Clonmore, Clontagh, Clontoner, Clonboy, and Anaghelty, plus the mill standing on the Comber, Lisdrom in Farnanagh, Aghenesh parsonage, Drumsnought rectory, the gurtine and the market and fairs at Clones. (D/DL E88)

1637　(May) Note of rents received from Clones manor, Co. Monaghan, listing 35 tenants. (D/DL E88)

1637　(1 July) A note of Viscount Ely's acquittance of £2,000 to Sir George Wentworth, paid to Sir William Ussher, Arthur Campion, Captain Smith, Mr Warburton, Walter White, Mr Wakefield, Mr Lake (the assignee of Thomas Clerke of London), and the assignee (un-named) of Edward Bass of London. (D/DL E87)

1637　(All Hallows) Certified copy (by Edward Aldrige) of two rentals for the Loftus lands in Co. Monaghan, at Hallowtide 1637. The first concerns the 'Panitearny' section of the Clones estate, and lists 14 tenants, *viz.* Edward Aldrich, Brian Stapleton, Robert Aldrich, Charles Campbell, Robert Johnson, Richard Cuttler, Nicholas Wilson, Margaret Farmore, Thomas Longhe, Mr Johnson, George Foster, Patrick Madder McDolane, John Bootkie, William O'Moore, James Hatton, and William Halliwood; there then appears a note signed by Paul Davis that the rental was shown to Robert Johnson on 4 Nov. 1637. The second is for an un-named parcel (also part of the Clones estate), and lists the rents of 13 tenants, *viz.* Mabel Richison, Luke Ward, 'the abbott O'Conlie', Edward Evers, Mortoe O'More, Mr Simpson, Mr Willoughby, Mr Burke, Richard O'Bracken, Nicholas Burne, the Bishop of Kilfenora, Matthew Browne and Thomas Grant; this too was shown to Robert Johnson by Paul Davis. (D/DL E87)

1637　(All Hallows) A note of rents received and rents overdue from Clones manor at Hallowtide 1637; 35 tenants have paid, two are in arrears. There then follows a list of payments made by Robert Johnson (the receiver) to various persons, *viz* Nicholas Burn, Sir Robert Loftus, Mr 'Idgram' [i.e. Ingram] for the customs, the Bishop of Kilfenora, and Robert Johnson himself. (D/DL E88)

1638　(16 May) Copy of a letter by Charles I to Lord Deputy Wentworth. (D/DL E91)[118]

1638　(May) Incomplete half-yearly rental for Clones manor ending May 1638, with most of the rent receipts missing. There then follows a note of four tenants who have failed to pay their rent, and details of how the receipts were made over to Sir George Wentworth and Robert Johnson, the latter requiring 10s 6d for making an affidavid against Lord Maguire and Mr Connell. (D/DL E88)

1640　(All Hallowtide) A rental for the manor of Clones, Co. Monaghan, giving a list of 30 tenants, as follows: *viz* Margaret Harmon, Mr Carr, Patrick Moder McDullan, William O'Moore, Mr Hamilton, William Halliwood, Abbott O'Conlye, John Montgomery, Widow Wallis, Mr Champenoune, Mr Sympson, Mr Willoughby, Mr Francis Sympson, Luke Ward, Richard Ramsbottom, Cahill Roe

---

[118] Published in Knowler (ed.), *Strafford Letters*, ii, p172.

O'Conly, John Hygate, Mr Fairfax, Matthew Browne, Anne Forster, John Armstrong, Christopher Armen, Patrick O'Mucklane, Robert Harper, James Dunghill, Samuel the tailor, James Wilfort, George Golding, James Anger and Philloney McEarney. Beside each name are notices of the rent due and rent paid, with comment on arrears, i.e. whether the outstanding sums were collected or forgiven due to various mitigating circumstances. The rental concludes with an account of how the money due at All Hallows 1640 was collected and disbursed by Charles Campbell over the following year down to 8 Aug. 1641. (2 copies, D/DL E87 and D/DL E88)

c1640   (n.d.) A rental for the Tohaghie lands for a whole year, which gives a list of 24 tenants, as follows: *viz* Matthew Blake, Robert Hovenden, Henry O'Neill, '2 of the Melvents', Edward O'Donnelly, Mr Campbell, Thomas Maxwell, Robert Maxwell, James Maxwell, Mr Gray, Shane O'Ranortie, Edmund McShane, John Britton, Matthew Urine, Patrick Branagan, Bryan O'Neill, Turlogh O'Connor, Donnogh McGranna, James Croyn, John Barkehy, Mewe ny Donnelly, and Tortagh O'Neill. (D/DL E87)

c1640   Undated list of rents due from twelve persons for houses in the town of Clones, followed by details of rents from the lands of Clonkerhill, Drumroe, Clonneall, Corragh and Rathgoland. (D/DL E88)

Family Papers (D/DL F)

c1640   Small bound volume of Latin exercises inscribed 'Ann Loftus' in faint red ink inside the front cover, made *circa* 1640 while she was being schooled in Ireland. In the first half of the book the exercises are brief observations on various countries and cities, while the second part of the volume has extracts from an anthology of the history of Rome in 20 neatly written chapters. (D/DL F106)

Legal Papers (D/DL L)

1536–1709   Eighteenth century history of the title to the rectory or parsonage of Clones, listing patents, commissions, feoffments, and other documents concerning the same from the reign of Henry VIII. The bundle includes a nineteenth century constat from the P.R.O.I. of letters patent, dated 13 May 1608, to William Brounker of various rectories and parishes, including Clones. (D/DL L55)[119]

1621–1675   Various legal documents arising from the case of Sir John Gifford v. Lord Chancellor Adam Loftus and Sir Edward Loftus, and cases concerning the Loftus family in the 1650s and 1670s (D/DL L56/13), as follows:[120]

  1621–50   Six documents concerning the case of Anne Loftus c1647–50, which make mention of many details of previous cases, marriage settlements, and other documents from 1621.[121]

  1621–75   Four documents arising from the case of Barrett v. Loftus in the 1670s, which give details of Lord Chancellor Loftus's marriage settlement for £1,750 with Sir Francis Rush in 1621, and also has

---

[119] These items form part of a larger bundle covering the period up to 1812, and arose out of an ongoing dispute with the Bishop of Clogher over the advowson of Clones. The individual items in the bundle are unnumbered.

[120] The bundle also includes further copies of two interrogatories from D/DL L56/9 below.

[121] Some copies of these items were published in H.M.C., *Various Collections III* (1904).

notes on the Lord Deputy and Council's decree of 1 Feb. 1638 in the Gifford v. Loftus case.

1636   (24 March) Articles of agreement between Lord Chancellor Loftus and his son, Sir Edward Loftus, reciting an earlier grant by same to same of the lands called the Lordship of 'Cryeustace' for the term of 1,000 years. These articles clarify that Sir Edward has agreed that the Lord Chancellor shall receive all issues and profits from the land during his natural life. Furthermore, the Lord Chancellor is empowered to change any details contained in the original grant during his life.

1637   (14 March) Answer of the Lord Chancellor Loftus to the petition of Sir John Gifford.[122]

1637   (23 March) Second answer of the Lord Chancellor to the petition of Sir John Gifford.[123]

1638   (12 July) Affidavit showing that Lord Chancellor Loftus received a warrant from Lord Dillon of Kilkenny West, dated 9 June 1638, to appear before the commission on the said case between Gifford and Loftus.

c1638   (n.d.) Addressed to the King, 'The humble petition of Adam Ld Viscount Loftus your Majesties Chancellor of Ireland now prisoner in ye Castle of Dublin'. Appeals that the case, recently acted upon by decree of the Lord Deputy and Council, be reopened. Argues strongly against the entire tenor of the decree. He has been imprisoned for six weeks.

1639   (12 July) The precipe and concord between Viscount Loftus of Ely and others unto Sir Robert Dillon and others, acknowledged by Sir Edward Loftus, and Jane his wife. Lists the holdings of the manor of Monasterevan and elsewhere in Co. Kildare, and Queen's and King's Cos.

1639   (18 Nov.) Notes entitled 'Time when the jointure should have been assured', which gives details of Sir Francis Rush's actions, etc. from Michaelmas 1621.

1641   (15 April) Inquisition post mortem into the estate of Sir Robert Loftus and Eleanor, his wife, particularly lands in Co. Monaghan [8 pages].

1641   (16 April) Further inquisition post mortem into the estate of Sir Robert Loftus and Eleanor, his wife, mainly relating to lands in Co. Monaghan, and including many deeds [46 pages].

17th cen.   (n.d.) Extracts from the Auditor's Office, which includes mention that William Brounker's grant was dated 13 May 1608. Also some details of the ownership of the monastery of Clones in 1641 (from an unnamed source) are given, which state that Thomas Fairfax was the incumbent of the rectory of Clones at £1 per annum, and Thomus Rush was the tenant of the monastery of Clones at £2 7s 6d per annum.[124]

1621–1675   A bundle of 29 items, almost all of which relate to the case of Barrett v. Loftus in the 1670s. However, these later documents include frequent reference to legal disputes from 1621. Only one item pre-dates 1641 (D/DL L56/11), as follows:

c1638   (n.d.) Brief concerning the Lord Chancellor's promise of £1,500 per annum to Sir Robert Loftus, and £200 per annum to Sir Edward Loftus during his life, listing three indentures of the

---

[122] A copy of this was published in *Ibid*.

[123] A copy of this was published in *Ibid*.

[124] These last details must come from a Crown rental rather than from the surveys of the 1650s.

Lord Chancellor covering the dates 1627–38. Following which is a page of evidence showing that the Lord Chancellor does not owe Sir Edward any more than £200 *per annum*.

1637   (7 March) Petition of Sir John Gifford to the Lord Deputy and Council. Discusses the marriage agreement of 14 years past between Loftus and Rush. Gifford wants to charge Loftus in court over this. (D/DL L56/14)[125]

1637–8   A bundle of eight items concerning the case of Sir John Gifford v. Lord Chancellor and Sir Edward Loftus. (D/DL L56/9)

1637   (2 August–27 Nov.) Interrogatories administered to witnesses produced on behalf of Sir John Gifford, citing the 18 questions to be answered. After which follows the full interrogatories of Sir William Cooley of Edenderry, King's Co.; Francis Hisson of Clonard, Queen's Co.; Katherine Prince of Goshell, King's Co.; Dame Mary, Lady Jephson; Sir Robert Meredith, Chancellor of the Exchequer; Sir Charles Coote the younger; Sir Charles Coote, bart., Privy Councillor; Sir George Wentworth; Christopher Wandesford, Master of the Rolls; and Anne, Lady Meredith, wife of Sir Robert Meredith [83 pages].

1637   (5 August–29 Nov.) Interrogatories on the part of the Lord Chancellor administered to witnesses produced on behalf of Sir John Gifford, citing the four questions to be answered. After which follows the full interrogatories of Katherine Prince of Goshell, King's Co.; Dame Mary, Lady Jephson; Sir William Cooley of Edenderry, King's Co.; Sir Robert Meredith, Chancellor of the Exchequer; Robert Johnson of Cloonesh, Co. Monaghan; Peirse Moore of Dublin; Edmund Wesley of Kildare; Morish Walsh of Kildare; Sir Charles Coote the younger; Henry Frend of Dunsink, Co. Dublin; Richard Ball of Doranstown, Co. Meath; Sir Charles Coote, bart., Privy Councillor; Nicholas Walsh, Vicar of Noraghmore, Co. Kildare; Sir George Wentworth; Christopher Wandesford, Master of the Rolls; Anne, Lady Meredith, wife of Sir Robert Meredith; Richard Fitz-gerald of Dublin; and Charles, Viscount Moore of Drogheda [48 pages].

1637   (4–27 November) Interrogatories administered to witnesses produced on behalf of Gifford, citing the eleven questions to be answered. After which follows the full interrogatories of Robert Johnson of Clonsigh, Co. Monaghan; Peirce Moore of Dublin; Henry Frend of Dunsinke, Co. Dublin; Richard Ball of Doranstown, Co. Meath; Sir George Wentworth; Alice Linsey, the relict of Arthur Linsey of Midleham Castle in Yorkshire; Anne, Lady Meredith, wife of Sir Robert Meredith; Richard Fitz-Gerald of Dublin; and Charles, Viscount Moore of Drogheda [28 pages].

1637   (22–24 November) Interrogatories administered to witnesses produced on behalf of Gifford, citing the four questions to be answered. After which follows the full interrogatories of Edmund Wesley of Kildare; Morish Walsh of Kildare; Sir Charles Coote the younger; Sir Charles Coote, bart., Privy Councillor; and Nicholas Walsh of Noraghmore, Co. Kildare [16 pages].

1637   (11–14 December) Interrogatories administered to witnesses produced on behalf of Lord Chancellor Loftus, citing the seven questions to be answered. Followed by the full interrogatories of Benjamin Robarts of Dublin; Michael Jones of Ballintogher,

---

[125] This bundle also includes three items dated in the 1670s, which give no details of events prior to 1641.

Queen's Co.; Ellinor Gray, wife of Thomas Gray of Coolnefora, Queen's Co.; Christopher White of Dublin; Thomas Gray of Coolnefora, Queen's Co.; Robert Gunter of Dublin; Robert Lalor of Dublin; Roger Griffith of Dromnagh, Co. Dublin; Anne Griffith, wife of Roger; Henry Parry of Dublin; Francis Dade of Dollardstown, Co. Kildare; John Page of Newhall, Co. Kildare; Jeremy Carter of Dublin; William Harris of Dublin; Lettice Loftus, daughter of the Lord Chancellor; Anne Gilbert, daughter of Sir William Gilbert; and Sir Thomas Meredith [50 pages].

1638   (13 April–21 July) Interrogatories administered to witnesses produced on behalf of Gifford, citing the original order for the same (dated 13 April) and the eleven questions to be answered. Followed by the full interrogatories (dated 13 April–21 July) of Roger Giles of Monesterevan, Co. Kildare; John Webster of Old Grange; Rowland Williams of Ushe, Co. Kildare; Patrick Hackett of Old Grange, Co. Kildare; Matthew Nangle of Ballysachs, Co. Kildare; Charles Dempsy of Killeen, King's Co.; Mortagh Slevin of Killpatrick, King's Co.; Daniell Daly of Grangebegg, Co. Kildare; Nicholas Welsh of Moilestowne, King's Co.; Teige O'Kerrine of Richardstown, King's Co.; Morrish fitz-Gerralt of Kilrush, Co. Kildare; Oliver O'Regan of Castlekeele, Co. Kildare; Patrick Doyne of Fanstowne, Co. Kildare; Daniell McNeile of the Garroone, Queen's Co.; Daniell McIvy of Clonnebegg, King's Co.; Kerne O'Higgin of Knockbarren, King's Co.; Art McCormick of Ballinehoyne, Queen's Co.; William Cleaburne, Dean of Kildare; and Anthony Spence of Dublin [55 pages].

1638   (7 June–21 July) Interrogatories administered to witnesses produced on behalf of Gifford, citing the original order for the same (dated 7 June) and the one question concerning particulars of the marriage to be answered. After which follows the full interrogatories (dated 21 July) of Sir William Cooley of Edenderry, King's Co; and Anne, Lady Meredith, wife of Sir Robert Meredith, Chancellor of the Exchequer.

1638   (20 June) Examination of witnesses, reciting appointment by Charles I of Sir James Ware and Sir Phillip Percivall to hear witnesses, depositions and examinations in the case between Gifford and the Lord Chancellor, and to enquire into particular matters of the case (appointment dated 1 June 1638). After which is appended the full interrogatories (based on three questions asked) of Henry Warren of Glanemuch, Co. Dublin; Simon Swayen, Vicar of Rathmichell; Sir George Wentworth; Thomas Clough; John Cosens; Donnell Murry; William Harris of Dublin; Roger Griffin of Dromnagh; Anne Griffin, wife of Roger; and Richard Ffont [26 pages].

1637–8   A bundle of eight items concerning the case of Sir John Gifford v. Lord Chancellor and Sir Edward Loftus. Seven of these items are copies of interrogatories listed in D/DL L56/9. The remaining item, which is undated (c1638), is a badly damaged treatise on the state of the case between Sir John Gifford and the Lord Chancellor [2 fols]. (D/DL L56/10)

1637–40   A bundle of four items, two of which are copies of documents calendared by the H.M.C., and there is a copy of an item from D/DL L56/13 (above). The final item is as follows (D/DL L56/15):

1640   (11 Oct.) Will of Sir Robert Loftus of Mellifont, Co. Louth, stating that he is to be buried in St. Patrick's, Dublin, and appointing Charles, Baron of Mellifont, his executor. Makes reference to excessive debts owed to him by Sir George Wentworth.

1637–75   A bundle of 24 items arising from the case of Sir John Gifford v. Lord Chancellor and Sir Edward Loftus, including two unrelated items from the 1670s. (D/DL L56/12)

1637   (9 Feb.–29 June) Copies of five answers of the Lord Chancellor and Sir Edward Loftus, one replication of Sir John Gifford, and the King's letter to the Lord Deputy and Council of 9 Feb., all of which have been calendared by the H.M.C. [11 items].[126]

1637   (4 July) Two copies of the rejoinder of the Lord Chancellor to the replication of Sir John Gifford, stating briefly that Gifford has said nothing new, and he has nothing further to add.

1638   (9 and 16 July) A certificate of Sir James Ware and Sir Paul Davys touching the arrears of £200 *per annum* and others sums owed by the Lord Chancellor to his sons, etc. With a detailed set of accounts of these arrearages covering the years 1622–37, leaving an overall arrearage of £3,179 6s 5d (being £1,357 19s 11d in arrears and a further £1,821 6s 6d in interest over those years). [5 fols].[127]

c1638   Two undated breviates made for Lord Chancellor Loftus on the state of the case against Sir John Gifford, which include detailed listings of all the court proceedings (petitions, answers, etc.) covering the period 1637–8.

c1638   'Answers to the Lord Chancellors reasons of his appeal to his Matie against the Decree of the Council Board'. Seven lengthy answers, principally dealing with the contentious marriage agreement.

c1638   Undated breviate made for the Lord Chancellor which gives annotated extracts of the evidence given by Sir John Gifford's witnesses [4 fols].

c1638   Extensive breviate made for the Lord Chancellor, which details every legal action, and gives abstracts of many witnesses' depositions in the case against Sir John Gifford [14 pages].

c1638   Breviate drawn up for the Lord Chancellor entitled 'The reasons that induced the Lord Chancellor of Ireland to appeal to his Matie from the Decree at the Councill board in Ireland, in the case wherein Sir John Gifford was plaintiff' [6 pages].

c1641   Petition of Lord Chancellor Loftus to the Lords assembled in the High Court of Parliament. The petition is countersigned by the Irish Privy Council (*viz.* Ormond, Dillon, etc.) with a note to the effect that Loftus was deeply oppressed by the late Earl of Strafford, particularly by Strafford's decree of 7 February 1637.

1638   (1 Feb.) Decree in the case of Sir John Gifford v. Lord Chancellor and Sir Edward Loftus, made by the Lord Deputy and Council.[128] (D/DL L56/8)

Miscellaneous (D/DL Z)

1587–1717   A schedule of 103 Irish deeds made in 1717 by Lord Dacre. This catalogue lists in detail those items catalogued as D/DL T28/1–103.

---

[126] A copy of this was published in H.M.C., *Various Collections III*; there are multiple copies of some items.

[127] There are two copies of this item, one in Roman numerals and the other in Arabic numerals.

[128] A copy of this was published in H.M.C., *Various Collections III*, p164.

However, 52 of the items are now missing, and this schedule is all that remains that gives details of their contents. The following are the entries made in the schedule to those items pre-dating 1641 which are now lost. (D/DL Z4)[129]

1606   (2 May) King's letter to the Lord Deputy, requiring a commission for finding out and setting apart bishop's lands granted to temporal lords and to stay passing the grants of abbey lands in the Cos. Monaghan and Fermanagh.[130]

1608   (1 June) Sale by William Brounker to Sir Francis Rush, for a certain sum of money (not given) of all his interest in the Abbey of Clones, Co. Monaghan.[131]

1614   (12 Oct.) Abstract of a King's letter directing a search and enquiry to be made for evidences belonging to the bishopric of Meath, and authorising the Lord Deputy and commissioners to determine all controversies relating to the lands of Clones and the claims of the Bishop of Clogher and Sir Francis Rush. Furthermore, it states that the Bishop should be awarded and put into possession of all he rightly owns.[132]

1616   (23 March) Award under the hands of the Lord Deputy, Chancellor, and Primate of Ireland, on direction of the above King's letter. The Bishops of Meath and Clogher are bound to each other in £2,000 to abide by said award. The award states that the 24 tates of the Abbey of Clones are to remain with Sir Francis Rush. The tates held by the Bishop are to remain with the bishopric of Clogher, and all impropriate parsonages held by Rush are to be relinquished. With many further details.[133]

1617   (13 March) King's letter reciting the above award, and discharging Sir Francis Rush from rent owed on six parsonages. Also confirming that Rush should enjoy the advowson of the parsonage of Clones, and enforcing the tenor of said award.[134]

1630   (19 Jan.) Inquisition post mortem after the death of Thomas Rush, detailing the property he owned in Co. Fermanagh (*viz* Lissdrumoe, the rectory and tithes of Agheroe, etc.). He died on 17 November 1629, and his three sisters are his co-heirs (Ellinor, married to Sir Robert Loftus, Mary, married to Sir Charles Coote, and Anne).[135]

1634   (Easter) Copy of a fine between (i) Francis, Lord Mountnorris, plaintiff, and (ii) Sir Robert Loftus and Ellinor his wife, Charles, Viscount Drogheda, Sir Edward Loftus, Sir George 'Goo:' and George Gifford, deforceants, of 15 messuages, 15 cottages, 300 acres of arable land, 40 acres of meadow, 140 acres of pasture and 100 acres of moor in the lands of Dunsink and Senblestown.[136]

1636   (24 March) Articles of agreement between Lord Chancellor Loftus and his son, Sir Edward Loftus, reciting grant of same to same (same date, see D/DL T28/25 below). These articles clarify

---

[129] The footnote to each item gives the reference number to the now missing original in the D/DL T28 series.
[130] D/DL T28/4
[131] D/DL T28/6
[132] D/DL T28/9
[133] D/DL T28/10
[134] D/DL T28/11
[135] D/DL T28/14
[136] D/DL T28/16

that Sir Edward has agreed that the Lord Chancellor shall receive all issues and profits from the land during his natural life. Further, the Lord Chancellor is empowered to change any details of the original grant during his life.[137]

1638   (1 Feb.) Decree in the case of Gifford v. Lord Chancellor and Sir Edward Loftus, made by the Lord Deputy and Council.[138]

1638   (17 July) Copy of an order of the Lord Deputy and Council, reciting a decree of 1 Feb. 1638, requiring the Lord Chancellor to pay £3,179 6s 5d to Sir John Gifford.[139]

1639   (11 June) Order of the Lord Deputy and Council discharging Sir John Gifford from making any reparation relating to a language suggested by Sir John [   ], and appointing a time for hearing the parties relating to the deficiency of said £200 per annum.[140]

1639   (13 June) Attested copy of a 'Dedmuns Polestatem' [sic] to Sir Edward Osborne and others, to take the several three last fines.[141]

1639   (12 July) Attested copy of a 'Dedmuns Polestatem' [sic] to Sir Edward Osborne, to take the precipes and concords of the said last three fines by Sir Edward Loftus and Jane his wife.[142]

1639   (Michaelmas) Copy of an indenture dated 27 July 1639, see D/DL T28/46 below.[143]

1639   (19 Nov.) Copy of the decree of the King and Council in England on Lord Chancellor Loftus's appeal. Declaring said appeal to be without any just cause and confirming the order and decree of 1 Feb. 1638 and commanding same to be put into execution.[144]

1640   (11 Oct.) Will of Sir Robert Loftus, making a reference that Sir George Wentworth had the keeping of all his writings.[145]

1641   (15 April) Copy of an inquisition post mortem into the estate of Sir Robert Loftus and Ellinor, his wife, in Co. Fermanagh (see below D/DL T28/54).[146]

1641   (16 April) Copy of an inquisition post mortem taken on the deaths of Sir Robert Loftus, Ellinor his wife and Henry Loftus, their son, enquiring into their estate in Co. Monaghan, reciting deeds, etc. (very detailed). Anne Loftus is the sole daughter and heiress of Sir Robert and Ellinor.[147]

c1640   Lord Loftus's commonplace book, containing a series of notes and transcripts of earlier documents concerning legal matters and precedents in Ireland, touching on the crown estate, the royal writ, tithes and the condition of church livings, etc. (D/DL Z9), as follows:

1549-50   (3 Edward VI) Transcript of a case in the court of Exchequer concerning John Geoffrey of Dublin and Piers Nugent.

1550-1   (4 Edward VI) Notes of cases transcribed by Loftus from the sixteenth century records of the Remembrancer of the Exchequer

---

[137] D/DL T28/26

[138] D/DL T28/32-3, two copies; A copy of this was published in the H.M.C. report, Various Collections III, p164.

[139] D/DL T28/35

[140] D/DL T28/41

[141] D/DL T28/42; Dedimus Potestatum.

[142] D/DL T28/45

[143] D/DL T28/47

[144] D/DL T28/49, 51, two copies.

[145] D/DL T28/53, another copy of this document can be found at D/DL L56/15 above.

[146] D/DL T28/55

[147] D/DL T28/56

re Barnaby Reilly of Dublin, merchant, and Simon Carpenter of same, citizen; Thomas Eustace, Viscount Baltinglass, and the townland of Rathfarnham, Co. Dublin; Edmund Blanchville of Blanchvillestown, Co. Kilkenny, and the rightful inheritance of Thomas, Earl of Ormond, at Lubbockstown; Thomas Tuite, tenant of the manor of Sonnaghe, Co. Westmeath; James Blake of Wardstown, Co. Meath, and Martin Blake of Athboy; Patrick Fin, Rector of Leixlip, Co. Kildare; James Walsh of Moreton and the Rector of Rathmore, Co. Kildare; Maurice Power fitz David and Peter Dobbin of Waterford; Richard Stanton of Dublin.

1552	(6 Edward VI) Notes of Exchequer cases regarding James[148], Rector of Balrath, Cos. Dublin and Meath; Reginald Talbot of Belgard, Co. Dublin; Richard Aylmer and others re the alienation of Dangen manor, Co. Meath; William Walsh of Polranken, Co. Wexford; Richard Synnott of Ballybrennan, Co. Wexford; William Talbot and Richard Burnett of Meath; Robert Preston of Balmadin, Co. Meath.
1553	(7 Edward VI) Notes of Exchequer cases re James Maconryke of Balrath, Co. Dublin; Hugh Goodacre, Archbishop of Armagh; John Bale, Bishop of Ossory; John Lyon of Kennockstown, Co. Meath; Thomas Clinche, Rector of Dunsany, Co. Meath.
1554–1558	(temp Philip and Mary) Notes of Exchequer cases concerning Henry Wise of Waterford.
1558–1603	A list of fee farm grants made in Ireland by Elizabeth I to Henry Draycott, Sir Richard Tinte, James Bath, Hugh McCallow, Walter Keating, Thomas Keating, Francis Cosby, Nicholas White, Moriertagh McLysagh McConnell O'More, Donald McGillpatrick, Arthur Comen, Thomas St. Leger, Hugh Lypiate, Hugh McDermott, George Delves, John Apprice, Robert Cowley, David Floyd, Walter Aphowell, Henry Cowley, Geoffrey Phillips, John Baynam, John Gill, Walter Hope, Andrew Skiddy, William Peppard, Sir Edmund Butler, John Whitney, the Earl of Kildare, Piers Hovenden, John Hovenden, Alexander Cosby, Thomas Fitzsimon, the town of Carlingford, Conor, Earl of Thomond, George Bourchier, Nicholas Harbert, the Earl of Ormond, John Fitzgerald fitz Edmund, Henry Harrington, Hubert Boye fitz Henry of Co. Galway, Rosse McMahon, Conyll O'Mulloy, Con McNeall Oge, George Gerland, Maurice, Lord Roche, Edmund fitz Thomas, Edmund Fitz Gibbon, Richard Grenville, Edward Gough, William Power, Thady McDermott MacCarthy and Edmund Barrett.
1565	(7 Eliz. I) Transcript of cases heard in the Exchequer regarding Patrick Nangle, Baron of Navan, and John Gallway of Limerick.
1568	(10 Eliz. I) Memorandum regarding the records of the realm of Ireland, and how they should be kept.
1568	(Easter) Memorandum concerning Nicholas Bermingham of Holyrath, collector of the subsidy in the barony of Castleknock, Co. Dublin.
1568	(13 Oct.) Government memorandum re the ruins of an old house containing a hospital at Carrickfergus.
1569	(20 March) Copy of a letter by Elizabeth I to Lord Deputy Sidney concerning the leasing of land to Sir John Plunkett, Baron of Louth, and others.
1570	(27 June) Memorandum concerning Andrew Brereton.

---

[148] Surname omitted in Ms.

1570	(n.d.) Memorandum re Roger Finglas of Porterstown, Co. Dublin.
1593	A list of 'Grants of Inheritance' made in 1593 to Tirlagh O'Byrne, Alexander Cosby, Nicholas Taaffe and Sir Henry Warren.
1612	(25 Feb.) Memorandum of the bond of Thomas Stoakes of Ballymaddin, Co. Kildare, to repair the church of Dowestown.
1621	(16 July) Memorandum of a bond concerning William Fitzgerald of Piercestown, Co. Westmeath.
1631	(17 May) The oaths of Richard Brett and Bryan McEver concerning the performance of a bond by Oliver Plunkett of Killeen (formerly of Kilmore).
1631	(7 July) Memorandum of the replication of George Andrews, Dean of Limerick and Chantor of St. Patrick's Cathedral, Dublin, re the state of the church of St. Andrew's in the City of Dublin.
1631	(9 July) The rejoinder of Sir Williams Reeves to Dean Andrews' replication.
1631	Extracts from the Irish state records regarding the protracted legal dispute between the Attorney General, Sir William Reeves, and Richard White and Christopher Plunkett of Co. Meath.
c1631	The oaths of Gerald and Christopher Plunkett regarding repairs to be done to the church, belfry and steeple of Barry, Co. Meath.
17th cen.	Lord Chancellor Loftus's copy of Sir Richard Bolton's declaration, setting forth how and by what means the laws and statutes of England came to be of force in Ireland.

Official Papers (D/DL O)

17th cen.	(n.d.) Petition of Thomas Gilly to the Chancellor, Chief Baron, and the rest of the Barons of the Exchequer of Ireland, which begins 'Humble petition of Tho: Gilly in restraint at Marshall Parris'. The catalogue gives a date of c1640 to this item, but it looks like it could be later. (D/DL O36/7)

Title Deeds and Leases (D/DL T)[149]

1587	(21 July) Letters patent of Elizabeth I showing how the crown title to the Abbey of Clones, Co. Monaghan, was found for the Queen by Henry Duke. (D/DL T28/1)
1587	(23 Sept.) Letters patent of Elizabeth I granting the Abbey of Clones, Co. Monaghan, to Henry Duke, to hold for 21 years, rent £4 10s. (D/DL T28/2)[150]
1603	(14 Sept.) Letters patent of James I, granting to Sir Francis Rush the Abbey of Clones for 21 years, rent £5. Recites patent to Henry Duke (above), and mentions that Rush married Duke's heiress, Mary. (D/DL T28/3)
1608	(13 May) Constat of a record in the office of the Master of the Rolls. Letters patent of James I granting to William Brounker the Abbey of Clones, to hold for ever in soccage. (D/DL T28/5)
1613	(27 Feb.) Warrant of the King's Commissioners to the Sheriff of Fermanagh to summon a jury of the freeholders on 15 April to enquire and return the title and claim of Sir Francis Rush to the

---

[149] A number of items in the D/DL T28 series are now missing or have been lost. Fortunately a schedule was made of them in 1717, see D/DL Z4 above.

[150] See *Cal. Fiants Ire.*, Eliz I, no.5042.

lands of the Abbey of Clones in Cos. Monaghan and Fermanagh. (D/DL T28/7)

1613   (12 April) Return to the King's Commissioners of an inquisition taken at Clones. This detailed inquisition lists lands held by the abbey of Clones, the Great Church at Clones, and the territory of Dartry in MacMahon's Country. After reciting many documents, it states that Sir Francis Rush is seized of all the land except 14 tates which are in the possession of the Bishop of Clogher (for which the Bishop paid a yearly rent to Henry Duke). (D/DL T28/8)

1623   (10 Nov.) Copy of the inquisition post mortem taken after the death of Sir Francis Rush, detailing the property he owned in Co. Fermanagh (*viz* Lissdromoe, the rectory and tithes of Agheroe, etc.). Thomas Rush is his son and heir, aged 15. (D/DL T28/12)

1627   (2 June) Feoffment in trust by (i) Adam, Lord Viscount Loftus of Ely, and Sir Robert Loftus, to (ii) Sir Richard Bolton, Sir Arthur Savage, Sir John Brereton, Edward Bolton, Arthur Ussher and Robert Meredith. (i) leases to (ii) all their estate in the manor of Monasterevan and lands of Killeene, Killpatrick and Kilbegg in King's Co., the manor and lands of Cegshogoroly, Fentesland, Borlitlea, etc. Co. Kildare, and Dromnagh, Co. Dublin. To hold for 99 years in trust to the following uses. The lands of Fontesland and Borlitlea to be held to the use of Sir Edward Loftus (the Viscount's second son). The other lands to the use of Viscount Loftus for his life, thereafter to the use of Sir Edward Loftus and the payment of Sarah's jointure (with many complex remainders). (D/DL T28/13)

1633   (Michaelmas) Copy of a fine in Co. Monaghan between (i) Charles, Viscount Moore of Drogheda, Sir Edward Loftus, Sir George St. George, and John Gifford, plaintiffs, and (ii) Sir Charles Coote, and Mary his wife, Edward Grimsby and Leonard Morlord, deforceants. Of a third part of the monastery of Clones, Co. Monaghan , a third of Lisdrome and Agheregh, Co. Fermanagh, and a third part of an unnamed estate in Co. Dublin (each listed in detail, including spiritualities). (D/DL T28/15)

1634   (21 Aug.) Feoffment by Lord Chancellor Loftus and Francis Dade, to Charles, Viscount Drogheda, James, Viscount Clandeboy, Maurice Eustace, Edward Bolton, and James Dudllen, reciting a deed of feoffment of 2 June 1627 (above, D/DL T28/13). Same lands to be held in trust to the same uses, with some minor alterations regarding Lady Loftus's dower and the jointure of Lady Ellinor Loftus. (D/DL T28/17–18, 2 copies)

1635   (Hilary, 10 Charles I) Copy of a fine between Viscount Moore of Drogheda and others, and Viscount Loftus of Ely and others, relating to land in King's Co. and Queen's Co. (D/DL T28/19)

1635   (2 March) Lease from Sir Robert Loftus and Dame Ellinor his wife, to Thomas Ingham of all the duty, tithes, tolls, etc., of the fairs of Clones. To hold for 21 years, rent £8 *per annum*. (D/DL T28/20)

1635   (2 June) Copy of Viscount Loftus's agreement to obtain £8,000 promised to be procured to him from the King by the Lord Deputy towards the discharge of the debts of his son, Sir Robert Loftus. (D/DL T28/21)

1635   (10 Nov.) Articles of agreement between (i) Sir Robert Loftus and Dame Ellinor his wife (one of the co-heiresses of Sir Francis Rush),

Anne Rushe (another of the co-heiresses of Sir Francis Rush), and (ii) Sir George Radcliffe and Sir George St. George. That (i) before the end of Hilary term next will levy a fine to (ii), of the monastery of Clones, with lands in Cos. Fermanagh, Monaghan, etc. to the use of Sir Robert and Ellinor and their heirs (with various remainders). Further, that John Gifford will receive a yearly rent charge of £200 from the estate. With other details. (D/DL T28/22–3, two copies)

1636	(Hilary, 11 Charles I) Copy of fine levied pursuant to the above articles of agreement dated 10 Nov. 1635.(D/DL T28/24)
1636	(24 March) Grant by Adam, Viscount Loftus of Ely to his son, Sir Edward Loftus, of his lands in the lordship or territory of Cryeustace and the manor of Galmorellerone and other lands in Co. Kildare. To be held for 1,000 years. (D/DL T28/25)
1636	(8 Oct.) Copy of an indenture between Viscount Loftus of Ely and Sir Edward Loftus, reciting several fines levied to Viscount Moore, Viscount Clandeboy and others of lands in Co. Kildare, and King's and Queen's Cos. Viscount Loftus now revokes the uses detailed in those fines, and limits the land to himself (for his life), and thereafter to his wife's jointure, and then to Sir Edward and his heirs. (D/DL T28/27–8, two copies)
1636	(12 October) Indenture between Viscount Loftus of Ely and Sir Edward Loftus, reciting a grant of same to same of the territory of Cryeustace and other lands, for 1,000 years. This indenture affirms that agreement. (D/DL T28/29)
1637	(3 Feb.) Lease from Sir Robert Loftus of Dublin, Dame Elinor, his wife, Sir George Wentworth and Dame Anne, his wife, to Robert Aldwich of Clones, Co. Monaghan, of tenements in the town of Clones, and the 'tates' of Clonedrigald, Killgorman, and Chappock. To hold the tenements for 41 years (rent 30s. stg) and the tates for 31 years (rent £40 stg). With extensive reservations. (D/DL T28/104)
1637	(3 Feb.) Indenture of a lease by same to Robert Johnson of Clones, re a house in the said town for 41 years without rent. (D/DL T29, un-numbered lease)
1637	(4 Feb.) Indenture of a lease by same to Charles Campbell of Shawvullogh, Co. Monaghan, re certain messuages in Clones, for 61 years at a rent of 30s (stg). (D/DL T29, un-numbered lease)
1637	(12 Feb.) Indenture of a lease by same to Richard Cuttler of Clones, merchant, re the lands of Kerne in Co. Monaghan, for 61 years, rent £19 19s 0d (stg). (D/DL T29, un-numbered lease)
1637	(14 Feb.) Indenture of a lease by same to Lieutenant Brian Stapleton of Newbrook, Co. Monaghan, re a mease and a mill in Clones, for 61 years at a rent of £57 10s 0d (stg). (D/DL T29, un-numbered lease)
1637	(15 Feb.) Indenture of a lease by same to Nicholas Willoughby of Carrowe, Co. Fermanagh, re Cloncumber and other lands in Co. Monaghan, for a term of 30 years, rent £30 (stg). (D/DL T29, un-numbered lease)
1637	(15 Feb.) Indenture of a lease by same to Luke Ward of Clones, re the lands of Tateanna-temple, Tullyevin, Ballynatappa, Annaghkilty and Drumcrue, Co. Monaghan, for 21 years at a rent of £65 (stg). (D/Dl T29, un-numbered lease)

1637	(20 Feb.) Indenture of a lease by same to John Cowy and Thomas Twigge of Drumadanning, Co. Cavan, re the lands of Rathgarlagh and Grangeboy in Clones, Co. Monaghan, for 21 years at a rent of £27 (stg). (D/DL T29, un-numbered lease)
1637	(20 Feb.) Indenture of a lease by same to Matthew Browne of Clones, gent., re part of Clones Castle lately in the possession of Nicholas Simpson, for 21 years without rent, with a clause specifying that he must repair and otherwise renovate the castle. (D/DL T29, un-numbered lease)
1637	(2 March) Indenture of a lease by same to Mabel Richardson of Clones, re a mease in the town, for 21 years at a rent of 30s (stg). (D/DL T29, un-numbered lease)
1637	(6 March) Indenture of a lease by same to John Lylle, clerk, re the lands of Lisdrom by Clones, for 30 years beginning in 1627, at a rent of £12 (stg). (D/DL T29, un-numbered lease)
1637	(16 March) Copy of the order of the Lord Deputy and Council on the petition of Sir John Gifford against Lord Chancellor Loftus. Ordering that all evidences, writings, conveyances, etc., relative to the case be produced, and that no further conveyances be executed on the lands in question. Furthermore, Sir Edward Loftus is to make his personal appearance. (D/DL T28/30)
1637	(17 March) Indenture of a lease by Sir Robert Loftus and Dame Ellen his wife, and Sir George Wentworth and his wife, of the first part, and Margaret and Thomas Fleming of Corin, Co. Monaghan, of the other, re Gortenenoune, for 21 years, rent £16 (stg). (D/DL T29, un-numbered lease)
1637	(7 April) Indenture of a lease by same to Nicholas Wilson of Clones, shoemaker, re the lands of Lothgallen, for 21 years at a rent of 30s (stg). (D/DL T29, un-numbered lease)
1637	(4 May) Indenture of a lease by same to Patrick Madder McDillon of Clones, yeoman, re the lands of Drum-macagarry, Co. Monaghan, for 21 years, rent £34 (stg). (D/DL T29, un-numbered)
1637	(6 June) Copy of the order of the Lord Deputy and Council, requiring Sir Edward Loftus to deliver to the Clerk of the Council a deed dated 24 March 1635. (D/DL T28/31)
1637	(7 June) Lease from Sir Robert Loftus of Dublin, Dame Elinor, his wife, Sir George Wentworth and Dame Anne, his wife, to William Moore of Croonagh, Co. Monaghan, of the tate called Croonagh and two parts of the tithes of the same. To hold for 21 years, rent £13 (stg). (D/DL T28/105)
1638	(1 Feb.) Decree in the case of Sir John Gifford v. Lord Chancellor and Sir Edward Loftus, made by the Lord Deputy and Council. (D/DL T28/34).[151]
1638–9	(14 Charles I) Copy of an indenture by Lord Chancellor Loftus, pursuant to a decree of 1 Feb. 1638, granting to Sir Robert Loftus and his successors, an annuity of £200 *per annum* out of his lands in Monasterevan, Co. Kildare, and elsewhere in Ireland. To hold during the several lives of the Lord Chancellor and Sir Robert. With a proviso that this shall be void if the decree is reversed or the Lord Chancellor's appeal is successful. (D/DL T28/36)

---

[151] A copy of this was published in the H.M.C. report, *Various Collections III*, p164.

1638–9   (14 Charles I) Copy of an indenture from Sir Robert Loftus, regarding several lands, to Lord Chancellor Loftus and Sir George Wentworth, to indemnify them against being bound with Sir Robert. (D/DL T28/37)

1639   (24 May) Copy of a writ of covenant between (i) Sir Robert Dillon, Sir Adam Loftus, Christopher Wandesford, Sir Philip Mainwaring, plaintiffs, and (ii) Adam, Viscount Loftus, and Sarah, his wife, Sir Robert Loftus, Sir Edward Loftus and Jane his wife, Sir Richard Bolton, Sam: Magart and Sir Edward Bolton, deforceants, of the manors of Galmoreston, Monasterevan, Coshogowly, Fontsland, the monastery of New Abbey, and many other lands (very detailed) in Co. Kildare, totalling 28,500 acres. (D/DL T28/38)

1639   (24 May) Copy of a writ of covenant between the same parties, of the manors of Monasterevan, Rossenellis, and many other lands (very detailed) in Queen's Co., totalling 16,000 acres. (D/DL T28/39)

1639   (24 May) Copy of a writ of covenant between the same parties of the manors of Monasterevan, Coshagaroly, Knockbarran, and many other lands (very detailed) in King's Co., totalling 18,000 acres. (D/DL T28/40)

1639   (June) Attested copy of a 'Dedmuns Polestatem' [sic] to Sir Edward Osborne to take the precipes and concords of the said last three fines by Sir Edward Loftus and others. (D/DL T28/43)

1639   (18 June) Order of the Lord Deputy and Council, reciting previous orders, committing Lord Chancellor Loftus to prison for default and sequestering his estate. (D/DL T28/44)

1639   (27 July) Indenture between Sir John Gifford and Lord Chancellor Loftus, reciting that by statute staple of same date the Lord Chancellor bound himself to Sir John Gifford in £4,000. This indenture states that this bond will be void on the Lord Chancellor permitting the rents, profits, etc., of his estate to be disposed of according to the orders of the Lord Deputy and Council, unless the King shall give order to the contrary. (D/DL T28/46)

1639   (Michaelmas) Exemplification under the Great Seal of Ireland, the seal of the Common Pleas, and the seal of the Exchequer, of the aforesaid three writs of covenant, the returns thereof, the *dedimus potestatum*, and other returns concerning same. (D/DL T28/48)

1639   (19 Nov.) Copy of the decree of the King and Council in England on Lord Chancellor Loftus's appeal. Declaring said appeal to be without any just cause and confirming the order and decree of 1 Feb. 1638 and commanding same to be put into execution. (D/DL T28/50, 52, two copies)

1641   (15 April) Copy of an inquisition post mortem on the deaths of Sir Robert Loftus (d. 25 Oct. 1640), Ellinor, his wife (d. 27 May 1639), and their son Henry Loftus (d. 9 Nov. 1640), reciting deeds concerning their estate in Co. Fermanagh (detailed). Anne Loftus is daughter and sole heiress of Sir Robert and Ellinor. (D/DL T28/54)

1641   (26 July) Receipt of £6 15s, paid by Anne Loftus, for fines on the two inquisitions post mortem into the estate of her parents (Sir Robert and Ellinor), by order of the Court of Wards. (D/DL T28/57)

GLOUCESTERSHIRE : County Record Office *
Clarence Row, Alvin Street, Gloucester GL1 3DW
Tel: (01452) 452 295
Fax: (01452) 426 378

LOOSE ITEMS

1599   Order to the High Constable to muster 36 soldiers at Stroud and levy £54 6s for the war in Ireland. Receipt endorsed by Richard Keble, servant to Lord Chandos, Lord Lieutenant of Gloucestershire. (D 149/M7/1)

1601   (6 Aug.) Letter from Lord Chandos to the Privy Council regarding 100 men impressed in Gloucestershire for service in Ireland, with details of coat and conduct money. (D 3552 TRS 202)[152]

1622   (16 Feb.) Nineteenth century transcript of a grant under letters patent of Kilbegan manor and monastery in MacGeoghan's country to Charles, Lord Lambert. The grant also includes other lands in Cos. Westmeath, Cavan and King's County. (D 2440, Hicks Beach Mss [uncatalogued], box 44)

1633   (July) Abstract of His Majesty's letters patent for the fishing of Great Britain and Ireland, which orders the establishment of a society for the same. The abstract is followed by a list of 38 persons (all English), headed by the Duchess of Buckingham, who had subscribed towards 'the advancement of the fishings upon his Majesty's coasts'. (D 2510/5)

COLLECTIONS

Berkeley MSS (ref. Berkeley)

The Record Office has access to this private collection. A number of letters of Irish interest, most notably those concerning the affairs of the 10th Earl of Ormond and the 4th Earl of Thomond, were calendared in I.H. Jeayes, *Descriptive catalogue of the charters and muniments ... at Berkeley Castle* (Bristol, 1892). These are available on microfilm in the Record Office. However, the following additional documents were discovered in the card index to the Berkeley deeds, which is available on request at the Record Office. The deeds themselves remain at Berkeley Castle:

1514   (13 March) Letter of attorney from Sir Maurice Berkeley to John Kite, Archbishop of Armagh, for entry onto his lands in Cos. Wexford, Kildare, etc., in Ireland. (Berkeley Ch. General 4940)

1517   Conveyance of lands by Margaret Butler, widow of Sir William Boleyn, daughter of Thomas, 7th Earl of Ormond, to Sir Thomas Boleyn of all her manors, etc., in England and Ireland. (Berkeley Ch. General 4611)

1534   (20 May) Lease (and counterpart) for 60 years by Piers Butler, Earl of Ossory, to Thomas, Lord Berkeley, of all his manors, etc., in Ireland. (Berkeley Ch. General 4685–6)

1569   (10 July) Instructions from Thomas Butler, Earl of Ormond, to John Archdekin, Treasurer of Cashel, re the maintenance of Elizabeth Berkeley, Countess of Ormond. (Berkeley Ch. General 5057)

---

[152] This item was purchased by the County R.O. from Sotheby & Co. in 1977.

Daunt & Stoughton MSS (ref. D 979)

1611–58	Diary and memoranda book of Thomas Daunt, containing many genealogical notes relating to the Daunt family, 1611–58, with notice of some births and deaths. It begins with his journey from Bretfieldstowne in Ireland to England in March 1611, and gets progressively more detailed as it continues [16 fols, badly damaged]. (D 979A/F2)
c1615	Judgement made at Waterford 'under his Majesties privy signet' in a dispute over title to Ballyellane, Co. Cork. Recites a bill of complaint against William Allarde and deeds dated 1613–15 which involve John Fitz Thomas of Cork, merchant [very poor condition]. (D 979A/T6)[153]
1638	(7 Sept.) Grant under letters patent of lands in Co. Cork to Thomas Daunt. (D 979A/T6)
1638	(5 Dec.) Petition of Thomas Daunt, esq., to Lord Deputy Wentworth and the Commissioners for Defective Titles, regarding the refusal of William Healing to contribute his share to the costs and damages incurred by Daunt. The judgement, in Daunt's favour, is given on the reverse. (D 979A/T6)
17th cen.	'A note of writings sent for Ireland, touching my land there', by Thomas Daunt, which gives a detailed list of estate papers concerning Boysestown and other lands in Co. Cork. Mentions his dealings with David Gallway, Philip Roche, Richard Myaghe, Lieutenant Harris and Mr. Skiddy. (D 979A/E9)

Messrs. Penley, Milward & Bayley, solicitors, MSS (ref. D 2078)

Boxes 4–7 of this accession contain another collection of papers relating to the Daunts and Stoughtons of Owlpen, which includes much further material on their Irish estate.

14th c.–1650	A small collection of deeds and leases relating to the Co. Cork estates of the Daunt family of Tracton Abbey (D 2078, Box 5/19, parcels 1–2), *viz*
1571	(14 March) Sale of lands at Gortwenmore in 'Rynewynchedyn', Co. Cork, by Richard and Redmond Nugent to Patrick Roche fitz Philip of Kinsale. (5/19, parcel 1)
1571	(14 March) Bond by Richard and Raymond Nugent of Rynewynchedyn to Patrick Roche of Kinsale, merchant, in the sum of £100 for the quiet possession of lands in Gortnenwore in Rynewynchedine. Witnesses: Davy Arthur, Jasper Browne and James Arthur. (5/19, parcel 2)
1571	(24 June) Quitclaim of the same lands, by the same parties. (5/19, parcel 1)
1584	(13 May) Statement of intent by William Wynchedan, alderman of Cork, regarding the interest of Elicia, daughter and heiress of James Wynchedan, in 'one villa called Baly ni Boysighe in Aghymartin', Co. Cork. Witnesses: John Coppinger, Philip Lynch, Philip Browne and Edward Lombard. (5/19, parcel 1)
1590	(20 Sept.) Will of Arthur Robins of Robins Rock, Co. Cork, by which he gave all his lands in the said county and various rights and services there to Arthur Hyde of Hyde Castle in the said county, to hold to Hyde, his heirs and assigns for ever. Other

---

[153] Almost half of this item has been eaten by a rodent.

bequests include 20s to the decayed church of Templehogan; £10 to his brother Alexander Robbins; to his servant Francis Hickford £6 13s 4d; to his horseboy John Roche 40s, and to Jane Whittington 20s. Probate 11 May 31 Eliz. Signed by Archbishop Loftus of Dublin and Ambrose Forth. (5/19, parcel 2)

1594 (7 May) Indenture between John Roche and James Roche, pursuant to the will of their father, Patrick Roche of Kinsale, merchant. Concerning Patrick's principal house in Kinsale, called 'the Rock of Kinsale', Dowle Castle and houses in Sisters Street in Kinsale. Witnesses: James Sarsfield and John Roche fitz Philip. (5/19, parcel 1)

1602 (1 Oct.) Grant by John Roche fitz Patrick of Kinsale to James Myaghe fitz Richard of the same, confirming to Myaghe a carucate of land called Killowny in Courcies country, and also a parcel of land called Parckynawll containing 40 acres in Kerrycurrihy, to hold to him and his heirs and assigns for ever; in consideration of an unspecified sum of money. (5/19, parcel 1)

1607 (17 March) Indenture between William Berkhead of Myloth Castle, Co. Cork, gent., and Thomas Daunt, reciting that Richard Myagh fitz Richard of Kinsale, in consideration of £26 16s 4d paid to him by Berkhead to the use of the said Daunt, had by his deed granted to Berkhead certain lands in Kerrycurrihy to hold in trust for Daunt; now this indenture witnesses that Berkhead has enfeoffed Daunt, his heirs and assigns for ever. Witnesses: Teige McDonogh and James Daunt. (5/19, parcel 2)

1607 (17 March) Sale by William Berkhead of Mylotes Castle, Co. Cork, to Thomas Daunt of Gortygreenan in the same county, of a bond of £100 dated 22 May 1605 by James Myaghe fitz Richard of Kinsale to Berkhead. (5/19, parcel 2)

1607 (12 April) Conveyance by Arthur Hyde to Sir Dominic Sarsfield of the townland of Renny in the cantred of Kinnalea, Co. Cork, by way of mortgage. Endorsed: discharged 8 April 1624. (5/19, parcel 1)

1607 (17 Oct.) Release of mortgage. James Myaghe of Kinsale grants to John Roche fitz Patrick of Cork, all the land mortgaged to him by the same Roche for a certain sum, now paid; to hold for ever. Witnesses: Donald MacShane, John Myagh, Owen O'Keefe. (5/19, parcel 1)

1607 (19 Oct.) John Roche fitz Patrick of Cork (late of Kinsale), in virtue of £52 paid to him by Thomas Daunt of Gortigrenan, has sold to Daunt certain lands, to hold to the said Daunt, his heirs and assigns for ever by way of mortgage; endorsed with a note of the same date by the attorney William Berkhead, that he had delivered seisin to Daunt. Witnesses: John Gillett, Donogh McShane, Thomas White, Conegore McMorrice and Thomas O'Closh. (5/19, parcel 1)

1608 (26 May) Bond of John Roche of Cork City to Thomas Daunt of Tracton Abbey, gent., in the sum of 200 marks, for the fulfilment of certain obligations set forth in a deed poll of the same date. (5/19, parcel 2)

1609 (25 April) Indenture between Arthur Hyde of Carriganeedy, Co. Cork, esq., and Matthew Harrys of Moyalls in the same county, witnessing that Hyde has demised and to farm let to Harrys the town and lands of Nohavale and Glangolane for 31 years at a rent of £6 in the first year and £6 13s 4d for every subsequent year. Witnesses: John [Bumer][154], R. Williams and Robert Hyde. (5/19, parcel 1)

1611   (13 July) Sale by Arthur Hide of Carriganedie, Co. Cork, to Henry Gold of Cork, merchant, in consideration of £60, lands in Noghwall [Nohoval], Glannykillen and Ballintreydine in Kinallea, Co. Cork. (5/19, parcel 1)

1612   (19 Dec.) Arthur Hyde acknowledges himself indebted to Sir Dominic Sarsfield in the sum of £20, which is to be added to another mortgage that he made to Sarsfield of the lands of Renny and Downgarret, making £60 in all. Witnesses: Robert Tyrry and John Williamson. (5/19, parcel 1)

1613   (8 Jan.) Sale by Dominick Roche fitz-William, alderman, and John Roche fitz-William, merchant, both of Cork, to Thomas Daunt of Bretfieldstown, Co. Cork, of their interests in the feoffment dated 24 Oct. 1595, by the late William Roche, alderman of Cork. In consideration of £15. (5/19, parcel 2)

1615   (1 April) Quitclaim by James Roche fitz-Patrick of Kinsale to Thomas Daunt of his interest in lands in Gortnygowenbegg. (5/19, parcel 1)

1621   (5 Sept.) Indenture between Matthew Harrys and James Daunt of Tracton Abbey, esq., witnessing that Harrys, in consideration of the sum hereafter mentioned grants and lets to Daunt certain land in the barony of Kinnalea for 2 ½ years and after at £32 rent *per annum* for the remainder of 21 years. (5/19, parcel 1)

c1622–5   Very badly mutilated item, evidently an inquisition post mortem into the estate of Thomas Daunt senior of Tracton Abbey, late deceased. The names of some of the jurors are discernible, including Thomas Nugent, Patrick Porsell, John Nugent, [ ] Roche of Killyane, and [ ] Douglas. (5/19, parcel 2)

1624   (12 May) Sale by Arthur Hide of Carrig Meady, Co. Cork, to Thomas Daunt of Tracton Abbey, in consideration of £460 of all his manors, lands, etc., in Neghowall [Nohoval] and Glankellan in the barony of Kinallea, in the said county. (5/19, parcel 2)

1624   (13 May) Bond of statute staple made by Hyde to Daunt in the sum of £800; signed by John Coppinger, Mayor of the Staple. Witnesses: Morris Roche (Constable), Patrick Lynch (Constable), and Francis Roche (Clerk of the Staple). (5/19, parcel 1)

1625   (20 Sept.) Declaration by Sir Arthur Hyde of Carriganeedy, Co. Cork, and Lady Helena his wife, that a fine was levied last Trinity term between Thomas Daunt, esq., plaintiff, and the said Sir Arthur and Lady Helena, defendants, of the castle, messuages and lands, etc., at Moghavally [Nohoval] and Glanagallan in the said county; with a warranty clause to Daunt, his heirs and assigns. Witnesses: Andrew Ketelby, Bar: Baker, Marcus Greame and Philip Ruinney. (5/19, parcel 1)

1628   (12 May) Declaration by Matthew Harrys of Noghovalle, Co. Cork, gent., stating that whereas Sir Arthur Hyde by his indenture dated 25 April 1609 granted to him the town and lands of Noghovalle and Glengelane for 31 years; now Harrys, in consideration of £100 paid to him by Thomas Daunt of Tracton Abbey has agreed to convey the said property to Frances and Catherine Daunt, daughters of the said Thomas, to their use during their lives and that of their assigns. (5/19, parcel 1)

---

[154] Unclear in Ms.

1628   (12 May) Bond of Matthew Harrys to Thomas Daunt in £200 for the fulfilment of the covenants in the preceding deed. (5/19, parcel 1)

14–19th cen. A lengthy file of translations made in the nineteenth century of old deeds concerning the Daunt estate (D 2078, Box 7/6), which while detailing the deeds given in Box 5/19 above, also mention the following items which are no longer extant:

1625   Exemplification of a fine between Thomas Daunt, plaintiff, and Arthur Hyde and Helena his wife, defendants, of the castle and lands of Noghovelly, Co. Cork (Feet of Fines 1° Charles I).

1638   (13 April) A schedule of the lands and hereditaments belonging to Thomas Daunt of Tracton Abbey, and his order of composition.

1638   (31 July) Document reciting that by letters patent Thomas Daunt, his heirs and assigns, had in consideration of the annual rent of £14 10s 2d, received from the crown the town and lands of Noghavalle, Glangullen, Renedungarret, Ballintryclew and Gortigennan in the barony of Kinnalea, Co. Cork, and other lands in the barony of Barrett's country in the said shire.

c1638   Outline of the conditions under which the Crown agreed to grant certain lands in Co. Cork to Thomas Daunt, reciting that he was required to pay rent; to settle four freeholders of English birth upon the premises, each of whom was to have £10 *per annum* worth of land; to settle another ten English families as under-tenants there; to maintain two horsemen and eight footmen continually upon the premises. Signed by Lord Deputy Wentworth and the Irish Council.

16th cen.   (n.d.) 'I Andrewe Skiddy, Alderman, doe acknowledge to have sould unto Edmund Worragh eighte hoggesheads of good salte beoffe packt in Burdeeaux casks, for the wch I have reced paiement from the said Edmund'. (D 2078, Box 6/9)

1638   (13 April) A schedule of the lands and hereditaments for which Thomas Daunt, esq., compounded, followed by an outline of the conditions under which the crown agrees to grant him certain lands in Co. Cork, signed by the Lord Deputy and Council [8pp]. (D 2078, Box 6/10–11)[155]

1638   (31 July) Translation made in 1793 of the grant of the manor of Noghavalle, Co. Cork, to Thomas Daunt by Charles I, whereby in consideration of the sum of £21 10s (stg) paid by Daunt into the hands of the Vice-Treasurer or General Receiver of Ireland, payable to the Crown by virtue of a composition agreement or concord entered into by the said Daunt at Dublin Castle, he is granted all the lands, villages, etc., of Noghavalle, Glenquillan, Renes *alias* Renny, Dungarrett, Ballynhaden *alias* Dredend, and Gortigrenna, all in the barony of Kinnalea; all the lands, etc., of Boysestown, Ballinanynybeg, Parkenynowle and Gortinownebegg in the barony of Kerrycurrihy, and also the lands, etc., of Bordenstown in the barony of Barrett's Country. To hold of the King's castle of Carrigrohan by common knight's service, with Bordenstown held of same by common socage, all for a yearly rent of £14 10s 2½d. (D 2078, Box 7/1)

---

[155] Although this comprises one item, the document was apparently broken up during sorting, and is now available out of sequence as two separate accessions, i.e. Box 6/11 = pp 1–2 and 7–8, and Box 6/10 = pp 3–6.

1639   (Trinity term) Verified copy by Henry Warren of the proceedings at the Crown Court in Cork against Thomas Daunt for non-payment of dues owed to the Exchequer, signed by Sir Richard Bolton [poor condition]. (D 2078, Box 6/12)

17th cen.   Evidence of witnesses in a boundary dispute, probably over land in Co. Cork [5 docs., damaged]. (D 2078, Box 6/15)[156]

Gloucester Borough Archives (ref. GBR)

1486–1648   Memoranda Book of the Corporation of Gloucester (GBR B2/1), which includes the following:

   1563   (20 Oct.) Warrant from Queen Elizabeth commanding all corporation officials to see that the Earl of Desmond is furnished with all necessary items, including sufficient shipping, and reasonably priced post horses, for himself and his family and servants, on his way into Ireland. The Queen specifically commands that officials are to treat the Earl with due regard and respect, especially considering 'his weakness'. Furthermore, the Queen states that Desmond has leave to go to Ireland, and once there he is to repair to the Earl of Sussex. (fol. 225r)

   c1580   (n.d.) 'The articles of Bristol against Gloucester'. This was one of many documents in a lengthy dispute between the two cities in 1580–2, concerning the elevation of Gloucester's status to that of a head port. These charges by Bristol include two articles concerning Ireland (articles 21 & 23) alleging that Irishmen are allowed to ship large quantities of corn out of Gloucester, and that victualling Irish troops would be more expensive for the government from Gloucester than from Bristol. (ff 85r–87r)

   c1580   (n.d.) The answer of the Mayor and Burgesses of Gloucester to the above. They state that 'the Irishmen neither can, nor can have any grain from Gloucester without licence', and they argue that it is up to the victuallers and purveyors where they get their commodities. Furthermore, they point out that most of Gloucester's small boats have continually been employed 'unto the service of Ireland'. (ff 87r–91r)

   c1581   (n.d.) Interrogatories to be administered to the witnesses on Gloucester's part, which includes a question (no. 19) asking about general trade between the Severn and Ireland. (ff 102v–104)

   c1581   (n.d.) Further interrogatories to be administered to witnesses on Gloucester's part, which includes three questions concerning Ireland. Firstly (no. 9), whether Bristol can supply sufficient quantities of grain to Cornwall, Wales and Ireland on its own. Secondly (no. 12), the quantity of small boats in Gloucester, and how many of them are employed in the Queen's service in Ireland, and thirdly (no. 15), whether all grain for victuals in Ireland are first laden on Gloucester's quays. (ff 104r–105v)

1565–1632   Gloucester City Minutes (GBR B3/1), which include one item relating to Ireland:

   1615   (17 Aug.) Case heard before the Common Council of the City concerning Henry Langford and Alderman Taylor, and £4 owed by Taylor to Langford. Taylor was to help Langford fund the 'frieght of a bark which he had then laden with commodities for Ireland'. Taylor lost the case. (ff 265v–267r)

---

[156] These items are falling to pieces, and are not available for consultation in the Record Office.

1586–1619 Gloucester Lieutenancy Records: Order & Letter Book (GBR H2/1), which includes several items of Irish interest, *viz*

1588 (4 Oct.) Names and origins of 25 soldiers from Gloucester City selected for H.M.'s service in Ireland, with a note that they are to be supplied with certain weapons as follows: ten with shot, five with bills, five with corselets and five with bows and arrows. (fol. 33v)

1588 (15 Sept.) Queen's instructions to the Lord Lieutenant of Co. Gloucester for the raising of 200 able men from the shire to be sent to Ireland. (fol. 33v)

1590 (9 Feb.) On this day in the college churchyard the Lord Lieutenant of the shire, Lord Chandos, took a view of the trained bands of 300 men bound for Ireland. The deputy commissioners were instructed to spend the next two days in applying the soldiers to their arms and supplying all deficits in their furnishings, 'by wch meanes all the armo^rs weare brought into good order & the men [made] in full redines' before being mustered prior to embarkation. There then follows details of the 25 men out of the 300 whom the city was to supply, with orders for taxation. (ff 49v–50v)

1590 (22 Feb.) Certificate by the City Commissioners addressed to Lord Chandos to the effect that the 25 men are ready for the voyage to Ireland. (fol. 50v)

1595 (March) 'About the myddell of Lent this yeare were C soldiers mustered out of the Countie of Glouc' for service into Ireland against the Rebellion of the Earl of Terone'. (ff 77v–79r)

1595 (Trinity term) At the Trinity term Quarter Sessions the High Sheriff of Gloucestershire and the rest of the Justices of the Peace prosecuted the Mayor and Aldermen of Gloucester for their portion of the troops to be raised for Ireland; recites that the Privy Council had required 60 foot and four horsemen from the city. There then ensues lengthy details of the case, whereby the city maintained that its charter prevented musters being held inside its liberties without special warrant. (ff 79v–81r)

1600 (25 June) Copy of a letter by Queen Elizabeth to Lord Chandos ordering the raising of 50 men in Gloucestershire for the war in Ireland. (fol. 82r)

1600 (26 June) Copy of the Privy Council's orders to Chandos re the same. (ff 83r–84v)

1616 (20 July) Copy of the King's letter for the supply of soldiers from the shire (15 muskets and 10 corselets) for the Irish foot bands. (fol. 87r)

1616 (31 July) Copy of the Privy Council's letter to the Lord Lieutenant of the shire, outlining the King's concern over the state of the armed forces in Ireland 'both in number and qualitie', and requiring 25 men to be levied in Co. Gloucester for service there. (ff 85v–86r)

1616 (4 Sept.) A true rate of levying within the City of Gloucester the sum of £18 for three soldiers to make up the number of soldiers in the decayed garrisons in Ireland, according to the rate of 6d a yard-land. (fol. 103r)

1616 (c9 Sept.) Note by John Jones that he received notice of the King's orders for the Irish troops from Sir William Cooke on 4 Sept. last, and on Tuesday next 11 Sept. he will present them properly furnished with arms and apparrel. (fol. 87r)

Gloucester Diocesan Records (ref. Diocesan)

1625	(1 August) Last will and testament of William Cecill of Bandon Bridge, Co. Cork, appointing his wife Margaret his sole executrix, and Thomas Atkinson and Michael Bull of Bandon Bridge the overseers. Leaves his main estates in Ireland and England to his eldest son, Richard, and smaller bequests of goods, money or property to his other children. Probate dated 7 September 1625. (Diocesan Wills, 1625, no. 220)
1636	(8 Oct.) Last will and testament of John Swanley of St. John's parish in Wexford, appointing his wife Elizabeth his sole executrix. Wishes to be buried in the churchyard of Selsker, and makes bequests to his children. Probate dated 21 April 1637. (Diocesan Wills, 1637, no. 78)
1637	(3 Jan.) Inventory of all the goods, chattels, and other property of John Swanley (see above) in the Diocese of Gloucester, taken by Henry Clifford, Edward Harmer, and William Watkins. Gives details of clothes, goods, leases of land, livestock, books and debts, totalling £556 18s 4d. (Diocesan Inventories, 1637, No. 7)

HAMPSHIRE : County Record Office *
Sussex Street, Winchester, Hampshire SO23 8TH
Tel: (01962) 846 154
Fax: (01962) 878 681

LOOSE ITEMS

1595	Order concerning a levy for the provision of horsemen for an expedition to Ireland. (W/K5/4 fol. 60)
1613	(31 May) Letter from Francis Kingsmill to Sir William Kingsmill, his brother, at Sidemountain. Parliament is entered into in Dublin with 'much confusion and difference between the English and Irish'. (19M61/1315)

COLLECTIONS

Coventry Collection (ref. 1M53)

This collection contains some Irish records of the Trenchard family, undertakers in the Munster plantation.[157]

1586	(27 June) Copy of letters of commission under the Great Seal to the Lord Deputy, Privy Council, and others, to divide up into seignories the lands in the province of Munster, forfeited by the rebellion of the Earl of Desmond. (1M53/1549)
1587–8	(n.d., 30 Eliz. I) Note of the commission to Sir John Norris and others to call before them persons with claims to escheated lands in Munster. (1M53/1550)
1607	(21 April) Copy of an order by the Lord Deputy and Commissioners for the seignory of Mount Trenchard, Co. Limerick, to be surveyed. (1M53/1551)

---

[157] There are many other documents concerning the English estates of the Trenchard family in this collection, which may include passing reference to their Irish affairs.

1608	(19 Nov.) Copy of an order that Francis Trenchard shall pay into the Exchequer as much rent as he has lately paid, and that no process shall issue against him for arrears. (1M53/1552)
c1610	(n.d.) Copy of a statement by Tirrelagh (*alias* Trelagh) McMahowne concerning Sangroly and Leagh. (1M53/1553)
c1610	(n.d.) Draft answer of Thomas Bolton, agent for Francis Trenchard, to the petition of Tirrelagh McMahon (above). (1M53/1554)
1612	(23 June) Certified copy of an Exchequer order concerning rents to be paid and sums owing to the Crown by Francis Trenchard. (1M53/1555)
1614	(20 April) Letter from Edmund Drewe at Lismakeere (?) to Francis Trenchard about expenses incurred against Mr. Riches. (1M53/1556)
1622	Draft certificate on the seignory of Corgrig *alias* Mount Trenchard, Co. Limerick, compiled by Trenchard's agent for the 1622 Commissioners' report on the state of the Munster plantation. It includes details of buildings, tenants and tenures, as well as a history of the title to the estate from the initial plantation grant. (1M53/1557)[158]
1623	(9 Jan.) List of the names of jurors for an inquisition post mortem after the death of Francis Trenchard. (1M53/1558)
1623	(9 Jan.) Inquisition post mortem (findings of the jury above) for Francis Trenchard, who died 10 May 1622, and was seized of the castle, towns, lands, etc., of Corgrig, Ballmecraige, Neleigh and Coppagh, Co. Limerick [4 fols]. (1M53/1559)
1624	(24 May) Letter from George Courtenay to Thomas Bolton, asking him to come and see him about a *scire facias* upon the seignory at the request of the Sir Richard Preston, Earl of Desmond. (1M53/1560)
1631	(Mich.) Instructions from Francis Trenchard to his uncle Bolton, his agent on his Irish estate. (1M53/1561)
1631–3	Statement of rents due from the seignory of Mount Trenchard, Co. Limerick. (1M53/1562)

Jervoise of Herriard MSS (ref. 44M69)

This is a large collection, much of which remains uncatalogued, with only box lists available as a guide. The following series have material relating to Ireland:

Miscellaneous (ref. 44M69/L)

1595	(27 March) Copy of letters patent to John Thornburgh, Bishop of Limerick, granting him the Deanery of York *in commendam*. (44M69/L/13/1)

Estate Accounts (ref. 44M69/E3)

This series of uncatalogued English estate accounts includes a volume of private notes and accounts relating to England and Ireland which belonged to Sir Henry Wallop, the Vice-Treasurer of Ireland from 1579 to 1599 (ref. 44M69/E3).[159] The

---

[158] This certificate, which contains details omitted in the Commissioners' summary report, is discussed in Michael MacCarthy-Morrogh, *The Munster Plantation* (Oxford, 1986), pp172–3.

[159] This reference refers to the box number. Individual items have not been catalogued. In his *Sources*, Hayes referred to a volume of Wallop's Treasurer-at-War accounts for 1579–80 that he believed was in

covering dates of the volume are 1584–96, and the items of Irish interest are as follows:

1584–96	Copies of letters from the chief governors of Ireland to Sir Henry Wallop, Treasurer-at-war, requesting him to make several payments to John Bleeke, Constable of Limerick Castle, and to the captain and men garrisoned there.
1584–8	Account of money paid to John Bleeke, Constable of Limerick Castle.
1591–2	Copies of instructions from Queen Elizabeth and the Lord Deputy about the revenues of the attainted lands of Munster in Ireland.
1592–5	Estimates of the annual charges on the revenues of Munster.
1595	Estimate of expenses for the army in Ireland.
1596	(11 Dec.) 'Noate of how many concordationnes William Auston brought me the 11th of December 1596 from Mr. Large'

Correspondence (ref. 44M69/E76–7)

These two uncatalogued boxes only include one item of Irish interest:

1580	Letter from Sir Pescal Brocas to Sir Henry Wallop, explaining that he has heard that Wallop will be testifying against him in an upcoming trial, and reminding Wallop that 'I met you in Hownsloe Heth, this last vackation, a little before your going into Ireland'. Brocas continues by relating all the evidence in his favour, and he claims that Wallop's information is not very strong and would only involve a wasted journey from Ireland. (44M69/E76)

Wallop Trust Papers (ref. 44M69/F14)

Although this box of uncatalogued material deals with the period in the late seventeenth century when the Jervoise family were involved in running the Wallop estate, it does include one item relating to Ireland prior to 1641, as follows:

1585	(20 July) Letters patent to Sir Henry Wallop, Treasurer-at-war, of the custody of the lands and castle of Corgrage with six carucates of land, and the lands of Nelegle, Ballinecrase, the castle of Ballilowrae with five carucates in the parish of Ballyrobert, Co. Limerick, and a castle called Cappagh in the parish of Longhkill, in the same county, parcel of the possessions of Gerald, late Earl of Desmond. To have and to hold the custody of the same during pleasure. (44M69/F14)[160]

Lieutenancy Papers (ref. 44M69/G5/)[161]

This large class of documents contains a great deal of information about the raising and equipping of troops in Hampshire, many of whom were bound for service in Ireland. Below is a list of only those items which make direct reference to Ireland, but there are many further documents in this class, which while

---

the Hampshire Record Office. There is a volume with this exact title in this box, but it refers purely to the administration of Wallop's English estate during his absence in Ireland, and the covering dates are in fact 1579–84.

[160] This patent does not appear in the published calendars of Fiants or Patent Rolls.

[161] 44M69/G5/ is the prefix given before the documents referred to below. For example, the first item's full reference number is 44M69/G5/XX.43

making no direct reference to Ireland, clearly concern troops which were to be sent there.[162]

1598	(14 August) List of captains and men of repute slain in Ireland. (XX.43)
1598	(31 Oct.) Letter from the Lord Lieutenant of Hampshire to Richard Poulet and other Justices and captains in the division of Basingstoke, re the levy of 300 men for service in Ireland. (XX.44)
1598	(6 Nov.) Document concerning the levying of men for service in the army in Ireland. (XX.45)
1598–1601	(6 Nov. 1598–11 Feb. 1601) Note of men levied in Co. Southampton for Ireland, with proportion money and conduct money. (XX.93)
1599	(27 Feb.) List of men taken at Basing Downe for Ireland. (XX.48)
1599	(2 March) Note of men appointed in Basingstoke division to go to Ireland. (XX.47)
1599	(6 March) Names of men impressed for Ireland. (XX.49)
1599	(5 June) Letter from the Deputy Lieutenant to the leading gentlemen of the divisions in Hampshire, concerning the supply of equipment for Ireland, together with an account of the same. In a volume of letters dated 1599. (XX.50)
1600	(27 June) Queen's letter to the Council re the provision of a company of horse for Ireland. (XX.89)
1600	(29 June) Council to Richard Poulet, requesting him to supply a light horse for Ireland. (XX.90)
1600	(29 June) Council to J.P.s in Co. Southampton to provide provisions for Ireland. (XX.95)
1600	(30 June) Deputy Lieutenant of Hampshire to Richard Poulet for the provision of 50 men for Ireland. (XX.93)
1600	(20 July) Bond of Thomas Smyth of Freefolk to serve as a light horseman in Ireland. (XX.94)
1600	(July) Account of conduct money for Ireland. (XX.93)
1600	(July) Return of contributions to pay and supply men for Ireland. (XX.96)
1601	(14 Jan.) Deputy Lieutenant to Richard Poulet for the provision of men for Ireland. (XX.93)
1601	(25 July) Proportion on Kingsclere division for paying 100 soldiers for Ireland. (XX.97)
1601	(31 Aug.) Richard Poulet's writ for levying the proportion on the occupants of Overton for soldiers for Ireland. (XX.98)
1628	(12 Aug.) Lord Lieutenant of Hampshire to the Deputy Lieutenant, for billeting 200 soldiers belonging to Colonel Crosby's company[163] in E. Meon. (XXXIX.33)

---

[162] They include a great many muster books for the companies of Captain Richard Poulet (for years 1596, 1598, 1600, 1607, 1612), Sir Thomas Jervoise (1616, 1618 etc.) and Captain Thomas Leigh (undated), as well as schedules of arms and many other documents. Though many of the troops were bound for the Netherlands, a great deal were also enlisted to serve in the Irish army.

[163] i.e. Sir Piers Crosby of Maryborough in Queen's County.

1628   (18 Aug.) Same to same, re the disorders among Crosby's Irish company, and also re an account for billeting. (XXXIX.33A)

1628   (22 Aug.) Deputy Lieutenant to Edward Lewes, to provide a billet for John Butler, an Irish captain. (XXXIX.34)

Temple (Palmerston) MSS (ref. 36M68)

1560   (27 Aug.) Copy of a translation of the pardon granted to Francis Agard for his alienation of Grange Gorman, Co. Dublin, and his other Irish estates. (36M68/159)

1560   (27 Aug.) Copy of a pardon of alienation for Francis Agard regarding Grange Gorman. (36M68/160)

1570–1748 Statement of the title of Henry, Lord Viscount Palmerston, to the manor and lands of Grange Gorman, including a schedule of deeds. (36M68/161)

16th cen.   A certified copy of the Queen's letter for Francis Agard, conferring on him an estate in fee farm at Grange Gorman. (36M68/158)

1626   (25 April) Inquisition before Anthony Dopping, feodary for Leinster, and Henry Kenny, commissioners to enquire into what lands Francis Agard of Grange Gorman held before his death on 11 October 1577, and who is his next heir. The estate was divided between his three daughters, Mabell, Cecilia and Maria. Mabell married William Agard, esq., and had two sons, Henry and John. On William's death she was next married to John King. On her death, her estate fell to Sir Henry Agard and his heirs; then in default of male heirs to his brother, who now legally holds the estate from the King. Enrolled in the Chancery of Ireland [attested copy dated 1838]. (36M68/157)

Wallop (Portsmouth) Collection (ref. 15M84)

1587   (25 July) Lease by Sir Henry Wallop to Nicholas Synnott fitz-Richard of Wexford, merchant, of a quarter of all the great and small tithes, alterages, offerings, profits, etc., in all the parishes, rectories, churches and chapels of the dissolved Abbey of Selsker, Co. Wexford,[164] except Beggeren, 'muche' Island, and Ilanekille. To hold for 21 years from 25 August 1582, at a rent of £24 8s (stg), £4 (Irish), and 30 pecks of port corn. (15M84/Box 57)

1598   (1 April) Letters patent granting license to Sir Henry Wallop to alienate the manor and friary of Enniscorthy, Co. Wexford, to Lodovic Brisket, Oliver Wallop, his son, and John Browne and Richard Hooper. (15M84/Box 57)

16th cen.   (c1584–99) Charter of exemplification, made at the request of Sir Henry Wallop, Vice-Treasurer of Ireland, of an enrolment of an indenture circa Henry III between the Bishop of Ferns, of the one part, and Philip de Prendergast and Matilda de Guerney, of the other, touching lands in Clone, Co. Wexford. (15M84/ Box 63)[165]

1611   (8 June) Copy of letters patent granting to Sir Henry Wallop the spiritualities of the abbey of Selsker (rent £101 13s 4d) and the

---

[164] For a list of these premises, see the Crown's 21-year lease to Wallop in 1587, *Cal. Fiants Ire.*, Eliz. I, no. 5115.

[165] The dating of this document is difficult, and all that can reliably be said is that Wallop is known to have begun purchasing land in Co. Wexford in 1584, and that he died in 1599.

manor and friary of Enniscorthy (rent £13 6s 4d), both in Co. Wexford, to be held forever in common socage. And also the lands Currignebruss, Co. Wexford, to be held for ever, by fealty only. (15M84/ Box 101)[166]

1621   (1 Dec.) Sale by Sir Francis Blundell to Sir Henry Wallop, of the manor of Blundell *alias* Templeshannon, Co. Wexford, in consideration of £1,350 (stg).[167] Wallop acquits Blundell of all possible penalties entailed in the patent, except in relation to building a house. (15M84/Box 57)

1634   (29 Dec.) Deed of feoffment by (1) Sir Henry Wallop, son and heir of Sir Henry Wallop of Enniscorthy, Co. Wexford, and Edward Avenal of Cliddersden, Co. Southampton, to (2) George Withers of Hall, in the parish of Dean, Co. Southampton, and John King of the same; of all his estates in Co. Wexford, to the use of the said Sir Henry Wallop. Recites earlier deeds of feoffment, crown grants and leases relating to the same property. (15M84/Box 63)

HAMPSHIRE : Southampton City Archives Office
Civic Centre, Southampton SO14 7LY
Tel: (01703) 832 251/223 855 ext. 2251

The Southampton Record Society (S.R.S.) has published a number of documents relating to Ireland in J. Rutherford (ed.), *The miscellaneous papers of Captain Thomas Stockwell, 1590–1614* (2 vols., S.R.S., xxxii–xxxiii, 1932–3). Thomas Stockwell was Sir Oliver Lambert's estate agent, and although most of his work entailed looking after Lambert's property in Southampton, he also needed to keep in contact with his master whenever the latter was absent in Ireland. As such, Stockwell's papers shed a great deal of light on Lambert's activities in Ireland, and they contain *inter alia* much general news about Irish affairs. The Stockwell papers are now part of the City's forfeited estates collection (SC4/6/1–198).[168] In addition, a second S.R.S. publication, R.C. Anderson (ed.), *Letters of the Fifteenth and Sixteenth Centuries*, (S.R.S., xxii, 1921), includes some letters regarding Irish prisoners in Southampton, as well as details of the dispute between Henry Ughtred and the Marquis of Winchester in 1587, when Ughtred journied to Munster. These items are now at SC2/9/2/1–145.[169]

    The report by the Historical Manuscripts Commission on the records of the town of Southampton (*11th Report*, App. III (1887), pp1–144) makes notice of two documents concerning Ireland. Of these, one is of especial interest, a book containing 'Notes and materials for the History of Ireland' (p6 of report), which was compiled in 1704. This item is now located at D/M 4/14, and is described as O'Flaherty's 'Ogygia vindicated'. The item forms part of the papers of William and Samuel Molyneux of Castle Dillon, many of which have been microfilmed for the National Library of Ireland.[170]

---

[166] For full details of this patent, see *Cal. Ir. Patent Rolls, James I*, pp198–9.

[167] For a list of these properties see Blundell's plantation grant, *Ibid*, p482.

[168] The last number in the reference sequence corresponds with the numbering in the S.R.S. publication. Some Stockwell papers can also be found in the University of Southampton Library (see below).

[169] The last number in the reference sequence corresponds with the numbering in the S.R.S. publication.

[170] N.L.I. n.2680–1 p.1586. Apart from some notes on the history of the manor of Castle Dillon (at ref. D/M 2/1), which gives the descent of the title to the estate from James I, this collection only begins in the late seventeenth century.

COLLECTIONS

The Port or Petty Customs Account Books of Southampton (ref. SC5/4)

This series is dated 1426–1601, and includes both exports and imports, and the places with which Southampton's merchants were trading. Each account book generally runs from Michaelmas to Michaelmas. Some of the earlier fifteenth century account books have been edited and published by D.B. Quinn for the S.R.S. (2 vols, xxxvii–xxxviii, 1937–8), and though prior to 1485, they contain a number of references to Irish merchants and shipping. It is likely that the unpublished account books for the later period contain Irish material as well.

Sessions Records (ref. SC9)

The Southampton Record Society has published a variety of examinations and depositions heard in the City's courts. See G.H. Hamilton (ed.), *The Book of Examinations and Depositions 1570–94* (S.R.S., xvi, 1914); R.C. Anderson (ed.), *The Book of Examinations 1601–2* (S.R.S., xxvi, 1926); and R.C. Anderson (ed.), *The Book of Examinations and Depositions 1622–44*, (4 vols, S.R.S., xxix, xxxi, xxxiv, xxxvi, 1929–36). Volume 3 of this last publication includes many references to Southampton's trade with Cork and Kinsale, and to the trial of Robert Keyes, a shoemaker from Cork. It is very likely that there are many other documents concerning Ireland in the unpublished examinations, and in other parts of the sessions records in general.

HAMPSHIRE : University of Southampton Library *
Highfield, Southampton SO9 5NH
Tel: (01703) 592 721/593 724
Fax: (01703) 593 007

LOOSE ITEMS

1601   (1 Oct.) Letter from John Walker [?] to Lieutenant Joseph at Sir Oliver Lambert's lodging at Thomas Court, asking for money and bonds owed to him by Lambert, when Lambert next comes to Dublin. Also news of the burning of 'Omaleye'. (Ms. 83/1/2)[171]

COLLECTIONS

Broadlands Estate Papers (ref. BR)

1583   (12 Aug.) Indenture tripartate between (1) Sir Henry Harrington and Dame Cecelia Agard, his wife, daughter and co-heir of Francis Agard, (2) William Agard of Foston, Co. Derby, and Mabell Agard, his wife, daughter and co-heir of Francis Agard, and (3) Henry Moore, son of Sir Edward Moore, and Mary Agard, his wife, daughter and co-heir of Francis Agard. The indenture details the partition tripartate of the entire estate of Francis Agard in Co. Wicklow and elsewhere. (BR 137/I/x)

---

[171] This item is part of a small bundle of four items which clearly became separated from the Stockwell papers in the Southampton City Archives Office (see above). It is not clear whether 'Omaleye' is meant to represent Offaly.

1621	(5 Jan.) Copy of an inquisition post mortem of John Allen fitz-William of Palmerstown, Co. Dublin [7 pages]. (BR 137/I/i)
1626	Copy of a mortgage from Donogh O'Connor Sligo to Lord Powerscourt, Lord Aungier, Sir Francis Annesley, and Sir William Parsons, of the lands of Cliftony [Cliffony?], Brenlater, Edenreagh, Castlegarran, Magherygelernon, Ballyfahyand, and Surragh *alias* Dannagh *alias* Carrowtenny in Co. Sligo, for the term of 99 years, at a rent of one grain of wheat. On condition that if Donogh pays Lord Powerscourt £470 before 1 May 1638, the said indenture shall be void. (BR 140/4)
1626	A letter from an antiquarian, James Burrow, in 1758, giving details of the death of Sir William Temple in Ireland in 1626 at the age of 72. (BR 7/34)
1636	(2 June) Bill of complaint to the Lord Chancellor by Matthew Allen against John Allen, regarding debts incurred from the mortgage of the lands of Palmerston. (BR 137/I/vi)
1636	(11 June) 'The joynt and severall answers of John Allen and Christopher Volden, def^{ts}, to the Bill of Mathew Allen, comp^{t}', relating to debts, and a mortgage of Palmerston for £1,500. (BR 137/I/ii)
1636	(2 Oct.) Lease by Matthew Allen of Palmerston to Laurence Dowdall of the lands of Grange and Scrowan, Co. Dublin, for 99 years, rent 10s. (BR 173/Bundle 5)
1636	(23 Nov.) Grant of an annuity by Matthew Allen of Palmerston to Thomas Wadding of Waterford, of £40 payable out of the lands of Palmerston, in consideration of £400 given. (BR 173/Bundle 5)
1637	(26 Nov.) Bond. Matthew Allen of Palmerston and Laurence Dowdall of Athlomny, Co. Meath, bound themselves to Thomas Wadding of Waterford. Wadding is to receive an annuity of £40 (stg) p.a. from lands in Palmerston, and a clause is included whereby failure to pay him his money will entitle Wadding to distrain the entire estate. (BR 173/Bundle 5)
1638	(21 Nov.) Judgement in Chancery in the case of Matthew Allen of Palmerston v. John Allen and Christopher Voleton. (BR 137/I/vii)
1640	(20 Jan.) Deed of mortgage by Matthew Allen of Palmerston, to Arthur White of Leixlip, Co. Kildare, of lands in Palmerston for 99 years. (BR 173/Bundle 5)
1640	(20 Jan.) Deed of mortgage as above, with counterpart. It also includes the principal which is £1,500. (BR 173/ Bundle 5)
1640	(21 Jan.) Lease from Arthur White of Leixlip to Matthew Allen, of lands in Palmerston for 41 years, at a rent of £150 (stg) p.a. [2 copies]. (BR 173/Bundle 5)
1640	(28 Jan.) Bond. Matthew Allen binds himself in £3,000 to Arthur White, before the Staple Court, to perform the covenants in the above mortgage. (BR 173/Bundle 5)
1640	(18 Nov.) Inquisition post mortem of Matthew Allen, of Palemerston, Co. Dublin [3 fols]. (BR 137/I/iii)

1641	(10 July) Deed of mortgage by Matthew Allen[172] of Palmerston to Arthur White of the lands of Palmerston, for 99 years, to commence at the end of the above term. In consideration of £500. (BR 173/Bundle 5)
17th cen.	Two documents dated 1685, regarding a dispute between Sir John Temple and Thomas Allen of Dunowny, Co. Wexford, which make reference to the following deeds (BR 137/I/iv,v),
1627	(25 June) Mortgage by Matthew Allen of Palmerston to John Allen, of the lands of Palmerston, at a rent of £80 yearly for eleven years.
1627	Matthew Allen binds himself in statute staple for £1,500.
1636	Further bills in the case of John Allen v. Matthew Allen, held in the court of Chancery in Dublin.
1639	(24 June) Chancery order to Matthew Allen to pay the outstanding sum of £886 11s 5d to John Allen.
1641	(28 Jan.) Final decision of the Court of Chancery in the preceding dispute.

Congleton, Barons Congleton MSS (ref. Congleton)

1597	(10 May) Lease by (1) Patrick Bremingham of Corballie, Co. Meath, gent; Richard Sedgrave of Killoylane, 2nd Baron of the Exchequer; George Tailor of Swords, esq; survivors to William Talbot, late of Malahide, Co. Dublin, deceased, co-feoffee to the said Richard and George, to (2) Nicholas Weston of Dublin, alderman; of a ruinous messuage and garden, with all its shops, houses, etc., in Winetavern Street in Dublin, for 99 years at £8 rent p.a. With a condition that (1) has the right of occasional residence. (Congleton Ms. 352/1)
1624	(7 Dec.) Letters patent to Richard Cassy of the City of Dublin, alderman, of lands and tenements in Dublin. (Congleton Ms. 354/1)
1626	Copy of a deed of feoffment by Nicholas White of Queen's County, to Walter Finglas, Walter Harding, Hugh Harding and Henry Starling, of all his lands in Rathloage and elsewhere in Queen's Co., to the use of his mother, Katherine Grace alias Harding, and after her death to the use of his wife, Dame Joyce Blundell, thereafter to his children, and then to his brother's heirs, etc. (Congleton Ms. 355/3)
1636	(29 June) Deed whereby Nicholas White of the City of London, authorises his mother, Katherine Grace of Maryborough in Queen's Co., 'to sett, lett, and dispose of the towns and lands of Rathleige in the said countie to her sole use, benifit and behoofe', for life. (Congleton Ms. 355/5)
1636	(29 June) Counterpart to the above by Katherine Grace, who acknowledges the lands of Rathleige, etc., and 'hereby assigne over the overseeing and manageing of all my goods and chattels whatsoever'. (Congleton Ms. 355/6)
1639	(7 Aug.) Lease by Christopher Forster, Mayor of Dublin, to Nicholas Lutterell, shoemaker, of one messuage or house, in Winetavern Street, Dublin. To be held for 21 years, at a rent of £17 (stg).[173] (Congleton Ms. 604)

---

[172] Presumably the son of the previous Matthew Allen.

[173] The rent is unclear, the document states 'seaven teend pounds ster.' This is most likley £17, rather than £7 10s or £7 0s 10d.

HEREFORD & WORCESTER : County Record Office, Hereford
The Old Barracks, Harold Street, Hereford HR1 2QX
Tel: (01432) 265 441

COLLECTIONS

Hereford Corporation MSS

The H.M.C. report on these archives (*13th Report*, App. IV, pp283–353) mentions three items of Irish interest. These are a 19 Nov. 1540 proclamation banning the import of Irish coins into England and Wales (p313), a 1552 examination of a wandering tailor who had come from Ireland (p318), and a pass dated 13 March 1602 signed by Sir Christopher St. Laurence (captain of 150 foot in Ireland) discharging Francis Voughan, a soldier, because he is badly wounded (p338–9). The archivist has told us that the city records, though sorted, have only received a summary list, and have not been given a detailed catalogue; hence we are not able to give the precise record office references to these items. They are probably part of the Bound Volumes of City Papers or the annual files of the Quarter Sessions Papers.

HEREFORD & WORCESTER : County Record Office, Worcester
County Hall, Spetchley Road, Worcester WR5 2NA
Tel: (01905) 766 351
Fax: (01905) 766 363

COLLECTIONS

Worcester Quarter Session Papers (ref. 110 BA 1)

The H.M.C. report on these records in *Various Collections*, i (1901), pp282–326, mentions a number of items relating to Ireland. Most concern veterans who had served in Ireland. In 1616 a veteran of the Nine Years War petitioned for relief, being no longer in receipt of his pension, and still suffering from a bullet lodged in his leg (p291). Another veteran, who had served for eleven years in Ireland petitioned for relief in 1617, because his landlord was about to evict him (p296), and in 1621 a soldier petitioned for a pass to go to the King's hospital in London to be treated for lameness which he acquired serving in Ireland (p303). There is at least one other document concerning Irish vagrants. In 1634 the Constable of Tredington reported that he had sent two vagrant Irish women back to Co. Cork, as directed by statute (p309). The quarter session papers include many more documents concerning the plight of veterans in the aftermath of the Nine Years War which were not mentioned in the H.M.C. report.

HERTFORDSHIRE : County Record Office
County Hall, Hertford SG13 8DE
Tel: (01992) 555 105
Fax: (01992) 555 113

LOOSE ITEMS

1628   Catalogue of the nobility of Ireland (including knights, baronets, etc.) created by James I and Charles I. (XII.B.31a)

1635   Copy of the sentence of the Council of War passed at Dublin upon Lord Mountnorris, and the petition of Mountnorris to the Irish Parliament. (XII.B.34)

1641   Account of Sir George Rawdon, in command of the Cavalry of Ulster during the 1641 rebellion, in a manuscript history of the Rawdon family. (79959 X)

1641–2   Receipt for William Cowper, repaying money disbursed for the maintenance of soldiers in Ireland. (D/EP F2)

17th cen. List of contributions for the distressed poor in Ireland. (VI.A.116)

KENT : County Archives Office, Maidstone *
County Hall, Maidstone, Kent ME14 1XQ
Tel: (01622) 694 363
Fax: (01622) 694 379

LOOSE ITEMS

1602   Letter from the Privy Council to Lord Cobham concerning the levying of 50 men from Kent. They are to be sent to Bristol for despatch to Ireland as reinforcements. (U601 011)

SMALL COLLECTIONS

Drury of Halstead MSS (ref. U1115)

1624   (April) Copy of the articles of agreement between the Earl of Leicester, the Earl of Clanricard, Lord Abergavenny, the J.P.s of Kent and the occupiers of land along the River Medway from Penshurst to Maidstone, and Michael Cole, gent. (U1115 014/8)

1629   (17 Feb.) Copy of a petition of the House of Lords to the Crown regarding their rights of precedence over Scottish and Irish peers. (U1115 017/5)

Sackville (Knole) MSS (ref. U269)

The Sackville collection is much smaller than it used to be having recently lost the Cranfield papers (given below), which were subtracted from it by the archivists to be treated as a separate collection. Despite the reduction in its size, however, it remains a potentially very valuable source for early modern Ireland, and it should be carefully checked, not least because it still contains a certain amount of Cranfield material, none of which has been properly catalogued.[174] The following list of Irish references should by no means be treated as the final word on the contents of the Sackville collection:

c1596   Portion of an order signed by Lord Burghley concerning arms for the troops in Ireland. (U269 O1)

c1620   Memorandum of a list of deeds of Cranfield's estate in Ireland and elsewhere made by John Bridgeman, some of which were missing. (U269 E510)

---

[174] Most of the collection has only received bundle or box listings. It is highly likely that the bundles catalogued A393–4, O290–1, O293–7, which are designated as the miscellaneous accounts and papers of Sir Lionel Cranfield and cover the period 1603–51, will contain references to Ireland. We, the authors, did not have enough time to make a search during our visit.

1622	Communication from the Commissioners of Courts of Justice in Ireland to the Privy Council, signed by 16 Commissioners including Thomas Crewe, Nathaniel Rich and Dudley Digges. (U269 O287)
1623–9	A volume of accounts of the farmers of the customs in Ireland, signed by Matthew de Renzi. (U269 O284)
c1631–8	Miscellaneous papers of Sir Lionel Cranfield, Earl of Middlesex, concerning Irish affairs (14 items). (U269 O292)
1640	Two documents concerning a dispute between the Earl of Middlesex and the Earl of Desmond, referred by the King to the Lord Keeper and the Attorney General for arbitration. (U269 L40)

LARGE COLLECTIONS

De L'Isle and Dudley (Penshurst) MSS (ref. U1475 O1–O49)[175]

The vast majority of this important collection has been published, either by Arthur Collins (ed.), *Letters & Memorials of State* (2 vols., London, 1746), or by the H.M.C., *De L'Isle & Dudley MSS* (6 vols., London, 1925–66). Moreover, a great part of the published material relates to Irish affairs, particularly to the career of Sir Henry Sidney as Vice-Treasurer and Lord Deputy of Ireland (1556–78), but in addition the later volumes of the H.M.C. series contain scattered references to companies of Irish soldiers serving Philip III of Spain on the Continent in the early seventeenth century. All of the documents which have been published, either by Collins or the H.M.C., can be consulted on microfilm in the British Library. Nevertheless, it has hitherto gone unnoticed that a large part of the De L'Isle and Dudley collection has long remained unpublished, probably due to the untimely death of Kingsmill, the archivist in charge of the H.M.C. calendar series. These unpublished manuscripts were not microfilmed by the British Library, and have not been used before.

c1550	Rules to be observed in setting up 'the Lord's Barn' in Limerick, made by the foundress [Latin, 8pp]. (O15/1)
1556	Copy made in 1556 of a medieval charter granting the liberty of Kerry to the Earl of Desmond. (O15/2)
1556–78	Miscellaneous undated bills, receipts, etc., including the charge of 'your Lordships last journey northward', which probably dates to 1566, as it mentions a payment of 12d to Shane O'Neill's messenger and gives details of Sidney's expenses when travelling through O'Molloy's country. In addition, the bundle contains a list of spices received by Cornellius Brenan of Roscarbery, merchant, and a document concerning a loan of £4 made to Sidney by Paul Turner of Wexford. (14 docs, O49/1–14)
1556–9	Two volumes of detailed household accounts, probably kept by Robert Holdiche, giving weekly accounts of expenditure passed by Sir Henry Sidney when Vice-Treasurer and Lord Justice of Ireland. Include references to several Dublin merchants, as well as to Sidney's expenses at Thomascourt, Co. Dublin, Kilkee, Co. Kildare, Leighlin Bridge, Co. Carlow, Stradbally in Queen's Co., and at Kilkenny, Thomastown, Wexford and Waterford. Some of the entries in Volume 1 refer to the purchase of boards in Co. Wexford for the construction of a portal in Lady Sidney's chamber at Kilkee Castle in February 1557. (O25/1–2)[176]

---

[175] The permission of Viscount L'Isle & Dudley is needed for access to this collection.

[176] The end paper of Volume 1 appears to be part of a fourteenth century devotional work.

1556–9   Bills, vouchers, accounts, receipts and warrants of Robert Holdiche as Deputy Treasurer of Ireland, steward of the household and paymaster to Sir Henry Sidney. These very miscellaneous papers are nearly all directed to Holdiche by Sir Henry and obviously form the basis of his accounts. They have been brought together from several bundles of loose bills and vouchers, and very few of the items are dated. They cover every aspect of Sidney's period of office as Vice-treasurer and include personal expenditure. (92 docs., O28)

1558   Robert Holdiche's book of 'Forren Paymentes', which includes details of payments to many of Sir Henry Sidney's servants, such as the clerk of the kitchen and the bailiff of husbandry. The book also lists the rewards given by Sidney to various messengers who brought packages to him, and contains several references to the charges of the Constable of Stradbally, John Henry. In addition, there are some accounts for Sidney's private and public affairs, including the cost of his westward journey and details of his debts and borrowings. (42pp, O21)

1559   Grant of a safe pardon to Michael Wallace of Ayr in Scotland, and others, merchants. (O15/22)

1565   Receipt and aquittance for £11,000 transferred to Ireland. (O15/3)

1566–73   Bills, receipts, warrants, etc., forming the basic documents of John Thomas's accounts. These include an account of moneys received for hides in 1566–9, an account of horses taken in 1571, and a bill submitted by Thomas Mighte in 1572. One document itemises the expenses of Sidney's westward journey in 1566, and mentions payments made to William Sidney, Jacques Wingfield, the Mayor of Limerick and Oliver Grace of Legan, Co. Kilkenny, among others. (37 docs, O39)

1567–78[177]   'A booke of sondrye private and particular reckoninges...', comprising notes of warrants, debts, allowances, bills, etc. Most of the entries concern Ireland, and include *inter alia* many references to Lord Deputy Sidney's private financial dealings, as well as containing details of money due to a company of galloglass commanded by Gerald Sutton and other sums outstanding to members of the Irish civil and military establishment. It is worth noting that Sidney's contact with the merchant community of Dublin is particularly well recorded in the volume, as are the financial problems of the Earl of Desmond and Sir John of Desmond. (1 vol., O46)

c1567   Note of Shane O'Neill's plate, which mentions 'the color of offes that Kinge Henry the viii gave owntto my father [Con Bacagh O'Neill]' when he was created 1st Earl of Tyrone in 1542. Before itemising Shane's plate, salt cannisters, spoons, basins, standing cups, etc., the document gives details of a number of gold chains which had apparently passed from the possession of O'Donnell, the Countess of Argyle and the Countess of Tyrone into Shane's hands. (O15/5)

1569–71   Notes of Irish rents, concerning lands at Cotlanstown and Ballymore. (O15/26)

c1570   Note of a request for money to be paid to Lady Tailboies. (O15/4)

---

[177] This volume is incorrectly dated 1575–8, one of the earliest entries detailing a warrant of 4 May, 1567, for the payment of the surgeon Patrick Bicton by the Vice-Treasurer, Sir William Fitzwilliam (fol. 5v).

c1570	Copies of an assignment of deeds to Sir Henry Sidney by John Chaloner of the Isle of Lambey. (2 copies, O15/6A,B)
c1570	Drafts of a commission to Sir John Perrot for the government and presidency of Munster. (2 docs, O15/7A,B)
c1570	List of ordnance and munitions remaining in Dublin Castle and being sent to Munster [4 fols, very faded]. (O15/8)
c1570	Charges done and disbursed by Patrick Goughe in connection with the ship the 'Carrick Sidney'. (12pp, O38)
1573	List of horsemen. (O15/24)
1574	Copy of the submission made at Cork by Gerald Fitzgerald, 14th Earl of Desmond. (O15/9)
1575	Report regarding the building of a tithe barn at Limerick, with eleven articles added. (4pp, O15/30)
c1575–8	A bundle of bills, receipts, warrants, etc., many of which are undated, including details of payments to a wide range of individuals, such as Sir Donough MacCarthy Reagh, Matthew Fitzharris of Mackmaine, Co. Wexford, and Captain Lloyd. There are also payments to unnamed merchants of Wicklow town for delivering four boat-loads of wood for the Lord Deputy's household in March 1577. (26 docs, O48/1–26)
1576–7	Loan made in 1576 by the town of Galway towards the cost of putting down the rebellion of John and Ullicke Bourke, sons of the Earl of Clanricard, endorsed with a receipt for £200 in 1577. (O15/10)
1576	List of the Lord Deputy's retinue, indicating the number of horses to be found. (O15/11)
c1576	Draft letter by Sidney to Thomas, 10th Earl of Ormond, allaying Ormond's suspicion that Sidney had encouraged the Baron of Upper Ossory, Barnaby Fitzpatrick, to attack his lands. (O15/28)
c1576	Draft letter from same to same, concerning Ormond's brother, Edward Butler of Ballinahinch, Co. Tipperary, whom Sidney hopes to advance 'bothe to some credit and living' in the Queen's service. (O15/29)
1577	Bonds concerning the seizure of French vessels. (2 docs, O15/13,14)
1577	(18 Nov.) Particulars of the manor and house of Tallaght, recited in a lease of the same to Lord Deputy Sidney by the Archbishop of Dublin, Adam Loftus. The document gives details of the manor house, which was surrounded by a moat, and of the demesne lands of Tallaght and Newtown, Co. Dublin. (O15/25)
1577	(Jan.–Sept.) Monthly stable accounts for horses and equipment. (7 docs, O47/1–7)
1578	(April) Draft of a letter from Edward Waterhouse to Elizabeth I, regarding the state of Ireland [12pp]. (O15/15)[178]
1578	(Sept.) Note of horses received from Christopher Wren on Sir Henry Sidney's return to England. (O15/16)

---

[178] For the letter as sent, see *C.S.P.I.*, 1574–85, p132.

1578   Lists of the Lord Deputy's servants returning from Ireland, with a note of their destinations and rewards given to them by their former master. (5 docs, O15/17–21)

1578   List of parcels delivered by John Leeke, including diaper, pewter, soap, spice, sweet meats, 'black-jacks', cloth and damask. (20pp, O15/23)

1578   List of presents received by Lord Deputy Sidney from Irish gentlemen at the feast of St. George. Nearly all of the presents came from the merchants and gentry of the Pale, the exceptions including the Corporation of Waterford and Edmund Fitzharris of Co. Wexford [1 small vol.]. (O15/27)

Cranfield Papers (ref. U269/1)

This vast collection was removed from the Sackville MSS (above) by the H.M.C. who planned to produce a calendar of the entire archive. The overwhelming majority of the documents concern the private and public career of Sir Lionel Cranfield, Lord Treasurer of England (1621–4), and 1st Earl of Middlesex. By 1966 some sections, comprising the business papers of Cranfield and his family, covering the dates 1551–1612, had appeared in print as H.M.C., *Sackville (Knole) MSS* (2 vols, London, 1942–66), edited by F.J. Fisher. At this point the H.M.C. concluded the series, leaving well over 90% of the entire collection unpublished.[179] Though the published material does contain some references to Ireland, the calendar as a whole is concerned more with Cranfield's role as a merchant, prior to his elevation to public office.

In fact, the entire collection comprises far in excess of 10,000 individual items,[180] most of which cover the period of this survey. The documents cover all aspects of Cranfield's career, with extensive sets of private correspondence and accounts, business papers, family and estate records, and a vast array of official papers. These official papers primarily concern Cranfield's period as Lord Treasurer of England (1621–4), and include extensive material concerning all aspects of his office, especially the Exchequer, customs administration, revenue, legal cases, the Virginia colony and Ireland. Thus this archive represents one of the largest private collections of any English official in the sixteenth or seventeenth centuries. Furthermore, the collection is only now receiving a complete (but highly summarised) listing.

Because the listing has not yet been finished, certain areas of the collection cannot be evaluated for this survey, thus making it impossible to ascertain and extract all the Irish material. Unfortunately, limited time, coupled with the enormity of the collection also precluded any independent searches by the authors; as a result, the ensuing guide should be treated with caution. Although the documents given below represent a large proportion of all the material relating to Ireland, many further items of Irish interest exist within the collection of which we have no details.

---

[179] See the prefatory note in Volume 2 (London, 1966).

[180] When the H.M.C. initially worked on the collection they gave reference numbers to over 10,000 items in the collection. However, they did not number all the items, particularly those records concerning Ireland and Cranfield's private and business correspondence.

Correspondence Business (ref. U269/1 CB)[181]

1620   Letter from William Burrell to Cranfield, rebutting accusations of Lord Boyle who had 'unconsionable dealings' with Mr. Bull, and regarding Irish business. (CB36)

1624   Letters from Sir Dudley Norton in Dublin to Cranfield, concerning letters from De Renzi, Cranfield's release from the tower, and other matters. (2 items, CB167)

1624–42   Letters from Sir Arthur Ingram to Cranfield, which include frequent reference to Cranfield's business in Ireland, and the Irish customs. (45 items, CB117)

1625–9   Letters from Richard Croshawe to Cranfield, mostly concerning the Earl of Desmond, including some letters sent from Ireland, Croshawe's account with Desmond 1618–22, and an account of the Earl's debts amounting to £13,777. (9 items, CB62)

1625–40   Letters from Henry Lovell to Cranfield, mostly concerning Ireland, particularly cases in the Irish Chancery, and mentioning the views of the Lord Deputy on various issues, etc. (14 items, CB140)

1629–38   Letters from Phillip Burlamachis to Cranfield, some of which relate to various business transactions in Ireland, and the bargain for the Irish customs. (25 items, CB33)

Correspondence Personal (ref. U269/1 CP)[182]

1622–33   Letters from Thomas and Elizabeth Hatton to Cranfield regarding Irish business and the Earl of Clare. (4 items, CP59)

1627–41   Letters from Arthur Brett to Cranfield regarding the Lord Deputy's firm government in Ireland, and other matters. (8 items, CP16/2)

Estate (ref. U269/1 E)

1625   Letter to Cranfield from Bevil Grenvile regarding conveyances of lands in Ireland (E340)

Legal (ref. U269/1 L)

c1630   Petition from Richard Gothorp to Thomas, Lord Coventry, for arrears owed from the Irish customs. (L33)

Official Exchequer (ref. U269/1 OE)

1619–21   Letters of John Parker, secretary to the Duke of Buckingham, to Cranfield, including reference to the trade commission for Ireland and many other matters. (9 items, OE544)

1619–24   Letters from Thomas, Earl of Kelly, to Cranfield, which mention Mr. Leckey's suit for lands in Ireland, and many other matters. (9 items, OE406)

---

[181] An unusual referencing system has been used. The letters do not receive individual reference numbers. Instead, the letters have been grouped together by correspondent. Each correspondent gets only a single reference number, irrespective of the quantity of letters he wrote. The catalogue for this section is currently being compiled, hence the list given here should be treated as partial.

[182] Again, the listing for this section is only partially completed, so that the items given here are only a fraction of what Irish material probably exists.

1620   List of the most pressing debts on ordinary revenue, with entries for ports, Ireland, castles, fees and pensions. (OE1383)

1621   Letter from Sir Henry Fane to Cranfield, relating news from court, and stating that Lord Falkland has been commanded to be ready for Ireland. (OE256)

1621   (11 Oct.) Remembrances for Cranfield concerning Crown Revenues, by Sir John Osborne, recommending that a book be made of all the yearly payments in England and Ireland [2 fols]. (OE540)

1621   Letter from Sir Henry Masters, at Doctors Commons, to the Duke of Buckingham, regarding the disposal of goods from a French ship wrecked off Galway in Ireland. (OE1062)

1621   Letter from James I to Mandeville and Sir Fulke Greville, with directions for money due to Lord Thomas Ridgeway for expenses as Treasurer-at-war and General Receiver in Ireland, to be allowed as deductions from his arrears. (OE1211)

1621   Letter from the Marquis of Buckingham to Sir Henry Marten regarding a French ship wrecked off Ireland and the cargo thereof. (OE1212)

1621–3   Letters of the Bishop of Lincoln to Cranfield, which discuss matters of trade and the Irish customs. (5 items, OE441)

c1621   Various letters, some dated 1621, of the Earl of Arundel and Surrey to Cranfield, which include discussion of the Irish business and that it has been settled as Cranfield wished. (OE23)

1622   Letters from Buckingham to Cranfield which relate to Sir Francis Blundell. They include a rebuke for delaying the business of the Mastership of the Wards in Ireland, as well as many other matters. (39 items, OE108)

1622   Letter from Sir John King to Cranfield pointing out some abuses practised in Ireland, and requesting part of his fees. (OE414)

1622   Certificate of the Mayor and Aldermen of Liverpool to Cranfield concerning the seizure of uncustomed goods bound for Ireland. (OE445)

1622   Petition of Robert Parkhurst and George Myne, Clerk of the Hanaper, to Cranfield, for a payment due to them from Lord Ridgeway, former Treasurer-at-War in Ireland. (OE554)

1622   Petition of the creditors of Brian O'Rourke to James I, which is referred to Cranfield for speedy repayment. (OE895)

1622   Expense of Sir Richard Houghton, including three years' troop maintenance in Ireland. (OE1386)

1622–3   Letters from Sir Thomas Roper to Cranfield which contain his suggestion for the payment of arrears from the Irish revenue. (2 items, OE617)

1622–3   Letters from Cranfield to the officers of the customs, which refer to the export of candles made from Irish tallow, and to the affairs of Sir Hugh Clotworthy, who is not to pay impost on plate and chattels taken to Ireland. Many other matters are also dealt with. (9 items, OE1104) c1622   Petition of Peter Moffelt of London and Thomas Collymore of Hamburgh, merchants, to Cranfield, for permission to export unsaleable Irish tallow to Hamburgh as candles. (OE496)

c1622   Petition of Owen, Procurator of the Court of Arches, to Cranfield, for letters of recommendation to the Lord Deputy of Ireland, re debt. (OE542)

c1622   Petitions of Grace Palmer, Cranfield's servant, to Cranfield, concerning the arrears of a pension due to Captain Fergus O'Donnell, for whom her husband is deeply engaged. (2 items, OE549)

c1622   Petition from Capt. Andrew Harper to the Privy Council, regarding his arrears as the owner of the post ships at Holyhead, for packets to Ireland. (OE1260)

1623   Petitions to Cranfield, concerning payment to Hugh Armstrong; maintenance of Bryan O'Rourke imprisoned in the Gatehouse; and payment to Sir James and Alexander MacDonnel from pensions. (OE22)

1623   Letters from Henry, Viscount Falkland, Lord Deputy of Ireland, to Cranfield, regarding the reprinting of the book of rates, the customs, and a petition on behalf of Sir Edward Herbot[183] (now living in Ireland) for the payment of his entertainments; also re the Lord President of Munster. (3 items, OE254)

1623   Petition of John Games to Cranfield for demise of reliefs and heriots in Ireland, and for a grant of arrears. (OE280)

1623   Petition of Isabell Gittrey to Cranfield to pay a provisions debt owed by Bryan O'Rourke, prisoner in the Gatehouse. (OE288)

1623   Petitions of Anne, widow of Francis Nash, to Cranfield. She has supplied £72 on bond to Bryan O'Rourke of Co. Leitrim for his maintenance. (2 items, OE517)

1623   (22 Jan.) 'The humble petition of the Creditors of Brian O'Rurke, esq., to the number of 30 persons and upwards', to Cranfield. (OE539)

1623   Petition of Christopher Phillipson to Cranfield for satisfaction of a debt owed by Brian O'Rourke, with an appended note in his favour by Cranfield to Sir Roger Pye. (OE570)

1623   Petition of Christopher Sharlock to Cranfield, for restitution of money seized at Minehead, and relating to voyages with a cargo of hides to Holland and Ireland. (OE656)

1623   Letter from Edward Turner to Cranfield, concerning his efforts supporting the suit of Sir Thomas Saville, and a proposed grant of land in Ireland worth £400 *per annum*. (OE743)

1623–4   12 Letters and Petitions by Brian O'Rourke to Cranfield, written from the Tower, relating to his debts, and the pension he is not receiving from the Exchequer (£240 outstanding). He is unable to pay off his debts until he receives the money. (12 items, OE538)

c1623   Letter from Cranfield to Sir Dudley Norton recommending William Owen who is going to Ireland. (OE1231)

---

[183] Sir Edward Herbert of Dora [Durrow] in King's Co.

1625–6	Two letters of Sir Henry Goodere to Cranfield, mentioning rumours of armadas against England and Ireland. (2 items, OE299)
c1627/8	Letter by Cranfield to his 'cosen', re conflicting mortgages on lands in Cos. Kilkenny and Tipperary made by the Earl of Desmond to Sir William Smith of London, and to Cranfield and Richard Croshawe in the 1620s. (OE 537)
17th cen.	(n.d.) Note of expenses incurred by Irish prisoners in the Tower of London, being Sir Cormac O'Neill, Sir Neil O'Donnell and Nachton O'Donnell. (OE1736)

Official Exchequer: Customs (ref. U269/1 OEc)

1614	Letter from William Singleton of Chester to Cranfield, requesting employment as a deputy and making reference to the deceits practised by Irish merchants. (OEc60)
1615	Three warrants, including for the repayment of the impost on satins from Ireland. (3 items, OEc65)
1619	Account of Irish Customs profits, with details of increases and decreases in various ports. (OEc134)
1623	Affidavit of London customs officers, that their authority was flouted when recording the goods of Irishmen at Holborn, Middlesex. (OEc241)

Official Exchequer: Trade (ref. U269/1 OEt)

1613–5	Letters from William Massam to Cranfield relating to the recovery of debt in Ireland, and other matters. (2 items, OEt46)
1614	Letter from Daniel Cooper to Cranfield, recommending his cousin for a licence and referring to the Irish customs. (OEt30)
1615	Letter from James Bagg of Plymouth to Cranfield, thanking him for his share in the Irish customs. (OEt25)

Official Ireland (ref. U269/1 Hi)[184]

1540[185]	Copy of a royal lease to Richard Grenville of the abbeys of Cork and Gill. (Hi188)
1586	Copy of a royal proclamation regulating the plantation of Munster, and its division into seignories, etc. (Hi225)
1598–1600	Account book of Sir George Carey, Treasurer-at-war in Ireland. (1 large volume, Hi1)
c1605	(n.d.) Memorandum on a debt of £32,000 by George Carey, late Treasurer-at-war. (Hi264)
1608	(18 May) Letter from the Earl of Salisbury to the Customs farmers of Chester regulating the trade with Dublin. (Hi127)
1608	Declaration of the account of Hercules Tirrell, Clerk of the Fines in the Province of Munster, for the years 1605–8 [4 fols]. (Hi15)

---

[184] Some of the following items were looked at by the authors, so this listing is slightly more detailed than the catalogue being produced by the Record Office.

[185] This date looks very dubious. Richard Grenville received a royal lease of these lands in 1589, see *Cal. Patent Rolls, Ire., Eliz. I*, p195.

1612 (22 Oct.) Tender for the Irish customs farm by Cranfield, John Suckling and three others, for a fine of £1,000 and an annual rent of £6,000. (Hi115)

1612–22 Letters from William Massam to Cranfield (23 items, Hi79), as follows:

1612–3 Suggestions for customs, which begs a share of the same; appointment of surveyors, Massam for all Ireland, Davenant for Munster; expressing grievance at the appointment of Davenant as surveyor of Munster; that he will be ruined unless supported by Cranfield's visit; offers a gift of orange and lemon trees received from Spain. (6 items)

1614 Gives lengthy account of the character of various Munster customs officials; transport of prohibited goods and Dublin burgesses; proclamation liberating transport of goods and subsequent recall, and the Lord Deputy's warrant freeing fishermen from the custom on salt; deliberations of the Irish Parliament over customs rates; Massam's wages; his wish to compound with his creditors; his loss of £2,000 in dealing with ordnance; the possible revenue of £7,000 from ports. (4 items)

1618–19 Maintenance of customs; fees and defalcations; Cogan boasts of controlling customs; disapproves of letting customs to natives, who never agree; stop of wool transport mitigated by licences; wool and cloth trade hindered by persons influential with the Council; poor return on the wine impost; details of customs evasion; offered Mr. Wood post as a waiter, who insists on a post as collector; complaint against Sir Arthur Ingram. (6 items)

1620–22 Requests increase in fees; yarn licence in Drogheda; ordnance sent to Spain; decline in wine impost; recommends accepting the offer by Irish merchants for a lease of the customs; encloses bills of exchange for receipts from Cranfield's lands in Munster; requests help in dealing with Sir Arthur Ingram; possible proceedings by Mr. Braban against the Earl of Desmond. (7 items)

1612–23 Title and estate papers concerning the seignory of Kinalmeaky and the monastery of Fermoy, which include a copy of the royal grant of the lands of Fermoy and elsewhere in Co. Cork to Sir Bernard Greville in 1612, the appointment of a steward on the same lands in 1622, and a conveyance by Cranfield to Sir George Horsey in 1623. (12 items, Hi186)

1613 (29 Dec.) Appointment of Leonard Martin as searcher for the port of Galway with a salary of £20 (stg) by Sir Arthur Ingram. Also articles of agreement between Leonard Martin and the Customs farmers relating to the collection of customs. (3 items, Hi194)

1613–19 Letters from John Pitt in Dublin to Cranfield, concerning; the poor return on customs, due to privileges granted; rates for Dublin and Limerick; silk and other goods sold at Dublin; false accusations against himself; has paid Sir Henry Docwra £600 a week; Trinity Guild in Dublin; is expecting money from certain ports; Sir George Elwick left confused accounts; excessive imports; account of an interview with the Lord Deputy. (5 items, Hi92)

1613–23 Letters from Sir Arthur Ingram to Cranfield which include: a bond of James Craig to Ingram, Cranfield and others over a share of the customs; a note on the powers of taxation granted to the Irish government in 8 Henry VIII [1516–7]; a request for advance payment; a recommendation of Sir Thomas Phillips, who has information; and a request for an answer to his letter about Sir Thomas Wentworth. (4 items, Hi70)

1614   Letters of Daniel Cooper in Waterford to Cranfield and George Lowe giving a report on the difficulty in collecting customs, and the fraud by Mr. Hynton, the Waterford customs official. The letters also concern Lord Hay's wine licence, and notes that the country people are treasonous and take advice from priests. (2 items, Hi47)

1614   Letters to Lord Deputy Chichester from James I, concerning the establishment of free schools in Ulster, and a warrant requiring his return to England. (2 items, Hi128)

1614   Petition of Richard Bishop and others, fishermen on the coast of Wexford, to Lord Deputy Chichester, to confirm their freedom from the duty on herrings caught on the coast, and on salt and beer brought from England. With the assent of the Lord Deputy and Council on the dorse (dated 17 September 1614). (Hi129)

1614–6   Irish Customs: Defalcations. (3 items, Hi1)

1614–22   Lists of commissioners for Ireland in 1614 and 1622. (3 items, Hi206)

c1614   (n.d.) Petition of William Doland to the customs farmers, relating to the appointment of Rawson and Robert Blake as Customers for Galway. (Hi136)

c1614   (n.d.) Proposals by William Massam for increasing the customs yield. (Hi232)

1615   (12 March) Letter from Anon[186] to the customs farmers, stating that he has sent Massam to the out ports for speedier collection. Also discusses the Mayors' delay in issuing the proclamations of the Lord Deputy, and mentions that the winter has been very harsh for cattle and corn. (Hi135)

1615   (16 March) Letter from James Craig in Dublin to Cranfield, giving details of the abuses practised by the Trinity Guild, and noting that Sir James Hamilton is reported willing to surrender his patent. (Hi50)

1615   Certificate of sums paid for the customs farmers on behalf of Sir Arthur Ingram. (Hi195)

1617   Abstract of exports, ports and commodities. (Hi2)

1617   Sums due to Cranfield, partly by assignment from Sir Arthur Ingram. (Hi3)

1617   Arrears on Lord Docwra's accounts due to almsmen, pensioners and others, with a similar note to the same effect. (2 items, Hi14)

1617   Report on wool, with advice against export licences. (Hi104)

1617   Agreement by the widow of Daniel Cooper to pay £27 yearly to Mary Cooper. (Hi196)

1617   Agreement by Cranfield to restore Robert Cogan as Surveyor General for 200 double sovereigns. (Hi197)

1617   Agreement for the furtherance of a suit to issue beer licences. (Hi226)

1617–22   General abstracts of accounts, estimates and arrears. (3 items, Hi16)

---

[186] Possibly Cranfield.

1617–23 Fines in the Presidency Court of Connaught, 1617–19, with a note by Lord Wilmot for 1620–22. (2 items, Hi20)

1617–24 Letters of Sir Richard Weston and Lord Chichester to Cranfield, concerning the business of Sir John Poyntz, and Cranfield's displeasure. Also regarding the large debt charged on Lord Grandison. (4 items, Hi106)

1618 (17 March) Letter from William Robinson to Cranfield, offering to do business for him in Ireland. (Hi93A)

1618 (Nov.) Letter from William Massam in Drogheda to Thomas Wood, stating that Mr. Calthorpe requests payment of a 20-year-old debt, and that he cannot rate customs at more than £10,000 a year because of a liability to defalcations. (Hi185)

1618 (11 Dec.) Draft warrant concerning grants to undertakers in Ulster. (Hi217)

1618 Letter from Robert Cogan in Dublin, to Cranfield, regarding his success in Chancery and the petty customs of Scotsmen. Also concerning complaints against Cranfield's local agent, and mentioning that merchants here are less encouraged than in England, particularly because of the trade restrictions on wool and hides. (Hi45)

1618 Letter from Robert Cogan and John Pitt in Dublin, to Cranfield, concerning a bill of exchange. They were forced to borrow £400. The debts of Robert Borwage in the west is £152. Mentions that the payment to Cranfield since the last dividend is £4,366. Also refers to Walter Wyle's debt, and to the efforts of the Lord Deputy to let the customs. (Hi46)

1618 Letter from Robert Cogan in Waterford to Richard Gaulthorpe in London concerning Massam's misleading statement about money, and the prejudicial restraints on wool and skins. Also gives a long account of a ship forced into port with excess cargo. (Hi149)

1618–23 Irish customs accounts, with receipts from 17 ports (summary). (2 items, Hi5)

1618–23 Letters from Sir Henry Docwra, Treasurer-at-war, to Cranfield, petitioning for payment of portage allowances, and discussing the false hopes raised by Sir William Steward for the payment of arrears. Also mentions that the Lord Deputy is summoned to England, and Docwra requests the payment of money assigned to him in London. (3 items, Hi54)

1618–23 Letters from James I to Cranfield, which discuss the grant of a share of the customs to Cranfield, and a former grant to Buckingham. The King also writes concerning a Privy Council order for a new rate on various goods, and mentions the dispatch of an agreed pardon. (3 items, Hi73)

c1618 Letters of Sir Richard Bingley (one dated 1618) to Cranfield, requesting Cranfield's help in his bid for either a royal pension or the office of Vice Admiral of Ireland, and discussing his services in transporting 1,300 unruly Irish from Ulster to Sweden. In addition Sir Richard states that he saved East India Company goods after shipwreck, and draws attention to Sir John Bingley's £2,000 tally for Sir Henry Docwra. (2 items, Hi32) c1618   Letters from Cranfield to Sir Henry Docwra, regarding the payment of arrears to Sir Edward Herbert, and the opinion or petition of Edward Baker, with a bill of exchange. (2 items, Hi138)

1619   Letter of Sir Nicholas Fortescue to Cranfield reporting the examination (apparently by the Privy Council in London) of complaints made by the Irish Council against a factor employed by Fortescue and Cranfield. Also discusses the question of erecting staple towns in Ireland. (Hi59)

1619   Letter from Lord Treasurer Suffolk to Sir Clement Edwards, and also a letter from Edwards to Cranfield, regarding the payment of customs into the Irish treasury. (2 items, Hi141)

1619–20   Accounts of the revenue and expenses of 17 ports. (3 items, Hi4)

1619–21[187] Letters and petitions from various individuals to James I, as follows: From Sir James Blunt with drafts of a warrant for the pay of captains (2 items); from Lord Ambigny and Sir Thomas Vavasour for the regulation of the tanning trade; from Thomas Dutton for the right to licence alehouses, with the case for regulation; from the Lord Deputy and Council with their opinion on the proposed Court of Wards; from Oliver St. John reporting the opinion of the Irish Council on measures against undertakers in Ulster for breach of contracts; from Sir William Harrington concerning the surrender of the captaincy of the O'Byrnes; from Sir Walter Tichborne for a grant of lands; from Brian O'Rourke for his release from prison and the restitution of his lands, reciting a grant of wardship to the Earl of Clanricard; and from Sir William Uvedale for surrender of a grant of the fines on ploughing by the tails of horses. (10 items, Hi162)

c1619   Summaries of agreements for the farm of the Irish customs (one dated 1619). (3 items, Hi199)

c1619   Paper showing the profits of the Court of Wards, 1616–1619. (Hi246)

1620   Letter from George Mole to Cranfield, with various observations before his journey to Ireland, and concerning the fall of prices and the shortage of ready money. He encloses a defence of the wool staplers. (Hi82)

1620–1   Draft warrants from James I to Grandison to build a customs house at Dublin, to examine the rate book, and to establish a Court of Wards. (2 items, Hi146)

c1620   Memorial of the royal title to the lands of Ely O'Carroll and Co. Longford. (Hi193)

1621   (Dec.) Four receipts signed by the Earl of Thomond, Lord President of Munster, for amounts received from the Lord Treasurer as assignee of the lands of Sir Bernard Grenville. (Hi18)

1621   Document concerning £950 due to Viscount Doncaster from eight participants in the farm of wines. (Hi19)

1621   Letter from Ralph Birchensha to Cranfield, offering to put his knowledge of Irish affairs at Cranfield's disposal. (Hi33)

1621   Petition of Lord Carew to Cranfield, for reimbursement of his expenses and payment for munitions. (Hi37)

---

[187] Some items are undated.

1621	Petitions of Sir Cormac O'Neill, Sir Neil O'Donnell and Nachton O'Donnell, prisoners in the Tower of London, to Cranfield, for their urgent relief as the Lieutenant of the Tower is not furnishing necessaries. They request an allowance of £5,000 *per annum*, their estates having been sequestered. (2 items, Hi86)
1621	Letter from the Earl of Cork at Lismore to Lord Carew, Master of the Ordnance, discussing the land of Sir Bernard Grenville which he had arranged to buy, but which is now desired by Cranfield. (Hi121)
1621	Letter, probably from Lord Mandeville to Lord Chichester, urging that the army be paid at least part of the money due, in order to avert unrest. (Hi130)
1621	Letter from the Privy Council to Viscount Grandison regarding money due and grants to be made to Sir Henry and Sir Thomas Dutton. (Hi148)
1621	Letter from the Lord Deputy and Council to the Privy Council, discussing the state of the plantations. (Hi177)
1621	Memorandum on accounts and the quarter share of Richard Galthorpe (*alias* Calthorpe). (Hi198)
1621	List made by Sir Francis Blundell of the royal salmon fisheries in Ulster withheld from the King. (Hi227)
1621	Note by Sir James Perrot of the revenue raised in Connaught by Sir John Perrot, Lord Deputy (1584–8). (Hi228)
1621–2	Letters from Sir Francis Gofton and Sir Richard Sutton to Cranfield, concerning various financial matters, particularly army wages, customs, pensions and fees. (2 items, Hi62)
1621–2	Letters from the Earl of Cork to Sir Dudley Norton enlisting Cranfield's help over a disputed title to Gill Abbey, which he intends to fortify. Also making an offer for the lands purchased by Cranfield from Sir Bernard Grenville, and discussing Grenville's agent in Fermoy, Co. Cork. There is a further letter from Cranfield to Norton discussing his bargain with the Earl of Cork. (5 items, Hi171)
1621–3	Estimated army pay arrears since 1619, with an abstract of army pay rates, addressed to Cranfield by Sir Francis Crofton and Sir Richard Sutton. (7 items, Hi12)
1621–3	Letters from Sir Francis Annesley to Cranfield, which discuss: an estimate of the Irish revenue; proposals for plantations; financial irregularities; a refusal to make entries in the Pell Office until commanded by the Lord Deputy; some payments to Lord Docwra, who objected to giving accounts; wants in the army due to the diversion of funds; and the new Chief Baron, his fees and perquisites. (5 items, Hi28)
1621–3	Letters of Viscount Grandison (the Lord Deputy), to Cranfield, which discuss: the charges against himself made by Sir Roger Jones; Cranfield's farm of the Irish customs; the non-payment of the army for two years, which should be settled before he leaves his post; Grandison's request for Cranfield's favour in two suits; and Grandison's request for directions on the allowances to Lord Deputies, quoting a precedent for the Munster presidency. (6 items, Hi63)

1621–3   Letters from Sir Dudley Norton to Cranfield (26 items, Hi85), as
           follows:

1621   Concerning the establishment of the Court of Wards in Ireland;
           Sir William Parsons desires the post but would not be a popular
           choice; the choice of the Archbishop of Armagh's successor;
           some reports of dissent against the new plantations, and Norton's
           own disapproval of the same; also regarding letters lost by
           shipwreck. (5 items)

1622   Has received no letters; letters from the Earl of Cork; the
           departure of Lord Grandison; a letter sent throughout Ireland
           concerning   the   intentions   of   the   Commissions;   a
           recommendation of Sir John Bingley; the proposed Court of
           Wards; the arrival of the new Lord Deputy; the retirement of the
           Commissioners from the plantations; the bad character of Sir
           Charles Coote; the directions required for the plantations; the
           praise of some of the Commissioners; Cranfield's good service in
           preserving the Commission of Wards; the differences with Lord
           Wilmot. (9 items)

1623   Intends sending £220; a communication with Lord Esmond on
           arrangements concerning the Earl of Desmond, and payments to
           Cranfield; the kidnapping of Sir Benjamin Thorneborough in
           Ulster; the dearth of coin and cattle; the arrears of army pay;
           news that Lord Docwra may buy Cranfield's land in Munster,
           and that the Earl of Desmond has agreed to sell; the reactions to
           the stay of pensions; the recommendations for suggestions by the
           Council of Ireland. (12 items)

1621–3   Letters from Viscount Wilmot to Cranfield, which concern: the
           government of Ireland, including the plantations and finance; Sir
           Dudley Digges to give his opinion of Wilmot, Jones and Norton,
           relative to Parliament; the payment of arrears should be separate
           from current expenses; some comments on the Commission; an
           argument to prevent fines from the Leitrim plantation being used to
           build a fortified town, claiming instead that the money should be
           used to pay the army; a claim that Munster is a flourishing province,
           Connaught merely Irish; the rumoured death of the Archbishop of
           Tuam; the first fruits are usually remitted, and some bishops have
           no residence; the fines of the Presidency Court cannot finance
           Connaught; the vast grants of royal land that are made to unworthy
           persons; the advice against further plantations. (10 items, Hi107)

c1621   Petitions of Richard Galthorpe (one dated 1621), a distressed
           orphan, to Cranfield, for payment of sums due for his father's share
           of the Irish customs. (3 items, Hi60)

c1621   Petition of Sir Robert Hide, gentleman pensioner, to Cranfield, for a
           grant of land promised to him by the King in 1619. (Hi66)

c1621   Letter from William Noye to Sir Bernard Grenville giving advice
           concerning the lands in Munster which Sir Bernard proposes to sell
           to Cranfield. (Hi151)

c1621   Estate papers (some dated 1621) relating to the lands of the Earl of
           Desmond in Cos. Kilkenny and Tipperary, and his financial
           dealings with Cranfield and Richard Croshaw, which include a fine
           between both parties, a note on their transactions, and a draft of a
           royal grant of revenue to Cranfield and Croshaw, Desmond having
           defaulted on a debt. (3 items, Hi189)

1622	(17 April) Letter from Florence MacCarthy to Cranfield, with information on some dealings in Munster land in which Cranfield has an interest. (Hi83)
1622	(29 April–3 June) Two letters from Sir William Jones and Sir Dudley Digges to Cranfield, in which they discuss enquiries into the state of the church, the revenue, the courts of justice and the plantations, and give suggestions for the reformation of the courts of justice and the revenue administration. (2 items, Hi75)
1622	(31 May) Letter from Sir Dudley Norton to the Earl of Cork, stating that Cranfield is willing to sell the land that he purchased from Sir Bernard Grenville. (Hi132)
1622	(May) Directions to the Sheriffs of Ireland from the Commissioners for Ireland ordering them to publish the terms of the Commission in their respective areas. (Hi160)
1622	(8 June) Abstract of five letters received by Cranfield from Ireland on 8 June relating to large-scale abuses. (Hi230)
1622	(13 June) Letter from the Lord Chancellor and Lord Justice of Ireland to Cranfield, regarding Sir Charles Coote's failure to account for moneys received by him. (Hi72)
1622	(13 June) Letter from the Lord Justices of Ireland to the Privy Council, relating to complaints against Sir Charles Coote, who is about to go to England leaving no accounts for Connaught. (Hi176)
1622	(22 June) Copy of an order of the Privy Council authorising Lord Deputy Falkland to take 100 quarters of wheat with him for his family and household, free of duty. (Hi201)
1622	(20 July) Draft letters of Cranfield to Sir Dudley Digges requesting him to enquire into church matters, and to devise reforms of abuses in the collection of royal revenue. Also Cranfield to Sir Francis Blundell, stressing the importance of improving the King's revenues in Ireland. (Hi139)
1622	(22–27 July) Proclamations by the Lord Justices and Council publishing the aims of the Irish Commission. (2 items, Hi213)
1622	(29 July) Letter from the Irish Commissioners to Cranfield, announcing their intention to inspect and visit the plantations, and stating that a certificate concerning the revenue is to be completed on their return to Dublin. (Hi71)
1622	(10 Nov.) Draft letter from Cranfield to the Lord Deputy and Commissioners, commanding the Commissioners to conclude their business and return to England. (Hi167)
1622	(20 Nov.) Letters from Cranfield to Sir Henry Holcroft, Chancellor of the Exchequer in Ireland, expressing his strong disapproval of the changes to be made in the Court of Wards. (2 items, Hi154)
1622	(29 Nov.) Letter from Sir Henry Holcroft to Cranfield, protesting that he did inform the Lord Admiral of Cranfield's opinions regarding the Irish Court of Wards. (Hi67)
1622	(6 Dec.) Letter from Matthew de Renzi to Cranfield, stating that the proceedings against the Earl of Desmond have been delayed by Mr. Massam's illness and Lord Esmond's promise to intercede. (Hi94)

1622   (7 Dec.) Note of Viscount Wilmot's proposals for reducing the cost of the Irish army. (Hi229)

1622   (17 Dec.) Letter from Cranfield to William Massam, ordering him to proceed with the Earl of Desmond's debts without delay. (Hi168)

1622   Wine imposts since 1615. (Hi6)

1622   Document showing the decline in receipts since 1620. (Hi7)

1622   Sums due to Lord Chichester as Governor of Carrickfergus. (Hi17)

1622   Letter from the Marquis of Buckingham to Cranfield, stating that Lord Cromwell in Ireland needs £80, and suggesting a payment to Richard Miller in Paternoster Row. (Hi35)

1622   Petition of Elinor, Countess Dowager of Desmond, to Cranfield, for payment of her pension granted to her by Queen Elizabeth, and for compensation for her jointure due from certain lands in Munster. (Hi52)

1622   Letters of Sir Dudley Digges in Dublin to Cranfield which discuss: his investigation into the royal revenue in Ireland; the complaints over the plantations and recusancy fines; the proceedings of the Irish Commission, the bishops and judges are slack in their answers; the grants in Ulster, being 16,200 acres for incumbents; the Lord Deputy very cooperative; the revenue statistics for 1615–17; the Commissioners to view the plantations. (7 items, Hi53)

1622   Letters from Richard Hadsor in Dublin, to Cranfield, regarding the complaints about plantations and dishonest sheriffs. Also he wishes to see a draft commission for Ireland, of which he is a protective member, and he excuses his delay in leaving Ireland. (3 items, Hi65)

1622   Letters from Sir William Jones to Cranfield, concerning his reluctance to serve on the Commission for Ireland, especially considering the expense and his dignity. Also requests an allowance for a clerk, and leave to return to England. (3 items, Hi74)

1622   Petition of Walter and Philip Percival to Cranfield, regarding the office of their father, the former Clerk of the Wards. (Hi89)

1622   Letter from George Richards to John Brereton, regarding cheese required for the Lord Deputy's household. (Hi118)

1622   Petition of Henry, Lord Docwra, to the Marquis of Buckingham, requesting a grant of land in Ossory lately declared for the King, to compensate the cut in his entertainment fee by the Commissioners. Also states that the army is short of money, and the arrears stand at £750,000. (Hi119)

1622   Letter from Sir James Perrot to Sir Arthur Ingram requesting a further meeting of the Commissioners before their instructions are signed. (Hi156)

1622   Letter to the Commissioners for Ireland from the nobility and gentry of Ireland, with a list of their grievances. (Hi159)

1622   Letter from John Brereton in Chester to John Jacob requesting a warrant to export cheese free of customs for the household of the Lord Deputy. (Hi161)

1622   Letter from Cranfield to the Earl of Kelly requesting the repayment of a loan, with an endorsed note of cases to be heard in Easter term. (Hi163A)

1622	Letters from Cranfield to Viscount Wilmot, requesting that he be kept informed of Irish affairs, and stating that he cannot yet advise on the fortifications for Connaught. (2 items, Hi184)
1622	Conveyance of the manor of Rynroyn, Co. Cork, to Cranfield. (Hi190)
1622	Draft instructions for the Commissioners for Ireland. (Hi207)
1622	Note of matters to be put to the Privy Council relative to the Irish Commission. (Hi208)
1622	Paper on the distribution of the revenue investigation between the various Commissioners for Ireland. (Hi209)
1622	List of matters for consideration relative to the Irish Commission. (Hi210)
1622	Notes of instructions by the Privy Council to the Irish Commission. (Hi211)
1622	Details of the plantations to be visited by various Commissioners. (Hi212)
1622	Note of orders by the Lord Deputy remitting rents. (Hi218)
1622	Project for supplying the navy with hemp and canvas from Ireland. (Hi232)
1622	Part of the instructions for the Commissioners for Ireland. (Hi270)
1622–3	Letters from Sir Francis Blundell to Cranfield, which discuss: a request of leave of absence to deal with petitions by the Irish; Sir Dudley Digges brings a letter; the abuses of the revenue system; the customs and the suspension of pensions; a request for appointment as Receiver of the Court of Wards; the intention to distinguish annual revenue from arrears, and to assign some arrears to pay debts; the debts to the army include £2,350 for Lord Chichester; the expenditure on Dublin Castle and the Royal house at Kilmaynham called Pheonix; the daily attendance on the Commissioners; the money diverted to the army; the pensioners will expect a similar payment to the army; the expenses exceeded official income; a request for an army company on the next vacancy; the Easter rents assigned to discharge the arrears; the Treasurer of the Wards received £24,259 and money borrowed from Lord Brabazon; many army captains would resign a third of their wages for payment of the remainder; Cranfield has made the Irish government solvent; the Lord Deputy has suspended payments to the army; Mr. Massam is unlikely to recover from illness; a request to be a member of the commission to pay the army; the payment of Lord Grandison's allowance; a request for Cranfield's help against a charge of acting against the King's interest. (17 items, Hi34)
1622–3	Letters by the Earl of Clanricard to Cranfield concerning the payment of his pension as Lord Lieutenant of Galway; compensation due to him was not properly paid for surrendering Connaught; his plea for discharge of arrears from money now in Ireland; his reconsidered decision to resign his company of foot, failing the payment of arrears. (4 items, Hi44)
1622–3	Letters from Sir James Perrot in Dublin to Cranfield, which discuss: a scheme to strengthen the army and reduce its expense; reports on the work of the Irish Commission, noting a lack of cooperation

among officials there; a request for secrecy about his opinions; defective titles and a proposal to lease land to Irishmen; a request for payment of his allowance; details of a private suit, and a plan regarding recusancy fines; a request for a grant of the tobacco impost in Ireland. (11 items, Hi91)

1622–3   Various letters to the Lord Deputy as follows: from James I with a warrant to pay Lord Grandison's expenses, and instructions for the revenue administration; from the Privy Council concerning the pension of Sir James Blount; and from the Earl of Thomond requesting payment of his pension as formerly. (4 items, Hi166)

1622–3   Letters from the Commissioners for Ireland to the Privy Council, reporting on their work and the complaints over the plantations. They recommend Hugh Cressey as a Judge. (2 items, Hi175)

1622–3   Letters from various individuals to Richard Willis, as follows: from Sir Francis Gofton listing Irish pensions to be paid despite the recent stay of pensions, and noting that rent arrears are to be certified by Sir Francis Blundell. Gofton also discusses his father, and a request for Blundell to pay a pension in Ireland to Sir Edward Herbert (4 items); from T. Dickenson with a copy of the contract required for the Irish Commissioners; from Lord Chichester stating that the soldiers press for payment; and from Sir John Bingley to remind Cranfield that Sir John Norton groans under delays. (7 items, Hi183)

1622–4   Letters of Sir Thomas Coventry to Cranfield, which concern: the need to speed up the business of the Court of Wards in Ireland; the Earl of Desmond's desire for a lease of royal mines in Cos. Kilkenny, Limerick and Tipperary; comments concerning the manor of Dungarvan, Co. Waterford, and Tracton Abbey; and a note and valuation of mines in Ireland. (4 items, Hi49)

1622–4   Letters from Cranfield to Sir Thomas Coventry, requesting his opinion on the instructions for the Irish Commissioners, and a draft warrant to prepare the terms for the customs sublet by Buckingham to Lord Caulfield and others. Also recommending a grant of a new customs lease to Viscount Andover, and concerning a draft warrant for a grant of old debts to Sir William Harrington in return for the surrender of his interest in the Byrnes Country. (4 items, Hi133)

1622–4   Small volume of proposals for a new book of customs rates made by the Irish Commissioners dated 1622, and a draft warrant for additions to the same dated 1624. (2 items, Hi200)

1622–9   Letters of Lord Deputy Falkland to Cranfield which discuss: soliciting funds on taking up his post; his surprise at Cranfield's interference with his plans to dispose of lands claimed by Phelim MacFeagh O'Byrne; a payment for Andrew Harper, Captain of the packet ships; his charges against Falkland relative to Greenwax; recusants and the wardship of Lord Folliot; the loss of his father's estate; his Irish service involves financial loss; his lack of support; his foot company and ordnance; the arrears due to Sir Thomas Roper; his effort for cloth manufacture in Dublin; the fishing in the west; the improvement of the customs revenue; the suppression of pirates; the encouragement of English colonies; his comments on Lord Docwra's request to divert money to pay the army; the maintenance of royal credit; the rebate to the governors of Co. Londonderry and their failure to maintain castles; a suggested administrative reform; beginning the Ossory plantation; an offer of £1,400 a year for the customs farm; Phelim MacFeagh O'Byrne's suit for the lands of Ranelagh and Cosha; his rebuttal of the charge of making grants on old warrants; defalcations produced by the wars; and referring Cranfield to De Renzi's customs accounts. (16 items, Hi58)

c1622   Letter of the Earl of Arundel and Surrey to Cranfield, with an urgent summons to attend the King; also discusses the fact that the Irish Commission is overdue, and notes the names of the Commissioners. (Hi30)

c1622   (n.d.) Letter from Lord Caulfield, Muster Master of the Ordnance, and Sir John King, Muster Master, to Lord Treasurer Cranfield, with an abstract of their petition for their fees to be paid from the Irish revenue, and concerning a petition of Lady Folliot for payment of her late husband's entertainments, and permission to compound for the wardship of her son. (Hi42)

c1622   (n.d.) Letter from Cranfield to the Marquis of Buckingham, giving draft comments on the proposals of Sir Thomas Roper to licence alehouses. (Hi120)

c1622   Letter from Cranfield to the Commissioners for Ireland, requesting their opinion on lands held by Mr. Sergeant Davies. (Hi158)

c1622   Memorandum by Sir Francis Blundell on the six plantations in Ireland, for the Irish Commission. (Hi221)

c1622   Note of enquiries relative to Londonderry. (Hi222)

c1622   Memorandum on the Ulster and Longford plantations, probably made for the Irish Commission. (Hi223)

c1622   Proposals of the Irish Commission for plantations. (Hi224)

c1622   Memorial by Viscount Wilmot, Lord President of Connaught, that the fines in his court fail to meet the costs of his government. (Hi248)

c1622   Summary of Mr. MacCarthy's petition asking for a grant of lands in Carbery, the manors of Seyskin, Mashnaglass, and Chingeall, and land demised to him by his father-in-law, the Earl of Clancarthy. (Hi253)

c1622   (n.d.) Note by Viscount Grandison regarding a letter to be written to Lord Docwra about the defalcations of the Irish Army. (Hi273)

c1622   (n.d.) List of the members of the Committees of the Council appointed to consider various Irish affairs. (Hi274)

1623   (27 Feb.) Letter from the Earl of Thomond to Cranfield, requesting that Sir Francis Blundell should be directed to pay his entertainments out of the Irish revenue. (Hi100)

1623   (1 April) Note of the way in which 15 lists for Ireland are to be commanded and disposed of by Sir Francis Blundell and other high officials. (Hi241)

1623   (7 May) Petition from Cormock MacDonnell, agent of the Dowager Countess of Desmond, to Cranfield, for money due to the Countess out of the Exchequer, to be paid either in England or Ireland. (Hi84)

1623   (25 July) Letter from Sir John King to Cranfield, giving his opinion on the present directions for paying the arrears of the army in

	Ireland, and pleading for payment of his fee as Muster Master. (Hi76)
1623	Abstract, estimates and certificates of the King's revenue. (4 items, Hi21)
1623	Details of the King's debts, with a note for their repayment. (3 items, Hi22)
1623	Public expenses; the army, civil officers, etc. (Hi23)
1623	Documents and accounts concerning Sir Francis Blundell, Vice-Treasurer and General Receiver of Ireland. (5 items, Hi24)
1623	Letters from Lord Chichester to Cranfield, in which he begs his favour relative to the Irish annuities; recommends Sir Robert King for the pleas in Connaught; petitions to compound for the wardship of Viscount Dillon's grandchild, and suggests a grant to Sir John King. (3 items, Hi43)
1623	Petition of William Geere, merchant, to Cranfield, for his intervention with the Lord Deputy against Thomas Turner of Dublin, merchant. (Hi61)
1623	Petition of Robert Lawley, merchant, to Cranfield for a conference in their dispute over the wool staple. (Hi77)
1623	Letters from Adam Loftus, Lord Chancellor of Ireland, to Cranfield, offering to surrender his pension for a place as Master of the Wards, and complaining that the fees due to him are small and payment unreliable. Also states that he has sent a petition for the restoration of his pension, and mentions the failure of his suit before the Board. (3 items, Hi78)
1623	Petition of Patrick O'Hanlon to Cranfield, for payment of his pension or else a grant of his fare to return to Ireland. (Hi87)
1623	Letters from Sir William Parsons to Cranfield which concern: his appointment as Master of the Wards, with a long account of the business thereof, including frauds; the rapid revenue improvement; the Spanish marriage, which excites expectation of religious liberty; the rebellious and barbarous Irish, and a suggested English army of 5,000; the English form to be imposed without malice or peculation; various earls who have smothered the tenures of six counties; a regular land tenure that could mitigate Irish disobedience; the nomadic Irish who are unfit for civil office, and use brehon law. (8 items, Hi88)
1623	Letter from Henry Pierse and others to Cranfield, regarding the poor state of Ulster, and requesting more time to increase the plantations. (Hi90)
1623	Letters from Sir Thomas Roper to Cranfield, concerning frauds in the survey of Ulster, and requesting an extension of his patent considering his difficulty in maintaining a company from the revenue of alehouse licences. (2 items, Hi96)
1623	Letter from Viscount Sarsfield in Dublin to Cranfield, regarding abbeys purchased by Cranfield. (Hi97)
1623	Letter from the Commissioners for the Vice-Treasurer's account to Cranfield, suggesting the suspension of pensions and other remedies for mitigating discontent. (Hi101)

1623   Letter from Thomas Roper to Nicholas Harman, Cranfield's secretary, concerning £1,000 due to Roper from Sir Francis Blundell. (Hi152)

1623   Letter from the Lord Deputy and Council to the Judges recommending houses of correction to discourage sturdy beggars. (Hi163)

1623   Letters from Cranfield to Adam Loftus, the Lord Chancellor of Ireland, requesting greater speed in the case involving Mr. Massam, and also reporting on the administration of justice. (2 items, Hi164)

1623   Letter from Cranfield to Sir Richard Monson, Treasurer of the Army, ordering him to pay the arrears of Sir Richard Morrison. (Hi169)

1623   Draft agreement by Cranfield for a farm of the Irish customs by Lord Caulfield and others, from the original grant to Buckingham. (Hi201A)

1623   Memoranda by Cranfield relative to the Irish Commission. (Hi214)

1623   Recommendations by the Irish Commissioners to encourage trade. (Hi215)

1623   Copy of a royal warrant to the Lord Deputy for the issue of new patents to the undertakers. (Hi219)

1623   Memorandum and notes on the inconvenience of escheats to the Crown, as the undertakers do not perform contracts, endorsed 'information of Sir William Wyndsor'. (2 items, Hi220)

1623   Instructions for escheators and feodaries. (Hi233)

1623   General warrant to supply post horses and shipping for the King's messenger. (Hi234)

1623   Memorandum of Lord Chichester's claim for money as certified by Docwra, also mentioning the embassy in Germany. (Hi235)

1623   Summary of articles in Chancery in the case of John and William Kildale against William Cliffe and others, concerning an arrest in contempt of the Royal Commission. (Hi236)

1623   List of ports in England and Ireland. (Hi237)

1623   'Private Memoranda' referring to the Lord Deputy, the payment of army arrears and other matters. (Hi238)

1623   Memorandum by Cranfield for various actions, including a review of arms. (Hi239)

1623   Survey of the provinces, with the tax revenue from each. (Hi240)

1623   Privy Council minute concerning the administration of fines for drawing ploughs by horses' tails. (Hi242)

1623   List of debts of the Countess of Kildare, including £1,700 to goldsmiths. (Hi243)

1623–4   Letters of Laurence, Lord Esmond to Cranfield mainly concerning his attempts to secure money owed to Cranfield by the Earl of Desmond, detailing his unsuccessful 14-day journey to persuade the Earls of Cork and Thomond to purchase part of the Desmond estate. Esmond has paid £1,760 to de Renzi (Cranfield's attorney) and Mr. Massam has assumed lands to secure the main debt of £7,000. There is a general shortage of money, the tenants are late with rent, and there is a difficulty securing a higher rent or selling land because of earlier favourable leases made by the 10th Earl of Ormond before 1614. Discusses the possibility of securing sales or mortgages on the estate to pay the debts, but despairs of finding a buyer. States that he will do no more on Desmond's behalf. Mentions his loyalty to the Earl of Arundel and to Cranfield. (5 items, Hi57)

1623–4   Letters of Cranfield to Lord Esmond, largely concerning his dealings with the Earl of Desmond, giving details of various lands and the rents due. Cranfield also states that De Renzi can receive the money, unless Esmond can safely remit by exchange, and that he has given no directions to take possession of the lands. (3 items, Hi142)

1623–7   Letters from Cranfield to Lord Deputy Falkland, recommending Edmund Hunter and William Geere, who are in dispute with the merchants of Cork and Dublin. Requests an account of land grants, and discusses the impossibility of clearing arrears, and that the payment of the army captains will be partly by the assignment of various debts. Mentions requests by Caulfield and Tichbrew, that ploughs are dragged by the tails of horses in Ireland, and that Falkland has misunderstood the £2,350 assigned to Lord Chichester. (7 items, Hi143)

1623–30   Disbursements for Cranfield and Richard Croshaw, prepared by Matthew de Renzi in Dublin. (2 items, Hi26)

1623–35   Letters from Cranfield to Matthew de Renzi, which mostly concern Cranfield's business with the Earl of Desmond, with details of mortgages, Desmond's lands, and Lord Esmond's role therein. Also discuss an enquiry into a possible heir to the Irish estate. Furthermore, Cranfield notes receipt of bills of exchange, the state of the customs, and his grievous treatment by the Duchess of Buckingham. (6 items, Hi178)

1623–41   Letters of the Earl of Cork to Cranfield, which discuss: his decision to decline the purchase of the Fennoy and Gilalby estates. He is in England after an absence of three years; and he seeks redress in the House of Lords for his great losses. (3 items, Hi48)

1623–45   Letters from Matthew de Renzi to Cranfield, which frequently concern rent collection on land conveyed to Cranfield by the Earl of Desmond as security for £7,000, and Cranfield's business concerning the Earl of Desmond's debts in general. The letters are also concerned with: customs returns; sending bills of exchange; payments on the authority of Burlamachi; de Renzi's stipend of £20; frequent robberies; his work on Cranfield's behalf; plantations in general, specifically the plantation of Connaught; the possibility of a foreign invasion, and a conspiracy to murder the English; his thanks for £100 bounty; Lord Somerset's share of the customs; the Lord Justice's favour to the Earl of Ormond; the Lord Justice's reluctance to grant warrants, in view of the tenants' poverty; the Earl of Cork's claim that his rents are £7,000 in arrears; Cork's insufficient power in the kingdom, which is best governed by one alone, with his own means; explanations on the accounts of the customs farmers, who have spent £2,213; more rumours of pirates; de Renzi's 29 year residence in Ireland; his work for Mr. Liske; the death of his father; his acrimonious conference with Lord Mulgrave; and many other matters. (69 items, Hi95)[188]

---

[188] Only one item post-dates 1641.

c1623   Letters of Sir Bernard Grenville to Cranfield (one dated 1623), requesting his favour in two suits, and discussing Cranfield's interest in the cantred of Kenalmeachin [Kinalmeaky]. (2 items, Hi64)

c1623   Letters from Cranfield to Sir Francis Blundell (some dated 1623) which discuss: the implementation of the Commission's recommendations; the warrant to pay an unspecified sum to Docwra; the abatement of a pension to Sir Richard Morrison; the general misery and want of wages; the expense at Dublin Castle; the reservations on accounts; the partial payment of the army arrears from the Easter rents; how Irish business is frequently considered by Buckingham; how Blundell's service in Ireland is expected to redeem his errors in England; how £2,137 is due to Lord Chichester as Governor of Carrickfergus, who will notably accept two thirds, so Cranfield urges prompt payment; the payment of arrears to Sir William Wyndsore; how Cranfield may send inspectors; the need to pay the army before settling arrears. (14 items, Hi117)

c1623   Letters from Cranfield to Sir Francis Gofton, requesting his opinion on the pensions of Lord Caulfield, Sir Richard Morrison, and Sir John King, claimed as exempt from the last instructions. (2 items, Hi150)

c1623   (n.d.) Note in the hand of Richard Willis of the judicial places that are vacant in Ireland, and notes by Cranfield on the customs and the government of Virginia. (Hi254)

c1623   (n.d.) Draft order concerning the arrears of the pension to Sir James Blunt. (Hi266)

c1623   (n.d.) Note of decisions for dealing with recusants before the Prince's journey to Spain prevented any progress. (Hi271)

1624   (March) Abstract of the 1622 Commission for Ireland and a draft of a new one, by Sir Edward Coke and others, addressed to the Lord Deputy, with notes. (Hi216)

1624   (6–7 August) Letter from the Earl of Desmond to Matthew de Renzi requesting him to forgo Cranfield's threat to enter his estate. Also a letter from the Countess of Desmond to Lord Esmond, asking him to write to De Renzi or Cranfield to persuade them not to enter Desmond's lands, promising to pay what is due. (2 items, Hi179)

1624   Extracts from the accounts of Lord Ridgeway, Treasurer-at-war. (Hi13)

1624   Letters from Lord Caulfield to Cranfield and Richard Willis, concerning printing errors in the book of rates, and port certificates for royal officers as well as customs farmers. (2 items, Hi39)

1624   Letter from Cranfield to Roger Brabant, regarding rents on the seignory of Kinalmeaky; the arrears are reserved to Cranfield. (Hi187)

1625   Letters from Thomas Wilson to Cranfield, with a detailed project for maintaining 4,000 soldiers by a levy of corn. (2 items, Hi108)

1626   Letter from John Mayle to Cranfield, reminding him of business to be concluded in the purchase of land. (Hi81)

1627   (16 Nov.) Letter from the Earl of Desmond to Sir Thomas Coventry, Lord Keeper, stating that he cannot attend due to illness, but will be in London in 10–12 days time. (Hi144)

1627–38   Letters of Thomas Dongan to Cranfield, mostly concerning transactions with the Earl of Desmond as follows: subpoenas for tenants and the leases made by the Earl of Desmond; his journey to Dunmore and Kilkenny and the obstinacy of tenants; Lord Esmond at Kilkenny and transactions with his agents; documents delivered to Desmond, who owes Cranfield £13,777; Cranfield's interest charges; the Earl's anger that Cranfield is ruining Lady Desmond; Mr. Smith's lease, which should be secured; documents left with the Master of the Rolls; the Lord Deputy's warrants; the attournments by tenants; the payment to the Duchess of Buckingham; a request to deliver a certificate to the King before Desmond obtains a copy. (11 items, Hi56)

c1627   (n.d.) Letter from Cranfield to Sir Endymion Porter, discussing an emotional conversation he had with the Earl of Desmond in Cranfield's garden. Cranfield dealt with him as a brother, lending him money to preserve his estate. (Hi173)

1628–9   Letters from Anon to Anon, with a copy of royal warrants dealing with the lands of the Earl of Desmond, and the £1,100 p.a. due to Cranfield and Richard Croshaw. The Earl and Countess are dead, and details of the provisions for their daughter, Elizabeth Preston, are given. There is also a draft letter (perhaps to the Lord Deputy) for the early payment of £600 to Matthew de Renzi. (5 items, Hi114)

1628–31   Tobacco imposts, with notes of royal grants. (4 items, Hi8)

1629   (10 Dec.) Letter from Cranfield to Sir George Shirley, Chief Justice, regarding the appointment of a rent collector. Also mentions that even though the Earl of Desmond is dead his unquiet spirit still walks. (Hi180)

1630   Letter from Sir Arthur Ingram to Anon, with an acknowledgement relative to the customs, involving Cranfield and Viscount Wentworth, of 1,000 marks. (Hi110)

1630   Letter from Sir Arthur Ingram and Mr. Burlamachi to Anon [probably Cranfield], concerning an offer for a lease of the customs, with detailed terms. (Hi111)

1631   Letters from Anon to Sir Robert Heath, regarding a warrant for a lease of the customs to Philip Burlamachi and Nicholas Harman. (3 items, Hi153)

c1631   Letter of Lord Caulfield, Roger Jones and others to Cranfield, concerning customs matters, and stating that Nicholas Harman has been appointed as the nominee of Cranfield, who is not expected to meddle further. Relates that there are small profits and a gloomy outlook because of the state of trade with Spain and other countries. (Hi40)

1633   (4 June) Letter from Matthew de Renzi in Dublin, to Captain John Millward in London, stating that the Chief Justice advocates favour to the Earl of Ormond, and noting that Ormond takes the principal and best rents. Thinks it is desirable to procure Royal Letters as a remedy. (Hi170)

1634   (20 Oct.) Letter from George Shirley in Dublin to Cranfield, concerning money due from the lands of the late Earl of Desmond. (Hi98)

1634	Letter from Lieutenant Colonel Peter Hone to Cranfield, requesting relief and transport to Ireland, and mentioning his 46 years in the army. Letter sent by the youngest of his eleven sons. (Hi68)
1634	Letter from Richard Isaack in Dublin to Henry Ayers, regarding his engagement in a law suit, and possible communication between Cranfield and the Lord Deputy. (Hi116)
1634	Petition of William Smith to Charles I concerning a debt of £1,550 secured on the lands of the late Earl of Desmond in Tipperary and Kilkenny, with relevant letters to Cranfield from Viscount Wentworth and to Wentworth from the King. (3 items, Hi124)
1634–5	Letters from Cranfield to Lord Deputy Wentworth, explaining the terms of a lease by Buckingham to Cranfield and others, in the name of the grantee's servants. Cranfield also states that he will defend himself against the scandalous petition of Mr. Smith, and he discusses the suit against the late Earl of Desmond, and mentions the executors of Mr. Croshaw. (2 items, Hi182)
1635	Letter from Edward Bagshaw in Dublin to Cranfield, regarding the impost on tobacco, and that his integrity has been challenged only once, by the Duchess of Buckingham. (Hi36)
1635	Letter from William Raylton (Lord Deputy Wentworth's secretary) to Cranfield, enclosing a letter from the Lord Deputy. (Hi93)
1635	Letters from Henry Smith to Cranfield requesting the expedition of Smith's suit with the Earl of Ormond and a composition with the Earl of Desmond. (2 items, Hi99)[189]
1636	Letter from the Lord Deputy and Council to Anon, regarding arrangements to collect the tobacco impost. (Hi113)
1637	Testimony of Nicholas Harman, Cranfield's trustee, regarding the terms of the customs farm. (Hi202)
1637–41	Unsigned petitions to Charles I and the Archbishop of Canterbury, re the enjoyment of the tobacco impost, from which the petitioner was ousted by Wentworth. (4 items, Hi123)
1638	Letter from John Coke to Lord Deputy Wentworth, relating to a lease of the tobacco impost. (Hi181)
17th cen.	(n.d.) Notes of customs rates to be improved on various commodities in 16 ports. (Hi9)
17th cen.	(n.d.) Fees to officials, with suggestions for improving collection. (Hi10)
17th cen.	(n.d.) Pensions and arrears due to Lord Folliot, Cranfield and Captain Titchbourne, and a note on the expenses of Lord Caulfield, addressed to Richard Willis. (2 items, Hi25)
17th cen.	(n.d.) Arrears of 'Concordations' [i.e. concordatums] made after a conference with Sir William Ussher. (Hi27)
17th cen.	(n.d.) Anonymous letters to Cranfield, which discuss: the grants to Lord Caulfield and Captain Titchborne; the drawing of ploughs by the tails of horses; a request for aid to obtain a patent for land with a defective title; the payment of £400 to Lord Cromwell for his foot company. (4 items, Hi29)

---

[189] It is not clear which Earl of Desmond is meant here, but it is probably Richard Preston.

17th cen.   (n.d.) Letters of Captain John Baylie to Cranfield regarding a grant of fishing rights. (2 items, Hi31)

17th cen.   (n.d.) Letter from John Carne, Customer of Bridgwater, to Cranfield, requesting permission to allow Irish fishermen to exchange fish for beans. (Hi38)

17th cen.   (n.d.) Letter of Lord Caulfield and Sir Henry Titchborne to Cranfield, with a proposition aimed at obtaining their arrears of pay. (Hi41)

17th cen.   (n.d.) Petition of Francis Dade, servant to the Irish Lord Chancellor, to Cranfield, to increase the rewards of the Chancellor, now only £300 a year and a few trifling perquisites. (Hi51)

17th cen.   (n.d.) Petition of Captain Fergus Donell to Cranfield for payment of his pension arrears of three and a half years, mentioning his voyage from Ireland. (Hi55)

17th cen.   (n.d.) Letter from Edmund Hunt, Customer of Cork, to Cranfield, with a memorial on the management of the tobacco impost. (Hi69)

17th cen.   (n.d.) Petition from Elizabeth Massam to Cranfield, concerning her late husband's property and his freedom from the wine impost. (Hi80)

17th cen.   (n.d.) Petition from Trinity College, Dublin, to Cranfield, for the payment of royal pension of £400 *per annum*. (Hi102)

17th cen.   (n.d.) Letter from the Ulster Undertakers to Cranfield, with various proposals including one for increased toleration of conformable natives. (Hi103)

17th cen.   (n.d.) Petition from Arthur Weale, merchant, to Cranfield, requesting the return of the impost on goods exported to Ireland. (Hi105)

17th cen.   (n.d.) Letters from Anon to Anon, concerning Cranfield's failure to repay £200, which is endorsed 'to be paid in Ireland'. Also regarding the customs, and the composition with the Duke of Buckingham. (2 items, Hi109)

17th cen.   (n.d.) Letter from John Mitward [? Millward] to Anon, requesting payment in England to Mitward and Sir Thomas Metham. (Hi112)

17th cen.   (n.d.) Petition from Christopher Grave, servant of Lord Caulfield, to Lord Carew, Master of the Ordnance, for payment of a sum granted to supply the store in Munster. (Hi122)

17th cen.   (n.d.) Petitions from Cranfield to Charles I, for hearing his case against the Earl of Desmond, who pleads sickness, and also the executors of Richard Croshaw. (3 items, Hi125)

17th cen.   (n.d.) Petition from Lady Mary Needham to Charles I for 500 acres called New Hagard near Trim, formerly the property of Alexander Jepson, executed for his role in a plot. (Hi126)

17th cen.   (n.d.) Petition from Laurence Lisle to the House of Commons, concerning his rights in the tobacco impost. (Hi131)

17th cen.   (n.d.) Letter from Alexander Spicer to Sir Thomas Coventry, Lord Keeper, stating that he has been presented to a rectory in the north of Ireland, but has been precluded from entry. (Hi134)

17th cen.   (n.d.) Letter from Lord Esmond to the Earl of Desmond, stating that he has the company of Francis Rush, and concerning the four years arrears in pay. (Hi137)

17th cen.   (n.d.) Letter from Nicholas Harman to the Earl of Dorset, concerning the harsh treatment of Cranfield over the Irish Customs, and the exactions demanded by the Duchess of Buckingham. (Hi140)

17th cen.   (n.d.) Letter from Cranfield to Lord Deputy Grandison, stating the royal intention to provide for the army. (Hi145)

17th cen.   (n.d.) Letter from Lord Treasurer Mandeville to Viscount Grandison, with instructions for army payment. (Hi147)

17th cen.   (n.d.) Letter from the Officers of the Court of Wards to Richard Hadsor, giving details of their work since the establishment of the Court. (Hi155)

17th cen.   (n.d.) Letter from the Privy Council to the Irish Council, with the form of a general order to assist the officers of the Court of Wards. (Hi157)

17th cen.   (n.d.) Letters from Cranfield to the Lord Deputy of Ireland, concerning the irregularities in the account of the Easter rents from the Vice-Treasurer, and Lord Caulfield's proposal for settling his arrears. Mention is also made of the expected vacancy in the archbishopric of Tuam, and that the Earl of Thomond has promised to present his case to the Lords. (4 items, Hi165)

17th cen.   (n.d.) Letter, probably from Cranfield, to Sir William Parsons, relating to the Court of Wards and Lady Folliot's son. (Hi172)

17th cen.   (n.d.) Petition from the Irish Customs farmers to the Privy Council, asking for redress in a dispute over the payment of stipends from their funds. (Hi174)

17th cen.   (n.d.) Note of Cranfield's lands in Limerick City and County, and in Co. Tipperary. (Hi191)

17th cen.   (n.d.) Particulars of crown grants to natives in Cos. Monaghan and Cavan. (Hi192)

17th cen.   (n.d.) Considerations for a new grant of the customs farm, apparently by Matthew de Renzi. (Hi203)

17th cen.   (n.d.) Draft warrant for Sir John Jephson to take plate and furniture (listed) to Ireland. (Hi204)

17th cen.   (n.d.) Summary of a proposed lease, relating to the customs farm. (Hi205)

17th cen.   (n.d.) Instructions for establishing the Court of Wards (Hi244)

17th cen.   (n.d.) Paper on the abuse of a grant of concealed wardships in the province of Connaught and Co. Clare. (Hi245)

17th cen.   (n.d.) Paper on the decision to establish the Court of Wards. (Hi247)

17th cen.   (n.d.) Survey of the forts of Castle Park and Kinsale. (Hi249)

17th cen.   (n.d.) Notes on the chiefry, or rent paid in money, beef and corn out of Co. Wicklow, endorsed 'Sir William Harrington his suit'. (Hi250)

17th cen.   (n.d.) List of undertakers for the Mint and of equipment to be brought from England, with a diagram showing a harp and crown. (Hi251)

17th cen.   (n.d.) Memorandum on the sale of unserviceable ordnance stores and Cranfield's proposals. (Hi252)

17th cen.   (n.d.) Memorandum by Cranfield on protecting the coast from pirates. (Hi255)

17th cen.   (n.d.) Brief notes by Cranfield on Londonderry. (Hi256)

17th cen.   (n.d.) Note of documents relating to revenue found in the State Papers Office, to be shown to the Lord Treasurer. (Hi257)

17th cen.   (n.d.) Brief notes by Cranfield on some proposed reforms. (3 items, Hi258)

17th cen.   (n.d.) Long memoranda on civil and church government. (Hi259)

17th cen.   (n.d.) Project to encourage the fishing industry, including selling pilchards in Mediterranean countries. (Hi260)

17th cen.   (n.d.) Memorial on Ireland by Sir John Bingley, desiring his appointment as Surveyor of the King's revenue. (Hi261)

17th cen.   (n.d.) Memorandum on the causes of the decay of trade. (Hi262)

17th cen.   (n.d.) Notes on providing salt, with a proposal to take its sale into the King's hands. (Hi263)

17th cen.   (n.d.) Memorial by Lord Docwra, Treasurer-at-war. (Hi265)

17th cen.   (n.d.) Recommendations, apparently by Sir Francis Annesley, for reducing expenses by abolishing offices and reducing the army. (Hi267)

17th cen.   (n.d.) Proposals by Richard Hodsall for increasing the revenue and establishing a mint. (2 items, Hi268)

17th cen.   (n.d.) Proposals by Lord Caulfield, Master of the Ordnance, to reform the Ordnance, and a note of decisions made therein. (2 items, Hi269)

17th cen.   (n.d.) Notes by Sir Francis Blundell on the settlement of Ulster and his services since becoming Vice-Treasurer. (2 items, Hi272)

17th cen.   (n.d.) Essay comparing Jugurtha with Hugh O'Neill, Earl of Tyrone. (Hi275)

Official Legal (ref. U269/1 OL)

1623   Letter from Lord Deputy Falkland in Dublin to Cranfield, regarding the wardship of his nephew, Edward Longueville. (OL14)

1624   Letter from Cranfield to Sir William Parsons, relating that the King desires a favourable consideration of Viscount Dillon's petition for the wardship of his grandchild and heir, and giving instructions for future wardships in Ireland. (OL40)

Official Navy (ref. U269/1 ON)

1622   Proposition of Sir Thomas Dutton for the maintenance of his ship *The Phoenix*, with an account of his service off the coast of Ireland, with particular reference to pirates. (ON11)

Official General (ref. U269/1 Oo)

1624–8	Letters from Richard Willis to Cranfield, which include a discussion of the provincial courts of Munster and Connaught, and many other topics. (11 items, Oo92)
1627	Letter from Cranfield to Sir Thomas Coventry, Lord Keeper, regarding the Earl of Desmond's pretended illness and claiming that he is only creating a delay so as to obtain the rents owed to Cranfield for himself. (Oo121)
17th cen.	(n.d.) Notes (apparently by Cranfield) for Parliament, covering a wide range of issues including the Irish customs. (Oo212)

Official Wardship (ref. U269/1 OW)

17th cen.	(n.d.) Ireland cloth of estate and other goods, from various tradesmen. (OW68)

KENT : Institute of Heraldic and Genealogical Studies
Northgate, Canterbury, Kent CT1 1BA
Tel: (01227) 768 664
Fax: (01227) 765 617

COLLECTIONS

Cullerton's Abstracts of Irish Wills

These are copies of abstracts of Irish wills in the Prerogative Court of Canterbury, made by the staff of Cullerton's Heraldic Office. In total there are 559 abstracts of wills. There is an index for the surnames in this collection, 'Irish Wills in the Prerogative Court of Canterbury' in *Family History*, xi (1980). The originals, which have extensive details for Ireland, can be found in the Public Record Office in London.

LANCASHIRE : County Record Office
Bow Lane, Preston PR1 2RE
Tel: (01772) 263 039
Fax: (01772) 263 050

LOOSE ITEMS

1486	Appointment of Lord Strange to the constableship of Wicklow Castle. (DDK 2/2)
1569	(18 July) Grant by the Lord Deputy and Council of the lands of Holywood Abbey, Co. Down, to John Potter. (DDTr, bundle 3, no. 175)
1628	Creation of Sir Robert Molyneux as Viscount Maryborough. (DDM 3/19)

COLLECTIONS

Tasburgh MSS (ref. DDGe)

1612	Copy of letters patent granting Conge Abbey, Co. Mayo, to Sir Robert Cressy. (DDGe Hall 1291)

1632   (20 Aug.) Copy of a feoffment from Sir Robert Cressy to Sir
          Thomas Rotherham, Sir Thomas Waynman [Wenman] and Sir
          Charles Coote, of the estate of Conge Abbey, Co. Mayo, to be held
          in trust to the sole use of Sir Robert Cressy and his heirs. (DDGe
          Hall 1292)

LANCASHIRE : Stonyhurst College Archives
Clitheroe, Lancashire BB7 9PZ
Tel: (01254) 826 345
Fax: (01254) 826 732

Most of the Jesuit archives relating to Ireland were transferred to the Irish
Province in 1868,[190] but a number of items still remain at Stonyhurst. *The Letters
and Dispatches of Richard Verstegan*, ed. A. Petti (Catholic Record Society, lii,
1959), include a number of items from Stonyhurst concerning news from Ulster
c1593–6 (ref. Collectanea B., 109, 117, 145, etc.; Anglia II, no.3, etc.). The
H.M.C. Report on the Stonyhurst MSS lists a few more of their holdings
(H.M.C., *3rd Report* (1872), App., pp 336–9), including an edition of a Catholic
tract published in Ireland in 1605, and a number of Latin descriptions of Ireland
of various dates.[191] The following were omitted from that report:

1577–1603   'Magna Persecutio in Hibernia', contained in a volume of Brussels
            transcripts. (A.IV,13 (i), p.79)[192]

17th cen.   (n.d.) 'De Compendio Annalium Hibernia Portei'. (A.LV,1.M, also
            referred to as Grene Col. M 84e)

LEICESTERSHIRE : County Record Office *
Long Street, Wigs Ton Magna, Leicester LE8 2AH
Tel: (0116) 257 1080
Fax: (0116) 257 1120

LOOSE ITEMS

1613   (16 Feb.) Privy Seal writ for a forced loan of £10 from John
          Loggins, gent., of Little Tew, Oxfordshire, which is to be used for
          the maintenance of forts and magazines in Ireland. Endorsed by Sir
          Thomas Spencer, with a receipt of same, 26 March 1613.
          (DG39/2040)

1628   'Funeral elegy, upon ye late Sad Departure ... [of] Lady Cicilia,
          Countesse of Londondery'. (DG5/970)

COLLECTIONS

Cave, Lords Bray of Stamford Hall MSS (ref. DE)

A large collection of material relating to the Touchets, earls of Castlehaven, has
recently been deposited in this Record Office, and is in the process of being

---

[190] Stonyhurst still has a list of the 36 items transferred to Ireland (ref. B.I, 5, p.29), of which 22 relate to
the period prior to 1641. The covering dates for these manuscripts is 1576–1698.
[191] The 1605 tract has reference A.IV, 1 C. (otherwise known as Grene Col. C); the other documents
referred to in the H.M.C. report can be found at A.IV, 11 & A.IV, 16.
[192] A similar transcript by Richard Cardwell is held in the Archives Department of the English Province of
the Society of Jesus in London (see below).

listed.[193] Part of this collection (DE 3128) relates to the trial in the early 1630s of Marvyn Touchet, 2nd Earl of Castlehaven, on various sexual and moral charges. These papers contain fifteen separate documents including the examinations of Castlehaven himself, Lady Audley, Henry Skipwith and several others. There are extensive depositions of his servants, including at least one Irishman, Florence Fitz-Patrick. Considering the explicit nature of these documents, they are under restricted access, and searchers should write to the County Archivist in advance of visiting to organise permission from the depositor.

Finch MSS (ref. DG7)

The papers of the Finch family of Burley-on-the-Hill have received considerable attention from the H.M.C., including a short listing in the *7th Report*, App., pp 511–8,[194] and a five-volume calendar (*Finch MSS*, Vols I–V). The first volume of this calendar covers the period 1537–1660, and includes a number of documents concerning Ireland during the sixteenth and seventeenth centuries. These items are now catalogued as DG7/Boxes 4982 and 4988.

Hartopp of Dalby Hall MSS (ref. 8D39)

1597   (13 July) Letters patent (enrolled in the Irish Chancery) leasing to Robert, Earl of Essex and Ewe, the manor of Evon, and lands in Evon, Oghill, Clonefideragh, Disertan, Killewerke, Clonekyne, Isawghtowne, etc., Co. Kildare, for 21 years, at a rent of £60 13s 6d, in consideration of the surrender of a former lease of the property. (8D39/1783)[195]

1611   (20 April) Marriage settlement between (1) George, Lord Audley, and (2) Sir Edward Cecil, son of Lord Exeter, Sir Henry Montague, and Sir Edward Noell of Brooke, Rutland. Reciting the intended marriage of (1) and Elizabeth Noell, sister of Sir Edward Noell, and stating that (1) has settled all his estates in England on the children of his former wife. Furthermore (1) quits any claim to the property or dower of Elizabeth Noell, and covenants that 3,000 acres in Omaygh, Co. Tyrone, and 2,500 acres in Oryer, Co. Armagh, Ireland, which are to be granted to (1) by the King, shall subsequently be settled on (1) and Elizabeth Noell and her heirs. Additionally, Elizabeth Noell is to enjoy Laughlyn House while she lives in Ireland. (8D39/778)

1611   (21 April) Gift by George, Lord Audley, to (2) above, of all his personal estate or property, goods, chattels, etc., in England and Ireland, in consideration of his love and affection for Elizabeth Noell, daughter of the late Sir Andrew Noell, and his intended marriage to her. (8D39/779)

1611   (20 July) Mortgage by the assignment of an annuity, by George, Lord Audley, to Nicholas Hooker of London, goldsmith. Reciting a grant of an annuity dated 1 June 1610 by Sir Mervin Tutchett to his father George, Lord Audley, of £500 yearly out of his property in England and Ireland. Lord Audley conveys the same to Hooker, in consideration of a sum of money, to be void if Audley pays £83 by 15 April next. (8D39/780)

---

[193] When visited, the part of this collection listed as DE 2399 was not catalogued or available for viewing. It is known to contain documents concerning lands in Co. Tipperary from the 1690s at least. It may well include earlier material.

[194] Many of the documents listed on pp514–7 are now lost or were destroyed by a fire in 1908.

[195] This item was calendared in *Cal. Patent Rolls, Ire., Eliz. I*, pp429–30.

1612   (12 March) Letters patent granting to George, Lord Audley, and Elizabeth, his wife, 2,000 acres in the barony of Orior, Co. Armagh; 2,000 acres in the barony of Omagh, Co. Tyrone; and a further 1,000 acres in Co. Tyrone. (8D39/781)

1619   (1 March) Marriage settlement between (1) the Countess Dowager of Castlehaven, widow of George, late Earl of Castlehaven, (2) Sir Piers Crosby of Tarbert, Co. Kerry, and (3) Lord Noell of Brooke, Sir Henry Montague, Lord Chief Justice of England, and Sir Edward Cecil. Reciting the intended marriage of (1) and (2), and recording that (2) is to have £1,500 from (1) as dower. (1) covenants to lease all her property in Armagh and Tyrone to (3) for 80 years at the rent of a peppercorn, and she grants them her personal estate in trust. (1) is to enjoy the rents and profits of her property, and (2) is to pay (3) for the benefit of (1) a yearly charge of £150. However, neither of these provisions is to be put into effect while (1) and (2) live together. (8D39/781)

Sherard, Lords Gretton of Stapleford Hall MSS (ref. DG40)

Part of this collection is entitled 'Irish Nobility and Parliamentary Attendance' and includes the following items:

1629   (28 June) Copy of proceedings in the Privy Council regarding a petition from certain aristocrats to the King about their precedence and standing. (DG40/544)

1634   (23 May) Printed proclamation for the holding of Parliament at Dublin, on 14 July 1634, and requiring all those who are entitled to be present to turn up there. (DG40/545)

1634   (24 May) Writ to attend the Parliament at Dublin on 14 July next issued to William, Lord Sherard. (DG40/546)

1634   (20 June) Note by William, Lord Sherard, that he received his Parliamentary writ 'for Ireland dispensation', and also a letter from Mr. Secretary Coke by the messenger, Mr. Stockdale. (DG40/548)

1634   (21 June) Receipt of Edward Stockdale to Lord Sherard on his payment of £6 12s for a dispensation not to attend the Parliament in Ireland. (DG40/547)

1634   (21 June) Copy of a proxy sent by Lord Sherard to the Parliament in Ireland. (DG40/549)

1634   (14 July) List of Irish peers in England summoned to the Parliament at Dublin. (DG40/550)

1634   (14 July) Copy of a list detailing the table of precedence for the procession of lords, together with a list of representatives of the Irish counties and boroughs in the Commons at the Parliament held in Dublin. (DG40/551)

1634   (24 Oct.) Copy of a memorandum of the Garter King of Arms, relating to the fees payable on presentation at Parliament. (DG40/557)

1634   (4 Nov.) Declaration that the nobility of Ireland not attending Parliament in Dublin should pay all fees due to officers as if they were present. (DG40/552)

1634   (15 Nov.) Copy of a table of fees which noblemen are to pay to the Clerk upon receiving their first writ of summons. (DG40/553)

1634	(18 Nov.) Copy of a table of fees that are payable to the Yeoman Usher by noblemen attending Parliament. (DG40/554)
1634	(18 Nov.) Copy of a table of fees that are payable to the Gentleman Usher, Black Rod, by noblemen attending Parliament. (DG40/555)
1634	(27 Nov.) Letter from William Raylton to Lord Sherard about the fees of the nobility attending Parliament in Ireland. (DG40/556)
1634	'A note of such Acts as have passed in this second session of Parliament in Ireland begun the fourth day of November in the tenth yeare of his Majesties Raigne'. (DG40/558)
1635	(12 Feb.) List of the Irish nobility, five of whom had paid their subsidies and seventeen who had not at this date. A note from the Treasury says that if they do not pay, extents are to be issued to levy the same amount on their lands. Also a list of the lords of Ireland, and of the lords of England and Ireland, who possessed no lands in Ireland. (DG40/559)
1635	(8 May) Receipt of William Raylton to Lord Sherard for fees paid to officers of the Parliament. (DG40/560)
1635	(4 June) Copy of the list of subsidies of the nobility, granted at the Dublin Parliament on 14 July 1634. (DG40/561)
1635	(4 June) Copy of an extract of the first subsidies to be paid by various earls, viscounts and barons, to the Crown. (DG40/562)
1635	(30 Oct.) Letter of Archbishop William Laud and others, to Lord Sherard, about paying his subsidies that were decided at the Irish Parliament, Sherard being assessed at £80. (DG40/563)
1635	(3 Nov.) Receipt of Edward Stockdale to Lord Sherard for £7 12s 9d in fees paid to the officers of arms for the Parliament of Ireland. (DG40/564)
c1635	Memorandum of the debt of William, Lord Sherard, that he owes four subsidies, each of £20, to the Crown, as assessed at the Parliament in Ireland on 14 July 1634. (DG40/565)
1636	The bill of the lawyer, Mr. Hillarey, for 'a supersedes to stopp execution for youre Irish subseties'. (DG40/566)
1636	(13 Feb.) Copy of an extent issued by the Barons of the Exchequer to obtain £80 from William, Lord Sherard, for his part of the sum assessed at Parliament in Dublin, 1634. (DG40/567)
1636	(26 Feb.) Summons to William, Lord Sherard, to attend court at Westminster, on pain of £100, with notes of his attendance, 23 June 1638. (DG40/568)
1636	(20 May) Synopsis of the Attorney General's remarks on the extents being issued to recoup the sums due the Crown for money levied by subsidies on the nobles of the Irish Parliament, and subsequently left unpaid by many of them. (DG40/569)
1636	(31 May) Writ to the Sheriff of Leicestershire to apprehend and hold William, Lord Sherard, until he has disgorged his debts of £40 to the Crown, due for his part of the subsidy assessed at the Irish Parliament of 14 July 1634. Orders an inquisition into Lord Sherard's property in Leicestershire. (DG40/571)
1636	(8 June) Receipt of William Raylton to Lord Sherard for £80 in subsidies due to the Crown. (DG40/570)

1636 (10 June) Extract from the Pipe Roll detailing the payment by Lord Sherard of his debt of £80 to the Crown. (DG40/572)

1636 (10 June) Receipt of the Pells, signed by Edward Wardour, for £80 for Irish taxes. (DG40/573)

1636 (31 Dec.) Letter from the Bishop of London and Francis Cottington to Lord Sherard requesting a speedy settlement of his debt of £80 to the Crown, and asking him to pay William Raylton, the agent of Lord Deputy Wentworth, in London. (DG40/574)

1637 (17 May) Copy of the Pells record of a receipt for £80, received from William, Lord Sherard, by Edward Wardour. (DG40/575)

1638 (13 June) Copy of William, Lord Sherard's, account and payment of £80 to the Crown *via* Sir Richard Roberts, with a note on the reverse side 'Look in the Pipe Office in Barbican whether theis subsidies be not for the same that are paid in by Sir Henry Skipwith, late Shreif of Leic.' (DG40/576)

1639 (8 Feb.) Letter from the Bishop of London and Francis Cottington to William, Lord Sherard, requesting that two overdue subsidies, amounting to £40, be paid to William Raylton, the agent of the Lord Deputy of Ireland. (DG40/577)

1640 (1 Feb.) Writ of summons to Lord Sherard to attend Parliament at Dublin Castle on 16 March 1640. (DG40/579)

1640 (6 Feb.) *Quietus* for the third of four subsidies levied at the Parliament in Dublin on 14 July 1634. (DG40/580)

1640 (6 Feb.) Receipt of George Wadland, late under-sheriff of Leics., to William, Lord Sherard, for £80 being the third of four subsidies taxed on him in the Irish Parliament of 14 July 1634. (DG40/581)

1640 (12 March) Draft appointment of a proxy for Lord Sherard, to attend Parliament in Dublin. (DG40/582)

1640 (16 March) Letter from Lord Sherard to Sir Francis Windebank, relating that 'I have sent you my proxie, having a blanke for the noblemans name in Ireland to be inserted'. Explains that he has had word from the Lord Lieutenant of Ireland that he should give his proxy to the 'Lord President of Connoe', a person that Sherard does not know. (DG40/622)[196]

1640 'March 1639[–40]. Fees to be paid for the Dispensation £7 12s'. (DG40/578)

c1640[197] Letter from [ ] to Lord Sherard imploring his aid with all others of 'our quallities', in a suggested plea to the King to treat his nobles less harshly. (DG40/583)

c1640 Copy of a petition of William, Lord Sherard, to the Crown to consider the case of Irish peerages as being no different from others. (DG40/584)

c1640 Petition of the nobles of Ireland to the King, deploring subsidies and their liability to serve as sheriffs and regretting their being denied

---

[196] This document is not catalogued with the other Irish Parliamentary papers, and appears elsewhere in the collection.

[197] The following items are undated but relate mainly to the 1640 Parliament, though some may concern the 1630s in general.

commissions, 'That being esteemed a Punishment for Romanists and great offenders' [2 copies]. (DG40/585)

c1640   Extract of Acts relating to the obligation of English peers to pay Irish subsidies [2 copies]. (DG40/586)

c1640   Treatise based on Acts of Parliament, that Ireland is a 'domynian annexed to England and not a distinct domynion'. (DG40/587)

c1640   Case that holders of Irish and French titles have held seats in Parliament by right of their English holdings and not by writ of summons, etc. (DG40/588)

c1640   Memorandum of the case of English nobles with Irish titles, with no lands or goods in Ireland, against paying Irish subsidies. (DG40/589)

c1640   'To be considered upon the Irish Lords'. Counsel's opinion for the Irish lords not paying the subsidy. (DG40/590)

c1640   Note of debts to the Crown by Viscounts Chaworth and Lumley, and Lords Fitzwilliam and Sherard. (DG40/591)

c1640   Note of a writ of extent issued out of the Court of Exchequer against William, Lord Sherard. (DG40/592)

c1640   'Records in the Tower to be Serched for. Goe to Mr. Collecke and give him somwhat for expeditcon'. (DG40/593)

c1640   (3 July) Copy of a note from the Sheriff of Leicestershire about the payment of Irish subsidies. (DG40/594)

LINCOLNSHIRE : County Archives Office *
St. Rumbold Street, Lincoln LN2 5AB
Tel: (01522) 525 158/526 204
Fax: (01522) 530 047

COLLECTIONS

Ancaster MSS (ref. ANC)

The correspondence in this collection has been calendared as H.M.C., *Ancaster MSS* (London, 1907), and it contains several letters concerning the survivors of the Spanish Armada who were shipwrecked on the west coast of Ireland in 1588. However, the calendar is partial, dealing exclusively with correspondence, and the following documents remain unpublished:

1555   Proclamation by Queen Mary and King Philip 'Mindyng to Roote Out and Extinguysh Al False Doctrine And Heresies' by banning the importation into England of all the works published by Luther, Zwingli, Calvin and others, including the bishop of Ossory, John Bale. (10 ANC/362)

1579–80   (17 Aug. 1579 – 5 Nov. 1580) The accounts of Sir William Pelham, Lord Justice of Ireland. The document is broken down into three chronological sections, the first covering the period when Pelham was Colonel of the royal forces in Leinster. This section makes particular mention of the costs which he incurred in furnishing and transporting 30 men with their armour, horses, tents, etc., to Ireland, and gives details of the replacement of horses that died while he was out on campaign against the rebels. The second section covers his charges as Lord Justice from 18 Aug. 1579 to 7

Sept. 1580, and the third details his expenses after he delivered the sword of state to the Lord Deputy, 7 Sept. – 5 Nov. 1580. In this third section the costs of his voyage home to England and his brief stay with his servants and followers on Lambay Island are itemised, and at the end it is shown that his disbursements exceeded his receipts by £2,300 17s 5d. (10 ANC/335)

c1630–1   Petition to the King by Robert Bertie, Earl of Lindsay, touching his heavy debts incurred in the royal service, and asking if he may be considered for employment as Lord Deputy of Ireland or Admiral of England. (10 ANC/341.1)

1640   (25 March) Letter by William Broxholme to Leonard Tompson written at Berwick, relating that more English troops are coming to Berwick to face the Scots, and making passing reference to Wentworth's return to Ireland. (3 ANC 8/1/13 (f))

Dudding Papers (ref. FL DUDDING 68–78)

This collection includes a number of deeds relating to Aslackby in Lincolnshire during the late sixteenth century to which Elizabeth Fitzgerald, Countess of Lincoln (the daughter of the 9th Earl of Kildare) was a party. They were published by Reginald C. Dudding, 'Some Aslackby Deeds', *Lincolnshire Notes & Queries*, xxiii (1934–5), pp133–46.

Market Deeping Parish Records (ref. Market Deeping parish)

The only item in this collection of any interest is the account book of the parish officers and the churchwarden, 1570–1647 (ref. Market Deeping parish 10), which has the following references to Ireland:

1602   Payments for the provision of armour, training and conduct of soldiers bound for Ireland.

1603   Money paid by the town bailiffs to maimed soldiers returned from the wars in Ireland.

LINCOLNSHIRE : Lincoln Cathedral Archives
c/o Lincolnshire Archives Office, St. Rumbold Street, Lincoln LN2 5AB

According to the H.M.C., *Guide to the Locations of Collections*, p38, the records held by this repository were deposited in the Lincolnshire Archives Office. However, when the Archives Office was visited in 1992 we were informed that much of the material appearing in the published catalogue still resides in the Cathedral. For researchers wishing to contact the Cathedral we advise that they first approach the Archives Office for assistance. Though we were unable to communicate directly with the Cathedral, the following item appears in a published catalogue by K. Major, *Handlist of the Records of the Bishops of Lincoln and of the Archdeacons of Lincoln and Stow* (1953):

James I   A treatise on the appropriations of the Parish Churches in Ireland and other matters [70pp]. (Miscellaneous Books no.1)[198]

---

[198] We would like to thank Kenneth Nicholls for bringing this item to our attention.

GREATER LONDON : Corporation of London Records Office *
P.O. Box 270, Guildhall, London EC2P 2EJ
Tel: (0171) 606 3030 ext. 1251
Fax: (0171) 332 1119

COLLECTIONS

City Corporation Records

The archives of this corporation are extensive, and are dealt with below under their respective sections.

Chamber Accounts 1535–1586 (ref. Chamber Accounts)

These two volumes (ref. Chamber Accounts 1 & 2) are the only sixteenth century City accounts surviving in the Record Office. Most of the material from both has been published by Betty R. Masters (ed.), *Chamber Accounts of the Sixteenth Century* (London Record Society, xx, 1984), which includes reference to the transportation of Irish beggars from the City in 1584.

City Cash Accounts (ref. City Cash)

This series of large volumes only commences in 1633, and the first four volumes cover the years 1633–43. Due to pressure of time, only the first volume could be checked when the Record Office was visited. The other three volumes probably contain similar material.

1633–5	City Cash Accounts Michaelmas 1633 – Michaelmas 1635. (City Cash Accounts 1/1)
1632–3	(Michaelmas to Michaelmas) Includes a list at the end of the account of outstanding debts owed to the City by many London companies who had not paid their shares in the Londonderry plantation scheme. The total outstanding was £604 5s. (fol. 93r)
1633–4	(Michaelmas to Michaelmas) Precisely the same details as above. (fol. 180r)
1634–5	(Michaelmas to Michaelmas) Includes the same details, except that the outstanding sum was £609 17s. (fol. 271v)

Common Council Journals (ref. Jor.)

This extensive collection consists of the original minutes and other proceedings of the Common Council. However, the corporation also kept contemporaneous fine-hand copies of exactly the same records; these, being the more legible source, are listed below (Letter Books).

Historical Papers (ref. Hist.)

1513–44	Calendar of Patent Rolls, Ireland, for the years 5, 6, 22, 24–35 Henry VIII [32pp]. (440A)[199]
1641	(25 Oct.) Copy of a letter, probably written by the Lord Justice, Sir William Parsons, giving a lengthy account of the 'conspiracy of the papists in Ireland to extirpate the English' [7ff]. (Vol. III, no. 99 [113A])
1641	(5 Nov.) Contemporary copy entitled 'Lettres from the Councill of Ireland relating the further proceedings of the rebells there' [5ff]. (Vol. III, no. 99 [113A]).

---

[199] It is not clear whether this item is merely a copy of *Cal. Patent Rolls, Ire., Henry VIII–Eliz. I*, or notes from the original documents.

Letter Books (ref. Letter Book)

This series of large volumes are exact contemporaneous copies of the Journals of the Common Council, but in fine clerk hand. There are indices to the Letter Books in the Record Office, but they are highly abbreviated, and much is left out. All Irish references that were found in the indices were followed up in the original volumes, and they are listed below. However, it is very probable that the indices omitted some material concerning Ireland, and as a result, the following list should not be taken as an exhaustive guide to all the Irish material.[200]

1542[201]   (6 Feb.) Proclamation in the City of London of King Henry VIII's title as King of Ireland. (Book Q, fol. 47r)

1580   (9 July) Assent by the Common Council to the request of the Queen for 300 men, supplied by the London companies, to be sent into service in Ireland. Followed by a list of each company and stating how many men the City will furnish. With a note (dated 15 July) appointing four men to survey the troops. (Book Z, fol. 72v–73v)

1580   (27 Sept.) Assent to the request of same for 500 men to be raised and sent to Ireland. With lengthy details of how much ordnance, apparel and weapons each soldier is to receive and how many men each company will contain. (Book Z, fol. 90)

1580   (5 Nov.) Order by the Mayor directed to the Exchequer to pay the Chamberlain of the City for coats furnished to 800 men. Lists the number of coats granted to each company, and notes that they are to be paid at 4s each. (Book Z, fol. 104v–105)

1598   (20 July) Assent to the request of the Queen dated 18 July for ten light horsemen and furnished horses for service in Ireland. With copy of the Privy Council's directions for same dated 16 July. (Book AA, fol. 196v–197)

1598   (26 Aug.) Assent to the request of the Queen and Privy Council to borrow £20,000 from the City for six months, to be used in suppressing the rebels in Ireland. With a list of each company and how much their share will be. (Book AA, fol. 198v)

1598   (13 Sept.) Assent to the Queen's letters patent for the raising of 300 troops in the City for service in Ireland, reciting the Privy Council's letter to the same effect, dated 28 August. This is followed by an order of Common Council to levy a fifteenth tax to pay for it. (Book AA, fol. 202v–204v)

1598   (29 Dec.) Assent to the request of the Queen to raise 600 troops for service in Ireland, reciting the Queen and Privy Council's letter of same date. (Book AA, fol. 225v–227v)

1599   (23 Feb.) Assent to the request of the Queen to raise 100 troops for service in Ireland, reciting the Queen's letter, dated 17 Feb., and the Privy Council's orders, dated 18 Feb., to the same effect. (Book AA, fol. 234v)

1599   (31 March) The Queen's proclamation 'declaring her princelie resolution in sending over of her army into the Realm of Ireland'. (Book AA, fol. 248r)

---

[200] These books are not letter books in the literal sense; the name given them probably derives from their reference numbering, which is by the letters of the alphabet.

[201] This item is dated 1540[-1] in the letter book, but must be a mistake for 1541[-2].

1600   (25 Jan.) Assent to the request of the Queen to raise 300 troops for service in Ireland, with lengthy details on pay, apparel, weapons, etc. Reciting the Queen's letter, dated 12 Jan., and the Privy Council's orders, dated 15 Jan., to same effect. (Book BB, fol. 22v–23v)

1608   (8 Oct.) Assent to the request of the King to raise £700 for the furnishing and sending of 250 soldiers to Ireland, reciting the King's letter, dated 23 May, and the Privy Council's orders, dated 25 May, to same effect. (Book CC, fol. 282r)

1609   (1 Aug.) Order to send John Broade, goldsmith, Hugh Hamersly, haberdasher, Robert Treswell, painter stainer, and John Rowley, draper, to Ireland to survey and assess the lands lately stipulated for plantation there. The charges are to be borne by the City. (Book DD, fol. 64v)

1609   (3 Aug.) Order that upon the suit of Hugh Hamersley (see previous item) he is discharged and spared of going to Ireland. John Munes, mercer, is appointed to travel in his place. (Book DD, fol. 65r)

1609   (2 Dec.) Upon hearing the report of the commissioners (above) on their survey of the plantation area, the Common Council orders the setting up of a committee to meet twice weekly on plantation affairs (lists 32 people to be on the committee, either aldermen or representatives of the companies). The committee to be especially directed by one of the following: Stephen Soame, John Garrard or Thomas Bennett, all aldermen. (Book DD, fol. 94v)

1609   (15 Dec.) Reading and approval of the first report of the Committee on Plantation (set up above). This detailed report deals with many aspects of the proposed plantation under four headings 1) 'What somes of money should be expended', 2) 'What land and privileges should be demanded', 3) 'What things should be performed', and 4) 'How all should be managed and ruled'. (Book DD, fol. 95v–97v)

1609   (22 Dec.) Decision based on the previous report, and the deliberations of the Privy Council, to increase the investment in Ulster from £15,000 to £20,000. (Book DD, fol. 99r)

1610   (8 Jan.) Order to form a committee to deal with and direct the collection of the £20,000 for the plantation. The Committee is to include various aldermen and company representatives, and the four commissioners sent to Ireland (see above). (Book DD, fol. 99v)

1610   (30 Jan.) Approval of a detailed agreement between the Privy Council and the various city plantation committees. With an enrolment of the agreement, dated 20 January. (Book DD, fol. 101v–104r)

1610   (9 March) Order to pay the first two payments, totalling £10,000, towards the plantation, and that done, some other course to be taken for taxing and levying the rest of the £20,000. (Book DD, fol. 125r)

1610   (7 June) Upon request by the Privy Council to the Company lately set up to deal with the plantation, to give them 2,000 acres set aside for the City, the Plantation Company referred the matter to the Common Council. The Council, after long deliberation, ordered that the Privy Council was to give assurances to grant the whole area to the City, and the Privy Council was not to receive the 2,000 acres. (Book DD, fol. 149r)

1610   (11 July) Order to form a committee to deal with the levying of £10,000 remaining for the plantation upon the City, and the raising of 10,000 quarters of corn. (Book DD, fol. 158r)

1610   (18 July) Order stipulating the City's new assessment, stating that this will affect the assessment towards the remaining £10,000 for Ireland, and the 10,000 quarters of corn. (Book DD, fol. 166r)

1610   (20 July) Reading in Common Council of the four articles required by the Privy Council upon the City's plantation estates in Ulster, particularly concerning the disputed 2,000 acres, the Bishop of Derry's tithes, the fishing rights and the termon lands. (Book DD, fol. 168r)

1610   (31 July) Order agreeing that the termon lands should be allowed to the Bishop of Derry, and left out of their assurance. (Book DD, fol. 168v)

1611   (14 Jan.) Order directing that the Governor, Deputy and Assistants of the lately enacted Plantation Company have full power in Ulster to let the City's fishing rights for a maximum of seven years. Order also taken to assemble the London companies to see if they will accept land in lieu of their investments, to plant at their own costs in Ulster, or whether they wish to refer the letting of their lands to the Plantation Company or the committees. (Book DD, fol. 213r)

1611   (17 Feb.) Order, upon the previous order, listing the shares of land in Ireland to be distributed to 18 companies, and ordering a time limit for the rest of the companies to signify their consent, or else their parts to be disposed of by the committees. (Book DD, fol. 238v)

1611   (8 April) Order appointing the officers of the Plantation Company, directing that all the officers (i.e. the Governor: William Cockayne, the Deputy: William Towerson, and the Assistants) shall continue in office for another year. Except John Rowley, draper (an Assistant) who is now in Ireland on the City's business, who is to be replaced by Edward Rotteram, draper. (Book DD, fol. 248v)

1611   (31 May) Order, upon the information of Governor Cockayne of the Plantation Company stating that he had too few Assistants, to increase the number of Assistants in the Company by eleven men (all named). (Book DD, fol. 279v)

1611   (10 July) Order, upon the information of Governor Cockayne that the initial £20,000 has nearly run out, to levy and tax a further £10,000 in the City towards the plantation in Ulster. (Book DD, fol. 295v)

1612   (6 March) Order appointing a new committee (members named) to join with former committees to examine all accounts concerning the plantation. (Book EE, fol. 32v)

1612   (11 July) Order to send out a precept to every company in the City for the speedy collection of the £5,000 remaining of the £10,000 granted towards the plantation in Ireland. (Book EE, fol. 52v)

1613   (8 Jan.) Order appointing the Governor, Deputy, Assistants and Treasurer of the Plantation Company. Cockayne to stay as Governor, against his wishes (other officers named). (Book EE, fol. 83r)

1613   (30 April) Order, upon the information of Governor Cockayne stating that they have run out of money and have used most of the

£3,000 lent to them by the Chamber of London, decreeing that £10,000 more should be levied and taxed in the City towards the plantation. (Book EE, fol. 115r)

1613   (July) Upon the request of the Privy Council to strengthen the walls of the City of Derry for better security, the Common Council, after much deliberation, orders that the houses and walls in Derry shall be built according to the original intentions and plans of the committees. (Book EE, fol. 135v)

1613   (July) Order sending Alderman George Smith of London and Mathias Springham, merchant taylor, Smith's assistant, to Ireland to assist with the plantation. (Book EE, fol. 136r)

1613   (8 Nov.) Reading of the report, dated 15 Oct., by Alderman Smith and Mr. Springham upon their return from Ireland, and a lengthy and detailed list of 'Abuses' and suggested 'Reformations'. With a note by the Common Council that the report was well liked and some further investigation would be required. (Book EE, fol. 174v–177v)

1613   (17 Dec.) Reading of a division made by Governor Cockayne and surveyed by Alderman Smith and Mr. Springham of all the companies' estates in Ireland, which includes a list of the amounts invested by each company, and a very detailed valuation and survey of the plantation area, divided into 12 allotments.[202] With an order to levy and raise a further £5,000 in the City towards the plantation. (Book EE, fol. 180v–188r)

1614   (17 Aug.) Reading of a report by Mathias Springham, assistant to Alderman Smith, on the agreements he concluded on his journey in Ireland, which gives a detailed account of all agreements, disbursements, etc. With an order of Common Council in general agreement with the same. (Book EE, fol. 245v)

1614   (17 Aug.) Order appointing the Governor, Deputy, Assistants and Treasurer of the Plantation Company. Alderman George Smith to replace Cockayne as Governor, with the names of the other officers. (Book EE, fol. 245v)

1614   (8 Dec.) Order that in addition to the documentation given to each company of their division in the plantation, each company should also receive details of the rates used to value the land in question. (Book FF, fol. 31v)

1615   (11 Jan.) Order taken to raise, levy and tax £7,500 on the City towards the plantation in Ireland, over and above the £45,000 already levied. (Book FF, fol. 38v)

1615   (5 May) Discussion on whether or not to build a keep at Coleraine, in consideration of the large circumference of the walls and the few inhabitants. Order taken that the Governor and other officers of the Plantation Company should make a report on the same and return it to the Common Council. (Book FF, fol. 80r)

1615   (5 May) Order appointing the Governor, Deputy, Assistants and Treasurer of the Plantation Company. Alderman George Smith to remain as Governor, and the other officers are also named. (Book FF, fol. 80v)

---

[202] This item has been published in T.W. Moody (ed.), 'Schedules of the Lands in Ulster allocated to the London Livery Companies, 1613', *Analecta Hibernica*, viii (1938), pp299–311.

1615   (15 July) Order appointing Alderman Thomas Bennett to be Governor of the Plantation Company in place of George Smith, deceased. Also an order appointing Adrian Moore, haberdasher, and Mathias Springham, merchant taylor, to join with nine others (named) to be auditors of the money expended by the City on the Irish plantation. (Book FF, fol. 102r)

1615   (6 Aug.) Order to raise, levy and tax a further £500 for the plantation in Ireland. (Book FF, fol. 104r)

1616   (27 Feb.) Receipt of a complaint presented to the King by John Wilkinson, Recorder of Coleraine, against the proceedings of the City of London's plantation in Ireland, with details of his complaints. (Book FF, fol. 161v)[203]

1616   (20 March) Order appointing the Governor, Deputy, Assistants, and Treasurer of the Plantation Company. Alderman Thomas Bennett to remain as Governor, with the names of the other officers. (Book FF, fol. 146v)

1616   (20 March) Upon the request of the Governor and the other officers of the Plantation Company to send persons into Ireland to survey the work of the plantation, order is taken to send John Williams, goldsmith, and Nicholas Leate, ironmonger. (Book FF, fol. 147r)

1616   (30 March) Order to appoint Thomas Westraye, grocer, and John Green, salter, as Assistants in the 'Society for the plantation in Ireland'[204] to replace two others (named). (Book FF, fol. 152r)

1616   (30 March) Order, upon the suit of John Williams and Nicholas Leate, discharging them from going to Ireland, and directing the Plantation Company to come up with replacements. (Book FF, fol. 152r)

1616   (4 May) Order to send Alderman Peter Probey, Governor of the Plantation Company, and Mathias Springham, his assistant, to Ireland in order to survey the plantation. (Book FF, fol. 157r)

1616   (1 Oct.) Reading in Common Council of the report of Alderman Peter Probey and Mathias Springham on their visit to Ulster, relating particularly to the cities of Derry and Coleraine. Listing in detail their instructions (38 questions), followed by their extensive answers to each question. (Book FF, fol. 204r–212r)

1617   (1 Aug.) Order appointing the Governor, Deputy, Assistants and Treasurer of the Plantation Company. Alderman Probey to remain as Governor, with the names of the other officers. (Book FF, fol. 301r)

1618   (30 April) Order appointing same. Probey remains as Governor. (Book GG, fol. 54r)

1619   (27 Aug.) Order appointing same. Probey remains as Governor. (Book GG, fol. 186r)

1620   (4 July) Order appointing same. Probey remains as Governor. (Book GG, fol. 259r)

---

[203] This is entered out of sequence after May 1616 in the Letter Book, and could be incorrectly dated.

[204] This is the first time that it is referred to as a Society, rather than a Company. Thereafter both terms are used interchangeably.

| 1621 | (28 Feb.) Order appointing same. Probey remains as Governor. (Book HH, fol. 26r) |

1621 | (28 Feb.) Order appointing same. Probey remains as Governor. (Book HH, fol. 26r)

1622 | (19 June) Order appointing same. Alderman Robert Johnson is appointed Governor. (Book HH, fol. 165v)

1622 | (27 June) This day Alderman John Gore, Alderman Allen and Alderman Dury were sworn in as Assistants for the plantation, having been appointed on 19 June. (Book HH, fol. 181v)

1622 | (4 July) This day Alderman Johnson, lately appointed Governor of the 'Society' was sworn in for the due execution thereof. (Book HH, fol. 181v)

1623 | (13 March) Order appointing the Governor, Deputy, Assistants and Treasurer of the Plantation Company. Johnson remains as Governor, with the names of the other officers. (Book HH, fol. 213v)

1623 | (11 October) Order appointing Edward Warner, merchant taylor, as Treasurer of the Plantation Society. (Book II, fol. 31v)

1623 | (11 October) Enrolment of a letter to the Governor and Society from the Lord Deputy and Council of Ireland, dated 1 Sept. 1623, proposing the building of a jail and stocks in Derry county. Order taken directing the Society to deliberate the matter. (Book II, fol. 31v)

1624 | (25 Feb.) Order appointing the Governor, Deputy, Assistants, and Treasurer of the Irish Society. Alderman Robert Johnson to remain as Governor, with names of other officers. (Book II, fol. 53v)

1624 | (2 June) Enrolment of a lengthy letter to the Common Council from the Privy Council concerning the defences of Londonderry, Culmore and Coleraine, with the detailed answer of the Common Council. (Book II, fol. 72v–75r)

1625 | (16 April) Order appointing the Governor, Deputy, Assistants, and Treasurer of the Irish Society. Sir Humphrey Handford, Alderman, is appointed Governor, with the names of other officers. (Book II, fol. 145r)

1626 | (8 June) Order appointing same. Alderman Robert Parkhurst is appointed Governor. (Book II, fol. 247r)

1627 | (7 April) Order that the Irish Society should continue in its functioning as before, until the next Council meeting. (Book KK, fol. 24v)

1627 | (24 May) Order appointing the Governor, Deputy, Assistants, and Treasurer of the Irish Society. Alderman Robert Parkhurst to remain as Governor, with the names of other officers. (Book KK, fol. 30r)

1628 | (6 March) Order appointing same. Parkhurst to remain as Governor. (Book KK, fol. 128v)

1629 | (2 March) Order appointing same. Parkhurst to remain as Governor. (Book KK, fol. 210r)

1630 | (7 Aug.) Order appointing same. Parkhurst to remain as Governor. (Book LL, fol. 54r)

1631 | (9 March) Order appointing same. Parkhurst to remain as Governor. (Book LL, fol. 90v)

1632   (9 April) Order appointing same. Parkhurst to remain as Governor. (Book LL, fol. 180r)

1633   (25 Feb.) Order appointing same. Parkhurst to remain as Governor. (Book MM, fol. 26r)

1634   (2 Oct.) Order appointing same. Parkhurst, now the Mayor-elect of London, is to remain as Governor. (Book MM, fol. 147r)

1636   (17 May) Order appointing same. Parkhurst to remain as Governor. With a detailed preamble, reciting a Star Chamber decree of Candlemas 1634 against the City and the Irish Society, which included the surrendering of the original plantation patent. Also reciting a petition of the Mayor and Aldermen to the King asking to be allowed to appoint officers to the Irish Society, with a reply by Secretary Windebank, dated 10 May 1636, saying that this would be acceptable and not against the tenor of the Star Chamber decree. (Book NN, fol. 33r–34r)

1636   (17 May) Order that a Council be held in a week on the 'great and weighty matters' concerning the £70,000 fine imposed on the City by decree of Star Chamber of Candlemas 1634 relative to the Ulster plantation. The Council believes that all members should be given time to acquaint themselves with the details of the matter. (Book NN, fol. 34r)

1636   (24 May) Order appointing a committee of 33 members (named), to be headed by Alderman Thomas Gardiner, to examine the matter of the £70,000 fine and to report to the Council on how this problem can be resolved. With a lengthy preamble, giving details of the charges made against the City in Star Chamber. (Book NN, fol. 36r)

1636   (23 June) Reading of the report of the above committee, stating that various proposals should be put to the King, including one that the City pay the King £100,000 over five years and in return get a number of demands fulfilled, primarily the overturning of the Star Chamber decree. (Book NN, fol. 42r–43r)

1637   (24 Jan.) Reading of a draft petition drawn up by the committee (above) to the King, seeking to persuade him to accept their offer of £100,000. With an order of Council that this petition is to be written in fine hand and sent. (Book NN, fol. 72r)

1637   (28 Feb.) Reading of the petition drawn up by the committee (above) to the King, pointing out that the King wants all fishing rights and another £20,000 above the £100,000 offered. With an order appointing a new committee to treat with the King's Commissioners, to be headed by the Lord Mayor, Edward Bromfield (other members listed). (Book NN, fol. 97r–98v)

1637   (28 Feb.) Order appointing the Governor, Deputy, Assistants, and Treasurer of the Irish Society. Lord Mayor Bromfield is appointed Governor, with the names of the other officers. (Book NN, fol. 99r)

1637   (9 March) Report by the committee (above) stating that the Companies have spent so much money already that they should surrender to the Crown what fishing and lands they now have, in return for their demands. Order by Council to proceed. (Book NN, fol. 100v)

1637   (21 March) Report by the committee that the above offer was made to the King, but he declared that what he wanted was merely the

£100,000 plus £12,500, and in return the City would get the fishing rights and everything else they demanded. With an order to proceed and for the committee to reach a common agreement with the King's Commissioners. (Book NN, fol. 110v)

1637 (22 June) Report that a resolution was made between the City and the King. The King accepts all the customs, fishing, land and other things offered by the City, and £12,500 in money, and in return accedes to the City's requests. (Book NN, fol. 134r)

1639 (24 Jan.) Enrolment of a letter to the Mayor and the 'late' Governor, Assistants and Deputy of the Irish Society by Sir John Bankes, Attorney General, dated 24 Dec. 1638, asking the Corporation and Society to deliver to the King all records and copies of acts of Common Council concerning the lands of the companies or the Society in Co. Londonderry. With an order of Council to comply with the above. (Book OO, fol. 123r)

1639 (24 Jan.) Order appointing six men (named) to take the accounts of Tristram Beresford, and others (unnamed) 'the cities agents and accomptants in or about the new plantation in the County of London Derry in Ireland'. (Book OO, fol. 123v)

1641 (7 Jan.) Report of the Recorder, stating that the Court of Aldermen appointed a committee to oversee all aspects of the Parliament touching the City's interests, to inform the Common Council of what transpired, and to lobby MPs on the City's behalf. The committee presents to the Council a draft petition to Parliament concerning the City's Irish lands (not recited). With an order approving the petition and allowing it to be submitted to Parliament once it is 'fair written'. (Book PP, fol. 13v)

1641 (31 Jan.) Presentation by the Recorder of a fair copy of the petition to Parliament, read in full, concerning many aspects of the plantation, particularly the City's dispute with the King. With an order to ascribe the names of the Mayor, Alderman, and Burgesses of the City to the petition, and ordering Alderman Wollaston to join the committee. (Book PP, fol. 14r–16r)

1641 (3 July) Report made by the Recorder that the Commons and the King have enquired into the petition, and it looks as though the City may be regranted all its land in Ulster, thus the committee asks for advice in their dealings. With an order to meet to discuss the matter. (Book QQ, fol. 5r)

1641 (21 Oct.) Reading into the Council minutes of the vote in favour of the City taken in the Commons about the City's petition concerning Londonderry, with the full text of the Commons' resolution. (Book QQ, fol. 7r–8r)

1641 (30 Nov.) Various documents recited concerning the entertainments provided by the City on the King's return from Scotland. Also that the King informed the City that with the Commons' vote, Londonderry would be restored to the City. (Book QQ, fol. 11v)

Remembrancia (ref. Remembrancia)

This has received a calendar, *Analytical Index to the Remembrancia 1579–1664*, ed. W.H. and H.C. Overall (London, 1878), which includes numerous references to Ireland and Irish lands. There are numerous documents concerning the levying of troops in the City for Ireland throughout 1580 (pp232–6), and again in 1601 (p245). Similarly, there are a substantial number of items concerning the progress of the Ulster plantation (pp172–5). Otherwise, there are only a few references to Irish vagrants in the City in 1629 (pp340, 362), and a document concerning the appointment of Mr. Auditor Phillips as a Commissioner for Ireland in 1623 (p415).

Reportories of the Court of Aldermen (ref. Rep.)

As with the Letter Books (above) this listing is based on the Record Office's indices. Though the list below is extensive, it should not be treated as complete.

1580	(12 July) Appointment of civic commissioners to make a survey of all the foreigners within the several wards of the City, and to allot out of them the number of 300 men to be sent to the service in Ireland. (Rep. 20, fol. 90)
1580	(29 Sept.) Order for three aldermen to meet that afternoon to take a view of the names of all the foreigners that are certified to provide men for the Irish service. (Rep. 20, fol. 117)
1580	(4 Oct.) The wardens of the several livery companies appointed for the furnishing of 200 soldiers for the war in Ireland (who were to be ready by 3 Oct.), are ordered to pay each soldier 8d per day. (Rep. 20, fol. 117v)
1580	(4 Oct.) The Chamberlain of London is instructed to repair to the Lord Treasurer of England to obtain his lordship's warrant for the repayment of certain sums disbursed by the City for the coat and conduct money of 500 soldiers for service in Ireland. (Rep. 20, fol. 117v)
1585	(27 July) Order that all poor unemployed persons in the City who have been pressed for the Queen's service in Ireland are to be paid 8d a day apiece. (Rep. 21, fol. 197v)
1587	(4 May) Order that two aldermen are to appear before the Privy Council for warrants 'For the conveyance of such Yrishe beggars as remayne w^thin and nere unto thys Cyttie to the Cyttie of Brystoll and thence to procure them to be transported into Ireland'. (Rep. 21, fol. 429v)
1587	(9 May) 'Yt is ordered that all suche Irishe roagues & vagabonds whyche now remayne wythin thys Cyttie and the freedom and lybertyes theareof or w^thin a myle compasse of the same, shalbe presentlye taken up and conveyed to the Cyttie of Brystoll and from thence into Ireland, at the chardge of thys Cyttie'. (Rep. 21, fol. 430v)
1587	(11 July) Appointment of three commissioners to peruse the accounts of Anthony Hall, skinner, touching his charges disbursed in conveying the Irish rogues from London to Bristol. (Rep. 21, fol. 452)
1600	(29 Feb.) Order that William Romney, haberdasher, shall pay unto Sir John Harte the sum of £300 in part payment for the coats and apparel of the soldiers lately sent on the Queen's service into Ireland. (Rep. 25, fol. 56v)
1600	(7 Aug.) Order that 350 men shall be raised by the City and sent to Chester for service in the war in Ireland, as required by the Queen's instructions. (Rep. 25, fol. 132v)

| 1606 | (7 March) William Rodes, who lately served as a drummer under Sir Henry Harrington in Ireland and was impressed in London, shall have the next pension which falls void. (Rep. 27, fol. 167) |

1606 | (7 March) William Rodes, who lately served as a drummer under Sir Henry Harrington in Ireland and was impressed in London, shall have the next pension which falls void. (Rep. 27, fol. 167)

1608 | (8 Sept.) It is ordered that John Gardiner, Treasurer for Martial Causes, shall pay to Jerome Heydon, ironmonger, the sum of £11 16s 6d to be by him given to the Mayor of Chester in recompense for money outlaid in supplying the needs of hose shoes and other necessaries to certain soldiers lately sent from London to embark for Ireland. (Rep. 28, fol. 269v)

1608 | (22 Nov.) The Bridgemasters are ordered to pay to Richard Strongitharne, ironmonger, the sum of £100, parcel of £240 owed to him for arms by him sold to the Committee for Martial Causes for the arming and furnishing of 250 soldiers for service in Ireland. (Rep. 28, fol. 303)

1609 | (1 July) Open reading in the City Court of a project recommended by the Privy Council re a plantation in the north parts of Ireland 'wth motives and reasons to induce and persuade this Cyttye of London to undertake plantation there'; followed by a court order that each livery company should nominate four experienced men to consider the scheme. (Rep. 29, fol. 52v)

1609 | (18 July) Because a committee of aldermen submitted an answer to the Privy Council regarding the proposed Ulster plantation before any discussions were held with the Irish government, order is made that time should be put aside for the preparation of a new answer. (Rep. 29, fol. 61v)

1609 | (22 July) 'Upon conference had wth the Commities appoynted for the plantacon in ireland it is ordered that p'cepts shalbe p'sently sent to the severall companies of this Cittye requiering them to call there companies togeather upon Wensday next to understand what every pticulr man will willingly adventure to the same'. (Rep. 29, fol. 64)

1609 | (22 Aug.) Order that £300 be allowed to the Chamberlain of the City for the costs of four persons appointed on 8 Aug. to survey the land in Ireland. (Rep. 29, fol. 72)

1609 | (28 Nov.) Order re the return from Ireland of John Brode, Robert Treswell, John Mun and John Rowley, the four Commissioners appointed by the Corporation to view the plantation there. The Chamberlain shall pay them a further £100 over and above the £300 already budgeted for their work in Ulster. (Rep. 29, ff 137v–138)

1609 | (30 Nov.) Order that Sir Thomas Bennett and 17 others shall meet at the Guildhall by 2 o'clock this afternoon to confer with the four commissioners lately sent to view the plantation in Ireland. (Rep. 29, fol. 138v)

1609 | (9 Dec.) Whereas the Chamberlain has disbursed £415 9s to the Ulster commissioners, it is ordered that the Bridgemasters of London shall repay him the said sum. (Rep. 29, fol. 149v)

1610 | (23 Jan.) Whereas the sum of £20,000 was by act of Common Council agreed to be disbursed by the City towards the Irish plantation, it is agreed that a new act should be prepared explaining how the money is to be raised by taxes from the companies of the City. (Rep. 29, fol. 164)

1610   (7 Feb.) It is ordered that precepts shall presently be sent to the companies of the City requiring them, before 10 Feb., to bring in a quarter of the money rated on them towards the Ulster plantation. (Rep. 29, fol. 171)

1610   (7 March) Precepts to the several companies to bring in the money as yet unpaid out of the first £5,000 due towards the plantation in Ulster. (Rep. 29, fol. 186v)

1610   (8 May) Edward Barnes and Thomas Thwayte, Wardens of the Company of Mercers, are committed prisoners by the City Court because they have failed to pay the Chamberlain the second instalment of the Irish money. (Rep. 29, fol. 219v)

1610   (5 June) It is ordered that there shall be a Common Council meeting held tomorrow for certain business concerning the plantation in Ireland. (Rep. 29, fol. 231)

1610   (7 June) Imprisonment of Owen Semper and Peter Ash, Wardens of the Company of Cooks, for failing to make payment of the money due for the Irish plantation and the building of new granaries at the Bridewell in London. (Rep. 29, fol. 235v)

1610   (15 June) Imprisonment of Roger Bellowey and Edward Emerson, Wardens of the Brewers Company, for same. (Rep. 29, fol. 250v)

1610   (15 June) Re-imprisonment of Owen Semper for refusing to pay £25 towards the Irish plantation. (Rep. 29, fol. 250v)

1610   (5 July) Imprisonment of Messrs Cockes and Booth, Wardens of the Company of Clothworkers, for same. (Rep. 29, fol. 253v)

1610   (5 July) Imprisonment of Messrs Smith and Langhorne, Wardens of the Company of Salters, for same. (Rep. 29, fol. 254)

1610   (9 July) It is ordered that the Chamberlain shall forthwith deliver £600 to the Treasurer appointed for the Irish business. (Rep. 29, fol. 260v)

1610   (27 July) Whereas at a court held on 19 July last it was ordered that the Chamberlain pay over £600 of the Irish money; now it is decided that he should deduct out of the said money the further sum of £415 9s 0d formerly disbursed to the four Ulster commissioners. (Rep. 29, fol. 264v)

1610   (7 Sept.) Whereas the Chamberlain has disbursed £1,015 9s for Ireland, it is nevertheless this day ordered that the said sum shall be forborne until collection be made of the last £5,000 from the several companies. (Rep. 29, fol. 274v–275)

1611   (9 April) The Chamberlain shall forthwith furnish the Governor appointed for the plantation in Ireland with the sum of £300, £400 or £500 for some few days. (Rep. 30, fol. 97)

1611   (7 June) Forasmuch as Alderman Cockayne, the Governor of the Irish plantation, has out of his own private purse disbursed a great sum of money towards the said plantation, it is ordered that the Chamberlain is to reimburse him in the sum of £986 11s 0d. (Rep. 30, fol. 126v)

1611   (11 June) Governor Cockayne is to be likewise paid the sum of £300 for his costs in effecting the plantation. (Rep. 30, fol. 130)

| 1611 | (19 Sept.) It is awarded that the Chamberlain shall presently lend unto the Governor and Assistants of the Irish plantation the sum of £200 which is to be immediately employed about those affairs. (Rep. 30, fol. 178) |

1611   (24 Oct.) Whereas Henry Smith, salter, late alderman, is charged by the Company of Salters at £33 6s 8d towards the Irish plantation, with which he is aggrieved, it is decided that forasmuch as the said Smith has been a worthy benefactor of the City his charge should be lowered to £20. (Rep. 30, fol. 206v)

1611   (7 Nov.) Order that the Chamberlain shall disburse £400 to the Governor and Assistants of the Irish plantation. (Rep. 30, fol. 212)

1611   (14 Nov.) The Chamberlain is likewise ordered to pay £700 to the same for the same. (Rep. 30, fol. 219v)

1612   (28 Jan.) It is ordered that at the next Common Council the court shall be moved to appoint auditors to audit the accounts concerning the Irish plantation. (Rep. 30, fol. 260v)

1612   (30 Jan.) Robert Fuller, Master of the Barber Surgeons, is imprisoned for refusing to pay the money proportioned upon the Company towards the Ulster plantation. (Rep. 30, fol. 263v)

1612   (12 March) Alderman Smith and Alderman Rotherham are ordered to accompany Alderman Cockayne the Governor, Mr Towres his deputy, and others of the committee appointed for the plantation business in Ireland, to the Star Chamber on Saturday next at 2 o'clock to confer with the King's Commissioners for Ireland about plantation affairs. (Rep. 30, fol. 293)

1612   (16 June) The matters contained in the petition of Rees Coytmore re the service which he is able to perform for the City about the Irish plantation are referred to the hearing of Sir John Summerton, Sir Thomas Middleton and others. (Rep. 30, fol. 331v)

1612   (2 July) The Chamberlain is ordered to pay to Governor Cockayne the sum of £1,000 towards the Irish plantation. (Rep. 30, fol. 344v)

1612   (21 July) The Chamberlain acknowledges receipt of five obligations, including two concerning Alderman Cockayne, the Governor of the plantation, one for £1,080 due on 16 June 1613, the other for £1,080 due on 26 May 1613. (Rep. 30, fol. 357)

1612   (21 July) The Chamberlain is ordered to deliver £100 to Governor Cockayne to add to the total of £1,000 lent hitherto, to be spent on the Irish lands. (Rep. 30, fol. 357)

1612   (15 Sept.) The Chamberlain is ordered to disburse all moneys that should have been taxed in the City upon the Coopers and Brownbakers towards the supply of £10,000 agreed for the Irish plantation. (Rep. 30, fol. 376)

1612   (17 Sept.) At this court William Towerson, skinner, Deputy for the plantation in Ireland, promised either this afternoon or within a few days to repay the Chamberlain the sum of £200, which appeared to be remaining in Towerson's hands after the closing of the account. (Rep. 30, fol. 377v)

1612   (22 Sept.) The Chamberlain acknowledges receipt of £200 from Towerson. (Rep. 30, fol. 378)

1612   (7 Oct.) The Chamberlain is ordered to pay the £200 he received from Towerson over to Mr. Mun, the Treasurer of the Irish plantation. (Rep. 30, fol. 390v)

1612   (19 Nov.) The Recorder of London, Sir Steven Soame, and others are required to meet and advise upon a petition to be presented to the Privy Council re certain plantation matters well known to the said committee. (Rep. 31, fol. 8v)

1612   (15 Dec.) Soame and others are again instructed to confer re the City's grievances concerning the Irish plantation and attend the Privy Council to answer the exceptions taken by the Lords of the Council to the same. (Rep. 31, fol. 21v)

1612   (15 Dec.) It is ordered that a Common Council shall be held on Friday 8 January next to resolve certain matters touching the Irish plantation. (Rep. 31, fol. 22)

1613   (23 Feb.) The City Chamberlain is ordered to forthwith lend to Governor Cockayne or Rowland Backhouse, the Treasurer for the Irish plantation, the sum of £600 to be expended in that service; the same to be allowed against the first moneys that shall be received of the livery companies towards the said colony. (Rep. 31, fol. 49v)

1613   (11 March) Order that Thomas Jones, esq., Mr. Dyes, the City Remembrancer, and Mr Hamlett, clerk, shall be present at the examination of the charter granted by the King to the City for the assurance of the new plantation in Ireland. (Rep. 31, fol. 60v)

1613   (11 March) Order that the Chamberlain shall lend Alderman Cockayne, Governor of the plantation, or the Treasurer, Mr Backhouse, the sum of £1,400 towards the said plantation. (Rep. 31, fol. 60v)

1613   (18 March) Order that Rowland Backhouse, Treasurer for the Irish plantation, shall take care that the charge about the passing of the assurance of the City's charter made by the King will be reasonably and sparingly disbursed; and that 20 nobles be given to Henry Wigmore, clerk to Mr Locksmith, for his pains engrossing the same. (Rep. 31, fol. 67v)

1613   (15 April) Order that the Chamberlain shall lend Governor Cockayne or Treasurer Backhouse £1,000, to be paid as well for the passing and dispatch of the great charter lately granted by the King as for other affairs re the Irish plantation. (rep. 31, fol. 79v)

1613   (18 May) This day an indenture of covenant was sealed with the Common Seal of the City whereby the Mayor and Commonalty do hereafter discharge the Master and Warden of the Company of Coopers of the repayment of £70 imposed upon them towards the plantation in Ireland. (Rep. 31, fol. 99)

1613   (30 July) Upon motion made at this court by certain of the committee appointed for Irish business and upon some other special causes, this court moves that it is thought fit that Clement Mosse of London, solicitor, shall go over into Ireland with Alderman Smyth and Mr Springham to attend them touching the plantation there. (Rep. 31, fol. 124v)

1613   (2 Aug.) This day the masters and wardens of several companies were covenanted to appear in court re the non-payment of their moneys due on 31 May into the Chamber for the 7th and 8th payments towards the plantation; upon appearance, the masters and wardens gave their answers and promised to make payment. (Rep. 31, fol. 148)

1613 (14 Sept.) Order that the Company of Cordwainers shall pay all outstanding money due for the plantation in Ireland before the next session of the court. (rep. 31, fol. 159)

1613 (11 Nov.) The four Wardens of the Cordwainers Company are committed to the Poultry Compter gaol for failing to pay into the Chamber of London all money due towards the Irish plantation. (Rep. 31 pt. 2, fol. 205v)

1613 (11 Nov.) Richard Welch, one of the Wardens of the Company of Fruiterers, is likewise committed for failure to pay same. (Rep. 31 pt. 2, fol. 206)

1614 (14 April) Precept for Irish Money to be forthwith sent to the companies to bring into the Chamber of London all money that should have been paid in February last and is yet unpaid, and the City Chamberlain to lend them money in the meantime to pay bills of exchange. (Rep. 31 pt. 2, fol. 296)

1614 (3 May) William Warman, one of the Wardens of the Cooks Company, is committed to the Newgate gaol for non-payment of moneys due towards the Irish plantation. (Rep. 31 pt. 2, fol. 300v)

1614 (27 Aug.) Upon the humble suit of the wardens of divers companies it is ordered by this court that the officers of each company shall attach the bodies of all persons free of each respective company that shall refuse to pay what they are assessed of towards the Irish plantation, and bring them before the Lord Mayor for contempt. (rep. 31 pt. 2, fol. 389)

1614 (3 Sept.) Whereas at the last Common Council held on 17 Aug., Alderman Smyth was elected Governor of the plantation in Ireland, Mr Stone, Deputy, Mr Backhouse, Treasurer, and seven others, Assistants; the oaths now administered to them shall be entered in the book of oaths. (Rep. 31 pt. 2, fol. 393v)

1614 (3 Sept.) Governor Smyth is lent £300 by the City Chamberlain to be spent about the plantation in Ulster; the sum to be repaid out of the money due from the companies. (Rep. 31 pt. 2, fol. 394)

1614 (13 Sept.) Alderman Leman, Mr Sheriff Bennett and Henry Garraway, lately elected as Assistants to the Society for the new plantation in Ireland, were this day sworn for the due execution of their places. (Rep. 31 pt. 2, fol. 399)

1614 (17 Sept.) John Gore, Maurice Abbott and George Needler, lately elected Assistants of the plantation, were likewise sworn. (Rep. 31 pt. 2, fol. 415)

1614 (11 Oct.) Francis Fuller, Adrian Moore and Thomas Barber, lately elected Assistants, likewise sworn. (Rep. 31 pt. 2, fol. 427)

1614 (10 Nov.) The Master and Wardens of the Plumbers Company are commanded to pay all money assessed on them towards the Irish plantation. (Rep. 32, fol. 5v)

1614 (14 Nov.) The Chamberlain is ordered to lend to the committee for the new plantation in Ireland the sum of £600, to be repaid out of the first moneys that shall be received from the livery companies. (Rep. 32, fol. 7)

1614 (22 Nov.) The Warden and Fellows of the Company of Woodmongers, upon pain of imprisonment, are ordered to pay the moneys they were assessed of towards the Irish plantation. (Rep. 32, fol. 11)

1614 (8 Dec.) Whereas at a Common Council meeting held on 17 Dec. 1613 a division of the lands in Ireland was made into seven several parcels and delivered to the companies, but the several rates at which the lands were valued was not delivered, now for divers considerations and especially to the intent that every company may know how the lands are now valued (which will be a good direction to them in the letting or disposing of their lands, and also so that it shall be known that the several proportions of land were made according to their value and that no company had any injustice in the said division), it is thus ordered that the values of any particular parcel shall be added unto them according to the rate which was set upon them by Alderman Smyth and others who did survey the same, and the same to be entered into the journal of the Common Council and thereupon to be delivered to the several companies. (Rep. 32, fol. 18v)

1615 (4 Jan.) A committee of four aldermen is ordered to meet and call before them the Governor and Assistants of the Irish plantation to discuss the matters in dispute between Sir John Jolles and the said Governor and Assistants. (Rep. 32, fol. 30)

1615 (7 Jan.) The Chamberlain is ordered to pay £400 as a loan to the Governor and Assistants of the plantation, over and above the £600 already lent; the interest rate on the total loan of £1,000 is to be 6%. (Rep. 32, fol. 30v)

1615 (7 Jan.) The Masters and Wardens of the Companies of Fruiterers and Cordwainers are ordered to pay their Irish money as assessed. (Rep. 32, fol. 31)

1615 (11 Jan.) Another committee is appointed to consider the differences between Sir John Jolles and the Governor and Assistants of the plantation in Ireland. (Rep. 32, fol. 33v)

1615 (1 Feb.) George Brasswell, one of the Wardens of the Company of Fruiterers, is committed to prison for failing to pay arrears due towards the Irish plantation. (Rep. 32, fol. 52v)

1615 (2 May) Another committee is appointed to consider the Jolles-Irish plantation dispute. (Rep. 32, fol. 103v)

1615 (23 Aug.) The Chamberlain is ordered to lend £500 for the Irish plantation to Governor Bennett, to be repaid out of the first moneys received towards it from the livery companies. (Rep. 32, fol. 165v)

1615 (31 Aug.) A committee is appointed to consider the cause of the Master and Wardens of the Plumbers Company, who have today promised to pay all arrears due by them towards the Irish plantation. (Rep. 32, fol. 167v)

1615 (7 Sept.) The Chamberlain is ordered to lend the sum of £1,000 to the Governor and Assistants of the plantation, to be disbursed towards the said colony; and to be repaid at an interest rate of 7%. (Rep. 32, fol. 169)

| 1615 | (26 Sept.) The Masters and Wardens of the Companies of Fruiterers, Scriveners and Woodmongers are ordered to appear in court regarding their failure to pay the moneys assessed on them towards the Ulster plantation. (Rep. 32, fol. 180v) |

1615   (20 Oct.) A committee is appointed to consider the cause of those companies that are behind in their payments towards the plantation. (Rep. 32, fol. 192)

1615   (24 Oct.) The chamberlain is ordered to lend a further £200 to Rowland Backhouse, Treasurer of the Irish plantation, at 7% interest. (Rep. 32, fol. 196)

1615   (5 Dec.) Philip Hore, one of the Wardens of the Company of Fruiterers, has promised to pay within the month the sum of £44 due towards the Irish plantation, and £7 due upon the last assessment, or else be committed in default. (Rep. 32, fol. 215v)

1615   (12 Dec.) Simon Kynsland and Samuel Calvert, Account-keeper and Secretary respectively to the Governor and Assistants of the Ulster plantation, were both here in open court sworn for the due execution of their said offices. (Rep. 32, fol. 218v)

1616   (8 Jan.) The Wardens of the Company of Joiners have promised to pay into the Chamber of London all money due by them towards the Irish plantation. (Rep. 32, fol. 226v)

1616   (23 Jan.) The Master and Wardens of the Company of Plumbers shall commit such of their company to prison who refuse to pay what they are assessed of towards the Ulster plantation. (Rep. 32, fol. 235v)

1616   (27 Jan.) Whereas certain complaints have been presented to the King by John Williamson, Recorder of Coleraine, against the proceedings of the City of London's plantation in Ireland, accusing the Governor and Assistants of the same of negligence, so Williamson was today brought before the City Court to certify the truth of his accusations. Captain Edward Diddington and others who lately returned from Coleraine were also present to hear his statement. After likewise hearing the testimony of the aforesaid Governor and Assistants, the court found Williamson's claims to be untrue and frivolous. To prevent any further accusations it is ordered that the Privy Council should be told the facts of the case. (Rep. 32, fol. 252v)

1616   (21 March) Alderman Barkham and Alderman Rotherham, lately elected Assistants of the plantation, were duly sworn into office today. (Rep. 32, fol. 266)

1616   (11 April) John Greene and Thomas Wefframe were likewise sworn in as Assistants. (Rep. 32, fol. 271v)

1616   (18 May) At the request of the Governor and Assistants of the plantation, Clement Mosse was authorised by the court to go into Ireland with the Governor and Matthew Springham to help them in their negotiations for the business there. When called to appear in court, Mosse asked to be spared the journey, but was eventually persuaded to go over. (Rep. 32, fol. 291v)

1616   (18 May) This day the exemplification of the Act of Common Council made to Alderman Probie [Probey] and Mr Springham touching their negotiations in Ireland, having been read and confirmed at the last court, was hereby sealed. (Rep. 32, fol. 292)

1616	(4 June) This day John Evans and two others of his fellow public notaries were imprisoned for failing to pay what they were assessed of towards the Irish plantation; they were committed to the Poultry Compter. (Rep. 32, fol. 296v)
1616	(11 June) The Chamberlain is ordered to pay £54 5s 0d to the Wardens of the Company of Ironmongers, being the rateable part of the moneys disbursed for the Irish plantation due by the Coopers Company, whose part this City has undertaken; the payment is made in recompense for certain building which the Ironmongers had done on their proportion. (Rep. 32, fol. 300)
1616	(20 June) The Chamberlain is ordered to pay the Treasurer of the Irish plantation the sum of £600 as a loan to be expended on affairs there; repayable at 7% interest, the same to be repaid out of the first moneys received from the livery companies. (Rep. 32, fol. 307v)
1616	(25 June) Gabriel Sheriff was called before the court for refusing to pay his due towards the Irish plantation; unless he pays the arrears (£3) he will face imprisonment. (Rep. 32, fol. 312)
1616	(1 July) The Wardens of the Company of Grocers are ordered to deduct out of the sum of £200 due by them towards the Irish plantation the sum of £69 18s 1d allowed them towards the charges by them expended in defence of a suit to the King in a dispute with the Apothecaries. (Rep. 32, fol. 322)
1616	(24 Sept.) The Chamberlain is ordered to lend £600 to Adrian Moore, Treasurer of the Irish plantation, at 8% interest, to be repaid out of the first moneys received from the livery companies. (Rep. 32, fol. 354)
1616	(3 Oct.) The Chamberlain is likewise authorised to lend a further £400 to Treasurer Moore towards the Irish colony, at 7% interest, etc. (Rep. 32, fol. 357v)
1616	(8 Oct.) Alderman William Gore was today sworn as one of the Assistants of the Irish plantation. (Rep. 32, fol. 361)
1616	(17 Oct.) Leonard Stone, grocer, is imprisoned for refusing to pay the money he was assessed of towards the Ulster plantation. (Rep. 32, fol. 367v)
1616	(8 Nov.) The Chamberlain is authorised to lend the Treasurer of the plantation in Ireland so much money as he needs to satisfy bills of exchange for moneys expended in the said plantation (not exceeding £1,700), to be repaid out of the first moneys received of the livery companies at 7% interest. (Rep. 33, fol. 15)
1616	(18 Dec.) Thomas Coventry, Recorder of London, was today sworn in as one of the Assistants of the Irish plantation. (Rep. 33, fol. 28)
1617	(11 Feb.) The Masters and Wardens of the Companies of Scriveners, Barber-Surgeons, Carpenters and Brewers were all warned to pay the moneys due to the Company of Ironmongers towards the Irish plantation. (Rep. 33, fol. 55)
1617	(8 April) Anthony Benn, Recorder of London, was today sworn in as one of the Assistants to the Society for the City's plantation in Ireland. (Rep. 33, fol. 84v)

1617	(20 May) George Travers, one of the Wardens of the Company of Poulterers, was ordered to pay £15 into the Chamber of London, arrears due towards the Irish plantation. (Rep. 33, fol. 106)
1617	(15 Aug.) This day Robert Buck and John Williams were sworn as Assistants for the Irish plantation. (Rep. 33, fol. 156)
1617	(18 Sept.) William Bonham, Roland Healing and John Halsey were likewise sworn. (Rep. 33, fol. 166v)
1618	(28 April) The Chamberlain is authorised to lend £500 towards the Irish plantation at 8% interest, repayment by the usual means. (Rep. 33, fol. 277)
1618	(5 May) Governor Adrian Proby and three of the Assistants of the Irish plantation were today sworn into office. (Rep. 33, fol. 285v)
1618	(7 May) Matthew Springham and three others were likewise sworn as Assistants. (Rep. 33, fol. 288)
1618	(23 May) Rowland Backhouse was today likewise sworn as Auditor for all the accounts of the Irish plantation. (Rep. 33, fol. 308v)
1618	(9 June) Samuel Armitage likewise sworn as an Assistant. (Rep. 33, fol. 319)
1618	(11 June) Martin Bond and Humphrey Harford likewise sworn as Auditors of the Irish plantation accounts. (Rep. 33, fol. 320v)
1618	(12 June) Alderman Hackett likewise sworn as an Assistant for the Irish plantation. (Rep. 33, fol. 322)
1618	(28 Sept.) The Governor and Assistants of the plantation are authorised to receive as a loan out of the Chamber of London the sum of £500 at 8% interest for six months. (Rep. 33, fol. 400v)
1618	(6 Oct.) Richard Martin, Recorder of London, was today sworn as an Assistant for the Irish plantation. (Rep. 33, fol. 403v)
1618	(29 Dec.) Mr Recorder likewise sworn. (Rep. 34, fol. 27)
1619	(5 Jan.) The Chamberlain is ordered to lend the Governor and Assistants of the plantation the sum of £200 at 8% interest for six months. (Rep. 34, fol. 27v)
1619	(7 Sept.) Mr Sheriff Hamersley, Richard Edwards, Jacob Pennington, Thomas Massam, Robert Parkhurst and William Palmer were today all sworn as Assistants to the Irish plantation. (Rep. 34, fol. 197v)
1619	(9 Sept.) William Canning likewise sworn. (Rep. 34, fol. 199v)
1619	(14 Sept.) Christopher Allison likewise sworn. (Rep. 34, fol. 203)
1619	(23 Sept.) Henry Slater likewise sworn. (Rep. 34, fol. 208)
1619	(5 Oct.) Alderman Johnson likewise sworn. (Rep. 34, fol. 212v)
1620	(7 March) The Chamberlain is authorised to seal a letter of attorney to Arthur Brittaine touching the Fishmongers' part of the lands in Ulster for the further managing of the same; he shall also set his hand to a letter from him and others to Mr Downing the late agent there re the previous accounts for the plantation. (Rep. 34, fol. 364)
1620	(8 July) Ralph Pinder, John Grane and Nicholas Crispe were today sworn as Assistants for the Irish plantation. (Rep. 34, fol. 503)

1621   (30 Jan.) Clement Mosse the City Solicitor was likewise sworn as Secretary for the Irish plantation. (Rep. 35, fol. 83v)

1621   (7 March) Alderman Deane, Samuel Goldsmith, John Broade, Peter Bradshaw, John Burrell and Ellis Crispe likewise sworn as Assistants. (Rep. 35, fol. 120v)

1621   (13 March) Christopher Cletherowe likewise sworn as Assistant. (Rep. 35, fol. 130)

1621   (15 March) John Hide likewise sworn. (Rep. 35, fol. 132)

1622   (27 June) John Gore, Alderman Allen and Alderman Dary likewise sworn. (Rep. 36, fol. 182v)

1622   (3 July) Samuel Armitage, Daniel Hills and John Harp likewise sworn. (Rep. 36, fol. 187)

1622   (4 July) Alderman Johnson was today sworn as Governor of the Society for the plantation in Ireland. (Rep. 36, fol. 188)

1622   (7 July) Simon Gibbons sworn as an Assistant. (Rep. 36, fol. 203)

1624   (1 March) Alderman Whitworth, John Highlord, Richard Robbins, Thomas Gwyere and William Whitwell likewise sworn as Assistants. (Rep. 38, fol. 77v)

1624   (2 March) Daniel Gorsuch likewise sworn. (Rep. 38, fol. 79)

1624   (25 May) This day upon reading certain writings from the Lords Commissioners re the demands made for the supply of arms and fortifications in Londonderry, Coleraine, and Castle Culmore, it is thought fit and so ordered by this court that Sir John Lemon [Leman] and ten others – or any five of them – joining with the Committee for the Irish plantation, shall diligently peruse the articles of agreement between the King and the City about the said plantation, and shall consider how to answer every particular of the said demands, and prepare the business in writing for the next meeting of the Common Council. (Rep. 38, fol. 129v)

1625   (3 May) On this day Sir Humphrey Handford was sworn as Governor of the Irish plantation, and Mr Alderman Deane, John Davis, William Essington, James Monger and John Aubrey likewise sworn in as Assistants. (Rep. 39, fol. 183v)

1625   (5 May) William Hanies is likewise sworn as an Assistant. (Rep. 39, fol. 187v)

1625   (1 Dec.) This day, upon the reading of an order of the Privy Council touching the sequestration of the rents and revenues of the lands and tenements of Londonderry, it was thought fit by this court that Alderman Johnson and the Deputy and Committee for the Irish plantation should forthwith consider what hitherto hath been done in answer to the Articles propounded and sent from the Lords regarding the said plantation, and consider what is further fit to be done in answer thereunto, and to prepare the same in time for the next Common Council. Alderman Johnson is entreated to fill the office of Governor of the plantation in place of Sir Humphrey Handford, deceased, until a new one is chosen. (Rep. 40, fol. 36v)

1626   (28 Feb.) Alderman Johnson, Alderman Whitmore, Alderman Raynton, Alderman Freeman and Alderman Parkhurst (or any three of them) are ordered to address themselves to the Earl of

Manchester, Lord President of the Privy Council, about the Irish plantation business. (Rep. 40, fol. 128v)

1626   (5 Sept.) On this day Alderman Parkhurst was sworn as Governor of the plantation in Ireland, and Thomas Langton, William Bowyer, Robert Gray and Richard Peate were likewise sworn as Assistants. (Rep. 40, fol. 350)

1627   (16 Jan.) This day was read the King's letter in recommendation of Captain Bingham for the keeping of Kilmore [i.e. Culmore] Castle in Ireland, now void by the death of Captain Baker; as Bingham has expressed his desire to accept the same, the court hereby grants him the post. (Rep. 41, fol. 74v)

1627   (7 March) Alderman Hammersley and six others (or any four of them) with Mr Stone, one of the City's standing counsel, are appointed to attend upon the Lords Commissioners tomorrow about the Irish business. (Rep. 41, fol. 143v)

1627   (31 May) Alderman Raynton, Alderman Freeman, Alderman Heiling, Alderman Cletheroe, John Wythers and Humphrey Brown were today all sworn as Assistants for the Irish plantation. (Rep. 41, fol. 233v)

1628   (29 March) Symon Lawrence, Roger Hemmings, Richard Davis, Thomas Bewley, William Redding and Thomas Leedam were likewise sworn. (Rep. 42, fol. 139v)

1628   (17 July) Sir Thomas Middleton and eight other members of the committee for the Irish plantation are ordered to attend upon the Privy Council tomorrow at 1 o'clock. (Rep. 42, fol. 243)

1628   (18 Nov.) Sir Heneage Smith and six others ordered to address themselves to the Earl of Marlborough about the sequestration of the rents of the City of London's lands in Ulster. (Rep. 43, fol. 24)

1629   (22 March) Alderman Hodges, Alderman Heylyn, Alderman Ffen, Robert Jefferies, William Middleton, Simon Yeoman, John Wollastone and Roger Drake were sworn as members of the committee for the Irish plantation. (Rep. 43, fol. 130v)

1630   (27 April) It is ordered that Sir Thomas Middleton, Sir Martin Lumley and Sir Robert Dury shall confer together re the affairs of the Irish plantation, and Alderman Parkhurst is likewise ordered to aid them therein. (Rep. 44, fol. 217)

1630   (23 Sept.) Richard Miller and Richard Pigott were sworn as Assistants for the Irish plantation. (Rep. 44, fol. 336v)

1630   (7 Oct.) John Babington was likewise sworn as an Assistant. (Rep. 44, fol. 344)

1630   (19 Oct.) John Hall was likewise sworn. (Rep. 44, fol. 360v)

1630   (20 Oct.) John Dike was likewise sworn. (Rep. 44, fol. 349)

1631   (15 April) Walter Drape was likewise sworn. (Rep. 45, fol. 259v)

1631   (10 July) Whereas Alderman Parkhurst has asked this court for a certificate under the seal of the Custom & Usage of London re the precedence among aldermen, in order to help quieten a dispute lately arisen among the aldermen of Dublin in Ireland, a certificate was this day read in court towards that purpose. (Rep. 45, fol. 448v)

1632	(3 May) Sir Maurice Abbott, alderman, and three others were this day sworn as Assistants for the Irish plantation. (Rep. 46, fol. 182v)
1632	(19 May) Richard Edwards was likewise sworn. (Rep. 46, fol. 202)
1632	(29 May) Richard Woodward was likewise sworn. (Rep. 46, fol. 204v)
1632	(31 May) John Wolverstone and Richard Turner were likewise sworn. (Rep. 46, fol. 211)
1632	(31 July) Statement by the Common Council on behalf of the several companies of Waxhandlers, Founders and Turners, stating how they were appointed with the Company of Haberdashers in the 4th proportion of land in Ulster. (Rep. 46, fol. 329)
1633	(20 March) Alderman Aboy, Mr Cutts, Mr Langley, Mr Hollingshed and others were today sworn as Assistants for the Irish plantation. (Rep. 47, fol. 153v)
1633	(24 April) Order that the City Recorder, Sir James Campbell, and others are to attend upon the Privy Council at 8 o'clock tomorrow morning re the Irish lands purchased by the City. (Rep. 47, fol. 203v)
1633	(30 April) Order that a report be drawn up about the dispute with the Crown over the City's lands in Ulster. (Rep. 47, fol. 206v)
1634	(23 Oct.) Edward Ditchfield, David Edwards and N. Rawlins were today sworn as Assistants for the Irish plantation. (Rep. 49, fol. 12)
1634	(13 Nov.) Mr Sacarroll, Thomas Witherall and Thomas Mustard were likewise sworn. (Rep. 49, fol. 13)
1634	(25 Nov.) Samuel Armitage was likewise sworn. (Rep. 49, fol. 29)
1635	(27 Jan.) Appointment of a committee (headed by Sir George Whitmore) to be present at a hearing of the cause of the Irish plantation tomorrow in the court of Star Chamber. (Rep. 49, fol. 65)
1635	(19 Feb.) The Chamberlain is ordered to pay the sum of £5 12s 0d to the Company of Ironmongers for their costs in the plantation. (Rep. 49, fol. 101)
1638	(25 Jan.) Appointment of the Recorder, Mr Stowe and Mr Pheasant to oversee and aid the companies in the surrender of their patents to the King, according to H.M.'s command. (Rep. 52, fol. 69)
1639	(12 Feb.) Mr Mosse, Controller of the Chamber, today produced the patent for the Irish lands granted by James I, as required by the Attorney General for King Charles's use; the court accordingly orders him to present it to the crown. (Rep. 53, fol. 104)
1641	(4 March) It is ordered that Alderman Pratt and Mr Parner shall this afternoon attend the debate in the House of Commons re the Irish lands. (Rep. 55, fol. 92v)
1641	(7 Oct.) It is ordered that the Chamberlain shall pay the Recorder £100 in consideration of his great pains in pursuing the cause of the Londonderry lands. (Rep. 55, fol. 202)
1641	(11 Nov.) Orders for the raising of £50,000 relief for Protestants in Ireland. (Rep. 55, fol. 223)
1641	(29 Nov.) Orders for the payment of £457 6s 8d into the Chamber of London for the like cause. (Rep. 55, fol. 230v)

1641   (29 Nov.) Order for the payment of £400 to the Victualler of the
            Navy and a further £1,000 to the Treasurer of the Army in Ireland.
            (Rep. 55, fol. 231v)

Records of the Irish Society

A number of items from this collection have been published by the I.M.C. in
T.W. Moody & J.G. Simms (eds.), *The Bishopric of Derry and the Irish Society
of London, 1602–1705*, i (1602–70) (Dublin, 1968).[205] Furthermore, much of this
collection has been microfilmed for the Public Record Office of Northern
Ireland.[206] However, most of the early records of this society were destroyed in
the Great Fire of London of 1666, and in a further fire in the Chamber of London
in 1786. Even so, one important document survived, albeit badly damaged, and is
now under highly restricted access. This is 'The Great Parchment Book' of 1639,
which contains contracts made between the royal commissioners and the tenants
on the lands of the Irish Society and the London Livery Companies in Ulster,
following the forfeiture of the estates to the Crown. There are in total about 165
folios in the document, most of which are extensively fire–damaged and often
illegible. It is now kept in six large boxes, and located at 667E–G.[207]

Though most of the original archives of the Society were destroyed, many
transcripts and other items are to be found amongst their records, as follows:

temp Eliz. I Four photograph copies of the map of Ulster by Baptisto Boazzio.
            (Irish Society Plans (2nd series).5)

c1600–11   Copies made by the Ordnance Office and others of various maps of
            Ulster, part of which is taken from British Library, Cotton Mss,
            Augustus I, Vol.2. (Irish Society Plans (3rd series).19)

1609–18   Volume of transcripts of documents, drawn up as evidence in a case
            of the Skinners Company v. the Irish Society, which includes copies
            of Common Council Orders, letters patent, minute books, deeds,
            correspondence, and other items from unnamed sources concerning
            the Londonderry plantation and the Skinners Company. (935 pages,
            Irish Society/B/5)

1609–1785   Extracts from the Journals of the Common Council, Reportories,
            and other City records concerning the Irish Society. (Irish Society
            Solicitor's Papers, Box 9.8)[208]

1609–1787   Nineteenth century copies of Common Council orders appointing
            the Governors, Deputies, and Assistants of the Irish Society. (Misc.
            Mss. 173.4)[209]

1611   Inquisition at Dungannon, Co. Tyrone. (Irish Society Solicitor's
            Papers, Box 12.6)

1611–1900   List of Governors of the Irish Society. (Research papers 1.26)

1613–49   One volume containing a seventeenth century transcript of James I's
            letters patent to the Irish Society, dated 29 March 1613, with an
            index referring to lands, privileges, powers, courts, liberties, etc.,
            granted to the Society and the Corporation of Londonderry. At the

---

[205] Some of these items can be found at Irish Society, Box 1.6.

[206] P.R.O.N.I. Mic.9A.

[207] Mr. R. Hunter has suggested that the original order of the folios in this book can be deduced from the
1641 rent returns by the King's receivers, Robert Whitfield and Charles Reade, P.R.O. SP 63/259. A copy
of this item is kept in the Record Office to facilitate such work.

[208] There is a similar document for the period 1609–37 in Irish Society Solicitor's Papers, Box 9.11.

[209] There is a similar document at Misc. Mss. 237.8.

end of the volume are five folios of accounts dated 1640–9 of an unnamed timber tradesman and carpenter, which contains numerous payments for the purchase of boards, and receipts for a variety of building works. Following this account is a smaller undated list entitled 'my Cosen Jam. Harrington his account of his expenses', which includes purchases of cloth, buttons, ribbon, and other items. (Irish Society/B/2)[210]

1613–1819   Volume entitled 'An abridgement of the principal matters contained in the Records belonging to the Hon. the Irish Society from its original incorporation till May 1819'. The first half of the volume is concerned with the period prior to 1641, and includes abstracts and references to letters patent, deeds, leases, petitions, court cases, London Common Council decisions, and many other documents.[211] The item is, however, a history and not a catalogue, and tends to merely make reference to the documents rather than transcribe them in full. (322 pages, Irish Society/B/4)

1617   (10 Sept.) Deed of sale by the Irish Society to the Warden and Commonalty of the Mystery of Goldsmiths, of the manor of Goldsmithshall. (Irish Society Solicitor's Papers Box 10.45/2)

c1629   Instructions to John Rowley, agent and receiver of the Irish Society in Ireland. (Irish Society Solicitor's Papers, Box 9.12)

1637–8   (13 Charles I) Partially translated *scire facias* and judgement thereon against the Irish Society and the twelve companies, with a table of analysis of James I's patent to the Society and the proceedings in the case, compiled c1832 [270 fols]. (Irish Society/J/1)

c1637   Draft pardon from the King to the City and the livery companies whereby they were discharged from the judgement of the Court of Star Chamber regarding the forfeiture of their estate. (Misc. Mss. 44.8)

17th cen.   (n.d.) Fragment of an early seventeenth century history of the Mercers' Company's involvement in the Ulster plantation, dealing with events from the beginning of the plantation until the Mercers' grant from the Irish Society on 15 April 1617. It shows that the Mercers paid a total of £1,524 towards the early stage of the plantation. This item is only one folio in length, and numbered pages 1 & 2, and was obviously originally part of a larger work. (Misc. Mss. 55.13)

GREATER LONDON : Dulwich College Library
College Road, London SE21 7LD
Tel: (0181) 693 3601
Fax: (0181) 693 6319

In G.F. Warner's *Catalogue of the MSS and Muniments of Alleyn's College of God's Gift at Dulwich* (London, 1881) the following entry appears in the diary

---

[210] There are many other copies of the 1613 patent in the collection, i.e. Irish Society/B/1; Misc. Mss. 222.3; Misc. Mss. 222.4.

[211] Many of the items in this volume were published in T.W. Moody & J.G. Simms (eds.), *The Bishopric of Derry and the Irish Society of London, 1602–1705*, i (1602–70) (Dublin, 1968).

and account book of Edward Alleyn for the period 29 Sept. 1617 to 1 Oct. 1622 (Ms. 4), under the date 7 July 1622: 'I dind att Detford w^t ye Countes of Kildare'.

GREATER LONDON : English Province of the Society of Jesus
114 Mount Street, London W1Y 6AH
Tel: (0171) 493 7811
Fax: (0171) 495 6685/499 0549

LOOSE ITEMS

1558–96	'Annals of Ireland', giving entries for 1558–72, 1578, 1582–4 and 1590–6. The entries for the years 1573–7, 1579–81, 1585–89 are blank [41 fols]. (19/1/6)
1577–1603	Transcript of 'Magna Supplicia a Persecutoribus aliquot Catholicorum in Hibernia', taken from the Cardwell Transcripts of the Belgian Archives [14 fols]. (Cardwell Transcripts, I, ff 49–62)[212]
1610	'Elucidatio aliqua circa missionem Hibernicanam', being transcripts of documents concerning the Jesuit mission to Ireland in 1610 [6 fols]. (Notes and Fragments – Fr Thorpe, ff. 29–34)
1641	'The Papists Rebellion in Ireland, anno 1641'. The account begins in 1641 and ends in 1643 [c113 pp]. (19/1/6)

GREATER LONDON : Greater London Record Office *
40 Northampton Road, London EC1R 0HB
Tel: (0171) 332 3824
Fax: (0171) 833 9136

LOOSE ITEMS

1562	(10 Jan.) Letter to Lord Robert Dudley, Master of the Queen's Horse, from Alexander Creak of St. Patrick's Dublin, asking his advice on the acceptance of the Bishopric of Meath [Creak was Bishop of Kildare 1560–1564].[213] (P92/SAV/1957)
1599–1600	(28 Dec.–29 May) Accounts of William Okey, Keeper of the Gatehouse Prison, Westminster, for food and lodging of prisoners. Countersigned by the Privy Council. Includes accounts of one Irish prisoner, as follows: 'Bernard O'Donell oweth for his dyett & lodging for 22 weeks at the rate of 10s. the week, £11; for his fuell at 14d the week for 13 weeks, 15s.2d.; for candles at 5d. the week, 5s.5d.; for washing at 4d. the week, 7s.4d. _____ £12 7s. 11d.' (JB/6–7)
1628	Order by Charles I for a tenth of the customs to be paid to Endymion Porter, Esq. (Acc 1128/185/6)
c1641	(29 Aug.) Letter from Lady Elizabeth Dillon to her husband Sir James Dillon (later 3rd Earl of Roscommon), concerning the

---

[212] The original of this is held in the Bibliotheque Royale, Brussels. It is also available on microfilm in Ireland, at N.L.I. n. 562, p. 816. There is a similar transcript in Stonyhurst College, Lancashire (see above).

[213] Creak wrote to Cecil on the same day, regarding the same issue, see E.P. Shirley (ed.), *Original Letters and Papers in Illustration of the History of the Church in Ireland during the Reigns of Edward VI, Mary, and Elizabeth* (London, 1851), pp104–5.

repayment of £100, the surrender of the Scottish army and the disbanding of the English army. (Acc. 2079/G2/1)

COLLECTIONS

Sessions Records

Some of these documents have been published by the Middlesex County Records Society in John Cordy Jeaffreson (ed.), *Middlesex County Records*, Vol. III [Old Series] (London, 1888) which includes one document relating to Ireland (p52) and the Star Chamber case concerning the Londonderry plantation in 1633. However, the vast majority of these records remain unpublished, but a typescript bound catalogue in the Record Office of 'Middlesex Sessions Rolls, Sessions Registers and Gaol Delivery Registers 1607–1612', includes two documents concerning Ireland, *viz*

1609   (20 Dec.) An affidavit concerning Thomas Davies of St. Allhallows the Great, London, clothworker, by his wife, stating that he is unable to appear without endangering his life, since he has gone into Ireland about 'the new planting there'. (Typescript, Vol. 3, p162)

1612   (28 May) Gaol Delivery made at Justice Hall in the Old Bailey, including, 'Not guilty: George Sprewle for stealing divers goods from the Lord Archbishop of Castile in Ireland'. (Typescript, Vol. 9, p223)

GREATER LONDON : Guildhall Library, Manuscripts Section *
Aldermanbury, London EC2P 2EJ
Tel: (0171) 332 1863
Fax: (0171) 600 3384

LOOSE ITEMS

1595   (9 March) Lease by Walter Kenetie [Kennedy] to Launcelot Money, both of Dublin, of lands at 'Oxmantoune Grene' in Dublin. (Ms. 18,776)

1613   (29 March) Translation of the charter granted to the Irish Society by James I [122 pp]. (Ms. 6760)

1637   (15 Aug.) Letters patent of a grant of lands in Cos. Leitrim, Longford and Roscommon to Brian Jones and others. On vellum, with a broken seal of Charles I. (Ms. 18,777)

COLLECTIONS

Archdeaconry Court of London Records (ref. Mss. 9,050–2)

This extensive collection of wills, administrations and other testamentary records has received a detailed catalogue by Marc Fitch (ed.), *Index to Testamentary Records in the Archdeaconry Court of London*, Vol. 1: (1363)–1649 (British Record Society, London, 1979). There are a number of references to Ireland and Irish people, as well as a few wills of Irish persons resident in London.

Baker's Company MSS (ref. Mss. 5,199–5,200)

1610–33   A book of accounts for the Irish estates of the Company of Skinners, 1610–33, giving details of 'Moneys disbursed towards the Plantacion' and 'Repayments made of the same disbursements' (ff 1–25). The volume also contains a 'Copie of the printed Booke, expressing the Condicions wch were to be observed by the Brittish undertakers of the Escheated Landes in Ulster in Ireland [1610]', as well as a copy of the lot which fell to the Company of Skinners upon the division of the City of London's land in Ireland, c1610. Thereafter, the volume has further accounts of moneys collected and paid towards the plantation, 1609-33, and notes regarding an intended lease to Captain Doddington in 1614. At the end there is an early seventeenth century version of the *Life of St. Clement*, with a contemporary drawing of the saint. (Ms. 5,199)

1610-18   A bound volume of transcripts of papers concerning the Ulster estate of the Baker's Company made c1772, beginning with an abstract of the title of the estate of the Skinner's Company, 1610. Thereafter, the volume provides a detailed account of the management of the estate, with copies of the minutes and proceedings of the Skinner's Company, 1610 – Sept., 1618. (Ms. 5,200, pp1-12)

Cook's Company MSS (ref. Ms. 3,115)

1610   Articles between the King and the City of London touching the plantation of the late Earl of Tyrone's lands in the province of Ulster within the realm of Ireland. (fol. 1r)

c1618   Disbursements of the Cook's Company regarding the plantation of Ulster, 1609-18. (fol. 3v)

1628   Rental of the land of the Company of Mercers in Ulster for the half-year ending at the feast of All Saints, 1628, with a certificate of the present state of the lands which mentions how much rent was actually received. (fol. 4v)

1630   (5 Nov.) Endorsed 'In the account of the company of Mercers land & their associates for the plantation in Ireland passed the 5th day of Nov. 1630'. (fol. 7r)

1631   (May) Rental of the Ulster estate of the Company of Mercers, for the half year ending May, 1631. (fol. 7v)

1631   (5 Nov.) The account of the Mercers' Irish estate for 1631. (fol. 7r)

1631-3   Endorsed 'The Irish Account: Rent out of Ireland in the years of Mr John Walthall and Mr Thomas Conles, warders of the company of Mercers, viz for 1631, 1632, 1633', which also includes payments made for the same account for the same years. (fol. 11r)

Fishmonger's Company MSS (various refs.)[214]

1592-1699   The Court Minutes of the Company of Fishmongers. A 26-volume typescript calendar is available for this series inside the Library, and the first three volumes cover the period up to 1647. Volume 1 contains a couple of notices concerning the raising of a loan from the Company towards the furnishing of soldiers bound for Ireland in 1595 and 1598 (Vol. 1, pp83 and 214), and Volume 2 mentions the provision of ammunition for the forts at Coleraine and Derry, etc., in the 1630s (Vol. 2, pp426 and 447). On the whole, however, nearly all of the pre-1641 entries deal with the management of the Fishmongers' estate in Ulster, containing numerous references to their agent and his accounts, as well as the raising of a subscription towards the plantation.

---

[214] Some of these records have been microfilmed for the P.R.O.N.I., Mic.9B.

1618   (20 Oct.) A nineteenth century copy of an indenture of a grant by the Society of the Governor and Assistants of the New Plantation in Ulster to George Downing of Wallworth, Co. Londonderry, gent., of the parcel of land called Ballytemple. (Ms. 7,275)

Grocer's Company MSS (ref. Ms. 9,912)[215]

1618   (18 Oct.) Creation of the manor of Grocers in Ireland by the Society of the Governors & Assistants in London of the new plantation in Ulster. (Ms. 9,912/no.1)

1618   (19 Oct.) Sale and release of the manor of Grocers in Co. Londonderry to the Company of Grocers by the same. (Ms. 9,912/no.2)

Ironmonger's Company MSS (various refs.)

1609-18   Transcript made in 1839 of British Library Add. Ms. 47,807, which contains a report on the Ironmongers' estate in Ulster, a short history of Ireland, the 1609 orders for the plantation and the details of the divisions between the companies. It also includes a survey made on 20 Sept. 1614 of the 7th Portion (the Ironmongers' portion) by Thomas Perkins, with similar details for 1616, and abstracts of company accounts regarding the plantation [87 fols]. (Ms. 17,276)

1609-1832   A lengthy report, drawn up in 1832, concerning the Irish estate of the Ironmongers Company, which deals *inter alia* with the Irish Society and the Irish affairs of the 12 great livery companies between 1609 and 1832. It contains numerous extracts from the Ironmongers' court minutes and correspondence about the manor of Lizard, Co. Londonderry [57 fols]. (Ms. 17,277)

1609-17   Minute Book of the Company of Ironmongers, which contains details of every meeting held by the Board, and includes a great deal of information about the lands in Ulster and how they were set, with occasional mention of the estate rentals and accounts, etc. [174 fols]. (Ms. 17,278/1)

1613-59   The Charter & Memoranda Book of the Irish estate of the Company of Ironmongers (Ms. 17,275), which includes the following :

1609   (May) Decision of the Common Council regarding the proposed plantation of Ulster. (fol. 165)

1613   (29 March) The King's grant that the City of Derry be hereafter an entire county called Londonderry, followed by a recital of the charter of the City of Londonderry, setting out the details of the plantation there. (ff 1–121)

1618   (15 Oct.) Creation of the manor of Lizard, Co. Londonderry. (ff 141 and 172)

1618   (16 Oct.) Grant by the Society of the Governors & Assistants in London of the New Plantation in Ulster of the lands of Ballimoore, etc., in Co. Londonderry, to George Canning. (ff 151 and 172)

1618   (16 Oct.) Grant by the same to William Canning of the town of Balleneffnoigh, Co. Londonderry. (fol. 160)

1618   (16 Oct.) Grant by the same to John Exhill of the town and lands of Talduffe, Co. Londonderry. (fol. 161)

1618   (16 Oct.) Grant by the same to Nathaniel Carrington of the town of Tawne Moore, etc., Co. Londonderry. (fol. 161)

---

[215] *Ibid.*

1618	(16 Oct.) Grant by the same to William Wilkes of land called Fiskall, etc., Co. Londonderry. (fol. 162)
1618	(16 Oct.) Grant by the same to Richard Thokeston of the town of Sissaboy, etc., Co. Londonderry. (fol. 162)
1618	(7 Nov.) A grant by the same to the Company of Ironmongers of an estate in Ireland, etc. (ff 123 and 173)
1619	(11 Aug.) A lease to George Canning of all the estate of the Ironmongers in Londonderry for 41 years at a rent of £150 p.a. (ff 130 and 174)
1623	(1 May) Grant to George Canning of a fair and a weekly market at Aghine. (fol. 134)
1632	(2 Feb.) Letters of attorney to Geoffrey Baker, Henry Flushe and others re lands in Co. Londonderry. (fol. 140)
1641	(26 Aug.) 'The case of London Derry: resolves upon the question'. (fol. 167)

1613–1724 A book of plans of the Ironmongers' Irish estate, comprising coloured maps of Lizard manor, Co. Londonderry, showing the divisions of holdings, 1613–14 and 1724 [1 vol.]. (Ms. 17,298)

1617–1729 A collection of 20 deeds relating to the Ironmongers' Irish estate (Ms. 17,292). Apart from further copies of the creation of the manor of Lizard, and the series of leases to George Canning, Richard Thokeston, William Wilkes and John Exhill in 1618 (as outlined in the entry for Ms. 17,275 above), this collection contains the following items for the pre-1641 period:

1618	(20 Jan.) Letter of attorney granted to George Canning by the Company of Ironmongers. (Ms. 17,292, no.3)
1618	(10 Feb.) Grant, assignment and quitclaim by the Company of Bowyers to the Company of Ironmongers of all their interest in certain lands in Ulster. (ibid, no. 2)
1618	(10 Feb.) Similar grant, assignment and quitclaim by the Company of Fletchers to the Ironmongers. (ibid, no.1)

Mason's Company MSS (ref. Mss. 5,325 and 5,328)

1609–1737 Extracts of orders re the Irish estates of the Company of Masons, giving details of letters, committee decisions, and payments, etc. Approximately 35 items cover the period before 1641. (Ms. 5,325)

1609–15 Mayoral precepts for the Irish estate of the Company of Masons, 1609–15, with receipts for payments to the Chamber of London for the same. This contains 24 items, all of which are receipts of money paid towards the plantation in Ulster. (Ms. 5,328)

St. Paul's Cathedral MSS (ref. Ms. 25,202)[216]

1580	A collection of 20 items relating to the provision by the Dean and Chapter of St. Paul's Cathedral of eight or nine light horsemen to fight in the Queen's service in Ireland in October 1580, as follows:
(1)	Undated and unsigned draft petition to the Privy Council by the Dean and Chapter of St Paul's Cathedral, in the hand of Dean Alexander Nowell, expressing doubts that the horses and armour will appear at Chester on the appointed day, and complaining of the high prices being charged for horses and armour.
(2)	Undated memorandum by an anonymous writer re the shortage of mail and daggers.

---

[216] St. Paul's press mark A55/48.

(3)   (6 Oct.) A letter by Robert Beale, Clerk of the Privy Council, to Dean Nowell, re his dealings with Brian Fitzwilliam over the horses and armour.

(4)   (6 Oct.) Same to same, adding further comments to Fitzwilliam's proposal to fully furnish the horsemen at £20 each.

(5)   (9 Oct.) Same to same, stating that the deal for the horses is completed.

(6)   (9 Oct.) Letter by Robert Tower, Prebendary of Wenlocksbarn, to Dean Nowell, concerning his enquiries for suitable horses for the Irish service.

(7)   Undated and unsigned detailed estimates for the cost of providing eight men with apparel according to the Privy Council's direction, and for the armour for eight light horsemen [3 pp].

(8)   'An estimate what the charges of the furniture of apparrell will stande in for a light horseman beside his horse'.

(9)   An undated note of how much Dean Nowell, Mr. Mullyns, Mr. Walkes and Mr Tower should each pay towards the cost of furnishing the eight horsemen.

(10)   (10–22 Oct.) Account of money laid out for the furniture of eight light horsemen, dated 10 Oct. 1580, with a further note of costs dated 22 Oct.

(11)   Account similar to above.

(12)   A rough draft account similar to above.

(13)   A note of 'Garments delivered to the Tailors for nine men, to whom they were delivered, and what parcels they bee, 1580'.

(14)   A note of apparel for one man.

(15)   A note of costs for making apparel.

(16)   A note that the soldiers Nicholas Wylton and Anthony Warde were commended by their captain, William Russell, and others, to receive apparel from the Dean and Chapter of St. Paul's.

(17)   An undated account by Richard Ratcliffe of expenses in furnishing the soldiers.

(18)   (c11 Oct.) A note of garments received from the tailors for nine soldiers.

(19)   An undated account by Richard Ratcliffe of 'what I have layed oute more than is conteyned in my other bill for the Deane and chapter of Pawles'.

(20)   The names of the nine men furnished by the Dean and Chapter of St. Paul's Cathedral for service in Ireland.

Vintner's Company MSS (ref. Ms. 15,534)

A collection of deeds concerning the Londonderry estate of the Vintners Company between 1619 and 1741, which includes the following pre-1641 items :

1619   (20 April) Lease of the manor of Loughinsholin by the Vintners Company to Baptist Jones of Vintnerstown, Co. Londonderry, esq., for 57 years at a rent of £120 p.a. (Ms. 15,534 LID. 1)

1619   (7 July) Assignment of the above lease by Sir Baptist Jones of Vintnerstown to William Emin, Thomas Baylie and Henry Frith, citizens and vintners, to hold the aforesaid manor in trust for the Vintners Company, which stands bound for Sir Baptist's debt of £1,000 to Elizabeth Feltham of London, widow. (Ms. 15,534 LID. 2)

1625   (21 July) Lease of Loughinsholin manor by the Vintners Company to Henry Conway of Vintnerstown, Co. Londonderry, esq., for 51 years at a rent of £120 p.a. (Ms. 15,534 LID. 3)

GREATER LONDON : House of Lords Record Office

House of Lords, London SW1A 0PW
Tel: (0171) 219 3074
Fax: (0171) 219 2570

The manuscripts of the House of Lords, for the period 1485–1641, have received a comprehensive and detailed calendar by the H.M.C. (*1st Report*, Appendix, pp1–10; *2nd Report*, App., pp106–9; *3rd Report*, App., pp1–36; *4th Report*, App., pp1–163). It is possible that there is further unpublished material relating to Ireland in the Record Office's extensive archive. For an introduction to their collections, see M.F. Bond, *Guide to the Records of Parliament* (London, 1971).

GREATER LONDON : Inner Temple Library

Inner Temple, London EC4Y 7HL
Tel: (0171) 797 8251
Fax: (0171) 797 8178

The H.M.C. detailed a number of items of Irish interest in their report on this archive's holdings, *11th Report*, Appendix VII, pp227–308. This list has been substantially updated and extended in J. Conway Davies, *Catalogue of Manuscripts in the Inner Temple*, 3 vols (Oxford, 1972). The following items concern Ireland:

COLLECTIONS

The Petyt Collection (ref. Petyt)

1296–16th c. 'Evidences and records proving the antiquity and precedency of the Lord Thomas fitz-Morris, Lord and Baron of Kirrie', with extracts from the close rolls of 25 Edward I, and later documents. (Ms. 538, Vol. 44, fol. 47)

1536   (6 May) Commission to Lord Leonard Grey, Lord Deputy of Ireland, to give the King's royal assent in Ireland. (Ms. 538, Vol. 6, fol. 1)

1540–1   Statute of 32 Henry VIII, c. 24, dissolving the Order of St. John of Jerusalem in England and Ireland. (Ms. 536, Vol. 10, fol. 282)

1545–1607 Collection of documents including 'Certain rolls in parchment dated 1545, being an indenture amongst other things touching the erection of a Mint for making of base money in Ireland, remaining in the custody of Sir Thomas Lake, Clerk of the Signet 1607'. Also a letter from the Lord Deputy of Ireland concerning the 'discommodities' arising because of the baseness of the Irish coin, dated 1550, and other documents on the same matter. (Ms. 538, Vol. 29, fol. 22ff)

1552   'A Display of Bastardy', a tract for maintaining the claim of the heir apparent of Sir Thomas Cusacke, sometime Lord Chancellor of Ireland, to his inheritance. With a paper addressed to the Lord Justices of the Irish Exchequer, and a paper addressed to Henry, Earl of Northumberland. (Ms. 538, Vol. 27, fols 149–61)[217]

---

[217] See *C.S.P.I.*, 1509–73, pp126–7.

1566 (12 April) Copy of a letter from Sir Henry Sidney, Lord Deputy of Ireland, to Phillip Sidney, his son, being then at school at Shrewsbury with Mr. Aston. (Ms. 538, Vol. 18, fol. 339)

c1570–91 A petition book containing 250 abstracts (Ms. 538, Vol. 10), which are largely undated, including the following which concern Ireland:

n.d. Thomas, Lord Buckhurst to Lord Deputy Fitzwilliam, regarding title to land and a 'reconciliation'. (fol. 9)

n.d. Petition in favour of the Surveyor General of Ireland. (fol. 11)

n.d. Petition concerning 'your office of Lord Governor of B[antry] in the realm of Ireland'. (fol. 15v)

n.d. Marginal note by Burghley to stay the suit against the sureties of one that is in the Queen's service out of Ireland. (fol. 43v)

n.d. Unsigned petition, probably by Fitzwilliam, to the Queen, for better allowance in consideration of his great charges. Mentions that he was assigned to the office of Treasurer-at-war in Ireland, and twice was Justice of Ireland. Refers to the time when Sir Henry Sidney was Lord Deputy. His charges have been above £2,000, largely as a result of payment from base coin. (fol. 59v)

n.d. Petition to the Queen for a lease in reversion in consideration of 30 years service in Ireland. (fol. 60)

n.d. Petition, parties unknown. 'I am bold upon my small acquaintance with you in Dublin in Ireland, being now in London, at the departure of my nephew Thomas Alford to serve under you in the Low Countries'. (fol. 62)

1575 (1 M[ ]) License for the transportation of yarn out of Ireland by the Queen to Lord Deputy Fitzwilliam. (fol. 67)

n.d. Letter addressed to the Lord Deputy of Ireland, thanking him for remitting a displeasure upon his request. (fol. 70)

1583–1636 Volume (Ms. 538, Vol. 51) containing a number of items concerning Ireland:

1583 (5 June) Letter from the Earl of Desmond to the Earl of Ormond, upon his false report of rebellion. (fol. 49)

1583 (11 Aug.) Letter from Sir Henry Wallop, Vice-Treasurer of Ireland, to the Queen, by way of apology to purge himself of some false rumours which have caused her displeasure. (fol. 49v)

1596 (20 Feb.) Letter to the Lord Deputy which includes an apology from the Lord President of Ireland [sic] about proceedings against Phelim Phlenk. (fol. 125)

c1596 (n.d.) Two letters to the Lord Deputy, one petitioning for a pension of 2s 6d per day. (fol. 126)

c1596–7 Ordinances to be put into execution for the reformation of sundry abuses and disorders used in the musters and payments of the Queen's army in Ireland, dated 39 Elizabeth I. (fol. 128)

1599 'A general bond voluntarily made by the good subjects of the Kingdom of Scotland to the Kings Majesty for the preservation of his person in the pursuit of his undoubted right to the crown of England and Ireland'. (fol. 41)

c1613 (n.d.) Complaint made by the Irish to James I, with a copy of the King's reply for the redress of the wrongs about which they complained. (fol. 143)

1627 (30 April) Speech made by the Lord Primate of Ireland before the Lord Deputy and the Great Assembly at Dublin Castle. (fol. 149)

1634 (15 July) Lord Deputy Wentworth's speech to the Irish Parliament. (fol. 152)

1634–5	Notes of the Acts passed in the Irish Parliament, listed by each of the four sessions. (fol. 158)
c1634–6	List of the archbishops, bishops, earls, viscounts, barons, baronets, counties, rivers, lakes, ports and harbours in Ireland, followed by a note that the royal revenues in Ireland are worth (besides casualties) £52,420 3s 6¼d. Also that the Lord Deputy earns at least £5,864 8s 11d from fees, lands in Kilmainham, rent corn, impost wine and other royal sources. (fol. 160)
1636	(25 June) The effect of Lord Mountnorris's speech at the Castle Chamber in Dublin, upon a case in which he had formerly been sentenced by court martial. (fol. 213)
1599	(15 Nov.) The proclamation of Hugh O'Neill, Earl of Tyrone, dated at Dungarvan. (Ms. 512, Vol. T, ff 259–261v)
1599	(n.d.) Copy of the Queen's letter to the Earl of Essex and the Irish Council, delivered at Dublin after Essex had left for England. (Ms. 538, Vol. 36, fol. 95)
1600	(10 March) Commission to take Sir George Carey's accounts (as Treasurer-at-war, Vice-Treasurer, and General Receiver of Ireland), the commissioners being Sir Thomas Egerton, Lord Buckhurst, the Earl of Nottingham, Sir Robert Cecil, Sir John Fortescue, Sir Robert Periam [Perham?], and Sir George Carey. (Ms. 538, Vol. 6, fol. 77)
1600	(10 March) Commission to enquire into the abuses perpetrated by the late Treasurer of Ireland, Sir Henry Wallop, and by various of his officers and ministers there. The Commissioners appointed are Sir Robert Napper, Chief Baron of the Irish Exchequer, Sir Anthony St. Leger, Sir George Fenton, Francis Gofton (one of the Auditors of Prests), and Richard Sutton (one of the Deputy Auditors of the English Exchequer). (Ms. 538, Vol. 6, fol. 81)
c1600	A copy of John Dymmok's 'A Treatice of Ireland'. (Ms. 538, Vol. 35, fol. 49–69v)[218]
1600–1	In a volume of abstracts of the proceedings in the Commons of England, 43 Elizabeth, and documents relative to those proceedings, is 'The copy of the Spanish General's letter for Ireland written to the Irish Catholics and showed by Mr. Secretary Cecil to the Parliament House on the [blank] day of [blank] at this mark'. (Ms. 537, Vol. 16, fol. 497)
1601	(12 Jan.) Queen's letter for raising 300 soldiers in London for service in Ireland, with a Privy Council letter to the like effect, dated 15 Jan. (Ms. 535, Vol. 2, fol. 371)
1601	(25 Nov.) Warrant to pay the Queen's debts in Ireland since 20 Elizabeth [1577–8], addressed to Lord Buckhurst and others. (Ms. 538, Vol. 6, fol. 113)
1609	(27 April) 'Mr. William Daniel's brief oration to the Irish upon their submission, according to my Lord Deputy's instructions', before the Council. (Ms. 538, Vol. 17, fol. 262)
1628	(8 Dec.) Copy of the apology of Viscount Falkland, Lord Deputy of Ireland, to the Privy Council, dated from Dublin. (Ms. 537, Vol. 27, fol. 341)

---

[218] This has been published by the Irish Archaeological Society, R. Butler (ed.), 'A Treatice of Ireland by John Dymmok', *Tracts Relating to Ireland*, ii (1842).

1629   (14 Feb.) Petition of the English Lords to the King against the precendency of the Irish and Scottish nobility, to which is attached their 'Reasons' dated 7 Feb. 1629. (Ms. 538, Vol. 44, ff 118–27v)

c1629   (n.d.) 'Touching precedency of the nobility of England and the nobility of Scotland and Ireland'. (Ms. 537, Vol. 37, fol. 26v)

1631   (23 April) The arraignment and trial of Mervin, Lord Audley and Earl of Castlehaven, at the King's Bench in Westminster, on charges of rape and sodomy. (Ms. 536, Vol. 8, fol. 352)

c1633   (n.d.) 'Orders made by the Lord Wentworth, Lord Deputy of Ireland, to be observed by his secretaries and Gentleman Ushers', eight articles. (Ms. 538, Vol. 20, fol. 691)

1634   (9 May) Letter from Wentworth to Sir Francis Windebank at Holyhead, written from Dublin Castle, about arrangements for conveying a package to him by post barque. (Ms. 538, Vol. 17, fol. 473)

1638   'Against the Lord Lieutenant [sic] of Ireland'. It begins: 'In our declaration we have joined with Canterbury, the Lord Lieutenant of Ireland, whose malice hath set all his wit and power on work to divide and do mischief against our Kirk and country'. (Ms. 538, Vol. 27, fols 46–51v)

17th cen.   (n.d.) Letter from John Hunt, Sergeant-at-Arms at the English Commons, to Peter Hill, Sergeant-at-Arms attending the Irish Commons, enclosing a list of the usual and accustomed fees in the Parliament in England. (Ms. 538, Vol. 14, fol. 198)

17th cen.   (n.d.) Two legal tracts. i) 'That the legislative power in Ireland doth belong to the King, by the advice of his Parliament of Ireland, not by his Parliament of England'; ii) 'Whether a statute made in the Parliament of England shall be of force in Ireland before it be enacted and approved in the Parliament of Ireland'. (Ms. 538, Vol. 18, fol. 445–8)

Miscellaneous MSS (ref. Miscellaneous)

c1575   (n.d.) Letter from Robert Roll to John Palgrave, Reader of the Inner Temple, stating that 'I am sorry that my Masters of the Bench would appoint no other to be steward of the Reader's drinking. For at this present I am wholly destitute of money by reason of the great charges I was at for my furniture ... If you will appoint me steward to lay out the money I will pay it him when I come out of Ireland again'. (Miscellaneous Ms. 30/8)

1588   Copy of 'Certain Advertisements out of Ireland concerning the losses and distresses happened to the Spanish Navy upon the West Coast of Ireland....' [10 fols]. Imprinted at London, by I. Vantrollier for Richard Field. (Miscellaneous Ms. 147/2)

1641   (9 Nov.) Order of the English House of Commons for the tendering of the oaths to Irish students and other suspected persons. Presumably this refers to students at the Inner Temple.[219]

---

[219] This item could not be located in J. Conway Davies' published catalogue, but was mentioned in the H.M.C. report as part of an unnumbered miscellaneous manuscript, see H.M.C., *11th Report*, App. VII, p307.

GREATER LONDON : Irish Genealogical Research Society Library
82 Eaton Square, London SW1W 9AJ

The Society has collected a large body of manuscript materials, mainly in the form of transcripts of public and private collections. These records have been listed in occasional publications in their journal *Irish Genealogist*, under the title 'Lists of accessions'. See *Irish Genealogist*, i (1937–42), pp28–31, 61–3, 91–4, 126–7, 160–1, 191–3, 224, 289, 322, 349; *ibid*, ii (1943–55), pp290–1, 322–3; *ibid*, iv (1968–73), pp53, 151–2, 375–6. Some transcripts are from privately held archives, making much of the documentation in this repository unique.

GREATER LONDON : Lambeth Palace Library *
Lambeth Palace, London SE1 7JU
Tel: (0171) 928 6222

LOOSE ITEMS

15–17th cen. A volume compiled c1476 containing notes and transcripts of over 50 papal bulls for the church in Ireland; throughout the text are marginal comments by Bishop John Bale of Ossory (c1552–63) and James Ussher, Lord Primate of Ireland (c1625–56). (Ms. 61)

1521   (10 Dec.) A volume entitled 'Clementinae' including notes on the foundation of a Franciscan convent at Roscrea, Co. Tipperary, in 1477. On the verso of the last leaf is a note concerning a conferment made by Maurice Fitzgerald, Archbishop of Cashel, *viz* 'Mem. quod decimo nous die mensis decemb. in domo d^{ni} Will. de Cassill Mauricius dei gr. Cassilens Archiep. conferebat et dedit priman tonsuram Rhoberto et Willemo Stapulton filius Patricii theobaldi Stapulton necnon et Redmundo filio d^{ni} Donati fillii Redmund preceptoris de Clonauly et dispensavit cum quolibet ipsorum ut possit ad minores ordines pervenire et simplex bene(fici)um optinere presentibus tunc Roberto Oflowan et mauricio filio doctoris phisice de Cloyn Philippo Oflowan et me Thoma Ohaly notario publico. A.D. m^o. cccccc^{mo}. xxi. Ind. x pontif. pape Leonis x anno ix'. (Ms. 46)

1585   (12 June) Copy of the last will and testament of Thomas Lancaster, Archbishop of Armagh, with note of probate, transcribed in 1890 by John Sarum from the original manuscript in the Dublin Public Record Office, which was subsequently lost in the 1922 fire. (Ms. 1396)

c1585   Seven letters by English antiquarians about the career of Archbishop Lancaster of Armagh, including more notes taken from published and unpublished sources. (Ms. 1812)

1599   A partial listing of the knights created in Ireland by the Earl of Essex in 1599; only prominent Englishmen are named. (Ms. 1371, fol. 113)

1612   Almanac for the year, calculated for Ireland by William Farmer, 'chirgion & practitioner in the mathematicall artes'. (Ms. 816)

1621   (11 March) Entry in the household accounts of Lady Middlesex to the effect that on this day Lord Chichester stayed to dinner at Chelsea. (Ms. 1228)

1621–2   (21 Jan. 1621–22 Sept. 1622) The household book of Sir Lionel Cranfield, Earl of Middlesex, which includes at the end a full list of all his servants and details of how they entered his service. A gentleman waiter at Chelsea named John Scly was hired on the recommendation of the Earl of Desmond, and Mr Price, the yeoman of the bottles, was likewise put forward by the Lord Deputy of Ireland, Viscount Falkland. In addition, three footmen of the stable – Thomas and Edmund Murphy and Piers Synnott – were also probably of Irish extraction. (Ms. 3361)

1637   (22 March) A volume containing a copy made for Archbishop Laud of the statutes of Trinity College, Dublin [66 pp]. (Ms. 730)

c1640   (n.d.) An Act for the dissolution of all superstitious chantries, guilds and fraternities in the kingdom of Ireland and vesting in the hands of the Crown the houses and fields thereof and all manner of messuages and other things heretofore belonging to them; and for appropriating part of the messuages, lands, tenements, etc., of the Guild of St. Anne within the Church of St. Audon's, Dublin, and the arrears of the same due since the commencement of the leases that were made thereof in the year 1636 by virtue of an act of council in that kingdom, and to continue for 60 years for the maintenance of the prebendary of St. Audon's. (Ms. 640, pp585–629)

COLLECTIONS

Bacon MSS (ref. Mss. 647–662)

1594–5   A volume of the correspondence of Anthony Bacon (Ms. 650), which contains a number of letters by Henry Gosnold, a government agent in Ireland,[220] as follows:

1594   (2 July) Letter from Henry Gosnold to Anthony Standen, thanking him for his kindness and apologising for not saying good-bye when he left London; he was upset at what his new occupation (in Ireland) would hold in store for him. (fol. 223)[221]

1594   (14 Sept.) Letter by Gosnold to Anthony Bacon, from Dublin, discussing his voyage to Ireland and giving his first impressions of the country and its people. He thinks it unlikely that all its inhabitants can be converted. (fol. 265)

1594   (26 Oct.) Same to same, from same, restating his love and friendship for Bacon. (fol. 291)

1594   (n.d.) Same to same, reporting the lack of provisions in Ireland, and praying for help. (fol. 353)

1595   (8 Jan.) Letter from Anthony Standen to Henry Gosnold, thanking Gosnold for remembering him to the Lord Deputy. (fol. 38)

1595   A similar volume of Bacon correspondence (Ms. 652), mainly for 1595, containing the following items of interest:

1595   (4 Oct.) Letter from Lord Deputy Russell to Sir Roger Williams, from Dublin, expressing his thanks for Williams' past kindness and also for his brother's affection. A few days ago a priest was captured at Drogheda while attempting to carry letters from Tyrone into Spain; the Irish chiefs are seeking Spanish help under the false pretence that they have taken up arms to defend the Catholic faith. The danger of a religious rallying cry is very great, for the Irish are a superstitious people and will surely

---

[220] It is worth noting that 2 other volumes in this collection (MSS 649 and 653) contain 12 more letters about Gosnold's activities in 1593 and 1596. Some of these may deal with Ireland, but such was the nature of Gosnold's employment – he was a spy – it is often far from clear where he was.

[221] There is a copy of this letter on fol. 243.

follow the rebels. Russell asks for any intelligence about Spanish interest in Ireland or of secret meetings between Spanish and Irish agents. (fol. 70)

1595 (18 Oct.) Letter from Anthony Bacon to Lord Deputy Russell, stating that he will assist Russell in any way he can. Reports that an English priest recently put ashore in England from Spain and willingly gave details to the Queen and to Bacon of the Spanish plans. The priest has agreed to continue passing on information to Bacon of Spanish activities in England, Ireland and elsewhere; Bacon will send the relevant data on to Russell. (fol. 87)

1595 (22 Nov.) Letter from the Earl of Tyrone to Lord Deputy Russell, from Dungannon, to further his pardon from the Queen. Tyrone is sorry for his past disloyalty; he is willing to pay a fine of 20,000 cows, yield up Blackwater fort, and to receive sheriffs in his territory, as delineated in his letters patent. (fol. 169)

1595 (18 Dec.) Letter from Lord Deputy Russell and the Irish Council to the Earl of Tyrone, proposing a conference with Tyrone and O'Donnell where the two chieftains shall submit and receive pardon for their offences. Complains that Monaghan fort was taken by Tyrone contrary to the terms of the cessation; it must be restored to the Crown. The conference should be held under the Queen's protection at Drogheda, which has better provisions than Dundalk. (fol. 275)

1595 (21 Dec.) Tyrone to the Lord Deputy and Council, stating that he has just received their letter and thanking them for their favour. Tyrone promises that he will refrain from meddling in Monaghan and will try to persuade O'Donnell to attend the coming peace conference. He favours prolonging the cease-fire. (fol. 273)

1595 (21 Dec.) Same to same, agreeing to a date for the peace conference to be held after the Christmas holidays. (fol. 274)

1595–6 Another volume of Bacon correspondence (Ms. 651), including a number of letters re government activities in Ireland, *viz*

1595 (2 Aug.) Letter from Lord Deputy Russell to Sir Roger Williams, from Dublin, thanking him for bringing the need for reinforcements to the Queen's attention. Deals briefly with his 'quick spirited' Frenchman[222] and his disagreements with Sir Richard Bingham, and goes on to discuss the shameful running away of Tyrone's troops. The government gave chase for five miles and killed a few of Tyrone's horse and foot; they would have killed 3,000 or 4,000 on French or Spanish terrain, but in Ireland the bogs and high mountains make such actions impossible. Asks that he be remembered to the Earl of Essex. (ff 291–2)

1596 (20 Jan.) Letter by Sir Henry Wallop and Sir Robert Gardiner to Lord Deputy Russell, reporting their parley with Tyrone and O'Donnell. (ff 5–6)[223]

1596 (21 Jan.) Same to same, enclosing a letter from the Irish chiefs [as below]. (fol. 7)[224]

1596 (21 Jan.) Letter from Tyrone and O'Donnell to the Royal Commissioners, Sir Henry Wallop and Sir Robert Gardiner,

---

[222] This was probably Anthony Standen, a government spy; for details about his earlier activities see Paul E.J. Hammer, 'An Elizabethan Spy Who Came in from the Cold: the Return of Anthony Standen to England in 1593', *Bulletin of the Institute of Historical Research*, lxv (October, 1992).

[223] See *Cal. Carew Mss.*, iii, pp138–9.

[224] *Ibid*, p141.

stating that they have concluded nothing yet and that they dislike the movement of troops in Cavan. (fol. 8)[225]

1596   A similar volume (Ms. 656), containing the following Irish references:

1596   (last of Feb., i.e. 29 Feb.) Letter from Lord Deputy Russell to Anthony Bacon, sending thanks for past favours and stating that he thinks the Crown has lost more men in the last cessation than it would have done in war, and in twice as much time. (fol. 339)

1596   ([ ] March) Letter from the Earl of Essex to Lord Deputy Russell, recommending a number of (un-named) people in Ireland, and bringing the case of Patrick Fox to the Deputy's special attention. (fol. 240)

c1596   (n.d.) 'News from Ireland', relating how the Crown forces under Captain Brett and Captain Chichester were attacked in the Curlews by the O'Connors, the McDermods and Bryan Oge. The royal army succeeded in stealing about 600 cows, losing only 5 men (all loyal Irish), while the rebels lost 22 men. Goes on to say that the Lord Deputy's company has killed over 120 rebels in the Curlews country, and the ensuing list of the dead and prisoners includes such prominent rebels as Bourke McRedmund, Shane Bourke McRedmund, Cough O'Madden, two sons of Owney O'Madden, Ammagh Duffe McLaughlin, Modder O'Madden and Hugh McTirlaugh Roe's son. Also reports that the Lord Deputy has taken Owny O'Madden's castle and put the garrison (being 17 shot) to the sword. (fol. 387)

1596   A similar volume (Ms. 655), with a few items of interest, as follows:
1596   (19 Jan.) The demands of Tyrone and O'Donnell presented to the Royal Commissioners, listing six grievances, beginning with liberty of conscience. (fol. 200)[226]

1596   (25 Jan.) Letter from the Royal Commissioners, Sir Henry Wallop and Sir Robert Gardiner, to the Lord Deputy and Council in Dublin, responding to the demands of Tyrone and O'Donnell. (ff 200v–201r)[227]

1596   (26 Jan.) Articles of agreement reached between the Royal Commissioners and Tyrone and O'Donnell concerning a cessation of arms. (fol. 201v)[228]

1596   (26 Jan.) Letter from Lord Deputy Russell to the Earl of Essex, from Dublin, expressing his concern over Spanish designs in Ireland, and reporting that the Royal Commissioners have received no satisfaction during their conference with the rebel leaders, though they expected no better. Philip O'Reilly has joined the traitors and has been accorded the title 'the O'Reilly' by them; Tyrone has made one Glasney MacCawley 'the Magennis' by tanistry, disinheriting Sir Hugh Magennis's son. Russell is convinced that all the Irish are party to this conspiracy; the country will be lost if he receives no reinforcements or supplies. He wants 300 horse. He has decided to keep the rebels' demand for religious freedom a secret as it is too dangerous to be made public in Ireland. (fol. 194)

---

[225] *Ibid*, p140.

[226] *Ibid*, pp133–4.

[227] *Ibid*, pp147–8.

[228] *Ibid*, p149.

1596   (29 Jan.) Letter from the royal commissioners to the Lord Deputy and Council, reporting problems with O'Donnell. (fol. 202r)[229]

1596   (9 Feb.) Letter from Henry Gosnold to Anthony Bacon, from Dublin (in French), expressing his gratitude for Bacon's previous letter. Reporting the impossible state of affairs in Ireland, and discussing the policy of granting pardons to the rebels. (fol. 7)

1596   A similar volume of Bacon correspondence (Ms. 660), which only includes one item concerning Ireland, *viz*

1596   (8 Dec.) Letter from Lord Deputy Russell to the Earl of Essex, from Dublin Castle, reporting rumours from the merchants of Waterford and New Ross that the Spanish are sending a new armada to Ireland. Tyrone has deployed most of his troops in Armagh and has broken all of his promises. Russell then gives a lengthy description of troop deployments and complains of Sir John Norris and Sir Geoffrey Fenton for feigning illness and doing nothing. (ff 228–9)

Beloe MSS (ref. Mss. 3256–73 & 3391)

1635–7 A volume of the papers of Sir John Bramston, Chief Justice of the King's Bench, 1615–53 (Ms. 3391), which was deposited with the Library by Mr M. Beloe after the main series of Beloe MSS (MSS 3256–73) were received. It contains the following Irish references:

1635   (22 Sept.) A letter from Lord Deputy Wentworth and the Irish Council to Bramston, from Dublin Castle, requiring him to answer the petition of James Spottiswood, Bishop of Clogher, against Lady Elizabeth Bramston re certain lands in Co. Fermanagh. (fol. 6)

1636   (23 Sept.) Letter from Sa: Mayart to Lady Elizabeth Bramston, from Dublin, touching the delivery of a confidential letter. (fol. 20)

1636   (29 Nov.) Letter from Sa: Mayart to Sir John Bramston, from same, re discussions held with the bishops of Derry and Clogher re the renewal of a lease by the latter prelate. (fol. 23)

1637   (4 March) Letter from John Bramhall, Bishop of Derry, to same, from same, re the renewal of a lease by the Bishop of Clogher to Lady Bramston and the unusual circumstances prevailing in Ulster when it was first granted. (fol. 10)

1637   (7 June) Same to same, from same, re the terms arranged with the tenants of the lands leased from the Bishop of Clogher. (fol. 29)

1638   (26 Feb.) Letter from [ ] Willoughby to same, from same, re the value of the lands leased from the Bishop of Clogher. (fol. 27)

1636–41 Another collection of the letters and papers of Sir John Bramston (Ms. 3263), which contains the following items of interest:

1636   (25 Feb.) Letter from Sir William Brabazon, 1st Earl of Meath, to his brother-in-law Sir John Bramston, advising him to purchase certain lands from Cecil Calvert, Lord Baltimore; John Bradbury will write to him more at large on his Irish business. (fol. 4)

1636   (7 May) Same to same, from Kilroderry, re the purchase of a lease from the Bishop of Derry, and describing difficulties in obtaining a place from Sir George Radcliffe. (fol. 13)

1636   (26 Sept.) Same to same, from same, discussing the purchase of lands at Harleston. (fol. 16)

---

[229] *Ibid*, pp158–9.

1638   (2 Sept.) Letter from Lord Deputy Wentworth to same, from Cosha, thanking Bramston for his assistance in a Star Chamber case against Sir Piers Crosby. (fol. 21)

1639   (12 April) Same to same, from Fairwood Park, protesting Wentworth's innocence of the charges brought against him by Sir Piers Crosby, which are to be heard in the Star Chamber next term. (fol. 27)

1641   (5 May) The articles of attainder of the Earl of Strafford, and the opinion of the judges that he was guilty of high treason. (ff 50–1)

1641   (27 June) A letter by the Earl of Meath to Elizabeth, wife of Sir John Bramston, written at Kilroderry, concerning the financial problems of the Earl's son in England, his own losses 'by extreme violence', and a suit against him in the Star Chamber. (fol. 52)

Carew MSS (various refs.)

Though the vast bulk of the Carew MSS were calendared in the nineteenth century by J.S. Brewer and W. Bullen (eds.), *Calendar of the Carew Manuscripts preserved in the Archiepiscopal Library at Lambeth* (6 vols, London, 1867–73), some items in the main Carew series in this archive were omitted and are detailed below (Mss. 606, 626 and 635). Furthermore, in the series of manuscripts entitled 'Lambeth Palace Mss', which cover the first 500 items in this repository, a number of additional items of Carew origin were found. These are also listed below.[230]

c1536–1610 Volume of miscellaneous documents concerning the Kavanaghs and Co. Carlow in general. It includes, amongst many other items, a copy of the 1543 treaty between Lord Deputy St. Leger and the MacMurrough as well as many genealogical abstracts and other material concerning that clan. (Ms. 606)[231]

1559–94   (Easter 1559 – 10 March 1594) A brief collection of such sums of money as were paid out of the Exchequer into Ireland and the Low Countries. (Ms. 247, pt. 1, ff 135r–138v)

1576   A narrative of the death in Ireland of Walter, Earl of Essex, which is followed by 'The song the Earle of Essex sange the night before he died'. (Ms. 250, ff 155r–159v)[232]

1582   (4 Feb.) Memorandum of a lease by the Company of the Battery and Mineworks to Alderman Martin and Mr Mytchell of all the Company's privileges in the realm of Ireland, for a term of 15 years at a rent of £60 p.a., 'which said lease is to be devided into xvi severall ptes to 16 named persons'. (Ms. 291, fol. 51r)

1582   (29 March) An estimate made by the Company of the Battery and Mineworks concerning its privileges in Ireland for mines of gold, silver, quicksilver and copper ore; its lessees, Messrs Martin and

---

[230] The material appearing in the published calendar can be consulted on microfilm in the National Library of Ireland and in the Boole Library, Special Collections, University College, Cork.

[231] The documents from this volume have been used by Kenneth Nicholls, 'The Kavanaghs, 1400–1700', *The Irish Genealogist*, v (1977–9), pp435–47, 573–80, 730–4, *ibid*, vi (1981), pp189–203, and also by Donal Moore, *'English Action, Irish Reaction' The MacMurrough Kavanaghs, 1530–1630* (Maynooth Historical Series, No. 4, 1987).

[232] There is another copy of this item at Ms. 251, ff 231r–238r. The song was published in J.P. Collier (ed.), 'Ancient Biographical Poems', *Camden Miscellany III* (Camden Society Vol. 61, 1854, London), pp19–20.

Mytchell, are expected to deliver 300 tons of copper and other stuffs to the Company. (Ms. 291, fol. 50v)

c1582   (n.d.) Memorandum concerning a good vein of copper ore at a place called Cashel, 'being a myle from Slaine ... and within 5 myles of Tredart [i.e. Drogheda]'. The document goes on to note that the land roundabout belongs to Francis Bath, who keeps two tons of copper ore in his house, and it reports a rumour that further store of copper ore may be found on Lord Slane's estate. (Ms. 291, fol. 52r)

1586–9   (Feb. 1586–March 1589) A note of the forces to be kept in readiness out of certain English counties for Ireland, prepared in Feb. 1586 and sent in March 1589. (Ms. 247, pt. 2, fol. 23r)

1588   (July) Projects on 'the discovery of the Spanishe Navie', including a clause relating that forces should be in readiness for service in Ireland. (Ms. 247, pt. 2, ff 20r–23)

1596   Edmund Spenser's 'View of the present state of Ireland discovered by way of dialogue between Eudoxus and Irenius'. This manuscript is said to contain some variations from the printed version [111 fols]. (Ms. 510)

1599   Laws and orders of war established for the good conduct of the service in Ireland, beginning 'Robert, Earl of Essex & Ewe, Earl Marshall of England ... to all the officers of the Armye and all Colonells, Captens, Officers and Souldiers of Companies, and all her Maties subjects and others, whome these lawes and orders ensuinge respectively and sevrally shall conserve'. (Ms. 247, pt. 2, ff 149r–153v)

1599   Copy of the correspondence between Sir Thomas Egerton, Lord Keeper, and the Earl of Essex while Essex was in Ireland. (Ms. 250, ff 181r–184)[233]

c1600   (n.d.) A project beginning 'It is gen'ally thought meete, That for mayntenance of her Maties warres in Ireland and the good of the Realme of England, there should be base money coyned for that service, Soe that nowe the question is alltogether whether the same should be of meere base money, or of base money wth some small myxture of Silver, And then whether the Sterling money nowe in Ireland should continewe Currant as nowe it dothe'. (Ms. 254, ff 283r–287r)

c1600   (n.d.) 'A proiect for Ireland, howe yor Matie maye give unto the Army theire full paye, wth high contentment, yet be a greate gayner thereby, and save the treasure issued in Ireland from beinge exhausted and exported into other conntreyes'. The author goes on to demonstrate how the minting of silver harps and copper money would work; among other things, he recommends that any soldiers leaving Ireland should pay their wages into the government bank at Dublin before they leave, receiving bills of exchange for use in London at the rate of 25s (Ir) = 19s (stg). (Ms. 254, ff 287r–296v)

c1600   (n.d.) 'A consideracon towchinge the Exchange betwixte England and Ireland, with an answer to such objections as may arise to it.' There is a marginal note [fol. 308v] to the first objection, viz: 'It shalbe a needeles feare for any man to thinke her Matie will coyne

---

[233] This has been printed in T. Birch, *Memoirs of the reign of Queen Elizabeth*, ii (London, 1754), pp384–8

any further quantytie of these new grotes than may suffice ye Irishe exchanges only: because her Maties losses shall exced an hundred fold any particular mans losse, yf her Maties revenewes (wch God forbyd) should be payed in such moneyes'. (Ms. 254, ff 304v–313v)

c1600   (n.d.) Certain objections made by some of the Privy Council appointed by the Queen to consider the project presented to her highness for the easing of the Irish exchanges, to which the projectors make their answers. (Ms. 254, ff 314r–319r)

1601–2   (1 April 1601–31 Dec. 1602) A brief estimate of the Queen's charges in ready money for the army and debts compounded for and paid in Ireland, over and besides victuals, apparel and munition. (Ms. 254, ff 328r–329r)

Eliz. I   (n.d.) A project made by Captain Edmund Hayes for a mint in Ireland, which also discusses the state of Irish trade and customs. (Ms. 254, ff 297r–301v)

Eliz. I   (n.d.) Hayes's discourse for the standard of Ireland, beginning 'The importante Consideracones wch moved her Matie to reforme the moneyes of Ireland and to reduce the same unto the Anncient standard of that conntrey'. (Ms. 254, ff 302r–304r)

Eliz. I   (n.d.) A project for Ireland, wherein the Queen is advised to allow £16,000 (stg) towards the cost of metals and workmen for the coining of £320,000 in base money for the said realm; according to a contemporary table of contents at the front of the volume, the scheme was rejected. (Ms. 254, ff 280v–282v)

Eliz. I   (n.d.) A project for reducing the Irish money from 12d to 8d, beginning 'where the Standard of Ireland is nowe at 3 ounces fyne, wch is after the rate of three pence sterlinge in every shillinge, It maye nowe by a newe proclamacon be ordered that noe man shall take any Coyne of that Standard, but after this rate, the xii^d for viii^d'. (Ms. 254, ff 320v–322r)

Eliz. I   (n.d.) A proclamation against counterfeit money in Ireland, beginning 'A motion for preventinge of Counterfett moneyes made beyonde the Seaes, that they shall not passe the Exchange in Ireland'. (Ms. 254, ff 322v–326v)

Eliz. I   (n.d.) A project for decrying the coin in Ireland, beginning 'It may nowe, by a newe proclamacon be ordered, That noe man shall take any coyne of that Standard, for more than double the inward vallue of sterling silver'. (Ms. 254, ff 326v–328r)

Eliz I   Volume of Irish historical tracts (269 fols), compiled in the sixteenth century. Includes a copy of the Book of Howth made for Mr. Edmund of Limerick City, James Fanning of Waterford, merchant, and William Roche; a contemporary copy of Edmund Campion's 'Two bokes of the historie of Irelande' with marginal notes by Dr. John Dee. Also includes copies of Giraldus Cambrensis, and a chronicle of Irish affairs 1316–70 and 1484–1579 compiled from Campion, Stanihurst and other sources. (Ms. 248)

James I   (n.d.) The opinion of Sir Richard Martin touching the base Irish monies, beginning with 'A false and foolishe accompt'. (Ms. 254, ff 319r–320v)

c1604–15   (n.d.) Copy of an account of the siege of Vobesco in Russia, by Lieutenant William Anderson, dedicated to Sir Arthur Chichester, Lord Deputy of Ireland. (Ms. 250, ff 463r–475) c1614–5   (n.d.) A volume of genealogies of leading Irish families, commencing with O'Brien of Thomond, Concomroe and Inchiquin. This is a very valuable source, as the entries often record marriages, illegitimate children and the dates and causes of death of important Irish lords not mentioned in other sources. (Ms. 626)[234]

c1614–5   (n.d.) Another volume of genealogies, similar to above. (Ms. 635)[235]

1621   (March) The project of Peter French of Galway, alderman, for renewing and establishing a mint in Ireland 'as in former tymes hath beene and may seem very expedient in this tyme of so well a settled peace, wth the meanes of supplying it wth convenient Stoare of Bullion (the materiall livelyhood thereof) from tyme to tyme, and the reasons annexed of the utility and good effects that it will produce'. (Ms. 255, ff 63r–67v)[236]

1627   A brief journal of the Duke of Buckingham's action against the French at the Isle of Rhe near Rochelle, which mentions first, that the Irish forces arrived on Monday 3 Sept. and second, that when the royal army withdrew early in October, the Irish regiment commanded by Sir Piers Crosby marched first in order of retreat. (Ms. 250, ff 431v and 433r)

c1627   Volume of Irish genealogy and heraldry entitled 'All the Erles, Viscounts and Barons of Ireland, created and made by vertue of there Majesties letters patent from King James and King Charles', with coats of arms, crests and mottoes. (Ms. 257)

Court of Faculties Muniment Books[237]

1541   (1 July) James Umfrey, Rector of St. Mary's of Painestown in the diocese of Meath, chaplain to the Lord Deputy of Ireland, Sir Anthony St. Leger, received a dispensation for holding pluralities. (Book A, 1543–9, p31)

1544   (25 Feb.) Thomas Belhouse of Westhamfeld in London diocese, chaplain to the Lady Elizabeth, Countess of Kildare, received a like dispensation. (Book A, 1543–9, p12)

1544   (17 May) Thomas Sweetnam, Vicar of Bradburn in the diocese of Coventry & Lichfield, chaplain to Robert, Bishop of Down & Connor in Ireland, received a like dispensation. (Book A, 1543–9, p27)

1572   (16 June) Richard Nangle, B.A., Vicar of Rathmore in the diocese of Dublin, received a like dispensation. (Book B, 1567–91, p66)

1572   (16 July) John Ball, LL.B., chancellor to Adam Loftus, Archbishop of Dublin, and Archdeacon of Glendalough in St. Patrick's Cathedral, Dublin, received a dispensation to hold a benefice or a cathedral preferment under lawful age or without ordination. (Book B, 1567–91, p11)

---

[234] The N.L.I. microfilm is in very poor condition and is difficult to read. A much better microfilm copy can be consulted in the Boole Library, Special Collections, University College, Cork.

[235] As with the previous entry, the microfilm copy in Cork is superior.

[236] The project is identical to that which French had addressed to the Privy Council two years before on 1 March 1619, which is published in Raymond Gillespie, 'Select Documents XLII: Peter French's petition for an Irish mint, 1619', *Irish Historical Studies*, xxv, no. 100 (Nov. 1987), pp413–20.

[237] The following items make specific reference to Ireland. However, it should be noted that the books also contain a great deal of information on the background of English clerics who came to Ireland.

1574   (20 Aug.) Lawrence Bryan *alias* Brian, perpetual Vicar of Cloncurry in the diocese of Kildare in Ireland, received a dispensation for pluralities. (Book B, 1567–91, p33)

1577   (15 Feb.) Roger Sowdon, B.A., chaplain to Lord Dunsany in Ireland, Vicar of Wynckleigh in the diocese of Exeter, received a dispensation to hold the rectory of Aspington in the same diocese. (Book B, 1567–91, p79)

1578   (17 Sept.) John Roberts, M.A., 'preacher of the word of God', chaplain to Lord Garret Fitzgerald, Rector of Swindon in the diocese of Gloucester, received a dispensation to hold the rectory of Rudford in the same diocese. (Book B, 1567–91, p74)

1591   (2 Aug.) Robert Richardson, B.A., Rector of Chiddeston in the diocese of Winchester, Precentor of Durham Cathedral, Prebendary of Trasgrave and Prebendary of Wexford in the diocese of Ferns in Ireland, received a dispensation for non-residence. (Book B, 1567–91, p20)

Fairhurst MSS (various refs.)

1561   Holograph manuscript by John Bale, Protestant Bishop of Ossory, entitled 'A retourne of James Canceller's raylinge boke upon hys owne heade, called the pathe of obedyence: to teach him hereafter how he shall sedicyously gyve forth a pernicyouse disobedyence against the crowne of thys realme, in stede of true obedyence'. (Ms. 2001)[238]

1580   (29 Sept.) Letter from Elizabeth I to John Whitgift, Bishop of Worcester, requiring the provision of horse and armour by the Bishop, Dean and Chapter and clergy for service in Ireland. (Ms. 2009, fol. 1)

1580   (29 Sept.) Letter from the Privy Council to the same, with instructions for the muster at Chester, including details of equipment to be provided. (Ms. 2009, fol. 3)

1596   (26 Feb.) Letter from Lord Burghley to Archbishop Whitgift, asking for a further certificate of musters of the clergy for service in Ireland to be sent to him. (Ms. 3470, fol. 173)

1596   (4 March) Letter from Archbishop Whitgift to the bishops of the province, requiring the dioceses to find in proportion 300 horsemen and 285 foot to muster at West Chester on 31 March for service in Ireland; equipment of horse and foot described in detail; those without cuirasses may buy them at Chester for 20s; the Irish service 'doeth little lesses importe England then if this realme itself were invaded' [copy]. (Ms. 2009, fol. 64)

1596   (8 March) Letter from William Redman, Bishop of Norwich, to Archbishop Whitgift, stating that musters cannot be raised in time; he can only raise 12 horse; the diocese is overrated 15 muskets and 50 calivers; and he hears of no company being raised by the laity. (Ms. 2009, fol. 66)

1596   (13 March) Letter from Archbishop Whitgift to Francis Willis, Dean of Worcester, and Arthur Purefey, Chancellor of the same, requiring obedience to the Queen's orders for Ireland. The diocese of Worcester has less cause to complain than any other, being only

---

[238] The Catholic writer James Canceller first published his treatise *The Path of obedience* in 1553.

charged with foot, and of the 150 certified only 45 are taken. Fines and sequestrations are to be raised on recalcitrants [copy]. (Ms. 2009, fol. 55)

1596 (13 March) Letter from same to Herbert Westfaling, Bishop of Hereford, asking him to likewise obey the Queen's orders for Ireland, and to deliver certificates of recalcitrants to the Privy Council without delay [copy]. (Ms. 2009, fol. 56)

1596 (13 March) Letter from same to William Chaderton, Bishop of Lincoln, urging him not to delay in forwarding the Irish soldiers, 'because the service is of great importance'; though the burden of the clergy is heavy, the times require it; those absent from the diocese must contribute [copy]. (Ms. 2009, fol. 58)

1596 (1 April) Letter from Archbishop Whitgift to Lord Burghley, sending letters from William James, Dean of Christ Church, and Mr Brincow, *custos spiritualitas*, from whom Whitgift has received a note of the condition of the horses and the names of the horsemen sent to Chester for service in Ireland. Defaulters such as Martin Culpepper, the Warden of New College, should receive an exemplary punishment [draft]. (Ms. 2009, fol. 70)

1596 (1 April) List of horse and foot to be sent to Ireland by each diocese in England. (Ms. 2009, fol. 90)

1596 (11 July) Letter from the Privy Council to Archbishop Whitgift, sending a schedule of dioceses which have sent incomplete or defective horse to Chester, whereby a third of the 300 due to be supplied by the clergy for the Irish wars are wanting; the Council orders that inquiries should be made, especially in the dioceses of Lincoln, Norwich, Llandaff, and all deficiencies must be made good by 10 Aug.; failing that, the sum of 20 marks per horse and £10 per petronel is to paid. (Ms. 2009, fol. 72)

1596 (9 Aug.) Letter from same to same, with directions for payment of sums due for Ireland from defaulting clergy. (Ms. 2009, fol. 74)

1596 (12 Aug.) Account by Sir John Stanhope, Treasurer of the Chamber, of the sums paid by the bishops and deans in England for the provision of horses for Ireland. (Ms. 2009, fol. 76)

1596 (20 Aug.) Letter from Lord Burghley to Archbishop Whitgift, requiring payment of certain sums for Ireland due from the dioceses of Norwich, Lincoln and Ely. (Ms. 2009, fol. 78)

1596 (16 Sept.) Letter from same to same, requiring payment of any sums raised from the clergy, as the Irish campaign is suspended for lack of money. (Ms. 2009, fol. 82)

1596 (2 Oct.) Letter from same to same, concerning the dispatch to Chester by the Bishop of Gloucester of horse instead of money 'contrarie to the corse of the other bishops', who all sent money towards the war in Ireland. (Ms. 2009, fol. 84)

1596 List of horse, petronels, muskets and calivers supplied by each diocese in England towards the war in Ireland. (Ms. 2009, ff 68–9)

1598 (16 July) Letter from the Privy Council to Archbishop Whitgift, requiring the bishops and clergy under his jurisdiction to furnish £30 for each of 20 horse for service in Ireland, the condition of horses supplied last time having been too poor for use; a further 10

	are being raised in York; recusants are to give relief to the bishops. (Ms. 2009, fol. 92)
1598	(18 July) Letter from Archbishop Whitgift [to Richard Bancroft, Bishop of London], informing him that he is assessed at two horses or £60, and the Dean of St. Paul's at £30 [copy]. (Ms. 2009, fol. 94)
1598	(18 July) Letter from same [to Sir Robert Cecil], stating that the clergy will take the new demand hard owing to the late burden of the Irish service and because they have recently paid the first part of a subsidy granted by Parliament in the hope of no more extraordinary charges; the money cannot be raised in the time allowed [copy]. (Ms. 2009, fol. 96)
c1598	Note by Archbishop Whitgift of soldiers raised by the English clergy in 1588 and 1595, and of the same sent to Ireland in 1596 and 1598. (Ms. 2009, ff 88–9)
1599	(Dec.) Statement of prayers said in various London churches for the recovery of the Earl of Essex from sickness that he contracted after his return from Ireland. (Ms. 3470, ff 216–218v)
16th cen.	Inspeximus made in the sixteenth century of the liberties granted to Waterford by Richard II; Latin copy. (Ms. 3475, ff 69–76)
c1600	(n.d.) Proposals for the government of Ireland. (Ms. 3472, ff 11–12)
1601	(7 Oct.) Letter from Elizabeth I to Archbishop Whitgift, requiring the clergy of the diocese of Canterbury to provide 45 light horse for service in Ireland, the Spaniards having landed in Munster. (Ms. 2009, fol. 141)
1601	(7 Oct.) Letter from the Privy Council to same, describing equipment of the horses and men to be provided by the clergy; they are to muster at Bristol; none are more fit to ride than men born in the north. (Ms. 2009, fol. 143)
1601	(after 7 Oct.) Letter from Whitgift to the Lords Lieutenants of the shires, instructing them to find men to ride the horses provided by the clergy for Ireland [copy]. (Ms. 2009, fol. 147)
1601	(9 Oct.) Letter from same to the bishops of the Province of Canterbury, with instructions for raising horses for Ireland [copy]. (Ms. 2009, fol. 149)
1601	(15 Oct.) Letter from the Privy Council to Archbishop Whitgift, stating that the Lords Lieutenant, etc., are, when requested, to provide men to ride the horses supplied by the clergy for the Irish campaign. (Ms. 2009, fol. 145)
1601	(1 Nov.) Letter from Donough O'Brien, 4th Earl of Thomond, to Archbishop Whitgift, complaining about the condition of the horses sent by the clergy. (Ms. 2009, fol. 151)
c1601	(29 Nov., no year given) Letter from Sir Robert Cecil to Archbishop Whitgift, stating that the Queen desires a voluntary contribution from the courts under Whitgift's jurisdiction and from persons of 'spiritual profession' for the war in Ireland about to be undertaken. (Ms. 2009, fol. 123)
1607	(Sept.) Copy of a letter from Ireland to an unidentified member of the Privy Council, giving an account of the flight of the earls of Tyrone and Tyrconnell. (Ms. 3472, fol. 81)

1613	Survey of the diocese of Cork and Ross by William Lyon, Bishop of Cork, Cloyne & Ross, arranged by deaneries, detailing the quality of the incumbent ministers and the condition of their churches. (Ms. 3472, ff 132–155)
1615	(15 Aug.) Letter addressed to Sir Dudley Carleton, English ambassador to Venice, written at Paris by Anthony Sergeans, giving news of overtures to Spain by an Irish friar named Thomas Stronge on behalf of most of the nobility of Munster in that kingdom. (Ms. 3472, fol. 161)
1622	(16 May) Certificate by Jonas Wheeler, Bishop of Ossory, of the state of his diocese, containing a survey of the parishes with the names of the incumbents; the condition of the churches and the value of the livings; notes on individual clergy, indicating their knowledge of Irish; articles of inquiry submitted to the Bishop with his answers; list of institutions since the burning of the records in Bishop Walsh's time;[239] account of lands and rents lost to the see since the accession of James I; account of property recovered, and a list of the grievances of the clergy of the diocese [64 pp]. (Ms. 2013)
1629	(25 April) Letters patent appointing Daniel Molyneux and Adam Ussher to the offices of King-of-Arms and Principal Herald of Ireland respectively. (Ms. 3474, ff 98–101)
1631	(17 July) Draft of a letter by John Selden, written on behalf of the Countess of Kent, to John Holles, 1st Earl of Clare, re private affairs. (Ms. 3513, fol. 14)
1631	Draft of a letter by John Selden, likewise written on the Countess of Kent's behalf, to Richard Burke, Earl of Clanricard & St. Albans, regarding the tenants of a mill in the forest of Dean. (Ms. 3513, fol. 13)
1636	(12 Feb. and 25 May) Orders for the payment of ship money to William Raylton, agent of the Lord Deputy, by Irish noblemen sent out of Ireland to reside in England, for two ships to guard the coast of Ireland. (Ms. 3472, fol. 241)
1638	(28 May) Letter by James Ussher, Archbishop of Armagh, to Henry Bourchier, 5th Earl of Bath, alluding to the delay in publishing *Britannicarum ecclesiarum antiquitates* because the printer, a Scot, ran away; goes on to discuss the loan of a manuscript from Sir Thomas Cotton and the publication of the works of Matthew Paris. (Ms. 2004, fol. 47)
1640	Memorandum re proceedings to be taken in 1648 by the Sheriff of Sussex against Richard, 1st Viscount Lumley of Waterford, for non-payment of subsidies in Ireland as demanded by the parliament held in 1640; Latin copy. (Ms. 3474, ff 138–53)
17th cen.	Notes by Sir Matthew Hale on classical and biblical chronology taken from manuscripts in the possession of James Ussher, Archbishop of Armagh [90 ff]. (Ms. 3487)

Gibson MSS (various refs.)

c1591	(n.d.) Petition by Morgan Colman for a continuation of his assistance; outlines his services since 1571 as writer of the Queen's letters, secretary to Sir William Drury and others in Ireland, and to

---

[239] Nicholas Walsh, Bishop of Ossory 1578–85.

Lord Willoughby in the Low Countries. Endorsed 'The Lord Keeper'.[240] (Ms. 932, fol. 33)

c1593   (n.d.) Copy of the terms by which an Irish rebel in Connaught agreed to submit to the Crown; refers to a lease made to Sir Thomas L'Estrange of the island of Aran, of which eight or more years have expired. Endorsed 'certaine demandes of a Traitor'. (Ms. 941, fol. 60)

c1596   (n.d.) Spanish copy of a letter from Juan d'Idiaquez, Secretary of State to Philip II, concerning affairs in England, Scotland and Ireland. (Ms. 941, fol. 146)

c1620   (n.d.) A list of the composition of the Committees for Irish Affairs, with the days and times of meeting. (Ms. 930, fol. 98)

1628   (8 Dec.) A letter by Lord Deputy Falkland to the Privy Council, written at Dublin Castle [5 ff]. (Ms. 929, fol. 59)[241]

1632   (23 June) The autobiography of Sir Richard Boyle, 1st Earl of Cork, recording his experiences down to his appointment as Lord Treasurer of Ireland in 1631 [3 ff]. (Ms. 929, ff 132–4)

1639   (7 Sept.) Proceedings at the Court of Castle Chamber, Dublin, for the censure of Henry Stewart and four others for refusing to take the oath for Scots living in Ireland. (Ms. 936, ff 213r–214r)[242]

Laud MSS (ref. Ms. 943)

1631   (2 Sept.) A letter to Laud by Mr Attorney William Noy re the recovery of the rectories and tithes in Ireland. (Ms. 943, pp529–34)

1635   An exact account of the improvements of the state of the Church of Ireland within the province of Armagh and the diocese of Cork since Sir Thomas Wentworth arrived as Lord Deputy; sent by Wentworth to Archbishop Laud. There are accounts for the dioceses of Clogher, Dromore, Kilmore, Ardagh, Derry, Raphoe, Down, Connor and Cork [part of Ms. missing]. (Ms. 943, pp523–8)

1637   (21 March) Letter by Archbishop Laud (as Chancellor of the University of Dublin) to Lord Deputy Wentworth, concerning the new charter and statutes procured and sent to the University. (Ms. 943, pp519–22)

1639   (22 Jan.) A full account of the improvements of the bishoprics and livings within the province of Armagh in Ireland, from the arrival of Lord Deputy Wentworth in 1633 to the end of 1638, with rentals of the several bishoprics at that time; sent to Laud by John Bramhall, Bishop of Derry. (Ms. 943, pp535–54)

Shrewsbury & Talbot MSS (ref. Mss. 694–710 & 3192–3206)

This collection is divided into two sections. The first, MSS 694–710, deals exclusively with the papers of the earls of Shrewsbury from the middle ages through to the seventeenth century; it was published as H.M.C., *Calendar of the*

---

[240] Probably Sir John Pickering, in whose service Colman was employed.

[241] Printed in J.T. Gilbert, *History of the Irish Confederation*, i, pp210–17.

[242] See *C.S.P.I.*, 1633–47, pp222, 251 and 325–6. Ms. 936 also contains a great many copies of documents by Francis Bacon including his letters to Thomas Jones, Archbishop of Dublin in 1618 (fol. 93) and Sir William Jones, Chief Justice in 1618 (fol. 94), both of which have been published in J. Spedding, R.L. Ellis, et. al. (eds.) *Works of Francis Bacon* (7 vols, London, 1857–74).

Shrewsbury & Talbot Papers, Vol. I: Shrewsbury MSS, ed. C. Jamison (London, 1966), and it contains a number of items of Irish interest, most notably some letters dealing with Thomas Butler, 10th Earl of Ormond. The second section, MSS 3192–3206, is devoted instead to the Talbot papers. These were previously held in the College of Arms, and were calendared as H.M.C., *Calendar of the Shrewsbury & Talbot Papers, Vol. II: Talbot MSS*, ed. G.R. Batho (London, 1971).

Wharton Mss (Mss. 577–595)

1555	(7 June) A bull of Pope Paul IV, 'Papae de erectione Hiberniae in Regnum'. (Ms. 577, pp84–5)
1555	(15 Oct.) Another bull of same, 'extendens Legationem Reginaldi Poli Cardinalis et quaecunque alia Legationes pro Regno Anglia datae ad Renum Hiberniae'. (Ms. 577, pp85–6)
1601	(20 Jan.) 'Litera Cynthi Cardinalis S. Georgii ad Ugonem Onaslium Ducem Exercitus Catholici in Hibernia'. (Ms. 577, pp86–7)
1601	(12 July) A bull of Pope Clement VIII, granting an indulgence to those who go in devotion to St. Gobonet's church in Muskerry, Co. Cork. (Ms. 577, pp87–8)
1623	Orders and directions of James I concerning the state of the Church of Ireland, its possessions, free schools, those of its lands that are given to charitable uses, the maintenance of its clergy, etc., in 39 articles. (Ms. 577, pp213–21)
1634	The Canons of the Synod of Dublin held in 1634; printed at Dublin in 1635. (Ms. 595, pp119–22)
17th cen.	(n.d.) 'Epistola William Bedell, Episcopi Kilmore, ad Gasporem (sic) Despotinum de Praedicationibus Jesuitarum apud Sinenses ...' (Ms. 595, pp55–6)

GREATER LONDON : Lincoln's Inn Library
Holborn, London WC2A 3TN
Tel: (0171) 242 4371
Fax: (0171) 831 1839

LOOSE ITEMS

1639	'Declaration of the House of Parliament of Ireland, 12 March 1638'.[243] (Misc. Ms. 366)

COLLECTIONS

The Hale MSS (ref. Hale Mss)

These were the private papers and manuscripts of Sir Matthew Hale, Chief Justice of the King's Bench, which he bequeathed to the Society in his will. They include many of John Selden's volumes. The following are of Irish interest :

Edward VI	Account of proceedings in the reign of Edward VI, concerning the Prior and Convent of Holy Trinity, Dublin. (Hale Ms. 42)[244]

---

[243] This date must be incorrect, as no parliament was sitting in Ireland in 1638–9.

[244] This item is mentioned in Hayes, *Sources*.

1618–9	Account of the censure of Verdon, a priest in Ireland, for scandalous words concerning the King, 16° James I. (Hale Ms. 11, Art. 21)
c1628	'The reasons used on the behalf of the rt. hon. George Earl of Shrewsbury and Waterford to prove that Sir Richard Lumley, knt., being lately created Viscount Lumley of Waterford, may not enjoy that title without wrong to the said Earl'. (Hale Ms. 12, Art. 48)
c1628	'The case between George Talbot Earl of Shrewsbury and Sir Richard Lumlie Viscount Lumley of Waterford, upon a reference to the Earl of Arundel, earl Marshal of England, and other commissioners'. (Hale Ms. 83, fol. 295)
1634	(9 April) Writ from Thomas, Viscount Wentworth, Lord Deputy of Ireland, transmitting into the Court of Chancery of England certain bills of things proposed in the next parliament in Ireland. (Hale Ms. 83, Art. 16, fol.102v)
17th cen.	A volume or common-place book of 'record matter' and antiquarian legal documents by John Selden. They are catalogued under various headings, including a section on Ireland, victuals for war, etc. Selden's notes are invaluable material for the study of law, as he often furnishes extra information regarding the published statutes that may not be available elsewhere. He also draws attention to some unpublished decisions, many of which have been lost. (Hale Ms. 86)
17th cen.	A geographical treatise of all the countries then known, 'Divinis et humanis rebus Julius Caesar singulariter instructus', with details on Ireland and Britain [21 fols]. (Hale Ms. 73, Art.3)

GREATER LONDON : National Maritime Museum *
Romney Road, Greenwich, London SE10 9NF
Tel: (0181) 858 4422 ext. 6722/6691
Fax: (0181) 312 6632

LOOSE ITEMS

1601	(13 Oct.) Letter from the Privy Council to John Temple. Discusses the recent arrival of the Spanish at Kinsale and notes that the Queen has ordered the raising of 5,000 men in England to go to Ireland to meet this threat. The Queen has also commanded that certain men of sufficient means should provide horsemen at their own charge, to save the Exchequer the cost. Thus Temple is ordered to furnish one horseman with a horse, and to send him to Bristol, to be there by 28 Oct. At the end of the letter, the Privy Council gives precise details of what Temple is to supply, *viz* 'A sufficient light horse or guelding, fitted with a morocco sadle of buffe or other good lether, and the rest of the furniture therto agreable, and that the man to serve on him to be armed with a good Curasse, and Caske, a Petronell furnished, a good swoord and dagger, and a horsmans cote of good cloth.' (AGC/6/1)
1601	A volume of naval notes by Sir Robert Cotton, including a transcript of the orders made by Elizabeth I to withstand the Spanish invasion of Ireland; she imposed a charge of horse and furniture upon the nobility and gentry and others of her ablest subjects 'wch was willingly p'formed accordingly by all'. (PLA 2, p.4)

1625   A list of the King's fleet in 1625, which includes details of a ship commanded by Captain Gilbert of Valentia, *The Reformation.* (PLA/P/17)

COLLECTIONS

Central Administration Documents (ref. CAD)

1598–9   Ordnance Office Accounts (CAD/C/3), unfoliated, with the following references to Ireland,

1599   (12 Jan.) A debenture made unto Richard Lentall for providing provisions, furnishings, etc. (listed in detail) to the ship called *The Antelope*, ready to sail to the coast of Ireland, under H.M.'s orders. Total £17 11s 8d.

1599   (12 Jan.) A debenture made unto Thomas Lyncon, as above for the ships called *The Cramona*, *The Adventure*, *The Charles*, *The Moon* and *The Some*. Total £30 16s 9d.

1599   (28 Jan.) A debenture made unto John Younge, master of a hoye called *The Gift of God*, for carrying powder and shott from the Tower warf to *The Antelope* and *The Adventure*. Total 33s 4d.

1599   (9 Feb.) Received from William Megges of London, merchant, lead for use as munition and shot in Ireland, worth £118 17s.

1599   (9 Feb.) Received from Henry Travers, servant unto William Tavendish, lead for like use in Ireland, worth £282 22d.

1599   (9 Feb.) Received from Richard Sleigh of London, merchant, lead for like use in Ireland, worth £139 18s 7d.

1599   (9 Feb.) Received from Nathaniel Wary of London, merchant, lead for like use in Ireland, worth £55 5s 10d.

1599   (9 Feb.) Received from John Slanye of London, merchant, lead for like use in Ireland, worth £116 14s 7d.

1599   (9 Feb.) Received from William Walltall of London, merchant, lead for like use in Ireland, worth £237 10s.

1599   (10 Feb.) Received from Adam Wood various types of boards and timber (listed in detail) for use as munitions in Ireland, worth £63 6s 8d.

1599   (10 Feb.) Received from Robert Savage of London, merchant, various types of boards and timber (listed in detail) for use as munitions in Ireland, worth £309.

1599   (10 Feb.) Received from Edmond Nevyll of London, merchant, two tons of English and Spanish Iron for use as munitions in Ireland, worth £26 13s 4d.

1599   (10 Feb.) Received from William Kettle, collarmaker, horse harnesses and white leather hides (listed in detail) for use in Ireland, worth £16 6s 6d.

Dartmouth Collection: Maps (ref. P/49)

These records form part of the archive of George Legg, Lord Dartmouth, and include two volumes, in several hands, of maps, plans and surveys of Ireland, dated 1580–1673, as follows:

1580   Water colour map of the 'battle of Smerwick', showing tents, ships and positions. (P/49/31)

c1587   Rough pen and ink sketch, with a description of Muskerry and other places, with some names of proprietors. (P/49/24)

1589   (28 Aug.) Survey of parts of Cos. Cork and Waterford for the Commissioners for the Munster plantation. Water colour on several sheets stitched together, giving place names, acreages, and names of some of the inhabitants. (P/49/29)

1589	(28 Aug.) Similar survey of Inchiquin 'containing in total 5,303 acres', in water colour, giving similar details. (P/49/39)
c1589	Similar survey of lands claimed by William Carter in right of his brother, Arthur, by a lease from Sir William Drury, in Co. Limerick, in water colour, with the like details as above. (P/49/23)
c1589	Map of the Munster plantation in colour, on vellum, showing the estates of the undertakers. (P/49/20)
c1589	Map of the Munster plantation in colour, on paper, showing the undertakers' estates, with a list of undertakers at the side. (P/49/22)
c1589	Unfinished water colour map of the Munster plantation, showing estates granted to undertakers. (P/49/27)
c1589	Unfinished colour map of Munster, giving details of fields and woods. (P/49/18)
c1590	Unfinished map of the north of Ireland, which was drawn to show the importance of settling a stronghold in Ulster against the activities of the Scottish. (P/49/5)
1594	Water colour map of Co. Fermanagh, by John Thomas, with place names and other details. (P/49/21)
c1595	Detailed water colour map of the north-east of Ireland, particularly 'that part of Ulster commonly called the Clande Boyes and for the great woods of the Dufferine', showing the necessity to have a garrison in the vicinity to stop Scottish mercenaries arriving. (P/49/25)
c1595	Unfinished coloured map of the north of Ireland, showing parts of Connaught, and marking the battle of Beleek (1594). (P/49/9)
1599	Pen and ink map of the Earl of Essex's Munster journey, showing the position of tents and giving the names of the leaders of the army. (P/49/37)
1599	Pen and ink map of the Earl of Essex's northern journey, with the same details as above. (P/49/34)
1599	Water colour map of Essex's northern journey, as above, but with fewer names. (P/49/35)
c1600	Unfinished coloured chart of the coast of the north of Ireland. (P/49/6)
c1600	Unfinished colour map of Lough Erne. (P/49/8)
16th cen.	Unfinished coloured map of the south-west coast, giving some place-names. (P/49/6a)
1601	Pen and ink map of the siege of Kinsale, giving the depth of the channel and the position of the English ships during the siege. (P/49/17)
c1601	Pen and ink plan of Kinsale (with some water colour) by Johannis Mansell, with key showing Princes Gate, St. Nicholas Gate, Cork Gate, the Church, the Market, the English town, the Fort, the Blockhouse, and other features. (P/49/16)

c1603   Water colour map with some decorations, entitled 'A true description of the Northwest parts of Ireland wherin is the most part of O'Donnell's country – part of Tirones, part of McGuyres, part of O'Rorkes, all the county of Sligo – part of McWilliams and part of the county of Roscommon truly collected and observed by Captain John Baxter, finished by Baptista Boazio'. (P/49/7)

General Records (ref. REC)

1592   (5 Feb.) Instructions from the Lord High Admiral to Captain Humphrey Reynolds, concerning an expedition to Ireland with the object of suppressing piracy, and arresting the ringleaders. Signed by Nottingham. (REC/1/8)

1599   (14 Feb.) Instructions from the Officers of the Navy, by order of Sir Thomas Mansfield, to Charles Blessington, Deputy Treasurer and Muster Master to the fleet setting out for Ireland, requiring him to take a muster of men in *The Antelope, The Adventure, The Charles, The Popinjay* and *The Moon*, with their flyboats. (REC/1/13)

1599   (14 Feb.) Additions to Charles Blessington's orders. i) To take and send to the officers of the Navy musters of the mariners of the 16 transports of munitions to Ireland, of 14 transports of soldiers from the Low Countries, and of mariners and boat carpenters of four other vessels. ii) To take note of the time these men spent in transport, their discharge of munitions, and to pay them accordingly, as they may cross to Rochelle, Bayonne or Bordeaux for their own benefit on the return journey. (REC/1/14)

1609   (13 Oct.) Warrant issued by Nottingham, Lord High Admiral, to Captain Humphrey Reynolds of H.M.'s pinnace, *The Moon*, ordering him to proceed to Ireland, and there arrest and imprison all such persons as have supplied, traded with, or helped pirates (near Baltimore creek haven or any other part) and charging all J.P.s and other local officers to assist him in this matter. (REC/1/32)

1610   (26 Jan.) Directions from Nottingham, Lord High Admiral, to Captain Humphrey Reynolds at Dartmouth, advising him that on the recommendation of Sir William Monson, he has been chosen to proceed to Ireland with [blank] months victuals and to return speedily to be ready for further employment. (REC/1/31)

c1640   (Nov.) An answer to the Lords Commissioners concerning certain accusations and proposals sent by the Lord Lieutenant of Ireland, giving, i) Accusations of dishonesty and corruption against H.M.'s ministers in England and certain purveyors in Ireland, with answers to same; ii) Suggestions for the defence of Ireland and for having a dockyard at Kinsale, with answers showing their impracticability. (REC/1/59)

General Series (ref. SER)

Eliz. I   A volume of miscellaneous copies of documents about the English Navy (SER. 135), which contains three items of interest:

  1588   A brief note of the English preparations against the Spanish Armada, which mentions that Sir Richard Bingham, Lord President of Connaught, was included on a special Council of War. (p.17)

  c1590   (n.d.) Instructions for Sir Richard Luson, stating that because the King of Spain intends to despatch a fleet to Ireland, Luson is directed to have special care 'to hinder the quiett passage of any such ffleete for yt kingdom [i.e. Ireland]'. (p.15)

c1594   (n.d.) Copy of the Queen's commission to Sir Francis Drake and the Lord President of Munster, Sir John Norris, to attack the Spanish at sea. (pp 22–3)

1618   Commissioners' report on the state of the Navy, which includes mention 'That the *Primrose* in Ireland maie be sold or disposed so as the services on that coast maie not be increased by her means'. (SER/133 fol. 16r)[245]

Leconfield MSS (ref. LEC)

Much of this collection has been published, including the documentation concerning Ireland. It includes a copy of Sir Henry Mainwaring's 'Of the beginnings, practices, and suppression of Pirates' written in 1617, which contains frequent mention of Irish piracy and the use of the Irish coastline by pirates in general. It has appeared in print as part of a larger work on Sir Henry, which includes an extensive biographical study, G.E. Manwaring & W.G. Perrin (eds.), *The Life and Works of Sir Henry Mainwaring* (2 vols, Navy Records Society Vols. 54 & 56, 1920–1).[246] The writings of Sir William Monson are also to be found in this collection, including a lengthy account of Sir Richard Leveson's command of the Navy off the Irish coast, particularly Kinsale, in 1601. This has also been published in M. Oppenheim (ed.), *The Naval Tracts of Sir William Monson in Six Books* (2 vols, Navy Records Society Vols. 22–3, 1902).[247]

Phillipps MSS (ref. PHB)

This collection, part of the manuscripts of Sir Thomas Phillips of Cheltenham, include a great many Spanish documents concerning the Armada in 1588. These items have been translated and published by George P.B. Naish (ed.), 'The Spanish Armada', *The Naval Miscellany IV* (Navy Records Society Vol. 92, 1952), pp1–84. They contain a copy of a letter from Phillip II to Cardinal Archduke Albert, 14 Sept. 1587, which discusses the impracticability of an Irish invasion because the English are guarding the coast with German cavalry. It goes on to state that the planned Armada against England must be kept secret, though if it is discovered it should be made to look as though it is bound for Ireland (pp7–11). The collection also includes Petruccio Ubaldino's narrative or account of the Armada, which mentions in some detail its fate on the Irish coast in 1588 (pp30–82).

GREATER LONDON : University of London Library *
Senate House, Malet Street, London WC1E 7HU
Tel: (0171) 636 8000 ext. 5030
Fax: (0171) 436 1494

LOOSE ITEMS

1576   Account of the death of the Earl of Essex in Ireland in 1576. (Ms. 312, ff 232–5)

---

[245] On fol. 3v it is recorded that the *The Primrose* is said to be 80 tons with ten men at harbour.

[246] Mainwaring's tract on piracy is to be found in Vol. 2 (i.e. Navy Records Society Vol. 56), pp9–49, the pages concerning Ireland being pp14–17, 33, 39–41, 46–8.

[247] The account concerning Sir Richard Leveson can be found in Vol. 2 (i.e. Navy Records Society Vol. 23), pp123–50.

1595	(cOct.) Instructions from the Earl of Essex to his agent/spy [Anthony?] Ersfield or Eversfield, sent to Paris to gather intelligence. Ordering him through various contacts to get regular information on France and in exchange he can give his informants details of England, Scotland and Ireland. Edward Reynolds will tell him what he can say re England, Scotland and Ireland. (Ms. 187, ff 11r–12r)
c1600	Volume of transcripts, made c1600, of the trials of William De La Pole, Duke of Suffolk (by Henry VI), and Sir John Cobham, 3rd Lord Cobham (by Richard II). States that the Duke of Suffolk was condemned to five years banishment, but was waylaid as he was crossing the Channel and captured and placed in a little boat. One of his captors, a knave of Ireland 'one of the lewdest men on board' took a rusty sword and smote off his head with half a dozen strokes. (Ms. 19)
1602	(22 Aug.) Letter from the Privy Council to Lord Treasurer Buckhurst authorising the payment of £140 to James Coles of London, to reimburse him for moneys he had paid to John Ratcliffe, Mayor of Chester, for the victualling and transport of troops from Chester to Dublin. (Ms. 382)
1617	Sir Francis Bacon's speech to Sir William Jones, Chief Justice of the King's Bench in Ireland. (Ms. 20, ff 193v–195v)
James I	(n.d.) 'The question concerning your Majesties prerogative in laying impositions upon merchandises', treatise by Sir John Davies, Attorney General of Ireland [101 fols]. (Ms. 25)
1634	(15 July) Contemporary copy of the speech made by Lord Deputy Wentworth to the Houses of Parliament in Dublin. (Ms. 290, ff 34r–46v)
1640–52	Copy of Clarendon's 'Short view of the state of Ireland from the year 1640 to the year 1652....' Being in essence a vindication of the 12th Earl and 1st Marquis of Ormond. (Ms. 45)

COLLECTIONS

Chalmers MSS (ref. Ms. 30)

A collection of transcripts of papers relating to Ireland, 1154–1791, primarily taken from the Public Record Office and the British Library by George Chalmers (1742–1825), as follows:

1550–1639	Notes taken from English Privy Council Journals concerning printing in Dublin, which have since been published.[248] (Ms. 30, fol. 26)
1618	(10 March) Privy Council order dismissing John Franchton from the post of H.M. Printer in Ireland, and appointing Felix Kingston to his place. (Ms. 30, fol. 23)
1626–69	List of the exports of Ireland by commodity and quantity for the years 1641, 1665 and 1669, with marginal notes of the figures for 1626, giving breakdowns by 57 commodities. (Ms. 30, fol. 30)
1626–69	Another copy of the same list. (Ms. 30, fol. 36)

---

[248] See J.R. Dasent et al (eds.), *Acts of the Privy Council*, 39 vols (1870–1964).

Fuller Collection (ref. Fuller)

This enormous collection of documents was made by the seal-and-antiquities collector, Captain A.W.F. Fuller, who managed to obtain a large number of manuscripts and seals dating from the thirteenth to the nineteenth centuries.[249] The collection is divided into a series of 35 boxes and seven cabinets. A detailed list exists for the items in the boxes (which contain only one document of Irish interest dated 1617, see below), but not for the cabinets. The cabinets contain over half the entire collection, and only a very rough list exists for Cabinet II, along with more detailed lists for parts of Cabinets I & V. Cabinet II contains two drawers of documents of Irish interest which are listed below, but because most of the archive is unlisted no access could be obtained to see if other Irish material was there. The Irish documentation found spans from 1339 to 1712. The entire collection is used by the University as a teaching archive, and given the highly varied nature of its contents it is probable that there is more material of Irish interest to be found elsewhere in the cabinets.[250]

Many of the following documents were almost definitely taken from the Browne MSS, the Coppinger MSS, the McCarthy of Carrignavar MSS, and the Sarsfield MSS. How Fuller got his hands on them is not at all clear, but Richard Caulfield published notes taken from them in his book *Kinsale* (Guildford, 1879), and in the pages of the *Gentlemans Magazine* in the 1860s. At this point they were still in private hands. Kenneth Nicholls has kindly given us details of the published versions of the following items and the original collections that they came from, which can be found in the footnotes to each entry.

1486   (19 July) Release by Henry White and others (named) to Maurice Ronan, burgess of Youghal, and his heirs and assigns, of a messuage in Youghal near the castle. (Cabinet II, Drawer 5/12)[251]

1488   (22 May) Lease by Maurice Oge Bran to James Bren, of one messuage in Fysherstreet in Kinsale. Term unclear, rent 12d. (Cabinet II, Drawer 5/13)[252]

1488   (29 Aug.) Grant by John fitz-Ricard fitz-Symon le Rede Baret, Lord of Cloyth Phylyb, to Eugenius MacKathraig of all his interest in the town of Donachaymoy, dated at Cork, with a long list of signatories (including 'Dyonisius', 'Oherllahy', etc.). On the dorse is written 'Richard Caulfield, Cork 3 Hen. VII'. (Cabinet II, Drawer 5/14)[253]

1489   (16 Nov.) Conveyance by Maurice Ronan, burgess of Kinsale, to James Barry and Margaret Yong, his wife, of one messuage with appurtenances in the town of Kinsale (with details of its location). (Cabinet II, Drawer 5/15)[254]

1490   (15 April) Conveyance by Maurice Ronan, burgess of Youghal, to Thomas O'Colan, burgess of Youghal, of his lands of Ballynm[ ]. (Cabinet II, Drawer 5/18)[255]

---

[249] For an introduction to this private collector, see Timothy J. McCann, 'Captain A.W.F. Fuller, 1882–1961, and the Fuller collection in the West Sussex Record Office', *West Sussex History*, 24 (1983).

[250] Drawer 6 of Cabinet II contains a very faded and mutilated document dated by the archivists as 1554. It appears to be an extract from a manorial roll, and reference is made to a place called Weston in M[ ]. It would appear to be of English origin, but it is not clear.

[251] From the Sarsfield Mss; Caulfield, *Gent. Mag.*, August 1864, p193.

[252] From the Browne Mss; Caulfield, *Kinsale*, p366.

[253] From the Carrignavar Mss, an abstract of which can be found in University College Cork, Ms. U.83/5, fol.11; see also W.F.T. Butler, *Gleanings from Irish History* (London, 1925), p112.

[254] Caulfield, *Kinsale*, p382.

[255] Probably from the Browne Mss; Caulfield, *Kinsale*, p366.

1490   (30 April) Letters of attorney from Maurice Ronan of the City of Cork to Thomas Pike, to deliver seisin to John Bouler (Bolter) of lands in the City of Cork. (Cabinet II, Drawer 5/16)[256]

1490   (30 April) Conveyance by Maurice Ronan of the City of Cork to John Bolter of various messuages and lands in the City of Cork. (Cabinet II, Drawer 5/17)[257]

1496   (3 Nov.) Letter of attorney from John Bolter to Philip [Maurice?] Ronayn regarding a burgage in the town of Kinsale and some property in the City of Cork. (Cabinet II, Drawer 5/20)[258]

1496   (8 Nov.) Release by John Bolter to Maurice Ronayn of all his tenements, messuages, lands, etc., in the City of Cork. (Cabinet II, Drawer 5/19)

1514   (15 Feb.) Conveyance by Edmund Tyrry of the City of Cork, to David fitz-John Creagh ['Crewach'] of a house in the City of Cork lately in the possession of Thomas fitz-John Melachlayn. (Cabinet II, Drawer 5/21)

1516   (1 May) Lease by Philip Barry, Lord of Kinaley, to Maurice Roche, in consideration of £20 paid to Philip, of the town of Ballymychille in the lordship of Kinaley. Term unclear, rent £20. (Cabinet II, Drawer 6/4)[259]

1518   (16 Oct.) Conveyance by John Pike, merchant of Youghal, to John Galvy and Eustace Ronan of Cork City of a house and garden in Youghal. (Cabinet II, Drawer 5/25)

1518   (21 Oct.) Conveyance by John Pike, merchant of Youghal, to John Galvy and others of a house and garden in Youghal. (Cabinet II, Drawer 5/24)[260]

1518   (22 Oct.) Conveyance by John Pyke, merchant of Youghal, to [   ] Plyn and Eustace Ronan of a house, garden and messuage in Youghal, late in the tenure of Anthony Pyke (with many other details). (Cabinet II, Drawer 5/22)

1521   (Mich) Grant by Peter Sarsfield to Gerald fitz-Philip Sarsfield of a weir in the port of the City of Cork called Tully moy, to have and hold for his life, and after his death to his heirs. With many conditions. (Cabinet II, Drawer 5/23)[261]

1522   (11 Nov.) Bond by John Ronan, burgess of Youghal, to Thomas Ronan, burgess of Kinsale, to satisfy William Walshe and Edmund Vuall, burgesses of Youghal (mentions Maurice Ronan). (Cabinet II, Drawer 5/26)[262]

1523   (22 April) Grant by Thomas Ronayn, burgess of Kinsale, to Philip Pownche, cleric, of a tenement in the City of Cork, on King's Street, with rent, the usual services and other customs due to Ronayn. (Cabinet II, Drawer 5/27)

---

[256] From the Sarsfield Mss; Caulfield, *Kinsale*, p382.
[257] *Ibid.*
[258] From the Sarsfield Mss; Caulfield, *Gent. Mag.*, April 1863, p452.
[259] From the Browne Mss; Caulfield, *Kinsale*, p367.
[260] From the Sarsfield Mss; Caulfield, *Gent. Mag.*, April 1863, p453–4.
[261] From the Sarsfield Mss; Caulfield, *Gent. Mag.*, March 1865, pp319–20.
[262] From the Sarsfield Mss; Caulfield, *Kinsale*, p385.

1525   (16 Jan.) Conveyance by Elina Coursy, widow, to Thomas Cormyk, burgess of Kinsale, of one messuage in Kinsale between the property of Edmund Martell and Richard Deynys. (Cabinet II, Drawer 5/28)[263]

1528   (10 Oct.) Lease by Thomas Ronan fitz-Morris of Cork, merchant, to Maurice Bren of the town of Youghal, of various lands and tenements in Youghal. Term unclear, rent 9s. (Cabinet II, Drawer 5/29)

1537   (30 April) Deed of William Wardolley [Werdown?] of Cork concerning lands in Ballinna and Shandon, with reference to Henry Wardolly and others. (Cabinet II, Drawer 5/30)[264]

1537   (30 April) Conveyance by William Wardolry [Werdown?] of Cork to Robert Wardolry of Cork, of lands in Shandon in Cork, with many details. (Cabinet II, Drawer 5/32)[265]

1538   (5 Sept.) Mortgage by Edmund Roche, son and heir of Milos Roche, to Thomas Ronan of Cork, of one half of the town called Kilmorymolagn and Ballyneroche for 3 marks (stg). (Cabinet II, Drawer 5/31)

1541   (15 Oct.) Conveyance by Philip Barry, Lord of Kinnalega, to Patrick Myagh, burgess of Kinsale, of one piece of land called Flemynoustrale in the land of Rincorry, in the lordship of Kinnalega, and of the advowson of Ynyssanan.(Cabinet II, Drawer 6/unnumbered transcript)[266]

1549   (23 March) Grant by the Bishop of Waterford and Lismore of the 'vacant' parsonage of Lisronaghe to 'Petro lvyet' [Piers Owhet], making mention of the threat posed by rebels to this parsonage. (Cabinet II, Drawer 6/5)[267]

1550   (26 Feb.) Lease by Thomas Ronan of the City of Cork to Michael [or Nicholas] Blake of Youghal, of one messuage in Youghal and its appurtenances. Rent 3s 4d. (Cabinet II, Drawer 5/33)[268]

1552   (29 Nov.) Conveyance by Phillip Barry, Lord of Kynalega, with the consent of Margaret Barry, to Richard Yonge of Kinsale, burgess, of one carucate of land called Balymichael in the lordship of Kynalega. Rent 23 marks. (Cabinet II, Drawer 5/34)[269]

1558   (3 Nov.) Grant by Gerald Coursy, Baron and Lord, to Henry Brown of Kinsale, merchant, of exemption from public office in Kinsale. (Cabinet II, Drawer 6/7)[270]

1562   (11 Sept.) Lease by James Ronan fitz-Thomas to William Gallway of Kinsale, burgess of one great messuage in Kinsale. To hold for 59 years, rent 6s. (Cabinet II, Drawer 6/8)[271]

---

[263] From the Browne Mss; Caulfield, *Kinsale*, p367.

[264] From the Coppinger Mss.

[265] *Ibid.*

[266] This information appears on a loose attachment in Drawer 6, probably written by Fuller. The original deed could not be found. However, the original deed was from the Browne Mss; Caulfield, *Kinsale*, p368.

[267] From the Coppinger Mss.

[268] From the Sarsfield Mss; Caulfield, *Gent. Mag.*, Aug. 1864, p194.

[269] From the Browne Mss; Caulfield, *Kinsale*, p369.

[270] From the Browne Mss; Caulfield, *Kinsale*, p369.

[271] From the Sarsfield Mss; Caulfield, *Kinsale*, p330.

1568   (31 March) Conveyance by John White, son and heir of James White of Kinsale, to Henry Browne of Kinsale, burgess, of one 'locum' in Kinsale. To hold for ever, rent 6d. (Cabinet II, Drawer 6/9)[272]

1576   (27 Sept.) Bond of Thomas Barry of Ryncorran *alias* Lord Barry Oge of Kynnalee, in £100 (stg) to Henry Browne of Kinsale, burgess. The condition is that Barry must (in consideration of a certain sum) give possession of Michelston containing one ploughland to Browne. Browne to pay rent of 5s (stg). (Cabinet II, Drawer 5/36)[273]

1577   (16 May) Lease by the Wardens and Proctors of the Cathedral Church of the Holy Trinity of the City of Waterford (with the consent of the mayor, sheriffs and citizens of same) to Edward Walsh fitz-James of Waterford, merchant, of a house called 'the Chantors Chamber'. To hold for 61 years, rent 12s. (Cabinet II, Drawer 5/35)[274]

1580   (22 Sept.) Conveyance by the Master, brethren and poor men of the Hospital of the Holy Ghost in Waterford, to John Lea fitz-Nicholas of Waterford, merchant, of 'one place within the church of the said Holy Ghoste for a buriall for the said John and his heirs, children wives and posteritie. The said place or grounde beginning right under the Alter call St. Brides Awl, and hence westwards in length 14 foot' and eight foot wide. (Cabinet II, Drawer 6/10)[275]

1584   (30 Sept.) Feoffment by Thomas Skiddy fitz-Richard of Cork City, to Edmund Tyrrey fitz-Edmund of Cork, alderman, and David Carroll of same, merchant, of all his possessions, lands, rents, weirs, revenues, etc., called Skiddy's Castle, a bakehouse, other houses, Ballibegg, 'Farryn ny clogey leghy' in Rathemore, Shandon, Skiddy's Acre, and other lands and services. To be held for ever in trust to the use of Thomas Skiddy and his heirs male, in default of which to Edmund Tyrry fitz-David and Margaret Skiddy, daughter to said Thomas, and their heirs male. (Cabinet II, Drawer 5/37)[276]

1596   (23 March) Lease by Thomas Sarsfield fitz-William of Cork City, alderman, to Moris Fox of same, husbandman, and Margaret his wife, of 'one garden to build a thatch house therein' between the lane to St. Catherine's churchyard, the Queen's highway, and two small gardens belonging to David Kealy and Philip Collaine. To hold for 21 years, rent 6s 8d (stg). (Cabinet II, Drawer 5/38)

1602   (20 Sept.) Lease by 'Sir' William Carroll, Archdeacon of the Cathedral Church of Lismore, to Robert Brennocke fitz-Thomas of Clonmel, yeoman, of the parsonage of Ballybealane in the diocese of Lismore in Co. Tipperary, and the rectories or parsonages of Kilmolashe and Kilrushe in the said diocese, in Co. Waterford. To hold for 61 years, rent £8 (Irish). (Cabinet II, Drawer 6/13)[277]

1610   (27 Jan.) Conveyance by Edmund Gallway, Mayor of Cork, and his trustees (named) to Morris Ronayne fitz-James of Cork, gent., of the

---

[272] From the Browne Mss; Caulfield, *Kinsale*, p371.

[273] From the Browne Mss. and not noticed by Caulfield.

[274] From the Coppinger Mss.

[275] From the Coppinger Mss.

[276] From the Sarsfield Mss; Caulfield, *Gent. Mag.*, Aug. 1865, p176.

[277] From the Coppinger Mss.

small thatch house now in the occupation of Dermod Callighan of Cork, butcher, and 'a voyed place' belonging to it, being without the south gate of the City of Cork. To hold for ever, appointing Christopher Gallway of Cork, merchant, as attorney to deliver possession. (Cabinet II, Drawer 6/14)

1617   (23 April) Quitclaim by James Prendergast to Nicholas Lea to mortgaged lands in Castlereagh, Co. Waterford. The mortgage was for £126 and made to John Bray, dated 4 May 1614; Nicholas Lea subsequently bought the mortgage from John Bray. The original mortgage also had a codicil that if Prendergast paid £300 in four years he could re-enter the lands. Now Nicholas Lea buys the release of the same for a further £300. (Box 27/2)[278]

GREATER LONDON : Victoria and Albert Museum *
South Kensington, London SW7 2RL
Tel: (0171) 938 8500
Fax: (0171) 938 8461

COLLECTIONS

The Forster Collection (ref. various)

1628   (15 Aug.) Letter written at Whitehall by Sir Edward Conway, Viscount Killulta, to the Lieutenant of the county of Southampton regarding the billeting of soldiers in Southampton, including a detachment of Irish troops. (48.G.1)

c1630   (3 Aug.) Letter from Viscount Dunluce to Lord Conway re private affairs, written at Welbecke, the seat of the Earl of Manchester. Dunluce claims he will live 'a happie, quiet and retired life', for the royal court was 'never more hard to be known nor less worthie of the curiositie' [3pp]. (48.G.2/1)

1632   (10 May) Letter from 'Geo: Jones maior Dublin' and others, to Lord Deputy Wentworth, reporting that they have heard from Sir Thady Duffe that Wentworth has agreed to support their petition and cause, and they thank him for his assistance. (48.G.2/1)

1632   (24 Sept.) Letter written at York by Lord Deputy Wentworth prior to his embarkation for Ireland, concerning the affairs of Sir David Fowlis, an English knight; probably addressed to the Earl of Carlisle [4 pages]. (48.G.23)

1640–45   Transcript of 'A Journal of the Parliament begun Novr. 3. Tuesday Anº Dom 1640, Anº 16º Caroli Regis, by Sir Simonds D'Ewes'; the journal ends on 3 Nov. 1645. The transcript is interleaved throughout with many notes by the historians John Forster and Thomas Carlyle [4 vols.]. (48.B.23–6)

1641   (16 Feb.) Copy of the articles and depositions presented against the Earl of Strafford, in the English House of Commons. (48.G.23)

1641   (Before May) Anonymous letter addressed to Rev. P. Bliss endorsed 'The Earle of Strafford characterised in a letter sent to a friend in the Country ... 1641', written before the Earl was executed. Of the charges against Strafford, the author says 'whether his Lopp bee guilty of high treason I cannot determyne. Sure it is many fowle

---

[278] From the Coppinger Mss.

things stick upon him by manifest proofes, which neither his friens nor all the fig-leaves in paradice can cover' [10pp]. (48.G.2)

1641   (After May) 'The Earle of Strafford his ellegiack poem, as it was pen'd by his owne hand a little before his death', printed in 1641 with woodcut ornaments, beginning 'Sate give me leave, and vexe my thoughts no more ....' (48.G.23)

GREATER LONDON : Westminster Abbey Muniment Room

Westminster Abbey, London SW1P 3PA
Tel: (0171) 222 5152 ext. 228
Fax: (0171) 233 2072

Although both H.M.C. reports on this archive's holdings (*First Report*, App., pp94–7; *Fourth Report*, App. pp171–99) mention Irish material, it all pre-dates 1485. Fortunately, however, there is at least one item for the period of this survey in the Muniment Room that the H.M.C. missed:

LOOSE ITEMS

1632   (24 March) Copy of part of a patent granting to the Duchess of Buckingham certain customs and dues on goods exported from and imported into Ireland, for 15 years, for £20,000. (Muniment 54116)

GREATER LONDON : Westminster Diocesan Archives

16A Abingdon Road, Kensington, London W8 6A4
Tel: (0171) 938 3580

These are the archives of the Roman Catholic Archbishop of Westminster. This repository was formed in 1907 from the records of the Catholic Diocese of Westminster, the Catholic Chapter of London at Spanish Place, Brompton Oratory, and other collections. The H.M.C.'s two reports on the precursors of this archive (*5th Report*, App., pp463–76)[279] include a few items of Irish interest from the seventeenth century. However, the best introduction to the collections held by this repository can be found in P. Hughes, 'Westminster archives', *Dublin Review*, cci (1937), pp300–10. The 'A' series of records, containing mainly official documents of the Catholic Church in England from 1501, is the most important for the study of Irish history. The index to this series has been microfilmed for the National Library.[280] There are, however, further documents concerning Ireland in the other series held by the repository.

GREATER LONDON : Dr. Williams's Library

14 Gordon Square, London WC1H 0AG
Tel: (0171) 387 3727
Fax: (0171) 388 1142

LOOSE ITEMS

1592   A collection of documents concerning the trial and judgement of Sir John Perrot. It includes 'The Arraignem^t' on 27 April 1592 (ff 2r–

---

[279] The reports deal with the collections of the Catholic Chapter of London, Spanish Place, and the Catholic Diocese of Westminster.

[280] N.L.I. microfilm n.5207, p.5311.

29v), and the 'Judgm^t', with details of most of the speeches against Perrot, and his defence (ff 30r–44v).[281] (Morice Mss. M.vii.)

1600–1695   A list of Irish archbishops and bishops, by diocese, with incomplete dates of consecration, translation, and death. The list would appear to have been largely compiled in the nineteenth century from purely printed sources, particularly Ware, and Wood's *Athenae Oxonienses*.[282] (Morice Mss. M.ix., ff 1r,2r–6r,8v)

GREATER MANCHESTER : Chetham's Library
Long Millgate, Manchester M3 1SB
Tel: (0161) 834 7961
Fax: (0161) 839 5797

LOOSE ITEMS

1640–52   'A short view of ye state and condition of Ireland from the year 1640 to this time [1652]; or a vindication of his late Majesty of blissed memory, our soveraigne King that now is, and their Majesties supreame minister instructed by them, for conducting the affairs of that kingdome, from the scandalls and culumnies cast on them by many scandallous pamphlets set forth in latin by anonimous writers, and particularly against a pamphlet lately published by the direction of a titular Bishop of Fernes, and composed by him.' (6701 (Mun.A.4.36))

COLLECTIONS

Irish History MSS (ref. 27909 (Mun.A.6.77))

One volume [631 fols], of miscellaneous documents including a number of descriptions of Ireland from the 1580s and 1590s, notes on the Irish peerage, court fees, petitions and other official material. Much of the volume is concerned with Irish religious foundations and the Church of Ireland under Charles I.[283] There are over 100 separate items, of which seven are sixteenth century and the rest are seventeenth century, up to 1663. The volume appears to have been compiled by both Dudley Loftus and Thomas Preston, Ulster King-at-Arms. There is a report on this volume with a detailed catalogue of its contents in H.M.C., *2nd Report* (1871), App., pp156–8.

GREATER MANCHESTER : The John Rylands University Library *
University of Manchester, 150 Deansgate, Manchester M3 3EH
Tel: (0161) 834 5343/6765
Fax: (0161) 834 5574

LOOSE ITEMS

1554   'A Dialogue between Death and the Patient', written originally in Irish by Denis O'Daly, in 1554. This copy includes both the original

---

[281] An almost identical copy was published in, *A Complete Collection of State Trials* (2nd ed., London, 1730), Vol.1, pp181–9. The printed version has a further paragraph at the end, missing from this copy.

[282] There is also a very incomplete listing of Irish bishops, only listing those for Achonry–Cashel (Morice Ms. M.x/1).

[283] N.L.I. microfilm, n.2814, p.1924.

| | Irish, and a copy of the English translation by John Collins in 1805.[284] (Irish Ms. 126) |

1560   (2 June) Sale by Rowling Billinge of Bagheggrig, Margaret his wife, and Elyn Billinge, widow, to John Payn, Treasurer of the Household of the Earl of Sussex, Lord Lieutenant of Ireland. (Rylands Charters No. 924)

1560   A volume of miscellaneous notes on Ireland which includes a deed in Irish by members of the MacClancy family dated 1560. (Irish Ms. 21)[285]

1613–1831   Lists of M.P.s elected to the Irish Parliament, by county. Some pre–1641 members are included. (English Ms. 333 [R.24457, Vol.V])[286]

1613–1776   'List of those Irish who died at the Irish College at Louvain', which includes 12 entries prior to 1641, including Francis MacDonnell, son of the Earl of Antrim, who died in 1636, and Edward Fleming 'proff.' who died in 1615. The list was compiled by Phillip Jean-Baptiste O'Kelly. (Irish Ms. 120, ff 41–6)[287]

c1628–9   A volume of documents concerning Parliament, which contains 'A petition against the precedence of the Scottish and Irish nobility' (fol. 69), and 'A copy of the Apology of the Lord Viscount Falkland, Lord Deputy of Ireland, to the Lords of H.M. Privy Council' (fol. 72). (English Ms. 942)

17th cen.   (n.d.) A volume entitled, 'A Looking Glass for the Reformed Church and State of Ireland, wherein may be Discerned the Effegies of Popery, with all the Traterous Conspiracyes of Irish Papists against the Crowne of England for about 200 yeares now Past', assigned by a note on p.1 to Robert Ware, son of Sir James Ware, the Irish antiquarian. (English Ms. 1029 [R.91695])[288]

COLLECTIONS

Boyle, Earl of Cork MSS (ref. English Ms. 887 [R. 77738])[289]

A volume of manuscripts, dating 1494–1753, including the following which are relevant to this survey:

1494–5   Extract of an Act of Parliament for Ireland, $10°$ Henry VII, prohibiting the office of Treasurer in that lordship from being hereditary. (fol. 90)

1631   (12 Oct.) Grant of the office of Lord High Treasurer of Ireland to Richard, Earl of Cork, with a salary of £30 p.a., to hold the same during pleasure. (fol. 91)

1632   The 'True Remembrances' of Richard, 1st Earl of Cork's; a short autobiography covering his career to 1630, including his dispute with Sir Henry Wallop in the 1590s, his purchase of the Raleigh estate, and many other events. (ff 22–7)

---

[284] This transcript was made by Michael Long of Cork in 1814.

[285] This item could not be found when we visited the Library, but it has fortunately been microfilmed for the N.L.I.: microfilm, n.2487, p.499.

[286] N.L.I. microfilm, n.4201, p.3872.

[287] N.L.I. microfilm, n.3539, p.3157.

[288] N.L.I. microfilm, n.4763, p.4751.

[289] N.L.I. microfilm, n.4762, p.4750.

1636   (14 May) The 1st Earl of Cork's 'Grand Settlement Septipartite',
             between (1) Richard, Earl of Cork, (2) Sir William Parsons, Sir
             John Browne, Sir William Fenton and Sir Percy Smith, (3) Sir
             Richard Boyle, Lord Dungarvan, son and heir of Lord Cork, (4) Sir
             L. Boyle, Viscount Boyle, (5) Sir Roger Boyle, Baron Broghill, (6)
             Francis Boyle, 4th son of Lord Cork, (7) Robert Boyle, 5th son of
             Lord Cork. Settling his entire estate, real and personal. (ff 31–87)

1641   The 1st Earl of Cork's 'Decree of Innocency' concerning the Irish
             rebellion of 1641. (ff 27–30)

MSS concerning the Calverts, Lords Baltimore (ref. Latin Ms. 326 [R. 38973])[290]

A volume of legal tracts, either compiled by or for the 2nd Baron Baltimore
c1668, entitled 'Questions of Lawe and affaires of state concernyng the
Kingdome of Ireland'. It includes the following items which contain detailed lists
of legal precedence prior to 1641:

1.   'That the Legislative power in Ireland doth belong to the Kinge by
             the advice of his Parliament of Ireland, not of his Parliament of
             England'. Legal notes covering the 15th–17th centuries.

2.   'This great question touching the quartering of soldiers in Ireland
             and hath reference to the statute of 18 Henry VI is a mixt and
             complicated question'. Legal notes covering the 15th–17th
             centuries.

3.   'That ye legislative power in Ireland doth belong to the Kinge by the
             advice of his Parliament of Ireland and not of his Parliament of
             England'. Legal notes covering the 13th–17th centuries.

4.   'Whether a statute made in the Parliament of England shall be of
             force in Ireland before it be enacted and approved in the Parliament
             of Ireland'. Legal notes covering the 14th–17th centuries.

5.   'Patent concerning Cecill Calvert Baron of Baltemore, son and heir
             of George Calvert', and what would appear to be notes by Calvert
             on this patent and patents in general, covering the 13th–17th
             centuries.

6–8.   Notes concerning mostly English legal cases, 14th–17th centuries.

Clerk of the Pells MSS (ref. Latin Mss. 244–7 [R. 38460])[291]

1622   (Easter) Volume of receipts by the Office of the Clerk of the Pells of
             Crown rents, reversions, wardships, compositions, casualties, fines
             for alienation, subsidies, etc., for the provinces of Connaught and
             Ulster [54 fols]. (Latin Ms. 244)

1622   (Easter) Volume of same, for the provinces of Leinster and Munster
             [101 fols]. (Latin Ms. 246)

1622   (Michaelmas) Volume of same, for the provinces of Connaught and
             Ulster [116 fols]. (Latin Ms. 245)

1622   (Michaelmas) Volume of same, for the provinces of Leinster and
             Munster [116 fols]. (Latin Ms. 247)

---

[290] N.L.I. microfilm, n.4765, p.4753.

[291] N.L.I. microfilm, n.4765, p.4753. These items were originally part of the Carew of Crowcombe Court
collection (now widely scattered), and were mentioned in the H.M.C.'s report on same, *4th Report*, App.,
p373. Other material from this collection was also found in Somerset County Record Office (see below).

Crawford Collection (ref. various)[292]

16th cen.   A volume of heraldic manuscripts, including an Irish armorial, and 'a very ancyent book of Armes in Golde contayning the coats of English and Irish race; Knightes of the Carpet made at the said mariage of Prince Arthur'.[293] (English Ms. 15 [Crawford 26])[294]

16th cen.   A volume of nineteenth century transcripts entitled 'Collectanea De Rebus Hibernicis I', which includes: 'The general hosting appointed to meet at the Hill of Tara on the 24th September 1593' (ff 146–63)[295], and the customs, rights and privileges of O'Kelly of Hy Many from a translation by John O'Donovan (fol. 85). (English Ms. 496 [Crawford Irish Coll. 54])[296]

1552–1606   A volume, as above, entitled 'Collectanea De Rebus Hibernicis II', which includes: 'A letter from the Chancellor [Sir Thomas Cusacke] to the Duke of Northumberland relating to the present state of Ireland 8th May 1552' (ff 4–73), 'A letter written by Sir John Davis, knt, Attorney General of Ireland to Robert, Earl of Salisbury touching the state of Monaghan, Fermanagh and Cavan .... Written Anno 1606' (ff 75–162). (English Ms. 497 [Crawford Irish Coll. 100])[297]

1567–1703   A volume, as above, entitled 'Collectanea De Rebus Hibernicis III', which includes: 'The rest of the letter by Sir John Davies in 1606' (ff 1–55), and the 'Inscription on the Old Bridge of Athlone', which relates that it was built in 1567 under the directions of Sir Henry Sidney, and took less than a year to complete. It also gives a brief description of the works of Peter Lewis, Clerk of Christ Church Cathedral in Dublin, who was steward to the Lord Deputy and oversaw many building projects, particularly in Dublin Castle. The inscription also reports that Shane O'Neill was overthrown and coign and livery was abolished (ff 166–7). (English Ms. 498 [Crawford Irish Coll. 99])[298]

1641–7   A Volume containing two documents: 'The state of the Kingdom before the rebellion of 1641' (pp 1–8), and 'The rebellion and Management of the ensuing war till the flight of the Marquis of Ormond to France in 1647' (pp 9–123). Both documents were written by a royalist supporter of Ormond. (English Ms. 505 [Crawford Irish Coll. 122])

Mainwaring of Peover Hall MSS (ref. Mainwaring Mss.)

This collection is very large and much of it remains uncatalogued; hence it may possibly contain further items relating to Ireland. Sadly, however, a thorough

---

[292] The Crawford manuscripts seem to have received at least two catalogue reference numbers, and we have included both in the entries for each item. The reference numbers which we have enclosed in square brackets are now obsolete, and the former number is the present reference. To avoid problems, enquiries to the repository should mention both numbers to be sure.

[293] i.e., Arthur, eldest son of Henry VII, married in 1501 to Catherine of Aragon.

[294] N.L.I. microfilm, n.4201, p.3872.

[295] A note states 'transcribed from the Mss. collections of Archbishop King in the Library of the Royal Dublin Society'.

[296] The volume has been microfilmed by the N.L.I., n.4761, p.4749.

[297] Both taken from a transcript of the Clogher MSS in the N.L.I. (Harris MSS). The letter by Davies is concluded in the following volume. The volume has been microfilmed by the N.L.I., n.4761, p.4749.

[298] Apparently the bridge was destroyed in 1844, prompting the author to transcribe this unique original foundation inscription. This volume has been microfilmed for the N.L.I., n.4762, p.4750.

trawl through its holdings may prove rather difficult as the series of original letters which cover the period prior to 1641, though still housed at this repository, have been misplaced. The three letters below are among the missing items, and the details given have been taken from the catalogue of the collection.

1587   (1 Aug.) 'Co. Limerick in the Province of Munster – A Particular of such Castles, houses, lands and other hereditments as are allocated unto Edmund Mannaring of the Springe in the countie of Chester, esq.' Lists property in the barony of Feadymore etc., Co. Limerick, with values, acreages ('after the rate of 428 acres english measure to the ploughland'), chief rents and other details. Attached are documents relating to the settlement of the estate in June and October 1588. (Mainwaring Mss. No. 390)

1604   (28 June) Order by the President and Council of Munster for the granting of livery to Sir Randle Mainwaring of certain castles and lands in Ireland. (Mainwaring Mss., Letters B. No.1)

1605   (3 July) Warrant to Sir Randle Mainwaring, Sheriff of Limerick, respecting the possession of Brouree, Co. Limerick. (Mainwaring Mss., Letters B. No.2)

1628   (7 Feb.) Letter from George Mainwaring to his father, Sir Randle. (Mainwaring Mss., Letters B. No.3)

Stanley of Hooton MSS (ref. Rylands Charters 1457–74, 1705)[299]

1576   (8 Oct.) Lease by Patrick, Bishop of Waterford and Lismore, to Sir William Drury, of the manor, castle, etc., of Lismore, for 61 years [and a copy]. (Rylands Charter No. 1457–8)

1584   (12 Jan.) Bond of Owen MacMeriertigh of Donygap, and Hugh MacMeriertagh, late Prior of Keylle in Kerry, to Sir William Stanley, Sheriff of Co. Cork. (Rylands Charter No. 1459)

1584   (16 May) Receipt from Anne Thickpenny, widow of John Thickpenny, to Sir William Stanley, for a year's rent for the castle of Lismore, etc. (Rylands Charter No. 1460)

1584   (30 Nov.) The same for a half year's rent. (Rylands Charter No. 1461)

1585   (10 June) The same for a half year's rent. (Rylands Charter No. 1462)

1585   (Oct.) The same for a half year's rent. (Rylands Charter No. 1463)

1585   (1 Dec.) Feoffment by Sir William Stanley to John Egerton the younger of Olton, Cheshire, Thomas Bunburie of Stanney, and John Poole of Poole; of the castle, etc., of Lismore, to the use of his wife and children. (Rylands Charter No. 1465)

1586   (13 May) Receipt from Anne Thickpenny, as above, for a half year's rent. (Rylands Charter No. 1464)

1587   (5 July) Copies of two letters from Peter Warbarton to [   ], regarding the passage of Sir William Stanley's lands in Ireland, with a note of the same date by Edward Mathewe to the effect that on 1 Dec. 1586 [1585][300] he was present at the sealing and delivering of the above feoffment (No. 1465) to John Egerton et al. (Rylands Charter No. 1466)

---

[299] Most of these items are on N.L.I. microfilm, n.4763, p.4751.

[300] The date of the feoffment in this letter is different from that of the feoffment itself.

c1587[301]   (n.d.) Petition of John Egerton of Olton, Cheshire, by his attorney, Edward Clegg, to the Lord Deputy and Council, regarding an order by the English Privy Council for restitution of goods seized from Lady Stanley in Ireland. He requests that Anthony Power, Sheriff of Co. Waterford, be empowered to make the restitution. (Rylands Charter No. 1469)

1587   (2 Sept.) Letter from the Lord Deputy to the Sheriff of Waterford, ordering him to make restitution of goods previously seized from Lady Stanley in Co. Waterford. (Rylands Charter No. 1705)

1587   (14 Oct.) Petition of John Egerton to the Lord Deputy and Council, requesting that Colthurst and Mawe, attorneys to Sir Walter Raleigh, repair to the Lord Deputy and show Sir Walter's alleged title to Lismore. (Rylands Charter No. 1470)

c1587–8   (n.d.) Answer of Sir Walter Raleigh, by his attorney Andrew Colthurst, to the bill of John Egerton, concerning title to the Lismore estate, and the purchase of corn there on 28 Aug. last from Anthony Power, Sheriff of Co. Waterford. (Rylands Charter No. 1471)

c1587–8   (n.d.) Reply of John Egerton to the above, relating to the title of lands in Lismore. (Rylands Charter No. 1472)

c1587–8   (n.d.) Note recording goods left with Mr. White in Waterford, delivered to him by Edward Clegg and John Russell. Lists a number of household wares. White then delivered these to Thomas Braban, a cooper in Chester. (Rylands Charter No. 1473)

1588   (Shrove Tuesday, i.e. 20 Feb.) Letter from Roger Wilbraham to Sir Rowland Stanley, John Egerton, John Poole, and Thomas Bunbury, regarding examinations relating to a lease made by the Bishop of Waterford and Lismore to Sir William Stanley. (Rylands Charter No. 1467)

1588   (24 Feb.) Letter from Anne Thickpenny to Lady Stanley, concerning enquiries in Dublin into Sir William Stanley's estate, and the hard dealing done to Lady Stanley by Sir Walter Raleigh. (Rylands Charter No. 1468)

16th cen.   (n.d.) Letter from William Stanley jnr. to his mother, Lady Stanley, with a tailor's bill. (Rylands Charter No. 1474)

MERSEYSIDE : Liverpool City Record Office

Central Library, William Brown Street, Liverpool L3 8EW
Tel: (0151) 225 5409/225 5417
Fax: (0151) 207 1342

COLLECTIONS

Liverpool Town Books (ref. 352 MIN/COU I 1/1–16)

These books record the proceedings of the Common Council and date from 1550 to 1835. Portions of the books, in varying degrees of detail, have appeared in print. Most of the material up to 1603 is contained in J.A. Twemlow's *Liverpool Town Books, 1550–1603* (2 vols, Liverpool, 1918–35). There is a large body of

---

[301] This document, though undated, obviously predates the following item.

documentation concerning Ireland in the sixteenth century in this publication, of a similar nature to that appearing in the Chester City Record Office (see above).[302] A great deal concerns trade, particularly the importation of Irish tallow, wool, fish and (unusually) wheat and other grain. There are references to merchants and trade from Dublin, Drogheda, Carrickfergus, Waterford and Wexford, including a merchants' bond in 1568 between factors from Ireland and Manchester (i, p498). There is also an interesting Assembly Order in 1592 demanding that Irish merchants attend church service on Sundays on pain of a fine (ii, p637). There is a similarly large quantity of material concerning the transportation and billeting of soldiers bound for Ireland, an issue that raised a number of problems for the Corporation. In October 1595 the Common Council ordered that ships transporting sick and diseased soldiers from Ireland should inform the Mayor before landing (ii, p702). In August 1601 the Corporation flatly refused to raise troops for Irish service, and there are a number of items concerning this dispute with the government (ii, pp795–7). Like Chester, the town was used for sending letters and messengers between the respective governments in Dublin and London, and there are a number of items concerning this activity.

The town books also contain a substantial number of documents concerning the colonisation schemes of Captain Thomas Smith and the Earl of Essex in east Ulster during the period 1572–4, most of which concern the trouble caused by the troops in their companies. There is a detailed account of the ships and personnel impressed for service by Essex and an account written late in 1573 on the failure of Essex's mission and the wrecking of *The Swanne* off the Irish coast (ii, pp44, 112–3, 119–24, 146–8, 179). There are a number of other items throughout the collection which concern many aspects of the town's relations with Ireland. There is a coroner's inquest into the death of a mariner aboard a ship from Drogheda; the ship was to be used for transporting part of Shane O'Neill's company in March 1562 (i, pp185–7). There are also details on the storm which affected Sir Henry Sidney's passage to Ireland in December 1565 (i, p291–4).

More selective extracts have been published for the seventeenth century in G. Chandler and E.K. Wilson's two books, *Liverpool under James I* (Liverpool, 1960) and *Liverpool under Charles I* (Liverpool, 1965). These include a number of references to Irish merchants and trade in general, including a list of ships stayed by the Mayor in 1639, under the government's directions to stop all Scottish shipping. This list includes a Scottish ship carrying goods belonging to Irish merchants, *The Content of Dunnagadee* in Ireland which was flying Scottish colours, and *The Providence of Strangford* owned by a Scottish man, John Ore (*Liverpool under Charles I*, p261).

Undoubtedly, the collection contains further Irish material not noticed in any of these volumes, particularly for the seventeenth century.

---

[302] See also F.J. Routledge, 'Liverpool and Irish Politics in the Sixteenth Century', *Mackay Miscellany* (Liverpool, 1914).

WEST MIDLANDS : Birmingham Central Library
Chamberlain Square, Birmingham B3 3HQ
Tel: (0121) 235 3586
Fax: (0121) 233 4458

COLLECTIONS

Coventry Papers (ref. DV 873–909)

This repository holds a large collection of the official papers of Sir Thomas Coventry, Lord Keeper of the Great Seal of England [1625–40]. They consist in the main of docquets of letters patent covering every aspect of his office and the Chancery in general. Though we have no specific references to Irish material in this collection, less than 10% of these records have been listed and indexed. There are over 18,000 individual items, and given the frequent notice of Irish people, lands and offices in the published English patent rolls for the sixteenth century, it would be remarkable if there was no material concerning Ireland in this collection.

NORFOLK : County Record Office
Gildengate House, Anglia Square, Norwich NR3 1AX
Tel: (01603) 761 349
Fax: (01603) 761885

LOOSE ITEMS

1641 A letter of 1654 by Sir Nicholas Le Strange to Miles Corbett referring to a suit concerning the Irish estate of the late Earl of Strafford at the time of his attainder in 1641. (Le Strange P20)

Charles I An undated petition of Henry Honyng to Charles I, asking for some reward for his services in settling King James's escheated lands in Ulster and in coming to England to announce to Queen Elizabeth the proposed invasion of Ireland by Spain. (Ms. 15669)

COLLECTIONS

Knyvett MSS (ref. KNY)

This includes letters dated 1598–1600 from Henry Knyvett to his brother, Sir Thomas, during Essex's expedition to Ireland (KNY 676–749). Of these 73 documents, at least one relates specifically to the progress of the war in Ireland.

NORTHAMPTONSHIRE : County Record Office *
Wootton Hall Park, Northampton NN4 8BQ
Tel: (01604) 762 129
Fax: (01604) 767 562

LOOSE ITEMS

1592 (8 June) Assignment of lands in Co. Cork, owned by the late Sir Richard Greville, by Bernard Greville of Stowe in Cornwall, esq., to John Greville, his brother. (G. 3228)

1599   Royal proclamation of Elizabeth I 'declaring her princely resolution in sending over of her army into the realm of Ireland'. Printed in London by the deputies of Christopher Barker. (Th. 522)

c1601   (12 Nov.) Letter from Sir Robert Cecil 'to my good L.', regarding the fleet in Cork and the death of the young Earl of Desmond. (D(F) 67)

1602   (7 Jan.) Letter from the Privy Council at Whitehall to the Sheriff and Commissioners of Northants, ordering them to raise 60 troops for service in Ireland. (YZ 4988)

1629   Indenture of agreement between (a) Charles Cokaine, esq. of London, (b) Henry, Earl of Thomond, and (c) William Cokayne, Matthew Craddock and Thomas Henchman, citizens of London. Relating to lands in the City of London, Yorkshire, Leicestershire, etc., and a previous marriage settlement between the Thomond family and Charles Cokaine. (YZ 5629)[303]

1632   (13 June) Agreement concerning the lands of Crosbie in the barony of Maryborough, Queen's Co., between Sir Piers Crosby and Henry, Earl of Marlborough [badly damaged]. (G. 3683)

1641   Undated 'List of such Irish Nobility as stand outlawed for high treason in the 1641 rebellion and of such as have their outlawries reverst, and Those outlawed for High treason since the King's Accession (1660)', by Daniel Wybraits. (I(L) 3340)

c1641   Undated item entitled 'Pasages concerning the Lord Deputy (Strafford) at his last convention'. (I.C. 3604)

COLLECTIONS

Cockayne MSS (ref. C)[304]

1599–1602   The account of John Jolles and William Cockayne, merchants, for victualling the forces in Ireland. A duplicate made in July 1604. (C. 2923)

1600   (24 March) Agreement concerning victuals for Ireland, between William Cockayne, citizen and skinner of London, and John Jolles, citizen and draper of same. (C. 2695)

1602   (13 Aug.) Assignment of the profits of the brewhouse and 'horsemyll' in Lough Foyle to William Cockayne by Robert Newcomen of Dublin, gent. (C. 2589)

1602   (14 Aug.) Agreement between Newcomen, Jolles and Cockayne, stating that Newcomen will pass the accounts for the three provinces of Leinster, Ulster and Connaught, and secure them for presentation to Her Majesty's auditors. (C. 3234)

1602   (Sept.–Oct.) Thomas Smyth's account for victualling the troops in Connaught. (C. 3218)

1602   Declaration by Christopher Lynch, Mayor of Galway, and others, re the bad meal provided by the victuallers in Connaught. (C. 3233)

---

[303] There is another copy of the 1629 Thomond–Cockayne marriage settlement amongst the Cockayne collection, listed below (ref. C. 2707).

[304] As well as the documents listed below, the collection also contains much miscellaneous genealogical material compiled by and for G.E. Cockayne for his *Complete Peerage*. For example manuscript C. 1973 is a copy by G.E.C. of a pedigree, certified in 1820 by the Ulster King-at-Arms, of the Fitzgeralds of Cloyne c1500–c1820.

1607   (16 Aug.) Quit-claim concerning the victualling of the forces in Ireland by Sir Robert Newcomen of Dublin to Cockayne and Jolles. (C. 2494)

1608   (13 May) Indenture of bargain and sale by Newcomen to Cockayne of the debts due on the Irish victualling accounts. (C. 2704)

1611   (1 April) Agreements concerning the fisheries on the River Bann, at Lough Foyle and 'Longhewater', between Jolles and Cockayne. (C. 2567)

1612   (Jan.–March) A list of salmon and eels sold [probably in Ireland] and the amount of money raised, with accounts, and a copy of Sir Thomas Phillips' bill for the fishing in the keeping of Sir John Jolles. (C. 2754)

1621–1799   An alphabetical list of Irish baronets, with dates of creation [printed]. (C. 825)

1627   (14 March) A letter by the Earl of Thomond to Viscount Savage, regarding his daughter, Mary O'Brien. (C. 2467)

1627   (6 July) Thomond to Charles Cockayne, from Bath, giving family news. (C. 2765)

1629   (20 Jan.) A manuscript book, compiled c1646–57, giving the abstract of title to various properties of Charles Cockayne, Viscount Cullen of Ireland. It deals primarily with his Northants estate, but also gives an abstract of his marriage settlement with Mary, daughter of the Earl of Thomond, made on 20 Jan. 1629. (C. 2707)

1633   (12 May) Thomond to Charles Cockayne, his son-in-law, re the payment of £3,000 by Cockayne. (C. 2445)

1634   (30 April) Thomond to Charles Cockayne, from Bunratty, concerning family affairs. (C. 2473)

1634   (26 June) Same to same, from Dublin. (C. 2435)

1634   (17 July) Boe Clanch to Charles Cockayne, from Dublin, concerning Cockayne family business. (C. 2471)

1634   (29 Sept.) Thomond to his daughter, Mary Cockayne *nee* O'Brien, re family affairs and attendance at the Irish parliament. (C. 2443)

1634   (7 Nov.) Thomond to Charles Cockayne, re money and family business. (C. 2450)

1635   (8 Dec.) Copy of a letter to the Earl of Thomond by his brother, concerning Lord Gerard's marriage settlement. (C. 2457)

c1635   Undated letter by Luke Rawson to Sir Barnaby O'Brien, from Bunratty, re financial matters. (C. 2476)

1636   (7 March) Barnaby O'Brien to Charles Cockayne, from London, mentioning Barnaby's brother lending money to Lord Gerard. (C. 2847)

1636   (10 March) Thomond to Charles Cockayne, regarding financial matters. (C. 2454)

1636   (4 April) Thomond to his daughter Mary, regarding a family marriage. (C. 2462)

1636   (10 Nov.) Thomond to Charles Cockayne, from Dublin, regarding the preferment of Bess and his wish for the same for Megg and the rest. (C. 2769) c1639   Undated letter by Charles Cockayne to 'Sweete', expressing his gratitude to the Earl of Thomond and the Lady Mary. (C. 2453)

c1640   (1 Nov.) John Horsey to Charles Cockayne, from Dublin, probably in regard to the Earl of Thomond. (C. 2465)

Finch Hatton MSS (ref. FH)

1173–1638   A volume of lists of deputies, chancellors and treasurers, etc., of Ireland, drawn up in the early seventeenth century, with a loose document signed by Sir James Ware, 1 July 1638. (FH 42)

1489   A copy made from the Book of Howth of the procession of the lords of Ireland at Greenwich following their summons to court by Henry VII after the battle of Stoke. (FH 229, ff 226–7)

c1543–85   Names of the earls and barons in Ireland created in 35 Henry VIII [1543–4], with another list noting the creation of Donal MacCarthy Mor as Earl of Clancare and Theobald Butler as Baron of Cahir by Elizabeth I. (FH 225, ff 244–5)

1573–88   (11 May, 15 Eliz.–14 Feb., 29 Eliz.) Document endorsed 'The Lord Ch: Hatton's Lands', giving the devolution of his estates, and mentioning his lands in Ireland. (FH 3473)[305]

c1598   Undated notes of settlement of the affairs of the late Sir Christopher Hatton after his death, with marginal comments. States that his Irish lands were sold for £1,600. (FH 3713)

1599   A volume of copies of correspondence, which includes two letters of Sir Thomas Egerton, Lord Chancellor and Keeper of the Great Seal of England, to Robert, Earl of Essex, Lord Lieutenant of Ireland, giving advice concerning the Queen and his campaign in Ireland. Also contains a letter written to Essex in Ireland by Lord Mountjoy. (FH 2381)

1599   (17 April) Endorsed 'An estimate of the estate of Ireland as yt standeth at this present; distracted and broken with these rebellions in the severall provinces thereof, together with the severall forces of the rebells in their particular territories and lykwise what castles and holds ar keapt for her Majesty in every province and particular country. This collection was debated and agreed upon in counsil and signed by the councill then present and so delivered to the rt. hon. Earl of Essex & Lord Leuten. and Governor Generall of this Realme of Ireland'. (FH 127)

1616   'Testimony of the worthy service performed by Captain James Bluntt at Kinsale in Ireland', signed by the lords of the Privy Council. (FH 26, no.94)

1617   Speech of Sir Francis Bacon when Sir William Jones was made Chief Justice of the King's Bench in Ireland, in which Bacon eulogises the previous incumbents of the post, Sir Robert Gardiner, Sir James Ley and Sir Humphrey Winch, and advises Jones to take especial care of the plantations in Ulster, Wexford and Longford. (FH 83, ff 7v–9v)

c1620   Undated project to keep pirates from the harbours in Ireland, with an estimate of how much this will cost the King. It deals in

---

[305] This item is misdated 1615–29 in an endorsement. The endorser confused the abbreviated references to the regnal years of Queen Elizabeth (11 May, anno 15–14 Feb., anno 29) with short-form calendar years.

particular with the need to defend Broadhaven, Valentia and Bearehaven. Reports that Mr Cormack has agreed to build a fort on his lands at Broadhaven with the Crown's support, and Mr Hussey and Mr Banester wish to have ten soldiers and £100 p.a. to protect Valentia. (FH 333, ff 13r–14r)

c1623   Creations of Irish peers by James I. (FH 8, fol. 7)

1627   (7 April) The King's letter to Lord Deputy Falkland regarding the Ulster King of Arms' request that funerals and visitations follow the same procedure in Ireland as in England. (FH 26, no. 15)

1628   (8 Dec.) A copy of Lord Deputy Falkland's apology to the lords of the Council. (FH 87, ff 38–55)

1634   (15 July) Speech of Lord Deputy Wentworth to both Houses of Parliament, given at Dublin Castle. Near-contemporary copy [6pp]. (FH 3702)

c1640   Declaration of the Houses of Parliament in Ireland, offering to help the King against the Scottish covenanters with a grant of subsidies. (FH 2889)

c1641   Petition to the English House of Commons by the gentry, freeholders and inhabitants of the County Palatine of Lancaster, which includes a suggestion that men and money be sent quickly to quell the rebellion in Ireland. (FH 2600)

Fitzwilliam (Milton) MSS (ref. F(M))

A large section of this collection represents the official papers of Sir William Fitzwilliam, Lord Deputy of Ireland [1571–5, 1588–94]. Much of the Irish material has received a listing in Charles McNeill, 'Fitzwilliam Manuscripts at Milton, England', *Analecta Hibernica*, iv (1932), pp287–326. However, there is more to be found in the other sections of the collection, as follows:

Correspondence (ref. F (M) C.)

1567   (11 June) William Fitzwilliam to Hugh Fitzwilliam, reporting the recent deaths of Shane O'Neill and Lord Dunboyne, and mentioning the imprisonment pending trial of the Earl of Desmond and Lord Power. (F (M) C. 27)[306]

1568   (14 July) Copy of the submission of Sir John of Desmond, knowing he has offended the Queen's laws in Ireland and begging for clemency. Signed and sealed at Havering before the Privy Council, and verified by Robert Beale. (F (M) C. 29)

1568   (14 July) Copy of the submission of Garret, Earl of Desmond, the details of which are the same as above. (F (M) C. 30)

1572   (2 May) Copy of the instructions of the Lord Deputy and Council of Ireland, as to the assessment on Co. Westmeath for provisioning the garrison. Also mentions the Lord President of Connaught. (F (M) C. 33)

1572   (3 June) Draft instructions of the Lord Deputy and Council relating to a cess of £860 to be charged on Cos. Meath, Dublin, Westmeath, Louth, Kildare and Wexford for the suppression of Rory Oge

---

[306] A transcript of and commentary on this letter can be found in Ciaran Brady, 'The killing of Shane O'Neill: some new evidence', in the *Irish Sword*, xv, no. 59 (Winter, 1982), pp116–23.

O'More and his accomplices. Shows the amounts for each county. Postscript about finding 100 men to serve with the Earl of Kildare. (F (M) C. 34)

1572   (19 July) Draft instructions of the same about the assessment on the five 'English counties' and Wexford. Endorsed with a memorandum by Fitzwilliam about a complaint by Walter Fowlam of Termonfeghan regarding cess charged on a 'betaghtown' which the Lord Primate says should be exempt. (F (M) C. 35)

1572   (30 Aug.) Draft instructions of the Lord Deputy to the Sheriff and others of Co. Dublin as to their assessment, and the demand that it be paid by September. (F (M) C. 36)

1572   (2 Oct.) Draft instructions of same to same, threatening to incarcerate defaulters from the cess in Dublin Castle, and giving full details of cess charges in the Pale counties and Wexford. (F (M) C. 37)

1572   (3 Oct.) Draft or copy of the instructions of the Lord Deputy, referring to the neglect in the collection of the cess, with a postscript authorising distraint for non-payment. (F (M) C. 38)

c1572   Undated 'humble request' of the Earl of Desmond, asking to be re-possessed of his own lands and those he has placed in mortgage, with advice concerning them written in the margin. Signed by the members of the Privy Council. (F (M) C. 39)

1573   (6 Jan.) Answer of the Earl of Desmond to articles delivered to him by the Queen and the lords of her Council. (F (M) C. 40)[307]

1573   (21 Jan.) Instructions from the Privy Council, responding to the replies of the Earl of Desmond, and stating that they do not mislike his answers to the first four articles, but they warn against acceding to his claims to farms and leases without further deliberation. (F (M) C. 41)[308]

1573   (23 Feb.) Copy of the submission of James Fitzmaurice and his associates before Sir John Perrot, Lord President of Munster, and others 'in the presence of a multitude in the church of Kylmalluck'. James and his confederates display their repentance for rebelling in 1569 with Sir Edmund Butler, etc. (F (M) C. 42)[309]

1573   (22 April) Draft articles of 'certain things from which the Earle of Desmond is to be restrained'. Refers to coign and livery, guns in his castles, black rent, the giving of horses and weapons to his followers, etc. (F (M) C. 43)

1573   (28 April) Copy of the answer of the Earl of Desmond to articles proposed by the Lord Deputy and Council, explaining that because his lands are surrounded by enemies, he needs ordnance for his defence, etc. (F (M) C. 44)

1574   (1 Jan.) Instructions of Queen Elizabeth to Lord Deputy Fitzwilliam, criticising him for not taking a stronger hand with the Earl of Desmond, especially after the seizure of Castlemaine. Orders that the Earl of Thomond should be restored to his castles. (F (M) C. 45)

1574   (18 May) Instructions of same to same, agreeing to the Earl of Desmond coming to England and submitting there. Orders

---

[307] *C.S.P.I.*, 1509–73, p492.

[308] *Ibid*, p493.

[309] *Ibid*, p496.

Fitzwilliam to be sterner in his dealings with the viscounts Roche and Barry. (F (M) C. 46)[310]

1574   (c15 June) Instructions of same to same, citing proof of the Earl of Desmond's continued crimes in Ireland, where he has captured Captain George Bourchier. The Queen is sending Sir William Drury over to advise Fitzwilliam on military matters. (F (M) C. 47)[311]

1574   (19 June) Instructions of the Council to Lord Deputy Fitzwilliam, advising him to send forces into Munster and make sure Cork and Kinsale remain loyal, and ordering him to take heed of the sons of the Earl of Clanricard and quieten Connaught. Also mentions Seckford the victualler. (F (M) C. 48)

1574   (2 Aug.) Instructions of Queen Elizabeth to same, referring to the Earl of Desmond's answers, which were rude and 'inconsiderate'. He argued about retention of his castles as if the Crown had not power to take his life and everything he possesses. Nevertheless, he is to be received into the royal mercy. (F (M) C. 50)[312]

1574   (16 Aug.) Instructions of the Council to same, re Fitzwilliam's dealings with Desmond. They marvel that the Pale should be so weak after so short a time, and find it very strange that Viscount Gormanstown and Lord Delvin have refused to subscribe to the proclamation of rebellion against Desmond. (F (M) C. 51)

1574   (2 Sept.) Copy of the submission of Gerald, Earl of Desmond, before Fitzwilliam and others of the Irish Council at Cork. (F (M) C. 52)[313]

1574   (19 Sept.) Letter of Desmond to Fitzwilliam. Commits himself and his causes to Fitzwilliam's direction, with a postscript asking that Mr Synnott be joined in commission with the others. (F (M) C. 53)

1574   (15 Oct.) Answer of Viscount Gormanston and the Baron of Delvin to the Lord Deputy and Council, explaining why they did not subscribe the proclamation against the Earl of Desmond. (F (M) C. 54)

1575   (29 July) Instructions of the Queen to Lord Deputy Fitzwilliam and the Earl of Essex, relating to the situation in Ulster, where it is understood that Tirlaugh Luineach O'Neill has been compounded with to attack Sorley Boy MacDonnell. (F (M) C. 55)

1580   (6 July) Letter from Roger Bodenham at San Lucar to William Fitzwilliam jnr., reporting that the Spanish hatred of the English is 'marvelous gret', and suggesting that Philip II hopes to engender a fear of Spanish attack in Ireland, England and Flanders so that he will be left alone to deal with Portugal. (F (M) C. 69)

1589   (4 March) Instructions from the Privy Council to the Lord Deputy of Ireland, relating to the collection of the revenue, the composition in Connaught, the need to abolish tanistry from the lands of the O'Tooles, the O'Byrnes and the Kavanaghs, and many other matters. (F (M) C. 89)

1591   (26 Oct.) Instructions of the Queen to Lord Deputy Fitzwilliam, relating to the Commission for Ecclesiastical Causes, the abuse of

---

[310] *C.S.P.I.*, 1574–85, p23.

[311] *Ibid*, p29.

[312] *Ibid*, p35.

[313] *Ibid*, p37.

martial law, and the activities of local administrators and governors, etc. Lengthy letter of state. (F (M) C. 92)

c1591 Undated comprehensive collection of notes on the case against Sir John Perrot in Ireland, including the following headings: disloyalty and discontentment shown by Perrot to the Queen in Ireland; Perrot's contempt of the Councils of England and Ireland; accusations, proofs and statements of witnesses (1585–91); references to Denis Roughan the priest and a letter to the King of Spain, etc. [58 pages, bound together in a book]. (F (M) C. 93)

1601 (5 Oct.) Letter from E. Mountagu to William Fitzwilliam jnr., relating to a levy of 50 men from Northants for service in Ireland. (F (M) C. 136)

Political Papers (ref. F (M) P.)

post-1558 Notes (probably by Sir Walter Mildmay) on the increase in the cost of Ireland, the Navy, the Ordnance, etc., after 1558. (F (M) P. 10)

1576 Speeches of Walter Devereux, Earl of Essex, while on his death bed. (F (M) P. 97)

1577 (11 April) Notes and jottings by Sir Walter Mildmay regarding expenses incurred by the Crown under various headings (Wardrobe, Navy, Ordnance, Admiralty, Ireland, Berwick, etc.). Endorsed, with a note concerning the descent of Philip II. (F (M) P. 9)

1580 (Dec.) Reasons why wines were cheaper in Scotland and Ireland than England, by F. Walsingham, Secretary of State. (F (M) P. 121)

General Series (ref. F (M))

1559 (15 Nov.) Inspeximus and exemplification made at the request of the Mayor and Bailiffs of the City of Limerick, of a decree by the Lord Justice and Irish Council, by which certain French ships had been seized at Limerick haven, it having been proved that they contained more artillery and ammunition than ships were entitled to when plying these shores. Witnessed at Dublin by the Earl of Sussex. (F (M) 2061)

1561 (20 Dec.) Letters patent appointing Sir William Fitzwilliam as Lord Justice of Ireland. (F (M) 2062)

1563 (24 July) Letters patent nominating and appointing Sir William Fitzwilliam to the office of Vice-Treasurer and Treasurer-at-wars in Ireland. (F (M) 2550)

1567 (4 Aug.) Indenture between Lord Deputy Sidney and Sir William Fitzwilliam, witnessing that Sidney had received £6,000 from Thomas Jenison, the Queen's Auditor for Ireland, and delivered the same to Fitzwilliam to be spent on the Irish service. (F (M) 2551)

1569 (14 June) Covenant between Vice-Treasurer Fitzwilliam and William Collier of Stephenstown, Co. Dublin, captain in the Queen's Irish forces, for the victualling of a band of footmen under his command between 24 May 1560 and 30 Nov. 1568. (F (M) 2552)

1569 (14 June) Bond by the aforesaid Collier to Fitzwilliam in £1,000 to observe the above covenant. (F (M) 1553)

1570 (14 March) Letters patent appointing the Earl of Leicester, Lord Howard of Effingham, Sir Francis Knollys, Sir William Cecil, John

Hanby and Thomas Jenson, to examine Sir William Fitzwilliam about the rendering of his accounts as Vice-Treasurer and Treasurer-at-wars in Ireland. (F (M) 2066)

1570–4 Four Pipe Roll acquittances for payment of what Sir William Fitzwilliam owed the Crown in bonds, in respect of his account as Treasurer-at-wars in Ireland. (F (M) 2067–70)

1571 (8 March) Lease of Crown property by Sir Henry Sidney, Lord Deputy of Ireland, to Richard Chichester, gent., of lands at Lusk, Swords, and Portrane, Co. Dublin, Tubber, Co. Kildare, and Dollogh and Grenoke, Co. Meath, for a term of 21 years at £4 5s 6d *per annum*. (F (M) 2072)

1571 (11 Dec.) Letters patent appointing Sir William Fitzwilliam as Lord Deputy of Ireland. (F (M) 2073)

1572 (2 June) Letters patent granting license to Sir William Fitzwiiliam to transport 300 barrels of butter and 200 weys of cheese yearly into Ireland for the better victualling of the garrison there. (F (M) 2074)

1572 (6 Oct.) Letters patent declaring that although Sir William Fitzwilliam has been found to owe the Queen £3,964 11s 0d, on examination of his Irish accounts, Her Majesty has decided to remit £1,000 of that sum in respect of his good service in that realm, and she grants that the balance may be paid off in instalments over the next 10 years. (F (M) 2075)

1572 (19 Oct.) Order by Lord Deputy Fitzwilliam to his servant Walter Brandrop to purchase 500 quarters of wheat and 500 quarters of malt in England for transportation into Ireland. (F (M) 2554)

1573 (15 Jan.) Letters patent to Lord Deputy Fitzwilliam, Lord Chancellor Weston, Vice-Treasurer Fitton, Chief Justice Plunkett, Chief Baron Dillon and Nicholas White, Master of the Rolls, to grant leases of the Queen's lands in Ireland, for terms of 21 years or less. (F (M) 2555)

1573 (10 July) Copy of a Crown lease to Richard Mainwaring, gent., of the ruined chapel of St. Lawrence by Ballyfermot, Co. Dublin, the rectory of Gilton, Co. Kildare, and lands in Rathergell and elsewhere in Ireland, for 21 years. (F (M) 2556)[314]

1575 (9 June) Will of Thomas Wingfield of Norwich, gent., made on the eve of his departure for Ireland, bequeathing all his lands, etc., in England and Ireland to his brother Anthony Wingfield of London, goldsmith, and leaving gifts of money to other members of his family. (F (M) 2165)

1588 (31 May) Will of Robert Browne of Peykirk, Northants, gent., 'beinge mynded, God wyllinge, to passe into Ireland, there to imploye myself in her Majesties service'. (F (M) 2168)

16th cen. Two fragments of a roll of accounts of money lent by the Irish nobility and others to Queen Elizabeth. (F (M) 2558)

1611 (15 Dec.) Privy Seal demanding a loan of £10 from John Price, gent., to be collected by Sir William Fitzwilliam for public services in Ireland. (F (M) 2092)

---

[314] This deed has been used as a cover or wrapper for other documents.

1620   (1 Dec.) Letters patent creating William Fitzwilliam of Milton, Northants, esq., Baron Fitzwilliam of Lifford, Co. Donegal, with particulars of the fees paid for the creation of a baron. (F (M) 2366)

Miscellaneous Papers (ref. F (M) M.)

1588   (20 June) Note of the debts of Sir William Fitzwilliam 'at his going to Ireland 1588'. (F (M) M. 386)

16th cen.   A note of the conquering and lands of Ireland, containing extracts from chronicles, and suggesting advantages and profits which the Queen can take in Ireland. (F (M) M. 122)

Miscellaneous Volumes (ref. F (M) Misc. Vols.)

16th cen.   A copy of an Irish chronicle in Latin belonging to the period 1162–1370 made in the late sixteenth century, endorsed 'Francisus Agard me possidet'. Only the back cover (vellum) remains. (F (M) Misc. Vols. 39)

O'Brien (Blatherwycke) Papers (ref. OBB)

1625   (30 April) Mortgage by Connor Crone O'Brien of Tobermally, Co. Clare, gent., and Mortagh O'Brien of Ballyassie, his son and heir, to Connor O'Keargyne, of lands in Kilonomona parish in the barony of Inchiquin, for £80 and five good calf-cows. (OBB 70)

1625   (30 April) Bond in £200 to perform the covenants in the above deed. (OBB 71)

1625   (29 June) Deed of sale by Connor O'Brien of Tobermally, of land in Drumcliffe parish in the barony of Islands, to Donough O'Brien fitz Conor of Lemeneagh, Co. Clare, gent. (OBB 72)

1628   (6 Nov.) Bond in £200 of Donnogh O'Brien fitz Teige of Ballyassie, Co. Clare, to Donough O'Brien of Lemeneagh, to procure assignments of lands in Tobermally. (OBB 73)

1630   (28 Sept.) Bond in £300 of Donough O'Brien of Lemeneagh, Murtagh Garriff O'Brien of Cahircorkane, Bryan O'Brien of Aghrua, Donald O'Brien Mac Dermot of Carowduff, and Loghlen Keogh O'Heher of Cahirmacumae, gents., to Thomas Thornton of Neadymirry and Mahowne MacNamara of Mayreaoke, gents., to secure the quiet possession of the quarter of land of Ardkearney in the barony of Bunratty, Co. Clare. (OBB 74)

1632   Feoffment by Donough O'Brien fitz Teige of Ballinaberry and Hugh McCrattyne of Caherogan, Co. Clare, gents., feoffees in trust of Donough O'Brien, to Donough O'Brien of Lemeneagh, of half a plowland at Tobermally. (OBB 75)

1633   (17 Aug.) Indenture of a lease by Conor Grone O'Brien of Tobermally, gent., to Edmund O'Hernane of Irish, yeoman, of a moiety of the uppermost half quarter of Tobermally, called Cnocktobermally, for 11 years at a rent of 45s p.a. (OBB 76)

1633   (18 Aug.) Deed of mortgage by Conor Grone O'Brien of Tobermally, gent., to Daniel Og O'Hernane of Irish, merchant, for £20, of a moiety of Cnocktobermally, together with the bond for the performance of the same. (OBB 77–8)

1635   (18 July) Indenture of a lease by Donough O'Brien Mc Conor Crone of Ballyassie, gent., to Edmund O'Hernane of Irish, yeoman, of a moiety of the upper half of Tobermally, for the term of 9 years. (OBB 79)

1635 (20 July) Deed indented concerning the mortgage by same to Daniel Og O'Hernane of Irish, gent., of a moiety of the upper half quarter of Tobermally, in consideration of the sum of £80 1s 6d, together with the counterpart of the same. (OBB 80–1)

1636–7 A deed poll of 31 Oct. 1678, which refers to a lease by Henry, Earl of Thomond, dated 2 March 1635/6, to James Mahon and Richard Arthur, merchants of the City of Limerick, concerning the castle, town and lands of Crattalaghmore and Portreyn in the barony of Bunratty, Co. Clare, which the Earl granted to them for the term of 98 years, in return for a red rose or a peppercorn. By deed dated 8 Aug. 1637, Mahon and Arthur assigned the same to Dr. Thomas Arthur, doctor of physic. (OBB 85)

1640 (5 Sept.) Bond by Conor O'Brien of Lemeneagh, gent., to Teige O'Kerine, in an unspecified sum, to perform covenants concerning the sale by Conor to Teige for £90 2s 0d of the town and lands of [? Ballyasbua] in the barony of Inchiquin, Co. Clare. (OBB 82)

1641 (29 June) Deed of attorney whereby Donough O'Brien *alias* Donough Mantagh O'Brien of Ballyassy, gent., names Conor O'Brien of Lemeneagh, gent., to act as his attorney to redeem the mortgage of the half quarter of Tobermally from Daniel Og O'Hernane for £105. (OBB 83)

1641 (29 June) Bond in £300 by said Donough to said Conor, promising to make an estate to Conor once the Tobermally lands are redeemed. (OBB 84)

Ormonde (Kilkenny) MSS (ref. O.K.)

This accession comprises in all approximately 3,000 documents relating to the English estates granted to the 1st and 2nd Dukes of Ormond, the Earl of Ossory and the Earl of Arran, in the late seventeenth century. They were preserved in the muniment room of the Butler family home at Kilkenny Castle until 1951, when the Marquess of Ormond obtained the sanction of the Irish government to sell his family papers. The National Library of Ireland, which acquired the deeds and papers relating to the Irish estate, did not express interest in the English material. Subsequently, when the English papers were offered to the British Library, it was feared that they would be split up among the record repositories of the 33 English counties to which they relate. To prevent this, the trustees of the Ormond family held negotiations through the offices of the British Museum to deposit the documents with the Northamptonshire Record Society, which then acted as the record office in the shire. Since the papers were formally deposited in Northants in 1951, about 491 documents have been catalogued, but the vast majority of the collection remains unlisted in 66 boxes. Not all of the items are English, and apart from some miscellaneous private papers concerning the Kilkenny estate during the eighteenth and nineteenth centuries, the following documents of relevance to the Irish lands before 1641 have been found among the catalogued material; undoubtedly there is further material among the uncatalogued boxes.

c1615 A contemporary copy of a letter by James I, in which the King agrees to grant a renewal of the liberty of Tipperary to Walter, Earl of Ormond, with an explanation of the extent of the Earl's liberties. (O.K. 416)

1625 (24 Nov.) Copy of a letter by Charles I to Lord Deputy Falkland, concerning a complaint by the Earl of Ormond that his records and evidences have been mislaid, which prevents him from contesting claims made in the Court of Wards over the amercements of divers persons' lands in Tipperary. The King agrees to stay the proceedings in the Court until the missing documents are found. Transcript made on 25 May 1626. (O.K. 437)

c1626   Fragment of an item giving the oath of Charles Walsh, servant of the Earl of Ormond, swearing that an unidentified document is a true copy. (O.K. 469)

1632   (11 Dec.) Copy of the judgement in a case concerning the manor of Thurles, Co. Tipperary, heard in the Court of Wards before Sir Richard Bolton. (O.K. 445)

Temple Stowe MSS (ref. T(S))

c1640   A feoffment in trust whereby Thomas Temple and Thomas Rous, in consideration of £5, grant the remainder of the farm of Baltinglass Abbey with its lands in Cos. Dublin and Wicklow to Lord and Lady Baltinglass. Recites an earlier deed re a grant of the estate by Thomas, Viscount Baltinglass, to Temple and Rous on 30 May 1637 [badly damaged]. (T(S) Box 7/3b/19)

1641   (2 June) Notes in the hand of Sir Peter Temple regarding 'howe I shuld macke lecis of all my landes to pay my dettes'. Begins by making a lease to his sons, Richard and John, and to his daughter Anne, Lady Baltinglass, of all such land as he had from his first wife, Anne Throckmorton, the old rent of which is to be paid to Lady Baltinglass. (T(S) Box 7/3b/11)

1654   A copy of the 'Civil Survey & Down Survey' for Co. Wexford, concerning the landownership there in 1641, made in the nineteenth century. (T(S) Box 45/1)[315]

Westmorland MSS (ref. Westmorland Mss.)

1576   (12 Jan.) A warrant for the discharge of the Earl of Kildare's two sons from the custody of Sir Walter Mildmay, with a note concerning Mildmay's delivery of the boys into the care of their cousin, George Garret, signed by their aunt, the Countess of Lincoln. (Box 2, parcel xii, no. 1, A5)

c1576   Undated letter to Mildmay from Lady Lincoln expressing her thanks for taking care of her nephews. (Box 2, parcel xii, no. 1, A8)

1596–1603   An undated treatise by Anthony Nixon entitled 'England's Hope against Irish Hate', concerning the rebellion of Hugh O'Neill, Earl of Tyrone [small bound vol., 45 fols.]. (Misc. Vol. 30)

1636   (20 July) A discharge to the Dowager Countess of Westmorland by Robert Needham, Viscount Kilmurry [Kilmorey] in Ireland, Lady Eleanor his wife, and Robert Needham, his son and heir apparent. (Box 6, parcel xi, no. 10)

---

[315] Unfortunately, this copy does not contain extracts from the missing section of the Wexford Civil Survey concerning the barony of Forth.

NOTTINGHAMSHIRE : County Archives Office *
Castle Meadow Road, Nottingham NG1 1AG
Tel: (0115) 950 4524

LOOSE ITEMS

1627	Molyneux pedigree, compiled in 1627 for Sir John Byran, showing his descent from Vivian Molyneux. (M. 5412)[316]
1628	(21 July) Royal letter under the signet to Lord Deputy Falkland, ordering him to issue a grant under the Great Seal of Ireland conferring a baronetcy on Adam Colclough of Tintern Abbey, Co. Wexford. Signed by the King, and endorsed with a note of enrolment on the Irish Chancery rolls, dated 13 Sept. 1628. (DD 683/3)

COLLECTIONS

Duke of Portland MSS (ref. DDP and DD 4P)

16th cen.	A group of nine documents dating between c1611 and 1629 relating to the interest held by Edward Alford and others in the manor of Bishop Burton, the rectory of Thorner, and the prebend of Saltmarsh, with other properties in Yorkshire; the rectories of Tedrington and Holne in Gloucestershire; and also in premises at Darlington, Co. Durham, all of which were granted to Thomas Butler, 10th Earl of Ormond, by the late Queen Elizabeth, in reward for his services. (DD 4P, 28/27–34)
1616	(21 July) Copy of an order in Council for the provision of 25 men from Derbyshire for service in the army in Ireland. (DDP 7/2)

NOTTINGHAMSHIRE : University of Nottingham Library *
University Park, Nottingham NG7 2RD
Tel: (0115) 951 5151/951 4565
Fax: (0115) 951 4558

LOOSE ITEMS

16th cen.	A bound volume entitled 'A brief collection of the greatest part of the life of Sir James Croft, Comptroller of the Household: and of the Privy Council to Queen Elizabeth, gathered by himself', which probably contains information re his period as Lord Deputy of Ireland, 1551–3. (Pw V/83)
17th cen.	A History of the Holles family, by Gervase Holles, which contains material regarding the military services performed in Ireland during the reign of Elizabeth I by Francis Holles, Sir Gervase Holles, and Sir John Holles, 1st Earl of Clare, who was knighted there in 1593. This item has been published, A.C. Wood (ed.), *Memorials of the Holles family, 1493–1656* (Camden Soc., 3rd series, lv, 1937). (Pw V/6)

COLLECTIONS

The Middleton (Willoughby of Wollaton Hall) Collection (ref. Mi.)

The main body of the Irish papers in this collection have been artificially divided into two sections, entitled 'Munster Plantation Papers' and 'Ulster Plantation

---

[316] We would like to thank Bríd McGrath for bringing this item to our attention.

Papers' respectively. The latter section is misleadingly named, referring as much to the Leix plantation and the manor of Galen Ridgeway, Queen's Co., as it does to Ulster. None of these items were included in the report on the collection in H.M.C., *Middleton MSS* (1911).

Munster Plantation Papers

c1584	Articles concerning Her Majesty's affairs for the disposing of her lands in Munster in Ireland, whereof it pleaseth Her Majesty to grant an estate to Englishmen, to them and their heirs for ever (15 articles); with a note of 'The farm or freeholders charge the first year' [4pp]. (Mi Da 57a)
c1584	The plot of Her Majesty's offer touching the peopling of Munster in Ireland [1p]. (Mi Da 57b)
16th cen.	A rough sketch map, entitled 'The distribution of 62 seigniories in Munster in Ireland' [1p]. (Mi Da 57e)
n.d.	(7 May) Letter to Percival Willoughby from his brother relating his experiences since landing at Youghal on 14 April. Mentions the recent death of Mr. Marrow, 'but the villain that slew him is according to his deserts hanged in chains', and part of his bowels burned in Cork City [2pp]. (Mi Da 57c)
n.d.	Another letter to Percival Willoughby, in which his correspondent details landing at Waterford on 17 Nov. on estate business, and reports travelling to the seigniory of Mr. Cuffe, who has dealt harshly with the tenants [3pp]. (Mi Da 57d)

Ulster Plantation Papers

c1610	Fragment of an undated letter to Sir Thomas Ridgeway, Vice-Treasurer of Ireland. (Mi Da 57/1 dd)
1611	(7–8 Dec.) Sir Thomas Ridgeway to Sir Percival Willoughby, regarding lands in Clogher barony, Co. Tyrone [1p]. (Mi Da 57/1 j)
1612	(27 Feb.) William Turvin to Mr. Anthony in London, re the passage of lands in Tyrone from Sir Percival Willoughby to Captain Leigh [1p.] (Mi Da 57/1 g).
1612	(4 May) Sir Thomas Ridgeway to Sir Percival Willoughby, concerning the Fenbragh estate in Tyrone [1p]. (Mi Da 57/1 ee)
1615	(13 July) Francis Willoughby to his mother, regarding his journey to London and his need of money towards travel to Ireland [1p]. (Mi Da 57/1 h)
1616	(12 March) Covenant by John Leigh to call his castle by the name of Castle Cassandra, as requested by Sir Francis Willoughby when he sold the manor of Ffaithnagh, Co. Tyrone, to Leigh. (Mi Da 57/1 m)
1622	(2 April) Indenture between (i) Thomas, Earl of Londonderry and Lady Cicilia, his Countess, (ii) Sir Robert Ridgeway, Dame Ellice, his wife, Edward and Mark-William Ridgeway, and (iii) Sir Simon Weston and Sir Francis Willoughby, regarding the provision of the manor of Galen Ridgeway, Queen's County, as jointure for Dame Ellice. (Mi Da 57/1 e)
c1630	Undated note of receipts of a half year's rent from the tenants of the manor of Galen Ridgeway, amounting to £60. (Mi Da 57/1 s)
1630	(22 May) Indenture concerning a bond of statute staple in the sum of £20,000 made at Kilkenny by Robert, Lord Ridgeway, and Sir

Simon Weston to ensure that they would pay maintenance money due to Edward and Mark-William Ridgeway. (Mi Da 57/1 f)

1631   (18 April) Copy of the provisos and conditions approved by Henry Staines, agent to Lord Ridgeway, in the matter of the recognizance of £20,000. (Mi Da 57/1 u)

1631   (10 Sept.) Verification by Robert Archer, Clerk of the Staple in Kilkenny, of a copy of another recognizance of statute staple taken by Lord Ridgeway for the honouring of debts and annuities to his brothers. (Mi Da 57/1 v)

1631   (10 Dec.) Indenture between (i) Lord Ridgeway and others and (ii) Mark-William his brother re an annuity of £120 out of Galen manor. (Mi Da 57/1 c)

1632   (10 March) Indenture whereby the lands of Kilrush, Ballynegery, Sampson's Court and Kilronan, parcels of Galen manor in Queen's County, are granted to Oliver Wheeler of Dunmore, Co. Kilkenny, and Edward Kingsmill of London, to hold to the use of Mark-William Ridgeway. A list of the tenants appears on the reverse. (Mi Da 57/1 d)

1633   (9 Sept.) Copy of an order made by Sir Richard Bolton and Sir Philip Percival in the Court of Wards concerning an inquisition post mortem recently held at Maryborough into the late Earl of Londonderry's estate. (Mi Da 57/1 bb)

1633   (15 Sept.) Copy of the annuity made to Mark-William Ridgeway in 1631, entered by Mr. Dopping in the Rolls Office. (Mi Da 57/1 p)

1633   (27 Sept.) Indenture between Lord Ridgeway and his brother, Peter Ridgeway of Ballinakill, re an annuity of £120 p.a. (Mi Da 57/1 b)

c1633   Undated note of rent receipts and payments made on behalf of Mark-William Ridgeway. (Mi Da 57/1 r)

1634   (11 Nov.) Letter of attorney by Mark-William Ridgeway of Ballinakill. (Mi Da 57/1 n)

c1635–6   Undated note concerning the claim made by Robert, 2nd Earl of Londonderry, to part of the territory of Idough, Co. Kilkenny. (Mi Da 57/1 o)

1636   (10 Feb.) A schedule of lands and hereditaments for which Robert, Lord Londonderry, compounded, and a copy of an order given by the Commissioners for Defective Titles regarding his estate. (Mi Da 57/1 t)

1638   Enrolment in Chancery of a recognizance made in Kilkenny by Robert, Lord Londonderry, concerning his obligations to his brothers. (Mi Da 57/1 a)

c1640   Undated notes concerning the possessions of Galen manor made by William Booth. (Mi Da 57/1 y)

c1640   Copy of Michael Cowley's opinion about a feoffment made by Thomas, late Earl of Londonderry, and others. (Mi Da 57/1 q)

c1640   Undated notes re the Londonderry estates. (Mi Da 57/1 x)

1641   (11 Aug.) Acknowledgement of the receipt of £14 by William Ford from Mark-William Ridgeway. (Mi Da 57/1 l)

1641   (2 April) Declaration and order by Sir Francis Willoughby regarding a grant in 1616 of an annual rent of 22s. to him by John Leigh of Omagh, Co. Tyrone. (Mi Da 57/1 i)

n.d.   Note of a half year's rent due from Galen manor. (Mi Da 57/1 w)

n.d.   Letter by Calcott Chambre, probably to Sir Percival Willoughby, reporting news from the Ulster estate, where Mr. Leigh has had trouble collecting the rent. (Mi Da 57/1 z)

n.d.   Receipt of £2 10s rent from Thomas Meredith, one of the tenants of Galen manor. (Mi Da 57/1 aa)

n.d.   Note of payments made regarding munitions and servants expenses. (Mi Da 57/1 cc)

n.d.   Thomas Selmony to Sir Percival Willoughby requesting that the bearer, a young soldier, be appointed to one of Willoughby's companies. (Mi Da 57/1 k)

Other Middleton Papers

In addition, there are a few more Irish items scattered throughout the rest of the collection:

1610   An account of the marriage in Dublin Castle of Francis Willoughby to a daughter of Sir Thomas Ridgeway, Vice-Treasurer of Ireland. (Mi LM 27, pp83–4)

1640   Papers concerning the settlement of affairs on the estate of the Earl of Londonderry in Queen's County [2 items]. (Mi Da 100, Mi 5/169/82)

Clifton Correspondence (ref. C1 C)

A large collection of letters written to Sir Gervase Clifton early in the seventeenth century, which contains the following items of Irish interest :

c1632–4   Undated letter from Frances Clifton to Sir Gervase Clifton describing her voyage to Dublin, where she met the Earl of Cork and Lady Dungarvan. (C1 C 115)

1632   (6 June) Robert Butler to same, mentioning that Lord Wentworth has not yet left for Ireland. (C1 C 58)

1632   (31 Oct.) Lettice, Baroness of Offaly, to same, regarding the Lord Deputy and Viscount Ranelagh. (C1 C 352)

1633   (30 Jan.) Robert Butler to same, re Lady Exeter's visit to Lord Wentworth's house, and also concerning Lord Falkland's money. (C1 C 59)

1633   (27 July) Wentworth to same, reporting his decision to make a treaty with the Earl of Cork. (C1 C 720)

1633   (9 Aug.) Thomas Benson to same, concerning his speeches with Wentworth in April. (C1 C 34)

1633   (19 Dec.) Henry, Lord Clifford, to same, regarding the affairs of Lords Wentworth, Cork and Ranelagh. (C1 C 706)

1634   (16 April) E. Clifford to same, reporting the good opinion formed of Lord Dungarvan. (C1 C 86)

1634   (9 May) Henry, Lord Clifford, to same, stating that he has sent his servant to the Earl of Cork in Ireland to receive the valuation of the lands passed to him by Lord Dungarvan. (C1 C 88)

1634	(27 June) Same to same, describing a party held at Skipton attended by Wentworth. (C1 C 708)
1634	(c June–July) Same to same, reporting news that Wentworth and the Earl of Cork have reached a conclusion. (C1 C 691)
1634	(26 Sept.) Lord Dungarvan to same, concerning his return to Ireland and his opinion of Wentworth. (C1 C 625)
1634	(26 Sept.) Lady Dungarvan to same, re her hearty welcome from Lord Cork and a civil one from the Lord Deputy. (C1 C 624)
1634	(27 Sept.) Hubert Cressy to same, including comments on the state of Ireland. (C1 C 142)
1634	(23 Oct.) George Butler to same, giving an account of a quarrel between Wentworth and Lord Cork. (C1 C 54)
1635	(14 Feb.) Henry, Lord Clifford, to same, stating that the Earl of Cork has gone to Dublin to answer the bill laid against him in Castle Chamber. (C1 C 696)
1635	(23 March) Sir Richard Tempest to same, asking for news of the health of Miss Clifton in Ireland. (C1 C 441)
1635	(April) Lady Dungarvan to same, re Clifton family affairs. (C1 C 155)
1635	(27 June) Robert Robotham to same, mentioning Lord Dunluce, Lady Dungarvan and also the Wentworth-Cork dispute. (C1 C 388)
1635	(12 July) Christopher Wandesford to same, regretting Clifton's absence from Ireland, and mentioning the Lord Deputy's progress through the country. (C1 C 604)
1635	(17 Aug.) Lady Dungarvan to same, referring to lords Clifford and Cork, who have gone to the Lord Deputy. (C1 C 627)
1635	(20 Aug.) Lord Dungarvan to same, from Portumna, re Lord Clifford's arrival in Ireland. (C1 C 626)
1635	(20 Aug.) Christopher Wandesford to same, re the state of Ireland. (C1 C 473)
c1635–6	Undated letter by Dru Cooper to same, re Lord Cork and the Bishop of Lismore. (C1 C 136)
1636	(6 July) Wentworth to same, hoping to meet Sir Gervase at Rufford, where he intends to attend upon the King. (C1 C 719)
1636	(26 Nov.) Christopher Wandesford to same, reporting his conversation with the Lord Deputy. (C1 C 474)
1636	(30 Nov.) Wentworth to same, re his passage to Ireland, Mr Wandesford and the Earl of Holland. (C1 C 486)
1637	(22 Feb.) Christopher Wandesford to same, praising the Lord Deputy. (C1 C 475)
1637	(24 Feb.) Wentworth to same, reporting the safe delivery of horses. (C1 C 718)
1637	(July) Christopher Wandesford to same, re his intention to marry his son to the second daughter of the Earl of Sunderland. (C1 C 476)
1638	(17 March) Henry, Lord Clifford, to same, re Lord Dungarvan and his wife. (C1 C 92)

1638   (8 Sept.) Wentworth to same, re the Lord Chancellor of Ireland, Lord Clifford and the misfortunes that have befallen the family of the late Earl of Clare. (C1 C 721)

1640   (15 July) Earl of Kingston to same, mentioning a rumour that the Earl of Strafford is to go to Ireland and that Mr Glanville, the great Chancery man, has become one of his servants. (C1 C 687)

OXFORDSHIRE : Oxfordshire Archives *
County Hall, New Road, Oxford OX1 1ND
Tel: (01865) 815 203/810 801
Fax: (01865) 810 187

COLLECTIONS

Dillon of Costello–Gallen Collection (ref. DIL)

1567   Map showing the territories of Irish princes and chieftains, the various septs subordinate to them, and also the districts in possession of Anglo-Irish lords. [19th cen. copy]. (DIL XX11/d/4)

1575–1601   A volume of transcripts of letters and documents relating to Captain Thomas Lee. Includes a number of items concerning his service in Ireland, all of which are taken from the State Paper series in the Public Record Office in London [c400 fols]. (DIL XXI/18)

16th cen.   Nineteenth century notes of Harold Dillon concerning the Dillon family during the sixteenth century. Includes a copy of a 1591 petition of Ellinor, wife of the future 1st Viscount Dillon, asking that her husband be released from the Tower. (DIL XXII/d/1a–n)[317]

1607   (29 Oct.) Bond of Captain William Yelverton in £100 to pay Owen Boyle £10 (stg), being the repayment on a mortgage of four years. (DIL XXII/b/11a)

1610   (19 July) Confirmation by the King to Sir Theobald Dillon of his hereditary lands and other lands he has bought, *viz* the manor of Killenfeghe, castle of Ballinakilty, manor of Glascorne, castle of Ballyneferagh, manor of Portlick, castle of Ballymullen, and other lands in Co. Westmeath, and, the manor of Gally, Co. Roscommon, manor of Castlemore, Kilcolman, Binfadda, Ballindore, Annagh, Monyen, Gallen and other lands in Co. Mayo [19th cen. copy]. (DIL XXII/b/2)[318]

1623   (16 March) Letters patent creating Sir Theobald Dillon of Costello-Gallen, Co. Mayo, Viscount Dillon of Costello-Gallen, for himself and his heirs male [a photographic copy]. (DIL XXII/b/3)[319]

Valentia MSS (ref. E6)

This collection represents the archive of the Annesleys of Bletchingdon, Viscounts Valentia. They inherited the Bletchingdon estate and some Irish property in 1737 at the death of the 5th Earl of Anglesey, and were made heir presumptive to that family's Irish titles in 1841 by the 2nd Earl of Mountnorris and 9th Viscount Valentia. Why so many early Irish deeds survive in this

---

[317] N.L.I. microfilm, n. 5208, p. 5312.
[318] Ibid.
[319] Ibid.

collection is not altogether clear. In 1949, after the death of the 12th Viscount, his heiresses agreed to deposit the archive in the Bodleian Library. In 1969 the owners formally agreed to transfer the collection to the Oxfordshire County Record Office.[320]

1594	Letters patent granting to Dermot MacMorish Kavanagh of Knockangarrow, the lands of Coolnaleen, Cronecromaghte, Clonynemannaghe, and Kilchome, Co. Wexford, late belonging to Griffin MacMurrough Kavanagh, attainted, and of the lands of Kilmichael, late belonging to Dermot O'Nittin, attainted, in accordance with letters under the sign manual, dated 1591.[321] (E6/7/1D/1)
1596	Bargain and sale by Robert Annesley of Mallow, Co. Cork, to Nicholas Burke of Limerick, alderman, of the castle, town and lands of Rathaverd *alias* Rathurd, and the town of Donaghmore, Co. Limerick. Reciting letters patent dated 1589. (E6/7/4D/1)
1610	Rough draft of a defeasance of a mortgage by Henry Atherton of Mountnorris, Co. Armagh (mortgagee) to Patrick Hanlon of Co. Armagh, gent. (mortgager), of lands in Co. Armagh. (E6/7/3D/1)
1611	Indenture concerning some mortgaged property between (1) Capt. Henry Atherton of Mountnorris, Edward Trevor of Narrow Water, Co. Down, and Henry's brother, Richard Atherton (guarantors), (2) Capt. Anthony Hawes of Newry (creditor), and (3) Patrick MacPhellym O'Hanlon (mortgager), regarding seven townlands in Orior barony, Co. Armagh, and reciting two bonds. (E6/7/3D/2)
1611	Lease by the King to Francis Annesley of the fort, castle, town, etc., of Mountnorris in O'Hanlon's country, Co. Armagh, for 21 years. (E6/7/3D/5)
1611	Bargain and sale, with a conditional covenant of conveyance, by Patrick O'Hanlon to Arthur Basset and Francis Annesley. O'Hanlon sells lands in Co. Armagh to Bassett. The deed recites letters patent of 1609, whereby O'Hanlon surrendered Mountnorris Castle with 300 acres to the King, on condition that it would be returned to him if not needed as a fortress. O'Hanlon conveys that reversion to Annesley. (E6/7/3D/3)
1611	Bond on statute staple made at Dublin by Patrick O'Hanlon of Co. Armagh to Francis Annesley, in the sum of £500 (stg), owed for wool and hides. O'Hanlon offers all his property, personal and real, as security. (E6/7/3D/6)
1613–16	Bargains and sales by Patrick O'Hanlon to Francis Annesley of the manor, lordship, castle, towns, lands etc., of Mountnorris, Co. Armagh. (E6/7/3D/7)
1613–1711	An eighteenth century document concerning lands in Cos. Armagh and Tyrone belonging to the Annesley family, which includes a schedule of leases made since 9° James I. (E6/7/9D/6, 8)
1614	Inquisition by Francis Annesley and other Commissioners, concerning the lordship, manor, lands, etc., of Mountnorris, Co.

[320] We would like to thank Dr. Darwall-Smith for sending, at short notice, the new reference numbers for the following items. He has recently been responsible for substantially recataloguing the entire collection. A copy of this new catalogue, which may include documents not noticed in the following list, is to be deposited with the National Archives in Dublin.

[321] See *Cal. Fiants Ire.*, Eliz I, no. 5862.

Armagh. Reciting letters patent of 1609 and 1612 relating to the premises, and listing all its parcels, lands, markets, fairs, etc. (E6/7/3D/8)

1615   Letters patent reciting letters patent of 1610 granting to Phelim MacHugh, Brian MacHugh and Cahir MacHugh O'Reilly, sons of Hugh O'Reilly, late of Ballaghanea, Tirlagh MacHugh MacBrian bane O'Reilly, Shane MacPhillips, Anthony Atkinson, and Francis Annesley, certain parcels of land, towns, etc., in the baronies of Tullyhaw, Castlerahan, and Clanmahon, Co. Cavan, and in the barony of Orior, Co. Armagh. (E6/7/3D/9)

1615   Letters patent reciting letters patent of 1610 granting to Edward Trevor, William Wilson, Sir Thomas Ridgeway, George Ridgeway, Sir Richard Wingfield, William Parsons, Charles Poynts, Philip Griffith, Marmaduke Whitchurch, John Hamilton, William Cole, Sir Francis Roe, and Robert Hamilton, lands in the baronies and territories of O'Nelan, Clanbrassill, and Orior, Co. Armagh, Lifford and Raphoe, Co. Donegal, Clogher and Dungannon, Co. Tyrone, Lurg and Magheryboy, Co. Fermanagh, and Tullyhunco, Co. Cavan. (E6/7/9D/1)

1615   Bargain and sale by John King of Bagotrath, and Sir Adam Loftus of Rathfarnham, Co. Dublin, to Francis Annesley, of the Priory of Termonfeighan, and all its lands, tithes, etc., in Cos. Louth and Armagh. Includes a clause that Annesley may have the estate after a term of 21 years (from 7° James I) if it is not then occupied as a fortress. (E6/7/9D/2)

1616   Bargain and sale (reciting letters patent/grant of the previous day) by Francis Edgeworth of Dublin, to Sir Francis Annesley, of land in Kinelarty *alias* MacCartans Country, Co. Down (also, counterpart of above). (E6/7/10D/1–2)

1616   Appointment by Annesley and Edgeworth of attorneys to receive livery of seisin, in the preceding sale. (E6/7/10D/3)

1617   Counterpart of a lease by Sir Francis Annesley to William Smyth of Ballenenghy, Co. Down, of the lands of Ballycloghmaghericatt, etc., Co. Down, for 21 years. (E6/7/10D/6)

1617   Bargain and sale by Phelim MacCartan of Ballenehinch, Co. Down, to Sir Francis Annesley, of lands in Killeaneartin *alias* Kinelarty *alias* MacCartans Country, Co. Down. (E6/7/10D/4)

1617   Exemplification of a fine, dated 1616, between Francis Annesley, plainant, and Roger Chamberlain of Nishrath, Co. Louth, deforciant, regarding lands in Clough and Kinelarty, Co. Down. (E6/7/10D/7)

1618   Letters patent granting to Patrick Peppard, Sir James Ware, Nicholas Masterson, Anthony *alias* Owny MacHugh Ballagh MacDonogh Kavanagh, Michael Synnott, Alexander Redmond, Walter Synnott, David MacPhelim, Tirlagh MacMoriertagh, Donogh MacMurtagh and Donell MacMurtagh, various lands in Co. Wexford, part of the plantation there.[322] (E6/7/1D/3)

1618   Letters patent granting to Art MacDermot Kavanagh *alias* Kinselagh, the lands of Kilmichael, Cooleteduffe, Ballingarry, Slewbracke, Creagh, Balliloghran, Coolecreagh, Kilpatricke and

---

[322] *Cal. Ir. Patent Rolls, James I,* p361.

Gorey, Co. Wexford, to be created the manor of Ballingarry, subject to the conditions of the Wexford plantation.[323] (E6/7/1D/5)

1618	Letters patent granting to Sir George Trevelyan the manor of Sampton, Co. Wexford.[324] (E6/7/1D/4)
1618	Letters patent granting to Francis Blundell the manor of Blundell *alias* Templeshannon, Co. Wexford.[325] (E6/7/1D/2)
1619	Letters patent granting to Sir Thomas Hibbotts the manor of Monisootagh, Co. Wexford.[326] (E6/7/1D/6)
1619	Copy of letters patent granting to Sir Francis Annesley various lands in Cos. Armagh, Tyrone, Down, and Wexford, including the sites of the nunneries of Templefartagh and Templebreed in the town of Armagh. (E6/7/3D/11)
1619	Exemplification of a fine, dated 1618, reciting a writ of precipe of 1617, between Sir Francis Annesley and Patrick O'Hanlon, regarding 4,800 acres in Co. Armagh. (E6/7/3D/12)
1620	Letters patent granting to Edmund Medhop the manor of Medhopall, Co. Wexford.[327] (E6/7/1D/7)
1620	Bargain and sale by Donogh Reogh O'Hagan to Sir Francis Annesley of part of the lands of Ballygorman, Co. Armagh. (E6/7/3D/13)
1621	Letters patent reciting a sign manual of 1619, granting to Sir Francis Annesley and Thomas, Lord Cromwell, lands in the counties of Mayo, Galway, Kildare and Dublin. (E6/7/9D/3)
1621	Exemplification of a fine of 1619, reciting a writ of precipe of 1619, between Sir Francis Annesley, plainant, and Richard Rolleston, gent., Elizabeth his wife, Arthur Rolleston and John Rolleston, gents., deforciants, regarding the manor of Teemore, Co. Armagh. (E6/7/3D/14)
1627	(20 Dec.) Feoffment in trust by Sir Francis Annesley to Sir James Hamilton, Viscount Clandeboy, Viscount Chichester, Sir Robert King, Charles Points (*alias* Poyntz) and Robert Dixon, of his entire estate in Cos. Wexford, Tyrone, Armagh and elsewhere in Ireland, and all his lands in England and Wales, to his use, and after his death to the use of his son, Arthur. Provided that if Sir Francis pays them 12d (stg) 'upon Strongbowes Toombe in Christchurch in Dublin', the deed is void. (E6/1/12/2)
1630	(25 Sept.) Letters patent granting to Francis, Lord Mountnorris, and his heirs and assigns for ever, the 'proportion of Teimore' in Co. Armagh [18th century copy]. (E6/1/12/1, fol. 4)
1630	Fiant for a grant to Francis, Baron Mountnorris, of the manor and lands in Teemore, and the concealed land in Ballygorman, Co. Armagh, the premises to be known as the manor of Mountnorris. The fiant was delivered to Chancery on 25 November. (E6/7/3D/15)
1630–50	Articles of agreement dated 1650, in which it is stated that Arthur Annesley was still owed the annual rent of £140 for the manor of

[323] *Ibid*, p390.
[324] *Ibid*, p359.
[325] *Ibid*, p482.
[326] *Ibid*, p448.
[327] *Ibid*, p482.

Monisootagh, Co. Wexford, by Lord Brabazon, for the year before the 1641 rebellion, and furthermore that £109 5s 9d still remained on the accounts of 'Mr Hull' of 13 July 1641. The following deeds are also recited (E6/1/12/7):

1630	(25 June) Statute staple of James Honarden, for moneys owed to Annesley (states that the remaining debt in 1650 was £80, and the case was before the Exchequer).
1630	(13 Aug.) Bond of Lord Barrymore for moneys owed to Annesley (states that the remaining debt in 1650 was £40 10s, and the case was before the Exchequer).[328]
1636	(14 Oct.) Settlement by Mountnorris to Barnewall and Hoile (see E6/7/9D/4 below).
1636	(Michaelmas) Bill or note under the hand of Lady Brabazon for payment of £50 to Lord Mountnorris.
1636	(9 Dec.) Bond of Archibold Erskine, Archibold Hamilton and Henry Manning, esqs., in £2,400, for the payment of £1,210 on 1 Oct. 1639, to Arthur Annesley.
1637[329]	(16 Jan.) Bond of Walter and John Straby of Dublin, merchants, in £200 for the payment of £102 10s on 17 June following to Randall Aldersey.
1637	(9 May) Bond of Roger Moore and Nicholas Barnewall in £400 for the payment of £210 on 17 Jan. following to Arthur Annesley.
1637	(29 Nov.) Bond of Oliver, Lord Louth, Sir Chistopher Bellew, and Nicholas Barnewall in £440 for the payment of £235 on 29 May following to Randall Aldersey.
1637	(11 Dec.) Statute staple. Thomas Masterson stands bound in £800 (with a defeasance dated the same day) for the payment of £455 14s 3d on 1 May following to Randall Aldersey.
1638	(4 May) Bond of Robert, Lord Dillon and James Dillon, his son, in £2,000, for the payment of £1,260 by 4 May 1639 to Arthur Annesley.
1638	(4 May) Bond of same to same, in £100 for the payment of £60 by the same date.
1638	(18 May) Bond of Richard Lane in £200, for the payment of £110 by 10 May 1639 to Arthur Annesley.
1638	(30 June) Bond of John, Lord Taaffe, Thomas, Lord Dillon, Theobald Taaffe, and Sir James Dillon, in £1,323 (stg), for the payment of £661 10s on 30 Sept. following to Arthur Annesley.
1638	(14 July) Bond of the Earl of Ormond and Donogh MacCarthy in £825 for the payment of £412 10s on 1 Nov. following to Arthur Annesley.
1638	(4 Dec.) Bond of Sir Archibold Hamilton and Sir Francis Hamilton in £660 for the payment of £363 on 1 Nov. 1639 to Arthur Annesley.

1633   Counterpart of a lease by Francis, Baron Mountnorris, to James Moore of Uloghren, and his son Francis Moore, of the lands of Cloghram *alias* Ballyclogher, Co. Down, for 21 years. (E6/7/10D/8)

1634   Counterpart of a lease by Francis, Baron Mountnorris, to Robert Warde of Dublin, Marie his wife, and Nicholas Warde his brother, of the lands of Cloghmagherecatt, Co. Down, for three lives. (E6/7/10D/9)

---

[328] As with the previous item, this figure could represent the entire debt or bond, or maybe only an outstanding portion.

[329] The date is either 1631[–2] or 1636[–7].

1635   Quitclaim by Jane Edgeworth, relict of Francis Edgeworth, of all her dower lands in Co. Down (not listed) to Francis, Baron Mountnorris. (E6/7/10D/10)

1636   (14 Oct.) Counterpart of a settlement/lease from Sir Francis Annesley, Baron Mountnorris, to Nicholas Barnewall of Turvy, Co. Dublin, and Josias Hoile (or Doyle), clerk, of his estates in Cos. Armagh, Tyrone and Wexford. Barnewall and Hoile shall enter the estates for two years following the death of Sir Francis, they shall make payments of £1,500 a piece to his daughters for their marriage portions, and they shall pay annuities of £66 13s 4d to his sons, and various annuities to his daughters, along with other conditions. (E6/7/9D/4)[330]

1637   Letters patent to Francis, Baron Mountnorris, Roger Chamberlaine (deceased), Phelim MacCartan, Jane, Baroness Mountnorris, and others, being a licence to alienate, and a pardon for previous alienations of 1616 and 1617, concerning land in Cloghmagherecat, Co. Down. (E6/7/10D/14)

1638   (3 April) Marriage settlement papers of Arthur Annesley, son and heir of Lord Mountnorris, and Elizabeth Altham, eldest daughter of Sir James Altham, deceased. The marriage portion includes the manors of Medhopall, Sampton, Monisotagh, Annesley and Clonevan, Co. Wexford, and Mountnorris in Co. Armagh. (E6/1/22/1–5)

1640   (4 June) Indenture tripartite between (1) Francis, Lord Mountnorris, and Lady Jane his wife, (2) Arthur Annesley, his son and heir apparent, (3) Sir Richard Phillips, Roger Lort, of Pembrokeshire, John White and Thomas Leeke, of London. (1) conveys to (2) all his estates in Ireland, England, and Wales, except his estates in Co. Down, on condition that (2) pays to (1) £4,000 and an annuity of £900. (3) to be allowed entry onto the estates if (2) does not fulfil these conditions. Includes several further details, and copies of earlier settlements. (E6/1/12/4)

1640   Fine raised on Francis, Lord Mountnorris's Irish estates (except in Co. Down), as part of the settlement dated 4 June, above, to convey them to his son and heir apparent, Arthur Annesley. (E6/1/12/3)

1640   (11 July) Quitclaim or release by Francis, Lord Mountnorris, on behalf of his daughters, Anna, Jane and Katherine, and his sons, John, Peter, George and William, to Arthur Annesley, his son and heir apparent, of all annuities out of his estates in Cos. Armagh, Tyrone and Wexford, proscribed in the settlement made for the aforesaid children dated 14 Oct. 1636 (see above), to commence from 24 June last past [two copies]. (E6/1/12/5–6)

1641   Fine (lease for 61 years from 1638) between Richard Fitz-Gerald, plainant, and George, Earl of Kildare, deforciant, on lands in Drinnanstown, Cloncurry, Cappanagid, Collioghmore, Colliaghbegg and Gary Cahir, all in Co. Kildare. (E6/7/8D/1)

17th cen.   An early eighteenth century rent roll of lands in Co. Wexford, including notes of deeds dating from 1639. (E6/7/6/1)

---

[330] This settlement appears frequently in documents throughout the period after 1641.

OXFORD UNIVERSITY : Balliol College Library
Oxford OX1 3BJ
Tel: (01865) 277 777
Fax: (01865) 277 803

The vast majority of this College's manuscript holdings have received an extensive listing in R.A.B. Mynors, *Catalogue of the Manuscripts of Balliol College, Oxford* (Oxford, 1963), and the following Irish documents have been noticed:

LOOSE ITEMS

1632   (23 June) Autobiography of Sir Richard Boyle, 1st Earl of Cork and Lord High Treasurer of Ireland, ending in 1631 [18th cen. copy, 8 fols]. (Ms. 341)[331]

17th cen.   Volume containing approximately 34 sermons preached by James Ussher, Archbishop of Armagh and Primate of Ireland, some of which are unfinished [557 fols]. (Ms. 259)[332]

COLLECTIONS

The Conroy Papers (ref. Conroy)

Since the publication of Mynors' catalogue the College has received the Conroy family papers, which include detailed genealogical tracts of the family's lineage and history. Most of the information relevant to this survey concerns Moylin O'Mulconry of Tullon, Co. Roscommon, who died in 1637, and his son and heir Thorna O'Mulconry (d.1647), both of whom were the lineal ancestors of the Conroys. (ref. 6.M & N; 9A.4, 5, 6, 7, 12, 13.5; 9B; 14B; etc.)[333]

OXFORD UNIVERSITY : Bodleian Library, Dept. of Western Manuscripts *
Broad Street, Oxford OX1 3BG
Tel: (01865) 277 158
Fax: (01865) 277 187

The Bodleian Library possesses a rich collection of manuscripts concerning the history of early modern Ireland, and a considerable number of them have appeared in print under the auspices of the Irish Manuscripts Commission, either in calendar form or as part of a detailed listing. Furthermore, the library has published two series of catalogues of its Western Manuscripts giving summary details of all its acquisitions to 1975.[334]

Though we have attempted to include all relevant manuscript material, we have especially tried to fill out details on items not noticed, or heavily summarised by the presently existing catalogues. Many of the library's larger collections concerning Ireland are well known to historians, and we have only

---

[331] This has been printed in *The Works of the Hon. Robert Boyle* (London, 1744) i, p1–4.

[332] Fifteen of these sermons (from this manuscript) have been published in vol. xiii of Usher's, *Works* (Dublin, 1847–64).

[333] For an introduction to this collection see Katherine Hudson and John Jones, *The Conroy Papers: A Guide* (Oxford, 1987).

[334] R. W. Hunt, F. Madan et al (eds.), A *Summary Catalogue of Western Manuscripts in the Bodleian Library at Oxford* (7 vols, Oxford, 1895–1953) and M. Clapinson & T.D. Rogers (eds.), *Summary Catalogue of Post-Medieval Western Manuscripts in the Bodleian Library Oxford: Acquisitions 1916–75* (3 vols, Oxford, 1991).

given short introductions to them, centering on what published catalogues are available to aid researchers. The Carte, Laud and Clarendon MSS are good examples, and we have only given them a limited amount of space in our listing. They deserve to receive a proper calendar, especially the Carte collection, the enormity of which precludes anything other than the most basic introduction here.

Given the size of the library's holding it is very likely that there is further material concerning Ireland buried in documents or collections which were not inspected by the authors

LOOSE ITEMS[335]

1155–1633   'Syllabus chartorum et literarum patentium de rebus Hibernicis ordine chronologico digestus, 1155–1633', with an index of people and places, compiled by Sir William Betham c1825. (Ms. Eng. hist. b. 123)[336]

1568   An account of Ireland by Giovanni Portinari entitled 'Trattato sopra il regno d'Irlanda', written in Italian and dedicated to Elizabeth I [bound, 107 fols]. (Ms. Ital. d. 13)[337]

1571   'The order and usage howe to keepe a Parliam^{t} in England in these dayes, Collected by John Vowell als Hooker, gent., one of the cittizens of the Citty of Exeter at the Parliam^{t} holden at Westm' A° Dn 1571 ... and ye same used in the Realme of Ireland'. (Ms. Eng. hist. c. 304, ff 167–79)

1575   (6 May) Certificate by Sir Peter Carew, Lord of the Barony of Idrone and Constable of Leighlin Bridge, Co. Carlow, that Anthony Rogers is resident with Sir Peter within Leighlin Castle, and should therefore be paid his annual pension out of the Exchequer in England. (Ms. Autog. d. 24, fol. 102)

1577   Two documents relating to the Catholic bishopric of Mayo, one in which Patrick O'Hely *alias* Patricius de Petra is recommended for the see, the other a copy of a letter by the Bishop of Mayo to Ferreira. (Ms. e. Mus. 156)

1584–8   A collection of documents apparently assembled by W. Johnes, secretary to Lord Deputy Perrot, which includes notes of sixteenth century legal precedents, a description of Ireland and of the Lord Deputy's household c1586, and material concerning the order of the household kept by Sir John Perrot while he was Lord Deputy, 1584–8. (Ms. Add. C. 39)

1586   (24 Jan.) Letter by Lord Burghley to Robert Petre, sending him the Privy Seal for Ireland and ordering him to make payments to Mr. Brabazon, Thomas Percivall, Lord Deputy Perrot, the Earl of Tyrone, Arthur Robbins, Henry Sheffield, Barnaby Googe, Sir William Fitzwilliam, Sir Henry Harrington's trumpeter, and John Powell, the victualler. (Ms. Eng. hist. c. 318, fol. 92)

1599   Journal of the movements of the Earl of Essex in Ireland in 1599, with copies of documents concerning his subsequent arraignment and execution. (Ms. Eng. hist. c. 121, ff 10–21)

---

[335] It is worth noting that Ms. Oxf. dioc. papers d. 105, contains several episcopal acts passed by the former Archbishop of Dublin, Hugh Curwin, who spent the last year or so of his life as Bishop of Oxford in 1567–8.

[336] N.L.I. microfilm, n.5903, p.6418.

[337] This item was purchased by the Bodleian on 2 April 1936, in an auction at Sotheby's.

1599   Copies of speeches made by members of the Privy Council in regard to the rebellion of the Earl of Tyrone and the proceedings of the Earl of Essex. (Ms. Eng. hist. c. 119)

16th cen.   Antiquarian notes concerning the marriage of Thomas Bourke to Honora O'Mulrian during the sixteenth century. Contains depositions of seven witnesses regarding the terms of the marriage, and makes mention of a dowry of 200 cows, 40 garrans, 8 chief horses, with plate and other household goods worth £100. (Ms. Eng. misc. c. 107, ff 38–9)

16th cen.   A summary of Edmund Spenser's 'View of the Present state of Ireland', termed 'Ireland's good'. (Ms. Eng. misc. f. 473, pp 51–66)

16th cen.   Copy of a description of Ireland in a volume of extracts and manuscripts made largely by William Lombarde, 1566-8. (Ms. Lat. hist. d. 2, fol. 63v)

16–19th cen. The correspondence of Richard Caulfield of Cork during the ninteenth century, which includes frequent transcripts of deeds and other records obtained by Caulfield whilst working on his histories of Cork, Kinsale and Youghal. The items are briefly discussed in Charles McNeill, 'Reports on Manuscripts in the Bodleian Library, Oxford', *Analecta Hibernica*, i (1930), pp8–11. (Ms. Eng. misc. e. 108)

1600   A volume of the speeches and orations of Sir Nicholas Bacon and other orators, compiled c1621, which includes the speeches of the Lords of the Council made in the Star Chamber concerning the recent expedition of the Earl of Essex into Ireland. (Ms. Eng. hist. d. 144, ff 44–51)

1600   A nineteenth century copy of Captain Josias Bodley's description of his journey to Lecale in Ulster. (Ms. Dm. 6. 8, pp 140–55)[338]

1600–33   Autograph theological and antiquarian collections by Dr James Ussher, Archbishop of Dublin, and others, arranged under 95 headings and including copies of letters by Ussher, William Bedell, Bishop of Kilmore, and others [English & Latin]. (Ms. Barlow 13)

1601   (20 Nov.) Certificate that Evererd Edmunds, the factor of John Jolles and William Cockayne, merchants, has laden '200 three quarters and 1 bushell of wheate, Winchester measure' aboard the *The Edward & John of Mevagefield*, which is bound for Dublin from Truro. The wheat is for the provision of the royal army in Ireland. (Ms. Eng. hist. c. 187, p. 7)

1602   (7 April) Order of the Privy Council to pay £25,000 (stg) to Sir George Carey, Master of the Exchequer in Ireland, for the exchange there. (Ms. Eng. hist. c. 318, fol. 95)

pre-1615   Pedigrees of the Butler, Fitzgerald, Molyneux and other Irish families, made by Roger Dodsworth before 1615. (Ms. Dodsw. 126)[339]

1616–42   Copies and abstracts of documents from the Irish State Paper series in the P.R.O. made in the nineteenth century by the historian Samuel R. Gardiner. (Mss. Eng. hist. d. 9, 11)[340]

---

[338] Published anonymously as 'Bodley's visit to Lecale', in *Ulster Journal of Archaeology*, 1st series, ii (1854). The original manuscript is in the British Library.

[339] There is also a c1645 pedigree of the Butlers made by Roger Dodsworth at Ms. Dodsw. 33.

[340] N.L.I. microfilm, n.5901, p.6416.

c1621   'Prima pars controversiarum quae inter Catholicos et hereticos Gormaristas sive Calvinistas et Arminianos ... controverti solent', by Peter Wadding. Transcribed by Simon Netterville at Antwerp in 1621. (Ms. e. Mus. 114)

1625–6   Seven sermons given in London by James Ussher, Archbishop of Armagh. Six of these took as their subject the text Heb. ix. 14, and were preached at Felsted, Bishopsgate Street, and Islington in 1625. The final sermon was given at Great St. Bartholomew's on 2 July 1636. Transcribed at the time by W.I. [145 ff]. (Ms. Eng. th. e. 25)

1629–39   (1 May, 1629 – 30 Nov., 1639) Abstracts of 20 letters to William Laud, Archbishop of Canterbury, by Archbishop Ussher. Aside from antiquarian matters, the letters (pp8–19) deal in general with such issues as the toleration of papists and the state of public morals. The principal people dealt with include Dr William Bedell, Bishop of Kilmore; Sir Charles Coote; the Bishop and Archdeacon of Derry, and the Dean of Cashel. In addition, the collection also includes (pp23–5) notes made early in the seventeenth century regarding the charter and statutes of Trinity College, Dublin, and copies of two letters to Laud (pp19–21) by Bishop Bedell in 1633 concerning complaints which had been made about Bedell's soft handling of papists in Co. Cavan. He defends his efforts to preach to them in their own tongue. The final abstract of Irish interest (pp25–6) includes a copy of a letter to Laud by Dr Bramhall, Bishop of Derry, re the scale of the improvements in the revenues of the Church of Ireland since Lord Deputy Wentworth's arrival, with a detailed listing of the income which the archdiocese of Armagh and the dioceses of Derry, Clogher, Raphoe, Ardagh, Down & Connor, Meath, Kilmore and Dromore could anticipate in 1638. (Ms. Sancroft 18, pp8–26)

1630   (18 Feb.) Letter to the Earl of Cork from Sir John Leeke, concerning general Irish affairs and news from England. (Ms. Percy. c. 1, ff 1–2)

c1631–41   A collection of ciphers used by Lord Deputy Strafford, as deciphered by the Rev. William Knowler in the eighteenth century. (Ms. Add. C. 276)

1633–5   (6 Sept. 1633–14 Jan. 1635) Register of warrants issued by the Lord Deputy of Ireland in cases brought before him. (Ms. Eng. hist. c. 304, ff 448–584)

1636–40   A bound volume containing transcripts of letters written by Christopher Wandesford to Sir George Radcliffe on general Irish affairs, together with a few other items (Ms. Add. C. 286),[341] as follows:

     1636   (26 March) Wandesford to Radcliffe, re Wandesford's visit to Carrick to attend the christening of Lord and Lady Ormond's newly-born son. (fol. 21)

     1636   (6 June) Same to same, discussing the patent held by John Browne for the manufacture of iron pots in Ireland, and re Wandesford's negotiations with the Earl of Ormond for the purchase of Idough, Co. Kilkenny. (fol. 1)

     1636   (6 June) Same to same, mentioning the affairs of George Carr, Mr Harris, William Raylton, and Mr Monke, etc. Wandesford also asks Radcliffe to see that the charges against Sir Thomas

---

[341] N.L.I. microfilm, n.5905, p.6420.

Esmond are fortified, and expresses the hope that Sir Piers Crosby will be stayed until the Lord Deputy arrives. (ff 2–3)

1636   (18 June) Same to same, expecting news of Radcliffe's safe landing soon, and noting that the Chief Baron is a little distempered following his accident. (fol. 5)

1636   (22 June) Same to same, reporting that the Chief Baron of the Exchequer is gone home to be cared for by his wife 'after the fall out of his Coach', and re some private matters, most notably Wandesford's efforts to acquire the territory of Idough. (ff 3–4)[342]

1636   (6 July) Same to same, re John Browne's stubborn refusal to part with his patent for the manufacture of iron pots, with a postscript re the examination of Mr Joyce from Wexford. (fol. 7)

1636   (19 July) Same to same, sending news of Sir Faithfull Fortescue, Sir Richard Plumleigh, Sir Beverley Newcomen, and Sir Philip Percival and his wife. (fol. 8)

1636   (9 Aug.) Same to same, stating that he is glad of the news of the Irish customs farm, and recommending a suit by Captain Pigott for the sergeantship of Munster, etc. (fol. 13)

1636   (17 Aug.) Same to same, stating that Miss Vane's mother will not agree to a match with the Wandesford family, and discussing the activities of Mr Wells in the matter. (ff 8–10)

1636   (17 Aug.) Unaddressed document endorsed 'The Lord Justice Wandesford his Instructions', giving further details of his efforts to arrange a marriage between his son and Mrs Elizabeth Vanes' daughter. (ff 10–12)

1636   (12 Sept.) Wandesford to Radcliffe, re his dealings with Lord Dillon, and sending his regards to Capt. Southworth. (ff 14–15)

1636   (22 Sept.) Same to same, re John Browne's agreement to sell his license for the manufacture of iron pots. (fol. 16)

1636   (3 Oct.) Same to same, regarding the acquisition of Idough, Lord Dillon's affairs, and John Browne's decision not to sell his license. (ff 17–18)

1636   (12 Oct.) Same to same, reporting that Lord Dillon has still not sent the writings to Mr. Sambadye, 'the reason I know not'. (fol. 18)

1636   (16 Oct.) Same to same, re Radcliffe's acquisition of land, the continuing problems with Lord Dillon, and the refusal of Mrs Vanes to send her daughter to Ireland. (ff 18–19)

1636   (27 Oct.) Same to same, declaring that he has given the Lord Deputy a full account of the business with Lord Dillon, and other matters. (ff 5–6)

1638   (23 June) Same to same, re opposition to Wandesford's title in Idough, and asking Radcliffe to speak with William Raylton about John Browne's second payment for the manufacturing license. (fol. 22)[343]

1638   (31 June) Same to same, concerning the poor health of Sir Richard Scott, who has gone to stay with Sir Thomas Rotherham. Wandesford also comments upon the good state of the army, to which several new officers have been appointed. He also reports on a recent court decision against old Mr. Harpole's administrators. (ff 23–4)[344]

---

[342] This was published in T.D. Whitaker (ed.) *The Life & Original Correspondence of Sir George Radcliffe* (London, 1810), pp 243–4.

[343] Published in *Ibid*, pp246–7.

[344] *Ibid*, p248.

1640	(12 June) Same to same, sending news of the death yesterday of the Attorney-General of Ireland, and also regarding the proceedings in the Irish House of Commons, with a postscript concerning the Earl of Ormond's query about despatching troops to Knockfergus. (ff 25–6)[345]
1640	(21 June) Same to same, re the Bishop of Derry's suit, and the appointment by convocation of the Archbishop of Tuam to proceed with the sentence against the Bishop of Killaloe's suffragan. Wandesford has appointed Lord Dillon and Lord Lowther to investigate the Bishop of Killaloe's allegation that Sir Richard Osborne and the M.P.s for the town of Waterford have plotted against him. (ff 26–8)
1640	(24 June) Same to same, expecting Radcliffe's return from London, and asking him to 'for God's sake bring us clere directionns about all things'. (fol. 29)
1640	(29 June) Same to same, concerning the improvement in Lord Strafford's health, and also dealing with the Bishop of Waterford's recent confinement, and the Vice-Treasurer's report of the 'slowness of the cumming in of Monyes'. (fol. 29)
1640	(28 July) Same to same, re the opinion of the Committee of Revenue in Ireland that the companies of horsemen cannot be paid their entertainment money, and the Treasurer's alarming comments about the state of the government finances. (fol. 30)
1640	(28 July) Copy of a letter written by Lord Deputy Wandesford and the Irish Council to the Earl of Strafford, re their inability to pay the army in Ireland. (ff 31–2)
1640	(7 Aug.) Wandesford to Radcliffe, regarding Sir Robert Parkhurst's business in Ireland, and the proceedings in the Irish Parliament. (fol. 33)
1640	(18 Aug.) Same to same, regarding the stay of the horsemen in their garrisons, and the collection of the subsidy, with a postscript about the transport of skins from Ireland. (fol. 35)
1640	(24 Aug.) Same to same, concerning the Bishop of Killaloe and Lord Strafford's health. (ff 33–4)
n.d.	Same to same, asking Radcliffe's advice about the arrival of *The Swallow* under Captain Kettleby for service towards Dumbarton, with a postscript stating that 'the provysyons of powder and the rest are arrived out of Holland'. (fol. 37)
n.d.	John Browne's answer to the propositions of the undertakers for the manufacture of iron pots and ordnance in Ireland. (ff 37–9)
1636–41	Collections of notes and documents on various matters, including the life of Sir Thomas Wentworth, Earl of Strafford, which contains the following (Ms. Eng. hist. c. 286):
1632	(21 Oct.) Copy of Lord Deputy Wentworth's letter to the Lords of the Privy Council, from York, re matters of state. (pp59–61)
1636	(25 July) Copy of a letter by Lord Deputy Wentworth to the Master of the Rolls, Christopher Wandesford, re general government affairs, part of which is in cipher. (pp53–9)
1639	(16 April) Copy of Wentworth to the Privy Council, re general affairs. (pp61–2)
n.d.	Notes on the life of Strafford (1593–1641). (pp 63–6)
1639–79	Copies of official letters written by Sir James Butler, 12th Earl and 1st Duke of Ormond, relating to Irish affairs, including some of his

---

[345] *Ibid*, p251.

correspondence with the Earl of Clanricard, 1641-3. (Ms. Eng. hist. c. 37)[346]

1640   Copy of the articles presented against the Earl of Strafford at his impeachment and trial. (Ms. Eng. hist. c. 284, fol. 154 onwards)

1641   (20 May–1 July) A small collection of newsletters written by Thomas Jenyson for Sir Rowland St. John (Ms. Eng. lett. c. 589),[347] which includes the following references to Irish affairs:

(20 May)   Jenyson notes that Sir George Radcliffe is 'to goe to Ireland to be tryed', and also reports a rumour that 'the Irish army ... shall have liberty to serve any forrayne prince', and states that the Earl of Leicester is to be made Lord Deputy. (fol. 34)

(3 June)   Jenyson sends news that the M.P. for Windsor has been imprisoned for scandalising the House of Commons over the impeachment of Strafford, and expresses his doubts over the wisdom of allowing 'so many Irish to serve the Spaniard'. (fol. 36)

(7 June)   'A rumour there is here of a powder plott under the Parliament house in Ireland that was ready to have taken, but that one of the plotters was touched in conscience and came distractedly into the house and revealed it'. (fol. 39)

(1 July)   Reports that last week in Parliament the new chief governor of Ireland, Lord Leicester, was accused of pocketing his mail before it had been registered by the Parliamentary Committee. (fol. 48)

17th cen.   'The life, deeds and death of Sir John Perrot, knt.', written in the seventeenth century. (Ms. Wood D. 33)

17th cen.   A miscellaneous collection of documents, mainly medieval, made by and on behalf of Archbishop Ussher of Dublin, which includes *inter alia* various manuscripts concerning the lands of the archdiocese of Armagh. (Mss. Add. A. 379–80 and Add. C. 296 and 299)[348]

17th cen.   More miscellaneous documents collected by Archbishop Ussher, mainly medieval in date. (Ms. Add. C. 301)[349]

17th cen.   Several collations of the Latin Psalter, with manuscript and printed editions, almost all in the hand of Archbishop Ussher, beginning (fol. 1) 'Collectio Psalteri a B. Hieronymo ex Hebrao conversi, et a Jac. Fabro Parisijs anno 1513 edit, cum alijs exemplaribus Mss[is] et impressis' [119 ff]. (Ms. Add. A. 91)

17th cen.   Seventeenth century copy of Sir John Davies' Question concerning impositions. (Ms. Add. A. 116)

17th cen.   Bound volume entitled 'traceings from the old map of Galway. To be Engraved. A.D. 1853'. There follows a fine tracing in pencil from a mid-seventeenth century picture-map of Galway City, showing details of mounted soldiers practising at a tilt, the town's bridges, fortified walls, its thoroughfares, etc. [14pp]. (Ms. Top. Ireland d. 6)

17th cen.   Biographical notice of Sir John Davies (1569–1626), Solicitor General of Ireland, by John Aubrey, made c1685. (Ms. Autog. d. 21, fol. 147)

---

[346] N.L.I. microfilm, n.5903, p.6418.

[347] Purchased at Sotheby's on 17 Dec. 1979.

[348] N.L.I. microfilm, n.5904, p.6198, n.6419 and p.6934.

[349] N.L.I. microfilm, n.5905, p.6420.

17th cen.   Pedigree of Sir William Pope, 1st Earl of Downe (1573–1631). (Ms. Pedigree Rolls 32)[350]

17th cen.   A collection of seventeenth century poetry, including lines upon the conviction of the Earl of Castlehaven (1631), beginning 'Rome's worst Philenis ...', and also verses on the Earl of Strafford's epitaph, apparently written by the Earl of Cleveland, beginning 'There lies life & valiant dust ...' (Ms. Eng. poet. e. 97)

17th cen.   An ordinary of arms of the Irish nobility, which includes the armorial bearings of such families as those of Plunkett, Dowdall, Dillon, Wise, Harrold, Wadding, Piphoe, Bath, Wellesley, Barnewall, etc. (Ms. Rylands c. 43)[351]

COLLECTIONS

Ashmolean MSS (ref. Ms. Ashmolean)

1542   (1 Oct.) The ceremony at Greenwich Palace for the creation of Con Baccagh O'Neill as 1st Earl of Tyrone. (Ms. Ashmolean 840)

c1542–62   Forms of the submission of Con O'Neill to Henry VIII in 1542 and Shane O'Neill to Elizabeth I in 1562, with the names of the noblemen present on the latter occasion. (Ms. Ashmolean 830)

1566   (7 July) 'R. Elizabethae literae patentes, quibus Nicholaum Narbon, alias Richmond, in Reger Armorum et principalem Heraldum tocuis regni nostri Hiberniae constituit, cognomine Uluester'. (Ms. Ashmolean 831)

1566   Warrant by the Queen for the Earl Marshal, the Duke of Norfolk, to create Richmond Herald a King of Arms by the name of Ireland. (Ms. Ashmolean 857)

c1588–91   Accusations presented against Sir John Perrot re his government of Ireland and other matters, with proofs. (Ms. Ashmolean 830)

c1599   A bound collection of miscellaneous papers containing copies of two undated letters by the Earl of Essex to Elizabeth I 'upon his Commaund to go for Ireland'. (Ms. Ashmolean 781, ff 82–3)[352]

16th cen.   Legal memoranda re the spiritual jurisdiction of Ireland, *temp* Elizabeth I, which goes on to outline the extent of the archdioceses of Armagh, Dublin and Cashel. It also contains a brief note of the temporal lords of Ireland. (Ms. Ashmolean 1144, ff 253–4)[353]

1621   Draft of a letter from James I to the Lord Deputy of Ireland, for confirming the Ulster undertakers in their estates on condition of a double rent, with a resolution of the Privy Council concerning the same. (Ms. Ashmolean 830)

1634   Letter from Thomas Preston, Ulster King of Arms, to the College of Heralds in London, asking them to search out precedents concerning the right of the officers of Arms to have hearses and

---

[350] The Bodleian purchased a collection of records concerning the Oxfordshire estates of the Pope family (c1559–1650) during an auction at Sotheby's on 29 Oct. 1975 (ref. Ms. Top. Oxon. c. 769–771).

[351] Purchased at Sotheby's on 6 Nov. 1899.

[352] The original manuscript is no longer available for inspection, having been very badly damaged over the years by the acidic corrosion of the ink. A photocopy made in 1988 (Ms. Ashmole 781*) is available instead, along with a negative microfilm (Ms. Film 579) which was made in 1963.

[353] The notes were probably written sometime between 1558 and 1583, as Garret, 14th Earl of Desmond (d. 1583) is listed along with his fellow lords.

palls used at funerals, which he requires to override the objections raised by the clergy in Ireland. (Ms. Ashmolean 836)

1656   Narrative of the life of the late Lord Primate of Ireland, Archbishop Ussher, addressed to Charles II by Dr Nicolas Bernard. (Ms. Ashmolean 829)

17th cen.   'Britannia, or a chorographicall description of the most florishing Kingdoms of England, Scotland & Ireland, written by W. Camden & Translated into English by R. Knolles'. The endorsement reads 'This being Mr William Camdens manuscript found in his owne library lock'r in a cupbord as a treasuer he much esteemed and sinc his death sufferd to se light'. (Ms. Ashmolean 849)

17th cen.   Arguments of place and precedence in the state of Ireland. (Ms. Ashmolean 857)

17th cen.   Lists of Irish nobility created by James I and Charles I. (Ms. Ashmolean 818)

17th cen.   Transcripts of letters patent creating peers in England and Ireland, collected in the later seventeenth century by Elias Ashmole. Among the few pre-1641 Irish creations which are mentioned are those for Sir William Brounker, as Viscount Brounker of Newcastle; Richard Vaughan, as Earl of Carbury; Richard Wingfield, as Viscount Powerscourt, and William Harvey, as Baron Harvey of Ross. (Ms. Ashmolean 832)

Bankes Papers (ref. Ms. Bankes)[354]

This collection, comprising the papers of Sir John Bankes, the Attorney General of England between 1634 and 1640, is kept in the New Bodleian Library, and contains the following material of Irish interest:

1601–2   Undated extract of expenses of the soldiers sent to Ostend and Ireland, 1601–2, endorsed by Bankes. (Bundle 25, no. 2)

1605   (20 March) Letters patent of James I granting an annuity of 6s. *per diem* to Captain William Stafford in reward for his good service to the late Queen in her wars in Ireland. (Bundle 43, no. 90)

c1613   The heads of the charter granted to the City of London and the Governor and Assistants of the new plantation in Ulster. (Bundle 41, no. 97)

1632   (19 July) Copy of royal letters patent for 'The Councell and Comonaltye of Fishing of Gt. Brittaine and Ireland'. (Bundle 41, no. 63)

1634   (29 June) Royal commission to Lord Deputy Wentworth and the Irish Council concerning defective titles. (Bundle 41, no. 40)

1634   (16 Oct.) Warrant to prepare a commission empowering Lord Deputy Wentworth to give the royal assent to Acts passed in the Irish Parliament. (Bundle 10, no. 8)

1634   (26 Oct.) Warrant to Attorney General Bankes to make alterations in several Irish Acts, and to Lord Keeper Coventry to put them under the Great Seal. (Bundle 10, no. 2)

---

[354] A useful outline of the manuscripts of Sir John Bankes is provided by Irvine Gray, 'The Lydney Park Papers', in *Quarterly Review*, cclxxxix (1951), pp55–67, and D.M. Barratt, 'The Bankes Papers: a first report', in *Bodleian Library Record*, iv (1952–3), pp313–23.

c1634 Undated note of compositions made upon the Commission of Defective Titles in Ireland, showing in each case the old rent and the increase. Signed with a note by Wentworth [7 fols]. (Bundle 37, no. 32)

1635 (14 Jan.) Warrant to prepare a commission as on 16 Oct. 1634 (Bundle 10, no. 8) above. (Bundle 10, no. 9)

1635 (17 Jan.) Warrant to Bankes and Coventry, similar to 26 Oct. 1634 (Bundle 10, no. 2) above. (Bundle 10, no. 10)

1635 (27 Feb.) Warrant to prepare a commission authorising the Lord Deputy of Ireland, 'after a full debate in Parlt there', to give the royal assent to certain Acts, and to prolong the parliamentary session if necessary. (Bundle 10, no. 6)

1635 (18 April) Warrant for a commission to continue the Irish Parliament by adjournment. (Bundle 57, no. 8)

1635 (3 June) Warrant for a grant to Christopher Wandesford, Sir George Radcliffe and Sir George Wentworth, of the wardship of the body and lands of William Wentworth, son and heir of Lord Deputy Wentworth, at the latter's nomination. (Bundle 55, no. 58)

1635 (23 June) Warrant to prepare a grant to Lord Maltravers and Sir Francis Crane for the privilege of making farthing tokens, specifying emblems to be stamped on them for England and Ireland, and giving the exchange rates between London and Dublin. A proclamation is also to be prepared to the same effect. (Bundle 11, no. 35)

1635 (26 June) Petition of John Sanderson, one of the King's coachmen, mentioning money levied in Denbighshire in Wales in 1602 for troops bound for Ireland. (Bundle 17, no. 68)

1635 (10 July) Warrant for the reduction of the duty on coal transported to Ireland. (Bundle 15, no. 2)

1635 (14 Aug.) Sealed warrant to levy taxes upon the Irish nobility living in England. (Bundle 43, no. 39)

1636 (10 April) Warrant for the imposition of duties on imported hops, gold and silver, and cattle from Ireland. (Bundle 43, no. 53)

1636 (9 Oct.) Sealed order of Council to release on bail Sir Piers Crosby, against whom a case is pending in Star Chamber. (Bundle 42, no. 29)

1638 (18 March) Warrant for a grant of the office of Captain of the King's Castle of Culmore in Londonderry to Colonel Robert Stewart. (Bundle 37, no. 15)

1638 (30 March) Schedule of 'Things desired by the City [of London] to be granted', containing 24 clauses, some of which relate to land in Ireland. (Bundle 48, no. 9)

1638 (18 June) Warrants for grants of lands in New England, with a note that 'all born there of English, Scottish or Irish parents shall be free denizens of England'. (Bundle 51, no. 37)

1638 (23 Aug.) Draft renewal of the commissions to Lord Deputy Wentworth and others to examine and compose for defective titles in Ireland [40 fols]. (Bundle 61, no. 4)

1638 (23 Aug.) Letter to Bankes from Secretary Coke, sending the draft received from Ireland for amending H.M. Commission for Defective

Titles (above), about which some recusant lawyers have 'raised scruples'. (Bundle 65, no. 27)

1639   (6 Oct.) Sealed order of the King in Council for an investigation of the charges brought against the Lord Chancellor of Ireland by William Weston. (Bundle 42, no. 77)

1639   (8 Oct.) Information of William Weston, esq., before Bankes, concerning presents corruptly given to Lord Chancellor Loftus in Ireland. (Bundle 18, no. 14)

1639   (16 Dec.) Warrant for the creation of the office of H.M.'s Receiver of Coleraine, and a grant of the same to Charles Reade. (Bundle 59, no. 3)

1639   (16 Dec.) Warrant for the creation of the office of H.M.'s Receiver of Derry, and a grant of the same to Robert Whitfield. (Bundle 66, no. 8)

c1639   Undated note of witnesses against the Lord Chancellor of Ireland, *viz* Nicholas Stephens of Dublin, Andrew and William Pallane of Dublin, Thomas Bolger of Kilkenny, Thomas Cusacke, a Dublin merchant, Sebastian Fleming of Drogheda, Sir Robert Meredith, then 'genetaine' to the Chancellor, and other parties whose names are not known. The list is signed by William Weston and John Bankes. (Bundle 41, no. 55)

1639–40   (1 Dec., 1639–27 March, 1640) Four documents pinned together, concerning the petitions addressed to the Lord Deputy by Walter Fitzharris of Co. Wexford, 'a poor distressed prisoner in the common wards of the Fleet'. (Bundle 51, nos. 46–9)

1640   (27 Jan.) Warrant for a commission to Lord Deputy Strafford to summon a Parliament in Ireland. (Bundle 55, no. 65)

1640   (28 Jan.) Letter to Bankes from Secretary Coke, stating that the King desires Bankes to peruse and make recommendations concerning Acts submitted by the Irish Parliament for the royal assent. (Bundle 65, no. 59)

1640   (7 Feb.) Opinion on several Irish bills, signed by Bankes, Sir Edward Herbert, Sir Ralph Whitfield and Sir Robert Heath. (Bundle 10, no. 12)

1640   (10 Feb.) Warrant to Bankes and the Lord Keeper, Sir John Finch, similar to that of 10 June 1640 (Bundle 10, no. 5) below. (Bundle 10, no. 11)

1640   (6 March) Warrant for the creation of the office of Auditor of H.M.'s Revenues in Londonderry and Coleraine, and a grant of the same to Robert Chambers. (Bundle 54, no. 31)

1640   (18 March) A list of 28 Acts for Ireland. (Bundle 52, no. 25)

1640   (22 March) Warrant to prepare a commission authorising the chief governor or governors of Ireland for the time being to pass certain Irish Acts, etc. (Bundle 10, no. 7)

1640   (25 March) Warrants to Bankes and Finch, similar to those of 10 June (Bundle 10, no. 5) below. (Bundle 10, no. 13)

1640   (March) Titles of Acts now transmitted out of Ireland, which lists 28 Acts, with marginal notes by Bankes. (Bundle 41, no. 21)

1640	(c2 April) Warrant for a grant of the office of Receiver of Londonderry to Robert Whitfield. (Bundle 59, no. 19)
1640	(8 June) Opinion on several Irish Bills, and recommendations for amendments, addressed to the King by Sir Ralph Whitfield and Sir Robert Heath, sergeants-at-law. (Bundle 10, no. 3)
1640	(9 June) Warrant signed by Sir Francis Windebank for levying to the King's use the money to be assessed upon the Irish nobility residing in England. (Bundle 10, no. 1)
1640	(10 June) Warrants to Bankes to make amendments in certain Irish Acts, and to Finch to pass them under the Great Seal, with a minute on the same sent to the King by Bankes. (Bundle 10, no. 5)
1640	(12 June) Warrant for a commission authorising the chief governor of Ireland to cause certain Bills to be considered in the Parliament there, etc. (Bundle 55, no. 36)
1640	(11 Sept.) Warrant authorising the Lord Deputy of Ireland to cause certain Bills to be considered in the Irish Parliament and to give the royal assent thereto, and to prolong the session of that Parliament. (Bundle 10, no. 4)
1640	(24 Sept.) Letter to Bankes from William Raylton, asking his advice about a passage in the Act to be passed for the subsidies of the clergy in Ireland. (Bundle 65, no. 69)
1640	(29 Sept.) Letter to same from the Irish Council, re the Act for the Plantation in Connaught. (Bundle 65, no. 70)
1640	(15 Nov.) Sealed order of the King in Council, for a proclamation to put into effect the motion of Parliament to make the ports of Ireland open and free for all H.M.'s subjects. (Bundle 42, no. 73)
1640	(Nov.) Certified copy of the Remonstrance of the Irish Parliament to the Lord Deputy, setting forth numerous grievances [3 fols]. (Bundle 60, no. 11)
1640	(17 Dec.) Orders of the Grand Committee of the House of Commons for Irish Affairs, for hearing Tristram Beresford's case, and summoning the Attorney General and H.M.'s former Commissioners for Londonderry to attend the hearing. (Bundle 60, nos. 13–14)
1640	(c30 Dec.) Warrant for a commission to Sir William Parsons and Sir John Borlase to be Justices and joint governors of Ireland in the absence of Lord Deputy Strafford, his deputy Christopher Wandesford being dead. (Bundle 55, no. 113)
1640	Undated copy of the petition of Ralph Freeman, John Stone and Tristram Beresford, addressed to the House of Commons, to be restored to their tenancy of lands in Londonderry, lost through the decree transferring Londonderry from the City of London to the Crown [4 fols]. (Bundle 60, no. 12)
1640	Copy of a contract between the Crown commissioners and Robert Harrington re lands in Co. Londonderry. (Bundle 40, no. 27)
c1640	Undated, unsigned and un-numbered memoranda concerning the petition of the City of Londonderry. (Bundle 28)
c1640	Undated extract by Robert Chambers regarding lands in Londonderry 'within the Grocers' proporcion'. (Bundle 15, no. 16)

c1640   Draft propositions made by Lord Kirkcudbright and Sir John Clotworthy on behalf of the lessees in Co. Londonderry (3 fols), which is endorsed with numerous rough notes. (Bundle 6, no. 6)

c1640   Undated and unsigned memorandum about the plantations in Connaught. (Bundle 55, no. 6)

1641   (8 Feb.–15 March) Rough memoranda in the hand of Bankes on various subjects, including Irish parliamentary Bills. (Bundle 50, nos. 54–6)

1641   (17 Feb.) Notes by Bankes concerning the Irish Parliament and other matters, which may be rough minutes of a Council meeting. (Bundle 50, no. 57)

c1641   Memorandum re the Commission of Grace for the Remedy of Defective Titles in Ireland. (Bundle 55, no. 9)

c1641   Rough memoranda by Bankes about the demands of the Irish committees. (Bundle 55, no. 37)

17th cen.   'The humble remonstrance of James Cusacke, esq., one of your Mats. learned Councel in Ireland, and special attorney appointed for the service of defective titles there', asking that he be rewarded for his services. (Bundle 50, no. 26)

17th cen.   Draft instructions for the Bishop of Londonderry and others. (Bundle 18, no. 23)

17th cen.   Undated and unsigned memoranda regarding 'The true state of Sir John Clotworthy his Business concerning his pension', and also about his lands in Ireland. (Bundle 15, no. 15 A–B)

17th cen.   Undated and unsigned statement with regard to the town of 'Dale' in Ireland. (Bundle 15, no. 17)

17th cen.   Statement by Francis Harris concerning speeches lately made by Sir John Inis which mentions horses being brought to the Scots from Ireland. (Bundle 18, no. 29)

17th cen.   Rough draft of a memorandum re the farm of wine licenses and 'strong waters' in Ireland. (Bundle 37, no. 10)

17th cen.   Undated and unsigned proposition concerning alehouses, for the advancement of the royal revenues in Ireland. (Bundle 48, no. 1)

17th cen.   'Notes concerninge Ireland', unsigned. (Bundle 55, no. 38)

Bodleian MSS (ref. Ms. Bodl.)

1611–41   A bound volume of letters to and from Thomas Lydyate (Ms. Bodl. 313) which contains the following Irish items:

    1611   (24 June) Lydyate's Address in Latin to Thomas Chaloner, mentioning Trinity College, Dublin, and ending 'Cest ria in reditu ex Hibernia'. (ff 28–9)

    1611   (9 Sept.) A letter to Lydyate by James Ussher, nephew to the Primate of Ireland, mentioning the Albigensians and the Waldensians, and asking Lydyate to search out a copy of Sanders' *De Schismate Anglicano*, etc. Ussher also desires him to 'write me out what be noted concerning Ireland in ye year 1542', and mentions Sir Robert Cotton's promise to transcribe certain letters for him concerning the consecration of archbishops of Dublin by the archbishops of Canterbury. (fol. 77)

1611   (4 Oct.) Another letter by Ussher to Lydyate concerning 'ye annuall stipend and ye proportion of lande lying aboute ye Schoole...whereby I resolve you may well make account of your fiftye poundes per annu', at the least'. Ussher ends by asking Lydyate to bring him a copy of the new translation of the Bible. (fol. 61)

1617   (Advent) A letter to Lydyate by James Ussher, Archbishop of Armagh, reporting his meeting with Robert Allen, who was bound for England, and requesting the delivery of some canonical texts. (fol. 52)

1617   (2 June) Same to same, in which Ussher mentions a lecture which he gave in Trinity College, Dublin, three or four years previously. (fol. 68)

1617   (8 July) Lydyate's reply to above, stating that he expects to see Ussher in England soon, and discussing the beginning of Artaxerxes' reign and other matters. (ff 68–9)

1619   Archbishop Ussher to Lydyate, sending thanks for the delivery of Lydyate's *Geminus* and *Albatepnius*, and discussing various other works [Torn and stained]. (fol. 59)

1641   (13 Nov.) Dr Robert Pinck to Lydyate, from New College, Oxford, mentioning the great desire which the Lord Primate of Ireland has to see Lydyate. (fol. 19)

n.d.   Lydyate to Archbishop Ussher, re Lydyate's *Geminus*, etc., which Ussher 'promised to returne to mee above a twelvemoneth since'. (fol. 88)

Carte MSS (ref. Ms. Carte)

Parts of the Carte collection, one of the largest and most important of the Library's holdings, have been published in Thomas Carte (ed.), *A collection of original letters and papers concerning affairs in England, from 1641–1660* (2 vols., 1739), and in C.W. Russell & J.P. Prendergast, *The Carte Manuscripts in the Bodleian Library, Oxford* (London, 1871). For the most part, however, the collection, comprising some of the letters and papers of the Butlers, earls and dukes of Ormond, the Southwells, and Sir William Fitzwilliam, the Elizabethan Lord Deputy of Ireland, has remained unpublished.[355] It is one of the most valuable sources for the study of seventeenth century Irish history, and there is a considerable quantity of sixteenth century documentation as well. The collection has been microfilmed for the National Library of Ireland, and research in Ireland is aided by a transcript of large parts of the material in the National Archives.[356] However, a word of caution, the transcripts are not complete. Only letters, commissions, treaties and royal instructions are included, omitting the large body of financial, military and other administrative documentation in the collection. Furthermore, only some of the early volumes were tackled by the transcribers, and much relevant material is to be found in later volumes. There are also transcripts of some of the Elizabethan and Jacobean correspondence dealing especially with Lord Deputy Fitzwilliam, Lord Deputy Chichester and the 10th Earl of Ormond in the Manuscript Department of Trinity College Library in Dublin (T.C.D. Ms. 1791).[357]

---

[355] There is a useful introduction to the collection in T. Duffus Hardy & J.S. Brewer (eds.), *Report to the Right Honourable the Master of the Rolls upon the Carte and Carew Papers in the Bodleian and Lambath Libraries* (London, 1864). The papers of Lord Deputy Fitzwilliam can be found in four volumes at Ms. Carte 55–58.

[356] For relevant microfilm numbers see Hayes, *Sources*; The N.A.I. transcripts can be found on open access on the shelves in the readers room.

[357] Taken from Vols. 1, 30, 55–8, 62 and 131 of the Carte MSS.

Cherry MSS (ref. Ms. Cherry)

c1637	Copies of various letters made in the seventeenth century by Archibald Cherry (Ms. Cherry 23), which include the following:
1637	(29 Oct.) Dr Samuel Ward to Archbishop Ussher, from London, re the rumour that Ussher was to come to England, and also about a manuscript copy of Ignatius which Ward has transcribed. With a postscript stating that the Bishop of Derry was today brought to meet the King by Archbishop Laud. (pp177–80)
n.d.	Same to same, in answer to Ussher's of 10 March last. Ward expresses concern over Ussher's recent injury 'by the ovthrow of yʳ Coach'. Also mentions the issues raised by the death of the Archbishop of Tuam. (pp 181–4)
17th cen.	An account of Archbishop Ussher's views on justification. (Ms. Cherry 19)

Clarendon MSS (ref. Ms. Clarendon)

This important collection has received an extensive listing in O. Ogle, W.H. Bliss, W. Dunn Macray and F.J. Routledge (eds.), *Calendar of the Clarendon State Papers* (5 vols, Oxford, 1869–1970). Although the overwhelming majority of the collection is concerned with the period of the English Civil War, the Commonwealth and the Restoration, there is still a sizeable quantity of documentation prior to 1641 (see *ibid*, i (1872), pp1–222). Of particular importance are the papers of Sir Humphrey May, who was responsible for much of the English government's Irish correspondence under James I. There are a number of letters from May to Lord Deputy Chichester and Francis Annesley. The collection contains an increasing number of Irish records through the 1630s, with a great deal on the early months of the 1641 rising. The following well known item does not appear to have been included in the published catalogues:

1640–52	Copy of Clarendon's 'Short view of the state of Ireland from the year 1640 to the year 1652....' being in essence a vindication of the 12th Earl of Ormond. (Ms. Clarendon 121)[358]

The Heyricke Papers (ref. uncatalogued)[359]

This collection of the papers of Sir William Heyricke, Teller of the Exchequer, 1616–24, comprises 16 bound volumes of Exchequer orders and receipts, together with a calendar and index (vol. 17) made in 1859 by Joseph Brutt. It contains *inter alia* approximately 30 separate references to Irish affairs, the vast majority of which are routine administrative payments to the Treasurers-at-war, Sir Thomas Ridgeway and Sir Henry Docwra. There are also some payments of coat and conduct money to officers appointed to bring troops to Ireland. Otherwise, the only unusual entries concern three payments made in June/July 1623 and March 1624 to Brian O'Rourke in reward for his special services to the King.

Jones MSS (ref. Ms. Jones)

1571	The transcript from which Sir James Ware published Edmund Campion's 'History of Ireland (1571)' in 1633. (Ms. Jones 6)
17th cen.	Undated observations concerning Ireland, by Sir C. Reynell, 'howe that barbarous Conntrie might be reduced to a better Civilitye'. The author goes on to treat of the four causes why Ireland has fallen to

---

[358] N.L.I. microfilm, n.5900, p.6415.

[359] The Heyricke collection was recently acquired by the Bodleian at auction. The collection was previously on loan to the Leicestershire County Record Office.

such a barbarous state, *viz* 'ffirst, those wantes in nature, wherein they are ordinarylie from theire Childhood nursed upp...; Secondly, the neglectinge of religion & Church disciplyn, wch in former tymes was established amongest them; Thirdly, the p'vertinge the course of Justice wthout wch noe commonwealth can be assured; ffurthly and lastly, the wante of observance in the disciplyne of warre...' (Ms. Jones 56, ff 28–34)

Laud MSS (ref. Ms. Laud)

This collection contains six volumes which were originally part of the manuscripts of Sir George Carew, the majority of which are now housed in Lambeth Palace Library in London (see above). These volumes (Mss. Laud 610–615) cover a wide range of topics concerning Ireland from the medieval period to the seventeenth century and are available on microfilm in the National Library of Ireland.[360] There is a listing of their contents in H.O. Coxe & R.W. Hunt (eds.), *Bodleian Library Quarto Catalogues: II Laudian Manuscripts* (2nd ed., Oxford, 1973), pp431–43 and a brief summary in T. Duffus Hardy & J.S. Brewer (eds.), *Report to the Right Honourable the Master of the Rolls upon the Carte and Carew Papers in the Bodleian and Lambath Libraries* (London, 1864). Four of the volumes contain manuscript material relevant to this survey (Mss. Laud 611–614). Of particular interest is an account of Sir Richard Edgecombe's mission to Ireland in 1488 (Ms. Laud 614, pp1v–37r) and a book detailing the allotment of land in Co. Monaghan by Lord Deputy Fitzwilliam in 1591 (Ms. Laud 611, ff 140–65). There are many documents concerning the Nine Years War in Ms. Laud 612, and a number of other political and administrative manuscripts throughout Mss. Laud 611–614.

Lyell MSS (ref. Ms. Lyell)

1588   (26 Nov.) Copy of a report by the Spanish Council of State in Madrid to Philip II concerning the continuation of the war with England following the failure of the Armada. The 'Cardinal' advocates that the next attack on England should be begun from Ireland, because 'the Irish in past years showed a desire to live under the shadow and protection of Your Majesty'. His opinion was disputed by the 'Prior', who argues that the King should attack England directly, considering the enormous cost of trying to secure Ireland first [Spanish, with English translation]. (Ms. Lyell empt. 60, pp 58–61)[361]

1618   A discourse of pirates, by Sir Henry Mainwaring, which contains a few comments on the problem in its Irish context, *viz* (fol. 2r) although pirates are most active on the coast of England, 'yet in proportion Ireland doth much exceed it, for that [it] may well bee called the Nurserie and Storehowse of pyrats in regard of the generall good intertaynment they receive there'. Mainwaring also notes (fol. 2v) that pirates get much better intelligence in Ireland of the whereabouts of the King's ships 'then contrarywise they shall

---

[360] N.L.I. microfilm, n.4213, p.3884; The first volume, Ms. Laud 610, contains entirely medieval documentation, and has been described by Myles Dillon in *Celtica*, v (1960), pp64–76 and *Ibid*, vi (1963), pp135–55.

[361] Part of a bound volume of transcripts entitled 'Documents about the Spanish Armada' which were made from the originals among the muniments of the Marquis of Cabra in Spain. There may be another copy of this document in the Archivo General de Simancas, *Seccion de Estado* 2851, which contains a series of discussions by the Council of State, 12–26 Nov. 1588, on the future conduct of policy towards England. See Colin Martin & Geoffrey Parker, *The Spanish Armada* (London, 1988), p263.

have of the pyrats'. He ends (fol. 17r) by recommending that one of the royal ships should patrol the Irish Sea between Milford and Dublin. (Ms. Lyell empt. 24)[362]

Nalson Collection (ref. Dep.c.152–176)

This collection, formerly part of the manuscripts of the dukes of Portland, was calendared by the H.M.C., *13th Report*, App I & II (*Portland MSS*, vols 1–2). The published calendar contains a number of documents concerning Ireland in 1641, including a copy of the King's letter of 3 April to the Lord Justices (p10 of Report, ref. c.165/8), and the Lord Justices' letter of 27 November to William Lenthall (p28, ref. c.153/3). There are a number of examinations which touch on the Irish army (pp19–22, ref. c.165/16,17 etc.), a letter from Sir Phelim O'Neill to Sir William Hamilton on 23 November (p28, ref. c.153/2), and the deposition of Captain Wintour's boy concerning the Irish rebellion in December (p28, ref. c.174/6). There are also a number of general references to affairs in Ireland. The collection is now housed in the New Bodleian Library.[363]

North MSS (ref. Ms. North)

1595	(10 Sept.) Grant by Sir John North of property in London and Essex to his younger sons, prior to his departure for Ireland. (c.27, no. 58)
1595	(10 Sept.) Two copies of a similar grant of jewellery and plate, etc., to his daughters, Elizabeth and Mary. (c.27, nos. 59–60)
1611	(4 June) Bond and receipt for £365 paid by William Morins to the Barons of the Exchequer for the upkeep of the troops in Ireland. (c.29, nos. 13–14)
1613	(5 June) Receipt by Edward Wardour, Baron of the Exchequer, of £365 from W. Morins for the support of 30 infantry in Ireland. (c.29, no. 20)
c1619	Undated document endorsed 'The precedent of the patent of creation of Barronnets', which makes reference to the plantation in Ulster. (a.2, fol. 150)[364]
1625	(19 Oct.) A project for making a contract for the King's Navy to guard the coasts of England and Ireland, apparently drawn up according to a plan made by Sir Robert Mansfield, Treasurer of the Navy. (b.1, fol. 15)
1628	(2–10 Oct.) Letters from Sir Thomas Pope to his father, Sir William Pope, K.B., regarding Sir William's creation as Earl of Downe, Viscount Lucan and Baron of Granard in the Irish peerage on 16 Oct. next. (c.7, fol. 114–21)[365]
1629	(24 Feb.) 'The reasons of ye higher House of Parliamᵗ preferred to ye King agst ye Irish Nobility, and agst Forraigne Titles'. Endorsed

---

[362] It has appeared in print as part of a larger work on Sir Henry, which includes an extensive biographical study, G.E. Manwaring & W.G. Perrin (eds.), *The Life and Works of Sir Henry Mainwaring* (2 vols, Navy Records Society Vols. 54 & 56, 1920–1). The treatise can be found in Vol. 2 (i.e. Navy Records Society Vol. 56), pp9–49.

[363] The references given at the end of each calendared entry in the H.M.C. report have since been changed. The references N.I – N.XXII are now catalogued as c.152 – c.175 in the New Bodleian Library.

[364] See *C.S.P.I., 1615–25*, pp258–60.

[365] Although there was a docquet given for the peerage of Granard on 4 Oct. 1628, this title was apparently never used (*Complete Peerage*).

'Parliamentary Papers & letters to the Earl of Downe, 1628[–9]'. (b.1, ff 53–6)

1629	(27 and 29 July) Two letters from Viscount Chaworth to Sir William Pope, concerning Pope's Irish peerage. (c.7, ff 111–13)
c1629	Part of an address by counsel in a case concerning the relative precedence of English and Irish peers. (b.1, fol. 64)
c1629	The petition of the Lords in Parliament to the King concerning the Scottish and Irish peers. (b.1, ff 65–6)
c1629	Answers of the Scottish and Irish peers to the statement by the English peers. (b.1, ff 69–74)
c1629	A petition by the nobility of Ireland. (b.1, fol. 80)
c1629	'The reasons of the Parlt for precedence of the Irish Nobility'. (b.1, ff 77–8)
c1629	A petition from the Scottish and Irish lords to the King. (b.1, ff 67–8)
c1629	The last petition of the Scottish and Irish peers to the King. (b.1, ff 81–2)
c1629	Copy of a speech by Charles I re the creation of earls, viscounts and barons among persons owning lands in Scotland or Ireland who would take precedence below English peers. (b.1, ff 60–3)
c1634	Undated notes concerning a loan of £1,000 made by Sir John North to Thomas, Viscount Lecale. (b.19, ff 178–9)
1641	(4 May) The Earl of Strafford's letter to the King, written in the Tower of London. Printed 4°, A.D. 1641. (North Printed, e.2, no.1)
1641	Undated draft, probably made in the eighteenth century, of a narrative of the proceedings in Parliament against the Earl of Strafford, leading up to the King's assent to the Bill of Attainder, and the Earl's subsequent execution. (b.1, ff 152–66)
c1641	The case of Lord Fingal, concerning his dispossession from his lands at Stirrupstown, Co. Meath, in 1641, and their coming to the hands of one Peppiot. Lord Fingal was subsequently unable to recover the estate, either in the Court of Common Pleas or in Chancery in Ireland. (b.22, fol. 6)[366]
17th cen.	Part of a charter granting to the Mayor and Commonalty of the City of Londonderry the right to elect their own sheriffs. (a.2, fol. 188)

Perrot MSS (ref. Ms. Perrot)

Most of the Irish material in this collection has been published by Charles McNeill (ed.), 'The Perrot Papers', *Analecta Hibernica*, xii (1943), pp1–65, which brought the letter-book of Sir John Perrot, Lord Deputy of Ireland, 1584–6 (Ms. Perrot 1) to public notice.[367] One further item of relevance is also to be found in this collection:

1620	(2 July) Notes taken of Dr Ussher's sermon at Temple Church. (Ms. Perrot 9)

---

[366] Lord Fingal had been outlawed from his estate in Co. Meath on 17 Nov. 1641 (*Complete Peerage*).
[367] There is a microfilm of the original at N.L.I. microfilm, n.5319–20, p.5428–9.

Rawlinson MSS (ref. Ms. Rawl.)

This large collection contains numerous documents concerning Ireland. Charles McNeill published a lengthy description and analysis of the sixteenth and seventeenth century material in his 'Reports on the Rawlinson Collection of Manuscripts Preserved in the Bodleian Library, Oxford', in *Analecta Hibernica*, i (1930), pp12–178, and, *ibid*, ii (1931), pp1–92. He also published in full Ms. Rawl. D. 657 being Lord Chancellor Gerard's notes of his report on Ireland (1577–8) in *Analecta Hibernica*, ii (1931), pp93–291. Most of the material of Irish interest has been microfilmed for the National Library of Ireland.[368] However, the following two items which are not part of the A–D series of the Rawlinson Mss, were not noticed in McNeill's work.

1634	(15 July) Copy of the speech by Lord Deputy Wentworth at the opening of the Parliament at Dublin. (Ms. Quarto Rawl. 550)
1639	Poems in English and Latin on the death of Henry O'Brien, 5th Earl of Thomond, by Robert Codrington. (Ms. Rawl. Poet. 96)

Selden MSS (ref. Ms. Selden)

1612–29	A bound volume entitled 'Sir Ed. Deni Collectanea',[369] which contains notes concerning various legal cases in the early seventeenth century (Ms. Selden Supra 125), including the following of Irish interest:
1612	(27 Nov.) Legal opinion of Thomas Fleming, Edward Coke, and Lawrence Tanfeld concerning the claim made by the Earl of Shrewsbury to the title and honour of the earldom of Waterford and barony of Dungarvan in Ireland. They argue that he is not so entitled. (fol. 31)
1621	Various jottings regarding Irish lords and their attendance at parliament, with notes from several statutes 1° Edward III–18° James I. (fol. 54r)
1625	(8 May) Legal memoranda re the title to the barony of Kinsale, which 'hath been in the Lords Curcy'. There then ensues a number of notes taken from the state records in Dublin Castle, and more significantly, an extract from court rolls in the possession of Richard Boyle, Bishop of Cork (1620–38), regarding the descent of the barony from the reign of Edward I to 1625. The jottings make passing reference to several deeds, bonds, feoffments, etc., which had been made by the Courcys of Kinsale between 1542 and 1625, but very little detail is given. It also includes comments on the privileges due to a viscount, and has a brief outline of the Courcy genealogy. (ff 18r–19v)
1626	Jottings regarding the office of Gauger in Ireland, and 'how farr the offic is ruled at the com' law'. (fol. 49)
1629	(5 July) Memorandum that the law shows clearly that the Earl of Clanricard ought to have precedence before the Earl of Thomond. (fol. 30)
n.d.	Notes concerning the liberties of the City of Dublin since 3° Edward IV, and also notes re the attainder of the Earl of Kildare in 1534/5. (fol. 61)

---

[368] See Hayes, *Sources* for N.L.I. microfilm numbers.

[369] Sir Edward Denny inherited a substantial plantation estate at Tralee, Co. Kerry.

Smith MSS (ref. Ms. Smith)

1591 Speech of Adam Loftus, Archbishop of Dublin and Lord Chancellor of Ireland, proposing the establishment of Trinity College, Dublin, followed by some notes and a copy of the foundation charter of the College. (Ms. Smith 21)

1591–7 Certified copies of letters written by Elizabeth I on behalf of Trinity College, Dublin. (Ms. Smith 20)[370]

1598 (31 Oct.) Copy of a letter by Philip II to Hugh O'Neill, Earl of Tyrone, and Hugh O'Donnell, concerning their rebellion in Ireland. (Ms. Smith 68)

1610–29 A bound volume containing biographical material on the life of Sir Robert Cotton (Ms. Smith 71), including transcripts of letters to him, the following of which are relevant to Irish affairs:

 1610 (14 April) Copy of a letter by Sir Oliver St. John to Cotton , from Dublin, stating that Ireland is presently quiet, 'where the Sword, thankes be to God, lyes still'. Furthermore, he is sure that the Ulster plantation 'will be the greatest good that ever came to this kingdom'. (pp63–5)

 1610 (17 Aug.) Same to same, from Dublin, discussing the forts at Galway, Limerick, Duncannon, Halbolyn beside Cork, and Castle Park near Kinsale. (p69)

 c1610 (n.d.) Same to same, complaining that all his friends in England have forgotten him, and stating that he is presently stuck in the remotest part of Ireland, 'almost altogether Irish, and in doubtfull times nearest to harmes, lying open to the Western Ocean, and the country full of fair havens'. (p67)[371]

 1622 (25 Jan.) Copy of a letter to Cotton by the Bishop of Meath, re the Irish saints and other matters. (pp115–6)

 1624 (21 Dec.) Same to same, reporting his ill health over the past three months, it having 'pleased God to visit mee with a quartan', and his eagerness to recommence his work on 'the history of the British, Scottish and Irish beyond the yeare 600'. (p131)

 1625 (4 May) Letter to Cotton by James Ussher, Archbishop of Armagh, concerning Ussher's copy of the Samaritan Pentateuch. (pp133–4)

 1625 (12 July) Same to same, discussing the Roman and Gallican psalters. (pp137–8)

 1625 (23 Sept.) Sir Henry Bourchier to same, from Limerick, re his promise to procure for Cotton 'a leiger-book of some Abbey for you, though they bee very rare in this kingdome'. He goes on to state that those which do exist are in the hands of the owners of the abbeys, and he mentions that 'divers Bishops have black books,...which one may use for a time, but to get them absolutely is a thing impossible, because for the most part they are their best evidence for their lands and possessions'. (p139)

 1626 (21 Jan.) Same to same, in which Bourchier reports his recent meeting with the Archbishop of Armagh. 'This poor countrey suffers much by the burthen of his Majesties armie, which, for

---

[370] N.L.I. microfilm, n.5900, p.6415.

[371] The position taken by this transcript in the volume (between the first two items listed above) would suggest an approximate dating of 1610.

the greater part, hath no other maintenance, but what it receives from the Country'. (pp143–4)

1627   (19 June) Sir James Ware to same, from Dublin, expressing gratitude for Cotton's kindness towards him during his recent sojourn in England. Sends Cotton 'as a small token of my love ... an old register of saint Mary Abbey by Dublin', and asks that in return Cotton will get him 'some old Irish Annales, which ... were with the Earle of Totnes'. (p147)

1627   (10 Dec.) William Bedell, Bishop of Kilmore, to same, re the Psalter of David 'written by Ricemarcus in the Irish hand', which is presently held by the Archbishop of Armagh 'to whom I sent it by Dr [Samuel] Warde'. (pp149–52)

1628   (22 March) James Ussher, Archbishop of Armagh, to same, from Drogheda, concerning the Samaritan Pentateuch, and also re James Ware, 'an industrious searcher of the antiquies in this Country'. (p159)

1629   (24 Feb.) Sir James Ware to same, sending an ancient Roman coin and a map of one of the baronies of Co. Longford. (p163)

1639   (6 Sept.) Copy of a letter by Archbishop Ussher to Patricio Junio (*alias* Patrick Young), in answer to Young's of 20 July, 'the first I had from you these many years'. Discusses Young's *Catena* upon Job and other scholarly matters. (Ms. Smith 75, ff 105–6)

Talbot de Malahide MSS (ref. Ms. Talbot)

This collection of documents springs from two sources. Not only does it include the extensive medieval and early modern deeds of the Talbot family, but as a result of two lengthy legal disputes during the nineteenth century (concerning the Talbot title and the admiralty of Malahide) documents from the Public Record Office in Dublin and elsewhere were copied to facilitate the case. J.T. Gilbert published a brief report on the collection for the H.M.C. (*8th Report* (1883), App. I, pp493–9) while it was still in private hands. The collection is housed in the New Bodleian Library, and includes the following items: [372]

Original Manuscripts

1485   Grant to Thomas Talbot of the admiralty of Malahide and other privileges. Extensively decorated. (Ms. Talbot a.1)

1487   (4 April) Draft of the deed below between William Bowden and Thomas Cusacke concerning the trusteeship of Thomas Talbot's property. (Ms. Talbot c.97/6)

1487   (6 April) Quitclaim by William Bowden of Malahide, feoffee of Thomas Talbot, to Thomas Cusacke, of all his rights over the manors and lands in Malahide, Hamondstown and Gariestown, Co. Dublin, and Louth, Asshe and Castlering, Co. Louth, that he had lately received as trustee from Talbot.[373] (Ms. Talbot c.97/7)[374]

1487   (4 Sept.) Peter Talbot, Lord of Malahide, grants to John Lyncoll, for life, a rent of 3s. out of land in the suburbs of Waterford. (Ms. Talbot c.88/21)

---

[372] The collection was formerly on deposit in the Library at Trinity College, Dublin, but was transferred to the Bodleian in 1977 as a gift from the Hon. Rose Talbot, sister of the 7th Baron. Apparently a draft calendar of this collection was compiled by the late Professor J. Otway-Ruthven.

[373] There are transcripts and translations of this document at Ms. Talbot b.15/72,73.

[374] Ibid Ms. Talbot c.6/13,14,15.

1488   (20 Aug.) Lease by Sir Peter Talbot and William Bowden, of a
          messuage in the town of Malahide, to Thomas Ball and Alice
          Hassarde, his wife. (Ms. Talbot b.49/5)[375]

1489   (1 March) Lease by Sir Peter Talbot and William Bowden of a
          messuage in Malahide, to William Broun of Swords and Johanna,
          his wife, for their lives or to the longer liver. (Ms. Talbot b.49/6)[376]

1491   (18 Feb.) Deed whereby Denis More and Joan Boyscher, his wife,
          appoint 'Sir' Edward Houth, chaplain, as their attorney to receive
          ten sheep and two lambs from Thomas Harrold of Howth. (Ms.
          Talbot c.96/2)

1491   (20 Sept.) Lease by Simon Rede of Mableystown, to Henry Bayly
          and Helena, his wife, of all his lands in Mableystown and one acre
          of arable land in Dreynam, for 'quinquaginta et novem' years, rent
          13s. 4d. (Ms. Talbot c.96/3)[377]

1495   (15 Jan.) Lease by Sir Peter Talbot, Elizabeth Buckley and William
          Bowden, to Thomas Ball of Malahide and Alson, his wife, of four
          acres of arable land, for their lives, rent 8s. (Ms. Talbot b.49/7)

1499   (28 July) Quitclaim by Richard Hewyen, chaplain, to Thomas
          Harroll and Joan Ball, his wife, of a messuage, five acres arable, and
          the Abbey Park in Adamstown, parish of Garriestown, Co. Dublin.
          (Ms. Talbot c.90/16)

1501   (12 Oct.) Conveyance by Edmund Roo of Garrieston, Co. Dublin,
          'workman', to Robert Nolt of Garrieston, of a messuage, eight acres
          arable, and the Abbey Park, in Adamstown, Co. Dublin, to hold for
          ever of the chief lord of the fee. (Ms. Talbot c.90/17)

1501   (12 Oct.) Edmund Roo of Garrieston appoints John Yonge his
          attorney to give seisin to Robert Nolt of the above lands in
          Adamstown. (Ms. Talbot c.90/18)

1501   (13 Oct.) Quitclaim by Edmund Roo to Robert Nolt of the above
          lands in Adamstown. (Ms. Talbot c.90/19)

1512   (14 May) Quitclaim by Edmund Roo of Garrieston, 'husbandman',
          to Robert Nolt of a messuage and a park in Garrieston. (Ms. Talbot
          c.90/20)

1513   (29 Feb.) Grant by Sir Peter Talbot to Elizabeth Buckley, widow, of
          an annuity of 20 marks for her life out of the demesne of Malahide.
          (Ms. Talbot b.49/8)

1515   (1 May) Lease by the proctors of Our Lady Church of Garrieston to
          Richard Byrford of Garrieston, tanner, of certain premises [ms.
          torn] for 41 years, rent 18s. 11d. (Ms. Talbot c.90/21)

1516   (17 Dec.) Sale by Richard Goldyng of Pierston Laundy, gent., John
          Laundy of Garrieston, yeoman, and Janet Laundy, to Robert Nolt of
          Garrieston, freeholder, of two houses in Garrieston for a certain sum
          of money (not stated). (Ms. Talbot c.90/22)

1516   (17 Dec.) Quitclaim by Richard Goldyng et al, to Robert Nolt of the
          above property in Garrieston. (Ms. Talbot c.90/23)

---

[375] There is a copy of this document at Ms. Talbot b.15/75.

[376] There is a copy and translation of this document at Ms. Talbot b.15/76a,b.

[377] There is a copy of this document at Ms. Talbot b.15/77.

1517 (12 Dec.) Lease by Sir Peter Talbot of Malahide to Sir John Fitz-Gerrot and Joan Talbot, his wife, of all his lands in Moreton, Aysshe, Billinston, and Carrickhagh, Co. Louth, to hold for their lives, rent 10 marks and 10 gallons of butter. Sir Peter also leases them the reversion of all his land which is presently let to James Gernon in Co. Louth, for their lives, rent 13 marks and 10 gallons of butter. (Ms. Talbot c.92/15)

1518 (19 Oct.) Sir Peter Talbot, Lord of Malahide, leases a house in Waterford to William Fagan of Waterford, for 61 years, rent 23s. 4d. (Ms. Talbot c.88/22)[378]

1520 (12 May) Lease by James Osborne, Prior of the house of St. John the Baptist without the Newgate of the City of Dublin, to James Rere of Dublin, merchant, of a messuage in Rochell Lane, Dublin, for 51 years, rent 2s. 8d. (Ms. Talbot c.96/4)

1526 ([ ] May) Deed between Nicholas H[ ] of Dublin, husbandman, and Thomas More of Adamstown, Co. Dublin, husbandman (rest of the document badly damaged and illegible). (Ms. Talbot c.97/15)

1532 (18 Jan.) Deed whereby Thomas Talbot of Malahide undertakes to pay 40 marks to Sir John Rawson, Prior of St. John of Jerusalem, and to the Treasurer (20 marks each) for a pardon of alienation. Unclear. (Ms. Talbot b.49/9)

1534 (25 Jan.) Deed relating to property in Waterford, badly damaged and mostly illegible. (Ms. Talbot c.88/23)

1536 (8 March) Lease by Thomas Elward, Prior of the house of St. John the Baptist without the Newgate of the City of Dublin, to John Candell of Dublin, merchant, of a messuage in Rochell Lane, Dublin, for 61 years, rent 2s. 8d. (Ms. Talbot c.96/5)

1538 (26 March) Lease by the Dean (Sir Edward Basnet) and Chapter of St. Patrick's Cathedral, to Robert Yans *alias* Dellman, of the tithes of Malahide Church, for 5 years, rent £11 6s. 8d., with the further conditions that he is to repair the chancel and pay the priest. (Ms. Talbot b.49/10)

1538 (31 Oct.) Grant by John Young to John Gerrot and Amy Young, daughter of John Young, in consideration of their marriage, of four acres of the park of Garrieston, and half a messuage and ten acres of arable land in Garrieston, to be held for ever. (Ms. Talbot c.90/24)

1542 (20 Aug.) Grant by Isote Nute, daughter and co-heiress of William Nute, late of Baldwynston, to James Nute of Garrieston, of land in Balyenyston, Co. Dublin. (Ms. Talbot c.90/25)

1548 (28 June) Bond by Thomas Plunkett, Rector of Moynalty, in £100 to Sir Thomas Talbot of Malahide, to vacate the parsonage when required by Talbot, in favour of Talbot's nominee, with various other conditions. (Ms. Talbot c.92/10)

1556 (28 Oct.) Grant by William Talbot to James White and Thomas Woodlock, chaplains, to the use of the Dean and Chapter of Holy Trinity, Waterford, of a messuage in Waterford. (Ms. Talbot c.88/24)

1557 (18 June) Robert Talbot of Belgarde, and his feoffees (named) lease Culverhouse Park, Co. Dublin, to Hugh Kennedy for 41 years, rent 25s 8d. (Ms. Talbot c.99/1)

---

[378] There is a copy of this document at Ms. Talbot b.15/82.

1560	(21 June) Grant by William Talbot of Malahide to James White and Thomas Woodlock, chaplains, of a messuage in Waterford, with a condition that they are to carry out the terms of his will. (Ms. Talbot c.88/25)
1560	(16 Sept.) Conveyance by Richard Smith *alias* Conwey and John Edwarde, to Nicholas Howth *alias* Saint Laurence and Alison Nolte, his wife, of all the lands in Garrieston and elsewhere in Co. Dublin which they had of the gift of the late James Nolte of Garrieston. (Ms. Talbot c.90/27)
1563	(13 Feb.) Lease by the Vicars Choral of St. Patrick's Cathedral to Hugh Kennedy, merchant, of an orchard and garden in New Street for 61 years, rent 20s. (Ms. Talbot c.99/2)
1564	(2 March) Letters Patent to James Sedgrave concerning Hoggs Monastery, Co. Dublin, and reciting earlier letters patent from 6° Edward VI. (Ms. Talbot c.96/6a)[379]
1567	(16 March) Lease by the Vicars Choral of the Cathedral church of St. Patrick's, Dublin, to John Lennan of Dublin, merchant, of a messuage in St. Patrick's Street, and an orchard and garden in the New Street, for 81 years after the determination of a similar lease to John Lennan dated 1562, rent £3. (Ms. Talbot c.96/6b)
1567	(17 July) Will and inventory of the goods of Hugh Kennedy of Dublin, merchant. Detailed. (Ms. Talbot c.99/3)
1569	(6 May) Grant by Nicholas Wade of Keneere, Co. Dublin, husbandman, Helen Gerrot, his wife, Marion Gerrot, Alison Garret, and Margaret Gerrot, to Ovin Russell of Rushe, gent., of all their lands in Garrieston, Co. Dublin. (Ms. Talbot c.90/26)
1592	(March) Certificate of admission of William Corbett of Lucan as a tenant in the manor of Newcastle Lyons, at a court held at Newcastle Lyons before Sir William Sarsfield, seneschal. (Ms. Talbot c.96/7)
1592	(20 July) Bond of Gilbert Talbot of Belgard, Co. Dublin, gent., in £300 (stg), to Nicholas Ball of Dublin, alderman. The conditions are that Talbot must lease Rochestown to Ball for 61 years. (Ms. Talbot c.93/2)
1592	(8 Aug.) Acknowledgement by Gilbert Talbot that he is indebted to Nicholas Ball, alderman, in the sum of £30. (Ms. Talbot c.93/3)
1593	(10 June) Release by Thomas Fleming and Peter Fitz-Gerrot, chaplains, Gilbert Talbot of Belgard, Richard Moyhill of Ballidonan, and Nicholas Roche, to George Caddell of Cadreeston, Thomas Hackett of Sutton, and Robert Cadell of Hartacketown, Co. Meath, of all actions relating to the manor of Belgard (specified in detail). (Ms. Talbot c.95/5)
1593	(8 Aug.) Agreement between Gilbert Talbot of Belgard and Nicholas Ball as to the lease of Rochestown for 61 years. (Ms. Talbot c.93/4)
1593	(20 Oct.) Lease by Gilbert Talbot to Nicholas Ball, of Rochestown for 61 years, rent £20 (stg), in consideration of the sum of £109 (stg). (Ms. Talbot c.93/5)

---

[379] See *Cal. Patent Rolls, Ire., Hen. VIII–Eliz. I*, pp281, 285, 292, 392–3, 485.

1593   (n.d.) Family settlement. Gilbert Talbot of Belgard settles his property on his mother, Elizabeth Golding, his wife, Marie, his eldest son, Robert (and whichever of the daughters of John Caddell of Moreton as he shall marry), his second son, John, third son, Reynold, and Peirce Talbot fitz-John and Thomas Talbot fitz-Robert (badly damaged in places). (Ms. Talbot b.38/1)

1594   (30 Nov.) Bond by Gilbert Talbot of Belgard, in £20, to give George, son of Hugh Kennedy, a lease for 61 years of Culverhouse Park at a rent of 26s 8d (Ms. Talbot c.99/4)

1598   (10 Nov.) Lease by Gilbert Talbot of Belgard, and his feoffees, to Robert Kennedy of Dublin, of the Culverhouse Park, Co. Dublin, for 61 years, rent 25s 8d (Ir.) or 20s (stg). (Ms. Talbot c.99/5)

1599   (1 Nov.) Sale by Gilbert Talbot of Belgard to Robert Kennedy, of Culverhouse Park near 'Burgan's gate', for a certain sum (not stated). (Ms Talbot c.99/6)

16th cen.   (n.d.) Lease by William [   ] to John Sampson of a messuage in [ ], rent £7 (very badly damaged). (Ms. Talbot c.97/14)

1600   (1 Dec.) Deed whereby John Cadell of Moreton, Co. Dublin, and Robert, his son and heir, sell for £300 (stg) an annuity of £20 (stg) to John Godinge, Thomas Allen, Thomas Long, merchants, and William Long, tanner. With a bond to repay the £300 if he defaults on the payment of £20 yearly. (Ms. Talbot c.96/8)

c1600   (n.d.) Notes of evidence for the jury in a lawsuit as to whether certain lands belong to Talbot of Rochestown or to [   ] of Lagnanston. Detailed, proving Rochestown is a manor and other points [2 fols]. (Ms. Talbot c.93/6)

1602   (5 July) Sale by Robert Barnewall, Lord Trimbleston, and his feoffees (named), to Sir John Talbot of Malahide and Nicholas Rely of Dublin, of the lands of Kylkarty *alias* Kylkearthy, Co. Meath, for £300 (stg), to be held in trust to the use of William Talbot of Dublin, esq., his heirs and assigns for ever. (Ms. Talbot c.92/11)[380]

1609   (31 May) Feoffment by Robert Kennedy to Phillip and Thomas Couran, James Walsh, gents, and Edward and George Arthur, merchants, of all his land in Clariston, Trim, Balboyton and elsewhere in Dublin, to the use of himself and his heirs male. (Ms. Talbot c.99/7)

1610   (12 Feb.) A schedule of new Crown rents for land granted to James Sedgrave by letters patent of 6 Edward VI, which are to be incorporated in a new grant (the old rents being undervalued). The lands involved are Cleereston, Michnanston, Ballyhack, Ballibyn and Ballikerock, Hogges Rathagane, St. John's without the Newgate, Ballifermot, Bartraston, etc. (Ms. Talbot c.96/9)

1610–11   Extract from the Great Roll of 8 James I, concerning money owed to or due from Robert Kennedy of Dublin, alderman. Damaged. (Ms. Talbot c.99/8)

1611   (12 Aug.) Robert Kennedy pays £140 to Thomas Long of Dublin, as the amount due on a mortgage of Rochestown. (Ms. Talbot c.99/9)

1612   (12 Oct.) Inquisition post mortem of Richard Longe, deceased, merchant of Dublin. Lists his lands in Baldwinston and Garrieston

---

[380] There is a copy of this document at Ms. Talbot b.16/18.

within the manor of Malahide, and other property in Dublin. (As an original I.P.M. it also includes the signatures of the jury). (Ms. Talbot c.90/28)

1612–13 Fragment of a writ of 10 James I. Apart from the date the remainder of the document has been obliterated. (Ms. Talbot c.99/16)

1613 (27 Feb.) Award of Richard Bolton, Recorder of the City of Dublin, and Peter Delahide, as to debts due by Robert Kennedy to John Cusacke, alderman. Damaged. (Ms. Talbot c.99/10)

1613 (1 March) Sale by Bartholomew Ball, executor of the last will of Nicholas Ball of Dublin, alderman, and Robert Ussher, of their interest in Rochestown, to Christopher White for the use of Robert Kennedy, reciting deeds dated 1593. (Ms. Talbot c.99/11)

1613 (6 Nov.) Probate of the will of Sir John Talbot, declaring that his property in Co. Louth 'should goe and remain as his father had appointed the same by his last will'. (Ms. Talbot c.61/1)[381]

1614 (12 Feb.) Sale by Robert Kennedy to Emmanuel Downing of the remainder of a lease of 16 yards of the wall and pavement in Castlestreet that Kennedy had received from the Corporation of Dublin for 61 years. In consideration of £16. (Ms. Talbot c.99/12)

1614 (20 April) Lease by Richard Talbot to Richard Mahone of land in Garrieston, *viz*, Stafford's Farm containing 50 acres, and Dalton's Park containing 4 acres, for 21 years paying 1s 6d (stg) rent for each acre of Stafford's Farm and 2s (stg) rent for each acre of Dalton's Park, and many other services and customs, with numerous conditions. (Ms. Talbot c.90/29)[382]

1614 (20 Aug.) Grant by Richard Talbot of Malahide to Patrick Ferroll of Louth and Andrew White, of his manors of Louth, Aishe and Castleringe in Co. Louth, and all his other lands in Co. Louth, to be held by Patrick Ferroll for one year, remainder to Andrew White, to be held to the use of said Richard Talbot. (Ms. Talbot c.92/16)

1614 (18 Nov.) Final concord between Simon Richens and Gerald White as to various lands in Garrieston. (Ms. Talbot c.90/30)[383]

1615 (5 Sept.) Inquisition post mortem for Thomas, 10th Earl of Ormond, of his Dublin City property, *viz*, 'Carbery house' in the parish of St. Nicholas. (This original I.P.M. includes the signatures of the jury and the escheator, Richard Browne). (Ms. Talbot c.96/10)

1618 (9 Jan.) Royal writ to John Cashel of Dundalk, directing him that Richard Talbot of Malahide is to be allowed to enjoy his estate of Malahide and lands in Co. Louth without being in any way disturbed. (Ms. Talbot c.92/17)[384]

1619 (1 March) Bond of Patrick English to George Plunkett, to lease him a house in Winetavern Street, Dublin, for 21 years, rent £12.[385] (Ms. Talbot c.96/11)

---

[381] A summary of the original will, dated 23 March, is at Ms. Talbot b.16/24.

[382] There is a copy of this document at Ms. Talbot b.16/31.

[383] Ibid, at Ms. Talbot b.16/32.

[384] Ibid, at Ms. Talbot b.16/33.

[385] On the reverse of this document is an undated list of goods and prices [10 entries] which would appear to be a late 17th century household account.

1621   (30 June) Sale by Matthew Tirrell, son and heir of the late Sir John Tirrell of Dublin, to Robert Kennedy of the remainder of a lease of a house in Rochelle Street. Recites many previous deeds. (Ms. Talbot c.99/13)

1621   (10 July) Grant by Robert Cheevers of Carmaghton in Drogheda to Bartholomew Brett and James Bath of Drogheda, merchants, of an annuity of £40 a year, for 41 years, for the use of Catherine Cheevers *alias* Talbot. (Ms. Talbot c.92/18)[386]

1623   (4 Jan.) Conveyance by Robert Russell of Deiname, and Bartholomew Russell of Seaton, Co. Dublin, to Richard Talbot of Malahide, of any rights they may have, including wrecks and fishing, in the arm of the sea adjoining Seaton. (Ms. Talbot c.95/6)[387]

1624   (18 Jan.) Deed whereby the Master *et al* of the Guild of St. Anne in the Church of St. Anthony's, Dublin, appoint Thomas Taylor of Dublin their attorney to recover arrears of rent from John Weston and the executors and assigns of Nicholas Weston. Reciting an earlier lease of 20 Feb. 1594 of the chamber called 'Sir George Browne's chamber' and other rooms and cellars (described in detail) in St. Anthony's College, granted by Walter Sedgrave, late Master, to John Weston, son and heir of Nicholas Weston, alderman, for 61 years, rent £5 10s. (Ms. Talbot c.96/12)

1625   (28 Sept.) Inquisition post mortem of Sir Theobald, 1st Viscount Dillon, endorsed 'This bundle belongs to Christopher Mapas' [61 fols]. (Ms. Talbot b.130)

1627   (19 April) Grant by Patrick Gough of Dublin, alderman, to his cousin Robert Leyns of Creboy, Co.Meath, gent., in consideration of a certain sum of money (not stated), of an annuity of £7 4s. (stg) out of his lands in St. Thomas Street and St. John's Lane and the College of St. Anne by St. Andrews Church and elsewhere (named). (Ms. Talbot c.96/13a)

1627   (20 April) Grant by Robert Leyns of Creboy, Co. Meath, to Phillip Conran of Dublin, merchant, of the above annuity of £7 4s., in consideration of a lease of a house in the College of St. Andrew's, Dublin, with certain conditions (detailed). (Ms. Talbot c.96/13b)

1628   (31 May) Pardon of alienation to Robert Talbot of Dardeston, William Talbot of Roberston, Sir William Talbot of Careton, Richard Talbot of Newhaggard, Donald Donnough, Robert Barnewall of Donbro, John Cusacke of Cousinston, Walter Travers of Ballikey, Christopher Walton of Drogheda, Nicholas Fitz-Williams of Baldangan, and Christopher, Baron of Howth, deceased, for lands in Garrieston, Louth, Baldangan, Bolleston, Leytown, etc. (Ms. Talbot c.97/8)

1628   (21 July) Sale by John Finglass of Colbarton, Co. Dublin, to John Malone of the lands of Baldwinston and Garrieston, in consideration of a certain sum of money (not stated). (Ms. Talbot c.90/31)

1628   (28 Nov.) Record of action: Recovery by Patrick Mapas of Dublin, merchant, against Thomas Arthur of Dublin, merchant, of five houses and gardens without the Newgate, Dublin (elaborately decorated). (Ms. Talbot c.100/1)

---

[386] There is a copy and translation of this document at Ms. Talbot b.16/34,35.
[387] There is a copy of this document at Ms. Talbot b.16/36.

1630	([ ] Feb.) Quitclaim by Sir William Talbot of Cartone and Robert Talbot of Dardeston to the feoffees of Richard Talbot (named), of all their interest in the Co. Louth and Dublin estates of Sir John Talbot. (Ms. Talbot c.97/9)
1632	(10 May) Feoffment by Robert Preston of Ballmadden and Thomas Laurence *alias* Howth, to Christopher Fitz-William of Merrion, Matthew Cusacke and Thomas Holms of Malahide, of lands in Garrieston, Baldwinston, Newton, and Tipperragane, to be held in trust to the use of Richard Talbot of Malahide. (Ms. Talbot c.90/32)
1634–40	(12 Aug. 1634–18 June 1640) Action in Chancery. John Kennedy of Dublin, gent. v. Edward Arthur of Dublin, alderman, Walter Kennedy, Patrick Kennedy, *et al.* Includes pleadings, answers, replications, rejoinders, examinations and decrees [57 fols]. (Ms. Talbot c.99/14)
1636	(16 July) Sale by Patrick Barnewall of Allardston, Co. Louth, John, his son and heir, Thomas Hamlen, merchant of Dublin, and William Hamlen of Smitherton, gent., to Christopher Kent of Garrieston and William Talbot and Thomas Johns of Malahide, of a house and 86 acres in Garrieston, to be held to the use of Richard Talbot of Malahide, in consideration of a certain sum of money (not stated) paid by Richard Talbot. (Ms. Talbot c.90/33)
1637	(25 May) Marriage settlement of John Talbot, son and heir of Richard Talbot of Malahide, and Lady Katherine Plunkett, daughter of the late Earl of Fingall. With conditions. (Ms. Talbot b.38/2)
1640	(26 July) Will of Richard Talbot of Malahide, esq., regarding his estates in Cos. Dublin and Louth. He appoints James Bathe, Richard Berrford and Robert Cheevers as his executors. (Ms. Talbot c.61/2)[388]
17th cen.	(n.d.) Replication of Sir John Talbot to the answer of Richard Talbot in a case in Chancery. This was apparently Richard Talbot's copy and contains his marginal notes throughout the document [3 fols].[389] (Ms. Talbot b.1/4)

Transcripts

The Talbot collection also has numerous transcripts and translations of the documents listed in the preceding section; these have been identified in the footnotes above. There are in addition a number of transcripts of published documents, and of manuscripts from the State Papers series in the Public Record Office and the Cotton Mss. in the British Library. These items have not been listed here. Instead we have listed the transcripts of records held by the Public Record Office in Dublin prior to 1922, as well as transcripts of other records whose origin is less clear.

13–18th cen.	Volume (118pp) of miscellaneous notes and genealogies compiled largely from the original documents above and the transcripts below; however, it may possibly have other details not noticed elsewhere.[390] (Ms. Talbot c.11)
1486	(24 July) The King takes seisin of the estates of Thomas Talbot of Malahide, esq., on his death, in Cos. Dublin, Meath, Louth, Kildare and elsewhere. (Ms. Talbot b.15/69–71)

---

[388] There are copies of this document at Ms. Talbot b.16/43,44.

[389] There is a copy of this item at Ms. Talbot b.16/17.

[390] This volume is very miscellaneous, sketchy at best. It was essentially a general note book, and includes a wide variety of extracts.

1496–7   (Hillary Term, 12 Henry VII) Decision of Court. Elizabeth, widow of Thomas Talbot, and William Bowden are acquitted of contempt of court [4 fols]. (Ms. Talbot b.15/78–9)

1496–7   (Easter, 12 Henry VII) Court proceedings relating to poundage due to the King in 11° Henry VII [1495–6]. The defendant (?) pleads that the Act granting poundage to the King was enrolled on the roll of 1° Richard III, and by it he, as a citizen of Dublin, was exempted from payment of poundage. Accordingly judgement went for the defendant. (Ms. Talbot c.8/14)

1498   (8 March) King's letter for the holding of a parliament in Ireland. (Ms. Talbot b.11/13)

1499   'Prelates, Peers and Commons of Ireland', which includes a list of the principal ecclesiastical and civil administrators in each county with a note of money owed. For example 'Lord Abbot of Dunbrody £6 13s. 4d.' (Ms. Talbot b.11/45)

c1500   (n.d.) 'The answer of Thomas Talbot to the title of the Mayor, Bailiffs, and citizens of the City of Dublin to certain small customs claimed in Malahide'. (Ms. Talbot c.5/28–29)

1508–9   (Easter Term, 24 Henry VII) Extract from 'Fines', including the payment by Sir Peter Talbot of Malahide of 40d for 'his homage to [be] respitted untill the Octave of Easter next to come by'. (Ms. Talbot b.15/80–1)

1515   (7 Oct.) Letters Patent (copied from the Exchequer Memoranda Rolls) granting to Gerald, Earl of Kildare, the customs, poundage, etc., of Strangford and Ardglass. (Ms. Talbot c.7/32–3)

1516   (12 June) King's letter for the holding of a Parliament in Ireland. (Ms. Talbot b.11/12)

1527   (Easter) Exchequer court proceedings concerning pleadings brought by Thomas Netterville of Douth, esq. [7pp]. (Ms. Talbot b.13/35)

1529–30   (Trinity Term, 21 Henry VIII) Court charge of contempt against Thomas, heir of Peter Talbot [5 fols]. (Ms. Talbot b.15/83–4)

1530   (22 Nov.) Inquisition post mortem into the estate of Peter Talbot, late of Malahide, who died on 10 July 1528, giving valuations and listing the jury. (Ms. Talbot b.15/85–87)[391]

1531   (19 Oct.) Abstract from the Exchequer Memoranda Rolls of a case regarding land in Balliva, Coyllaghe, and the Hill of Owerston, heard before Patrick Finglass, Chief Baron of the Exchequer. (Ms. Talbot b.15/88)

1531   (Oct.) Writs to the Sheriffs of Cos. Dublin and Meath for hostings to be held on each manor. (Ms. Talbot b.11/39)

1531   (Michaelmas) Exchequer court proceedings. Thomas Talbot pleads that by patent of Edward IV he is exempt from serving as sheriff [3 fols]. (Ms. Talbot b.15/89–90; c.6/16–18)

1531   (Michaelmas) Proffers list (from the Exchequer Memoranda Rolls), including sheriffs for the cities of Dublin and Drogheda, and the counties of Meath, Dublin, Louth, Cork, Cross of Tipperary, Waterford, Limerick and Kilkenny. (Ms. Talbot c.6/19–20)

---

[391] See Griffith, *Cal. Inq. Dublin*, p31.

1532	(Easter) Proffers list, as above, giving names for the same places. (Ms. Talbot c.6/21–22)
1533	(Easter) Proffers list, as above, giving names for the same places. (Ms. Talbot c.6/23–24)
1535	(13 Sept.) Letters patent conferring the title of Baron of Curraghmore on Sir Richard Power. (Ms. Talbot b.11/19–20)
1535	(3 Oct.) King's letter to grant the title of Viscount Thurles to James Butler, and that of Viscount Grane to Lord Leonard Grey. (Ms. Talbot b.13/6)
1537	(17 Oct.) Inquisition into the estate of George St. Leger, son and heir of Anne St. Leger, heiress of the late Thomas Butler, 7th Earl of Ormond, in Cos. Dublin and Kildare [3 fols]. (Ms. Talbot b.15/91)[392]
1540	(5 Nov.) King's letter regarding O'Connor, the priory of Kilmainham and Sir Osborne Etchingham (Ms. Talbot b.13/7)
1540–1	Extract from the patent rolls (32 & 33 Henry VIII) reciting a letter from Henry VIII to the Lord Deputy touching the division of Meath and other matters [6pp]. (Ms. Talbot b.15/92)[393]
1541	(15 June) Letters patent conferring the title of Baron of Louth on Oliver Plunket. (Ms. Talbot b.11/32)
1541	(17 June) Letters patent conferring the title of Baron of Carbury on William Bermingham. (Ms. Talbot b.11/31)
1541	(30 June) Letters patent conferring the title of Viscount Baltinglass on Thomas Eustace. (Ms. Talbot b.11/29)
1541	(June) List of those lords spiritual and temporal who attended parliament. It also includes the names of those individuals who attended as observers. (Ms. Talbot b.12/3–4)
1543	(1 July) Letters patent making Murrough O'Brien the 1st Earl of Thomond and Baron of Inchiquin. (Ms. Talbot b.11/18)
1543	(1 July) Letters patent making Donough O'Brien the 1st Baron of Ibracken. (Ms. Talbot b.11/17)
1549	(26 and 29 Dec.) Recognition of the fealty and good works of Sir Francis Bryan, Marshal of the Army, making him a Privy Councillor in Ireland, and his oath (29 Dec.) taken before Sir John Allen. (Ms. Talbot b.16/1)
1553	(1 Mary) Inquisition post mortem into the estate of Sir Thomas Talbot of Malahide, reciting the will of his father, Sir Peter. (Ms. Talbot b.16/2–4)[394]
1559	(3 July) Letters patent appointing Thomas, Earl of Sussex, as Lord Deputy of Ireland. (Ms. Talbot b.11/2)
1560	(11 Jan.) List of those elected to the Irish House of Commons, by county. (Ms. Talbot b.16/5)
1563	(Hillary) Copy of the endorsement on a charter of Edward IV, that it was pleaded and allowed in Hillary 5° Elizabeth I on behalf of William Talbot of Malahide.[395] (Ms. Talbot c.6/25)

[392] *Ibid*, p57–8.
[393] See *Cal. Patent Rolls, Ire., Hen. VIII–Eliz. I*, pp78–9.
[394] See Griffith, *Cal. Inq. Dublin*, pp138–9.

| 1568 | (28 Feb.) Letters patent (taken from the Exchequer Memoranda Rolls) regarding the surrender of the lands of Lord Bremingham and Sir William Burke. (Ms. Talbot b.16/7–8) |

| 1568 | (Michaelmas) Exchequer memoranda of the Queen's letter regarding Edmund Langan, the Earl of Clanricard, the Mayor of Dublin, Sir William Sarsfield, and others. (Ms. Talbot b.11/23–4) |

| 1569 | (20 March) Translation of the charter of Carrickfergus, from an inspeximus dated Michaelmas 29° Elizabeth I. (Ms. Talbot c.8/16) |

| 1578 | (27 Aug.) Letters patent granting to Ralph Grimesditch a lease of the customs revenue of Dublin port. (Ms. Talbot c.6/50,52) |

| 1583 | (6 May) Letters patent conferring the title of Baron of Cahir on Theobald Butler. (Ms. Talbot b.11/28) |

| 1585 | (26 April) Lists of lords spiritual and temporal, knights and burgesses attending parliament, and the 'Orders to be kept and observed in the Lower or common house of Parliament' which gives the nine rules for attendants. (Ms. Talbot b.16/9–10) |

| 1585 | (10 Dec.) Inquisition post mortem into the estates of Gerald, Lord Courcy [1 fol.]. (Ms. Talbot b.16/39a) |

| 1585–6 | (28° Elizabeth) Verdict against the Corporation of Naas before the Barons of the Exchequer (very incomplete). (Ms. Talbot c.8/17) |

| 1586 | (Trinity Term) Extensive transcript of a case heard in the Exchequer concerning court cases in Co. Kildare regarding alienation, intrusion etc. [14 pp]. (Ms. Talbot 16/11) |

| 1590 | (Trinity) Enrolment in the Exchequer Memoranda Rolls of two statutes of 28° Henry VIII confirming all privileges, customs, etc., previously granted by the earls of Shrewsbury to the borough and liberty of Wexford. (Ms. Talbot b.13/36) |

| 1595 | (17 June) Inquisition post mortem taken at Drogheda into the estates of Sir Christopher St. Lawrence, Baron Howth, who died on 24 Oct. 1589 [6pp]. (Ms. Talbot b.16/12) |

| 1595 | (Michaelmas) Exchequer court proceedings, regarding a petition by Edmund Britt of Inistioge, Co. Kilkenny, concerning that borough's freedom from composition and an earlier decree of the Barons in support of this [8pp]. (Ms. Talbot b.10/38) |

| 1596 | (3 Feb.) Inquisition post mortem taken at Dublin into the estates of Sir Christopher St. Lawrence, Baron Howth, who died on 24 Oct. 1589 [6pp]. (Ms. Talbot b.16/13)[396] |

| 1596 | (5 May) Inquisition post mortem into the estates of William Talbot, late of Malahide, Co. Dublin, who died on 4 Feb. 1596, reciting his will in full [11 fols]. (Ms. Talbot b.16/14–16)[397] |

| 1596 | (2 Aug.) Letters patent granting to Patrick Finglas the wardship of Richard Talbot of Malahide. (Ms. Talbot c.6/27–8) |

| 1599–1657 | Inquisition post mortem, dated 20 Oct. 1657, into the estates of David, Viscount Buttevant, which includes transcripts of many deeds dating from 1599 onwards [5 fols]. (Ms. Talbot b.16/48) |

---

[395] A full transcript of the charter in question is at Ms. Talbot c.6/26.

[396] See Griffith, *Cal. Inq. Dublin*, pp298–9, 302.

[397] *Ibid*, pp303–4.

1603	(cMarch) Notes taken from the Patent Rolls on the procedure for the appointment of a Lord Deputy on the death of Queen Elizabeth I. (Ms. Talbot b.11/42–4)
1603	(7 Nov.) Letters patent appointing Robert Kinsman as Searcher of the ports of Derry and Ballyshannon. (Ms. Talbot c.7/45)
1603	(11 Nov.) Letters patent granting to Richard Bingley a lease of the customs revenue of the ports of Derry and Ballyshannon. (Ms. Talbot c.7/44)
1604	(23 July) Inquisition post mortem into the estates of Patrick Plunket, Lord Dunsany, who died on 17 March 1602, which recites earlier inquisitions and gives valuations [19 fols]. (Ms. Talbot b.16/19)
1604	(3 Dec.) Inquisition post mortem into the estates of David Roche, Lord Roche and Viscount Fermoy [3 fols]. (Ms. Talbot b.16/20)
1604	(7 Dec.) Inquisition post mortem into the estates of Lord Courcy [6 fols]. (Ms. Talbot b.16/21)
1605	(26 June) Letters patent granting to Captain Roger Langford a lease of the customs revenue of the port of Knockfergus. (Ms. Talbot c.7/40)
1605	(27 Sept.) Sale by Thomas Luttrell of Luttrellstown, Co. Dublin, esq., to Bartholomew Kent of Daneston, gent., of all his possessions in Luttrellstown, Kelliston, Shermollin, Ballistron, etc., in Co. Dublin, Dunboyne, Kilbrena, Keneston, etc., in Co. Meath, and Leixlip, Donamore, etc., in Co. Kildare, in consideration of a certain sum of money (not stated), to hold for ever as of the chief lord of the fee [8pp]. (Ms. Talbot b.16/22)[398]
1606	(10 July) King's letter setting out the terms of a commission for a general enquiry into all the charters, grants and customs enjoyed by corporations and individuals in Ireland [4 fols]. (Ms. Talbot c.5/31)
1606	(Michaelmas) Exchequer court proceedings. Information brought by Sir John Davies as to the manor of Ardglass, and pleadings thereupon wherein the customs, tonnage, and poundage taken in that port under a grant from Henry VIII to the Earl of Kildare are set forth. (Ms. Talbot b.16/23)
1607	(10 Feb.) King's letter regarding customs and giving directions respecting the collectors of customs. (Ms. Talbot c.6/31)
1607	(14 Nov.) Letter from the King to Lord Deputy Chichester concerning customs, tonnage and poundage. (Ms. Talbot c.6/33)
1607	(21 Dec.) Letters patent granting to George Grimesditch a lease of the customs revenue of Dublin port. (Ms. Talbot c.6/49,51)
1608	(9 Jan.) Letter from Richard Hadsor to the Earl of Salisbury discussing Lord Chancellor Gerrard's question in Dyer's Reports for 20 Eliz. [1577–8], that an Irish peer can only be tried in Ireland, and not in England. (Ms. Talbot b.11/25)
1609	(3 March) Letter from the King to Lord Deputy Chichester relating to town charters and customs. (Ms. Talbot c.6/35)

---

[398] This would seem to be a transcript of an original family manuscript, which could not be located in the collection.

1609	(29 March) Letter from the King to Sir John Davies concerning the customs and his office as Attorney General. (Ms. Talbot c.5/33)
1609	(3 Aug.) Transcript of the charter granted to Wexford Corporation [25pp]. (Ms. Talbot b.13/1)
1610	(11 March) King's letter regarding the customs of the towns and cities of Dublin, Waterford, Cork, Drogheda, Galway, Wexford, New Ross, Youghal, Kinsale, Knockfergus, etc., and a final settlement thereunto. (Ms. Talbot c.5/32)
1610	(6 June) Letters patent appointing Anthony and John Stroughton as Collectors of the customs at Dublin and Drogheda. (Ms. Talbot c.5/38b; c.6/46)
c1610	(n.d.) 'The names of all and singular the ports within the several provinces of Leinster, Munster and Connaught', and the customs officers for the ports with their pay. Includes details for all ports except Drogheda. (Ms. Talbot c.5/34–6)[399]
1611	(18 March) Letter from the King to Lord Deputy Chichester regarding the Irish customs and the claims of various corporations. (Ms. Talbot c.5/37)
1611	(10 Oct.) Appointment by Colly Phillips and George Grimesditch of Richard Heath as their Deputy Searcher for the port of Dublin. (Ms. Talbot c.8/19)
1612	(11 Feb.) Letters patent granting to Sir James Hamilton the customs revenue of various ports in Ulster. (Ms. Talbot c.7/41–2)
1612	(8 July) Letters patent appointing George Grimesditch as Collector, Customer and Receiver of all the customs and imposts in the ports of Dublin City, Skerries, Malahide and Wicklow. (Ms. Talbot c.5/38a; c.6/53–6)
1612	(25 Nov.) Remonstrances to the King against the proceedings of the Irish government signed by Christopher, Lord Slane, as one of the ancient peers of Ireland and a member of the Great Council. (Ms. Talbot b.12/8)
1612–3	Transcripts and extracts of inquisitions post mortem into the estates of Gerald Fitzgerald, late Earl of Kildare, which makes mention of Viscount Gormanstown, Robert, Baron of Trimbleston, Sir Christopher Plunkett of Dunsoglin, and Patrick Barnewall of Crikston. Most of the extracts are concerned with Richard Talbot of Malahide. (Ms. Talbot b.16/25, 27)
1613	(6 March) King's letter for the holding of a parliament in Ireland. (Ms. Talbot b.11/11)
1613	(25 March) Translation of the charter granted to Coleraine [15pp]. (Ms. Talbot c.8/21)
1613	(28 March) Letter from the King to Lord Deputy Chichester regarding precedence between the Barons of Delvin and Killyne, and giving Chichester authority to resolve all issues of precedence in the forthcoming parliament. (Ms. Talbot b.16/28–9)
1613	(April) Writ of summons issued for holding a parliament in Ireland addressed by the King to the Sheriffs. (Ms. Talbot b.16/26)

---

[399] Transcript taken from manuscripts held by the Chief Remembrancers Office.

| 1616 | (17 Jan.) Report by the Commissioners on the question of precedency between Lords Kerry and Slane. (Ms. Talbot b.12/9) |

1616   (10 Aug.) Letters patent appointing Ralph Bradish and Edward Leigh as Collectors of the customs at Dublin city, Skerries, Malahide and Wicklow. At the end there is a list of searchers for Dublin for the years 1507–1761. (Ms. Talbot c.5/39)

1616–74   List and notes of searchers and collectors for the ports of Ardglass, Coleraine, Derry and Strangford. Compiled from various unnamed sources. (Ms. Talbot c.5/40)

1618   (22 April) King's letter concerning Athlone Corporation. (Ms. Talbot c.8/22)

1618   (23 May) Abstracts of the Crown lease to the Duke of Buckingham of the customs of Ireland. (Ms. Talbot c.5/43; c.6/57–8)

1619   (11 July) Decision by the King regarding the Earl of Kildare's estates [16pp]. (Ms. Talbot b.12/15–16)

1619   (29 July) Letter from the King to Lord Deputy St. John concerning the customs, Sir James Hamilton, the Countess of Kildare and the composition. (Ms. Talbot c.5/44; c.6/59)

1620   (12 Feb.) Letter from the King to Lord Deputy St. John regarding the customs farm, victuals, the Countess of Kildare's claim to the customs of Lecale, and customs houses in Ireland. (Ms. Talbot c.5/45; c.6/60)

1620   (16 Feb.) Adjudication of the Lord Deputy and Privy Council of Ireland upon the claim made by the Earl of Kildare to the customs of Lecale. (Ms. Talbot c.7/35)

1620   (26 June) King's letter on behalf of Robert Digby and Lady Lettice Fitzgerald, giving award as to the barony of Offaly. (Ms. Talbot b.12/11)

1620   (5 July) Adjudication of the King concerning the estates of Thomas, 10th Earl of Ormond, deceased. Very detailed [52pp]. (Ms. Talbot b.12/14,17)

1620   (Michaelmas) Exchequer court proceedings against the Corporation of Athlone [35pp]. (Ms. Talbot b.13/37; c.8/20)

1620   'The General Charges of his Mts Customs in the Kingdom of Ireland, viz from the 25th March ano 1619 unto the 25th March ano 1620', with a particularly detailed listing of the charges of the port of Dublin [4pp]. (Ms. Talbot c.6/62)

1622   (July) Will of Peter Talbot of Rathdowne. Summary only. (Ms. Talbot b.16/37)

1624   (25 Jan.) Letter from Lord Deputy Falkland to the Privy Council regarding the passing of patents for the creation of noblemen and bishops. (Ms. Talbot b.13/13)

1626   'The Charges of his Mts Customes in the Kingdom of Ireland both ordinarie and extraordinarie for half year viz from the 29th September 1625 to the 25th March 1626', for the port of Dublin only. (Ms. Talbot c.6/63)

1626   (5 April) Inquisition post mortem into the estates of John, Lord Courcy [1 fol.]. (Ms. Talbot b.16/39b)

1626	(18 June) Letter from Dominick, Lord Kinsale, to Lord Conway, Secretary of State, concerning the title of Baron of Kinsale. With an enclosure setting out why Lord Courcy's claim to the Barony of Kinsale is false. (Ms. Talbot b.12/20–1)
1626–27	Petitions, letters, notes of evidence and the final decree of the Commissioners in London affirming the Barony of Kinsale to the heir male [12 fols]. (Ms. Talbot b.12/27)
1626–1761	Transcripts of documents in a case before the Attorney General in 1761 concerning the title of Baron of Kinsale. Many of the documents cited cover the period 1626–41. (Ms. Talbot b.10/21 etc.)
1627	(16 Feb.) Letter from Lord Deputy Falkland to the Privy Council stating that Lord Kinsale had sent over a power of attorney to answer Lord Courcy's claim to the Barony of Kinsale. (Ms. Talbot b.12/22)
1627	(19 Feb.) Letter from Lord Kinsale to Lord Conway regarding the title of Baron of Kinsale. (Ms. Talbot b.12/23)
1627	(9 May) Letter from the King to the Lord Deputy and Council on behalf of Lord Courcy. (Ms. Talbot b.12/24)
1628	(4 March) Copy of a clause in the patent enrolled in the Irish Chancery conferring the titles of Baron Chaworth of Trym and Viscount Chaworth of Armagh on Sir George Chaworth. (Ms. Talbot b.16/40)[400]
1628	(23 Aug.) Letters patent conferring the titles of Earl of St. Albans in the peerage of England and Viscount of Galway and Baron of Immanay in the peerage of Ireland on Richard, Earl of Clanricard. (Ms. Talbot b.11/22)
1629	(5 Aug.) Letters patent conferring the title of Baron Fitzwilliam of Merrion on Thomas Fitzwilliam. (Ms. Talbot b.11/26)
1634	(12 March) Will of Sir William Talbot of Cartoun, bart., in full [4pp]. (Ms. Talbot b.16/42)[401]
1634	(13 May) King's letter for the holding of a parliament in Ireland. (Ms. Talbot b.11/10)
1634	(20 June) Letter from the King to Lord Deputy Wentworth giving him authority to settle issues of precedence in the forthcoming Irish Parliament. (Ms. Talbot b.11/9)
1636	(Trinity) Exchequer court proceedings against George, Earl of Kildare, for the customs of Strangford and Ardglass [5pp]. (Ms. Talbot c.7/36–7)
1639	(Michaelmas) Exchequer court proceedings as to Richard Talbot's claim to the admiralty of Malahide, with the judgement against the Crown in Talbot's favour [13pp]. (Ms. Talbot c.6/64–5)
1640	(13 Jan.) Letters patent appointing Thomas, Earl of Strafford, as Lord Lieutenant of Ireland. (Ms. Talbot b.11/1)
1640	(11 Nov.) Inquisition post mortem into the Co. Dublin estates of Richard Talbot of Malahide, who died on 29 July 1640. (Ms. Talbot b.16/45–6)

---

[400] See *Cal. Patent Rolls, Ire., Charles I*, p423.
[401] There are also extracts from this will at Ms. Talbot b.16/41.

Tanner MSS (ref. Ms. Tanner)

Charles McNeill published *The Tanner Letters* (I.M.C., Dublin, 1943), in which he pruned the extensive Tanner collection of its Irish material.[402] Though the majority of the collection is concerned with the 1641–60 period, there are a number of documents pre-dating this. Of particular interest are the Bedell papers for the reign of Charles I, and there are even a number of sixteenth century manuscripts scattered throughout the collection.

Willis MSS (ref. Ms. Willis)

1592   A collection of English historical papers, including details of the trial of Sir John Perrot at Westminster Hall. (Ms. Willis 58, ff 245–9 and 263–305)

c1620   A treatise by Sir John Davies on the King's right to impose taxes. (Ms. Willis 57)

OXFORD UNIVERSITY : Christ Church College Library
Oxford OX1 1DP
Tel: (01865) 276 169

A catalogue of this College's manuscript collection was compiled in 1867, G.W. Kitchin, *Catalogus Codicum Mss. qui in Bibliotheca Ædis Christi apud Oxonienses Adservantur*, in which the following volume with Irish material was noted:

LOOSE ITEMS

1533–1700   Volume entitled 'Collectanea Ecclesiastica 1533–1700' (ref. Ms. 290), containing the following three items of Irish interest. However, the college librarian has informed us that these documents are merely late seventeenth century transcripts from Henry Foulis, *The History of Romish Treasons and Usurptions* (2nd ed., London, 1681), compiled for the use of William Wake, subsequently Archbishop of Canterbury.[403]

c1580   'The Pope's indulgence to stir up the Irish' [6 fols]. (Ms. 290, no.35)

1601   'The Spanish General's letter to the Irish' [8 fols]. (Ms. 290, no.40)

1603   'Opinion of the Popish Universities on the Irish Rebellion' [10 fols]. (Ms. 290, no.41)

OXFORD UNIVERSITY : The Codrington Library, All Souls College
Oxford OX1 4AL
Tel: (01865) 279 379

Although a catalogue by H.O. Coxe for this College's collection is unavailable in Ireland[404] – and as a result was not consulted by us – the college librarian is aware of the following items:

---

[402] Most of the published Tanner MSS are on microfilm in N.L.I., see Hayes, *Sources* for microfilm numbers.

[403] The transcripts are from pages 306, 484–5 and 491–4 of that work.

[404] For some reason the Trinity College, Dublin, copy of Coxe's *Catalogus Codicum Mss. ... Oxoniensibus* (1852), does not contain the section for All Souls College, though it was included in the

LOOSE ITEMS

1603   (10 April) Letter from Mr. Butler to the Earl of Ormond concerning
            Italy. (Ms. 155, fol. 13v)

1628   (9 Sept.) 'Parliament in Ireland' signed by Robert Hadson [?
            Hadsor], Henry Holcroft, William Jones, and Francis Annesley.
            (Ms. 204, p141)

1634   'Dr. Rives his animadversions upon the Commission to the Bp. in
            Ireland together with those of John Lamb', dated 1634. (Ms.
            204, p43)

1640   Articles of impeachment against Thomas Wentworth, Earl of
            Strafford, Lord Lieutenant of Ireland. (Ms. 181, fol. 195)

17th cen.   'Sir George Radcliffe on superiors and subjection' from a Ms. of
            Archbishop Ussher. (Ms. 256, fol. 203)

17th cen.   (10 June) 'Irish Grievances'. (Ms. 204, p153)

n.d.   'Notes to be considered of the recovering of the realm of Ireland'.
            (Ms. 155, fol. 58)

n.d.   'The manner of holding parliaments in France, Scotland and
            Ireland'. (Ms. 202, fol. 46v)

OXFORD UNIVERSITY : Corpus Christi College Library
Merton Street, Oxford OX1 4JF
Tel: (01865) 276 700
Fax: (01865) 793 121

The catalogue by Coxe includes the following items, to which a few more details
have been added:

LOOSE ITEMS

1592–1684   Notes by William Fulman of the Chancellors, Vice-Chancellors and
            Provosts of Trinity College, Dublin [2 fols]. (Ms. 315b, ff 356–7)

17th cen.   A list of Chancellors, Vice-Chancellors and Provosts of Trinity
            College, Dublin. (Ms. 319, fol. 204)

OXFORD UNIVERSITY : Exeter College Library
Oxford OX1 3DP
Tel: (01865) 279 621
Fax: (01865) 279 630

The listing by Coxe of the College's manuscript holdings includes the following
items, to which nothing new has been added:

LOOSE ITEMS

1586   (27 June) The Queen's letters respecting the plantation of the
            province of Munster after the rebellion of the Earl of Desmond, at

---

publication (see P. Morgan, *Oxford Libraries outside the Bodliean: A Guide* (Oxford, 1980)). The index
for Coxe's work, however, which also covers the missing All Souls section, includes numerous references
to Ireland, and Irish people, amongst the All Souls manuscripts. As such the librarian's notes, listed above,
probably only represent a part of the College's holdings concerning Ireland.

the end of which there is a copy of a letter of the 'undertakers' of the plantation to deliver certain lands to Andrew Reade. (Ms. 141, no.1)

16th cen.   (n.d.) A discourse on the government of Ireland and the character of the people. Begins with, 'At soche time as the meere Irishe of Ireland seemed to have bin in the height of their strength...' [20 fols]. (Ms. 154, no.2)[405]

1613–15   Abstract of the proceedings of the Parliament in Ireland. The inscription begins, 'Statuta, ordinationes, acta et provisiones edita in quodam parliamento illustrissimi principis domini nostri Jacobi....' [40 fols]. (Ms. 155, no.15)

1621   Report of the Commissioners appointed to inquire into the regulation of abuses in Ireland. (Ms. 174, no.5)

1622   Account or register of the proceedings of the Commissioners appointed to inquire into the state of the church, Crown revenues, courts of law, plantations, etc., in Ireland [1 vol, 69 fols]. (Ms. 95)[406]

1623   An establishment account expressing the number of all officers, general bands, companies of foot, and warders in forts and castles, appointed to serve in Ireland, with their entertainments and wages by the day, month and year. To begin from 1 April 1623, paid for by the Treasurer-at-war [11 fols]. (Ms. 96)

OXFORD UNIVERSITY : Queen's College Library
High Street, Oxford OX1 4AW
Tel: (01865) 279 121

At present we have received no reply from this College, but Coxe's catalogue includes the following items concerning Ireland, though his dating is often suspect:

LOOSE ITEMS

c1620–30   A volume of manuscripts concerning the nobility (Ms. 122), which includes :

    c1622   Nobility of Ireland, being Englishmen and residents of England. (Ms. 122, no. k)

    c1624   Concerning the ancestors and descendants of Thomas, Earl of Arundel, and the Lady Alathea, his wife, in Ireland. (Ms. 122, no. cc)

    1625   Instructions for Mr. Preston, Portcullis Pursuivant of Arms, being sent into Ireland in 1625. (Ms. 122, no.aa)

    c1625   Order for settling the fees of the Irish nobility to officers in England. (Ms. 122, no. z)

1625   Lord Deputy Falkland's query as to the share of pirates' goods to be had of the captains of King's ships. (Ms. 155, no.29)

---

[405] This document appears in a volume of sixteenth century tracts, and is probably contemporaneous with the rest of the volume's contents.

[406] N.L.I. microfilm, n.3477, p.3095.

c1628   Touching the Earl of Shrewsbury's title to the earldom of Waterford. (Ms. 155, no.18)[407]

17th cen.   In a volume of legal documents compiled in 1677 there is an undated tract entitled 'Whether a lord of Ireland committing treason there may be tried in England', which includes legal precedents predating 1641. (Ms. 157, no.18)

17th cen.   Arms of Irish and other noblemen with some pedigrees [1 vol, 116 fols]. (Ms. 81)

n.d.   A document entitled 'Convivium Hibernicum', with an inscription that reads, 'O Deus bone, quid ego in me susepi ?'. (Ms. 130, no.9)

COLLECTIONS

Bacon MSS (ref. Ms. 32)

A volume entitled 'Bacon Mss' which contains some letters relating to Ireland, *viz*

1599   Francis Bacon to the Earl of Essex, to take upon him the care of Irish business, when Cecil is in France. (Ms. 32, no.1d)

1599   Same to same, on the first treaty with Tyrone. (Ms. 32, no.1e)

1599   Same to same, advice on Essex's going to Ireland. (Ms. 32, no.1f)

1599   Essex to the Queen, on his command to go to Ireland. (Ms. 32, no.6)

OXFORD UNIVERSITY : University College Library *
c/o The Bodleian Library, Broad Street, Oxford OX1 3BG

This college's collection is presently housed at the Bodleian Library. Researchers should prefix the manuscript numbers with 'University College' when corresponding with the Bodleian.

LOOSE ITEMS

1599   (n.d.) Letter from the Earl of Essex to the Queen on his command to go into Ireland, describing the order as 'banishment ... into the cursedsd of all other Countries'. (Ms. 152, p122)

1599   (n.d.) Letter from Queen Elizabeth to the Earl of Essex and the Council of Ireland, reproaching him for his inactivity and his dealings with Ulster. (Ms. 152, p33–38)

1640   A volume entitled 'State and Parliamentary Papers', which includes a number of speeches, declarations, petitions and articles about the attainder of Lord Lieutenant Strafford (fols 26v, 27r, 28v, 29r, 29v, 30r, 30v, 36r) and the impeachment of Deputy Lieutenant Radcliffe (fol. 43r). (Ms. 83)

COLLECTIONS

Carew MSS (ref. Ms. 103)

A volume [160 fols] of documents relating to Ireland (Ms. 103), formerly in the collection of Sir George Carew, as follows:[408]

---

[407] This probably relates to the same case against Viscount Lumley of Waterford, as appears in Lincoln's Inn Library, Hale Ms. 12 & 83 (see above).

[408] N.L.I. microfilm n. 5491, p. 5658. The majority of the Carew MSS are housed in Lambeth Palace Library, London (see above).

15th cen.	Extracts from a chronicle, written in Irish, dealing with events after 1467 (ff 53r–56v)[409]
c1500	Extracts from a chronicle, written in Irish, containing largely genealogical notes. (ff 30r–42r)
1575	A rental, for one year, of the lands granted by Edward VI to Sir Nicholas Bagenal, Marshal of the Army in Ireland. Including the lordship of Newry, Co. Down (drawn up by Randolph Brereton, Constable of Newry Castle), the lordship of Mourne and Green Castle (by Hugh Lewes, Constable of Green Castle), and the lordship of Carlingford and Cowley (by Richard Aphewe, Constable of Carlingford). The rentals list each individual tenant, his holdings and rent paid, as well as other forms of income on the estate arising from spiritualities, mills, town customs, herriots, etc. (ff 115v–142r)[410]
16th cen.	Extracts from an Irish genealogy. (ff 43r–47v)
1600	A discourse on the government of the province of Munster addressed to Sir George Carew, Lord President of Munster. Begins 'I presume, my verie good Lord...'. (ff 159r–161v)
c1600	'A discourse for the reformation of Ireland', addressed to 'the Queenes most excellent Majestie. I have founde the chardge that your Majestie committed unto me...', recommending what should be done once the rebellion is over. (ff 99r–113r)
c1603–8	A genealogy written in Irish beginning with Donal MacCarthy, Earl of Clancare, and tracing all the septs and branches of the MacCarthys, back to Adam. This is followed by genealogies of O'Brien, MacConmara and other families derived from Cas and Cian, as well as O'Neill, O'Donnell and other septs. A reference to Rory O'Donnell, Earl of Tyrconnell, is the latest entry, giving the entire document a date of 1603–1608.[411] (fols 3v–27v)
1608	'The rates of merchandizes as they are set down in the Book of Rates for the Custom and Subsidy of Poundage...', which includes lists of goods with their rateable value. Printed pamphlet, Dublin. (fols 73r–80r)
1608	'A Collection of such orders and conditions as are to be observed by the Undertakers, upon the distribution and plantation of the Escheated lands in Ulster'. Printed pamphlet, London. (fols 81r–89v)
1610	'Conditions to be observed by the British Undertakers of the Escheated lands in Ulster'. Printed pamphlet, London. (fols 92r–98r)
n.d.	An Irish poem. (fols 58r–60r)
n.d	A list of names starting with 'Jenken Conwey, esquer, Daniell Ferris, gent, Daniell Oge McDaniell McCormack, gent, Owna McFerris, gent [etc.]'. Including in total 18 names of predominantly

---

[409] This document has been published with a commentary by Brian O'Cuiv, 'A fragment of Irish annals', *Celtica*, xiv (1981).

[410] This has been published by Harold O'Sullivan, 'A 1575 Rent Roll, with Contemporaneous Maps, of the Bagenal estate in the Carlingford Lough district', *Co. Louth Archaeological & Historical Journal*, xxi, no.1 (1985), pp31–47.

[411] O'Donnell was made an earl in 1603 and died in 1608.

Gaelic-Irish form. It would seem to be a list of Co. Kerry landowners.[412] (fol 61r)

SHROPSHIRE : County Record Office *
Castle Gates, Shrewsbury SY1 2AQ
Tel: (01743) 255 350
Fax: (01743) 255 355

LOOSE ITEMS

17th cen.   Copy of the 1689 pedigree of the Sandford family, which records details of the marriage *circa* 1620 of Francis, son and heir of Arthur Sandford of Sandford in Salop., esq., to Elizabeth, daughter of Calcott Chambre of Shillelagh, Co. Wicklow. (465/1021)

COLLECTIONS

Shrewsbury Corporation MSS

Many of the Corporation muniments, which were deposited in the County Record Office in 1975, were given a brief listing and analysis in H.M.C., *15th Report*, App. X, pp1–65, where 13 items of Irish interest are mentioned. Dealing primarily with the levying of troops during the Elizabethan wars, most of the documents referred to were taken from the Corporation's Miscellaneous Papers, with the remnant coming either from Municipal Register III or the Bailiff's Account for February 1613. There is no doubt that a lot more material remains undiscovered, particularly among the Trained Bands & Musters Papers.[413]

Sandford of Sandford Correspondence (ref. S.R.O. 2)

This collection includes a number of letters from Calcott Chambre to his son-in-law, Francis Sandford, relating to the administration of their estate at Carnew, Co. Wicklow, and other Irish business.

1627   (2 May) Calcott Chambre to Francis Sandford, re the presentation of his accounts and the organisation of their interest in the timber trade in Wicklow. Also gives directions for dealing with the wife of Felix Duff, Edmund Duff, and other Irish tenants. (2/284)

1627   (10 Nov.) Same to same, stating that he intends to travel to Dublin soon, and reporting a flood at Enniscorthy, Co. Wexford. (2/285)

1628   (22 Feb.) Same to same, asking if he should send a ship laden with salt to Dublin or Wexford. (2/286)

1628   (23 Feb.) Same to same, reporting that Lord Chancellor Loftus has desired some does to furnish his park, and repeating his question about the shipment of salt. (2/287)

1628   (28 May) Same to same, offering advice about the unreliability of their partners, Edward Ponton and Edmond McMorthogh, who are only out for themselves, and ordering that John Falkener be removed from his employment. (2/288)

---

[412] The name 'Jenken Conway esqer' appears alone on fol. 52r, which might indicate that the volume was in his possession at some point.

[413] Some of the Trained Bands & Musters Papers were published in the early volumes of the Transactions of the Shropshire Archaeological Society.

1628   (2 June) Same to same, concerning their dealings with Jacobson Garretson, master of *The Fox of Herne*, and Jacob Johnson, master of *The St Jacob of Aberslete*. (2/289)

1629   (21 Jan.) Same to same, complimenting Sandford on his handling of the petitions presented to the Lord Deputy against him by his brother and Teige McDonnell. (2/290)

1629   (30 Jan.) Same to same, giving further details about McDonnell's charges, and also mentioning earlier troubles with the Earl of Cork. (2/291)

1629   (20 May) Same to same, concerning the pipestave business in Leinster, and Chambre's meeting with Sir James Carroll. (2/292)

1631   (26 May) Same to same, with regard to news received from John Madden about the 'strange passage' between Sandford and the auditors, who were instructed to put down several hundred pounds as being due to Mr Farrell. Chambre suggests that Sandford has really used the money to pay for his own debts. (2/293)

1632   (22 Sept.) Same to same, regarding the cost of timber work desired by the Earl of Cork, and reporting that Sir Charles Cook the collier wants to send miners to dig for ironstone on the Irish estate. (2/294)

1632   (9 Aug.) John Maule to Sandford, intreating Sandford to pay him his money or else he will put Sandford's bond in suit. (2/295)

1641   (12 Jan.) Bond of Francis Sandford of Graines, Co. Dublin, esq., to Robert Milles and Peter Bythell of Dublin, merchants, in the sum of £60, stating that if John Sympole of Eightfild, Co. Salop., hosier, does not pay William Sutton of Chester £32 before 25 Jan. next, Sandford will do so. (2/296)

SOMERSET : County Record Office *
Obridge Road, Taunton TA2 7PU
Tel: (01823) 337 600
Fax: (01823) 325 402

LOOSE ITEMS

1572   A copy of a map of Ulster (1 roll). (DD/SAS/C/2402/44)

c1590   Paper draft of a grant (under the Great Seal of England) to Hellen fitz Edmund Gibbon, of the castle and lands of Kilblaine in Munster, forfeited by her uncle, Thomas MacShane MacMorris *alias* Thomas ne Skartye, attainted for high treason in the Munster rebellion, and subsequently found to be innocent; with a direction to Lord Deputy Fitzwilliam to restore her in blood at the next parliament, and to obtain the surrender of the property granted to Hugh Cuffe. (DD/PO/15)

16th cen.   (n.d.) Grant by Edmund Spenser of Kilcoman, esq., to 'Mr. Henry' of the keeping of his wood in Ballygamin, etc. (DD/SAS/M15)

1607   Names of those pressed for service in Ireland, which lists 30 names from the six hundreds in southern Somerset. (DD/HI/459)

COLLECTIONS

Bridgwater Borough: Water Bailliff's Accounts (ref. D/B/bw)

Several of the pre-1500 accounts have been published by the Somerset Record Society, Vols. 48, 53, 58, 60 and 70. There are 89 accounts for the period after 1500 (covering the years 1503–1640), none of which have been published. The documents include receipts for moorage, cranage, keyadge, and other town customs. For example, in 1565 *The George of Wexford* was charged 5s. for keyadge (D/B/bw/1465), and on 14 October 1606 a Mr. Turner (of Wexford) was charged 12d. for cranage for landing six tons of iron (D/B/bw/1490). There are numerous references to Irish merchants and Irish boats, reflecting Bridgwater's prominent place in Anglo-Irish trade during the early modern period.

Carew of Crowcombe MSS (ref. DD/TB)

Though most of the material in this collection relating to Ireland was sold to the Public Record Office, London (PRO 30/5), the John Ryland's University Library (see above) and Trinity College, Dublin, one further item stayed with the family until they deposited their remaining documents in Somerset Record Office. This item was not mentioned in the H.M.C.'s report on the collection (*4th Report*, App., pp368–74).

1594	(7 August) 'A sommary colleccon made of the estate of the realme [Ireland] as yt standeth at this present', being a description of the country signed by the outgoing Lord Deputy, Sir William Fitzwilliam, and the Council, and delivered to Sir William Russell at his swearing in as the new Lord Deputy on 11 August. The description centres on the state of Ulster, giving an area-by-area report on the state of the rebellion there. The principal concern is Fermanagh, Monaghan and the heavily besieged government fort at Enniskillen. There is also a lengthy report on the activities of Feagh MacHugh O'Byrne and Walter Reagh in Leinster. There are two postscripts at the end. The first, by Stephan Segar, Constable of Dublin Castle, and dated 9 August 1594, is a note of the pledges remaining in his care (being those for Sir John O'Dogherty and Feagh MacHugh O'Byrne). The second is a brief report by the Council, dated 11 August, on Maguire's defeat of the relief army, under Sir Henry Duke and Sir Edward Herbert, *en route* to Enniskillen on 7 August [8pp]. (DD/TB/56/51/8)

Mildmay MSS (ref. DD/MI)

1600	(3 April) Letter from George Carew, in Dublin, to his uncle George Harvey, in London, regarding his 'business' and the differences between Pallfryman and some of the officers [?of the Ordnance]. (DD/MI/Box 18/57)
1600	Plan of the deployment of troops at the capture of Glin Castle entitled 'The Castle of Glin taken by her Ma[ts] forces under the command of y[e] right Honorable S[r] George Carew knight, L. President of Munster y[e] 7 & 8 July, 1600'. It is a very well preserved colour plan (52cm × 40cm), including a fine depiction of Glin Castle. (DD/MI/Box 17/Map)
1601	Copies of four documents relating to troops bound for Ireland (DD/MI/Box 18/44), *viz*,

1601	(29 July) Warrant and instructions for Captain Skipwith to take charge of the embarkation of 100 men from Bristol, levied for service in Ireland.
1601	(31 July) Letter from the Privy Council to the City of Bristol requiring it to afford assistance in the embarkation of 895 men to Ireland.
1601	(15 Aug.) Receipt for the arms, etc., needed to furnish 100 men, sent by the captains (8 signatures) to George Harvie, Deputy Lieutenant of the Ordnance, and John Limewraye, Surveyor of the same.
1601	(15 Aug.) Note that the arms were delivered to the several captains. Signed: John Hopkins, Mayor, Samuel Norton.
1601	(6 Oct.) Copy of a letter from the Queen to the Lieutenant of the Ordnance in the Tower of London, and in his absence to his deputy, George Harvey, to provide cannoniers for service in Ireland. (DD/MI/Box 18/46)
1634	(11 Dec.) Copy of a royal letter to the Lord Deputy of Ireland, regarding a favour to be granted to Sir Thomas Edmondes, Treasurer of the Household. (DD/MI/Box 18/27)

Phelips of Montacute MSS (ref. DD/PH)

Many documents of Irish interest in this collection were listed in the H.M.C.'s report in 1872 (*3rd Report*, Appendix, pp281–7), particularly a bound volume of letters, dated 1585–1600, of the Lord Lieutenant of Somerset, which includes documents concerning the levying of troops for Ireland (p286b of report, now DD/PH/220). There is one further item relating to Ireland, not listed by the H.M.C.:

17th cen.	A document, probably written c1685, entitled 'A prospect of Popery or a short view of the cruelties, treasons and massacres committed by the Papists since the beginning of Queen Mary's reign'. In includes a number of references to Ireland, including the 1641 rising.

Somerset Quarter Sessions Records (ref. Q/SR)

This series contains some documentation concerning Irish vagrants in the early seventeenth century. A.L. Beier in his book, *Masterless Men* (London, 1985), gives details from these records (ref. Q/SR 62/38–42) about the transportation of a shipload of vagrants from Ireland in 1630 by Maurice Keysons *alias* Curry in *The Peter of Dungarvan*. Keysons was arrested and admitted that he regularly transported Irish people to England, charging 4s. per head for the service (see *Masterless Men*, p63). Though the authors could locate no other references in a brief search, this series undoubtedly contains further Irish material.

Trevelyan (Wolseley) of Nettlecombe MSS (ref. DD/WO)

Many of the documents concerning Ireland in this huge collection have been published by the Camden Society, J. Payne Collier (ed.), *Trevelyan Papers* (3 vols, Camden Soc., 1st series, Vols 67, 84, 105, London, 1857–72),[414] and more recently by the Somerset Record Office, Mary Siraunt (ed.), *The Trevelyan*

---

[414] The items in Volume 3 can be largely found in DD/WO/Box 54/Bundle 1, Box 55/Bundle 2, and Box 56/Bundles 4 & 5; the few tracts concerning Ireland in Vol. 2 are now at Box 55/Bundle 1.

Letters to 1840 (Somerset R.O., 1990).[415] They include many letters and other documents concerning Sir George Trevelyan, Lord Deputy Chichester, Bishop Montgomery of Derry and Meath, Lord Deputy Mountjoy, and general news from Ireland. However, many items still remain to be published, as follows:

1550–1640	A bundle of nineteenth century transcripts of documents (DD/WO/55/9), including:
1550	Copy of a plan of Carrickfergus (taken from the *History of Carrickfergus*, 1848)
1612	Copy of a drawing of Joymount, erected by Sir Arthur Chichester, from the British Library.
1614	Copy of the funeral entry of Susan Steyning, wife of Bishop Montgomery, from the Ulster Office.
1618	(6 April) Inquisition post mortem of Thomas Russell of Carickfergus.
1620	Funeral entry of Bishop Montgomery, from the Ulster Office.
1624	(23 March) Inquisition post mortem of Sir George Trevelyan of Sampton, Co. Wexford.
1625	(12 Aug.) Inquisition post mortem of [ ] of Antrim.
1625	Funeral entry of Sir Arthur Chichester, from the Ulster Office.
1630	Funeral entry of Sir Hugh Culme, from the Ulster Office.
1632	(29 March) Inquisition post mortem of Arthur, Lord Chichester.
1636	(9 May) Funeral entry of Walter Cottell [*alias* Cottle] of New Ross, from the Ulster Office.
1636	Funeral entry of Sir Edward Harris of Dromny, from the Ulster Office.
1637	Funeral entry of Phillip Culme, from the Ulster Office.
1639	Funeral entry of Mary, Dowager Baroness of Kercubright, from the Ulster Office.
1640	Funeral entry of Sir Arthur Bassett of Belfast, from the Ulster Office.
17th cen.	Copies of the Down Survey maps for parts of Coleraine.
17th cen.	Miscellaneous extracts from the patent rolls regarding Bishop Montgomery, Sir George Trevelyan, and the Willoughbys.

1593   (26 Feb.) 'The description of certain persons expected to come into the realme from the pts beyond the seas for some dangerous practycces to be attempted here'. Includes the physical descriptions of ten Irishmen (Alexander Rocheford, Thomas Don, William Caddle, Mallachias Fullam, Hugh O'Reilly, John Doyne, Donell O'Brien, Denys Conor, William Thomson, and James Ralley), for example 'Alexander Rocheford an Ireshman of 26 years of age, a tal man of stature; he hath latelie had the small pox, a flaxon bearde, the hair of his head browne'. The others include similar details, with special emphasis on distinguishing facial scars. (DD/WO/56/6)

1593–1604   Ten letters from George Montgomery to John Willoughby, prior to his appointment as Bishop of Derry. (DD/WO/54/8)

1599   (5 March) Letter from Gilbert Collynes to Mr. Willoughby, stating that 'Sir George Carie is shortly to go to Ireland'. (DD/WO/54/6)

1604   (12 Feb.) Letter from Richard Carey to Mr. Willoughby, discussing the health of his brother, the Lord Deputy of Ireland. (DD/WO/54/6)

---

[415] In her appendix, Siraunt includes various letters that she could not locate in the main collection, but had been published by the Camden Society. These documents have recently been deposited by the Trevelyans' solicitor (ref. DD/DH) and remain unlisted.

1604	(3 Aug.) Letter from George Carey to Gilbert Collans, giving news about Ireland, and discussing personal affairs. (DD/WO/54/6)[416]
1606	(4 July) Receipt of payment by Bishop Montgomery to William Willoughby. (DD/WO/54/8)
1606	(12 July) Letter from Bishop Montgomery of Derry to Edward Predeaux concerning his estate, and Nicholas Willoughby. (DD/WO/54/4/7)
1606	(16 July) Letter from Bishop Montgomery to John Willoughby, about his English estates and his family. (DD/WO/54/8)
c1606	(24 July) Letter from Susanna Montgomery (wife of Bishop Montgomery) to her brother, John Willoughby, discussing her travels to and from Ireland. (DD/WO/54/8)
1606	(22 Aug.) Letter from Bishop Montgomery to John Willoughby, regarding Willoughby's brothers who are in Ireland. (DD/WO/54/8)
1608	(13 Nov.) Letter from Bishop Montgomery to John Willoughby, regarding his family's unhappiness with his settling in Ireland. (DD/WO/54/8)
1608	(29 Nov.) Same to same, stating that selling his English estates would pay for his expenses in Ireland. (DD/WO/54/8)
1608–14	Documents concerning the English estates (Manor of Whitwell) of George, Bishop of Derry [3 items]. (DD/WO/31/11/2–4)
1609	(13 May) Letter from Phillip Willoughby to John Willoughby, regarding the proceedings of George, Bishop of Derry, in Ireland. (DD/WO/54/8)
1609	(30 May) Letter from Bishop Montgomery to John Willoughby, regarding his estates in England and other financial dealings. (DD/WO/54/8)
1609	(20 July) Same to same, discussing the erection of bishoprics in Ulster 'to the form of the foundation of the Bishoprics of England'. He believes it will take a whole winter's work. (DD/WO/54/8)
1610	(2 Oct.) Letter from Bishop Montgomery to John Willoughby, about his English estates. (DD/WO/54/8)
1618	(20 Oct.) Letter from Bishop Montgomery to John Willoughby, regarding family affairs, his activities in Ireland, and many other matters [4 fols]. (DD/WO/54/8)
1618	(21 Nov.) Letter from George, Bishop of Meath, to John Willoughby, discussing his plan to purchase 'things' and land in Ireland; needs the money owed to him. Asks that it be sent to Ireland without delay. He can have the merchants of Dublin collect the money from Willoughby any time. (DD/WO/54/8)[417]
1618	(20 Dec.) List of documents, etc., in Bishop Montgomery's case, sent to John Willoughby. (DD/WO/54/4/9)

---

[416] There are some other letters between George and Edward Carey and the Willoughbys bearing the same reference number which discuss purely personal matters, and do not seem to relate to Ireland.

[417] This document could be dated 1618 or 1628.

1618   (22 Dec.) Letter from Robert More to John Willoughby concerning
            the offer of an estate by Bishop George Montgomery.
            (DD/WO/54/4/8)

1618   (22 Dec.) Letter from George, Bishop of Meath, to his sister,
            Margaret Willoughby, regarding a farm to be let to his family.
            (DD/WO/54/8)

1618-63   Papers relating to Sir George Trevelyan's estates in Ireland, which
            includes a 'Cathalogue' of his estates in Co. Wexford, and a
            document relating that he made a 60 year lease of the premises to
            his wife, to commence at his death. (DD/WO/54/2/14)

1619   (12 Jan.) Letter from the Bishop of Exeter to Bishop George
            Montgomery concerning his title to an estate. (DD/WO/54/4/10)

1619   (27 Jan.) Letter from Bishop Montgomery to John Willoughby,
            discussing the £600 he needs, as per his letter of 21 Nov. 1618.
            (DD/WO/54/8)

1620   (6 Nov.) Letter from John Willoughby to Bishop George
            Montgomery of Meath, relating to a loan John made to his brother
            Phillip, through George. Asks that as punishment George not give
            the money to Phillip. (DD/WO/54/8)

1622   (1 Feb.) Conveyance by Nicholas Willoughby and Phillip Steyning
            of Ireland, to Hugh Culme of Cloghe and John Barnet of Monaghan,
            of lands in Roskerne, Co. Fermanagh, part of the late estate of
            Bishop Montgomery. (DD/WO/57/3/19)

STAFFORDSHIRE : County Record Office *
County Buildings, Eastgate Street, Stafford ST16 2LZ
Tel: (01785) 223121 etx. 8373/8380

LOOSE ITEMS

1578   (18 June) Letter from Henry, Lord Berkeley, to Thomas Paget
            asking for his favour on behalf of John Butler,[418] his man, suitor to
            Widow Sheppard of Stapewill. (D603/K/1/4/32)

1630   (Feb.) Royal writ directed to William, Lord Fitzwilliam, regarding
            the Irish administration [Latin]. (D603/O/6/2)

1641   A narration of the proceedings against Thomas Wentworth, Earl of
            Strafford, including numerous references to Ireland [1 vol.].
            (D661/20/2)

COLLECTIONS

Bagot (Stafford) MSS (ref. D(W)1721 & D3260)

The Bagot papers received a listing by the H.M.C. in 1874 (*4th Report*,
Appendix, pp325–44). Although most of the documents concerning Ireland were
sold between 1945 and 1955 to the Folger Shakespeare Library in Washington,
the remaining papers deposited in this Record Office include two volumes of
nineteenth century transcripts of letters then at Blithfield, covering the period
1570–1602 (D(W) 1721/3/290, D3260/1). The items concerning Ireland appear

---

[418] Probably from Ireland.

to have been fully dealt with by the H.M.C., and include letters from Richard Broughton to Richard Bagot in 1576, regarding the 1st Earl of Essex's journeys in Ireland, and his fatal illness. The letters relate that Essex 'suspected his drink was not the best', because a page and a gentleman who had been drinking with Essex had also fallen ill (D(W) 1721/3/290/39). Other letters from the 1590s give news from Ireland during the Nine Years War.

Sutherland (Leveson) MSS (ref. D593, D868)

This collection comprises the papers of Admiral Sir Richard Leveson, who commanded the English navy on the coast of Munster during the battle of Kinsale in 1601. Most of the items relating to Ireland have been listed by the H.M.C. in 1876 (*5th Report*, Appendix, pp135–214), and these papers are now to be found at D868/1–10. However there is one further item relating to Ireland,

c1613–4 (15 March) Letter from Henry, Lord Cobham, to Sir John Leveson at Halling, Kent, asking for help concerning his negotiations with the Countess of Kildare. (D593/Add/5/6)

SUFFOLK : County Record Office, Ipswich
Gatacre Road, Ipswich IP1 2LQ
Tel: (01473) 264 541

LOOSE ITEMS

1632 Will and executorship papers of Capt. James Waughope of Co. Down, who died in Muscovy. (S1/1/77.6,43,44)

COLLECTIONS

Purcell–Fitzgerald MSS (ref. HB 56)

This largely unlisted collection holds one box of records concerning the family's Irish estate. The pre-1641 documents in that box are itemised below. According to the archivist the reference numbers are temporary and will be changed once a full catalogue of the collection is completed. A systematic search of this collection would probably yield further Irish material.

1610 Final concord (Wyse family) of a messuage in Waterford. (HB 56)

1639 Charles I's charter to Waterford. (HB 56)

1639 Royal grant of the castle and town of Rochestowne to Nicholas Wyse. (HB 56)

SURREY : Guildford Muniment Room *
Castle Arch, Guildford GU1 3SX
Tel: (01483) 573 942

COLLECTIONS

The Bray Collection (ref. 52 and 85)

1576 Eye witness account (incomplete) of the sickness and death in Dublin of Walter Devereux, Earl of Essex. (52/7/8(1))

1641   (9 Oct.) Letter from Sir Edward Nicholas to Mr. Treasurer (i.e. Sir
              Henry Vane), discussing the state of troops in Ireland, the plague
              and general Irish affairs. (52/2/19(18))

1641   (9 Oct.) Letter from Sir Edward Nicholas to the Justices and
              Council in Ireland, stating that he received their recent report, and
              will be able to do all in their favour. (52/2/19(20))

1641   (27 Oct.) Letter from Sir Edward Nicholas to Mr. Treasurer, with
              brief notes on earlier packages, and comments about the Parliament
              of Ireland and its affairs. (85/5/2(23))

The Loseley MSS (ref. LM)

Although a large number of items from the Loseley collection were sold to the
Folger Shakespeare Library earlier this century, the main bulk of the papers
mentioned in the H.M.C., *7th Report* (1879) were deposited in Guildford Record
Office in 1950.[419] Of the nine items relating to Irish affairs between 1597 and
1608 which are contained in the Report, seven are presently held by the office or
are still at Loseley Park. The two missing items are the letters of 1597 and 6 Oct.
1601 respectively. In addition the Record Office received a fresh batch of
uncatalogued correspondence and other documents in 1971, which contain some
further papers of Irish interest, as follows:

1576   Parts of an account of the death in Ireland of Walter Devereux, Earl
              of Essex, including his speech the night before he died, *viz* 'I knowe
              my tyme is in the hands of God ... I have talked wth him often tymes
              synce I was sycke to my great joye. I will heare noe more of this lyf'.
              Probably written by Thomas Churchyard. (LM 1854)

1582   (8 May) Certificate given by Sir William Morgan, a captain in
              Ireland, to Walter Power, a soldier lately in his service, requiring all
              sheriffs, mayors, etc., to allow him to move freely from place to
              place in search of work. (LM 1746)

1582   (21 July) 'A note of all such as are at this present remaining
              prisoners in the Marshalsey being committed for their disobedience
              in Religion', including, '17. Walter Taylor of Ireland'. (LM
              1085/11)

1588   (30 July) The examination of Tristram Winshead, an English
              Catholic, regarding the Spanish plans to send an armada against
              England. Among other things he stated that several years
              previously, 'when Sir John Arundell was first trobled, he [Arundell]
              went into Ireland & so into France, Germanie and Italie'. (LM
              1329/370)[420]

1589   (27 July) A discourse by Maurice Fitzgerald, the White Knight's
              son, outlining the state of the Low Countries and what is intended
              by Philip II and the Duke of Parma touching England and France,
              beginning 'first he saiethe that he went over out of Ireland as page
              to S^r Wm Stanley, and hath contynewed wth him ever since, untill
              about viii moneths paste, at [which] ...[421] tyme upon the departure

---

[419] An early catalogue of the material in this collection was published in 1836, and includes a few
scattered references to people in early modern Ireland, A. J. Kemp (ed.), *The Loseley Manuscripts*
(London, 1836).

[420] Remarkably, this item was described as 'of no interest' in the old Record Office catalogue, and no
details of its contents were given.

[421] Ms torn.

of dyvers of the Irishe from [Stanley] ...[422] (who went to the service in France) he also lost him [i.e. Fitzgerald], S[r] Wm beinge very angrie wth his departure, and inquisityth to know whither he did determyne his iorney, and this examynate saide he wolde goe to france and Spaigne. Since w[ch] tyme he saithe he hathe ... [been] in the Duke's co'te at Brussells wth one Mr John Lacie an Irisheman, untill aboute xiiii dayes paste. He sayethe that at his comynge to the Dukes Co'te he founde theare wth him the Lo: Pagett & his brethren, Mr Throgmorten and his brother, Mr Henrye Poole (who saith he ought to be k. of England), and one Mr Morgan, all well intertayned by the Duke ... he sawe also the Earle of Westmorland at Antwerpe.' Fitzgerald goes on to describe the actions of the Spanish army in the Netherlands and gives details of how Philip II was preparing a new armada. (LM 1896)

1597   (6 June) Roll giving the names and dwelling places of about 100 men from all parts of Surrey who were bound for Ireland, apparently under the command of Captain Oliver St. John. (LM 1330/46)

1601   A brief declaration of the overthrow given by Lord Deputy Mountjoy to the Irish rebels and Spaniards near the town of Kinsale in Munster [3pp], beginning 'Tyrone accompanyed wth O'Donnell, O'Rorke, Magynyse, McMahone, Randall McSurley, Redmund Bourke, O'Conor Slygoes brother and Terrell, wth the cheyfe force and in effecte all the rebels in Irland, being drawen into Monnster and joyned wth the Spanyards that landed at Castlehaven, who brought to Tyrones campe syxe ensignes of Spanyards, And the greatest pte of the Irishry in Monnster, who beinge revolted, were wyned wth them and enterteyned in the kynges paye in generall Companyes and under their Awne lords, resolved to releive the Spanyards in the towne of Kynsale, and to that purpose set downe the 21 of december a myle and a half from the towne, betwene the Englishe Campe and Cork, etc. ...' The author of the manuscript estimated that after the battle there were 1,200 of the Irish lying dead about the battlefield, and 800 of them injured. (LM 1844)

1615–16   Expenses of prisoners in the Tower of London for food, clothes, tobacco, etc., which includes the costs of Sir Cormac O'Neill, Sir Donell O'Kane, Sir Niall O'Donnell, Nectan O'Donnell, and Francis Coppinger, amongst others. (LM 1087/1/5)[423]

1616   (8 April) Copy of articles of agreement between Sir Robert McLellan, Baronet, and Adrian Moore of London, esq., with regard to land in Ulster fallen to the Haberdasher's lot. Sir Robert is to build a village, and to 'plant and people the country with British Tennants'. Includes details of rent, etc. (LM 349/117)

1619–23   (1 April 1619–31 March 1623) Extract from the accounts of Henry, Lord Docwra, Baron of Culmore, Treasurer-at-Wars in Ireland, regarding the entertainment of Sir Richard Morrison, Governor of Wexford and Waterford, and for the entertainment of his companies of horsemen and footmen. Total: £2,608 16s 3d. (LM 1083/47/6)

---

[422] Ibid.

[423] The reasons for the incarceration of Sir Niall and Nectan O'Donnell are given in the Lord Deputy's letter to the Lord Privy Seal on 24 Sept. 1612 (R. Dudley Edwards (ed.), 'The Chichester Letter-Book', in *Analecta Hibernica*, viii (1938), pp45–6).

1628   (1 Jan. – 29 July) An account book for the billeting of troops at Guildford, which includes at the end details of money paid to various soldiers, including three Irishmen, *viz* Thomas Butler, John Brennan, and Dennis Folan, who each received 2s for four days. (LM 1330/73)

1635   'The relation of the proceedings against me, Francis, Lord Mountnorris, H.M.'s Vice-Treasurer and General Receiver and Treasurer at War in Ireland', together with an imperfect draft. (LM 1331/49)

17th cen.   Document concerning the Gresham family of Cos. Wexford and Waterford. (LM 1083/47/6)[424]

The Middleton Papers (ref. 145 and 1248)

Parts of this holding, comprising ten volumes of political papers dated 1627–1765, were microfilmed for the National Library of Ireland. However there are a great many further records concerning Ireland in the rest of the collection. The following list includes all relevant material found (whether microfilmed for the N.L.I. or not) though given the fact that the collection is only partially listed, it is likely to contain more.

1430–1705	Schedule of conveyances (145/box 94/1) which give few details,[425]
1630	(20 May) Mortgage by 'Fitzgerald and others' (not named) to 'Rice' of Corabby, Ballybane, etc.
1632	(3 Nov.) Grant by 'Sir John Fitzgerald and others' (not named) to Walter White of Castleredmond.

1608   (15 May) Copy of the surrender of Sir John fitz-Edmund Fitzgerald of all his lands, rents, services, etc., in the manors of Kilmacleynin, Cahirmone, in the barony of Imokilly and elsewhere in Cos. Cork and Kerry, to the King, to hold for ever. Thereafter follows the King's regrant to Fitzgerald, to be held for ever, by knights service. (145/box 94/1)

1628–92	Schedules of leases now expired (3 copies, 145/box 94/1) including,
1628	(9 July) Lease by Sir Arthur Hyde to John Horsey, of the castle, town and lands of Agherosse, Farrensemerene, Templemolagg, for 99 years.
1628	(20 July) Lease by John Horsey to Edward Horsey of the lands of Agherosse, Farrensmerene and Templemalagnie, for 99 years.

1631   (20 March) Bond of Statute Staple between (i) Richard and William Kent of Cork City, merchants, and (ii) Robert Tyrny, William Hore and William Sarsfield, all of Cork City, before Edmund Martell, Mayor of the Cork Staple. Bond in £70 (stg) of the goods of the Kents. (145/box 94/1)

1636   Two leases of lands at Johnstown, Co. Cork, between Maurice, Lord Roche of Fermoy, and several members of the Fennell family. (145/box 95)[426]

---

[424] This item could not be located by the Record Office, but is probably of late 17th century origin.

[425] Only one item predates 1485. See B.C. Donovan & David Edwards, 'British sources for Irish history before 1485', in *Analecta Hibernica*, xxxvii (forthcoming).

[426] These items could not be located in the Record Office. At present there is only a rough box list for this large collection, and it is easily possible that we overlooked them in our search.

1637 (20 Nov.) Sale by Christopher Walter fitz-John of the City of Cork, gent., Edmund Martell, Alderman of Cork, Morris Roche fitz-Patrick of Cork, gent., feoffees in trust to said Christopher, to Francis Coppinger of Cork, gent., reciting that Thomas Sarsfield mortgaged to Christopher the lands of Ballyrosine and elsewhere in the barony of Barrymore, Co. Cork, for £400 (stg) and entered a bond on the same in £800 on 20 Dec. 1635. Now Christopher sells his interest in the mortgage to Coppinger for £400 (stg). (145/box 95/2)[427]

1638 Deed concerning an annuity out of Glanevre between Lord Fermoy and Valentine Harding of Cork. (145/box 95)[428]

1638–1770 Abstracts of title to the Co. Cork estate, including a list of deeds made between 1638 and 1770. (145/box 102/bundle 15)[429]

1640 (Nov.) Articles of the charges brought against the Earl of Strafford, part of a collection of parliamentary and political papers which also has 'Brief notes of Parliamentary debates' in Dec. 1640, which may have other references to the Strafford trial. (1248/1/1 (f)–(g))[430]

17th cen. Notes of the trials of Sir Francis Annesley, Lord Mountnorris, and the Earl of Strafford, Lord Lieutenant of Ireland, probably made by Sir Alan Brodrick. (1248/9/1 (a))[431]

EAST SUSSEX : County Record Office
The Maltings, Castle Precincts, Lewes BN7 1YT
Tel: (01273) 482 349
Fax: (01273) 482 341

LOOSE ITEMS

1603 (19 June) Request signed by the Privy Council for the payment of £1,487 10s. to John Wood for the provision of victuals for his Majesty's forces in the province of Munster in Ireland. (Additional De La Warr Mss, 533)

1638 (Michaelmas) Deposition and memorandum of Edward Shirley of Midhurst, 14 Nov. 1637. Relates to the lands (all in England) of Henry Norton, late of Westham, a recusant. We are told that Norton died on 31 May 1627, and was buried the next day in the Parish Church of Freshford in Co. Kilkenny, Ireland. (SAU 1321)

COLLECTIONS

Rye Corporation MSS: Clerk's Correspondence (ref. RYE47).

Much of this was calendared by the H.M.C. in 1892 (*13th Report*, Appendix IV, pp1–246), and includes a number of references to Ireland. Particularly, the theft

---

[427] According to a N.L.I. special list of this collection, Box 95 should include another deed concerning Ballyrosine dated *temp* Elizabeth I. We would like to thank Kenneth Nicholls for bringing this to our attention. We were, however, unable to find the document in question.
[428] These items could not be located in the Record Office.
[429] Ibid.
[430] N.L.I. microfilm, p.7279.
[431] N.L.I. microfilm, p.7285.

by Capt. Peerse of £60 from an Irishman at Rye in 1581 (p78), and an order, dated 1624, by the Privy Council to the Lord Warden of the Cinque Ports to examine all Irishmen entering the country, because so many are 'imployed in the service of forraine princes' (p170). There are some remaining bundles which were not calendared by the H.M.C., and have not yet been listed. It is possible there are further Irish references still to be found in these.

Trevor of Glynde Place Archives (ref. GLY)

This collection has received a comprehensive listing in R.F. Dell (ed.), *The Glynde Place Archives* (Lewes, 1964), which includes the following items:[432]

1591–1619	Correspondence of Sir Richard Trevor with his brother Sir John Trevor I, about various matters including the Irish wars, 1591–5 [1 bundle, 17 letters]. (GLY 551)
1621	(19 Jan.) Letters patent granting a lease for 21 years to Sir Thomas Lake, Sir John Trevor, Sir Marmaduke Darrell, and Sir Thomas Bludder, of the impost of 5s. per chaldron and all customs on coal shipped from England and Wales to places abroad, including Scotland and Ireland. (GLY 387)
1625	(30 April) Letters under the Privy Seal confirming the exemption of coals shipped to Ireland from the impost of 5s. and the allowance to farmers on that account. (GLY 388)
1638–9	Copy of a declaration regarding the impost on coal shipped to Ireland, as 2s. per chaldron, by Abraham Perrot. (GLY 436, ff.131–7)
1640	(19 Aug.) Bond in £3,000 by Sir John Trevor II, to pay £1,500 to Sir Thomas Wenman, Sheriff of Tuam in Ireland, Sir Thomas Trevor, and Sir William Masham, by 15 Dec. 1641. (GLY 619)

WEST SUSSEX : County Record Office
County Hall, Chichester PO19 1RN
Tel: (01243) 533 911
Fax: (01243) 777 952

COLLECTIONS

Petworth House Archives

The West Sussex Record Office administers this important collection of papers of the Lords Egremont. It contains a large number of records concerning the Thomond and Orrery families for the period covered by this survey. A microfilm copy of the nineteenth century catalogue of Irish material in the Thomond papers is in the National Library of Ireland.[433] However, the collection remains on restricted access, and is still physically housed at Petworth. The Record Office makes fortnightly visits there, and will bring back items for consultation by searchers. Enquiries should be made well in advance of visiting the repository as there are no facilities for viewing the documents at Petworth itself. Consequently, being a private collection, it is outside the parameters of this book.

---

[432] There are further Trevor MSS in the Clwyd County Record Office, Ruthin, in Wales (see below).

[433] N.L.I. microfilm, n.4770, p.4767; some seventeenth century (mostly post-1641) material from this collection has also been microfilmed for the N.L.I., n.4770–2, p.4767–9.

WARWICKSHIRE : County Record Office *
Priory Park, Cape Road, Warwick CV34 4JS
Tel: (01926) 412 735
Fax: (01926) 412 509

LOOSE ITEMS

1599 (Dec.) Letter to the Earl of Essex from his mother, the Countess of Leicester, concerning Essex's absence from court and his disgrace after his return from Ireland. This is the sole Irish reference in the letter-book of the Earl of Essex, c1595–1600, which remains in the private possession of the Finch-Knightley family at Packington. It is available on microfilm in the Record Office. (Mi 229)[434]

COLLECTIONS

Fielding of Newnham Paddox Papers (ref. CR 2017)

1641 (27 July) Lewis Boyle, Viscount Kynalmeaky, to his brother-in-law at court, stating that he has sent a cast of merlins to George Fielding, Earl of Desmond, and the Countess his wife. (C2/133)

1641 (4 Oct.) Same to same, being a friendly note that 'The least Word from you shall present you the fairest wolfe dog in Ireland'. (C2/134)

Greville of Warwick Castle MSS (ref. CR 1886)

1596 (17 Nov.) Orders for furnishing horses and horsemen for Ireland. (2613)

1598 (4 Nov.) Orders regarding the dispatch of 100 troops from Warwickshire to Ireland, signed by Sir Thomas Egerton. (2614)

1598 (29 Nov.) Letter from the Privy Council to [ ], ordering a levy of 100 men from Co. Warwick for service in Galway in Ireland. (2619)

1599 (17 June) Letter from Captain Jobson to [ ], concerning the furnishing of troops for Ireland. (2620)

1599 (1 July) Letter to Sir Foulke Greville and Sir John Conway from S. Marolls, acknowledging that 100 men from Warwickshire have arrived at Chester on their way to Ireland, except for '8 persons ranne away, one there having the French disease and three others sick, by the way in all twelve absent'. (2616)

1599 (10 Aug.) Letter to Sir F. Greville from the Privy Council, sending a warrant to deliver armour for light horses and lances to Thomas Throckmorton. (2617)

1600 Part of a Navy account for the years 1598–1600 which has several references to English ships in service on the Irish coast in 1600, including an estimate of the cost of ten ships and barques which were employed at Sligo on or about 19 March that year (fol. 5) [badly torn]. (2678)

---

[434] This letter has been printed in W.B. Devereux, *Lives and Letters of the Devereuxs, 1540–1646* (2 vols., London, 1853), i, p495.

Seymour of Ragley (Hertford) MSS (ref. CR 114A)

Since the papers of the marquess of Hertford were deposited in this Record Office, the following items of Irish interest, which were overlooked in the H.M.C. report on the collection (*4th Report* (1874), App., pp251–4), have come to light:

1628	(16 Feb.) Letter to Viscount Conway from Lord Docwra, concerning the payment of troops who have not had their wages for some months, dated at Dublin. (114A/792)
1631–5	A group of documents including the ensuing Irish material (114A/769), *viz*
1632	(Lady Day) The English rents of Viscountess Conway.
1632	(Nov.) Two accounts 'with my Lady Viscountess Conway' which mention rents from Ireland.
1633	(April) An account of money received from Ireland by Katherine, Viscountess Conway, 1631–3.
1633	(April) Estimate of the annual revenues of Lord Conway, which states that 'The land in Ireland are about £2,000'.
1633	(May) A list of Lord Conway's debts.
1633	(3 Aug.) Endorsed 'Plate received 3rd Aug. 1633 at Dublin from Mr Vyner'.
1635	(April–May) Two accounts of Lady Conway's Irish money.
1632	(Aug.) 'A note of such evidences, deeds and writings belonging to the right honorable the Lord Viscount Conway and Killulta as remayne now at London'. This lengthy document contains details of 21 Irish deeds on ff 7–8 (114A/770), *viz*
1618	(27 May) The counterpart of Sir Foulke Conway and Lady Conway's bargain and sale of the Manor of Thrilsborles and other lands in Carmarthenshire to Lord Danvers.
1618	(24 June) A lease from Sir Foulke Conway to Edward Reade for 21 years of so much of Killulta as was worth £900 p.a., for the securing of the said Mr Reade from such debts as he stood engaged for on behalf of Sir F. Conway.
1618	(1 July) Lease by Sir F. Conway to Sir Faithful Fortescue, Foulke Reade and Richard Reade, of all his lands in Ireland in trust for 21 years after his death.
1623	(24 April) The counterpart of Sir F. Conway's mortgage of certain lands in Ireland for £1,000 to Lord Chichester.
1624	(19 Nov.) Letters of administration of Sir F. Conway's goods granted to the Lady Amy Conway in Ireland.
1626	(28 June) Letters of administration of Sir F. Conway's goods granted to Lord Conway in Ireland.
1626	(3 Dec.) A bond of £80 from Lady A. Conway to pay Lord Conway £40 on 4 June next.
1627	(16 Jan.) An arbitration submitted to by Lord Conway and Viscount Clandeboy concerning some questions at variance between them.
1627	(8 Feb.) A copy of a release from Lord Chichester of the lands mortgaged to him by Sir F. Conway.
1627	(9 March) Lord Conway's letter of attorney to Sir Faithful Fortescue and others to dispose of his affairs in Ireland.
1627	(10 July) Security made by John Spoake of certain lands in Lancashire for the payment of £103 to Lord Conway, with a bond of performance.
1627	(18 Aug.) Deed poll concerning Mr. Spouner and others who stand bound for 'his Lordship' for several sums in Ireland.

1627	(23 Nov.) Copy of the King's warrant to the Attorney General to prepare a patent for Lord Conway's lands in Ireland.
1628	(22 April) Articles of agreement between Lady A. Conway and Lord Conway.
1628	(1 May) Lady A. Conway's release of all her interest in the lands mortgaged by her husband, Sir F. Conway, to Lord Chichester.
1628	(6 May) A release (enrolled) from Lady A. Conway to Lord Conway of a bond deposited in the Lord Keeper's hands for the performance of certain articles.
1628	(6 May) Lady A. Conway's lease of her third in Ireland to Lord Conway for £400 p.a.
1628	(7 May) Copy of a bond of £500 from 'his Lordship' to perform covenants and articles entered into on 22 April (above).
1628	(23 July) Counterpart of Marmen Debbs lease.
1628	(27 Dec.) Counterpart of a grant of Ballendory to divers feoffees for the settling of £30 p.a. on the Minister of Lisnegarvey church.
1629	(2 May) Counterpart of Mr. Neld's lease of lands in Ireland, and another deed declaring the intention of that lease to secure to him £100 p.a. or £400.

1634   (30 May) Order by Lord Deputy Wentworth in the case between Lord Conway and Lady A. Conway, relict of Sir F. Conway, in which Lady Amy is barred from further claims on the Irish estate, as she has already received £6,500 and a jointure of £400 p.a. (114A/787)

Shirley of Ettington Hall MSS (ref. CR 229)

Nearly all of the Shirley family's Irish estate papers were deposited in the Public Record Office of Northern Ireland in 1981, and a detailed listing of the material can be found in 'Report on Private Collections, no. 142', in *Analecta Hibernica*, no. 20 (1958), pp 259–78. The only item of interest which remains in the Warwickshire Record Office is a nineteenth century copy of the royal letters patent and grant to Robert Devereux, 3rd Earl of Essex, of lands in Farney, dated 28 May 1620 (CR 229/7/3).[435]

WARWICKSHIRE : Shakespeare Birthplace Trust Records Office
The Shakespeare Centre, Henley Street, Stratford-upon-Avon CV37 6QW
Tel: (01789) 204 016
Fax: (01789) 296 083

Apart from the single following item, this repository also holds a few documents concerning the levying of troops for service in Ireland, for which we have obtained no further details.

LOOSE ITEMS

1604   (Feb.) Settlement on the marriage of Humphrey Packington of Chaddesley Corbett, Co. Worcester, and Dame Bridget, formerly

---

[435] Some documents about Farney from this collection (dated 1735–1814) appeared in Patrick J. Duffy, 'Maps of Farney in Longleat, Wiltshire, and Warwick County Record Office', *Clogher Record*, xii (1987), pp369–71; and idem, 'Remarks on viewing the estate of John Shirley, Esquire, situate at Carrickmacross in the barony of Farney, in the county of Monaghan, Ireland', *Clogher Record*, xii (1987), pp300–4.

wife of Sir Thomas Norryes, with mention of the Priory House of Bullybegge (? Ballybeg, Co. Cork) and the rectory and advowson of the same. (DR 5/1382)

WILTSHIRE : County Record Office *
County Hall, Trowbridge BA14 8JG
Tel: (01225) 713 138

COLLECTIONS

Marquis of Ailesbury MSS

This collection was extensively calendared in H.M.C., *Fifteenth Report*, App. VII, pp152–306, where only one document of Irish interest is given, being a letter to the Earl of Strafford by Charles I dated 2 March 1640, concerning the estate in Munster of Sir John Bingley's widow (p155).

Quarter Sessions Records

Much of the material in these documents has been listed by the H.M.C., *Various Collections*, i (1901), pp65–176, where a number of items of Irish interest can be found. Most of the items concern soldiers who had served in Ireland and were now seeking a pension. Some of these men had also been arrested for vagrancy and theft. Overall the H.M.C. list contains about thirty entries relating to these veterans, as well as a petition of 1641 by a tailor from New Sarum requesting relief for his losses when a cargo of his cattle bound for Ireland was lost in a storm near the Isle of Man on 22 August 1639 (p108). However, the H.M.C. report was selective and this collection is likely to contain further documents concerning Ireland

Rumbold MSS (ref. 413)

1628   (23 June) Warrant under the sign manual concerning the reversion of the clerkship of the Crown and the clerkship of the Hanaper of Chancery in Ireland, granted to Sir Edward Nicholas. (413/497)

1631   Seventeenth century copy of documents concerning the trial of the Earl of Castlehaven. (413/401)[436]

Troyte–Bullock MSS (ref. 865)

The only accession of Irish interest in this collection is the commonplace book of John Clavell (865/502), a colourful character who visited Ireland at least twice between 1633 and 1636.[437] The book affords some unique glimpses of the social life enjoyed by the Irish ruling elite at the time, and it also contains love poems for Clavell's English and Irish mistresses as well as copies of letters written to his uncle from Ireland, *viz*

1632   (Dec.) 'An introduction to the sword dance at Christmas 1632 at my Lord Barries in Ireland', which gives an account of the performance of a masque in the castle prior to the dance. (p13)

---

[436] A number of original depositions and examinations from this trial are held in the Cave, Lords Bray of Stamford Hall MSS (ref. DE) in the Leicestershire County Record Office (see above).
[437] According to the *Dictionary of National Biography*, John Clavell (1603–42) was probably the author of *The Soddered Citizen*. For a summary of his life and writings, see John Pafford, 'John Clavell', *Somerset Notes & Queries* (Sept., 1986), and for a more detailed treatment see Pafford's recent biography, *John Clavell 1601–43: Highwayman, Author, Lawyer, Doctor* (Oxford, 1993).

1633	(27 Sept.) 'A copy of the Earle of Barrimores Letter to my uncle Sir William Clavell at my first coming here'. Among other things, Barrymore informs Sir William that 'many of the best powers in the realm', including the Earls of Cork and Ormond and Lord Chancellor Loftus, have been impressed by the reformation of his nephew John Clavell's character. (p60)
1633	(25 Nov.) Sir W. Clavell to the Earl of Barrymore, thanking the Earl for his help in persuading his nephew to stop behaving wildly. (p60)
1633	(7 Dec.) George Kirke to the Lord Chancellor of Ireland, Sir Adam Loftus, warning him not to show too much favour to John Clavell. (p58)
1634	(3 July) Copy of a letter written by John Clavell to his uncle, Sir William. (p50)
1634	(14 Dec.) 'I landed in Ireland the second time on Sunday about 2 o'clock in the afternoon, being the 14th of December 1634'. (p49)
1634	(20 Dec.) Clavell to his uncle, reporting that he has just landed in Ireland. Suggests that his uncle should get the King to write to Lord Deputy Wentworth about their problem. (p48)
1634	'An Epitaph on the incomparable young Ladie Elizabeth Fitzgerald, eldest daughter to the Earl of Kildare, who died of a lingering consumption in the 4th year of her age 1634'. (p18)
1635	(31 Jan.) Same to same, stating that he has brought his father's land claims and his dispute with Sir Walter Coppinger before the Lord Deputy. (p47)
1635	(1 July) Lord Chancellor Loftus to Sir W. Clavell, discussing the reformation of his nephew John, and the young wards in Ireland whom he might marry. (p46)
c1635	'A funerall poem sacred to the memorie of the truely noble and most accomplished gentleman Sir Warham St. Liger, knight'. (p19)
1636	(2 Aug.) Petition, probably to Lord Deputy Wentworth, by John Clavell, outlining the 'insufferable wrongs' which he has endured in Ireland at the hands of 'old Baker who did comb in with Dillon to defraud me of my lands of Charigralan', and requests that Sir Walter Coppinger be brought to justice for wrongfully entering upon the estate. (p35)
n.d.	Prose poem from John Clavell to his Irish mistress ('cruell miss') after an argument. (p62)
n.d.	'J.C. his Epigram' concerning Alice, his Irish mistress, and Miss Green, his English one. (p59)
n.d.	Undated letter from J. Clavell to his uncle, discussing the 'weighty cause' why he must return to Ireland, and asking for money for apparel, etc. (p54)
n.d.	Another letter similar to above. (p51)
n.d.	Same to same, re Mr Baker and the leases of the Irish lands. (p44)
n.d.	A note 'To the happy and applauded match of the worthie Mr Clavell and his loving bedfellow Isabella'. (p23)

EAST YORKSHIRE : County Archives & Records Service
County Hall, Beverley, North Humberside HU17 9BA
Tel: (01482) 885 007
Fax: (01482) 885 063

LOOSE ITEMS

1631   (16 Jan.) Bond of £1,000 by Sir Walter Butler, Earl of Ormond and
             Ossory, to Robert Lylles, citizen of Limerick, for the performance of
             covenants. Recites an assignment to Lylles by Earl Walter, James,
             Viscount Thurles, and Richard Comerford jnr., of Dangenmore, Co.
             Kilkenny, gent., of the rectories of Stradbally, Killingarriff,
             Kilmurry and Luddenburg. Witnessed by John Butler, John Harte,
             and Charles Walshe. (DDC 132/15)

17th cen.   An undated map of Bantry Bay, showing vague details of Whiddy
             Island, Blackrock and Balgobben.[438] (DDCC (2))

NORTH YORKSHIRE : The Borthwick Institute of Historical Research
University of York, St. Anthony's Hall, Peasholme Green, York YO1 2PW
Tel: (01904) 642 315

According to the archivist there are scattered references amongst the
archiepiscopal records to the activities of Irish bishops and to English clerics
holding Irish preferments. For an introduction to the type of records held by this
repository searchers should first consult D.M. Smith, *A Guide to the Archive
Collections in the Borthwick Institute of Historical Research* (York, 1973), and
D.M. Smith, *A Supplementary Guide to the Archive Collections in the Borthwick
Institute of Historical Research* (York, 1980).

NORTH YORKSHIRE : City of York Archives Office
Archives Department, Art Gallery Building, Exhibition Square, York YO1 2EW
Tel: (01904) 551 879
Fax: (01904) 654 981

COLLECTIONS

City of York Military Papers (ref. E40)

1579   (19 Aug.) Letter from the Earl of Huntingdon to the Lord Mayor of
             York, concerning the furnishing of four light horsemen for service
             in Ireland. (no. 4)

1579   (Aug.) Order by Robert Creplying, Mayor of York, to the constables
             and parishioners of the 'Trinities in Goodromgayte' to assess 24s 4d
             towards the furniture of four horsemen bound for Ireland. There are
             returns for Tockwith, Dringhouses, Over Poppleton and St. Dennis.
             (nos. 5–6)

1579   (Aug.) Draft certificate of the Mayor to the Earl of Huntingdon
             concerning the four light horsemen above. (no. 7)

---

[438] The map is primarily concerned with the island, which is divided into parcels labelled by letters of the
alphabet. This would suggest that it is a late seventeenth century copy of the Down Survey.

SOUTH YORKSHIRE : Sheffield Archives *
52 Shoreham Street, Sheffield S1 4SP
Tel: (0114) 273 4756
Fax: (0114) 273 5009

LOOSE ITEMS

1632   Letters of attorney granted concerning property belonging to Lady
Elizabeth Cromwell, wife of Thomas, 1st Viscount Lecale.
(O.D. 1015)

1634   (23 July) Bill of complaint by George Bradshaw, citizen of London,
against Amy, widow and executrix of his uncle, Peter Bradshaw,
late merchant-tailor and citizen of same, which mentions *inter alia*
that in 1628–9 George was employed by his uncle in the
management of his estate in Ireland. George claims £60 for the cost
of his two journeys to Ireland. (Bowles Deeds, G.1)[439]

1639   (5 April) Letter from York by Leonard Pinckney to Stephen Bright,
Bailiff of Hallamshire, which mentions that Lord Clifford is
presently in Carlisle with 500 soldiers lately sent out of Ireland to
help quell the Scots. (BR 204)

1641   (11 May) Letter from the Earl of Strafford to his lady in Ireland
[printed]. (PHC 421)

SMALL COLLECTIONS

Bacon–Frank MSS (ref. BFM)

1638   Articles of agreement (not completed) between Cressy Tasburgh and
Richard Harbred, concerning the payment of £1,000, purchase
money for the site of Conge Abbey, Co. Mayo, which was bought by
Harbred. A valuation and particular of the lands is annexed
[partially legible]. (BFM 531B (E2))

1639   Counterpart of an assignment of the lands of Conge Abbey to
Richard Harbred of Wistowe in Yorkshire by Sir Thomas
Rotherham of Dublin, member of the Irish Council, for a certain
sum of money. (BFM 531A (E3))

Bagshawe Papers (ref. Bag. C)

1618   (6 May) Mortgage of the castle, town and lands of Bearnahealy, Co.
Cork, to William Younge of Kinsale, burgess, by Thomas Gogaine
fitz William of Bearnahealy, Edmund Oge, son of Edmund Swayne
of Dunverskye, and Thomas Russell of Ballyea, trustees for Thomas
and William. (Bag. C. 2581)

1630   (3 May) Assignment of the above mortgage to Charles McTeige
MacCarthy. (Bag. C. 2582)

Messrs Newman & Bond (Solicitors) MSS (ref. NBC)

1641   Copy of the settlement of the Irish estate of the Earl of Strafford to
various trustees, made in the nineteenth century. (NBC 576 (1–3))

---

[439] This document was found in the search room, in an old calendar of the Bowles deeds, and can be found
on p215. The archivists at Sheffield City Archives are unsure of the modern reference number for this
item, and advise searchers to refer to the old calendar when making enquiries.

17th cen.   Extracts from a grant to the Earl of Strafford by Charles I, giving an extent of the manors of Newcastle, Wicklow and Fairwood Park. (NBC 575)

LARGE COLLECTIONS

Wentworth Woodhouse Muniments (ref. WWM)

This vast collection, comprising the papers of Sir Thomas Wentworth, 1st Earl of Strafford and Lord Deputy of Ireland (1633–41), is one of the most important sources for the history of early seventeenth century Ireland. The archives include over 2,800 holograph letters mostly addressed to Wentworth, a number of letter books of his own correspondence, and a further 16 volumes of manuscript material. A large proportion of the documentation concerns Ireland. Though the political papers in this collection are well known, and many are on microfilm in the National Library of Ireland, historians have relied for too long on William Knowler's *The Earl of Strafforde's Letters and Despatches* (2 vols, London, 1739). Though much of the Strafford correspondence was included in this publication, a great deal of material, especially that concerning Ireland, was omitted. This was often a conscious decision on Knowler's part, for he worked under the direction of Wentworth's great-grandson the 1st Earl of Rockingham, who controlled access to the papers and wished Knowler to portray Wentworth in the best possible light. Not only are key letters concerning Ireland left out, particularly those concerning Wentworth's financial dealings and his actions against Lord Mountnorris, but Knowler often edited the letters he published cutting out sentences and paragraphs which he felt might be damaging to the memory of his patron's ancestor. All the Strafford Papers (formerly ref. Str. P, now WWM Str. P) have recently been microfilmed, and are available for purchase in 20 reels. The accompanying guide to this, *Crown Servants, Series One: The Papers of Thomas Wentworth, 1st Earl of Strafford 1593–1641, from Sheffield City Libraries* (Adam Matthew Publications, 1994), gives a comprehensive introduction to the collection, and an up-to-date index of correspondents.[440]

The collection also contains a number of deeds concerning Wentworth's financial transactions whilst in Ireland. Furthermore, in 1987, Sheffield City Library received another large deposit of manuscripts from Wentworth Woodhouse (ref. WWM Add.) which are dealt with separately below.[441]

Deeds (ref. WWM D)

Though the majority of the Wentworth deeds concerning Ireland were not deposited until 1987 (see below, ref. WWM Add.) there are a number of Irish documents to be found in the general series of deeds, as follows:

1577–1639   A collection of 38 deeds relating to the estate at Naas, Co. Kildare, particularly the site and lands of the dissolved monastery of St John of Jerusalem, as well as Clinton's Court, Hallwaistown and Gingerstown, and various messuages within the liberties of Naas. Among the parties to the leases and conveyances of the Elizabethan period are Thomas, 10th Earl of Ormond, Christopher Flattisbury, Walter Harrold, Nicholas Ball and Christopher Nolan, all of Dublin, Edward Missett of Dowdingstown, Peter Lewes of Naas, William Eustace of Castle Marten, Co. Kildare, and Tirlagh O'Byrne of

---

[440] An older, often misleading, index can be found among the National Library of Ireland Special Lists (N.L.I. Special List No. 51) on the open shelves in the Manuscript Reading Room.

[441] The correspondence of Wentworth and his father relating to English affairs has been published, J.P. Cooper (ed.), *Wentworth Papers, 1597–1628* (Camden Society, 4th series, xii, 1973).

Borris, Co. Carlow. The seventeenth century deeds deal either with transactions between the burgesses of Naas, or else with the acquisition of the Wentworth estate through the activities of Sir George Radcliffe, William Billingsley and Bartholomew Peisley. (WWM D 1448–1485(b))

1577–1618   A packet containing three royal grants under letters patent of property in Ireland, England and Wales. The Irish items concern lands at Carnew, Cosha, Kilcoman and Preban, Co. Wicklow, and Curraghwyehin and Curragharinne, Co. Tipperary, which were granted to Francis Edgeworth and Calcott Chambre early in the seventeenth century. (WWM D 1486–7 and D 1520)

1618–86   A packet containing five deeds relating to lands in Wales, Yorkshire and Ireland. The pre-1641 Irish material comprises a 1636 letter of attorney granted by Robert Bennett of Dublin, alderman, to Thomas Bennett of Johnstown, Co. Dublin, to prosecute his claims against Matthew Aylmer, late of Newtown Clayne, Co. Kildare, and a writ dated 5 Dec. 1636, addressed to the Sheriff of Co. Kildare, to deliver rents due from lands at Newtown and Horestown to the aforementioned Robert Bennett. (WWM D 1787–91, esp. 1788–9)

1628–69   A packet containing five royal grants under letters patent of the following: the manor of Moyglare, Co. Meath, to Sir Luke Delahide in 1628; a grant of free warren throughout eight parishes in Co. Wicklow to William, Earl of Meath, in 1634; lands at Newcastle, Shillelagh, Carnew, Wicklow, Tooreboy and Corbally, Co. Wicklow, to Sir George Carr and others in 1641; and a warrant of the King dated 8 June 1641, ordering that the money and goods of the late Earl of Strafford be placed in the safe custody of the Earl's trustees. (WWM D 1488–91 and D 1521)

Strafford Papers (ref. WWM Str. P)

This entire series, comprising the papers of Sir Thomas Wentworth, 1st Earl of Strafford, has recently been recatalogued and microfilmed. A comprehensive introduction to its contents can be found in the guide to the microfilm *Crown Servants, Series One* aforementioned (p274 above). This guide also contains the most complete index of correspondents available.

Because Sir Thomas Wentworth was Lord Deputy of Ireland for most of the period covered by these documents, nearly all the volumes in this series contain documents concerning Ireland. However, given the enormous size of the collection we have not listed individual items. Instead, as an example of the range of subjects and people which appear in the various books of holograph letters, we have included full lists of correspondents for two volumes (WWM Str. P 13–14). Many of the volumes listed below are on microfilm in the N.L.I., the reference to which can be found in the accompanying footnotes.[442]

1559–1601   Copies of instructions to Lords Deputy of Ireland and other Irish officials. (WWM Str. P 43)

1585–1645   A large collection of records covering a wide range of topics, entitled 'Miscellaneous State Papers Parts I–VII'. Most concern

---

[442] For those who are familiar with this collection it is worth noting that the series has been modestly recatalogued. Firstly, henceforth the correct reference should include the WWM prefix to each item. Secondly, the division of sections into 'a' and 'b' parts (e.g. WWM Str. P 20a and 20b) has been largely done away with (except in the cases of WWM Str. P 10–11), and lastly most items are now individually numbered, replacing the often erroneous folio and page numbers of yore.

Ireland and Wentworth's period as Lord Deputy, but also include a number of transcripts of documentary material prior to the appointment of Wentworth as Lord Deputy. The 482 items in this section are broken down as follows: general Irish affairs (items 80–141); Irish revenues (items 142–164); the establishment of a mint in Ireland (items 165–71); Irish customs and trade regulations (items 172–208); the Irish navy (items 209–232); the army in Ireland (items 233–274); land and plantations in Ireland (items 275–318); revenues and plantation in Athlone (items 319–336); Irish industry and trade (items 337–350); Irish petitions and case papers of private persons unconnected with official matters (items 351–427); the Foulis case (items 428–432); Youghal College, Trinity College and the Earl of Cork (items 433–442); the Mountnorris case (items 443–459); the case of Nicholas Stephans (item 460); the Piers Crosby case (items 461–74); the case of Lord Chancellor Loftus (items 475–7); the imposts on wines (items 478–80), and unspecified plans (items 481–2) [482 items]. (WWM Str. P 24–5)

1603–39   Copies of commissions and instructions to Wentworth and previous Lords Deputy of Ireland, including copies of various Commissions for Defective Titles in Ireland [14 items]. (WWM Str. P 23)

1611–32   Letter book of Wentworth's correspondence, as Lord Deputy, with officials and leading personages in Ireland, preparatory to his arrival in Dublin. This is preceded by copies of various instructions to previous Lords Deputy, 1611–28 [97 fols]. (WWM Str. P 1)[443]

1611–40   Miscellaneous collection of letters and speeches by Wentworth, many of which are addressed to his family. Also includes letters to Sir Edward Stanhope, Richard Marris (his steward), William Raylton, Sir George Radcliffe and others [215 items]. (WWM Str. P 21)[444]

1614–48   Miscellaneous bundle of documents which contains a few references to Ireland, including 'Improvements in ye Bishopricks and other ecclessiastical livings since my being Deputy within ye province of Ulster' dated 1636; a survey of the government of Ireland and a list of propositions concerning the government of Ireland addressed to the King in 1631; two letters from Wentworth to the Vice-Treasurer of Ireland, Sir Adam Loftus; a letter from Lord Lorne dated 1638; an undated document concerning directions for establishing a plantation in Ireland; and a number of narratives of events concerning the life of Strafford [19 items]. (WWM Str. P 34)

1625–39   Personal letters to Wentworth, mainly from his second wife, members of the Holles and Clifford families, and other relatives and personal friends [165 items]. (WWM Str. P 22)[445]

1627–33   (April 1627–March 1633) Letters to Wentworth [318 items]. (WWM Str. P 12)[446]

1627–39   Letters to Wentworth, with a few items sent to William Raylton, Sir John Coke, Sir Henry Marten and the Earl of Cork (29 March 1636–23 March 1637). In addition, there are petitions by Lord

---

[443] N.L.I. microfilm, n.3230, p.2850.
[444] Ibid, n.3918, p.3589.
[445] Ibid.
[446] N.L.I. microfilm, n.3914, p.3585.

Lambert, Lady Mountnorris, the Earl of Carlisle's creditors, and Thomas Elliott, as well as an extract from an intercepted letter by the rector of the Irish College at Rouen in France. At the end of the volume there is a series of letters sent to Wentworth from Lord Clifford and Christopher Wandesford for the period 1627–39 [262 items]. (WWM Str. P 16)[447]

1630–9   Letters to Wentworth and other documents relating to Irish ecclesiastical affairs, including letters from various Irish bishops, Archbishop Laud, and some personal notes from English ecclesiastics. Furthermore there are a number of other documents including petitions from Irish bishops, particularly a petition from the Archbishop of Tuam and the clergy of the province of Connaught for augmentation of the revenues of the church there. There is also a petition, dated 1633, from the Protestant inhabitants of Co. Cavan relating to the moneys collected there towards the maintenance of the army. There are some notes about ecclesiastical cases, especially the case of the benefice of Taghboine [Taughboyne, Co. Donegal] in 1634 and the monastery of Connall. Other matters dealt with include the affairs of Youghal College, Trinity College, Luke Plunkett, and John Bramhall, Bishop of Derry, and the state of the diocese of Down in 1634. Furthermore there is a statement about disputes between the secular and regular [Roman Catholic] clergy in Ireland which contains a list of Catholic clerics about Dublin in 1633. The collection also includes an undated map of Baltimore [83 items]. (WWM Str. P 20/100–182)[448]

1631–1772   Miscellaneous papers including letters to Wentworth from Charles I and Queen Henrietta Maria dating 1633–41 (items 2–47); letters concerning Wentworth's acceptance of the Deputyship of Ireland and other Irish matters (items 48–53); documents concerning the Earl's trial and death (items 54–69); and a number of letters by Knowler and the 1st Marquis of Rockingham concerning the publication of Strafford's political papers which include a few transcripts of letters by Strafford (items 70–85) and other miscellaneous items [91 items]. (WWM Str. P 40)[449]

1631–55   Miscellaneous Irish affairs and a survey of Wentworth's Irish estate, including warrants for tobacco, c1655. (WWM Str. P 41)

1632–8   (February 1632–August 1638) Copies of royal letters under the signet, warrants etc. [356pp]. (WWM Str. P 4)[450]

1633–4   (2 April 1633–April 1634) Letters to Lord Deputy Wentworth on a wide variety of matters, from the following people: the Earl of Carlisle (12 letters); Sir John Coke (11 letters); Henry Percy and Captain Richard Plumleigh (9 letters each); Sir Edward Osborne, Richard Osbaldston, and the Earl of Arundel (8 letters each); the Earl of Portland (7 letters); Lord Goring, Sir Arthur Ingram, Lord Cottington, Sir John Borlace, and Sir Francis Windebank (6 letters each); John Melton, Sir John Gibson and J. Okehampton (5 letters

---

[447] Ibid, n.3916, p.3587, and the letters to Clifford and Wandesford are at n.3917, p.3588.

[448] The rest of this section dating from 1546 is concerned with the administration of the Wentworth estate in England. The old catalogue division between Str. P 20a and 20b no longer applies. N.L.I. microfilm, n.3917, p.3588.

[449] Ibid, n.3918, p.3589.

[450] Ibid, n.3231, p.2851.

each); Joshua Gosnold (4 letters); the Earl of Newcastle, the Lords of the Admiralty, Michael Wentworth, Sir William Pennyman, Captain Thomas James, Sir Gervase Clifton, G. Garrard, Sir William St. Leger, and George Kirke (3 letters each); the Earl of Bridgwater, Lord Wilmot, the Earl of Cleveland, the Earl of Castlehaven, Sir William Saville, Sir Robert Aiten, Henry Wentworth, Lady Cottington, the Earl of Exeter, Sir Simon Weston, and Sir George Wentworth (2 letters each); Tobie Craddock, Sir George Radcliffe, the Earl of Cork, Lady Elizabeth Wentworth, Sir Philip Mainwaring, Henry Cressy, Sir John Hotham, Sir John Veel, Richard Hutton, Lord Fairfax, Peter Middleton, the Archbishop of York, George Butler, the Commissioners for Alehouses in Co. Clare, Mrs Hutton,[451] Anthony Stafford and Henry Masterson, the Earl of Leicester, Lady Leicester, Lord Savage, Sir Guy Palmes, Elizabeth of Bohemia, Thomas Little, William Robinson, Lady Carew, the Earl of Ancrum, Dr Simon Baskerville, the Archbishop of Canterbury, the Earl of Danby, the Prince of Orange, Sir William Boswell, William Merricke, John Atkinson, the Earl of Suffolk, Sir Edward Wingfield, Endymion Porter, Sir William Slingsby, Robert Parkhurst, King Charles I, Lord Baltimore, Sir Barnaby O'Brien, Sir Robert Mansell, Sir John Vaughan, Robert, Earl of Londonderry, Ralph Freeman, Dr J. Wickham, Samuel Van Paine at Arnim, the Sovereign of Kinsale,[452] the Earl of Thomond, Sir Thomas Coventry, Lady Mary Jephson, Sir Henry Slingsby, the Lords of the Privy Council, Sir Robert Heath, Lord Weston, Sir Ralph Hansby, the Earl of Manchester, and Sir John Lowther (1 letter each). In addition to the correspondence, there are several other items of interest, including a note of the receipts from the customs impost; 'The name of the Company of the *John of Lysbone* staid in the Harbour of Timoleague'; Sir George Wentworth's journal of business conducted by him at Court on behalf of his brother, dated March 1633; and notes on various petitions [235 items]. (WWM Str. P 13)[453]

1633–5   (May 1633–1635) Letter book of Wentworth's correspondence with the royal secretaries Coke and Windebank [270pp]. (WWM Str. P 5)[454]

1633–6   (May 1633–Mar. 1636) Letter book of Wentworth's correspondence with a number of people, including the Earl of Carlisle, the Commissioners for the Admiralty, the Bishop of London, Lady Clifford, the Earl of Leicester, Lord Clifford, Lord Goring, the Lord Marshal Arundel, Lord Willmot and the Earl of Newcastle [435pp]. (WWM Str. P 8)[455]

1633–7   Letter book of Wentworth's correspondence with the Spanish resident, Signor Nicolades, and with John Taylor and Captain Plumbleigh concerning Spanish trade, shipping and pirates, July 1633–Dec. 1636. Bound in with this volume is a book of letters to and from Coke and Windebank, 1634–7 [399pp].(WWM Str. P 9)[456]

---

[451] I.e. Lord Deputy Wentworth's sister.
[452] William Goolde.
[453] N.L.I. microfilm, n.3914, p.3585. The last letter in this volume is dated 'April 1634'.
[454] Ibid, n.3231, p.2851.
[455] Ibid, n.3233, p.2853.
[456] Ibid.

1633–40   Letter book of Wentworth's correspondence with Archbishop Laud for the period Nov. 1633–Nov. 1636 [366pp]. Bound in at the end is another volume of correspondence with the royal secretaries, Coke and Windebank, from February 1638–July 1640 [47pp]. (WWM Str. P 6)[457]

1633–40   (June 1633–April 1640) Letter book of Wentworth's correspondence with Charles I, Cottington and Weston [343pp & 110pp]. (WWM Str. P 3)[458]

1634–5   (20 Feb. 1634–21 March 1635) Although nearly all of the letters in this volume are addressed to Wentworth, there are also a couple of letters to Sir Philip Mainwaring and Sir Robert Pye. The correspondents are as follows: Sir John Coke (23 letters); the Earl of Carlisle (14 letters); the Earl of Portland (12 letters); Sir Francis Windebank and George Garrard (10 letters each); the Earl of Arundel and Lord Cottington (9 letters each); Lord Goring, George Kirke, and Sir John Borlace (7 letters each); the Duke of Lennox (6 letters); the Earl of Danby, Sir John Bingley, and the Lords of the Privy Council (5 letters each); Henry Percy, Thomas, Viscount Lecale, Lady Mary Jephson, Lord Conway, Sir William Slingsby, the Lord Commissioners of the Admiralty, Thomas Messingham at Paris,[459] and Sir Richard Plumleigh (4 letters each); William Robinson, Endymion Porter, Lord Baltimore, the Earl of Dorset, John Melton, Richard Osbaldston, Sir Edward Osborne, Lord Chaworth, and Sir William Pennyman (3 letters each); Captain John Gifford, the Earl of Newcastle, Sir John Gibson, Lord Wilmot, Viscount Wimbledon, Lord Docwra, Sir John Finch, the Earl of Bristol, Sir Thomas Rowe, Sir Arthur Ingram, John Wood, Lady Carew, Sir William St. Leger, the Earl of Westmeath, George Goring, Henry Wentworth, the Earl of Leicester, Sir Robert Aiten, the Earl of Exeter, Lord Weston, John Atkinson, and Sir Francis Seymour (2 letters each); the Earl of Mar, Sir James Hay, Andrew Stewart, Lady Anne Russell, Lord Esmond, Viscount Say & Seale, Sir William Power, Richard Hadsor, Lady Kerry & Lixnaw, George Butler, Captain Thomas Stafford, Sir William Balfour, Robert Adair, Chief Justice Thomas Richardson, Sir Thomas Edmonds, the Earl of Kildare, Sir John King, Michael Hopwood, the Earl of Antrim, Lord Chichester, Sir John Bourchier, A. Stafford, James Frey, the Earl of Middlesex, Hugh, Lord Iveagh, Sir Bazil Brooke, the Earl of Bridgwater, the Earl of Morton, Sir Simon Weston, Sir Sampson Darrell, the Earl of Cleveland, the Earl of Pembroke, Richard Bourchier, Lord Mohun, James Howell, the Earl of Ancrum, Sir John Bankes, the Earl of Kinnoule, the Earl of Nithsdale, Sir Arthur Hopton, Lord Strange, William Noye, P. Maule, John Taylor, the Countess of Exeter, Sir Ralph Hansby, Captain Thomas James, Sir Philip Burlamachi, Edward Rhodes, J. Okehampton, Lord Dungarvan, Sir Henry Wallop, Sir Robert Heath, the Mayor of Limerick,[460] Viscount Savage, the Earl of Castlehaven, John Denny, Lord Powerscourt, Sir Edward Wingfield, Lord Grandison, Sir Thomas Somerset of Cashel, Lord Lambert, Sir Hammon Le Strange, Sir Guy Palmes, Roger Palmer, Lord

---

[457] N.L.I. microfilm, n.3232, p.2852.
[458] Ibid, n.3230, p.2850.
[459] Messingham was Superior of the Irish College in Paris.
[460] Thomas Meade.

Valentia, Sir John Jephson, the Earl of Hertford, H. Morgan & John Johnstone, from Galway, the Earl of Lindsey, Samuel Van Paine at Arnim, and the Earl of Ormond (1 letter each). The collection also contains several other documents of value, such as a copy of an intercepted letter written by Owen Roe O'Neill regarding Irish soldiers in service on the Continent. There are also some notes about the proposed plantation in Connaught. In addition, there are a number of petitions presented to the King, etc., by the Earl of Clanricard, Sir James Oughterlong, Theobald, Lord Bourke of Brittas, Robert Calcott, late of the Isle of Man, Alexander Balfour, Edmund Spiring of Malahide, Co. Dublin, and John Wood [342 items]. (WWM Str. P 14)[461]

1635–6   (25 March 1635–23 March 1636) A collection of letters to Lord Deputy Wentworth on general affairs, which also has a few scattered items addressed to Sir John Bankes, Sir George Radcliffe, William Raylton, Sir Gerald Lowther, Sir Nathaniel Catelin and Sir Lucas Dillon. Aside from the correspondence, the collection includes the depositions of Lord Moore and Sir Robert Loftus on 12 Dec. 1635; an examination of Henry Gall, master of the barque *The Peter of Waterford*; a number of petitions by Richard Headon, Abraham Chamberlain of London, William Howard, Philip Darrell, and Thomas, Lord Cromwell of Lecale; notes on erecting a mint in Ireland; details of the King's ships on the Irish coast, and memoranda concerning the affairs of Sir William Balfour [367 items]. (WWM Str. P 15)[462]

1636–9   (Nov. 1636–May 1639) Letter book of Wentworth's correspondence with Archbishop Laud [191pp]. (WWM Str. P 7)[463]

1637   (August–December) Letter book of Wentworth's correspondence with the royal secretaries Coke and Windebank [16pp]. (WWM Str. P 11(B))[464]

1637–8   (25 March 1637–24 March 1638) Letters to Wentworth, which also contains a few scattered letters addressed to Lord Goring and William Raylton, as well as five petitions addressed to King Charles and Lord Deputy Wentworth, etc., by Walter Bourke of Turlough, Co. Mayo, William Perkins, Sir George Malby, Robert Parrington, and Sir James Hay. One of the most unusual items in the volume is a certificate by members of the crew of *The Patrick of Dublin* dated 10 July 1637, which concerns the appalling condition of the beer provided for them by the captain of the ship; it was 'not ffitt for men to drink, which we finde to bee the brewars ffault'. Finally, the miscellaneous material contains, among other things, ten extracts taken from letters out of Germany and France, a certificate on behalf of Captain Rowland Waters by the Earl of Denbigh and Viscount Wimbledon, instructions by the English Privy Council for Thomas Kettleby, Captain of H.M.'s ship *The Swallow*, employed to guard the coast of Ireland, as well as several copies of documents on various matters [325 items]. (WWM Str. P 17)[465]

---

[461] The first 170 letters in this series are available on N.L.I. microfilm, n.3914, p.3585, while the remaining 172 items have been placed on a separate reel, n.3915, p.3586.

[462] Ibid, n.3915, p.3586.

[463] Ibid, n.3232, p.2852.

[464] Ibid, n.3234, p.2854.

[465] Ibid, n.3916, p.3587.

1637–9 (April 1637–Sept. 1639) Letter book of Wentworth's correspondence with numerous individuals including Sir James Hay, the Earl of Marr, the Earls of Leicester, Holland, St. Albans and Northumberland, Lord Willmot, Sir Henry Vane, the Lord Keeper Coventry, the Duke of Lennox, the Bishop of Down and the Marquis of Hamilton [364pp]. (WWM Str. P 10(A))[466]

1637–40 (Sept. 1637–April 1640) Letter book of Wentworth's correspondence with numerous people, though much is addressed to the secretaries Coke and Windebank [335pp]. (WWM Str. P 11(A))[467]

1638 Book of arms of Wentworth, endorsed 'Richard Gascoigne etat 59, 27 maii Jamnunc in Hibernia 1638'. (WWM Str. P 39)

1638–9 (26 March 1638–23 March 1639) Letters addressed to Lord Deputy Wentworth. Two of the letters in the volume are addressed to Lady Bingley and John Harrison. Apart from correspondence, the collection also contains a copy of Sir John Bingley's will (dated 28 March 1638), petitions by Laurence Archer and Mrs Frances Fuller, and also a note of the inhabitants of King's County. There is also a memo by William Raylton concerning the scandalous petition by Laurence Archer linking the Lord Deputy with the 'blood of Robert Esmond, late dweller and merchant of Wexford' [188 items]. (WWM Str. P 18)[468]

1638–40 (July 1638–April 1640) Letter book of miscellaneous correspondence of Wentworth with Lord Cottington, Sir Henry Vane, the Lord Admiral and the Lord Keeper, amongst others [152pp]. (WWM Str. P 10(B))[469]

1639 (March–November) Letters addressed to Lord Deputy Wentworth [134 items]. (WWM Str. P 19)[470]

1640 (Jan.) Collection of autograph verses being 'a new years gift for Sir William Wentworth', from his fellow students at Trinity College, Dublin. (WWM Str. P 38)[471]

1640–1 Letters and many other documents relating to the Earl of Strafford's impeachment, attainder, trial and execution. Includes the journal of the proceedings of both Houses of Parliament, November 1640–May 1641. (WWM Str. P 35–7)

Wentworth Woodhouse Additional Muniments (ref. WWM Add)

Another large group of documents from Wentworth Woodhouse was deposited in Sheffield City Library in 1987. Though much remains uncatalogued, at least two sections concern Ireland. The first is a small collection of papers relating to the Irish customs and other matters, and the second a large collection of deeds concerning Strafford's Irish estate:

---

[466] Ibid, n.3234, p.2854.
[467] Ibid.
[468] N.L.I. microfilm, n.3917, p.3588.
[469] Ibid, n.3234, p.2854.
[470] Ibid, n.3917, p.3588.
[471] A list of the signatories to this document was published in T.U. Sadleir & H.M. Watson, 'A record of 17th century alumni', in *Hermathena*, lxxxix (1957).

Irish Customs Papers (WWM Add, Box 126/20/1–14)

1509	(20 April) A seventeenth century copy of the inspeximus made anno 1° Henry VIII of King John's charter to the City of Dublin. (Box 126/20/2)
1548	(21 April) A seventeenth century copy of the charter granted by Edward VI to the City of Dublin. (Box 126/20/1)
c1604–15	Endorsed 'Orders for ye officers of ye Customs in Ireland' made in the time of Lord Deputy Chichester. (Box 126/20/14)
1628–34	A true list of the levies for the army in Munster, with accounts of money raised for every quarter between 1 April 1628, and 1 Sept. 1634. It gives details of charges upon the counties of Cork, Limerick, Tipperary, Waterford, and Kerry, and the towns of Youghal, Kilmallock, Cashel, Clonmel, Kinsale, Fethard, Carrick-on-Suir, Dungarvan, and Dingle, as well as upon church lands in the province [large roll]. (Box 126/20/3)
1637	(17 June) Letter from James Travers to William Raylton concerning the customs in Ireland and a case re land in England. (Box 126/20/7)
1637	(9 Dec.) Endorsed 'Copy of the Lord Duke of Lenox his acquittance for £2,000', which he received from W. Raylton as part of a larger sum due to him for the surrender of the lease of the customs of Ireland. (Box 126/20/4)
1638[472]	(5 Feb.) Endorsed 'Draught of a replication concerning ye custome Business: under Mr Attorney of ye wards his hand'. (Box 126/20/12)
1638	(14 Feb.) Endorsed 'Coppie of the rejoynder of the Earl of Pembroke, Lord Duke of Lenox, etc., concerning the Irish Customs'. The copy was made on 17 Feb. (Box 126/20/9)
1638	(15 Feb.) Endorsed 'Coppie of the Rejoynder of the Earl of Antrim and the Lady Duchesse of Buckingham: Concerning the Irish Customs' to the replication of Rowland Wandesford, Attorney of the Court of Wards & Liveries. (Box 126/20/13)
1638	(16 Feb.) Endorsed 'Coppie of an order in the Court of Wards for a comission to examine witnesses concerning the lease of the Irish Customs'. (Box 126/20/8)
1638	(19 Feb.) Endorsed 'Interrogatories for witnesses on his Ma^ts behalf in the Court of Wards: Concerning ye Irish Customs', listing 12 questions on a large parchment. (Box 126/20/5)
1638	(19 Feb.) Endorsed 'Interrogatories concerning the Irish Customs' [7pp]. (Box 126/20/11)
1638	(23 Feb.) Letter from W. Raylton to Thomas Rowe, asking him to inform Lord Cottington of a meeting the next day regarding the return of the commission about the lease of the Irish customs. Rowe's reply is on the reverse. (Box 126/20/6)
1638	(1 March) Endorsed 'Addittional Interrogatorries concerning the Irish Customs'. (Box 126/20/10)

---

[472] All of the following eight items are dated 1637 (old style) in the originals.

Irish Deeds (ref. WWM Add)

This collection contains over 400 items concerning the Wentworth Irish estate 1387–1759. They mainly date 1580–1640, indeed over a third are 1630–40 in date. The collection is broken down into the following bundles of documents :

1407–1759   Deeds relating to Donore, Co. Kildare, and some documents dealing with the escheated lands of the Earl of Clancare in Munster, nearly all of which pre-date 1641. There are three items dating from the reign of Henry VII concerning the estate of Philip Britt of Donore, as well as a few deeds *temp* Henry VIII which refer to the transactions between Henry Wogan and his wife, Joan Britt, with William Oge de Geralduns (*alias* Fitzgerald). The later items include a copy of an inquisition post mortem held at Clonmel in 1635 into the Tipperary estate of William Dongan of Dublin, and they also make mention of William Dermott, Chancellor of Christ Church, Dublin, in 1571, Nicholas Harbert of Harbertstown in King's County, Robert Ashe, merchant, William Brouncker[473], Nicholas Wogan of Rathcoffy, Co. Kildare, Thomas Luttrell of Luttrellstown, Co. Dublin, Sir William Taafe, Edward McBrian O'Farrell of Lisshenure, Co. Longford, and many others [29 items]. (Brown Parcel 5, Box 2, Bundle 1)

1429–1523   A bundle of ten ancient deeds relating to land in Co. Kildare, particularly the area about Newtown and Oldtown in the feudal barony of Tymy. Four of the documents cover the early Tudor period, beginning with a quitclaim dated Oct. 1487, by John Fensame of Killadowen to Philip Byrtt (*alias* Britt) of Donore, Co. Kildare, of all his possessions in le Oldton. The subsequent items deal with a grant of property in the region by Henry Wogan and John Britt to John MacWilliam Oge in July 1509, and a deed of gift by Gerald Wellesley of Dengyn, esq., to Philip, the son and heir of Maurice Richardisson, lord of Kilmahik, Co. Kildare, in 1523 [10 items]. (Brown Parcel 5, Box 1, Bundle 1)

1523–1689   Deeds concerning Newtown and other lands at Oldtown, Donore, and Gingerstown, etc., Co. Kildare. The bundle commences with a seventeenth century schedule of deeds for the period 1523–1638, and continues with a document about the sale of property in Newtown to Sir Nicholas White, Master of the Rolls, by Thomas, son and heir of John Chaloner of Lambay, Co. Dublin, gent., in 1587. Other items include two declarations of uses, dated 1595 and 1604 respectively, and among the chief parties to the early seventeenth century deeds are William Fitzgerald of Oldtown, Richard Wellesley of Old Connall, Thomas Hussey, Robert Meredith, Valerian Wellesley[474], Gerald Aylmer, John Aylmer, and Thomas and Gerald Fitzgerald [10 items]. (Bundle 5, Box 1, small bundle of deeds)[475]

1571–1685   Deeds relating to the attainted or escheated lands of Christopher Eustace in Cos. Kildare and Dublin, and those of the Earl of Clancare in Munster. Includes documents relating to Sir Thomas Roper, Viscount Baltinglass, Sir Henry Power, Sir Henry

---

[473] The son and heir of Sir Henry Brouncker.

[474] His name is given as Wesley in this and other documents in the collection.

[475] Although Parcel 5, Box 1, etc., would have been more consistent with the nomenclature adopted for the other sections of the collection, this is the reference given in the catalogue.

Brouncker, Robert Parkhurst, Sir William Anderson, Sir George Herbert, Garret Baxter, Robert Bennett, Florence MacCarthy, Matthew Aylmer, James, Bishop of Clogher, and many others. Apart from the Dublin, Kildare, Cork and Kerry references, the bundle also contains some deeds relating to property in Co. Sligo, and two deeds relating to Calcott Chambre and the Shillelagh estate [41 items]. (Brown Parcel 1, Box 2, Loose deeds)

1581–1738   Deeds relating to the Strafford family and to their lands in Cos. Kildare and Wicklow, nearly all of which appertain to the period after 1641. The earliest item, dated May 1581, gives an exemplification of a common recovery between Gerald Wellesley, plaintiff, and Maurice Walshe, defendant. Other documents of interest include a 1637 agreement between Sir Charles Coote and Robert Plandon, as well as a contemporary copy of an entry in the gaol delivery rolls for Wicklow in 1628, which details a case regarding the rustling of cattle by Teige, Edmund and Shane McDonnell, who were burned in the hand for their offence [23 items]. (Brown Parcel 5, Box 1, Bundle 2)

1596–1645   Papers concerning the estates of George, Earl of Kildare, dealing with his grant of a lease of various lands at Maynooth and elsewhere in Co. Kildare to Ambrose Losse and James Fitzgerald in 1633, and the Earl's bond in the sum of £1,000 to George Carleton in 1635. The other Co. Kildare deeds in the bundle relate to the Milottestown estate acquired by William Archbold between 1617 and 1638, and a mortgage of Rathcoffy and other lands in the shire by Nicholas Wogan in 1637. In addition, there are three documents regarding Lord Deputy Wentworth's attempts to secure a lease of the manor of Glaslough in Co. Monaghan from the Dean of Clogher, Robert Barkley [23 items]. (Brown Parcel 3, Bundle 2)

1597–1680   Legal papers relating to the estates at Naas, Co. Kildare and Carnew, Co. Wicklow, mostly pre-dating 1641. The earliest item is a 1597 exemplification of common recovery between 1. John Fitzgerald of Blackhall and Thomas Wogan of Newhall, Co. Kildare, gents., and 2. Lady Margaret Butler, widow, and Gerald Fitzgerald, gent. The bundle also contains a c1640 schedule of the lands belonging to the manor of Kildare, as well as a final concord of 1636 in a case between Sir Adam Loftus and Thomas Newcomen, plaintiffs, and Richard Bealing, Michael Springham, Morgan Cullone, Joan McEnny Byrne and divers others, over a large tract of land in Co. Wicklow. The other documents make reference to William, Earl of Meath, Thomas, Viscount Baltinglass, John McMurtagh Byrne, Joshua Carpenter, Edward, Lord Brabazon, George Carr, Thomas Little, Henry Wentworth, and Calcott Chambre, amongst others [13 items]. (Brown Parcel 5, Box 3, Bundle 1)

1603–36   Deeds relating to the manor, castle and rectory of Newcastle, Co. Wicklow, which give details of the passage of the lands from Sir William Harrington to James Hay, Earl of Carlisle, through the Earl's intermediaries, Sir Edward Moseley, Arthur Jarvis and Humphrey Salwey. The bundle also has an inspeximus of a lease made by Carlisle in 1636 of the dissolved abbey of Wicklow and the manor of Kilpoole, Co. Wicklow [9 items]. (Brown Parcel 2, Bundle 1)

1603–40   Papers concerning lands in Sigginstown and Naas, Co. Kildare, and
           Shillelagh, Co. Wicklow. Parties to the deeds include Matthew
           Handcock, Walter Scurlock, Edward Brian O'Farrell, Calcott
           Chambre, John McMurtagh O'Byrne, Thomas, Lord Baltinglass,
           Henry Stokes, Laurence, Lord Esmond, Anthony Colclough, Cahir
           O'Byrne, Hugh McFellan O'Byrne and Phelim McGerald O'Byrne
           [8 items]. (Brown Parcel 4, Bundle 1)

1606–68   Papers relating to the acquisition of lands in Co. Sligo in 1638–40
           by Lord Deputy Wentworth's agent, Sir Philip Percival. Other
           notable documents in this bundle include four earlier deeds dated
           1606–9 concerning lands in the baronies of Carbury and Tireragh,
           Co. Sligo, which belonged to Sir Donough O'Connor Sligo, and
           there are a further six deeds regarding the transactions of Daniel
           O'Connor[476] with Brian McTeige Keigh, Andreas Crean, Dormice
           McCranny, Connor McBrehmile and Robuck O'Crean between
           1610 and 1628. Apart from the Sligo material, there are a few
           miscellaneous items, one of which is a bond of 1630 between
           Thomas Dunn, Sir Piers Crosby and Lord Baltinglass [31 items].
           (Brown Parcel 1, Box 1, Bundle 1)

1610–28   Legal papers and leases relating to the estate in Naas, Co. Kildare,
           belonging to Walter Segrave of Dublin, alderman, and his son,
           Henry Segrave of Little Cabbragh, Co. Dublin. The bundle includes
           the final concords in a dispute with David Toole and Gerald Woolfe
           of Naas, merchants, in 1610, and another with Henry Greenwood
           alias Harrington, dated 1614. The final item is a 1628 deed of
           bargain and sale with William Archbold [5 items]. (Brown Parcel 5,
           Box 2, Bundle 2)

1616–37   Deeds concerning Newtown, and also lands at Oldtown, Cappocke,
           and Ballykennan, all in Co. Kildare. The documents refer to Gerald
           Aylmer of Donada and several members of the Aylmer family,
           William Rochford, James and Christopher Eustace, Nicholas White,
           Elizabeth Wogan, Valerian Wellesley, Robert Meredith, Richard
           Cusacke, William Billingsley, Sir Paul Davis and Sir George
           Radcliffe [11 items]. (Brown Parcel 4, Bundle 2)

1617–57   This bundle of deeds relating to the Strafford estate in Co. Wicklow
           has a number of documents which pre-date Wentworth's
           involvement in the region, including a deed of bargain and sale by
           Sir Richard Greame to Murtagh and John McConohor O'Byrne in
           1619. Several of the items concern the lands of Thomas, Lord
           Baltinglass, and William Graham, and recipients of leases include
           William, Earl of Meath, Richard Claybrooke, Teige McDonnell,
           John Nutton, Philip Fearnley and Sir George Wentworth [18 items].
           (Brown Parcel 3, Bundle 3)

1617–80   Deeds concerning Naas, Co. Kildare. Apart from the usual
           documents dealing with Lord Deputy Wentworth's agents and
           intermediaries, the bundle contains a clutch of items about William
           Archbold, including his purchase of property from Patrick Gwen,
           William Crowe, Elias Flood, James Ware, James Flattisbury, James
           Kerdiffe and others, between 1617 and 1638 [17 items]. (Brown
           Parcel 4, Bundle 3)

---

[476] *Alias* Donnell or Donald. His name is most frequently given in the documents as Daniel.

1618–53   Deeds relating to the manor and estate at Cloghamon, Co. Wexford, belonging to Sir George Calvert, Lord Baltimore, which include two letters relating to the estate, as well as several leases and a note of receipts for payment of subsidies due to him in 1639. Among those dealt with in the documents are Nathaniel Hewett, Thomas Crofton, Ralph Smith, Nicholas Codd, George Carr and William Swanton, and there is a copy of a royal grant under letters patent confirming to Gerald Fitzgerald the lands lately held by his father, dated 1619 [17 items]. (Brown Parcel 4, Loose deeds)

1626–87   Deeds concerning the Strafford estate in Co. Sligo. This bundle includes details of the disputes in 1637 between Teige O'Connor and John French, and in 1638 between James and Patrick French. There is also a volume of building accounts for Sligo dated 1638–9. Other items concern the dowry due to Dame Sarah O'Connor *alias* McDonnell, sister of Randall, Earl of Antrim, and her dispute with Miles Bourke, 2nd Viscount Mayo. Among the principal parties to the remaining pre-1641 documents in the package are Donogh O'Connor, Owen McDermott, Walter and Andrew Creane, Francis Peisley, Geoffrey French, Richard Fagan, Edmund McJordan, Sir George Radcliffe and Sir Philip Percival [44 items]. (Brown Parcel 1, Box 1, Bundle 2)

1627–64   A bundle of deeds relating primarily to the Co. Wicklow estate of the Chambre family, especially their lands in the barony of Shillelagh. The package contains documents concerning their dealings with William, Lord Brabazon, Edward Deane of Kilkenny, Sir Cyprian Horsfall, David McTeige Kavanagh, Sir George Radcliffe, William Billingsley, Francis Sandford, James Fynes[477], John Crewe[478], Sir Philip Percival, and Job Ward of Newland, Co. Wexford, between 1627 and 1638 [20 items]. (Brown Parcel 2, Bundle 3)

1627–69   Apparently an original bundle, this contains a couple of documents relating to a marriage settlement between Sir Donogh O'Connor Sligo and Dame Sarah McDonnell, daughter of the Earl of Antrim, in 1627. Some of the other Co. Sligo papers deal with the running of O'Connor Sligo's estate, and a mortgage by Henry and Walter Creane of lands in the barony of Carbury to Geoffrey French in 1633. There are also a few deeds relating to the activities of Lord Baltinglass, Henry Masterson, John McMurtagh Byrne, John Johnson, and William and Thomas Graham in Co. Wicklow [21 items]. (Brown Parcel 3, Bundle 1)

1627–1670 A bundle of royal grants under letters patent, including a grant of 1627 to Sir William Parsons, Baronet, of the estate of the dissolved monastery of St. John the Baptist near Naas, with its possessions in Cos. Kildare and Wicklow. The other pre-1641 items comprise grants to Sir Thomas Wentworth of the offices of Lord Deputy and Governor General of Ireland, and another regarding the wardship of his son and heir [5 items]. (Brown Parcel 5, Box 2, Bundle 4)

1629–69   A package of documents concerning the acquisition of Shillelagh, Co. Wicklow, by Sir Philip Percival acting on behalf of Lord Deputy Wentworth. Because the Wentworth family's title to the territory

---

[477] James was the eldest son and heir of William, Viscount Say & Seale, and together with his younger brother Nathaniel Fynes, he was a frequent party to deeds concerning the Chambre estate in Wicklow.

[478] John was the eldest son and heir of Sir Thomas Crewe, Sergeant-at-law to Charles I.

was later called into question, the bundle contains several statements made after 1641 by various witnesses to the principal transactions which had taken place in the late 1630s. In addition, the bundle has a number of items relating to the marriage portion of £5,000 owed by Calcott Chambre of Carnew to the Earl of Meath, for the marriage of his daughter Mary Chambre to Sir Edward Brabazon, as well as a lease of the manor of Knockreah by Sir Adam Loftus to Joshua Carpenter and Henry Wentworth in 1639 [34 items]. (Brown Parcel 2, Bundle 4)

1636–1695   A bundle of seventeenth century legal papers. Except for a 1637 grant to Calcott Chambre of a fair at Carnew, Co. Wicklow, all of these documents appertain to the post-1641 period. Nonetheless, although the second item in the bundle is dated 1668, it contains a good deal of information about the condition of the Strafford estate before the 1641 rebellion, and refers *inter alia* to the late Lord Deputy's dealings over the manor of Moyglare and the territory of Idough, Co. Kilkenny [15 items]. (Brown Parcel 5, Box 3, Bundle 2)

1637–8   A complete copy of the case of James Fynes and John Case, defendants, in a bill of complaint brought by Calcott Chambre of Carnew, as well as other deeds relating to Chambre's land in Cos. Wicklow, Dublin, Wexford and Carlow [5 items]. (Brown Parcel 2, Bundle 2)

SOUTH YORKSHIRE : University of Sheffield Library
Western Bank, Sheffield S10 2TN
Tel: (0114) 276 8555 ext. 4343
Fax: (0114) 273 9826

COLLECTIONS

Hartlib Collection

According to the archivist, there are some letters dated from Dublin, pre-1641, in this collection. Unfortunately however, we can give no further details. Under an award from the British Academy the entire collection is presently being transcribed and edited. When this work is completed any Irish material should be easily located.

WEST YORKSHIRE : Bradford District Archives *
15 Canal Road, Bradford BD1 4AT
Tel: (01274) 731 931
Fax: (01274) 734 013

COLLECTIONS[479]

Hopkinson MSS (ref. 32D86)

This accession comprises the papers of the seventeenth century antiquarian, John Hopkinson, and the following references to Ireland have been listed in the catalogue to the collection:

---

[479] The Wilson of Eshton Hall MSS which were given a short report in H.M.C., *3rd Report*, App., pp293–300, have been deposited largely in this archive. However, the few items concerning Ireland could not be located, and it is possible that they were not deposited here.

1551–2   (20 Dec. 1551–22 Aug. 1552) Copies of letters by Edward VI to Barnaby Fitzpatrick, eldest son and heir of the 1st Baron of Upper Ossory in Ireland, written to him while he was absent at the French Court. (32D86/19)[480]

1596   (2 Dec.) Copy of the Privy Council's letter to Lord Darcy, ordering him to send the 400 troops raised in Yorkshire to the port of Chester for embarkation to Ireland. (32D86/32, ff 108r–9r)

16th cen.   A copy of 'Greensleeves', *alias* 'Leicester's Commonwealth', in which the allegation is made that Sir Robert Dudley, Earl of Leicester, tried to have the Earl of Ormond (and many other rivals) murdered. (32D86/32, ff 1–100)[481]

1601   (28 April) Copy of a letter by the Privy Council to the Archbishop of York, asking him to oversee the levying of soldiers to be sent as reinforcements to Ireland. (32D86/32, ff 127r–8r)

1601   (3 May) Copy of a letter by the Lord Lieutenant of Yorkshire, Thomas, Lord Burghley, ordering the levying and provisioning of horses for service in Ireland. (32D86/32, ff 128v–9v)

1640   Copy of a letter from the Lord Deputy of Ireland, the Earl of Strafford, to William Saville, for disbanding his regiment, which was stationed in Yorkshire. (32D86/28)

1641   Notes and writings on the impeachment of the Earl of Strafford. (32D86/27)

17th cen.   A collection of arms of the nobility, which contains (ff 79–106) a list of the Irish peerage drawn up *temp* Charles II, mentioning all noble creations since the fourteenth century. The volume also includes genealogical notes for the Butlers of Ormond (ff 121–2) and the Darcy family of Ireland (fol. 127), showing their inter-relationship with the Talbots, earls of Shrewsbury. (32D86/10)

Spencer Stanhope MSS (ref. Sp St)

1600   A copy of Captain Josias Bodley's account of his journey into Lecale in Ulster, written in Latin. (Sp St /11/5/4/1, ff 38r–42r)[482]

c1625   An Irish tithing table, being a true copy of the order by Charles I for the payment of tithes for the maintenance of the Church of Ireland in Ulster. The document goes on to describe the various Easter offerings in some detail, e.g. 'every Married couple is to paie yearely att Ester to the Minister 4d sterlinge, and every single man or woman likwise 2d ster.' Similar tithes were also charged at christenings, weddings, churchings of women, burials, mortuaries, etc. Probably written shortly after 17 July 1625. (Sp St /11/5/4/1, ff 42v–3v)

---

[480] These items have been published in J. Nichols (ed.), *The Literary Remains of Edward VI* (London, 1857). There are also nineteenth century copies of these letters in the National Library of Ireland, Ms. 4320.

[481] This controversial text, possibly written by the English Jesuit Robert Parsons, was suppressed by the London Privy Council as soon as it appeared; see D.C. Peck, 'Government suppression of English Catholic Books: the case of 'Leicester's Commonwealth'', in *Library Quarterly*, xlii, pt.2 (1977). In 1904 F.J. Burgoyne republished it from a lost manuscript version as *An Elizabethan Manuscript at Alnwick Castle* (London).

[482] This well-known document was published anonymously as 'Bodley's visit to Lecale', in *Ulster Journal of Archaeology*, 1st series, ii (1854). The original manuscript is in the British Library.

1638   (1 Aug.) Grant by Edward, Lord Conway of Killulta, to John Stanhope of Gray's Inn, of the office of steward of his manors of Killultagh and Derrivolgie (*alias* Felough) in Cos. Antrim and Down, to hold at pleasure of the grantor. Latin. (Sp St/4/4/1)

1640   (3 March) A letter sent from Dublin by John Tallis to 'Noble Mr Hartwell', in which he discusses his financial dealings with Mr Rawdon[483] and other people. Tallis also states that during the recent Christmas holidays he sent a commission of the peace to John Stanhope, and reports the news that 'the lo: Leutents tryall was certenly put of untill Wensday the 23 of the last moneth'. (Sp St/5/2/7)

1640   (25 April) Sir William Parsons' letter to 'my good cosen' concerning a warrant for the payment of £10 and the money claimed by Mr Alford, and discussing family affairs. Among other things, Parsons recommends the bearer, Moses Hill, 'eldest sonn To my sonn[-in-law] Arthur Hill, ... his father is a sweet kind frend to us all'. (Sp St/6/1/7)

1640   (24 Nov.) Assignment of a lease between (1) Henry Spencer the elder of Enisloghlin, Co. Antrim, esq., and George Rawdon of Brookehill in the same county, esq., of the one part, and (2) John Stanhope of Layganaine, gent., of the other, of the town and lands of Magheresunske in Antrim. To hold to the use of the executors of Marmaduke Dobb,[484] late of Lisnegarvey, for 21 years at a rent of £40 (stg) p.a. Witnessed by Edward McFillmony, Denis Doyne and Anthony Ibbetson. (Sp St/4/4/2)

1641   (30 Oct.) Letter to Walter Stanhope from his son John Stanhope, telling him of his escape from the Irish rebels, with only the clothes on his back. His wife and daughter died of smallpox, and he fears his Irish estate is lost. Endorsed in a later hand 'fathers Letter to grandfather of his flight from ye Irish rebellion'. There are two nineteenth century copies attached, one of which is printed. (Sp St/6/1/8)

c1641–2   Undated complaint of John Stanhope of Lisnegarvey, Co. Antrim, listing his losses sustained at the hands of the rebels in the last rebellion there. (Sp St/10/5/1)[485]

17th cen.   Undated list of nine Irish maxims, entitled 'Old English rules for purchasinge landes', which begins 'Who soe will be wise in p'chasinge lett them consider these pointes followeinge: 1. ffurst, see that the land be cleare in the title of the seller'. (Sp St/11/5/4/1, fol. 43v)

17th cen.   A list of towns in Ireland, giving their distances from Lisnegarvey (Lisburn) and Whitehaven, *viz* Castlereagh, Newtown, Egermount, Gosford, etc. (Sp St/15/8)

---

[483] Probably George Rawdon of Brookehill, Co. Antrim, who was closely related to John Stanhope, the chief subject of the documents.

[484] One of Lord Conway's tenants.

[485] Although this item is misdated in the catalogue as 23 Oct., 1641 (the date of the outbreak of the Ulster rising), it is clear that it was written some time afterwards. It was probably written in 1642, when most of the 1641 depositions were first made. Indeed, it is worth noting that on 19 May 1642 one of John Stanhope's servants made a deposition to the Commissioners at Dublin (Sp St/10/5/2).

WEST YORKSHIRE : The Brotherton Library, University of Leeds
Leeds LS2 9JT
Tel: (0113) 233 5518
Fax: (0113) 233 5561

LOOSE ITEMS

1623   (25 Sept.) Letter to Sir Henry Marten by Richard Fisher, from
Farmon, Co. Cork. Fisher has bought the position of Attorney
General of Munster for £300 but is pressed by debts in England and
thus is unable to complete the payment. He asks for a loan of £30
for two or three years without interest. This is the sole item
predating 1641 of Irish interest among the Henry Marten Papers,
and was previously described in H.M.C. *13th Report*, App. IV
(1892), p384, where it was misdated. (Henry Marten Papers, vol.
92, Political & Miscellaneous, i, 1600–50, fol. 8)[486]

WEST YORKSHIRE : Leeds District Archives *
Chapeltown Road, Sheepscar, Leeds LS7 3AP
Tel: (0113) 262 8839
Fax: (0113) 262 4707

COLLECTIONS

Temple Newsam MSS (TN/PO)

Although a calendar of part of the collection appeared in H.M.C., *Various
Collections VIII* (London, 1913) under the title 'Wood MSS', occasionally the
description of items is inadequate or misleading, and a considerable number of
documents about the Irish customs farm were omitted. The list below attempts to
fill out some of the H.M.C. entries as well as itemise the new material, but it is
not a comprehensive inventory of all the Irish references; it should be read
together with the printed calendar, which is still a very useful guide to the
collection as a whole. There are four sections of papers exclusively concerning
Ireland (General Accounts, Correspondence, Legal and Administrative, and
Tallow) and there are a few other items which concern Ireland amongst the
family's 'English' manuscripts, *viz*:[487]

General Accounts (ref. TN/PO 7/I)

1611–38   A bundle of loose sheets of draft accounts, containing the accounts
of Sir Arthur Ingram re his share of the Irish customs farm,
payments to various people out of the customs revenue, defalcations
allowed, and a comparison of old and new customs rates with
reasons for an increase. (TN/PO 7/I/23)

1612–15   (Michaelmas 1612–Michaelmas 1615) Three port books for
Coleraine, the last of which covers the period Sept. 1614 –
Michaelmas 1615, and was not mentioned in the H.M.C. report.
(TN/PO 7/I/1a–c)

---

[486] The collection forms part of the papers of Sir Henry Marten, Judge of the Prerogative Court and of the
Admiralty, and his son Henry Marten the regicide.
[487] Most of the items with the prefix TN/PO 7 can be found on microfilm in the N.L.I., n.3274, p.2892.

1612–15   (Michaelmas 1612–Michaelmas 1615) Four port books for Londonderry, one of which deals with the period Michaelmas 1613 – 24 March 1614, and was overlooked in the H.M.C. report. (TN/PO 7/I/4a–d)

1613–15   Accounts of the farmers of the Irish customs received by the Pells Office, which give details of when the half-yearly rents of the farm were paid into the Exchequer, as well as the amounts which were paid direct to other patentees, pensioners, etc. (TN/PO 7/I/6)

1613–36   A bundle of miscellaneous papers (TN/PO 7/I/24), containing the following :

1613/14   A list of debenture holders.

1615   Petition of Katherine Heskett that she be allowed the half-year's salary due to her late husband, Christopher Heskett, Collector of Customs for Drogheda, Dundalk and Carlingford.

1617   Receipt for an annuity of £150 from Bridget, Countess Dowager of Tyrconnell.

1627   Letter to Sir Arthur Ingram from the Earl of Clare.

1636   Note of the money owed by Matthew Trott, committed by the Sheriff of Dublin for debt.

n.d.   Petition of Sir James Oughterlong for a license to sell tobacco in Ireland.

1614–15   (18 Jan. 1614–Michaelmas 1615) Three port books for Strangford, Ardglass, Killough and Dundrum, the latter two of which were omitted from the H.M.C. report, and cover the period Michaelmas 1614 – Michaelmas 1615. (TN/PO 7/I/2a–c)

1614–17   (1 May 1614–22 April 1617) A bundle of 81 debentures for the payment of salaries to the customs officers in Ireland, which contain payments to the following: Ralph Bradish, Customer and Collector at Dublin, Skerries, and Malahide; Randall Brwyn and Thomas Jarry, Searchers of Youghal and Dungarvan; Matthew Butler, Searcher for Waterford, New Ross, Drogheda, Dundalk and Carlingford; Thomas Cave, Controller for Dublin and the port of 'Franchess'; William Cayme, Searcher for Cork; John Challenor, Controller of Drogheda; Robert Cogan, Surveyor-General of all the Customs in Ireland; Nicholas Cross and Edward Cross, Searchers of Galway; Francis Dixon, Searcher of Wexford and Arklow; Charles Grimsditch, Searcher of Limerick; George Grimsditch, Collector of Customs for Dublin, Skerries, Malahide and Wicklow; Richard Heath and Colin Phillips, Searchers for Dublin, Skerries, Malahide and Wicklow; Christopher Heskett, Collector of Customs for Drogheda, Dundalk and Carlingford; Edward Hinton, Collector of Customs for Waterford and New Ross; John Howe, Searcher for Kinsale; Edmund Hunt, Collector of Customs at Cork; Samuel Johnson, Controller of Customs for Cork, Limerick, Youghal, Dungarvan, Kinsale and Dingle; Nicholas Lee, Controller and Collector for Waterford and New Ross; William Lewellyn, Customer, Collector and Receiver of the Customs at Youghal and Dungarvan; Robert Master, Controller of Waterford and New Ross; Richard Mitton, Customer and Collector for Wexford and Arklow; Edward Mottram, Customer of Waterford and New Ross; David Myagh, Customer of Kinsale; Sir Dudley Norton, one of the principal Secretaries of State for Ireland, for his salary of £200 p.a. to be paid out of the customs revenue; William Perry, Customer for Limerick; Anthony Staughton, Collector for Dublin and Drogheda;

John Staughton, Customer, Collector and Receiver for Drogheda, Dundalk and Carlingford; John Taylor, Customer, Collector and Receiver for Galway; Thomas Tring, Searcher for Drogheda, Dundalk and Carlingford; Gerald Trant, Collector and Receiver of Customs for Dingle (*alias* Dinglecoush), and Richard Wollaston, Controller for Drogheda. (TN/PO 7/I/25 (1)–(81))

1614	(9 May) Appraisement of goods shipped from Ireland to London in *The Pearle*. (TN/PO 7/I/5)
1615	(20 May) Warrant by the Earl of Suffolk to Mr Bingley, for the farmers of the Irish customs to strike a tally for their half-year's rent. (TN/PO 7/I/8)
1615	(Michaelmas) Rough copy of a list of the sums of money paid in Ireland (salaries, etc.) and allowed in the half-yearly account of the farmers of the customs. (TN/PO 7/I/7)
1618	(12 Jan.) *Quietus Est* by the King's Privy Seal directed to the Lord Treasurer of England and others, subsequently enrolled among the Memoranda of the Exchequer in Ireland with the Remembrancer there, being the Exchequer's receipt to the farmers of the Irish customs for the half-yearly rent of £4,000 (Ir.) from Ladyday to Michaelmas 1617. (TN/PO 7/I/10)
1618	(12 Jan.) *Quietus Est* for the half-year Michaelmas, 1617 – Ladyday, 1618. (TN/PO 7/I/11)
1618	(24 April) The substance of the three half-yearly accounts of money paid into the Exchequer by the Irish customs farmers for Easter and Michaelmas 1616, and Easter 1617, drawn up by William Marwood, with the Lord Deputy's certificate that no defalcations were allowed. (TN/PO 7/I/13)
1618	(15 May) *Quietus Est* for £27,000 owed by the farmers aforesaid for 4½ year's rent from Ladyday 1613 to Michaelmas 1617 [Ink badly flaked]. (TN/PO 7/I/12)
1618	(22 June) Receipt for £2,311 17s 2¼d paid into the Exchequer for the half-year ended Ladyday 1617. (TN/PO 7/I/14)
1618	Note of bills of exchange to be sent to England, amounting to £1,953. (TN/PO 7/I/15)
1625–30	Account of money collected (totals only) according to the Auditor's books for each year 1625–30 inclusive, with estimated improvements above what is 'collected by the old Book of Rates' on cattle, hides, wool, yarn, tallow, butter, herrings, pilchards, salt, rugs and wines. (TN/PO 7/I/16)
1626	(9 Feb.) Two certificates issued by the Receipt of Pells showing what amounts were allowed for defalcations on the Irish customs farm for 1614 and 1616 [Parchment roll, Latin]. (TN/PO 7/I/6a–b)
1627	(16 Jan.) Warrant by the Earl of Suffolk to Sir John Bingley, for a tally to be struck at the Exchequer against the rent due on Ladyday from the farmers of the customs in Ireland, for the sum of £554 payable to Sir John Spillman for jewels delivered to the King. (TN/PO 7/I/17)
1632	(14 Nov.) List of goods belonging to Nicholas Kenny of Dublin, alderman, which were seized for his failure to register them in the Customs House. (TN/PO 7/I/20)

1632–5   Small bundle of Collectors' draft papers showing the total amounts collected from Irish ports between 1632 and 1635, drawn up every six months. (TN/PO 7/I/18)

1634–7   Four accounts between Sir George Radcliffe and Sir Arthur Ingram re the Irish customs farm. (TN/PO 7/I/21a–d)

1636   Two copies of a list giving the amounts by which each port was in arrears with its payments to the customs farmers. (TN/PO 7/I/22a–b)

Correspondence (ref. TN/PO 7/II)

1630   (30 June) Earl of Middlesex to Sir Arthur Ingram, regarding the attitude of the Earl of Mulgrave to the Irish customs. (TN/PO 7/II/12)

1632   (21 July) Thomas Somerset to same, from Waterford, requesting that John Stephens be restored to his place as a customs officer at Waterford. (TN/PO 7/II/27)

1632   (13 Oct.) Earl of Cork to same, complaining that Lord Mountnorris 'expresses himself with a very high hand in the matter of customs', and begs favour for the bearer, Edmund Hunt, a customer who has been dismissed from his office through jealousy. (TN/PO 7/II/9)

1632   (31 Dec.) Robert Cogan to same, enclosing accounts of money collected from all the ports for the half year. He explains that he could not send the accounts earlier for the lack of a trustworthy messenger, and complains that the sum of £250 which was due to himself had been disallowed by the auditors. (TN/PO 7/II/3)

c1632   Incomplete draft letter from Sir Arthur Ingram to 'Cousin Cogan', acknowledging two letters and complaining of the treatment of Lord Mountnorris, and commissioning Sir George Radcliffe to look into the matter. (TN/PO 7/II/10)

c1632   Draft of a letter by Ingram, encouraging his un-named correspondent to work diligently in the collection of the Irish customs and work amicably with his cousin, Robert Cogan. (TN/PO 7/II/11)

1633   (29 July) Sir George Radcliffe to Sir Arthur Ingram the elder, re routine work in collecting the customs. Lord Mountnorris is still receiving money from all the ports, but Sir George will soon take it all into his hands. (TN/PO 7/II/14)

1633   (10 Oct.) Sir George Radcliffe to same, giving an account of money payable to Ingram as his share of the half-yearly profits, and also stating his reasons for not employing Mr Trott as a waiter. (TN/PO 7/II/15)

1633   (31 Dec.) Sir George Radcliffe to same, enclosing an account of income from the customs for the half-year ended Michaelmas last, and mentioning that Robert Cogan had 'put away his interest' to Mr Norton. (TN/PO 7/II/13)

1634   (3 March) Robert Cogan to same, requesting the speedy payment of money due to him so that he can return to England for the sake of his health. (TN/PO 7/II/8)

1635   (6 July) Sir George Wentworth to same, re private affairs between them, and re Sir Arthur's offer to sell one-third of his share of the Irish customs. (TN/PO 7/II/28)

1635   (15 July) Sir George Radcliffe to Ingram the elder, from Boyle Abbey, re money to be paid to Sir William Russell, and reporting that 'Your servant Barbon is dead'. (TN/PO 7/II/19)

1635   (4 Nov.) Same to same, acknowledging the receipt of letters and giving his reasons for the dismissal of a waiter who was suspected of tearing a leaf out of the customs' book and allowing a ship to land at a prohibited place. (TN/PO 7/II/20)

1637   (2 Jan.) Same to same, stating that the accounts are settled, and thanking Ingram for his 'good ale and muskadine, when they come we will drink your health and make your welkin roare. And singe old Jasper Blitham songe.' (TN/PO 7/II/21)

1637   (7 Aug.) Same to same, re the taking of bonds and getting in securities on the accounts. 'The ship that brought your muskadine had the plague in her.' (TN/PO 7/II/22)

1638   (26 Feb.) Same to same, complaining of the dishonesty of Robert Cogan, and referring to the purchase of a share in alum mines and other matters. (TN/PO 7/II/23)

1638   (23 April) Same to same, re the amount of the customs profits sent to him and certain deductions made, and the alum business. 'I will provide Matthew Trott a place for your sake.' (TN/PO 7/II/24)

Legal & Administrative Papers (ref. TN/PO 7/III)

1500–1618   A book containing copies of various acts, indentures, etc., concerning the Irish customs (TN/PO 7/III/1), as follows:

     1500   An Act for Poundage in Ireland, setting forth the rates of duties payable on all merchandise.

     1613   Grant of the great and small customs of Ireland to Sir Arthur Ingram, Martin Freeman, Richard Lowe and Richard Calthorpe.

     1618   Surrender by Sir Lionel Cranfield, and the persons named above, of all their interest in the collection of Irish customs, including the duties on wines.

     1618   Grant of all the Irish customs to the above farmers for one year without payment of rent in return for their surrender of 4 years of the lease.

1607–9   Schedule of instruments relating to the transference of shares in the lease of the Irish customs. (TN/PO 7/III/2)

1612   (22 Oct.) Copy of the undertaking by Sir John Swinnerton, John Suckling, Lionel Cranfield, George Lowe and John Mayle, to pay £6,000 p.a. for the farm of the Irish customs, and a fine of £1,000, on the same conditions offered by Sir Arthur Ingram on his overture, whereby he offered £6,000 p.a. for 11 years. (TN/PO 7/III/3)

1613   (12 Nov.) Warrant from the Lord Deputy to the Customer of Galway to allow 120 tons of beef and pork to be exported by John French and Partners at 8s per ton. (TN/PO 7/III/5)

1613	Draft letters of concordatum to the Treasurer to repay Robert Cogan and John Pitt certain money out of the customs revenue. (TN/PO 7/III/6)
1613–32	Memorandum of the various leases of the Irish customs and of offers which had been refused, previously listed inadequately in the H.M.C. report. (TN/PO 7/III/7)
1613–32	Schedule of the leases of the customs of Ireland from 11° James I to 7° Charles I. (TN/PO 7/III/8)
1614	(28 Feb.) Letters of attorney from William Long of Dublin appointing Robert Cogan his attorney to receive £250 from Sir Thomas Ridgeway, Vice-Treasurer of Ireland. (TN/PO 7/III/9)
1614	(Aug.) Warrant to the farmers of the Irish customs to pay the pension due to the late Earl of Northampton for his surrender of a grant of the customs on starch, to Roger Pennell. (TN/PO 7/III/10)
1614	(12 Sept.) Warrant from the Lord Deputy to Robert Cogan to pay £100 to Captain Thomas Button to victual his ship, *The Phoenix*. (TN/PO 7/III/12)
1614–15	Three documents concerning the legal dispute between Sir Arthur Ingram and the Earl of Northampton, part of which concerned an annuity of £3,000 payable to Northampton out of the customs of Ireland, and mentioning a Privy Seal obtained by the Countess of Northampton for the sum of £750 to be paid to her by the Irish customs farmers. (TN/PO 7/III/33–5)
1618	(12 Jan.) Copy of a warrant under Privy Seal sent to the Earl of Suffolk, Lord Deputy St. John and others, that the rent of £6,000 reserved for the lease of the Irish customs be paid into the Exchequer at Dublin because of the difficulty in transporting sums of money to England. Also a note of reasons against this procedure. (TN/PO 7/III/13)[488]
1618	(15 May) Draft surrender by the farmers of the Irish customs (Sir Lionel Cranfield, Sir Arthur Ingram, George Lowe and Richard Calthorpe) of all their interest in the great and petty customs and the duty on wines brought to Irish ports, granted to them by letters patent dated 22 July 1613, with another draft of the same. (TN/PO 7/III/14)
1618	(20 May) Order for the Attorney General to report on the case where Robert Cogan, John Pitt and William Massam, agents of the farmers of the Irish customs, claimed that the customs of Strangford and Ardglass were in the hands of the Countess of Kildare, and that her lessees have lowered the duties there to draw shipping away from the neighbouring ports. (TN/PO 7/III/36)
1624	(10 Nov.) Letter from Edmund Sadler to Sir Arthur Ingram, requesting an appointment in connection with the accounts for impositions on logwood and starch for 1607 and the farmers' lease of 1611. (TN/PO 7/III/31)
1624	A statement of the rents due upon the farm of the Irish customs paid to the King, certified by Thomas Waad in answer to 'one Mr Sadler, who had informed sundry times against the same.' (TN/PO 7/III/15)

---

[488] This item was inadequately calendared in H.M.C., *Various Collections VIII* (London, 1913), p192.

c1626   Three documents concerning a case in Chancery between Sir William Pitt and Sir Arthur Ingram. Pitt alleges in a bill of complaint that Ingram has unlawfully tried to transfer the cost of a payment of £100 made in 1615 to Sir Thomas Coach onto him, although it should have been paid out of Ingram's share of the Irish customs farm. Then follows the answer of the defendant, and Pitt's replication. (TN/PO 7/III/37–9)

1631   (8 July) Warrant to draw up a lease of the Irish customs for 15 years, in favour of Nicholas Harman and Richard Mills, beginning Michaelmas next, at a rent of £14,000 p.a. and a fine of £10,000. The lessees are to have defalcations out of their rents for annuities, pensions, etc. (TN/PO 7/III/16)

1631   (19 July) Draft memorandum of an agreement re defalcations amounting to £3,300 to be divided between Robert Cogan and John Williams. (TN/PO 7/III/17)

c1632   A book containing copies of three deeds (TN/PO 7/III/18), as follows:

1632   (24 March) Letters patent of a lease of the customs of the ports of Ireland to Katherine, Duchess of Buckingham, reciting the Book of Rates for the Irish customs of 11° James I, the additions thereto of 21° James I, the new Book of Rates of 1624 and the reinforcement of the 10 March 1632. She is to hold the customs farm for a term of 15 years for a rent of £11,050 p.a. and a fine of £20,000. If she suffers any loss of revenue by any act of the King, such amount is to be defalked out of the annual rent.

1632   (26 March) Assignment from Katherine, Duchess of Buckingham, to Francis, Lord Mountnorris, Sir Arthur Ingram the younger, George Radcliffe of York and Robert Cogan of Chiswicke in Middlesex, of her interest in the letters patent above, for £4,500 p.a. until 2 Feb. 1646, the assignees to be responsible for the annual rent of £11,050.

1632   (21 April) Letters patent authorising payment of £3,300 to Sir Arthur Ingram the elder, and confirming the above assignment, with a covenant that out of the first two years' payments they might retain £3,300 for him as a defalcation, £1,000 of which should have been paid to Robert Cogan for his fees as Surveyor-General of the Customs, unpaid for 10 years.

1632   (21 April) A copy of the clause in the above relating to the £3,300. (TN/PO 7/III/19)

1632   (Before 25 June) Petition of Sir Edward Bagshaw, Customer and Collector for Dublin, to the Lord Justices of Ireland, complaining that Robert Cogan had presented a petition for a warrant to restrain him and others from collecting the customs. Bagshaw requests that the warrant should not be granted to Cogan as Lord Mountnorris is daily expected to return to Ireland, when the matter will be solved. (TN/PO 7/III/41)

1632   (25 June) Order for Robert Cogan to appear at the Council Board in Dublin the following afternoon to answer Sir Edward Bagshaw's petition above. (TN/PO 7/III/42)

1632   (27 Aug.) Draft appointment of Lord Ranelagh to act for one of the customs farmers in Ireland. (TN/PO 7/III/20)

1632 (22 Nov.) Regulations for keeping a Register of Seizures and Forfeited Bonds, with letters of introduction to Lord Mountnorris and Robert Cogan to appoint the bearer, Edmund Hunt, as Registrar. (TN/PO 7/III/21)

1635 Note made by Sir George Radcliffe concerning arrears on the Irish customs. (TN/PO 7/III/22)

c1635 A vindication by the Lord Deputy of his motives in accepting a share in the farm of the Irish customs, giving a resumé of the various leases of the same from 1613 onwards and the circumstances which led to his becoming one of the partners. (TN/PO 7/III/24)

1636 (Hillary Term) Replication of Sir John Banks, Attorney General of England, reaffirming all he stated in his information in his case against Sir William Pitt, Sir Arthur Ingram, Francis Morris and Francis Phillips. (TN/PO 7/III/40)

17th cen. A draft undertaking by Robert Cogan to conduct the Irish affairs in the interest of his partners and accept what salary they name from year to year. (TN/PO 7/III/23)

17th cen. Five draft papers, each containing a copy of the offer made by the farmers for the farm of the Irish customs, all of which are undated, but at least one was drawn up by Robert Cogan and submitted to Sir Arthur Ingram the younger. (TN/PO 7/III/25)

Tallow (ref. TN/PO 7/IV)

c1633 An anonymous treatise setting forth the reasons against royal approval of the project put forward regarding the sale of tallow in Ireland, which would hinder the cattle trade and prove detrimental to the owners of small barques who trade in hides, beef and tallow, etc. [6 ff, double foolscap]. (TN/PO 7/IV)

Stray references found elsewhere in the collection

1634–40 Seven accounts of the customs charged on coal exported from every port in England and Wales, which contain frequent references to Irish ships, their port of registration, etc. (TN/PO 6/VI/4–10)

1637 (10 June) Assignment between (1) Charles I, (2) Sir Arthur Ingram the younger and Roger Norton of London, and (3) Sir Adam Loftus, Vice-Treasurer of Ireland, and Sir Robert Meredith, Chancellor of the Exchequer in Ireland, whereby (2) sell their share of the Irish customs farm to (3), with instructions from the King that (3) should continue paying rent for the farm as (2) had done. (TN/PO 6/II/9)

1641 (7 Feb.) Counterpart of articles of agreement between (1) James, Earl of Suffolk and Henry, Earl of Holland, and (2) George, Lord Stuart de Aubigney and Katherine, his wife, stating that whereas James, Duke of Lennox, had promised to settle premises called Magavelin, Co. Donegal, on the said Lord de Aubigney, his brother, and whereas the Earl of Suffolk had promised £6,000 as a marriage portion to his sister Katherine, Lady de Aubigney, £2,000 of which had been paid, it was agreed that Suffolk and Holland should pay the remaining £4,000 within 20 days after Lord de Aubigney had settled the above estate on his wife. (TN/DZ/58)

WEST YORKSHIRE : Yorkshire Archaeological Society *
Claremont, 23 Clarendon Road, Leeds LS2 9NZ
Tel: (0113) 245 6362

LOOSE ITEMS

1599   Unsigned memorandum concerning the preparation of Spanish
            shipping to be used against England, and the English counter-
            measures to be adopted. The memorandum also mentions the forces
            under the Earl of Essex in Ireland. Endorsed 'Newes from Mr
            Levyn Seman'. (DD56/L3)

c1600   'A brief and perfect description of Ireland', in a volume of material
            primarily concerning the history of Richmondshire, compiled 1600–
            1607. (MS. 436)

COLLECTIONS

Genealogical Miscellanea (ref. MS. 514)

In 1896 the Irish antiquarian, R. Langrishe, wrote to Miss Collins at Kilburton
vicarage in Yorkshire, concerning his ancestors, the Horsfalls of Inishnag, Co.
Kilkenny, who hailed originally from the Halifax area. He enclosed a transcript
of two documents from the Public Record Office in Dublin (one of which was
subsequently lost in the fire of 1922),[489] as follows:

1595   (6 Oct.) Substance of the last will and testament of Roger Dalton of
            Knocknamona Castle, Co. Waterford, bequeathing to his 2nd wife,
            Alison, during her life, the profits of the seigniory in the Munster
            plantation which he purchased from Sir Christopher Hatton's heir,
            and itemising various other bequests to his friends and to members
            of his family. At the end, Dalton lists a number of debts which were
            due to him from Ralph Graye, James Eirgsye, and Jasper Mayne.
            (MS. 514/S)

1603   (20 Nov.) Summary of a Bill and Decree of Chancery in Ireland, in
            a case between Cyprian Horsfall and Alyson, the widow of Roger
            Dalton. It recites that according to an agreement dated 1 July 1601,
            Alyson promised to give Horsfall's fiancee, Jane Dalton, the portion
            bequeathed to her by her father. Though Horsfall was subsequently
            married to Jane at Knocknamona on 15 July 1601, he did not
            receive any of her portion before her death in 1603. (MS. 514/S)[490]

The Duke of Leeds MSS (ref. DD5)

1638   Deed concerning the proposed marriage between Elizabeth,
            daughter of the Earl of Sunderland, and George, eldest son and heir
            of Christopher Wandesford, Master of the Rolls in Ireland [fragile].
            (DD5/13/unsorted III)

c1638   A bound volume containing the advice of C. Wandesford to his son
            and heir for the regulation of the conduct of his whole life [83pp].
            This was published by T. Comber in 1727. The book also contains
            'A prayer composed by the Rt. Hon. Sir Christopher Wandesford,
            Lord Deputy of Ireland, who deceased Dec. ye 3rd Anno 1640 in
            Ireland' [8pp]. (DD5/12/33)

---

[489] Langrishe also enclosed a copy of the 1637 funeral certificate of Oliver Grace of Inchmore, Co.
Kilkenny, from the funeral entries among the Betham MSS in the British Museum.
[490] Although the bill has not survived, the substance of the decree can be found in the National Archives of
Ireland, Ms. R.C. 6/1: Repertory to Chancery Decrees, Vol. I, 1536–1624, p271.

1641	(23 Feb.) William Wandesford to Sir Edward Osborne, from Dublin, re the poor state of the affairs of the late Lord Deputy Wandesford, who died £3,000 in debt. (DD5/38/2, letter no. 36 of a bundle sent to Osborne re Wandesford family affairs, 1640–7)
1641	(1 May) Lady Alice Wandesford to her brother, Sir Edward Osborne, from Dublin, regarding the wardship of her son George and the problem over the disputed claims to Idough, Co. Kilkenny. (DD5/38/2, no. 48)
1641	(12 May) Same to same, with regard to 'these disordered times' and Strafford's trial. She is doubtful if her annuity out of the manor of Castlecomer, Co. Kilkenny, will be paid, as the tenants cannot at present be compelled to pay their rent, and she complains of her poverty. (DD5/38/2, no. 1)
1641	(26 June) Same to same, reporting a petition that has been presented in the Irish Parliament about her late husband's affairs, and describing her problem in finding a suitable wife in Ireland for her son George. (DD5/38/2, no. 2)
1641	(29 June) John Burniston to same, sending news that William Wandesford is setting out today for Ireland, and that George Wandesford has been taken out of college at Oxford. (DD5/38/2, no. 40)
1641	(6 July) Same to same, stating that several Irish causes submitted by Mr [Richard] Butler at Westminster are being remitted into Ireland. (DD5/38/2, no. 45)
1641	(27 July) Same to same, from London, reporting that Mr Butler has recommenced his petition to the Parliament about the lands of Idough, Co. Kilkenny. (DD5/38/2, no. 33)
1641	(20 Aug.) Lady Alice Wandesford to same, stating that her son George is presently 'entertained in my Lord [Raby]'s family'. (DD5/38/2, no.3)
1641	(29 Aug.) William Wandesford to same, concerning the cause of Idough now depending in the English Parliament. (DD5/38/2, no. 38)
1641	(5 Sept.) Same to same, from Castlecomer, re the efforts of Lord Arundel and Mr Butler to undermine the Wandesfords' title to Idough. (DD5/38/2, no. 43)
1641	(24 Sept.) Same to same, reporting that the Earl of Arundel intends to bring his claim to the lordship of Idough before the Irish Parliament. (DD5/38/2, no. 37)
1641	(28 Sept.) Lady Alice Wandesford to same, hoping that Osborne will watch over young George Wandesford while he is in England, and discussing George's marriage prospects. (DD5/38/2, no.8)
1641	(8 Oct.) Same to same, sending news of her conference with Sir George Wentworth over her son's prospects, and expressing her low opinion of Irish men, who 'are given to drink'. (DD5/38/2, no. 7)
1641	(15 Dec.) William Wandesford to same, enclosing a bill for the clothes and apparel of his nephew George from the draper, amounting to £8 11s 3d. (DD5/38/2, no. 46)
c1641	A schedule of the debts of the late Lord Deputy Wandesford. (DD5/38/2, no. 35)

ISLE OF MAN

ISLE OF MAN : The Manx Museum Library
Kingswood Grove, Douglas, Isle of Man IM1 3LY
Tel: (01624) 675 522
Fax: (01624) 661 899

Although the staff informed us that they could find no records specifically concerning Ireland, a recent PhD thesis by J.R. Dickinson, 'Aspects of the Isle of Man in the Seventeenth Century' (University of Liverpool, 1991) shows the range of Irish documentation held by the Manx Museum. In the bibliography to his thesis, Dr. Dickinson lists the various local government records which still survive for the period under review. There is a great deal in the archives illustrating the close economic ties between the island and Ireland. Of particular importance are a series of 'Ingates and Outgates' (or port books) for Douglas beginning in 1570. There is frequent reference to Irish ships and merchants, and ships travelling to and from Ireland among these papers. There is additional Irish material to be found among the other administrative records. The court records include Exchequer Books from 1580 (ref. Lib.Scacc.), Chancery Books from 1578 (ref. Lib.Canc.) and Books of Pleas from 1496 (ref. Lib.Plit.). There are also a series of bundles of 'Receipts and Disbursements' starting in 1579. Unfortunately none of these records have been catalogued or indexed, but given the Isle of Man's links with Ireland, the repository could hold a rich collection of Irish sources.[491]

---

[491] We would like to thank Dr. Raymond Gillespie for bringing Dickinson's thesis to our attention.

SCOTLAND

LOTHIAN : Edinburgh City Archives *
City Chambers, High Street, Edinburgh EH1 1YJ
Tel: (0131) 529 4614
Fax: (0131) 529 7477

LOOSE ITEMS

1610   (26 July) A long and detailed account of the trial before the Vice-Admiral of Scotland[492] and his deputies of 30 English pirates led by William Randell and John Parkins who operated along the Irish and Scottish coastlines from their base at Long Island in Roaringwater Bay, near Fastnet, 'ane plaice of resort of all Pirates and opin Roberis'. (reference unknown)[493]

1614   (12 April) Letters patent issued under the Great Seal of England and directed to the Lord High Treasurers of England and Ireland and all collectors and comptrollers of customs and other duties within those kingdoms, commanding that no great or petty customs, imposts, fees, entry silver, or other charges should hereafter be taken or exacted by any officers of England or Ireland from Scotsmen or Scottish ships, than is usually received from Englishmen and Irishmen, etc. (Historical Charter 79)

COLLECTIONS

Council Records (ref. Council Records)

The City archives contain 14 volumes of Edinburgh Council Records covering the period from 7 Oct. 1551–16 Aug. 1644 (vols. 2–15 inclusive). Comprising for the most part the minutes and enactments of the Town Council, mention of Ireland is understandably scarce, and Irish affairs are very rarely dealt with in the series of calendars which were published by the Scottish Burgh Record Society. For example, only a couple of references to the economic contact between Scotland and Ireland can be found in Marguerite Wood (ed.), *Extracts from the Records of the Burgh of Edinburgh, 1626–41* (Edinburgh, 1936).[494] Unfortunately, it is very difficult to ascertain how many more Irish references remain among the unpublished material, for the index to the series in the City Archives Office is hopelessly inadequate, only producing one new piece of information, given below. Suffice it to say that a good deal of Irish material probably remains undiscovered among the Council Records.

1641–2   (4 and 23 Feb.) Act for raising a voluntary contribution at all the church doors for the relief of the distressed Irish Protestants who

---

[492] Sir James Wemyis of Bogie.

[493] Luckily, the item has been published in full in Robert Pitcairn, *Ancient Criminal Trials of Scotland* (Bannatyne Club, 1833), pp102–8, where it is stated to have been taken from 'an Official Extract preserved in the Charter-Room of the City of Edinburgh'. We would like to thank Mr Graham Hopner of the Dumbarton Public Library for drawing our attention to this reference.

[494] On pp72 and 205. Other references to Ireland can be found elsewhere in the series, i.e. in J.D. Marwick (ed.), *Extracts from the Records of the Burgh of Edinburgh, 1573–89* (Edinburgh, 1882), p531; Marguerite Wood (ed.), *Ibid, 1589–1603* (Edinburgh, 1927), pp7, 16, 135 and 155, and M. Wood (ed.), *Ibid, 1604–26* (Edinburgh, 1931), p85.

had fled to Edinburgh after the outbreak of the rebellion in Ulster in October 1641 'to avoid the barbarous cruelty of the Natives', together with an act ordering that all of the money raised for the poor Irish immigrants be delivered to George Suttie. (Vol. 15, pp221 and 223)

The Moses Bundles (ref. Moses bundle)

1625	(11 Aug.) Disposition of John Mitchelhill, minister at Balliephilip in Ireland, son and heir of the late John Mitchelhill, burgess of Edinburgh, merchant, with the consent of Laurence Henryson, merchant, in favour of Barbara Gilchrist, widow of the said John Mitchelhill, for property in the City of Edinburgh, immediately east of the Tolbooth. (Bundle 4, no. 152)
1626	(23 July) Copy of a royal grant to James Primrose, burgess of Cobros, of an exclusive 21-year license to publish the treatise entitled *God and the King* in Scotland. Recites that the treatise, explaining the oath of allegiance, is universally taught in England and Ireland as a means to preserve young minds against the doctrines of the Jesuits. The King expects all householders and anyone who can read to buy the book. (Bundle 6, no. 216)
1637	(24 April) Disposition by Sir Alexander Hamilton, sometime of Innerwick in Scotland and now of Ballincreiff in Ireland, and Patrick Hamilton, minister at Innerwick, with the consent of Paul Ronnald of Killileagh, Co. Down, in favour of John Sydserff for a tenement on the south side of the High Street in Edinburgh. Registered on 24 May following. (Bundle 18, no. 725)
1637	(16 Aug.) Disposition by William Strang, minister at Attalie in Ireland, with the consent of his wife, Christian Strang, in favour of John Sloan, burgess of Edinburgh, merchant, for property on the north side of the High Street in Edinburgh. Registered on 24 August following. (Bundle 18, no. 738)
1637	(16 Aug.) Disposition of same, also with the consent of his wife, in favour of John Mitchell, burgess of Edinburgh, baker, and others, for another piece of property on the north side of the High Street. Registered on 27 April 1638. (Bundle 19, no. 773)
1641	(2 Nov.) Draft report of the Committee as to forces to be sent from Scotland to help in the suppression of the Irish rebellion. The number of 10,000 men is suggested, of whom 2,800 were to be Highlanders drawn from the shires nearest Ireland; their selection was to be left in the hands of those who knew the Highlands and Islands well and have most power in those parts. The generals are to be appointed by the King and Parliament. A list of shires and the proportion of men to be levied by each is appended. (Bundle 24, no. 996)

LOTHIAN : Edinburgh University Library *
George Square, Edinburgh EH8 9LJ
Tel: (0131) 650 3412
Fax: (0131) 650 6863

LOOSE ITEMS

15th cen. Photostat of an undated letter probably written in the late fifteenth century by Sir James Ormond to H. Dycon' and N. Potter, farmers. (Ms. Phot. 1368)

1526   (20 Aug.) A copy of a fragment of an agreement between MacEochagan *alias* Mageoghegan and 'An Sindach', dated 1526, beginning 'duthaidh an hSionnuigh ar caitheamh re ceart dfhaghail do'n hSionnach....' (O'Donnell Ms. K., viii)[495]

1571–1640 A large bound volume containing a collection of transcripts made in the eighteenth century of manuscripts concerning the relations of France with England and Scotland between 1292 and 1644 (Ms. Dc. 1. 41),[496] which includes the following references to Ireland:

1571   (28 May) Letter addressed to the French King from London by his ambassador to England, Monsieur De La Mothe Fenelon, which mentions the lands granted to Sir Peter Carew in Idrone by Elizabeth I and the efforts being made by Sir Thomas Stuckley to raise support in Spain for an attack on Ireland. (fol. 112v)

1604   (24 July) A copy of the treaty between Philip III of Spain and James I of England, clause 11 of which guarantees safe commerce to the merchants of England, Scotland and Ireland in the Spanish realm, with the like guarantee for Spanish merchants in King James's dominions, etc. (fol. 424r–v)

1640   Undated document mentioning Ireland, which deals with the subsidy being levied by the Crown for the maintenance of its army against the Scots. (fol. 162r–v)

1580–1   Microfilm containing transcripts of the accounts of the Earl and Countess of Argyle, 1577–1613, including under 1580–1 'Item to the Lady Kyntyris man and maltman directit to Irland at my Ladeyis command 4iij^s iiij^d'. (Ms. Mic. M. 663)[497]

1608   (July) A volume entitled 'Melvini Epistolae', including 'A short confutation of D. Downans [bishop of Derry] apologetik sermon maid for the dignitie of the episcopall office' by Andro Melvine (*alias* Andrew Melville) [11pp]. (Ms. Dc. 6. 45)[498]

1634–6   (4 Nov. 1634–21 July 1636) A large volume of transcripts of the dictates and lectures of Francis Le Rees, probably given at Paris University, as taken down by John Grace. The subject matter covers logic, physics and philosophy, and includes *inter alia* a commentary on Aristotle's 'Organum', etc. Inside the back cover is inscribed

[495] The O'Donnell collection contains many other items which seem to be transcripts from the Gaelic Annals and other printed sources as published in the nineteenth century by John O'Donovan and his circle. The item referred to above was published in full, both in English and Irish, by John O'Donovan (ed.), 'Covenant between Mageoghegan and the Fox, with brief historical Notices of the two Families', *Miscellany* (Irish Archaeological Society), i (1846), pp179–97.

[496] The volume was compiled *circa* 1765 for Charles Mackie, the then Professor of History in Edinburgh University.

[497] The transcripts were taken verbatim from the originals in the Argyll Charter Chest in Inverary Castle and the microfilm may very well include further Irish references not noticed during our search.

[498] A transcript of this manuscript can be found at Ms. La. III. 373.

'Monsieur Dermitio Dwier student hibernoyis ou colledge de la marsh soyt, Don a Paris in Frannce, Irlandae'. (Ms. Dc. 4. 39)

1640-1　　(Aug. 1640–June 1641) Transactions of the Committee of Estates of Scotland (Ms. Dc. 4. 16), including the following references of Irish interest:

1640　　　(5 Sept.) Petition of the English lords and gentlemen to the King, in which they mention 'the great mischeife that may fall upon the Kingdom' if the reports of the bringing into England of Irish foot soldiers is true. (fol. 4v)

1641　　　(24 March) Letter to the Committee from the Commissioners at London, mentioning the charges which have been brought against Strafford, the Lord Lieutenant of Ireland. (fol. 89r)

1641　　　(29 March) Document entitled 'Concerning Commerce and Trade', setting down conditions to govern trade between England, Scotland and Ireland. (ff 90v–91r)

1641　　　(cMarch) Document entitled 'Concerning certaine incendiaries of the Scottish nation in Ireland', which mentions Mr Corbett, a 'minister fugitive' and his 'reproachfull pamphletts'. It goes on to attack the sermons of the bishops of Down and Raphoe, and lists others who should be punished for their behaviour, particularly Dr Robert Blair, who wrote 'a book called Episcopacie not abjured in Ireland'. (fol. 92r)

COLLECTIONS

Laing MSS (ref. La.)

This extensive accession was partially calendared in H.M.C., *Laing MSS* (2 vols., London, 1928), which dealt mainly with sections I and II of the collection. In addition, sections III and IV were given a summary listing in G.K. Hall, *Index to the MSS in the University of Edinburgh Library* (3 vols., Boston, 1964–81). However, in some cases the descriptions which are given to items in the collection are inaccurate or partial, and a more detailed listing of these items is given below.[499]

c1594-9　　Notes made by J. Barrett in 1816 on the careers of Sir James Fullerton and Sir James Hamilton at Trinity College, Dublin, following their election as fellows c1594. The jottings begin by noting that in April 1595 Hamilton was sent to collect the profits due to the College from a commendam which it had received after the death of the Archbishop of Tuam, William Lally, and it is also noted that in August 1596 Fullerton, the College Bursar, paid Hamilton £20 to travel to Munster, etc. Many more details are given up to c1599 [2pp]. (La. II. 646/24)

1604-15　　Bound volume beginning with a genealogy of the earls of Donegal compiled in 1760, which includes an extensive entry for Sir Arthur Chichester, Lord Deputy of Ireland 1604–15, together with a detailed commentary on his period in office, e.g. 'In 1605, under Sir Arthur's government, the Old Violent Customs of Tainistry, and the inconvenient Law of dividing all Freehold Estates amongst all the Sons, called Gavelkind, were abolished by Judgement of the Court of King's Bench '. The genealogy also gives detailed entries for Sir Arthur's brothers, the Ulster planters Sir Edward and Sir Thomas Chichester, and notes the violent death of another brother, Sir John.

---

[499] It is worth mentioning that the 1614 clothes account for Sir Claud Hamilton (published in some detail in H.M.C., *Laing MSS*, i (1928), p135ff) has been missing since 1961.

The rest of the volume comprises a series of lengthy transcripts from the chronicles of William Farmer, 1612–15, which seem primarily to have been made so that the reader would appreciate the importance of the 1613–15 Irish Parliament over which Lord Deputy Chichester presided [1 vol, 128pp]. (La. III. 250)[500]

1608   (29 July) Prohibition of transporting fugitives and rebels from Ireland to Scotland, under pain of death, contained in a volume of transcripts from the 'Buikis of Secret Counsell' for the period 1561–1636. (La. III. 399, p59)

1612–29   A volume of rentals and accounts for the Irish estate of Sir Claud Hamilton (La. II. 5), containing the following:

1612–3   (1 Nov. 1612–1 Nov. 1613) 'The Rentall of the proportionn of Killenye and Eden perteineing to umquhile Sir Claud Hamiltonn, kny^t and possessed be the tenentis underwryttin, from Alhallowtyde 1612 till allhallowtyde 1613'. The document records details of the leasing of the lands of Stranabege, Tirecarnoan, Drummin, Sparing, Eden, Menecronye, Diriconvoe, Ruskye, Gartbaghe, Arhyolan, Stranagalvolye, Drine, Lismerwe, Monykennan, Lait, Cloncull, Killenye, Aughtermoye, Conglan, Conye, Gortecassill, Colloquhillye, Literbrait, Loghar, Clanapogahe, Dirrikella, Lisnecreage, Moydell, Glenlark, Benneleallye, Avistevodan, Killecurrye and Lisvolemetn'mene. The charges of rent in kind as well as rent in cash are given for each tenant, who are named as Patrick grome O'Dufferie, David Paine, Rorie O'Neill, Brian O'Neill and Harry Mergaghe's sons, Schawn O'Neill, Hugh McGuigne, Claud Hamilton, Phelim O'Dufferie, Dane Buy McKanellye, Neill grome McKeommnye, Rory McKeolgan, Hugh dow O'Duffereine, Coconnaghe O'Dufferie, Don Moder McConor, and Shaen McConnoer. (ff 2–3)

1613–5   A further two rentals, for All Hallows 1613–All Hallows 1614, and ditto for 1614–15. (ff 4–6)

1613–5   'Ane Compt maid and gevin up be Sir George Hamilton, knycht, Quhereintill he charged himself w^t the debtie of the Lands off Eden and Killenye perteineing to umq^l Sir Claud Hamilton, kny^t, his brother germane, 1613, 1614 and 1615, as is^{est} specifet'. (fol. 7)

1613–5   An account of discharges from the Irish rent, May 1613 – Nov. 1615, which gives details of various payments to James Elphinstone in Scotland, James Hamilton, John Ogilvie, Gilbert McCrackan and others, as well as itemising the debts due to Sir Claud by Brian Crone O'Dufferie and other Irish tenants. (ff 7–8)

1613–5   'Ane compt maid and gevin up to John Fleymeing to the right honorable the Erle of Abercorn in name off unq^{ll} Sir Claud Hamilton his heyres, And to Sir William Stewart, kny^t, off the lands off Monnterleny whereintill he charged himself w^t the rents off the firsaid landis fra Allhallowday 1613 till alhallowday 1615, being two years, etc.' (ff 11–2)

1616–7   An account of the rents from Monterleny and elsewhere in Ireland pertaining to Sir Claud Hamilton, 1616–17, with details of the discharge of the same, signed by William Hamilton.

---

[500] Farmer's chronicle of the Parliament has been published in John Lodge, *Desiderata Curiosa Hibernica* (Dublin, 1772). The rest of the chronicle has been published in C. Litton Falkiner, 'William Farmer's Chronicles of Ireland from 1594 to 1613', *English Historical Review*, xxii (1907), pp104–130 & 527–552.

Endorsed 'Sir George Hamiltonne' Compt off the Rent of Ireland'. (ff 13–14)

1616–7 Another copy of the same, endorsed 'the furst copy'. (ff 15–16)

c1616 An inventory of the goods and chattels of the late Sir Claud Hamilton, who died on 19 October 1614, with an endorsement at the end that an account was to be made of all his goods, etc., and of his cattle which were 'sauld in Ireland'. The inventory lists all of his swords, hosiery, drapery, salt cellars, etc. (ff 17–22)

1618–9 Sir George Hamilton's account for the Irish lands, Oct. 1618 – Aug. 1619, referring to payments made to estate officials, etc., with extensive notes re the correct steps which Sir George should take in the management of the estate. (ff 23–4)

1621 A similar account by Sir George Hamilton for 1621. (ff 25–6)

1629 An account of extraordinary expenditure, including payments for the servants' dinner, beer, ale, miscellaneous foodstuffs, and for smoking pipes, 1629. (ff 27–9)

1629 Sir William Hamilton's account, dated 31 June 1629, giving further details of payments for beer, mutton, etc., signed by John Ogilvie. (fol. 30)

c1629 Three more accounts of ordinary expenditure on food, etc., c1629. (ff 31–6)

c1628 Notes in Latin of the transactions of James VI & I, addressed to Charles I by Alexander Hay, which includes two entries re Ireland, one stating 'Hibernia Broccres et Brimores, et qui prius rebelles tunc pacati Anglorum obedientie emuli regii occurunt eigz obviam se submine dant', the other 'In Hibernia aute belta que totos quingentos plus minus annos vigebant, in felia regis ad coronum Anglia aditu penitus extincta fuint, etc.' (La. III. 219)

c1634–41 The commonplace book of Thomas Bowdler, entitled 'Thomas Bowdler his booke written wth his owne bloode 1634', which includes copies of various speeches made in the House of Commons in England concerning the attainder of the Earl of Strafford in 1640–1. More unusually, the book also contains an epitaph for Strafford, and a note entitled 'Newes from a private freind', c1640, which mentions that 'the Deputy of Ireland was in great solemnity created Earl of Strafford and Lo: Lieu. Gen. of Ireland'. (La. III. 532)

1636 (11 Aug.) Eighteenth century transcript of 'A conference between Dr. Henry Leslie, Bishop of Downe, and Dr John Bramhall, Bishop of Derry, on the one hand, and Mr James Hamilton on the other, ... [as held] 11th August, 1636' [35pp]. (La. III. 536)

1640 (13 April–5 May) An account of the proceedings in the English House of Commons [162pp], which contains a lengthy version of the Lord Keeper's speech on 13 April, including his comments on the reformed state of Ireland, as well as details of the Speaker's address to the King on 15 April which similarly drew attention to the progress of good civility in Ireland. (La. III. 384)

1640–1 (3 Nov. 1640–25 Feb. 1641) Speeches by Charles I, the Speaker of the House and others in the English Parliament (La. III. 764), including as follows:

no. 18 'To the very right honorable the Lord Deputy, the humble remonstrance of the knights, citizens & burgesses in [the Irish] Parliament assembled', listing their 15 chief grievances with the government of the country (8ff).

no. 20	'A petition delivered to the Lords of the Upper House of Parliament against the Deputy of Ireland for causing the hanging of a gentleman contrary to law' (2ff).
no. 21	'A message sent from the House of Commons and delivered by Mr Pym to the Lords of the Upper House of Parliament', regarding the information they have received about traitorous actions by the Lord Lieutenant of Ireland, the Earl of Strafford (1 fol.).
no. 22	'November 24th 1640, The extent of my Lord Lieutenant's charge of treason', listing seven articles brought against him (2ff).
no. 25	'Mr Pym his speech against the Lord Lieutenant of Ireland was read Nov: Anno Dom' 1640' (5ff).
no. 26	'The Accusation and impeachment of Sir George Radcliffe, Deputy to the Lord Lieutenant of Ireland by the Commons of this present parliament assembled, charging him with high treason' (1 fol.).
no. 27	'After reading of the articles against Sir George Radcliffe a short speech was delivered by Mr Pym to this effect the 31st December 1640' (1 fol.).
no. 28	'To the rt. hon. the Lords spiritual and temporal in the high court of Parliament assembled. The humble petition of Thomas, Earl of Strafford, his Ma^ts Lieutenant General of Ireland' (2ff).
17th cen.	The autobiography of Robert Blair (1593–1666), Scottish covenanter and former Presbyterian minister of Bangor in Ulster. (La. III. 268)[501]
17th cen.	'An Argument upon the Question of Impositions, Digested and divided into sundry chapters by [Sir John Davies] his Ma^ts Attorney General of Ireland', containing 33 chapters in all, with a dedicatory epistle to James I written by Davies [70pp]. (La. III. 398)
17th cen.	A collection of the works of Sir John Davies, containing poetry, prose and psalms translated into verse, most of which were written down after 1624, but including some items effected before that date. (La. III. 444)[502]

LOTHIAN : Scottish Catholic Archives
Columba House, 16 Drummond Place, Edinburgh EH3 6PL
Tel: (0131) 556 3661

Though the only specific reference to Ireland in this repository is listed below, it is likely it contains further sources concerning the activities of Irish churchmen on the continent. Mark Dilworth, the archivist for this repository, used a number of records held here in the compilation of his book on Scottish (often Irish) monasteries in Germany 1576–1697, *The Scots in Franconia* (Edinburgh, 1974). He particularly used the Ratisbon MSS, Schotten–Kloster MSS and the Blair letters. Though most of the material post-dates 1641, it is possible that there is earlier documentation in these collections as well.

LOOSE ITEMS

c1574–8	(12 July) Letter from the exiled Bishop of Cashel, in Rome, to Archbishop James Beaton, in Paris, commending Alexander Seton

---

[501] This was published in T. McCrie (ed.), *The Life of Mr Robert Blair* (Woodrow Soc., 1848).
[502] Published in Robert Krueger (ed.), *The Poems of Sir John Davies* (Oxford, 1975).

(later Earl of Dunfermline) who is studying theology in Rome and is about to journey to Scotland and back. (JB 2/6/14)[503]

STRATHCLYDE : Argyll & Bute District Archives
Kilmory, Lochgilphead, Argyll PA31 8RT
Tel: (01546) 604 120
Fax: (01546) 604 138

Though this repository informed us that there were no relevant records in their collections, the following item was found in a catalogue held by the Strathclyde Regional Archives in Glasgow (see below). That catalogue stated that this item was now held by the Argyll District Archives, with the reference T.D. 40/5. It is possible that this information is incorrect, or that the reference is no longer valid.[504]

LOOSE ITEMS

1640   (28 Dec.) Copy of the accusations presented against the Archbishop of Canterbury, the Lord Lieutenant of Ireland, and the Earl of Argyll, given into the English House of Commons by the Scottish Commissioners, and read in both Houses. Subscribed Ad: Blaire. (T.D. 40/5)

STRATHCLYDE : Ayr Burgh Archives *
Carnegie Library, 12 Main Street, Ayr KA8 8ED
Tel: (01292) 286 385
Fax: (01292) 611 593

COLLECTIONS

Burgh Accounts (ref. B6/25)

The only volume in this series which dates back to the sixteenth and early seventeenth centuries, known as The Book of the Common Good of Ayr (B6/25/1), has been published in G.S. Pryde (ed.), Ayr Burgh Accounts, 1534–1624 (Edinburgh, 1937). It contains several references to economic contact between Scotland and Ireland, as well as a couple of items giving details of Englishmen landing on the Scottish coast during the Nine Years' War.

Burgh Court Books (ref. B6/12)

1548   (15 Oct.) Order by the Burgh Court that John Wilson of Ireland and four of the town officers be remunerated for their labours on behalf of the town. (B6/12/2, p61)

Council Books (ref. B6/11)

1591   (8 April) Declaration in the Burgh Court regarding the 'lamentabill apprehensionn of Sᴿ Bryane O'Rorak one of ye lords of Connoght in

---

[503] This item comes from the important collection, held by this repository, of the papers of James Beaton, Archbishop of Glasgow and Scottish ambassador in France. It is possible that there are further Irish references to be found in these records. For an introduction to the collection see Mark Dilworth, 'Archbishop Beaton's Papers in the Scottish Catholic Archives', The Innes Review, xxxiv (1983), pp3–8.

[504] It is worth stating that the most important collection of records concerning Ireland to be found in Argyll is the privately held archives of the Dukes of Argyll. Enquiries about this collection should be addressed to the Chief Executive of the Clan Campbell Society, Inveraray Castle, Inveraray, Argyll, who is in charge of those records.

Irland'. The Town Council discusses the question of his liberty, and record his expenses as £24 (Scots). (B6/11/2, fol. 105v)

1602   (22 Feb.) Order by the Town Council that 'John Grave and William Dobyne, merchant boyis in Carrickfergus in Irland', shall have their barque and merchandise confiscated and forfeited, having broken the acts and statutes of the burgh when selling hides in the town. (B6/11/3, fol. 444v)

1617   (14 July) A series of entries recording the admission of the following persons from Ireland as free burgesses of the town of Ayr: Arthur, Lord Chichester of Belfast, and Lord High Treasurer of Ireland; Sir Humphrey May, Secretary of State for Ireland; Sir Randall MacDonnell, Lord of Antrim; Sir Arthur Bassett; Sir Faithfull Fortescue; Sir James Ogill, Sir William Layke, Sir John Fenton, and Henry Convey, servants to Lord Chichester; Robert Bysse, gent.; Andrew Boyd, servant to the Earl of Abercorn; Arthur Cavenagh; William White of Dublin, merchant; Sir James Hamilton of Bangor, and James Pennycuik, his servant, etc. (B6/11/4, ff 583v–586v)

1632   (5 Jan.) Admission of Master Hugh Montgomery, probably the son of Hugh, Viscount Ards, as a free burgess of the town. (B6/11/4, fol. 834v)

Burgh Registers (ref. B6/29)

The sole item of Irish interest in this series is The Cocket Book of Ayr (B6/29/1), which covers the period 20 September 1577 – 3 August 1632.[505] This is an unfoliated volume of 278 pages containing daily entries of ships leaving Ayr port. Each entry gives the date, the name of the merchant and master, the cargo aboard, and the name of the ship (often with its port of origin). For example 'Ultimo Maii 1586. John Wadding Irland man in Wasfurd merchand of the bark callit the katherine of Wascheford ressauit coquet of xvi twns of colis and payit his dew custume therfoir.' There are over 46 entries relating specifically to Irish ships, mostly from Wexford and Dublin, but also from Carrickfergus, Drogheda, Carlingford, Derry and some of the smaller Ulster ports. Most Irish ships left Ayr with coal, herrings, wine and salt, amongst other items. There are also occasional mentions of Irish produce being re-exported from Ayr, for example on 22 December 1625 an Ayr boat listed in its cargo 'Ireland butter'. Though the source is invaluable in charting Irish trade, the entries do not include the port or country of destination, thus making it difficult to assess the overall level of Irish trade with Ayr.[506]

STRATHCLYDE : Dumbarton District Library *
Strathleven Place, Dumbarton G82 1BD
Tel: (01389) 33273/63129
Fax: (01389) 33018

COLLECTIONS

Burgh Council Minutes (ref. 1/1/1)

1631   (28 Jan.) Entry in a volume of Town Council Minutes for 1627–41, that Robert Millar and John Lochlarne, servants 'under ye erle of

---

[505] There are two gaps in the volume, from 26 Oct. 1577–16 Sept. 1581, and 2 June 1598–17 June 1600.

[506] For an introduction to this document see R. MacKenzie, *Ayr's Export Trade at the end of the 16th Century* (Ayrshire Monographs, April 1988).

Antrim', confess to bringing over a bark from Ireland laden with oats and selling the same to unfreemen, contrary to an Act of Parliament. The Town Court ordains that Millar and Lochlarne must sell all 'there salt & timbr in hand' to cover the cost of their fine. (1/1/1, unpaginated)

Burgh Shipping Register (ref. 1/3/105)

1598–1607	Bound volume entitled the Dumbarton Shipping Register, 1597–1658 (1/3/105), which has the following references to trade with Irish merchants:
1598	(7 Nov.) Thomas Belloth and Michael Belloth [? Bellew], merchants of Ireland, entered Dumbarton in the boat called *The Andru of Rochelle*, carrying a cargo of salt. (p18)
1598	(22 Nov.) Another entry concerning *The Andru of Rochelle*, bearing Thomas Belloth and Richard Belloth, both Irishmen. (pp19–20)[507]
1607	(16 April) The barque called *The Marie of Stradaffe* in Ireland, bearing Nicholas Coulie of the same, entered the harbour, laden with '13 barrels of Aittes and 16 barrels of Beir'. (p82)

STRATHCLYDE : Glasgow University Library *
Hillhead Street, Glasgow G12 8QE
Tel: (0141) 339 8855 ext. 6767
Fax: (0141) 330 4952

LOOSE ITEMS

c1610	A lengthy report (49pp) addressed to James I by an unidentified 'traveller' concerning the state of the fishing industry in Britain, which makes the following references to the fisheries in Ireland (Ms. Eving 19):
p1	The observation that Holland has 2,000 ships, which is more than England, Scotland, Ireland, Spain, Portugal, Italy, Denmark, Poland, Sweden and Russia put together.
p12	A comment that the coasts of England, Scotland and Ireland are very rich in fish compared with the coasts of Spain and France.
pp29–30	'All over the coast of Ireland, Galloway, Sligo and the coast of Connaught to Balishanan the Baude and the North of Ireland, Lougefeilde, Knockfergus, Strangford there is stoore and variety of fish beside the multitude of codd, linge, herringe, salmons, seales, porpouses, whirlepoole and doggfish'. 'In the north of Ireland not far from Dunagall there are such multitude of herring as is hardly to be believed so large that 3 herring make a yard in length'. 'From Carlingford to Dundalk the Bay of Dublin to Waxford Waterford, Bearehaven, Crookhaven and so round about the coast of Ireland the like variety of fish aboundantly'.
p34	'Theis people of Ireland and round about the coast of England after they have been at sea and brought home their vessells full of fish will not go to sea again for more alt they are spent and they in debt, viz untill necessity compell them.'

---

[507] It is unclear from the wording whether the merchants were unloading fresh goods for sale in Dumbarton or departing for Ireland.

c1628   A volume of heraldic armorials, including 'The armes of the nobilitie of Ireland as they were created', which gives the coats of arms of 34 Irish peers in colour. (Ms. Hepburn Q. 23)[508]

1630–7   A small bound volume of documents concerning Scottish Presbyterianism, including an item apparently written by John McClelland entitled 'The ministers of Irland with whom I had aquentance and conversed with from the year 1630 to the year 1637, some whereof were there=after ministers in Scotland'. The author proceeds to give a lengthy description of the career of Robert Blair, the Presbyterian minister at Bangor, before going on to provide an account of Robert Cunningham, minister at Holywood, Josias Welch, minister at Templepatrick, George Dunbar, 'minister at Inver neeir Loathreigan in Irland', Andrew Stewart, minister at Donagar [Donegore?], Henry Calbert, minister at Oldston, John Ridge, 'ane Englishman at Antrum', James Hamilton, nephew of Lord Clandeboye, and Edward Brue [Bruce?], minister at Becadisland [Broadisland?]. (Ms. Murray 70, pp171–87)

1638–42   A book compiled by John Robertson which 'containeth a relation of Severall passages that fell out in Brittaine betwixt Anno° 1638 and 1642'. It includes a commentary on the Black Oath which was administered to the Scottish settlers in Ulster by Lord Deputy Wentworth in 1639, as well as a few general references to the efforts made by the Irish government to supply forces to help the King against the Covenanters in Scotland. (Ms. Gen. 1117)[509]

COLLECTIONS

Hunter MSS (ref. MS Hunter)

These manuscripts include two volumes of Elizabethan warrants for proclamations (MS Hunter 3 [S.1.3], and 380 [V.1.17]), relating to all aspects of government, including Ireland. The following are those which relate to Irish affairs.

1564   (14 July) Royal warrant to grant satisfaction to a petition of Edward Fitzgarret and Dame Agnes, his wife, who implored the Queen's help. (Ms. Hunter 380, no. 13)

1569   (27 June) Royal warrant regarding a case between Humphrey Wallronde, one of the six clerks of the Chancery in England, and Sir John Pollard, Lord President of Munster. The Queen notes that since Pollard has gone to Ireland Wallronde has unfairly increased his efforts during his absence to gain possession of the profits of a parsonage in Somerset. She grants an injunction to stay the case so long as Pollard remains 'in special service in Ireland'. (Ms. Hunter 380, no. 9)

1570   (2 May) Royal warrant addressed to the Lord Keeper of the Great Seal, Sir Nicholas Bacon, sending him certain bills and titles for the next session of the Irish Parliament, as follows: (1) 'An act that such cloth and stuffe as shalbe wrought of the wooles, flockes, lynen yarn, etc., ... shalbe transported for merchandise only by the merchants within [e]very the staple cities and towns of this realm,

---

[508] This item was bequeathed to the Library by Dr Charles A. Hepburn in 1973.

[509] The volume is unpaginated after fol. 210, but the relevant references to Ireland can be found within the last forty pages.

etc.'; (2) 'An explanation of the act made in a session of this parliament for the staying of wool, flockes, tallow and other wares and commodities, etc.'; (3) 'An act authorizing the Prymate of Ardmagh to sett his lands and possessions in the Irish Pale for years without the assent of his chapter'; (4) 'An act for the attainder of John Fitz-Gerald, called in his life the White Knight'; (5) 'An act for the attainder of Thomas Quem'forde of Ballimaka [Co. Kilkenny]'. The Queen's meaning is that the bills be returned to Ireland to the Lord Justice with her royal assent. For this purpose she gives Bacon warrant to draw up the acts with the Great Seal to be sent to Ireland 'in manner & form as in the like cases hath been used and accustomed'. (Ms. Hunter 3, no. 58)

1571   (22 June) Royal warrant addressed to Lord Keeper Bacon, as above, to transmit the following acts: (1) 'An act authorising the Governor for the time being by advise of the more part of the privy counsail ... to grant letters patent to the Irish and degenerate men of English name of their lands, yielding to her ma^tie certain reservacions'; (2) 'Act for the attainder of all such as be or shalbe indighted of treason, petie treason, murder, robbery, rape, or felon[y] committed since the first day of April 1569 to the last day of April 1571, etc.'; (3) An Act for the creation of free schools'; (4) 'An Act that exemplicacions shalbe of the same effort and strength as the record matter exemplified should be'; (5) 'An act for limitation of prescription'; (6) 'An act for the abolishing of extorte takinge meat drink victual and other refecions'; (7) 'An act that such cloth as shalbe wrought of the wool flocks and woolen yarn of the realm and such work as shalbe made of the shepefell, etc., ... shalbe staple ware and transported only by merchant staplers'; (8) 'An act for the establishing of the standard of measure for corn within certain shires of thius realm'; (9) 'An act for spuall parsons to be residing upon their spiritual promocyons and livings'. (Ms. Hunter 3, no. 53)

1617   'The Lord Keeper's speech to Sir William Jones, Chief Justice of the King's Bench in Ireland'. (Ms. Hunter 506, no. 13)

STRATHCLYDE : Strathclyde Regional Archives *
Mitchell Library, North Street, Glasgow G3 7DN
Tel: (0141) 227 2401
Fax: (0141) 226 8452

LOOSE ITEMS

1617   (19 Nov.) A notice that 'Mr Thomas Boyd declairit that John Muir was gone to Ireland and could not proceid with the censures of the kirk against him till his returne'. (Glasgow Presbytery Records, Original Records, ii, 142b)[510]

COLLECTIONS

Glasgow Burgh Records

The Minute Books of the Town Council would seem to be the only series of manuscripts among the Burgh Records which contain regular mention of

---

[510] Unfortunately, when the Regional Archive was visited, the catalogue to the Presbytery Records was not available for consultation. The reference given above was found among the typed extracts from the series made in 1988 by a local historian, Alaistair R. Hill (ref. TD 1134).

Glasgow's links with Ireland during the early modern period.[511] A few of these references have appeared in print in *Extracts from the Records of the Burgh of Glasgow*, 1573–1642 (Scottish Burgh Records Soc., 1876), and *Ibid*, 1630–1662 (1881), but the vast majority remain unpublished. The reader is asked to note that the list which follows below is only a partial guide to the unprinted material.

1581–6   (16 May 1581–27 April 1586) The Minute Book of the Town Council of Glasgow (Ms. C1/1/2), which contains the following Irish references:[512]

1581   (20 Aug.) Action and claim brought by Thomas Scote against Archibald Habbison, stating that 8 or 9 years ago Scote paid Habbison £10 (Scots) to bring back hides and other goods from his voyage into Ireland. Habbison has refused to deliver the merchandise, and the Town Court gives him 15 days to pay. (fol. 18v).

1582   (2 Dec.) William Cranforde binds himself to pay John MacCynnes the sum of 11 marks (Scots), collected by Cranforde on MacCynes's behalf from 'one Ireland man' (fol. 57r).

1583   (7 Jan.) General reference to the trade in Irish hides (fol. 60r).

1583   (7 Aug.) Reference made to Irish trade (fol. 96v).[513]

1583   (9 Aug.) Statement that while conveying goods in a ship out of Ireland, William Anderson and others were seized and held captive by Richard Cod, officer, acting at the instance of Eliot, Matthew and Andrew Wessom, friends to Matthew Trummyll in Ireland (fol. 97r).

1583   (15 Oct.) Bond by Andrew Stark and others (named) to pay all sums of money due to Steven Robertson of Glasgow, merchant, for goods imported from Ireland (fol. 106r).

1583   (17 Oct.) John Stellord and David MacThidine, burgesses of Glasgow, covenant to pay Robert Boyd of same, merchant, the sum of £113 (Scots) for importing 14 hogsheads of wine and 10 barrels of salt out of the ports of Ireland (fol. 106v).

1583   (4 Nov.) Agreement by Lady Agnes O'Neill to pay the ransom of £40 (stg) demanded by 'Enoehaugh [i.e. Donough] O'Donald' in Ireland, and giving further details of the case mentioned on 9 August (above). (fol. 110v).

1583   (19 Nov.) Mention of Irish hides imported into Glasgow (fol. 112v).

1583   (25 Nov.) Agreement between John Wessom and [   ] concerning the purchase of hides from Ireland (fol. 113r).

1584   (13 May) James Boddup agrees to repay £30 (Scots) to Elizabeth Graham at his return out of Ireland (fol. 132r).

1584   (18 May) Agreement by Robert Stenard to deliver goods purchased in Ireland, including wine and salmon, to Adam Alla'e (fol. 132r).

1584   (2 Dec.) Agreement concerning a dispute over the importation of goods worth £4 (Scots) from various parts of Ireland (fol. 168v).

---

[511] A quick look at the following manuscripts failed to produce any relevant material: the Act Books of the Dean of Guild Court for 1605–22 and 1638–53 (Mss. B4/1/1,3), and a volume of extracts from the Docquetted Minutes of the Trades House and Collectors' Accounts for 1605–78 (Ms. T–TH/1/2). Nevertheless, there is every reason to expect that a more thorough search through these and other sources will uncover further Irish references.

[512] The authors would like to thank Dr James McGrath of the University of Strathclyde for supplying a list of the contents of this volume.

[513] This entry is very difficult to read.

1585	(23 March) Statement by William Hamilton agreeing to import goods worth £25 (Scots) from Ireland for George Elphinston (fol. 180r).
1585	(30 April) David Flemyng and John Allane agree to deliver goods worth £58 (Scots), including Irish hides, to Robert Flemyng (fol. 183v).
1585	(29 Nov.) Reference to trade with Ireland [faded] (fol. 203r).
1585	(Dec.) David Flemyng and John Allane agree to deliver wine out of Ireland worth £65 (Scots) to William Flemyng. (fol. 205v).
1586	(April) Reference to trade with Ireland [Ms. badly torn and faded]. (fol. 218r).
1605–10	Glasgow Corporation Act Book, 1605–10 (Ms. C1/1/6), which contains the following Irish references among the Corporation accounts for the financial year Whit Sunday 1605–Whit Sunday 1606:
fol. 105r	'Item – gifen at command of John andrissonne and Thomas Mr, ballies, ye tent of Junij to ane puir soldart yt come out of Irland 3s. 4d'.
Ibid	'Item – yt same day gifn at com'and of ye balleis to and uyr suldart yt come out of Ireland 3s.4d'.
1609–13	(16 Jan. 1609–28 Aug. 1613) Glasgow Town Council Minute Book (Ms. C1/1/7), which has the following reference of Irish interest:
1610	(11 Dec.) Payment 'to fo' men for the expenses in transporting of for Ireland men to lynly qu conforinent ye naivand £20'. (fol. 94v)

Maxwell of Pollok Papers (ref. T–PM)

Much of this family's correspondence was published by William Fraser, *Memoirs of the Maxwells of Pollok*, 2 vols (Edinburgh, 1863), and the many references to Ireland relate chiefly to Sir John Maxwell of Pollok; the Earl of Nithsdale; Claud Hamilton, Lord Strabane; Sir Alexander Hamilton and the Earl of Abercorn. These published items are held at reference T–PM/110. However, there are many other documents concerning Ireland in this vast collection which have not been published. The following list includes all those references to Ireland which could be found in the Record Office's catalogue of the unpublished material, with some further notes from the originals. Undoubtedly, there are other documents of Irish interest in the collection which have not been noticed in the catalogue.[514]

1621	(28 March) Letter from A[ ] Hamilton to Sir John Maxwell, regarding information from Ireland that a Mr. McKnachtan of Argyll is employed by Lord Boyle to entreat with the King on behalf of an Englishman also called Boyle for an office in Ireland. He does not think McKnachtan will 'do us that wrang' as he is an old friend of his father, but if the recipient knows anything of this he is asked to tell the Marquis of Hamilton of it. (T–PM/113/168)
1622	(27 Nov.) Letter from James Patonne to Sir John Maxwell, concerning legal business. A footnote adds that the Earl of Nithsdale's lands in Ireland have passed to the Duke of Buckingham's youngest brother, who has been made a viscount and

---

[514] There are over 400 unpublished letters predating 1641, and the catalogue is often vague or obscure. For example, there are many letters between the Earl of Nithsdale and Sir John Maxwell concerning financial matters, but few details are given. It is likely that this correspondence would include further references to Nithsdale's estates and his general activities in Ireland.

that there are rumours that 'the king cost them to him'. (T–PM/113/171)

1628   (22 Dec.) Letter from J[   ] Maxwell to Sir John Maxwell. He has heard that the Earl of Nithsdale has obtained certain lands in Ireland as a gift from the King, but their extent he does not know, but feels that Sir John should know, and also that the Earl will soon be home. (T–PM/113/189)

c1628   (n.d.) Letter from John Maxwell of Barsill to Sir John Maxwell. The Earl of Nithsdale has gone to court in London to petition the King for a gift of various privileges (detailed) over 'the first planters of Ireland'. To this end Nithsdale has employed John Maxwell of Logane in Ireland who is well known to the Lord Deputy, who has been able to get 'the allowance of the council of Ireland in suficient writ'. Nithsdale's suit 'is thought to be the greatest sute that ever was obteint of his majestys father or of himself'. (T–PM/113/852)

1630   (3 June) Summons. Robert, Earl of Nithsdale and the Lord Advocate v. Sir John Maxwell of Pollok. Diligence at the defender's instance against Archibald Heygait, former Town Clerk of Glasgow, and Robert Boyd, formerly in Clerkland, now in Ireland, as havers of writs (unspecified). The action is for exhibition of writs of the defender's lands. (T–PM/107/4/45)

1631   (18 Nov.) Letter from William Cochrane at Edinburgh to Sir John Maxwell of Pollok setting an appointment between the Lord Strabane and the Lord Traquair to meet Sir John and Andrew Stirling of Law with his men at Kilpatrick Kirk at sundown on the following Thursday. (T–PM/113/17)

1631   (30 Dec.) Transcript of a letter from William Maxwell to Sir John Maxwell, mentions that 'Our Chief [Nithsdale] his Irish suite goethe on to contentment and I think his lordship be gone for court before this tyme'.(T– PM/113/549)

1632[515]   (28 Jan.) [   ] Maxwell to Sir John Maxwell, concerning the turbulent nature of English politics, fear of a French invasion and Spanish involvement in Ireland, 'we hear great rumours of raising armes for the Irish service but nothing as yit done'. (T–PM/113/226)

1633   (30 May) Letter from Elizabeth, Countess of Nithsdale, to Sir John Maxwell, relating that the King is on his way to Edinburgh, and her son is joining him at Berwick, having been shown great favour by the King who has spoken to the Lord Deputy of Ireland about him. (T–PM/113/234)

1634   (31 Jan.) Letter from Robert, Earl of Nithsdale to Sir John Maxwell, acknowledging Sir John's letter asking for payment on outstanding annual rents. Nithsdale replies 'it is not in my power to furnish money for I mynd shortly to go to Ireland, after my return I shall take such course as you may have satisfaction'. (T–PM/113/948)

1634   (6 Sept.) Letter from Elizabeth, Countess of Nithsdale, to Sir John Maxwell, regarding the management of her estate, and that there is a rumour that her son, Robert, has taken ship from Dublin to London. (T–PM/113/94)

---

[515] This date is damaged, it could be 1642.

1634   (19 Dec.) Letter from the Laird of Knockdolian to Sir John Maxwell, mentioning that 'Ower chieff' [Nithsdale?] has written to him concerning his business dealings in Ireland. (T–PM/113/250)

1635   (10 Jan.) Letter from [David] Watson to Sir John Maxwell, regarding John Bayae who spent three years in the service of his uncle the Archbishop of Cashel in Ireland. Bayae now hopes to go to France in the service of Sir William Hamilton, to learn the use of arms and the French tongue. Asks Sir John to write to Sir William on behalf of Bayae. (T–PM/113/252)

1635   (12 Nov.) Letter from Sir John Cochran to Sir John Maxwell, asking for advice 'to assist me to a settling in that business betwixt the earle of Abercorn and his brother My Lord of Strabane'. (T–PM/113/257)

1637   (3 Aug.) Letter from Robert, Earl of Nithsdale to Sir John Maxwell, concerning the 'many years' annuities owed to Sir John. Nithsdale explains that he has not received the money from Ireland that he expected and that 'I look not to have it till it be executed by the laws of that kingdom which goeth on with a slow paise'. (T–PM/113/274)

1637   (28 Oct.) Letter from Robert, Earl of Nithsdale to Sir John Maxwell, discussing debts, and that he is going to 'court to make som bargain for what I have been about in Ireland, by the which I shall be free of my greatest burdens', amongst which will be his payment of owed money to Sir John. (T–PM/113/951)

1640   (6 Feb.) Execution of summons on letters of poinding and apprising raised at the instance of William Cootts, Treasurer of Glasgow, against Mr. John Maxwell, formerly one of the ministers of the burgh, of various lands in Glasgow. For payment of £1,000 plus £200 expenses and penalty. Refers to Maxwell having fled to Ireland. (T–PM/107/11/18)[516]

1641[517]   (6 Feb.) Letter from Sir William Cochrane to Sir John Maxwell, mentioning that 'two of our regiments mairches to Ireland this week'. (T–PM/113/284)

---

[516] There are further documents in this case at T–PM/107/11/19–20, 28.

[517] The original date for this document was 1642, but was changed contemporaneously to 1641. The document almost certainly dates from 1642, and the contemporary confusion probably had much to do with the growing use of 1 Jan. (rather than 25 March) as the beginning of the year. For the sake of thoroughness we have included this document.

WALES

CLWYD : County Record Office (Flintshire)
The Old Rectory, Hawarden, Deeside, Clwyd CH5 3NR
Tel: (01244) 532 364
Fax: (01244) 538 344

LOOSE ITEMS

1610   Abstract of title (1610–1827) including letters patent to Richard, Earl of Clanricard, for lands at Park, Co. Galway, 19 July 1610. (D/BC/1646)

17th cen.   (n.d.) Survey/rental of the estate of Lady Aungier in Cos. Leitrim and Sligo [1 fol.]. (D/NA/1074)

CLWYD : County Record Office (Denbighshire)
46 Clwyd Street, Ruthin, Clwyd LL15 1HP
Tel: (01824) 703 077
Fax: (01824) 705 180

COLLECTIONS

Trevor of Brynkinalt MSS (ref. D/BK)

1575   (20 March) Feoffment by Gerald Coursy, commonly called MacPatrick of Crichcursagh, Co. Cork, to Robert Myaghe, Richard Roche, Philip Roche Fitz James, and John Baree *alias* Barry of Kinsale, of a parcel of land at Rinroane, Co. Cork. (D/BK/I/80)

1612   (8 July) Letters patent granting to Henry Beecher the castle of Mahowne and lands of Kynalmekie in Co. Cork for a consideration of £20. Coloured illumination. (D/BK/I/60)

1613   (18 Nov.) Feoffment by William MacRobert Barry of Ardohuoigg, Co. Cork, to Edmund oge MacSweeny, gent., and Teig Rieogh O'Cnoghuire, yeoman, both of Balliclohie, Co. Cork, of lands in Kilmoclynine, Co. Cork. (D/BK/I/72)

1620   (12 Feb.) Exemplification of a fine at Cork, between (1) Nicholas Brown, attorney for MacEdmond MacSwyny, gent., and (2) Robert Sweete, attorney for Sir John Fitz Edmond Fitzgerald, and Thomas Murry, concerning the right and custody of one castle, 50 messuages and 2,560 acres of land in Killmaclynyne, Co. Cork. (D/BK/I/73)

1620   (10 July) Defeasance between (1) John Delaware, merchant, and Thomas Talbott, gent., both of London, and (2) Sir Thomas Roper of Ropers Rest near Dublin. Declaration that if (2) pays (1) sums totalling £2,100, then (2) will be released from a bond in £2,000. (D/BK/I/484)

1620   (10 July) Statute staple in £2,000 by Thomas Roper of Dublin, to John Delaware and Thomas Talbott, of London. (D/BK/I/485)

1624   (21 Dec.) Lease from John Jephson of Moyalloe, Co. Cork, to Stephen Keene of the same, innholder; of the lands of Dromsligah in Moyalloe, Co. Cork. For 99 years, at a rent of £28 p.a., with the surrender of a former lease. (D/BK/I/61)

1630   (14 May) Feoffment by (1) John Barry *alias* MacRobiston, gent., Edmund Oge MacSweeny, gent., and Teige Riegh Croghmir, yeoman, all of Ballycloghie, Co. Cork, to (2) John Burly of Kilcolman and Phillip Barry of Drynagh, Co. Cork, gents., of the castle and lands of Killmoclynine in Orrerie, Co. Cork. (D/BK/I/74)

1631   (30 Sept.) Feoffment by Richard, Earl of Cork, to Sir William Fenton of Michelstowne, Co. Cork, and Sir Randle Clayton of Cork, of various lands in Co. Cork. (D/BK/I/81)

1632   (2 June) Power of attorney granted by (1) James Fitz Nicholas Barry of Anagh, Co. Cork, and Melaghlin MacAwliffe of Castle MacAwliffe, Co. Cork, to (2) Richard, Earl of Cork. To receive payments from mortgagees of properties in cos. Cork and Kerry. (D/BK/I/219)

1633   (15 Feb.) Mortgage by Walter White of Cork, merchant, to Sir Robert Tynte of Ballyreinane, Co. Cork, of the castle and lands of Castleredmond, Co. Cork, for £500. (D/BK/I/62)

1636   (20 Dec.) Grant by James Magrath of Kullewoer, Co. Donegal, esq., to George Clearke of Dublin, merchant, of an annuity of £52 issuing out of lands in Tormon-Magrath, Co. Donegal, in consideration of the surrender of a former annuity. (D/BK/I/99)

1636   (22 Dec.) Defeasance by George Clearke of Dublin, merchant, to James Magrath of Kullemor, Co. Donegal, and Tirlagh Magrath, his son and heir apparent, that if Magrath performs the covenants of a bond, then that bond to be void. (D/BK/I/486)

1636–1762 One bundle of deeds, correspondence, financial and legal papers of the Hamilton, Leslie, Broderick and Trevor families of Co. Armagh, which includes a copy of the will of Sir Edward Trevor, 'now prisoner here in the Newry', dated 1641. (D/BK/I/487)

1638   (21 Feb.) Quitclaim by Robert Cusacke of Rathgar, Co. Dublin, esq., and Alice, his wife, to Michael Doyne of Knockirne, Co. Antrim, esq., and Mabell, his wife, of lands at Ballynehattie and Ballyvulvallye, Co. Down, in consideration of £120. (D/BK/I/124)

1638   (1 April) Covenant to suffer a common recovery by David, Earl of Barrymore, to Sir William Fenton of Michelstown, Co. Cork, and Sir Piercy Smith of Ballyneta, Co. Waterford, upon various lands in Co. Cork. (D/BK/I/82)

1638   (1 Nov.) Feoffment by Owen MacQuaid of Lurugh Lynstie, Co. Tyrone, gent., to Sir Philip Percival of Dublin, and William Billingsley of Dublin, of lands at Killyconaghan and Kaliffe, Co. Monaghan. (D/BK/I/198)

DYFED : Pembrokeshire Record Office
The Castle, Haverfordwest, Dyfed SA61 2EF
Tel: (01437) 763 703

COLLECTIONS[518]

Haverfordwest Borough Muniments

The manuscripts in this series prior to 1660 have received an extensive calendar in B.G. Charles (ed.), *Calendar of the Records of the Borough of Haverfordwest 1539–1660* (Cardiff, 1967). They include a 1540 case heard before the Mayor and Justice of Haverfordwest concerning an illegal shipment of grain from Milford Haven destined for Waterford or New Ross and for the use of Irish rebels (p20). There are also documents concerning the transportation of troops to Ireland in 1600 (p42) and a 1609 receipt for payment of 20s given to Mr. Trendall, a preacher whom Sir James Perrot brought out of Ireland (p43). At the end of the book there is a comprehensive calendar of the borough's financial accounts for the period 1563–1600 which include frequent mention of Irish goods and people.

SOUTH GLAMORGAN : Glamorgan Record Office *
County Hall, King Edward VII Avenue, Cathays Park, Cardiff CF1 3NE
Tel: (01222) 780 282
Fax: (01222) 780 027

COLLECTIONS

Clayton Papers (ref. CL)

This deposit was originally part of the larger Clayton Papers, now widely dispersed throughout England, Ireland and the U.S.A. For an introduction to the original collection, with details of the location of the various sections which have been scattered, see Frank T. Melton, 'The Clayton Papers', *Bulletin of the Institute of Historical Research*, lii (1979), pp91–9. Further pre-1641 material was found in the Clayton deposit in the Essex County Record Office (see above).[519]

1635   (7 July) Articles of agreement made between (i) Phillip, Earl of
             Pembroke and Montgomery, and (ii) Randall MacDonell, Lord
             Viscount Dunluce, and Katherine, Duchess of Buckingham, wife of
             Lord Dunluce. Reciting previous articles of agreement dated 9 July
             1634, between the same parties, made on the intended (and since
             then solemnised) marriage of Charles Herbert, son of the Earl of
             Pembroke, and Mary Villiers, daughter of the Duchess of
             Buckingham. Whereby the said Duchess agreed to settle £20,000 on
             her daughter as a marriage portion, to be paid out of her annual
             income received from the Irish customs, and a further £5,000 from a
             legacy of the Earl of Rutland. To which sum the said Earl of
             Pembroke agreed to add £15,000, the total amount to be settled on

---

[518] In B.E. & K.A. Howells (eds.), *Pembrokeshire Life: 1572–1843* (Pembrokeshire Record Society, i, 1972), p2–4, reference is made to a 1595 letter from a number of Pembroke gents to members of the Privy Council concerning the defences at Milford Haven. The letter describes how the port could be used as a victualling base by the Spanish when invading Ireland. The item is given the reference Bronwydd Ms. 3, ff 96–7. Though the Howells do not give the name of the repository which holds this item, it is likely that it comes from records in the National Library of Wales.

[519] This collection is in the process of being relisted and renumbered, hence the reference numbers given for each item will eventually be superseded.

the said Lord Herbert and Lady Mary, and their heirs. By this agreement it is noted that the manner of securing payment of the said sums was not convenient, and that the previous agreement should be amended and that the moneys should be expended on the purchase of lands in fee simple to be conveyed to trustees for the Lord Herbert and Lady Mary. (CL/Deeds I/188)

1638   (26 April) Brief in the Court of Wards in the case of the Attorney General (on behalf of the King), plaintiff, v. the Earl of Antrim and the Duchess of Buckingham, his wife, the Earl of Pembroke, the Earl of Rutland, the Duke of Buckingham, Lord Francis Villiers, Lady Mary Herbert, Sir Edward Hales and Sir Robert Pye, defendants. The breviat contains the information and answers of each of the above defendants, the replication, rejoinder and proofs on behalf of the plaintiff and defendents, in a case concerning the administration of trust moneys derived from the Irish Customs (granted by Charles I to the Duchess of Buckingham in 1632 for 15 years) and the wardship of the Duke of Buckingham. The breviat recites many assignments, agreements and confirmations made by the Duchess and the Earl of Pembroke and Sir Robert Pye (trustees for the Duchess and her children) concerning the income of £4,550 p.a. derived by the Duchess from the assignment of the lease of the Irish Customs to Lord Mountnorris, Sir Arthur Ingram, Sir George Radcliffe and Robert Cogan. (CL/Deeds I/198)

Merrick, Button and Gwinneth Collection (ref. CL/BRA 247)

1604   (28 March) Letters patent granting an annuity of 6s 8d per day to Captain Thomas Button, until another annuity of 6s per day which had previously been granted to Button (but which had since been granted to Captain Robert Jemyson, as it had been presumed that said Button had died on a voyage to the West Indies) fell vacant. This annuity (of 6s) had been granted to Button by letters patent dated 27 May 1603, for being in the King's service on the coast of Ireland. Enrolled in the office of the Auditor of Ireland, 12 February 1615. (CL/BRA 247/364)

1620   ([ ] February) Indenture between King James I and Patrick Myagh fitz-James of Kinsale, Co. Cork, gent., son and heir of James Myagh fitz-Richard, late of Kinsale, decd. Reciting lease of 27 April 1598 by James Myagh fitz-Richard to Anthony Dillon of Castlepark, Co. Cork, gent., of the house of Castlepark and the adjoining 40 acres, for 31 years (no rent given). Also reciting a deed dated 19 February 1608 whereby Anthony Dillon assigned his interest in the above to King James I. Now Patrick Myagh leases to James I the above in consideration of 'obedience' and 'the better defence of this Kingdom against foreign invasion' and a sum of money (not stated). Term and rent of lease not given. (CL/BRA 247/409)[520]

1622   (9 April) Agreement between Sir Charles MacCarthy of Blarney, Co. Cork, and Sir Thomas Button of Lawrenny, Pembrokeshire, whereby Sir Thomas promised that he would endeavour to get Sir Charles created a baron and viscount of Ireland before the 31 May 1622, or at the latest by the 24 August 1622. Sir Charles to be created Baron of Muskerry and Viscount of Kinsale, or if not successful in this, to be created Baron of Blarney and Viscount Muskerry. The title to be made out to Sir Charles and his heirs

---

[520] This item was formerly catalogued as CL MS 4.770.

male, in default of which to his brother, Teige, and his heirs male. In consideration of which, Sir Charles undertakes to defray the expenses and pay Sir Thomas Button the sum of £2,300. (CL/BRA 247/407)

WEST GLAMORGAN : University of Swansea Library *
Singleton Park, Swansea SA2 8PP
Tel: (01792) 205 678 ext. 4048
Fax: (01792) 295 851

COLLECTIONS

Corporation of Swansea Records

The entire early records of the corporation are now on deposit in the University Library. After some examination, the only series of corporation records which appear to have references to Ireland are the following two volumes of Common Attorney's Accounts, which begin in 1617. These account books cover all income and expenditure in the town for each year, from Michaelmas to Michaelmas. In fact the income side of the account includes itemised listings of receipts of various port charges (halledge, keyadge, etc.) on each merchant arriving in Swansea. However, detailed as these entries may be, they rarely include the domicile of the merchant or ship involved, so that it is likely there are further references to Ireland which are not immediately apparent.

1617–35   Common Attorney's account book. Yearly accounts, from Michaelmas to Michaelmas. (Swansea Corporation Records, C.1)

    1625–6   Received from an Irishman for halledge of Iron that John Rosser bought ... 1s 2d. (p83)

    1628–9   Paid to three Irish gentlemen, with the consent of the Portrieve, on the 5 August ... 3s. (p118)
            Paid to Walter Barry of Galway, with the consent of the Portrieve, on the 13 August ... 1s 6d. (p118)
            Paid to four or five Irishmen, with the consent of the Portrieve, on the 17 August ... 6d. (p118)
            Paid to one Irishman and his wife and small children, who live in Jenkin Sparot's house, with the consent of the Portrieve, on the 16 September ... 2s. (p119)

    1629–30   Paid to three Irishmen for their supper at William Leweling's, with the consent of the Portrieve, on the 9 December ... 1s 6d. (p129)
            Paid towards the relief of eight Irish persons 'which travelled by a pass from parish to parish', with the consent of the Portrieve, on the 13 June ... 1s. (p131)

    1630–1   Paid to two 'little Irish children', on the 16 April ... 2d. (p144)
            Paid to John Williams, constable, to give to three Irishmen, with the consent of the Portrieve, on the 8 June ... 1s 6d. (p145)
            Paid to two Irishmen, with the consent of the Portrieve, on the 9 June ... 1s. (p145)
            Paid to John Carye, Irishman, going out of town, with the consent of the Portrieve, on the 26 June ... 1s. (p145)
            Paid to three Irishmen and women, with the consent of the Portrieve, on the 27 June ... 1s. (p145)
            Paid to the 'Jupshons' going out of town and to four Irishmen, and paid for their lodging, with the consent of the Portrieve, on the 28 June ... 5s. (p145)

1631–2   Paid to Christopher Gould, and Irishmen, by the appointment of the Portrieve … 1s. (p151)
Paid to a poor Irishman, by the appointment of the Portrieve … 6d. (p151)

1635–62   Common Attorney's account book. Yearly accounts from Michaelmas to Michaelmas. (Swansea Corporation Records, C.2)

1637–8   Received from an Irishman for throwing of ballast at the eastern side of the Pier … 2s 6d. (p16)
Received from Christopher Fleming, an Irish merchant, for throwing of ballast … 1s 6d. (p16)

1638–9   Received from Thomas Poolle, an Irish man, for throwing of stones on the quay … 1s 6d. (p20)

1639–40   Received from an Irishman for throwing of 'Axen in the Peare' … 2s. (p26)

GWYNEDD : Caernarfon Area Record Office
County Offices, Victoria Dock, Caernarfon LL55 1SH
Tel: (01286) 679 095
Fax: (01286) 679 637

LOOSE ITEMS

c1618   Volume of legal forms belonging to Thomas Dutton, a magistrate or clerk of the peace for Co. Donegal. The archivist describes it as a precedent book designed to allow a magistrate to perform his duties by setting out the legal formats for recognizances and the like. Though it does not mention specific cases, each type of form is set out as a Co. Donegal document, with the county name appearing in the top left-hand margin [20pp]. (XQP/106)[521]

COLLECTIONS

Quarter Sessions Papers (ref. XQS)

This series, which begins in 1541, includes numerous references to travel to Ireland, and Irishmen figure among the lists of criminals, paupers and vagrants who came to the magistrates' attention from time to time. This was largely because Caernarfon was on the main sea-road from Holyhead. The series has not yet received a comprehensive listing, and hence we are unable to give any specific references.

GWYNEDD : University College of North Wales Library *
Bangor, Gwynedd LL57 2DG
Tel: (01248) 351 151 ext. 2966
Fax: (01248) 370 576

LOOSE ITEMS

1625   (17 May) Copy of an order by John Williams, Bishop of Lincoln and Lord Chancellor of England to John Trefusis, Thomas Polwheile, John Coke and Sampson Bloye, or any two of them, to determine

---

[521] Captain Thomas Dutton was a settler in the Ulster Plantation. His estate, called Rosses, contained 2,000 acres in Co. Donegal. See George Hill, *The Plantation in Ulster* (Belfast, 1877), pp501–2.

and rectify a dispute between two Irish merchants, Marcus Linch and George Skerrett. The Bishop explains that he received a petition from the two merchants, and says that if they cannot solve the dispute, it should be returned to Chancery. (Baron Hill MSS, no. 52)

COLLECTIONS

Penrhyn MSS

1542 (8 July) Doom and Award, relating to the estates of Edward Griffith of Penrhyn, a captain in Ireland in the 1530s, who died of dysentry at Dublin on 11 March 1541. The document gives details of his death, as a prelude to a major dispute between Griffith's three daughters and co-heiresses, and his brother, over the inheritance to his huge Welsh estate in Anglesey and Caernarfon. (uncatalogued)[522]

1607 (cSept.) Letter from Osmund Oliver to Pyrs Griffith of Penrhyn. Osmund states that Sir Oliver Lambert stayed with him on his way to London, and told Osmund that the Earl of Tyrone 'with divers others both women and chyllderin are fled to the Kynge of Spayne'. He refers to the fact that Tyrone's eldest son is known as a 'great commander', but feels that the Earl's flight will bring 'shame and conffusion' to the King of Spain's allies. (uncatalogued)

Plas Newydd MSS

This collection contains the Welsh estate papers of Sir Nicholas and Sir Henry Bagenal, Marshals of the Army in Ireland, and Arthur Bagenal of Newry, Co. Down, during the years 1577–1638. There are a total of 23 items (Series IV/8475; Series V/1426–1461), most of which relate purely to the administration of their Welsh lands, but the following are of more specific interest to Ireland:

1596 (1 June) Deed of Covenant, (1) Sir Henry Bagenal, Marshal of the Army in Ireland; (2) Maurice Griffith of Porthamel, and Robert Griffith, his son and heir; relating to the marriage of either Arthur Bagenal or Griffith Bagenal (1st and 2nd sons of Sir Henry) and Jane Griffith, daughter of Robert Griffith. (Series V/1428)

1603 (5 Feb.–5 July) Two documents concerning the marriage of Arthur Bagenal of Newry and Magdalen Trevor, daughter of Sir Richard Trevor; and the agreements and bond between Sir John Savage and Sir Richard Trevor concerning the marriage of Anne Bagenal, daughter of Sir Henry Bagenal. (Series V/1438–9)[523]

1611 (20 March) Articles of agreement between Pierce Griffith of Penrhyn and Arthur Bagenal and Magdelan, his wife. Griffith agrees to join in sale with Bagenal of lands to the value of £4,000 in Wales, the estate of Sir Henry Bagenal, deceased. The proceeds of the sale to be disposed of for the defraying of debts, particularly in paying the marriage portion of 1,000 marks to his sister, Anne Bagenal, and for the 'charges in repairing the castles and houses of the said Arthur Bagenal in Ireland, Wales and elsewhere'. Griffith

---

[522] Edward Griffith's will can be found among the Prerogative Court of Canterbury wills in the Public Record Office, London. One of his daughters, Ellen, married Sir Nicholas Bagenal, who thus inherited part of the vast Griffith estate (see Plas Newydd MSS in this library).

[523] See under Cheshire County Record Office, Cholmondeley of Cholmondeley Collection, refs. DCH/E/304–9 and DCH/O/31, for details of the dispute over these marriages between Trevor and Savage in 1612.

is to convey the residue of the lands to Sir Arthur Chichester, Lord Deputy of Ireland, Sir Richard Trevor and Evan Lloyd in trust to the use of Arthur Bagenal and Magdalen and their heirs. (Series V/1441–2)

1617   (28 June) Letters patent, being a special livery to Arthur Bagenal, as son and heir of Sir Henry Bagenal, deceased, granting him possession of all the lands in Ireland, Wales and England, held of the King by his said father. (Series V/1445)

INDEX OF PERSONS
(including ship names)

INDEX OF PLACES